The
original edition
of this book con-
tained oversized maps.
PDF files of these maps
can be downloaded from
www.elibron.com/maps

THE AUTOBIOGRAPHY OF SIR HENRY MORTON STANLEY

Elibron Classics
www.elibron.com

Elibron Classics series.

ISBN 1-4212-6987-2 (paperback)
ISBN 1-4212-6986-4 (hardcover)

This Elibron Classics Replica Edition is an unabridged facsimile of the edition published by Sampson Low, Marston and Co., Ltd., London.

THE AUTOBIOGRAPHY OF SIR HENRY MORTON STANLEY

HENRY M. STANLEY, 1890

THE AUTOBIOGRAPHY OF SIR HENRY MORTON STANLEY, G.C.B.,

D.C.L., (Oxford and Durham), LL.D., (Cambridge and Edinburgh), etc.; Doctor of Philosophy of the University of Halle; Honorary Member of The Royal Geographical Society, and the Geographical Societies of The Royal Scottish, Manchester, etc.; Gold Medallist of The Royal Geographical Society of London; Gold Medallist of Paris, Italy, Sweden, and Antwerp Geographical Societies, etc.; Grand Cordon of the Medjidie; Grand Commander of the Osmanlie; Grand Cordon of the Order of the Congo; Grand Commander of the Order of Leopold; Star of Zanzibar; Star of Service on the Congo; etc., etc.

EDITED BY HIS WIFE,

DOROTHY STANLEY.

WITH SIXTEEN ILLUSTRATIONS, MAP, AND ONE FACSIMILE LETTER.

THIRD EDITION.

LONDON:

SAMPSON LOW, MARSTON AND CO., LTD.,

100, SOUTHWARK STREET, S.E

REPRINTED FROM AMERICAN PLATES BY
WILLIAM CLOWES AND SONS, LIMITED, LONDON

EDITOR'S PREFACE

IN giving to the world this Autobiography of my husband's early years, I am carrying out his wishes. Unfortunately, the Autobiography was left unfinished. I am, however, able to give very full extracts from his journals, letters, and private note-books, in which, day by day, he jotted down observations and reflections.

My best introduction is the following passage from a letter he wrote to me on November 30, 1893: —

'I should like to write out a rough draft, as it were, of my life. The polishing could take care of itself, or you could do it, when the time comes. Were I suddenly to be called away, how little, after all, the world would know of me! My African life has been fairly described, but only as it affected those whom I served, or those who might be concerned. The inner existence, the *me*, what does anybody know of? nay, you may well ask, what do I know? But, granted that I know little of my real self, still, I am the best evidence for myself. And though, when I have quitted this world, it will matter nothing to me what people say of me, up to the moment of death we should strive to leave behind us something which can either comfort, amuse, instruct, or benefit the living; and though I cannot do either, except in a small degree, even that little should be given.

'Just endeavour to imagine yourself in personal view of all the poor boys in these islands, English, Scotch, Welsh, and Irish, and also all the poor boys in Canada, the States, and our Colonies; regarding them as we regard those in the schools we visit in Lambeth, or at Cadoxton, we would see some hundreds, perhaps thousands, to whom we would instinctively turn, and wish we had the power to say something that would encourage them in their careers.

'That is just how I feel. Not all who hear are influenced by precept, and not all who see, change because of example. But as I am not singular in anything that I know of, there must be a goodly number of boys who are penetrable, and it is for these penetrable intelligences, and assimilative organizations, that I would care to leave the truthful record of my life. For I believe the story of my efforts, struggles, sufferings, and failures, of the work done, and the work left undone, — I believe this story would help others. If my life had been merely frivolous, a life of purposeless drifting, why, then silence were better. But it has not been so, and therefore my life can teach some lessons, and give encouragement to others.'

The pathos of this Autobiography lies in the deprivations and denials of those early years, here recorded for the first time. Yet these sufferings, as he came to realise, were shaping and fitting him for the great work he was to perform; and his training and experiences were perhaps the finest a man could have had, since, day by day, he was being educated for the life that lay before him. Stanley writes: —

'It can be understood how invaluable such a career and such a training, with its compulsory lessons, was to me, as a preparation for the tremendous tasks which awaited me.'

A boy of intense and passionate feelings, the longing for home, love, friends, and encouragement, at times amounted to pain; yet all these natural blessings were denied him; he received no affection from parents, no shelter of home, no kindness or help of friends, excepting from his adopted father, who died soon after befriending the lonely boy. Baffled and bruised at every turn, yet 'the strong pulse of youth vindicates its right to gladness, even here.' Orphaned, homeless, friendless, destitute, he nevertheless was rich in self-reliance and self-control, with a trust in God which never failed him. And so Stanley grew to greatness, a greatness which cannot be fully measured by his contemporaries. As a key to Stanley's life, it may be mentioned that one of his earliest and dearest wishes, often expressed to me in secret, was, by his personal character and the character of his work in every stage of his career, to obliterate the stigma of pauperism which had been so deeply branded into his very soul by the Poor-Law methods, and which in most cases is so lifelong in its blasting effects on those who would strive to rise, ever so little, from such a Slough of Despond. So that, when he had achieved fame as an explorer, he craved, far more than this, a recognition by the

English and American Public of the high endeavour which was the result of a real nobility of character and aim.

The ungenerous conduct displayed towards Stanley by a portion of the Press and Public would have been truly extraordinary, but for the historical treatment of Columbus and other great explorers into the Unknown. Stanley was not only violently attacked on his return from every expedition, but it was, for instance, insinuated that he had not discovered Livingstone, while some even dared to denounce, as forgeries, the autograph letters brought home from Livingstone to his children, notwithstanding their own assurance to the contrary. This reception produced, therefore, a bitter disappointment, only to be appreciated by the reader when he has completed this survey of Stanley's splendid personality.

That Stanley sought no financial benefit by exploiting Africa, as he might legitimately have done, is borne out by the fact that instead of becoming a multi-millionaire, as the result of his vast achievements, and his unique influence with the native chiefs, the actual sources of his income were almost entirely literary. This is indicated in the text.

Accepting Free Trade as a policy, the blindness of the British Nation to the value of additional colonies, and the indifference, not only of successive Governments, but of the various Chambers of Commerce, and the industrial community generally, whose business instincts might have been expected to develop greater foresight, were a source of the deepest concern and disappointment to Stanley; for it meant the loss to England both of the whole of the present Congo Free State, and, later, of the monopoly of the Congo Railway, now one of the most profitable in the world. The determined opposition for long exhibited to the acquisition of Uganda and British East Africa was also, for a time, a great anxiety to him.

It may also be pointed out here that all that is now German East Africa was explored and opened up to commerce and civilisation by British explorers, Livingstone, Burton, Speke, and Stanley. Thus England threw away what individual Empire-builders had won for the realm. The obvious advantages and paramount necessity to a Free-Trade country of having vast new markets of its own are sufficiently apparent, whatever views are held on the difficult Fiscal Question.

Canon Hensley Henson, in 1907, preached a remarkable sermon at St. Margaret's Church, Westminster, on St. Paul; and the following passage struck me as being, in some respects, not inapplicable to Stanley: —

'St. Paul, in after years, when he could form some estimate of the effect of his vision, came to think that it represented the climax of a long course of Providential action; his ancestry, character, training, experiences, seemed to him, in retrospect, so wonderfully adapted to the work which he had been led to undertake, that he felt compelled to ascribe all to the overruling Providence of God; that no less a Power than God Himself had been active in his life; and the singular congruity of his earlier experiences with the requirements of his later work, confirmed the impression.'

'Such men,' wrote the Rev. W. Hughes, Missionary on the Congo, 'as Dr. Livingstone and Henry M. Stanley, who went to Africa to prepare the way and open up that vast and wealthy country, that the light of civilisation and the Gospel might enter therein, are men created for their work, set apart, and sent out by Divine Providence, which over-rules everything that it may promote the good of man, and show forth His own glory. No one who has always lived in a civilised country can conceive what these two men have accomplished.'

The following striking picture of Stanley, from an article in 'Blackwood's Magazine,' may well be given here: —

'If the history of modern discovery has a moment comparable for dramatic interest to that in which Columbus turned his prow westward, and sailed into space, to link for ever the destinies of two hemispheres, it is the one in which a roving white man, in the far heart of Africa, set his face down the current of a mighty river, and committed himself to its waters, determined, for weal or woe, to track their course to the sea. The Genoese navigator, indeed, who divined and dared an unknown world, staked the whole future of humanity on his bold intuition, but posterity may one day trace results scarcely less momentous to the resolve of the intrepid explorer who launched his canoe on the Congo at Nyangwe, to win a second great inheritance for mankind.

'The exploration of the great, moving highway of Africa makes an epoch in the discovery of Africa, closing the era of desultory and isolated research, and opening that of combined, steady effort towards a definite, though distant, goal. That goal is the opening-up of the vast Equatorial region to direct intercourse with Europe.'

I will now close my preface with St. Paul's words, because they so wonderfully apply to Stanley:—

> In journeyings often, in perils of waters,
> In perils of robbers, in perils by mine own countrymen, in perils by the heathen,
> In perils in the city, in perils in the wilderness, in perils in the sea,
> In perils among false brethren;
> In weariness and painfulness, in watchings often,
> In hunger and thirst, in fastings often,
> In cold and nakedness.
>
> . . . .
>
> If I must needs glory, I will glory of the things that concern my weakness.
>
> (II Corinthians, Chap. xi, 26, 27, 30.)

The first nine chapters of the book are the Autobiography, covering the early years of Stanley's life. In the remaining chapters, the aim has been to make him the narrator and interpreter of his own actions. This has been done, wherever possible, by interweaving, into a connected narrative, strands gathered from his unpublished writings.

These materials consist, first, of journals and note-books. For many years he kept a line-a-day diary; through some periods, especially during his explorations, he wrote a full journal; and at a later period he kept note-books, as well as a journal, for jotting down, sometimes a personal retrospect, sometimes a comment on the society about him, or a philosophical reflection.

The material includes, next, a number of lectures, upon his various explorations; these he prepared with great care, but they were never published. They were written after he had published the books covering the same travels; and in the lectures we have the story told in a more condensed and colloquial way. Finally, there are his letters; in those to acquaintances, and even to friends, Stanley was always reserved about himself, and his feelings; I have therefore used only a few of those written to me, during our married life.

In some parts of the book, a thread of editorial explanation connects the passages by Stanley's hand; and for some periods, where the original material was fragmentary, the main narrative is editorial.

The use of the large type signifies that Stanley is the writer; the smaller type indicates the editor's hand.

I would here record my deep gratitude to Mr. George S. Merriam, of Springfield, Massachusetts, U. S. A., for the invaluable help and advice he has given me; and also to Mr. Henry S. Wellcome, Stanley's much-valued friend, for the great encouragement and sympathy he has shown me throughout the preparation of this book for the press.

Mr. Sidney Low's beautiful tribute, I republish, by kind permission of Messrs. Smith and Elder, from the 'Cornhill Magazine,' of July, 1904.

Finally, I would draw attention to the map of Africa placed at the end of this volume: Stanley carefully superintended the making of it by the great map-maker, Mr. John Bolton, at Messrs. Stanford's. It was Mr. Bolton's suggestion that I should put the small outline map of England beside it to indicate, by comparison, the relative size of that portion of Africa which is included in the larger map.

D. S.

CONTENTS

ILLUSTRATIONS

INTRODUCTION TO THE AUTOBIOGRAPHY

THERE is no reason now for withholding the history of my early years, nothing to prevent my stating every fact about myself. I am now declining in vitality. My hard life in Africa, many fevers, many privations, much physical and mental suffering, bring me close to the period of infirmities. My prospects now cannot be blasted by gibes, nor advancement thwarted by prejudice. I stand in no man's way. Therefore, without fear of consequences, or danger to my pride and reserve, I can lay bare all circumstances which have attended me from the dawn of consciousness to this present period of indifference.

I may tell how I came into existence, and how that existence was moulded by contact with others; how my nature developed under varying influences, and what, after life's severe tests, is the final outcome of it. I may tell how, from the soft, tender atom in the cradle, I became a football to Chance, till I grew in hardihood, and learned how to repel kicks; how I was taught to observe the moods and humours of that large mass of human beings who flitted by me.

As I have been in the habit of confining myself to myself, my reserve has been repugnant to gossip in every shape or form, and I have ever been the least likely person to hear anything evil of others, because, when the weakness or eccentricity of a casual acquaintance happened to be a topic, I have made it a principle to modify, if I could not change it. In this book I am not translating from a diary, nor is it the harvest of a journal, but it consists of backward glances at my own life, as memory unrolls the past to me. My inclination, as a young man, was always to find congenial souls to whom I could attach myself in friendship, not cling to for support, friends on whom I could thoroughly rely, and to whom I could trustfully turn for sympathy, and the exchange of thoughts. But, unfortunately, those to whom in my trustful age I ventured to consign the secret hopes and interests of my heart, invariably betrayed me. In some bitter moods I have thought that the sweetest parts of the Bible are wholly inapplicable to actual humanity, for no power, it appeared to me, could ever transform grown-up human beings so as to be worthy of heavenly blessings.

'Little children, love one another,' says divine St. John. Ah! yes, while we are children, we are capable of loving; our love is as that of Angels, and we are not far below them in purity, despite our trivial errors and fantasies; for however we err, we still can love. But when I emerged from childhood, and learned by experience that there was no love for me, born, so to say, fatherless, spurned and disowned by my mother, beaten almost to death by my teacher and guardian, fed on the bread of bitterness, how was I to believe in Love?

I was met by Hate in all its degrees, and not I alone. Look into the halls of legislation, of religious communities, of justice; look into the Press, any market-place, meeting-house, or walk of life, and answer the question, as to your own soul, 'Where shall I find Love?'

See what a change forty years have wrought in me. When a child, I loved him who so much as smiled at me; the partner of my little bed, my play-fellow, the stranger boy who visited me; nay, as a flower attracts the bee, it only needed the glance of a human face, to begin regarding it with love. Mere increase of years has changed all that. Never can I recall that state of innocence, any more than I can rekindle the celestial spark, for it was extinguished with the expansion of intellect and by my experience of mankind. While my heart, it may be, is as tender as ever to the right person, it is subject to my intellect, which has become so fastidious and nice in its choice, that only one in a million is pronounced worthy of it.

No doubt there will be much self-betrayal in these pages, and he who can read between the lines, as a physiognomist would read character, will not find it difficult to read me. But then, this is the purpose of an Autobiography, and all will agree that it must be much more authentic than any record made of me by another man. Indeed, I wish to appear without disguise, as regards manners and opinions, habits and characteristics.

If a nation can be said to be happy which has no history, that man is also happy whose uneventful life has not brought him into prominence, and who has nothing to record but the passing of years between the cradle and the grave. But I was not sent into the world to be happy, nor to search for happiness. I was sent for a special work. Now, from innocent boyhood and trustful youth, I have advanced to some height whence I can look down, pityingly; as a father I can look down upon that young man, Myself, with a chastened pride; he has done well, he might have done better, but his life has been a fulfilment, since he has finished the work he was sent to do.

Amen.

PART I

AUTOBIOGRAPHY

THROUGH THE WORLD

THE AUTOBIOGRAPHY OF SIR HENRY MORTON STANLEY

CHAPTER I

THE WORKHOUSE

IT is said that one of the patrician Mostyns, of North Wales, possesses a written pedigree forty feet long, to prove the claim of his family to a direct descent from Adam. Though no doubt much of this extraordinary genealogy is fabulous, it allows all of us plebeians a reasonable hope to believe that we are also descended from that venerated ancestor of our common humanity. The time has been when patrician families fondly believed their first progenitor had come direct from Heaven, and we baser creatures had to be content with an earthly sire.

I can prove as ancient a descent for myself, though the names of my intermediate progenitors between Adam and my grandfathers, Moses and John, have not been preserved. My family belonged to a class always strangely indifferent to written pedigrees, which relied more on oral traditions, the preserving of which has been mostly the duties of females, on account of their superior fluency of speech, and their disposition to cling to their family hearth. My earliest pains were caused by the endless rehearsal of family history to which my nurse was addicted; for soon after sunset each evening she would insist on taking me before some neighbour's fire, where I would meet about a dozen dames from the Castle Row, prepared to indulge in their usual entertainment of recitations from their stock of unwritten folklore. After a ceremonious greeting and kindly interchange of civil enquiries about each other's health and affairs, they would soon drift into more serious matter. I have a vague idea that much of it bordered on the uncanny and awful, but I retain a strong impression that most of their conversations related to the past and present of their respective families, courtships, marriages, and deaths being prime events. I also remember that there were many long pauses, during which I could hear a chorus of sympathetic sighs. The episodes which drew these from their affectionate breasts are quite forgotten, but those sighs haunt me still.

Such families as were clustered in front of the Green of Denbigh Castle were an exceedingly primitive folk, with far less regard for ancient ancestry than the Bedouin of the Desert. Indeed, I doubt whether any tradesman or farmer in our parts could say who was his great-great-grandfather, or whether one yeoman out of a hundred could tell who was his ancestor of two hundred years back. As King Cazembe said to Livingstone, the 'Seeker of Rivers,' 'We let the streams run on, and do not enquire whence they rise or whither they flow.'

So these simple Welsh people would answer if questioned about their ancestors, 'We are born and die, and, beyond that, none of us care who were before us, or who shall come after us.'

My personal recollections do not extend beyond the time I lay in the cradle; so that all that precedes this period I have been obliged to take upon trust. Mind and body have grown together, and both will decay according to the tasks or burdens imposed on them. But strange, half-formed ideas glide vaguely into the mind, sometimes, and then I seem not far from a tangible and intelligent view into a distant age. Sometimes the turn of a phrase, a sentence in a book, the first faint outline of a scene, a face like, yet unlike, one whom I knew, an incident, will send my mind searching swiftly down the long-reaching aisles, extending far into remote, pre-personal periods, trying to discover the connection, to forge again the long-broken link, or to re-knit the severed strand.

My father I never knew. I was in my 'teens' before I learned that he had died within a few weeks after my birth. Up to a certain date in the early Forties, all is profound darkness to me. Then, as I woke from sleep one day, a brief period of consciousness suddenly dawned upon my faculties. There was an indefinable murmur about me, some unintelligible views floated before my senses, light flashed upon the spirit, and I entered into being.

At what age I first received these dim, but indelible, impressions, I cannot guess. It must have been in helpless

THE COTTAGE WHERE HENRY M. STANLEY WAS BORN

infancy, for I seem to have passed, subsequently, through a long age of dreams, wherein countless vague experiences, emotions, and acts occurred which, though indefinable, left shadowy traces on my memory. During such a mechanical stage of existence it was not possible for me to distinguish between dreams and realities.

I fancy I see a white ceiling, and square joists, with meat-hooks attached to them, a round, pink human face, the frill of a cap, a bit of bright ribbon; but, before I am able to grasp the meaning of what I see, I have lapsed into unconsciousness again. After an immeasurable time, the faculties seem to be re-awakened, and I can distinguish tones, and am aware that I can see, hear, and feel, and that I am in my cradle. It is close by a wooden staircase, and my eyes follow its length up, and then down; I catch sight of a house-fly, and then another, and their buzz and movements become absorbing. Presently a woman advances, bends over me a moment, then lifts me up in her arms, and from a great height I survey my world.

There is a settle of dark wood, a bit of carving at the end of it; there is a black, shiny chimney; a red coal-fire, with one spluttering jet of flame, and waving soot-flakes; there is a hissing black kettle, and a thread of vapour from the nozzle; a bright copper bed-warmer suspended to the wall; a display of coloured plates, mainly blue, with Chinese pictures on them, arranged over a polished dresser; there is an uneven flagstone floor; a window with diamond panes set in lead; a burnished white table, with two deep drawers in it; a curious old clock, with intensely red flowers above, and chains and weights below it; and, lastly, I see a door cut into two halves, the upper one being wide open, through which I gain my first view of sky and space. This last is a sight worth seeing, and I open my eyes roundly to take stock of this pearly space and its drifting fleece as seen through the door, and my attention is divided between the sky and the tick-tack of the clock, while forced to speculate what the white day and the pearly void mean.

There follows a transition into another state of conscious being wherein I appear to have wings, and to be soaring up to the roof of a great hall, and sailing from corner to corner, like a humming bee on a tour of exploration; and, the roof presently being removed, I launch out with wings outspread, joyous and free, until I lose myself in the unknowable, to emerge, sometime after, in my own cradle-nest at the foot of the wooden stairs.

And thus, for an unknown stretch of time, I endure my days without apparent object, but quietly observant, and an inarticulate witness of a multitude of small events; and thus I waited, and watched, and dreamed, surrendering myself to my state, undisturbed, unaffected, unresisting, borne along by Time until I could stand and take a larger and more deliberate survey of the strange things done around me. In process of time, however, my tongue learns to form words, and to enter upon its duties, and it is not long before intelligence begins to peep out and to retain durably the sense of existence.

One of the first things I remember is to have been gravely told that I had come from London in a band-box, and to have been assured that all babies came from the same place. It satisfied my curiosity for several years as to the cause of my coming; but, later, I was informed that my mother had hastened to her parents from London to be delivered of me; and that, after recovery, she had gone back to the Metropolis, leaving me in the charge of my grandfather, Moses Parry, who lived within the precincts of Denbigh Castle.

Forty years of my life have passed, and this delving into my earliest years appears to me like an exhumation of Pompeii, buried for centuries under the scoriæ, lava, and volcanic dust of Vesuvius. To the man of the Nineteenth Century, who paces the recovered streets and byeways of Pompeii, how strange seem the relics of the far distant life! Just so appear to me the little fatherless babe, and the orphaned child.

Up to a certain time I could remember well every incident connected with those days; but now I look at the child with wonder, and can scarcely credit that out of that child I grew. How quaint that bib and tucker, that short frock, the fat legs, the dimpled cheeks, the clear, bright, grey eyes, the gaping wonderment at the sight of a stranger; and I have to brush by the stupefied memories of a lifetime!

When I attempt to arrest one of the fleeting views of these early stages of my life, the foremost image which presents itself is that of my grandfather's house, a white-washed cottage, situated at the extreme left of the Castle, with a long garden at the back, at the far end of which was the slaughter-house where my Uncle Moses pole-axed calves, and prepared their carcasses for the market; and the next is of myself, in bib and tucker, between grandfather's knees, having my fingers guided, as I trace the alphabet letters on a slate. I seem to hear, even yet, the encouraging words of the old man, 'Thou wilt be a man yet before thy mother, my man of men.'

It was then, I believe, that I first felt what it was to be vain. I was proud to believe that, though women might be taller, stronger, and older than I, there lay a future before me that the most powerful women could never hope to win. It was then also I gathered that a child's first duty was to make haste to be a man, in order that I might attain that highest human dignity.

My grandfather appears to me as a stout old gentleman, clad in corduroy breeches, dark stockings, and long Melton coat, with a clean-shaven face, rather round, and lit up by humorous grey eyes. He and I occupied the top floor, which had an independent entrance from the garden. The lower rooms were inhabited by my uncles, Moses and Thomas. By-and-bye, there came a change. My strong, one-armed Uncle Moses married a woman named Kitty, a flaxen-haired, fair girl of a decided temper; and after that event we seldom descended to the lower apartments.

I have a vivid remembrance of Sunday evenings at a Wesleyan chapel, on account of the tortures which I endured. The large galleried building, crowded with fervid worshippers, and the deep murmur of 'Amens,' the pious ejaculations, are well remembered, as well as the warm atmosphere and curious scent of lavender which soon caused an unconquerable drowsiness in me. Within a short time my head began to nod heavily, to the great danger of my neck, and the resolute effort I made to overcome this sleepiness, to avoid the reproaches of my grandfather, who affected to be shocked at my extraordinary behaviour, caused the conflict with nature to be so painful that it has been impossible for me to forget the chapel and its scenes.

After passing my fourth year there came an afternoon when, to my dismay and fright, a pitcher with which I was sent for water fell from my hands and was broken. My grandfather came to the garden door on hearing the crash, and, viewing what had happened, lifted his forefinger menacingly and said, 'Very well, Shonin, my lad, when I return, thou shalt have a sound whipping. You naughty boy!'

A tragedy, however, intervened to prevent this punishment. It appears that he was in a hurry to attend to some work in a field that day, and, while there, fell down dead. The neighbours announced that he had died through the 'visitation of God,' which was their usual way of explaining any sudden fatality of this kind. He was aged 84. His tomb at Whitchurch declares the event to have occurred in 1847.

Soon after, I was transferred to the care of an ancient couple who lived at the other end of the Castle, named Richard and Jenny Price, keepers of the Bowling Green, into which one of the courts of the old Castle had been converted. The rate for my maintenance was fixed at half-a-crown a week, which my two uncles agreed to pay to the Prices. Old Richard Price, besides being a gamekeeper, was Sexton of Whitchurch, and Verger of St. David's. His wife Jenny, a stout and buxom old lady, is remembered by me mostly for her associations with 'peas-pudding,' for which I had a special aversion, and for her resolute insistence that, whether I liked it or not, I should eat it.

Other memories of this period are also unforgettable for the pains connected with them, — such as the soap-lather in my Saturday evening tub, and the nightly visits of Sarah Price, the daughter of the house, to her friends at Castle Row, where she would gossip to such a late hour that I always suffered from intolerable fidgets. Mothers of the present day will understand how hard it is for a child of four or five years old to remain awake long after sunset, and that it was cruel ignorance on the part of Sarah to keep me up until ten o'clock every night, to listen to her prosy stories of ghosts and graves. Sarah's description of a devil, a curious creature with horns on his head, with hoofed feet and a long tail, was wont to make me shiver with fright. She was equally graphic and minute in her descriptions of witches, ghosts, fairies, giants and dwarfs, kidnappers and hobgoblins, bugaboos, and other terrific monsters, against whose extraordinary powers it behoved me to be always on guard. The dark night was especially haunted by them, and the ingle-nook by a bright fire was then the safest place for children.

If the grown folk had not all shared Sarah's belief in these gruesome creatures, I might perhaps have doubted they existed; but I remember to have seen them huddle closer to the fire, look warily over their shoulders at the shadows, as though they lay in wait for a casual bit of darkness to pounce upon them and carry them off to the ghostly limbo. Had Sarah but known how pain impresses the memory of a child, it is probable that she would have put me to bed rather than have taken me with her, as a witness of her folly and ignorant credulity. She believed herself to be very level-headed, and, indeed, by her acquaintances she was esteemed as a sensible and clever woman; but, as she infected me with many silly fears, I am now inclined to believe that both she and her neighbours were sadly deficient in common-sense.

One effect of these interminable ghost-stories was visible one evening when I went to fetch some water from the Castle well. It appeared to me that I saw on this occasion a tall, black spectre, standing astride of the Castle well. I took it at first to be the shadow of a tree, but tracing it upward I saw a man's head which seemed to reach the sky. I gazed at it a short time, unable to move or cry out; then the phantom seemed to be advancing upon me, fear put wings to my feet, and I turned and ran, screaming, and never once halted until I had found a safe hiding-place under my bed. The dreadful vision of that ghost haunted me for years, and for a long time I made it a rule not to retire until I had looked under the bed, lest, when asleep, ghosts and kidnappers might come and carry me off. The belief that the darkness was infested by evil agencies and ferocious visitants hostile to little boys I owe to Sarah's silly garrulity at Castle Row.

I am under the impression that during the day, for a portion of this period, I was sent to an infant's school, where there was a terrible old lady who is associated in my mind with spectacles and a birch rod; but I have no particular incident connected with it to make it definite.

Richard Price and his wife Jenny seem to have, at last, become dismayed at my increasing appetite, and to have demanded a higher rate for my maintenance. As both my uncles had in the mean time married, and through the influence of their wives declined to be at further charge for me, the old couple resolved to send me to the Workhouse. Consequently Dick Price, the son, took me by the hand one day, Saturday, February 20th, 1847, and, under the pretence that we were going to Aunt Mary at Fynnon Beuno, induced me to accompany him on a long journey.

The way seemed interminable and tedious, but he did his best to relieve my fatigue with false cajolings and treacherous endearments. At last Dick set me down from his shoulders before an immense stone building, and, passing through tall iron gates, he pulled at a bell, which I could hear clanging noisily in the distant interior. A sombre-faced stranger appeared at the door, who, despite my remonstrances, seized me by the hand, and drew me within, while Dick tried to sooth my fears with glib promises that he was only going to bring Aunt Mary to me. The door closed on him, and, with the echoing sound, I experienced for the first time the awful feeling of utter desolateness.

The great building with the iron gates and innumerable windows, into which I had been so treacherously taken, was the St. Asaph Union Workhouse. It is an institution to which the aged poor and superfluous children of that parish are taken, to relieve the respectabilities of the obnoxious sight of extreme poverty, and because civilisation knows no better method of disposing of the infirm and helpless than by imprisoning them within its walls.

Once within, the aged are subjected to stern rules and useless tasks, while the children are chastised and disciplined in a manner that is contrary to justice and charity. To the aged it is a house of slow death, to the young it is a house of torture. Paupers are the failures of society, and the doom of such is that they shall be taken to eke out the rest of their miserable existence within the walls of the Workhouse, to pick oakum.

The sexes are lodged in separate wards enclosed by high walls, and every door is locked, and barred, and guarded, to preserve that austere morality for which these institutions are famous. That the piteous condition of these unfortunates may not arouse any sympathy in the casual visitor, the outcasts are clad in fustian suits, or striped cotton dresses, in which uniform garb they become undistinguishable, and excite no interest. Their only fault was that they had become old, or so enfeebled by toil and sickness that they could no longer sustain themselves, and this is so heinous and grave in Christian England that it is punished by the loss of their liberty, and they are made slaves.

At one time in English history such wretches were left to die by the wayside; at another time, they incurred the suspicion of being witches, and were either drowned or burnt; but in the reign of Queen Victoria the dull-witted nation has conceived it to be more humane to confine them in a prison, separate husband from wife, parent from child, and mete out to each inmate a daily task, and keep old and young under the strictest surveillance. At six in the morning they are all roused from sleep; and at 8 o'clock at night they are penned up in their dormitories. Bread, gruel, rice, and potatoes compose principally their fare, after being nicely weighed and measured. On Saturdays each person must undergo a thorough scrubbing, and on Sundays they must submit to two sermons, which treat of things never practised, and patiently kneel during a prayer as long as a sermon, in the evening.

It is a fearful fate, that of a British outcast, because the punishment afflicts the mind and breaks the heart. It is worse than that which overtakes the felonious convict, because it appears so unmerited, and so contrary to that which the poor have a right to expect from a Christian and civilised people.

Ages hence the nation will be wiser, and devise something more suited to the merits of the veteran toilers. It will convert these magnificent and spacious buildings into model houses for the poor, on the flat system, which may be done at little expense. The cruel walls which deprive the inmates of their liberty will be demolished, and the courts will be converted into grassy plats edged by flowering bushes. The stupid restraints on the aged will be abolished, husbands and wives will be housed together, their children will be restored to them after school hours. The bachelors and spinsters will dwell apart, the orphans will be placed in orphanages, the idiots in asylums, and the able-bodied tramp and idler in penitentiaries, and these costly structures will lose their present opprobrious character.

But now, as in 1847, the destitute aged and the orphans, the vagabonds and the idiots, are gathered into these institutions, and located in their respective wards according to age and sex. In that of St. Asaph the four wards meet in an octagonal central house, which contains the offices of the institution, and is the residence of the governor and matron.

It took me some time to learn the unimportance of tears in a workhouse. Hitherto tears had brought me relief in one shape or another, but from this time forth they availed nothing. James Francis, the one-handed schoolmaster into whose stern grasp Dick Price had resigned me, was little disposed to soften the blow dealt my sensibilities by treachery. Though forty-five years have passed since that dreadful evening, my resentment has not a whit abated. Dick's guile was well meant, no doubt, but I then learned for the first time that one's professed friend can smile while preparing to deal a mortal blow, and that a man can mask evil with a show of goodness. It would have been far better for me if Dick, being stronger than I, had employed compulsion, instead of shattering my confidence and planting the first seeds of distrust in a child's heart.

Francis, soured by misfortune, brutal of temper, and callous of heart, through years of control over children, was not a man to understand the cause of my inconsolable grief. Nor did he try. Time, however, alleviated my affliction, and the lapse of uncounted days, bringing their quota of smarts and pains, tended to harden the mind for life's great task of suffering. No Greek helot or dark slave ever underwent such discipline as the boys of St. Asaph under the heavy masterful hand of James Francis. The ready back-slap in the face, the stunning clout over the ear, the strong blow with the open palm on alternate cheeks, which knocked our senses into confusion, were so frequent that it is a marvel we ever recovered them again. Whatever might be the nature of the offence, or merely because his irritable mood required vent, our poor heads were cuffed, and slapped, and pounded, until we lay speechless and streaming with blood. But though a tremendously rough and reckless striker with his fist or hand, such blows were preferable to deliberate punishment with the birch, ruler, or cane, which, with cool malice, he inflicted. These instruments were always kept ready at hand. It simply depended upon how far the victim was from him, or how great was his fury, as to which he would choose to castigate us with. If we happened to be called up to him to recite our lessons, then the bony hand flew mercilessly about our faces and heads, or rammed us in the stomachs until our convulsions became alarming. If, while at the desk, he was reading to us, he addressed a question to some boy, the slightest error in reply would either be followed by a stinging blow from the ruler, or a thwack with his blackthorn. If a series of errors were discovered in our lessons, then a vindictive scourging of the offender followed, until he was exhausted, or our lacerated bodies could bear no more.[1]

My first flogging is well remembered, and illustrates the man's temper and nature thoroughly, and proves that we were more unfortunate than vicious. It was a Sunday evening in the early part of 1849. Francis was reading aloud to us the 41st chapter of Genesis, preliminary to dismissing us to our dormitory. There was much reference in the chapter to Joseph, who had been sold as a slave by his brothers, and had been promoted to high rank by Pharaoh. In order to test our attention, he suddenly looked up and demanded of me who it was that had interpreted the dream of the King. With a proud confidence I promptly replied, —

'Jophes, sir.'

'Who?'

'Jophes, sir.'

'Joseph, you mean.'

'Yes, sir, Jophes.'

Despite his repeated stern shouts of 'Joseph,' I as often replied 'Jophes,' wondering more and more at his rising

[1] James Francis had been a working collier at Mold until he met with an accident which deprived him of his left hand. As he had some education he was appointed Master of St. Asaph Union, where he remained during many years. He became more and more savage, and, at last, it was discovered he had lost his reason, and he died in a mad-house. — D. S.

wrath, and wherein lay the difference between the two names.

He grew tired at last, and laying hold of a new birch rod he ordered me to unbreech, upon which I turned marble-white, and for a moment was as one that is palsied, for my mind was struggling between astonishment, terror, and doubt as to whether my ears had heard aright, and why I was chosen to be the victim of his anger. This hesitation increased his wrath, and while I was still inwardly in a turmoil he advanced upon me, and rudely tore down my nether garment and administered a forceful shower of blows, with such thrilling effect that I was bruised and bloodied all over, and could not stand for a time. During the hour that followed I remained as much perplexed at the difference between 'Jophes' and 'Joseph' as at the peculiar character of the agonising pains I suffered. For some weeks I was under the impression that the scourging was less due to my error than to some mysterious connection it might have with Genesis.

With such a passionate teacher it may be imagined that we children increased his displeasure times without number. The restlessness of childhood, and nature's infirmities, contributed endless causes for correction. The unquiet feet, the lively tongues, defects of memory, listlessness, the effects of the climate, all sufficed to provoke his irritation, and to cause us to be summarily castigated with birch or stick, or pummelled without mercy.

Day after day little wretches would be flung down on the stone floor in writhing heaps, or stood, with blinking eyes and humped backs, to receive the shock of the ebony ruler, or were sent pirouetting across the school from a ruffianly kick, while the rest suffered from a sympathetic terror during such exhibitions, for none knew what moment he might be called to endure the like. Every hour of our lives we lived and breathed in mortal fear of the cruel hand and blighting glare of one so easily frenzied.

The second memorable whipping I received was during the autumn of 1851, the year of Rhuddlan Eisteddfod. Cholera was reported to be in the country, and I believe we were forbidden to eat fruit of any kind. Some weeks, however, after the edict had been issued, I and the most scholarly boy in the school were sent on an errand to the Cathedral town. When returning, we caught sight of a bunch of blackberries on the other side of a hedge, and, wholly oblivious of the consequences, we climbed over a gate into the field and feasted on the delicious fruit, and, of course, stained our fingers and lips. On reporting ourselves to Francis, it was evident by the way he gazed at us both that he guessed what we had been doing, but he said nothing, and we retired from him with a sense of relief. About half an hour after we all had been dismissed to our dormitory, and we were all quiet abed, the master's tramp was heard on the stairs, and when he appeared at the door he had a birch as large as a broom in his hand.

He stood long enough to remind us all that he had expressly forbidden us to eat any fruit from stall or hedge because of the sickness that was in the country; then, giving a swishing blow in the air with his birch, he advanced to my bed and with one hand plucked me out of bed, and forthwith administered a punishment so dreadful that blackberries suggested birching ever afterwards. He next went to the bed of the scholar George, who hitherto had escaped the experience he was now to undergo, because of his remarkable abilities. George, being new to the exquisite pain of flagellation, writhed and struggled to such an extent that he exasperated the master, and received double punishment, and his back, breast, and legs were covered with wounds.

The hard tasks imposed upon us, such as sweeping the playground with brooms more suited to giants than little children, the washing of the slated floors when one was stiff from caning, the hoeing of frost-bound ground, when every stroke on it caused the nerves to quiver, the thinly-clad body all the while exposed to a searching wind; the compelling us to commit whole pages to memory during the evening; in these, and scores of other ways, our treatment was ferocious and stupid.

Under such treatment as these examples describe, who could have supposed that any of the St. Asaph waifs would ever have developed into anything resembling respectable manhood? Yet several of these poor lads have since risen to receive a large measure of respect from Society. One of them has become a wealthy merchant, another is a vicar, a third is a colonial lawyer, and a fourth is a person of distinction in a South African State.

It is true that, though unfortunate in early infancy, many of these children were of sound, vigorous stock, and descended from people who had once been eminently respectable; and the diet, though meagre, was nourishing; but the inhuman discipline, the excessive confinement to school, ought to have dwarfed their bodies, crushed their spirits, and made them hopelessly imbecile.

Up to the eleventh year of age we all appeared to be of the same mould, and of a very level mediocrity. We were of the same cowed, submissive aspect, and were a mere flock of cropped little oddities, eating at the same table, rising from bed and retiring at the same minute, subject to the same ruthless discipline, and receiving the same lessons. There were four classes of us, and the grade of intelligence in each class was so alike that one might predict with certainty what year the infant of the fourth class would be promoted to a place in the first. Favoritism was impossible, for no boy possessed means, grace, or influence to mollify or placate such a monster as Francis. Clad in that uninteresting garb of squalid fustian, with hair mown close to the skull, brow-beaten and mauled indiscriminately, a god might have passed unnoticed by the average visitor. But as each boy verged on his eleventh year his aptitudes became more marked, and he became distinguished by a certain individuality of character and spirit.

The number of boys in our school averaged thirty, but out of that number only five could be picked out as possessing qualities rivalling those of the average clever boys of the best public schools. One named 'Toomis' was a born mathematician, another was famous for retentiveness of memory. George Williams was unusually distinguished for quick comprehension, while Billy, with his big head and lofty brow, astonished Her Majesty's Inspector, who prophesied great things of him in the future, while I, though not particularly brilliant in any special thing that I can remember, held my own as head of the school.

When the Eisteddfod was held at Rhuddlan in 1851, I was the one chosen to represent the genius of the school; but, soon after the nomination, I fell ill of measles, and Toomis succeeded to the honour. Apropos of this: exactly forty years later I was invited to preside over one of the meetings of the Eisteddfod, held at Swansea, but as I was preparing for this honour, a fall at Mürren, Switzerland, resulted in the fracture of my left leg, which rendered my appearance impossible.

The other boys in the school consisted of the dunces, the indolent, the malingerers, the would-be truants, the dull, the noisy, the fat-witted majority, just six times more numerous than the naturally-able boys. This proportion of one in six is very common in the world. In ships that I have sailed in, among the military companions with whom I have campaigned, among the blacks and the whites of my African expeditions, in the House of Commons, and in Congress, the leaven of one in six seemed to be required to keep things rightly going.

When Bishop Vowler Short — who had once been tutor to Cardinal Newman — appeared on his annual visit to the school, he was heard to express high approval of the attainments of some of the boys in the first class, and, after honouring them with valuable souvenirs, graciously blessed them.

When Captain Leigh Thomas, the Chairman of the Board of Guardians, who was a local magnate, and of Indian distinction — being descended from that Captain George Thomas, who, in the last century, rose from obscurity to the rank of an Indian prince in North-West India — visited us, he pointed out to Francis promising traits in several of the head boys, and was not too proud to pat us on the head, and elevate us by kind encouragements with a hope that there were bright rewards in store for some of us for our manifest abilities.

Her Majesty's Inspector of Schools on his tour of inspection professed to discover in some of our boys the signs of unusual intelligence, and, calling one up to him, felt his head and his temples, and then turned round to Francis, and declared, in our acute hearing, that he felt assured 'that boy would be a prodigy of learning if he went on.'

Our parson — Mr. Smalley, of Cwm — unbent one day to examine us on Scripture History, and one boy so astonished him by his wonderful memory, and quick and correct answers, that he exclaimed, 'Why, Francis, you have quite a young Erasmus here.'

The famous Hicks Owen, of Rhyllon, examined us in geography one time, and was pleased to say, on concluding, that some of us knew far more geography than he knew himself, and that to prevent being shamed by us he would have to study his gazetteers and atlas before he ventured among us a second time.

The auditor of the Board, after testing Toomis's proficiency in mathematics, laughingly called him young Babbage, and a lightning calculator.

Such commendation was a great encouragement and stimulus. The rarity of it, I suppose, impressed it on our minds, and the sweetness of the praise had a more penetrating effect than blame or bruise.

The difference between our school and the public grammar school of the period lay in the fact that our instruction was principally religious and industrial, while in the other it was mainly secular and physical. The aim of the Guardians appeared to be the making of commonplace farmers, tradesmen, and mechanics, and instead of the gymnasium, our muscles were practised in spade industry, gardening, tailoring, and joiner's work.

Our outdoor games were of a gentle and innocent kind, and only pursued when the weather prohibited the use of the hoe and spade. We instinctively chased humble-bees, daddy-long-legs, we played with cowslip-balls, wove chains of dandelion flowers, and made chaplets of buttercups. The oldsters, through some mysterious connection with the outside boy-world, became acquainted with spring-tops, tip-cat, kite-flying, hop-scotch, and marbles, leap-frog, hen-and-chickens, and follow-my-leader. Through some means, the art of telling the time by thistledown, and of divining by blowing the tassel, had been introduced among us. We sometimes played hide-and-seek, and excited ourselves by mild gambling with stones. At rare intervals we blackened one another's eyes, but, from fear of consequences, our quarrels were more often settled by wrestling, when the victor might indulge his spleen by thumping the fallen without marking the face. We were firm believers in nocturnal visitants, and in the magic of the rhyme,

'Rain, rain, go to Spain,
Sun, sun, come again.'

The mimetic power was early developed in me. The school-teacher, and various country persons, the old porter even, were mimicked well enough to draw the applause of my school-mates.

We joyfully looked forward to the coming of May, which always preceded the season of sunshine and outdoor play on the lush green plats outside of the walls. We faithfully observed St. Valentine's Day, the 29th of May, the 5th of November, and the 30th of January, for the names of Guy Fawkes, and Charles I and II, were well known to us. Good Friday was always a gloomy day with us, and Easter was solemn; but Christmas became associated with pudding, toffee, and apples, and was the most welcome day in the year.

We were Church folk, and were swayed by her festivals. Most of us could repeat the Morning Service from memory, a few knew the Collects and Psalms by heart, for they had been given to us so frequently as tasks because of their sub-divisions, and because it was deemed necessary to keep us constantly occupied; and as, morning and evening, we performed our devotions, we grew marvellously familiar with Sacred History.

Our school was a little world in miniature. Most of those now prominent in my recollection had been foreshadowed by traits which distinguished my school-mates. The small creatures were faithful prototypes of scores of adults I have since met in various parts of the world. If they have not met with their deserts, good, bad, or indifferent, it must be because of their lack, or misuse, of opportunities, or accident. There were some among them good enough for heaven, there were others who seemed wholly vile. Even at that early age I held a belief that some of them would become heroes and saints, and would be world-famous, while there were two or three whom I regarded as too despicable for human intercourse. Time, however, has proved me to have been wrong. My saint occupies an average place among common men, my hero is lost in the deep silence, my criminals are probably as good yeomen as could be wished, my ideals of imbecility are modest citizens, but from among the unobserved flock have emerged two or three to note and worth.

Meantime, remote and secluded from the world without our gates, which rode in fine chariots, or sat in glory on the roof of the 'Jellamanjosy' coach, or strode free along the Queen's highway, we vegetated within the high walls surrounding our home of lowliness. We could take no part in public rejoicings, or grieve in its sorrows; we knew no Royal or State occasions, shared in no jubilant celebrations, and were equally ignorant of public panics and disturbances, as of the pomp and woes of war. In the Crimea there might be a million of men gathered together to play at the dangerous game of cannon-balls, and to batter one another into shapeless fragments; London might roar day and night with its thunderous traffic; Birmingham might be suffocating under the fumes of its furnaces; and Manchester might vibrate under the force of its accumulated mechanisms, — to us it mattered as little as though we were in another planet.

Year after year we noted the passing of the seasons by the budding blossoms, the flight of bees, the corn which changed from green to gold, the fall and whirl of leaves, followed soon after by white snow, and blasts of nipping winds, which stiffened our muscles, and sent us shivering to the fire.

The little shops near and in St. Asaph had somehow the air of large-hearted benevolence, which I never knew to be realised. How often I tried to peep in, that I might understand the ways of these singular people, having by right divine the privilege of dispensing to all men unlimited stores of food and clothing! How I envied the grocer's boy, who could dig his hands at his pleasure into inexhaustible barrels of currants and boxes of raisins, and the plenteous loaves of white fragrant sugar, or the smart youth with the blue necktie, who might wear any gorgeous robe he chose, for I believed it was only his modesty which prevented him from appearing in crimson, or yellow, silk and satin!

We had reason to believe that the great world outside contained lower depths of misery than anything experienced by us; for, now and then, we caught glimpses of horrid, unkempt vagrants as they came to the porter's lodge for a lodging; and, during our visits to St. Asaph, we could not enter the town without being impressed with the squalor of the Irish Square, which made us glad that we were not so disreputable as the ragged urchins of that sordid locality. Little as we were aware of it, our minds were becoming soiled by prejudices, just as our boots were stained with the greasy mud of that neighbourhood. The repulsiveness of the Square, and the insolence of the smutty-faced, bare-footed *gamins*, made us believe that Irishmen and Roman Catholics were barbarians and idolaters, and when, losing patience with their yelping clamour, we turned to resent their attacks, and saw them skurry to their kennels, we believed ourselves justified in the opinion that the young brats knew nothing of fair fighting. Once this opinion became fixed, no amount of argument would avail to prove its injustice.

Probably the very morning that I had had to bide the brunt of their savage rudeness, and had been disgusted with their ugliness, had seen me superintending the cleaning of our dormitory, with a zeal inspired by my firm belief that before we could be called good, we must be clean, within and without, and that our hearts, our persons, and our dwellings, should be without stain. How I came to manifest the passion of a fanatic for order and cleanliness I know not, yet when it was my turn to clean up and make the beds, I was seized with a consuming desire to exhibit everything at its best, to arrange the beds without a single crease or pucker, to make the folds with mathematical exactness, to dust and polish cupboards and window-sills until they were speckless, and to make the flagstones shine like mirrors. 'There,' I would say to my companions detailed for these duties, my eyes sparkling with pride, 'that is the way to wash a floor. Let us make the beds fit for princes to sleep in'; and hard after this triumph of order and neatness I would perhaps be despatched to the town to have every sense offended by the miracles of dirt and disorder in and around the Irish Square. No wonder that we felt unmitigated scorn for Irish habits and ways!

There were two or three boys, even among us, whom we should have exiled among the Irish had we the power. We felt it to be degradation to be near them at school. One was remarkable for a pasty complexion, small, piggish eyes, white eyelashes, and carroty hair. Another had projecting gooseberry eyes, which suggested that they might fall from him some day, as from a bush. His stubborn soul could endure thumping without bellowing, though a tear or two would trickle. His mouth was like that of a beast, and garnished with great, jagged teeth; and, altogether, he was so unlovely as to shock every sense in us. Between Francis and ourselves, they had a hard time of it; and I often wonder how fate has disposed of them during this long interval.

When I reached my eleventh year, the king of the school for beauty and amiability was a boy of about my own age, named Willie Roberts. Some of us believed that he belonged to a very superior class to our own. His coal-black hair curled in profusion over a delicately moulded face of milky whiteness. His eyes were soft and limpid, and he walked with a carriage which tempted imitation. Beyond these indications of him I remember but little, for just then I fell ill with some childish malady which necessitated my removal to the infirmary, where I lay for weeks. But as I was becoming convalescent I was startled by a rumour that he had suddenly died.

When I heard that his body was in the dead-house I felt stricken with a sense of irreparable loss. As the infirmary opened upon the court-yard which contained our *morgue*, some of the boys suggested that it might be possible to view him, and, prompted by a fearful curiosity to know what death was like, we availed ourselves of a favourable opportunity, and entered the house with quaking hearts. The body lay on a black bier, and, covered with a sheet, appeared uncommonly long for a boy. One of the boldest drew the cloth aside, and at the sight of the waxen face with its awful fixity we all started back, gazing at it as if spell-bound. There was something grand in its superb disregard of the chill and gloom of the building, and in the holy calm of the features. It was the face of our dear Willie, with whom we had played, and yet not the same, for an inexplicable aloofness had come over it. We yearned to cry out to him to wake, but dared not, for the solemnity of his face was appalling.

Presently the sheet was drawn further away, and we then saw what one of us had insinuated might be seen. The body was livid, and showed scores of dark weals. One glance was enough, and, hastily covering it, we withdrew, with minds confirmed in the opinion that signs of violence would appear after death as testimonies against him who was guilty of it. After what we had seen, it would have been difficult for anyone to have removed from our minds the impression that Francis was accountable for Willie's death.

For weeks after this my first thought in the morning was of Willie's dead face, and, in consequence, I could not help looking into every face with something of pity that mankind should be born for death and burial in the cold remorseless earth. When I re-entered the school I found myself curiously regarding Francis, and wondering that he was so insensible to the miserable fate in store for him, and that he could be so pitiless in his cruelty to his fellow-sufferers. What would he say, I thought, when the Judge, who would come to judge the quick and the dead, would ask him, 'What hast thou done to thy brother Willie?'

Some time after Willie's death, George, the scholar, and I became as chummy as twin brothers. He was not so amiable as Willie, but we believed him to be severely good, and far more learned, by which he obtained our respect. He was not a zealous friend, and after some intimacy with him I was often chilled with what appeared to be selfishness in him. It may have been that I was too exacting, but I certainly thought that it was not in his nature to be scrupulous in the keeping of the pact of chumship. If a cake or an apple was to be divided into two, an uneasy feeling came over me that he took pains to pick out the larger half, and in any dispute with other boys George was not so resolutely insistent on my behalf as the vow of brotherhood demanded. After a few weeks of effort to make inward apologies for his laxity and backwardness, it was forced upon me that he was by nature indifferent to his obligations, and it was agreed that each should be a friend unto himself for the future. There was no quarrel, however, but we parted with mutual respect.

About this period I came across a pious romance — the title of which is forgotten — relating to three young brothers or friends, — one of whom I remember was named Enoch, — who for their perfect piety were attended by a Guardian Angel. They had set out on travels through a land which must have been subtropical, from its luxurious vegetation and its beflowered scenes; but whatever might be the perils they encountered, or the temptations that beset them, the unseen guardian was always near them, and made them strong, confident, and victorious. The stories of Joseph, David, and Daniel, and the three brave youths at Babylon had powerfully affected me, but, unfortunately, their associations with tasks and rods had marred their attractions. My delight in saintly Enoch and his friends was unalloyed by any such bitter memories. The story was also written in an easy every-day language, and the scenes were laid in a country wherein God's presence was still felt. God had departed from Canaan, and He had cast off Israel, and now His protection was vouchsafed to all the children of men without distinction, and only piety and prayer were needed to secure His aid in times of distress.

Above the fireplaces in the schoolroom, the two dormitories, and dining-hall, were tacked painted iron sheets which were inscribed with appropriate Scriptural texts. We had Bible lessons morning and evening, collects and gospels to commit to memory. Our shelves held a fair collection of religious literature, — memoirs of Wesley, Fletcher, lives of Bunyan, Fox, Milton, and others of less note, sermons, and commentaries. Twice on Sunday we had full services, and after supper the porter of the establishment, who was a Methodist of super-fervid zeal, would treat us to a lengthy and noisy prayer, which, as I think of it now, was rather a tedious string of adjurations to, and incriminations of the Almighty, than a supplication for grace to the Creator.

But all these religious exercises and literature had not such direct immediate effect as this romantic novelette. I now conceived God to be a very real personage, as active to-day as in Biblical periods in His supervision of mundane concerns. I fancied God's Presence visible in many small events, but, to obtain the Divine interposition in one's favour, it was necessary to earnestly solicit it, and to be worthy of it by perfect sinlessness. Here was a great difficulty. It was not possible to be wholly free from sin in our circumstances. I observed that our seniors, though they punctiliously went through the forms of prayer, were none of them blameless. They were cruelly unkind, they were unjust in their punishments, they were censorious without cause, and most ungentle. They asked for

God's forgiveness for their trespasses, but were relentless in their condemnation of the smallest fault we committed. When I came to think of that beast Will Thomas, and that imp Davies, and that tale-bearer and mischief-maker Williams, my gorge rose against them, and I felt that the circumstances of Enoch's life were not like mine.

However, I made a grand effort to free myself from my vanity and pride. I compelled myself for a season to make the sacrifices demanded of me. I championed ugly Will against his oppressors, and suppressed my scorn of Davies. I strove to like Williams, though I feared he was incorrigible. I sought to surprise each of them with good offices, and in the process endured much contumely, because human beings are so prone to misconstrue one's actions. I rose at midnight to wrestle in secret with my wicked self, and, while my school-fellows sweetly reposed, I was on my knees, laying my heart bare before Him who knows all things, vowing that the next day should be a witness of my sincerity, and that I would have no fear of derision for attempts at well-doing. I would promise to abstain from wishing for more food, and, to show how I despised the stomach and its pains, I would divide one meal out of the three among my neighbours; half my suet pudding should be given to Ffoulkes, who was afflicted with greed, and, if ever I possessed anything that excited the envy of another, I would at once surrender it. Greater proof than these of my resolve to be perfect I thought I could not show, and when I had done my part, I hoped to see the sign of God's favour in milder treatment by Francis.

I cannot recollect that the season which I devoted to the subjection of self witnessed the lenity which I anticipated, or that it had any effect beyond a feeling of physical weakness; but, indirectly, I am not sure that it was wholly without gain. Without the faith which supported me, I might never have thought of experimenting on Will and practising it on myself, my dislikes, and passions, and placing them at the service of those I had despised; and I am inclined to think that the feeling of friendlessness was soothed. It was a comfort to know that though without a parent, relation, or friend on earth to turn to, I had a Father in Heaven before Whom I was the equal of the mightiest.

I believed in the immediate presence of Angels who were deputed to attend us for our protection, that the emissaries of the Evil One ranged about during the darkness of the night, seeking to wreak their spite against those averse to them, and I believed that the frightful dreams from which we sometimes suffered were due to their machinations.

Sometimes I woke up in the middle of the night, after a tremendous struggle with a nightmare, and, gaspingly looking out, fancied I saw the evil spirits crowding the darkness and sailing about like huge fantastic microbes, or standing, shadowy-grey, at the foot of the bed. I would rub my eyes hard for a clearer vision, and I would observe them retreat against the cold bare walls. Within, all was terror and confusion, entreaties to Heaven for protection, admonition respecting some neglect of prayer, or coldness in devotion; and I would rise from bed on being thus informed of the remedy, and indulge in the sacred theft of prayer with the humbleness due from a little child praying to the Universal Father and Creator.

If, by accident, I was discovered, the day following was certain to be one of torture, an opprobrious nickname, or bitter gibe, taunts, immodest expressions or gestures; every kind of conspiracy would be made to excite the demon that lurks within every human breast, so that by night, what with hate of my fellows, burning anger at their atrocious conduct, remorse for having succumbed to rage at their wicked practices, I had collapsed from my virtuous state, to be again brought to my sense of inborn sinfulness by some nightly visitation, or a curious gush of tearful repentance, and an agony of longing for the love of some human being.

The religious convictions of my childhood were too intense and real to omit recalling them. Often it appeared as though it were wholly useless to struggle against evil, yet there was an infinitesimal improvement in each stage. The character was becoming more and more developed. The temper was becoming firmer. Experience was teaching me something of that great lesson of life which enables one to view more calmly lapses of condition.

Thus there are two things for which I feel grateful to this strange institution of St. Asaph. My fellow-man had denied to me the charm of affection, and the bliss of a home, but through his charity I had learned to know God by faith, as the Father of the fatherless, and I had been taught to read. It is impossible that in a Christian land like Wales I could have avoided contracting some knowledge of the Creator, but the knowledge which is gained by hearing is very different from that which comes from feeling. Nor is it likely that I would have remained altogether ignorant of letters. Being as I was, however, the circumstances of my environment necessarily focussed my attention on religion, and my utterly friendless state drove me to seek the comfort guaranteed by it.

It would be impossible to reveal myself, according to the general promise involved in the title of this book, if I were to be silent regarding my religious convictions. Were I to remain silent, the true key to the actions of my life would be missing. Or, rather, let me try to put the matter more clearly: the secret influence which inspired what good I may have done in life, for the same reason prevented me from doing evil, curbed passion, guided me when the fires of youth, licentious company, irreverent mates, and a multitude of strange circumstances must have driven me into a confirmed state of wickedness.

I was therefore grateful, after all, for the implanting of religious principles in me by the Biblical education given me in the Union. The fear of doing wrong intentionally, the feeling of reverence, the impulse of charity, the possession of a conscience, are all due to this. Without this teaching I should have been little superior to the African savage. It has been the driving power for good, the arrestor of evil. It has given me an acute and perceptive monitor, able by its own delicacy to perceive evil no matter how deceptive its guise. It has formed a magnet by which to steer more straightly than I could otherwise have done.

My belief that there was a God, overseeing every action, observing and remembering, has come often between me and evil. Often when sorely tempted, came the sudden strength to say, 'No, I *will* not, it will be wicked; not criminal, but sinful; God sees me.' It is precisely for this strength that I am grateful. Reason would not have been sufficient to restrain me from yielding to temptation. It required a conscience, and a religious conviction created it. That same inward monitor has restrained me from uttering idle words, from deceiving my fellow-creatures with false promises, and from hastily condemning them without sufficient evidence, from listening to slanders, and from joining with them, from yielding to vindictiveness; it has softened a nature that without its silent and gentle admonitions would, I am sure, be much worse than it is. I do not claim that it has always been successful, — far from it, — but I am grateful for what it has done; and this feeling, so long as I possess it, will induce me to hope that it will ever remain with me, a restraining power, a monitor to do my duty to my Creator, and to my fellow-men.

Whether these religious convictions would have continued with me had I lived the life of the city is another question. I think not. At least, not in sufficient force. A journalist's life in New York does not give time for reflection or introspection.

Religion grew deep roots in me in the solitude of Africa, so that it became my mentor in civilization, my director, my spiritual guide. With religious conviction we can make real and substantial progress; it gives body, pith, and marrow; without it, so-called progress is empty and impermanent, — for without the thought of God we are tossed about on a sea of uncertainty; for what is our earth compared with the vast universe of worlds in unmeasurable space? But above all the vastness of infinity, of which the thoughts of the wisest men can extend to but an infinitesimal fraction, is the Divine and Almighty Intellect which ordered all this; and to Him I turn, — the Source of the highest energy, the Generator of the principle of duty.

In the adults' ward at St. Asaph was a harmless imbecile, named John Holywell, who had been a resident of the house for about a score of years. He was now over fifty, and was likely to remain until his body was conveyed to a pauper's grave. As his fate, so mine promised, except that I could pray and read.

Tyranny of the grossest kind lashed and scowled at us every waking hour, but even Will Thomas possessed something that I had not. He had relations who occasionally visited him with gifts; but I was alone, none ever came to see me.

I must have been twelve ere I knew that a mother was

indispensable to every child. To most boys of twelve such a simple fact must have been obvious, but as my grandsire and nurse had sufficed for my earliest wants, the necessity for a mother had not been manifest to me. Now that I was told my mother had entered the house with two children, my first feeling was one of exultation that I also had a mother, and a half-brother and a half-sister, and the next was one of curiosity to know what they were like, and whether their appearance portended a change in my condition.

Francis came up to me during the dinner-hour, when all the inmates were assembled, and, pointing out a tall woman with an oval face, and a great coil of dark hair behind her head, asked me if I recognised her.

'No, Sir,' I replied.

'What, do you not know your own mother?'

I started, with a burning face, and directed a shy glance at her, and perceived she was regarding me with a look of cool, critical scrutiny. I had expected to feel a gush of tenderness towards her, but her expression was so chilling that the valves of my heart closed as with a snap. 'Honour thy father and mother,' had been repeated by me a thousand times, but this loveless parent required no honour from me. After a few weeks' residence my mother departed, taking her little boy with her, but the girl was left in the institution; and, such is the system prevailing, though we met in the same hall for months, she remained as a stranger to me.

Among the notable incidents of this age was the suicide of the Governor, who through some mental strain ended his life with a razor. Then there was a burglary, or an attempt at one, in our schoolroom. We found one morning that one of the windows had been forced open, the poker lay on the table, and there were traces of the bookshelves and desks having been ransacked. After that, handsome Harry Ogden, who had been sent to Kinmel on an errand, returned highly intoxicated, which made us boys marvel at his audacity. Then Barney Williams, one of the cleverest boys in the school, was detected stealing stamps from the Master's letters, which offence was brought to the notice of the Guardians, and was punished by a public birching, as much, we believed, to the satisfaction of Francis as to the anguish of poor Barney.

Bishop Short having presented to us some skeleton drawings and views of cathedrals, I took to copying them, and in a few months had acquired such excellence that my reputation spread wide in our circle. Francis affected to believe that I was destined for a 'limner.' The Bishop rewarded me with a Bible bearing his autograph. Miss Smalley, of Cwm, presented me with a drawing-book and pencils, and I was introduced to a number of notabilities around as the 'artist' of the school. Other small accomplishments tended to bring me into prominence. My recitations were much admired. On our annual holidays I was selected to lead the choir of glee-singers, and, after the Government Inspector's examinations, I was pronounced to be the most advanced pupil.

I have no idea of my personal appearance at this time, but I remember to have heard some comments from bystanders as we bathed at Rhyl which made me blush violently, also Captain Thomas saying that it would be of vast benefit to me if I were put under a garden-roller. An old blacksmith of Denbigh, as I passed him one day, asked me if I was not the grandson of Moses Parry, and on my admitting it, pretended that I could not belong to the big-boned Parry breed; while one that stood by him terrified me by saying that I would be in prime order for eating, after a month's stuffing on raisins and sweeties. From an early age I contracted an intense dislike to these wretched personalities.

In process of time my classmates, who had grown with me, and been promoted simultaneously with myself, and now filled the first form, began to be taken away by their relatives, or entered service. Benjie Phillips became a page of Captain Thomas. When we saw him arrayed in his beautiful livery, George, the scholar, and I thought fortune most unkind and indiscriminating; but, looking backward, both of us must confess that, like fools, we knew not what was good for us. Fortune had reserved us for other work, but before we should be called we were fated to be tried a little more.

> 'Time teaches us that oft One Higher,
> Unasked, a happier lot bestows
> Than if each blighted dream's desire
> Had blossomed as the rose.'

Barney was the next to leave. Toomis, the calculator, found

employment with the Whiteley of the neighbourhood; and, finally, George, the scholar, was claimed by an uncle to be prepared for the ministry.

When, in 1856, the time came for Francis's annual visit to his friends at Mold, he appointed me his deputy over the school. On the very first day of his absence, a boy named David, my especial *bête noire* on the play-ground, and whose malice was a source of trouble to me, thought fit to question my fitness for the post, and persisted in noisy demonstrations against my authority. For a while the serious nature of a conflict with one who had often proved himself my superior in strength restrained me from noticing his breach of order. The sharp-witted boys of the first class observed this reluctance, and rightly accounted for it. They also soon became insolently boisterous, and I had to cry 'Silence!' as imperiously as possible. There was an instant's hush from habit at the word, but, overcoming their first fear, and prompted by mischievous David, the buzz was resumed, and soon became intolerable.

I strode up in front of David, and ordered him to take his stand at the Dunce's corner, which he scornfully declined at once. He dared me to compel him, and added biting words about my puny strength and impudence. Instinctively, the school felt that an exciting struggle was impending, and suspended their restlessness. I was forced to accept David's challenge, but when his sinewy arms embraced me I would gladly have compromised with him had my pride permitted, for the unbending rigidity of his stiff back was terrifying to think of. We contended breathlessly for some time, but, finally, I succeeded in kicking his stubborn pins from under him, and he fell heavily undermost. In a few seconds I rode in triumph over his prostrate form, and demanded his submission, which he sullenly refused. Dicky, more friendly than the others, came forward at the call with a woollen muffler, and with his assistance I made David captive, and after binding the tense arms conducted him to the opprobrious corner, where he was left to meditate, with two others similarly guilty. From the hour when the heroic whelp, David, was subdued, my authority was undisputed. Often since have I learned how necessary is the application of force for the establishment of order. There comes a time when pleading is of no avail.

Not many weeks after Francis had returned from Mold, an event occurred which had a lasting influence on my life. But for the stupid and brutal scene which brought it about, I might eventually have been apprenticed to some trade or another, and would have mildewed in Wales, because, with some knowledge of my disposition, I require great cause to break away from associations. Unknown to myself, and unperceived by anyone else, I had arrived at the parting of the ways. Unconsciously I had contracted ideas about dignity, and the promise of manhood was manifest in the first buds of pride, courage, and resolution; but our school-master, exposed to moods of savage temper, and arbitrary from habit, had failed to notice the change.

In May, 1856, a new deal table had been ordered for the school, and some heedless urchin had dented its surface by standing on it, which so provoked Francis that he fell into a furious rage, and uttered terrific threats with the air of one resolved on massacre. He seized a birch which, as yet, had not been bloodied, and, striding furiously up to the first class, he demanded to know the culprit. It was a question that most of us would have preferred to answer straight off; but we were all absolutely ignorant that any damage had been made, and probably the author of it was equally unaware of it. No one could remember to have seen anyone standing on the table, and in what other manner mere dents had been impressed in the soft deal wood was inexplicable. We all answered accordingly.

'Very well, then,' said he, 'the entire class will be flogged, and, if confession is not made, I will proceed with the second, and afterwards with the third. Unbutton.'

He commenced at the foot of the class, and there was the usual yelling, and writhing, and shedding of showers of tears. One or two of David's oaken fibre submitted to the lacerating strokes with a silent squirm or two, and now it was fast approaching my turn; but instead of the old timidity and other symptoms of terror, I felt myself hardening for resistance. He stood before me vindictively glaring, his spectacles intensifying the gleam of his eyes.

'How is this?' he cried savagely. 'Not ready yet? Strip, sir, this minute; I mean to stop this abominable and barefaced lying.'

'I did not lie, sir. I know nothing of it.'

'Silence, sir. Down with your clothes.'

'Never again,' I shouted, marvelling at my own audacity.

The words had scarcely escaped me ere I found myself swung upward into the air by the collar of my jacket, and flung into a nerveless heap on the bench. Then the passionate brute pummelled me in the stomach until I fell backward, gasping for breath. Again I was lifted, and dashed on the bench with a shock that almost broke my spine. What little sense was left in me after these repeated shocks made me aware that I was smitten on the cheeks, right and left, and that soon nothing would be left of me but a mass of shattered nerves and bruised muscles.

Recovering my breath, finally, from the pounding in the stomach, I aimed a vigorous kick at the cruel Master as he stooped to me, and, by chance, the booted foot smashed his glasses, and almost blinded him with their splinters. Starting backward with the excruciating pain, he contrived to stumble over a bench, and the back of his head struck the stone floor; but, as he was in the act of falling, I had bounded to my feet, and possessed myself of his blackthorn. Armed with this, I rushed at the prostrate form, and struck him at random over his body, until I was called to a sense of what I was doing by the stirless way he received the thrashing.

I was exceedingly puzzled what to do now. My rage had vanished, and, instead of triumph, there came a feeling that, perhaps, I ought to have endured, instead of resisting. Some one suggested that he had better be carried to his study, and we accordingly dragged him along the floor to the Master's private room, and I remember well how some of the infants in the fourth room commenced to howl with unreasoning terror.

After the door had been closed on him, a dead silence, comparatively, followed. My wits were engaged in unravelling a way out of the curious dilemma in which I found myself. The overthrow of the Master before the school appeared to indicate a new state of things. Having successfully resisted once, it involved a continued resistance, for one would die before submitting again. My friend Mose asked me in a whisper if I knew what was to happen. Was the Master dead? The hideous suggestion changed the whole aspect of my thoughts. My heart began to beat, as my imagination conjured up unknown consequences of the outrage to authority; and I was in a mood to listen to the promptings of Mose that we should abscond. I assented to his proposal, but, first, I sent a boy to find out the condition of the Master, and was relieved to find that he was bathing his face.

Mose and I instantly left the school, for the ostensible purpose of washing the blood from my face; but, as a fact, we climbed over the garden-wall and dropped into Conway's field, and thence hastened through the high corn in the Bodfari direction, as though pursued by bloodhounds.

This, then, was the result of the folly and tyranny of Francis. Boys are curious creatures, innocent as angels, proud as princes, spirited as heroes, vain as peacocks, stubborn as donkeys, silly as colts, and emotional as girls. The budding reason is so young and tender that it is unable to govern such composite creatures. Much may be done with kindness, as much may be done with benevolent justice, but undeserved cruelty is almost sure to ruin them.

We ran away with a boundless belief that beyond the walls lay the peopled South that was next to Heaven for happiness. The singing birds, the rolling coaches, the tides of joyous intercourse, the family groups, the happy hearths, the smiling welcome of our kind, all lay beyond the gates, and these we fled to meet, with the innocence of kids.

CHAPTER II

ADRIFT

WHATEVER innocent trust I may have entertained, that beyond the walled domain of the Union House I should meet with glad friends, was doomed to an early disappointment. I had often dreamed of a world that was next to Heaven for happiness. Many a long summer evening I had spent looking out of our windows upon the radiant vale of Clwyd, and the distant lines of hills which rose beyond leafy Cefn, exciting my imagination by the recital to myself of fanciful delights, which I believed to exist beyond the far horizon. The tides of humanity, as they swept gaily over the highroad in view of our gates, had seemed very beautiful and happy; but, at the first contact with the highly privileged people whom we met on the turnpike, they did not appear so gracious to me. Whether they rolled-by in carriages, or sat on the coach, enjoyed the air at the cottage-door, or smashed stones by the road-side, drove swift gigs, or tramped afoot like ourselves, all alike were harsh and forbidding. Even lads of our own age and frocked children assailed us with scorn and abuse.

It impressed itself on me that we were outcasts. We wore the Workhouse livery, and this revealed the sphere we belonged to, to all who met us. Beings in that garb had no business on the public road! We were clearly trespassers. What with the guilty feeling of having absconded, and outraging the public sense by our appearance in scenes where we were undoubted aliens, we began to feel exceedingly uncomfortable, and shrank from the view of every one.

As night approached, other anxieties troubled us sorely. Where should we sleep? How should we subsist? We could not remain always in hiding. The sun was about setting when we came across a disused lime-kiln. We crept through the arch into the open bowl-like interior. By cuddling together, we could just find room in the bottom to sleep; but, as it was still daylight, our feet could be seen through the opening of the arch by the passers-by, and we should be taken prisoners. We therefore had to lean on the sides of the kiln until the darkness came, before we could forget our misery in sleep. In this awkward position we waited silently for the darkness.

Our limbs ached with fatigue, our spirits were dejected. In about an hour, probably, it would be dark; but in such a mood, what a time to wait! Many illusions disappeared. Nothing of what I had seen through the Workhouse windows was real. I had been all the time dreaming, having taken too seriously facts which had been sugared with pleasantness for our childish minds. The world was ugly, cruel, and hard, and all grown-up people were liars. From my nurse and old women, my head had been crammed with ghost stories, and I had become a believer in signs, omens, auguries, and fetishism, transmitted to me by foolish peasants from our tattooed ancestors, until the clear glass of my mind had been blurred; and, as the darkness settled over me, memories of its spectral inhabitants came trooping to the surface. I fancied I saw images of those beings who haunt the dark when unguarded by lock and bolt. Through the top and arch of the kiln, we were open to their assaults. I became nervously watchful, and, the more I strained my eyes, the more I fancied I could see flaming imps acting a ceaseless pantomime of malice. Once or twice I thought I felt the whiff of ghostly wings, and my terror caused a feeling of suffocation. The only safe thing to do was to talk, tell stories to each other, that the accursed spirits might know we were awake and fearless. I continued awake by this method until the sky began to pale before the advancing dawn, when I softly dropped into sleep, and so passed the most uneasy night I remember.

With the sunrise, we rose, stiff and hungry, to resume our flight. By preference, we clung to the lanes, as being the safest for fugitives who wore the parish uniform; but, near Corwen, our aching vitals compelled us to brave the publicity of the pike road. We halted, at last, before a stone cottage, at the door of which a stout and motherly old woman stooped over a wash-tub resting on a three-legged stool. Her frilled cap looked very white and clean. A flaxen-haired baby sat astride of the door-sill, beating a tom-tom with a piece of china-ware. Our desperately famished state overcame our shyness, and we asked for a piece of bread. The woman braced herself up, and, giving us a compassionate look, said, 'You seem poorly, children. Surely you don't belong to these parts?'

'No, ma'am, we belong to St. Asaph.'

'Oh, yes. You are from the Workhouse.'

'Yes, ma'am.'

She invited us cordially to enter, and, opening a cupboard that was under the stairs, drew out a loaf. She cut off thick slices, smeared them with butter and treacle, and, filling two large mugs with buttermilk, set them before us, and bade us 'eat and welcome.'

After such kindness it was not difficult to win our confidence. I well remember how the homely clock, with its face crowned at the top with staring red flowers, ticked loudly during the pauses of our narrative, and how the minute-hand flung itself recklessly round the dial; how, near the door, the wash-tub became covered with a scum as the soap-bubbles exploded one by one; how the good woman suckled her babe to sleep, as we talked. The coloured picture of that cottage stands out unfading in my memory, despite the varied accumulations of so many years.

Having been strengthened by food, and comforted with friendly advice, we decided it would be best to push on towards Denbigh. Night overtook us, and we sought the lee of a haystack in a field, too tired to fear ghosts; and, early next day, drew near the castled town we both loved so well.

We reached the foot of High Street, and looked with envy at the shop-boys. We could not help peeping at the bright shop-windows which exposed such varied wealth, and admiring those singularly-favoured people, who were able to dispense such assortments of luxuries among their friends.

Beyond the market-place Mose led the way up a narrow lane leading towards Castle Green, and, shortly, turned in into a dingy stone house near a bakery. After mounting some steps we were confronted by a woman who, as soon as she rested her eyes upon my companion, lifted her hands up, and cried out in affectionate Welsh,—

'Why bless their little hearts! How tired they look! Come in, dears, both of you!'

When Mose crossed the threshold he was received with a sounding kiss, and became the object of copious endearments. He was hugged convulsively in the maternal bosom, patted on the back, his hair was frizzled by maternal fingers, and I knew not whether the mother was weeping or laughing, for tears poured over smiles, in streams. The exhibition of fond love was not without its effect on me, for I learned how a mother should behave to her boy.

A glow of comfort warmed our hearts as she bustled about the kitchen, intent upon unusual hospitality. She relieved us of our caps, dusted a polished chair for each of us with her apron, and set them in the snug ingle-corners, laughing and weeping alternately, and sending waves of emotion careering over us out of sheer sympathy. She burned to talk, but reminded herself, by starts, of our necessities, making us smile at her self-reproaches, her hurried attempts to snatch the food from the shelves of her dresser, and her evident intention to be bountiful. She, finally, arranged a table, and, from a new tin-loaf, cut out generous breadths, on which she dropped circles of black treacle, and pressed them into our hands. After piling other lavishly-buttered slices on a plate near by, the boiling water was poured over the tea, and not until she had seen us well engaged on her bounties did she slacken her haste. Then, bringing a high-backed chair between us, she laid one hand on the other in her lap, and exclaimed, —

'Dear heart alive, how you have grown, Mose, my lad! It makes my heart thump to see you so beautiful and clever-looking. Are not you very clever now? And don't you know just everything, writing and ciphering, and all that, you know? But what is the matter, children? How is it you have come to Denbigh? Have you been sent on errands, or have you run away? Don't be bashful, but tell me truly.'

When Mose had related the incidents which brought about our sudden departure from St. Asaph, a look of anxiety came across her face. Then she asked who I was.

I announced, 'I am the grandson of Moses Parry, of the Castle, on my mother's side, and of John Rowlands, of Llys, on my father's side.'

'Oh, indeed,' she said gravely, nodding her head up and down. 'I knew them both well, for when your grandfather,

Moses Parry, was rich and lived at Plâs Bigot, I was a servant girl in his service. That was a grand time for him. I have seen as many as forty people sit at the old man's table; the family, servants, and farm-hands all together. The family sat at one end. Then came the big salt-cellar, and below it the servants of the house and work-people were ranged on the two sides. A fine houseful we had always, too, and a finer family could not be seen in the Vale of Clwyd. Let me see; there was John, the eldest son, Moses, and Thomas, and there were the daughters, Mary, Maria, and a young girl called Elizabeth. Which of these was your mother? Not Mary, I warrant.'

'My mother's name is Elizabeth,' I replied.

'So! I think I remember something about her, and your father was the eldest son of John Rowlands, of Llys! Well, I wonder! It seems strange now how we lose count of people whom at one time in our young days we knew well. And old John Rowlands is your grandfather! Dear heart alive!

'I remember the burial of the old man, Moses Parry, very well. He died suddenly in a field. I was at the funeral, and saw him buried at Whitchurch. It was my duty, you know, and a fine funeral it was, too. Poor old man! It was a great come-down in the world from the great house at Plâs Bigot to that little cottage at the Castle. Did you think of going to see old John Rowlands?'

'Yes, I thought of him, and of Uncle Moses and Thomas, and of my cousin Moses Owen, who keeps a school at Brynford, near Holywell.'

'Well, I don't wish to discourage you; but those who know John Rowlands would tell you there was little hope of help from *him*. However, the Llys is not above a good hour's walk, and you could see him first. It might turn out better than we expect.'

'Why, is he so poor, then?'

'Poor! Oh no, John Rowlands is rich enough. He has two big farms, and is a very prosperous man, but he is severe, cross, and bitter. His eldest son, John, who, I suppose, was your father, died many years ago, thirteen or fourteen years, I should think. There are two daughters living with him, and they might be kind to you. No, it will be no harm to try the old man. He will not eat you, anyway, and something must be done for you.'

From this good woman I received more information relating to my family than I had ever heard previously. It has remained fresher in my memory than events of last week. At a later period I questioned Aunt Maria, of Liverpool, upon these matters, and she confirmed their accuracy.

The next morning, after a refreshing rest, I set out for the Llys, Llanrhaidr. I have but a faint recollection of its appearance, though I remember a big farm-yard, and fat stock-horses, pigs, cackling geese, and fowls. My mind was too much preoccupied with the image of a severe and sour old man, said to be my father's father, to take note of buildings and scenery.

Nothing is clear to me but the interview, and the appearance of two figures, my grandfather and myself. It is quite unforgettable.

I see myself standing in the kitchen of the Llys, cap in hand, facing a stern-looking, pink-complexioned, rather stout, old gentleman, in a brownish suit, knee-breeches, and bluish-grey stockings. He is sitting at ease on a wooden settee, the back of which rises several inches higher than his head, and he is smoking a long clay pipe.

I remember that he asked who I was, and what I wanted, in a lazy, indifferent way, and that he never ceased smoking while he heard me, and that, when I concluded, he took his pipe from his mouth, reversed it, and with the mouth-piece pointing to the door, he said, 'Very well. You can go back the same way you came. I can do nothing for you, and have nothing to give you.'

The words were few; the action was simple. I have forgotten a million of things, probably, but there are some few pictures and some few phrases that one can never forget. The insolent, cold-blooded manner impressed them on my memory, and if I have recalled the scene once, it has been recalled a thousand times.

I was back with Mose before noon, and his mother said, 'Oh, well, I see how it is. You have failed. The hard-hearted old man would not receive you.'

In the afternoon, I paid a visit to Uncle Moses, who was

now a prosperous butcher. Flaxen-haired Kitty, whose appearance in the dim time when I was an infant had caused my expulsion from the house of my grandfather, received me with reserve. They gave me a meal; but married people, with a houseful of children, do not care to be troubled with the visits of poor relations, and the meaning conveyed by their manner was not difficult to interpret.

I next visited the 'Golden Lion,' kept by Uncle Thomas; but here also, the house was full; and early on the following morning I was on my way to Brynford, to interview Moses Owen, the school-master.

Brynford is a hamlet situate in the midst of a moory waste, about half an hour from Holywell, and about five minutes' walk from Denbigh. The district is mostly given up to lead-mining. I stopped in front of a new National Schoolhouse, and the master's residence. My cousin was my last chance. If he refused his aid, my fate must necessarily be that of a young vagabond, for Wales is a poor country for the homeless and friendless.

I was admitted by a buxom woman of decided temper, whose first view of me was with an ill-concealed frown. But as I requested to see Mr. Owen, the school-master, she invited me in, gazing curiously at the strange garb of what she took to be a new pupil.

On being shown to the parlour, a tall, severe, ascetic young man of twenty-two or twenty-three years demanded my business. As he listened to me, an amused smile came to his face, and, when I had concluded, he reassumed his pedagogic severity, and cross-examined me in my studies. Though he gave me several hard questions which I was unable to answer, he appeared pleased, and finally agreed to employ me as pupil-teacher — payment to be in clothing, board, and lodging.

'But I cannot take you as you are. You will have to go to my mother's at Tremeirchion, who will see that you are properly equipped for our school with decent clothing, and in about a month you can return to me and prove what you are worth.'

Thus I entered on my first stage in the world.

Within three hours, on the following day, I entered the

straggling and ancient village of Tremeirchion. It lies scattered along a hillside, about three miles from St. Asaph, and four from Denbigh. In a remote time its humble founders had been constrained to build their cabins on this rocky waste at the outskirts of rich estates and fat farms, but ultimately their cabins had been replaced by slate-roofed cottages, and an ale-house or two, and as many shops for the sale of peasant necessaries were added. About the XIIth Century a small church was built, and a 'God's Acre' attached to it, which was planted with yew for the protection of the building from the gales,[1] and the whole was surrounded by a wall. Later on, when the appearance of Wesley had disturbed the litigious and discontented Welsh peasantry, a couple of chapels rose up.

Beyond the village, and after descending the hillside about a mile, past fir groves, and the leafy woods of Brynbella Hall, I came to the foot of the hill, and at a few yards from the road-side stood the inn, grocery-shop, and farm-house known as Ffynnon Beuno, — St. Beuno's Spring, or Well.

At the back of the house ran a narrow valley which terminated in the Craig Fawr (Great Rock). Near the front was a lodge and gate, leading to Brynbella Hall, well hidden by a tall, rook-haunted wood. The great house was once occupied by Mrs. Thrale, Dr. Johnson's friend.

Tremeirchion, literally translated, means the Maiden's Town, and was so named from a convent which stood in its vicinity, and was supposed to be the refuge chosen by St. Winifred, when she retired with a company of virgins after her revivification by good St. Beuno at Holywell. Compared with the famous spring of St. Winifred's at Holywell, that of St. Beuno is a modest affair, and boasts of no virtues beyond purity and sweetness. The water is collected in a stone tank adjoining the house of Ffynnon Beuno, and is allowed to escape, for the benefit of the villagers, through the open mouth of a rude representation of a human head, which is affixed in the front wall.

The externals of Ffynnon Beuno favourably impressed me. The sign over the door informed the public that Mary Owen

[1] In the preamble to the last Statute of Edward I, it is narrated that yew-trees were used for that purpose.

FYYNNON BEUNO

kept open house for the entertainment of man and beast, and sold groceries, tobacco, ale, and spirituous liquors, and, it might have added, milk, and butter, poultry, and sheep. As I walked towards the door I prayed inwardly that my aunt would be as gracious to me as I believed the owner of the cosy establishment ought to be.

She stood in the centre of her kitchen floor, as I handed her son's letter to her. The contents surprised and annoyed her. Though there was no scorn in her reception of me, I yet felt instinctively that she would rather not have received the news. The announcement was too sudden and precipitate to please a mother who, until now, had been a law to her favourite son. She took her own time to express herself. She asked me how I had found her house, whether I was hungry and tired, quietly observing me the while. She set before me an abundance of choice food. Her pattens signalled her movements in the pantry, dairy, shop, and beer-cellar; but I knew she was thinking of me, and the letter from her son. Each time she came in to add some dish to the fare she was spreading for me, I felt her searching eyes on me. This was an ominous beginning, and made me feel subdued as I sat in the shadow of the ingle-nook.

Some neighbours came in to quench their thirst with my aunt's brewing, and from my place I could not fail to hear snatches of the conversation, most of which related to me. My aunt was relieving herself of her grievance, by which I discovered that her sense of prudence had been offended by my cousin Moses' rash act.

'At his age,' she said, 'to take upon himself the keep and education of a growing boy! He will be marrying himself shortly, and will have children enough of his own to bring up. Why should he bother himself about other people's children? I say, "do what you can for your own, and let other people do for their families the same." I don't like this whim of Moses' at all. In the first place, it is disrespect to me, his mother, who has striven hard to establish him in life; and, in the second place, it is extravagant, and every penny that that boy will cost him must be a loss to the family that he will have to look after in the course of a few years,' etc., etc.

Poor Aunt Mary! She made me feel mean and depressed at the time, but I understand it all now. She had inherited the instincts of economy, and the calamities which had overtaken her father, and reduced his family from affluence to poverty, had taught her wisdom. From these circumstances she had long ago learned that only thrift, calculation, and contrivance, can prevent the most respectable family from declining to that poverty which leads to the workhouse. She knew that money meant much to poor folk, and that the only way to make money in her condition of life was to make the most of her resources, keep whatever she could scrape from the proceeds of industry; and, acting on those principles, she was an enemy to all imprudence and improvidence, waste and extravagance. As she could not invoke the law to hinder young couples from the folly of early marriage, she could disown them, even though they were her nearest relatives, and suffer them, unassisted, to bear the punishment due to the unwise. For mothers in her position, she knew of no other course, and necessity left no choice. The scraps of complaint which I heard enabled me to interpret her thoughts and actions towards me henceforth. When I saw the bony, narrow face, dark with vexations, and the way she jerked a tankard or a plate from the table, or flapped vigorously her duster, I knew that I was at the bottom of her trouble.

Her husband had died three years before, leaving her with the care of four sons. As her sons approached manhood, her responsibility increased. So far she had done admirably. Edward, the eldest, was a railway official at Morley, where in time his abilities must necessarily secure him promotion. Her second son, Moses, had graduated with honours at Carnarvon College, and was now the teacher of a National School at Brynford. Such a distinguished scholar, and one consumingly zealous in all that belonged to his profession, could not fail to have a brilliant future. John, the third son, was a lad of eighteen, on the eve of entering the railway service, as a clerk. David, the youngest, a lad of thirteen, was destined by his mother to assist her with the farm.

Before I left Ffynnon Beuno for school, I had abundant opportunities to inform myself of the low estimate formed of me by the neighbours. My aunt was so honest and candid that she admitted them fully into her confidence respecting me, and these sympathetic gossips, while they drank the home-brewed ale, expressed freely to one another their opinions of me, regardless whose ears might hear.

It was through these — especially Hugh, the blacksmith, and John, the butcher — that I was informed that I was the son of Aunt Mary's youngest sister, who had left her home early, for service in London, and had thereby grievously offended her family. In straying to London, in spite of family advice, my mother had committed a capital offence. She had, moreover, become the mother of three children, and had thereby shown herself to be a graceless and thriftless creature.

'Now,' said they, turning to me, 'you will know what to expect if you offend your aunt. With us the rule is "every family for itself, and God for us all." Mrs. Owen is a very good woman, but she will stand no nonsense. You don't belong to her, and you will be turned out of the house the minute you forget yourself. So look out, my boy.'

A young boy cannot be expected to penetrate into the secret motives of his elders, but, though his understanding may be dull, the constant iteration of hints will not fail in the end to sharpen his intelligence. Thus it was that I came to perceive that my condition had not been bettered much by my abrupt exit from St. Asaph. If in one I had suffered physical slavery, I was now about to suffer moral slavery. I say it in no resentful sense, but as a fact. I saw that I was to be subject to an anxious woman's temper, whose petulance would not be controlled by any tenderness for me. She was the undisputed mistress of her household, and those who were of it could only remain with her by uncomplaining submissiveness. This feeling of dependence on other people's favour, and the sense that my condition was never to be other than the singer of their virtues, greatly troubled me at times.

There are some, by nature proud, who patient in all else, demand
but this:
To love and be beloved, with gentleness; and being scorned,
What wonder if they die, some living death! — SHELLEY.

To her own children, Aunt Mary was the best of mothers. Had I received but a tithe of her affection, I fear that, like an ass partial to his crib, I should have become too home-loving ever to leave. As Jacob served Laban, I would have served aunt for years, for a mere smile, but she had not interest enough in me to study my disposition, or to suspect that the silent boy with a somewhat dogged look could be so touched by emotion. What I might have become with gracious treatment her youngest son David became. He clung to his mother's hearth, and eventually married the daughter of Jones, of Hurblas, by whom he had a large family. All his life he remained profoundly ignorant that beyond his natal nook the universe pulsed deep and strong, but, as the saying is, 'Home-keeping youth hath ever homely wits,' and gain and honour are not for those who cling to their fireside.

Throughout the working week Aunt Mary's face betrayed the fretfulness occasioned by her many cares. She was a veritable specimen of the Martha type, and, according to her nature, all her thoughts were bent upon industry and its proceeds. She took gloomy views of her financial affairs, and was prone to be in ill-humour, which was vented in saying disagreeable things to her servants. The damp hollow in which her house stood, between a brook and a well, hills and deep woods, probably was accountable for much of this. Her face was thin and sharp, and showed traces of bad health, as well as of anxiety. The querulous voice and frequent sighing proved that she suffered in body and thought. But on Sunday she was a model of propriety and decorum, and a beautiful motherliness often shone in her eyes, and not a trace of anxiety could be seen in her face. The next day, however, she would be transformed. The mind which governed the estate recovered all its alertness. It seemed as if the Sabbath cap and silk dress had some sedative influence on her, for when they were put away in lavender, and the Monday gown had been put on, she resumed her asperity. Like a stern general about to commence battle, she issued her orders to David about matters connected with the farm. No detail of byre or barn, seed or stock, field or fold, was omitted. David repeated them to me, and I conveyed them to Dobbin, the pony, Brindle, the cow, and her patient sisters, and to Pryn, the terrier.

From Monday's early breakfast to the Saturday tea, every creature at Ffynnon Beuno understood the peremptory law that each was to work. Our food was unstinted, and of superior quality. Never since have I tasted such divine bread, or such savoury meat, and the Sunday dinner was unsurpassable. If my aunt expected us to labour for her with all our might, no one could complain of being starved, or being ill-fed. What labour could a small, ignorant boy give for such bounties? I trimmed hedges, attended the sheep, cleared the byre, fed the stock, swept the farm-yard, cut and stacked fuel, drove Dobbin to Rhyl station for coal, or to Denbigh for beer, or to Mostyn for groceries — the odd jobs that may be done on a farm are innumerable.

Jane, the maid, was not averse to profiting by my help in churning, or milking, or preparing the oven for the week's baking. David, though a year younger than I was, used me as his fag. From him I learned how to mow, plough, and sow, to drive, ride, shear sheep, and mix pig-swill. I came to love the farm, its odour of kine and sweet fodder, the humours of the cattle and sheep, and, though often oppressed by the sense that I was the one unloved creature at Ffynnon Beuno, my days were not altogether unhappy.

At the end of a month, my school-outfit was ready, and David and I were driven by my aunt in her green shandry to Brynford.

School-life commenced the next day, and I was duly appointed monitor of the second class. In some subjects, a few of the head boys of the National School were more advanced than I was, but in history, geography, and composition I was superior.

The school closed at four o'clock, and from tea-time till our supper of porridge and milk — which Moses Owen affected, from his belief in the bone-making properties of oatmeal — was ready, I was kept indoors to learn Euclid, Algebra, and Latin, and Grammar. As my cousin possessed a fair library of solid literature, I soon made sensible progress, as, with his system of tuition, and my eager desire to acquit myself to his satisfaction, I could not fail to do.

Moses Owen was infatuated about books, and, had his health permitted, he would doubtless, in time, have been heard of in the world. At least, such was the opinion of those qualified to judge. He was, however, of delicate constitution, like many slender, overgrown youths, and his health required careful watching. His residence being new, and exposed to the winds blowing over the moory waste, the damp was perceptible in the weeping walls and the mouldy wall-paper, and he was often subject to fits of lassitude and weakness; but when in tone, he showed all the energy of his mother, and was indefatigable in teaching me. At meal-times he was always cross-examining me on the subject of my tasks, his conversation was highly scholastic, and, when out walking with him, I was treated to lectures. Fed by such methods and stimulated to think, I became infected with a passion for books, and for eighteen hours out of the twenty-four I was wholly engrossed with them. When, a couple of months later, I stood up for examination among the head pupils, my progress was conspicuous.

In time, all friendship with any schoolfellow at Brynford was impossible. Most of the boys were uncongenial through their incurable loutishness. Few of them were cleanly or orderly, and their ideas of what was right differed from mine. They were vilely irreligious, and to my astonishment acted as though they believed manliness to consist of bare-faced profanity. Most of them snuffled abominably, while as to being tidy and neat, no savages could have shown greater indifference. It would be easier to transform apes into men, than to make such natures gentle. They all appeared to have become acquainted with my antecedents, and their general behaviour towards me was not dissimilar to that which the unconvicted show towards the 'ticket-of-leave.' The gentlest retort was followed by expressions which reminded me of my ignoble origin. Often they did not wait to be provoked, but indulged their natural malice as from divine privilege. The effect of it was to drive me within my own shell, and to impress the lesson on me that I was forever banned by having been an inmate of the Workhouse. I was neither grieved nor resentful for this, because I had no dignity or vanity which could be wounded; and, being confined to my own thoughts, I obtained more leisure for observation, and there was less occasion for speech.

My cousin, also, was too imperious and exacting to leave me much time for brooding, and, to one of my temperament, moping is disagreeable. When, however, a few of our neighbours' children condescended, for want of other company, to solicit mine for hunting nests among the furze, or for a battle in the pools, or to explore an abandoned lead-shaft, the restlessness latent in all boys was provoked in me, and I remember several enjoyable Saturday afternoons.

Accomplished as my cousin Moses appears to have been in literature, he was too young to know much about human nature. After months of indefatigable tuition, he relaxed in his efforts. He began to affect a disbelief in my advancement, and to indulge in scorn of my progress. My short-comings were now the theme of his discourses, each time we met. My task became heavier and longer, his sarcasms sharper, and his manner more provoking. As I owed a home to him I was debarred from retorting. He did not stoop to the vulgar punishment of birching or caning, but inflicted moral torture by a peculiar gift of language. His cutting words were more painful to bear than any amount of physical castigation; their effect bewildered me and made me more despairing, and I think his unkindness increased as my helpless dependency on him was made more manifest. It frequently happens that as the dependent becomes humbler the tyrant becomes harsher, for the spirit taken from one seems to be converted into force in the other.

Aunt Mary, during all this period, had been regularly visiting her son once a week with fresh home-supplies, and, by observing the change in my cousin after one of these visits, I suspected that her wishes were gradually perverting his original intentions towards me. Moses was absolute over his brother David and myself, but when Aunt appeared it was obvious, even to me, that, however great her respect for his talents was, his personality sank in the presence of her masterful spirit. The stronger nature of his mother ruled him as completely at Brynford as when he was a tiny boy at home. In the same way that his mother showed her pride in her son Moses, her son was proud of his mother's fine qualities, her wise management of her property and business, and the esteem she won from all who came near her, as an honourable, far-seeing, and right-judging woman.

A pity it is that Moses did not pursue the shorter and

nobler course with me. It was but due to his mother that her wishes should prevail, but by hesitating, and gradually working himself into a dislike of me, he deprived me of the sweet memory of his goodness. Had he but called me and said, 'I am too poor to play the benevolent cousin longer, and we must part,' and sent me off there and then, I should have lived to honour him for his straightforwardness, and to remember with gratitude that, as long as he was able to, he was graciously beneficent. But, with every spoonful of food I ate, I had to endure a worded sting that left a rankling sore. I was 'a dolt, a born imbecile, and incorrigible dunce.'

When the tears commenced to fall, the invectives poured on my bent head. I was 'a disgrace to him, a blockhead, an idiot.' If, wearying of this, I armed myself with a stony impassiveness, he would vary his charges and say, 'I had hoped to make a man of you, but you are bound to remain a clodhopper; your stupidity is monstrous, perfectly monstrous!' He would push back his chair from the table, and with fierce, brow-beating glances exclaim, 'Your head must be full of mud instead of brains. Seven hours for one proposition! I never knew the equal of this numskull. I can endure no more of this. You must go back whence you came. You are good for nothing but to cobble paupers' boots,' etc., etc.

It would be difficult to decide whether I, becoming more and more confused by this wholly-unlooked-for violence, and confounded by a growing belief in my worthlessness, or Moses, tired with his self-imposed task of teaching his unfortunate cousin, deserved the more pity. Had I been in his place, and believed my protégé to be the matchless dunce he described me to be, I could never have had the heart to bait him to despair, but would have sought an occupation for him more suited for his capacities. Moses appears to have required time to heat himself thoroughly for such a resolve, and, in his desire for a proper pretence, he was becoming cruel.

So from this time he was mute about my merits. I was the object of incessant disparagement and reproaches, and the feeling of this acted as a weighty clog on my efforts. The excellence which the Owenses, Pritchards, and Joneses of the school might aspire to was to be denied me. My spiritual, intellectual, and bodily functions were to be stimulated with birch, boot, and bluster; for in no other way could one so dense as I be affected. The pain at last became intolerable, and I was again drawing perilously near revolt. But Moses saw nothing, and continued to shower his wordy arrows, which perpetually stung and caused inward bleeding.

I used to think that Moses was a grand scholar, but I got to believe that he had never been a boy. That towering intellect of his was not due to education, it came to him with his mother's milk. Yet I was unable to understand, when I reflected on the severity of his manner, how the Lord Bishop of St. Asaph — who was a Prince of the Church, and was three times older than Moses — could unbend so far as to challenge us Workhouse boys to a race over his lawn, and would laugh and be as frisky as any of us. The stones of the highway would sooner rise and smile than Moses Owen would relax the kill-joy mask he wore at this period.

At last, after a course of nine months' tuition, I received permission to visit Ffynnon Beuno, and I was never recalled to Brynford. Though my aunt never forgot that she ought to be rid of me as soon as possible, there was no hardship in doing chores for her at the farm. When she was gracious, as she often was, she amply compensated me for any inward sufferings inflicted during her severe week-day mood. She was an exacting mistress, and an unsympathetic relative, though, in every other sense, she was a most estimable woman. But what I lacked most to make my youth complete in its joy was affection.

Tremeirchion is only a hamlet overlooking the Vale of Clwyd, inhabited by tradesmen, farm-employees, and navvies, and their families; but my impression is that though the Vale contains a large number of landed proprietors, few of them are prouder than the occupants of the hamlet. Sarah Ellis, who rented a cottage from my aunt at the grand rate of 30 shillings a year, carried herself more majestically than any royal person I have since seen, and seemed to be always impressing her dignity on one. There was Mr. Jones, of Hurblas, Jones, of Tynewydd, Jones, of Craig Fawr, Hugh, the blacksmith, Sam Ellis, the navvy — they are revived in my mind now, and I fail to see what cause they had of being so inordinately haughty as I remember them to have been. Then there was my aunt — she was proud, David was proud — they were all exceedingly proud in Tremeirchion. I am reminded how they despised all foreigners, hated the Sassenach, and disparaged their neighbours, and how each thought his, or her, state, manners, or family to be superior to any other. Yet, if their condition was not humble, where shall we look for humbleness? But I am doubtless wrong in calling this opinionative habit 'pride'; perhaps 'prejudice' would describe it, the prejudice born of ignorance, and fostered in a small, untravelled community, which knew nothing of the broad, sunny lands beyond the fog-damp Vale. The North-Welsh are a compound of opposites, — exclusive as Spaniards, vindictive as Corsicans, conservative as Osmanlis; sensible in business, but not enterprising; quarrelsome, but law-abiding; devout, but litigious; industrious and thrifty, but not rich; loyal, but discontented.

Our tavern-kitchen on a Saturday night was a good school for the study of the North Welsh yeoman and peasant, for then it used to be full of big-boned men, dressed in velveteen coats and knee-breeches, who drank like troopers, and stormed like madmen. The farmer, butcher, tailor, shoemaker, navvy, game-keeper, and a 'gent' or two held high carnival during the last hours of the working week; and David and rosy-cheeked Jane and myself had to trot briskly in the service of supplying these mighty topers with foaming ale.

The first quart made them sociable, the second made them noisily merry. Tom Davies, the long-limbed tailor, would then be called for a song, and, after a deal of persuasion, he would condescend, in spite of his hoarseness, to give us 'Rule Britannia,' or the 'March of the Men of Harlech,' the chorus of which would be of such stupendous volume that the bacon flitches above swung to the measure. If, while under the influence of the ale and the patriotic song, the French had happened to invade the Vale of Clwyd, I do believe that if the topers could have got within arm's length of them the French would have had a bad time of it.

Then another singer would treat us to 'The Maid of Llangollen,' which soothed the ardent tempers heated by the late valorous thoughts; or John Jones, the butcher, envious of the applause won by Tom Davies, would rise and ring out the

HENRY M. STANLEY, AT 15

strain, 'To the West, where the mighty Mizzourah,' which gave us the vision of a wide and free land awaiting the emigrant, and an enormous river flowing between silent shores to the sea. More beer would be called for by the exulting men, while eyes spoke to eyes of enchanted feelings, and of happy hearts. Courage was high at this juncture, waistcoats would be unbuttoned for easy breathing, content flushed each honest face, the foaming ale and kitchen fire were so inspiring!

After ten, the spirits of our customers would be still more exalted, for they were deep in the third quart! All the combativeness of the Welsh nature then was at white heat. This would be the time for Dick Griffiths — wooden-legged Dick — to indulge in sarcasm at the expense of the fiery butcher; and for Sam Ellis, the black-browed navvy, to rise and challenge them both to a bout of fisticuffs; and then would follow sad scenes of violence, for John, who was gamey as a bantam-cock, would square off at the word.

But, at this critical moment, Aunt Mary would leave her shop-counter, and walk solemnly into the kitchen, and, with a few commands, calm the fiery souls. Dick would be bustled out ignominiously, as he was too irascible for peace after half-past ten. Sam would be warned of dreadful consequences if he lifted his voice again; while as for John Jones, the butcher, it was pitiful to see how craven he became at sight of a woman's uplifted forefinger. Thus did the men waste their spare time in gossip, and smoking, and drinking — which involved a waste of their spare cash, or the surplus left in their pockets after the purchase of absolute necessities. The gossip injured men's morals, as the smoking deadened their intellects, and the beer disturbed their lives. The cottage and farm fireside has received greater praise than it deserves, for if we think of the malice, ill-nature, and filthy or idle gossip vacuous minds find pleasure in, it will be seen that there is another side to the picture, and that not a flattering one.

This chapter might be expanded to a book, if I were to dwell on too many details of this period. It was crowded with small felicities notwithstanding myriads of slights. During the prostrating fevers of Africa, memory loved to amuse itself with its incidents. It had been my signal misfortune to have been considered as the last in the village, and every churl was but too willing to remind me of it. My aunt was nothing loth to subdue any ebullience of spirit with the mention of the fact that I was only a temporary visitor, and my cousin David was quick, as boys generally are, to point out how ill it became me to forget it, while Jane used it as an effective weapon to crush any symptom of manliness. But, with a boy's gaiety and healthful spirit, I flung all thoughts of these miseries aside, so that there were times when I enjoyed hearty romps with David, hunted for rabbits, and burrowed in the caves, or made dams across the brook, with the memory of which I have whiled many a lonely hour in African solitudes.

Aunt Mary had so often impressed it on me that I was shortly to leave, and worry in the outer world for myself, that my imagination while with the sheep on Craig Fawr, or at church, was engaged in drawing fanciful pictures of the destiny awaiting me. My favourite spot was on the rocky summit of the Craig. There the soul of 'Childe Roland' gradually expanded into maturity. There he dreamed dreams of the life to come. There I enjoyed a breezy freedom, and had a wide prospect of the rich Vale of Clwyd, — from the seashore at Rhyl to the castled town of Denbigh, — and between me and the sky nothing intervened. There was I happiest, withdrawn from contact with the cold-hearted, selfish world, with only the sheep and my own thoughts for company. There I could be myself, unrestrained. My loudest shout could not be heard by man, my wildest thought was free. The rolling clouds above me had a charm indescribable, they seemed to carry my spirit with them to see the huge, round world, in some far-off corner of which, invisible to everyone but God, I was to work out my particular task.

At such a time, Enoch's glorious and sweet life would be recalled in the lovely land of flowers and sunshine, and it would not be long before I would feel inspired to imitate his holy blamelessness, and, rising to my feet, I would gather stones, and raise a column to witness my vows, like Jacob in the patriarchal days. Those hours on the top of the Craig were not wholly without their influence. They left on the mind remembrances of a secret compact with the All-seeing God, Who heard, through rushing clouds and space, the love-

"CRAIG FAWR" FROM THE FARM

less boy's prayer and promise; and, when provoked, they often came between me and offence.

Finally, another aunt came to visit us from Liverpool; and, therewith, the first phase of my future was shaped. When she had gathered the intentions of her sister towards me, she ventured upon the confident statement that her husband — Uncle Tom, as he came to be known to me — was able to launch me upon a career which would lead to affluence and honour. He had such great influence with a Mr. Winter — Manager of a Liverpool Insurance Office — that my future was assured. After several debates between the two sisters, Aunt Mary was persuaded that I had but to land in Liverpool to be permanently established in a highly-prosperous business.

After Aunt Maria's departure, a letter from her husband arrived which substantiated all she had said, and urged the necessity of an early decision, as such a vacancy could not be left long unfilled. It only needed this to hurry Aunt Mary in procuring for me the proper outfit, which she was resolved should be as complete as if it were for one of her own children.

When the day of departure at last came, my feelings were violently wrenched; certainly some fibres of my affection were being torn, else why that feeling of awful desolation? It may appear odd that I wept copiously at leaving Ffynnon Beuno, where there were none who could have wept for me, had they tried ever so hard. Nevertheless, when one image after the other of the snug farm-house and lovely neighbourhood, the Craig Fawr, the fields, the woods, the caves, the brook, crowded into my mind, I was sorely tempted to pray for a little delay. It is probably well that I did not, and it was better for my health that my affections were with inanimate nature and not with persons, for, otherwise, it would have been a calamity. Wordsworth finely describes the feeling that moved me in the lines, —

> 'These hills,
> Which were his living being, even more
> Than his own blood . . . had laid
> Strong hold upon his affections, were to him
> A pleasurable feeling of blind love.'

As the little packet-steamer bore us towards Liverpool, and the shores of Wales receded from view, the sight of the melancholy sea and cold sky seemed in fit sympathy with the heavy burden which lay on my heart. They stirred up such oppressive fancies that I regarded myself as the most miserable being in existence, deprived of even a right to love the land that I was born in. I said to myself, 'I have done no harm to any living soul, yet if I but get attached to a field, all conspire to tear me away from it, and send me wandering like a vagabond over the unknown.'

Who can describe that sadness? Anguish racked me, and a keen sense of woe and utter beggary so whelmed the mind that my ears became dead to words, my eyes blind to all colours, save that which sympathised with the gloom within. No gold or silver had I, nor land, nor any right even to such small share as might be measured for my grave; but my memory was rich with pleasant thoughts, stored with scenic beauties. Oh! place me on the summit of the Craig again, and let me sit in peace, and my happy thoughts will fly out, one by one, and bring the smile to my face, and make me proof against the misery of orphanage and the wintry cold of the world; there my treasures, which to me were all-sufficing, wearied me not with their weight or keeping, were of no bulk to kindle covetousness, or strike the spark of envy, and were close-hidden within the soul. Often as I have left English shores since, the terrible dejection of spirit of that day has ever recurred to my mind.

When about half-way across the Dee estuary, I was astonished at seeing many great and grand ships sailing, under towers of bellying canvas, over the far-reaching sea, towards some world not our own. Not long after there appeared on the horizon clouds of smoke, out of which, presently, wound a large city. There I saw distinctly masses of houses, immensely tall chimneys, towers, lengths of walls, and groves of ship's-masts.

My rustic intelligence was diverted by the attempt to comprehend what this sight could mean. Was this Liverpool, this monstrous aggregation of buildings, and gloomy home of ships? Before I could answer the question satisfactorily, Liverpool was all around me: it had grown, unperceived by me, into a land covered by numberless structures of surpassing vastness and height, and spread on either side of our course. We sped along a huge sea-wall, which raised its grim front as high as a castle, and before us was a mighty river; on either side there was an immeasurable length of shore, crowded with houses of all sorts; and when I looked astern, the two lines with their wonders of buildings ran far out towards the sea, whence we had so swiftly come.

Before my distracted mind could arrange the multitude of impressions which were thronging on me, my aunt, who had sat through all unmoved and silent, touched me on the shoulder and bade me follow her ashore. Mechanically, I obeyed, and stepped out on a floating stage which was sufficiently spacious to accommodate a whole town-full of people; and, walking over an iron bridge, we gained the top of the colossal wall, among such a number of human beings that I became speechless with fear and amazement.

Entering a carriage, we drove along past high walls that imprisoned the shipping, through an atmosphere impregnated with fumes of pitch and tar, and streets whose roar of traffic was deafening. My ears could distinguish clinks of iron, grinding roll of wheels, tramp of iron-shod hoofs, but there was a hubbub around them all which was loud and strenuous, of which I could make nothing, save that it was awful and absorbing. Fresh from the slumbering existence of a quiet country home, my nerves tingled under the influence of the ceaseless crash and clamour. The universal restlessness visible out of the carriage windows, and the medley of noises, were so overwhelming that from pure distraction and an impressive sense of littleness in the midst of such a mighty Babel, every intelligent faculty was suspended.

The tremendous power of this aggregate force so fiercely astir, made me feel so limp and helpless that again I was tempted to implore my aunt to return with me to the peace of Tremeirchion. But I refused the cowardly impulse, and, before my total collapse, the carriage stopped at an hotel. We were received by such smiling and obliging strangers that my confidence was restored. The comfort visible everywhere, and the composed demeanour of my aunt and her friends, were most soothing.

In the evening, Aunt Maria appeared, and her warm greetings served to dissipate all traces of my late panic, and even infused a trifle of exaltation, that my insignificant self was henceforth to be considered as one of the many-throated army which had made Liverpool so terrible to a youthful rustic. She was pressed to stay for a nine-o'clock supper, but when she rose to depart I was by no means reluctant to brave the terror of the street. Aunt Mary slipped a sovereign into my hand, stood, over a minute, still and solemn, then bade me be a good boy and make haste to get rich. I was taken away, and I never saw her again.

The streets no longer resounded with the startling hurly-burly of the day. At a quick trot we drove through miles of lighted ways, and by endless ranges of ill-lit buildings. Once I caught a glimpse of a spacious market, aglow with gas-lights, where the view of innumerable carcases reminded me of the wonderful populousness of the great city; but beyond it lay the peaceful region of a sleeping people. At about the middle of this quieter part the cab halted, and we descended before the door of No. 22, Roscommon Street.

My precious box, with its Liverpool outfit, was carried into the house, and a second later I was in the arms of cheery 'Uncle Tom.' In expectation of my coming there was quite a large party assembled. There was my irrepressible cousin, Mary Parkinson, with her husband, tall John Parkinson, the cabinet-maker, a brave, strong, and kindly fellow. There were also my cousins Teddy and Kate, and Gerard, Morris, and others.

Cousin Mary was an independent young woman, and, like all women conscious of good looks, sure of her position in a small circle; but, important as she might be, she was but secondary to Uncle Tom, her father. He was the central figure in the gathering, and his sentiments were a law to his household. He stood in the forefront, of medium size, corpulent, rubicund, and so genial, it was impossible to withstand him.

'My word, laddy! thou art a fine boy! Why, I had no idea they could raise such as thou in Wales. What hast been living on to get so plump and round — cheeks like apples, and eyes like stars? Well, of all! — I say, Mary, John, my dears, why are ye standing mute? Give the laddy here a Lancashire welcome! Buss him, wench! He is thy first cousin. Teddy, my lad, come up and let me make thee acquainted with thy cousin. Kate, step forward, put up thy mouth, dear; there, that is right! Now welcome, a thousand times, to Liverpool, my boy! This is a grand old city, and thou art her youngest citizen,' etc., etc.

He was so breezy and bluff of speech, and so confident of great things for me in Liverpool, that I forgot I was in the city of noise and smoke, as well as my first dread of it. He was the first of his type I ever met. He had the heartiness and rollickness of the traditional 'sea-dog,' as sound in fibre as he was impervious to care. No presence could daunt him or subdue his unabashed frankness. He was like that fellow

'Who having been praised for bluntness doth affect
A saucy roughness.
He cannot flatter, he!
An honest mind and plain, — he must speak truth;
An they will take it, so; if not, he 's plain.'

Uncle Tom was a man of fair education, and had once occupied a responsible post in the railway service. It was through his influence that Edward Owen had found a position in it, and I presume that the memory of that had influenced Aunt Mary in committing me to his care. Uncle Tom must have been found wanting in some respects, for he had descended in the scale of life, while his protégé, Edward, was now mounting rapidly. He now was a poor 'cottoner,' at a pound a week, with which he had to support himself and large family. His fault — if fault it may be called — may be guessed by the fact that, while his family was increasing, he had rashly undertaken to burden himself with the care of a boy of my age, while the slightest accident or indisposition would leave him wholly without means to support anybody. His heart was altogether too easily expansive for one of his condition. Had his means permitted, he would have kept perpetual holiday with his friends, he so loved good cheer and genial fellowship. He was over-contented with himself and others; and too willing to become surety for anyone who appeared to possess good-humour and good-nature; and, through that disposition, which is fatal to a man of family, he continued to fall lower and lower, until his precarious wages barely sufficed for the week's wants.

During the first few days I did little more than tramp through the streets of Liverpool from Everton to the Docks, with Teddy Morris, aged 12, as a guide, who showed me the wonders of the city with the air of an important shareholder glorying in his happy investments. The spirit of his father in regard to its splendour and wealth had taken possession of him, and so much was I impressed with what he said to me, that, had a later comer questioned me about Liverpool, I should doubtless have expressed the conviction that its grandeur was due in a great measure to the presence of Uncle Tom and his son Teddy.

The day came when Uncle Tom took me to interview Mr. Winter, through whose influence I was to lay the foundation of that promised prosperity that was to be mine. I had donned my new Eton suit for the first time, and my hair shone with macassar. Such an important personage as Mr. Winter could only live among the plutocracy of Everton Heights; and thither we wended, with hope and gladness in our eyes.

Years ago, when Uncle Tom was in affluent circumstances, he had befriended Mr. Winter in some way that had made that gentleman pledge himself to repay his kindness. He was about to test the sincerity of his professions by soliciting his influence on behalf of his wife's nephew.

We were received with a profuse show of friendship, and such civilities that they seemed obsequious to me when I compared the sheen of Mr. Winter's black clothes with the fluffy jacket on Uncle Tom's shoulders. The gentleman took out his spotless kerchief and affected to dust the chair before placing it before his visitor, and anxiously inquired about the health of good Mrs. Morris and her divine children. When he came finally to touch upon my affairs, I was rendered quite emotional with pride by the compliments he showered upon me.

Mrs. Winter, an extremely genteel person in long curls, presently appeared upon the scene, and after cooing with her spouse and exchanging affectionate embraces, was introduced to us. But, though we were present, husband and wife had such an attraction for each other that they could not refrain from resuming their endearments. My cheeks burned with shame as I heard them call one another, 'My sweetie, darling love, blessed dearie,' and the like; but Uncle Tom was hugely delighted, and took it all as a matter of course. In Wales, however, married people did not conduct themselves so grossly in public.

When we rose to go away, Mr. Winter resumed his earnest and benevolent manner to us, and begged my uncle to call on him next morning at nine sharp, and he would be sure to hear of something favourable. While returning home down the slope from Everton, Uncle Tom was most emphatic in declaring that 'dear old Winter was a born gentleman, a dear, kind heart, and excellent old soul,' and that I might consider myself as a 'made man.' Exultations at my prospects inclined me to echo my uncle's sentiments, and to express my belief that Mrs. Winter was like a saint, with her dove-like eyes and pretty ringlets, though in some recess of me was something of a disdain for those mawkish endearments of which I had been an unwilling witness. These subjects occupied us all the way back to No. 22, Roscommon Street, upon entering which we revealed all that had happened to Aunt Maria, and made her participate in the delights of hope.

Twenty times during the month did Uncle Thomas and I travel up to Everton Heights, and the oftener we called on Mr. and Mrs. Winter, the less assured we became of the correctness of our first impressions. These visits cost Uncle Tom, who ought to have been at work checking the cotton bales, seventy shillings, which he could ill afford to lose. The pair at every occasion met us with exquisite politeness, and their cooing by-plays recurred regularly, he affectionate beyond words, she standing with drooping head, and meek sense of unworthiness, as he poured over her the oil of sweetness.

The visits had been gradually becoming more and more tedious to us, for what may have been gratification to them was nauseous to disappointed people, until at the end of the twenty-first visit Uncle Tom burst out uncontrollably with, 'Now, d—n it all! Stop that, Winter. You are nothing but an artful humbug. In God's name, man, what pleasure can you find in this eternal lying? Confound you, I say, for a d—d old rascal and hypocrite! I can't stand any more of this devilish snivelling. I shall be smothered if I stay here longer. Come, boy, let's get out of this, we will have no more of this canting fraud.'

Instinct had prepared me somewhat for this violent explosion, but I was shocked at its force when it occurred. It deepened my belief that my uncle was a downright, honest, and valiant man; and I respected the righteousness of his anger, but I was bound to be grieved by his profanity. He fumed all the way home at the *farceur*, and yet comforted himself and me, saying, 'Never mind, laddie! We 'll get along somehow without the help of that sweep.'

Aunt Maria's conduct when we reached home was the beginning of a new experience. She called me aside and borrowed my gold sovereign, for, as she put it, 'Uncle Tom has now been out of work for over three weeks, because, you know, it was necessary to call every day on the false friend, who fed him with hopes. He is awfully distressed and put out, and I must get him a good meal or two to put spirit into him. In a day or two he will be all right.'

On Monday morning of the next week she borrowed my Eton suit, and took it to the place of the three gilt balls. The Monday after, she took my overcoat to the same place, and then I knew that the family was in great trouble. The knowledge of this was, I think, the first real sharpener of my faculties. Previously, I had a keen sight, and acute hearing, but that was all: there had been no effect on the reason. I have often wondered that I was so slow of understanding things which had been obvious to little Teddy from the first.

I now walked the streets with a different object than sightseeing. Shop windows were scrutinised for the legend 'Boy wanted.' I offered my services scores of times, and received for answer that I was either too young, too little, not smart enough, or I was too late; but one day, after a score of refusals, I obtained my first employment at a haberdasher's in London Road, at five shillings a week; and my duties were to last from seven in the morning until nine at night, and to consist of shop-sweeping, lamp-trimming, window-polishing, etc.

As London Road was some distance from Roscommon Street, I had to rise before six o'clock, by which I enjoyed the company of uncle, who at this hour prepared his own morning meal. At such times he was in the best of moods. He made the most savoury coffee, and was more generous than aunt with the bread and butter. He was unvaryingly sanguine of my ultimate success in life. He would say, 'Aye, laddie, thou 'ilt come out all right in the end. It 's a little hard at first, I know, but better times are coming, take my word for it'; and he would cite numerous instances of men in Liverpool, who, beginning at the lowest step, had risen by dint of perseverance and patience to fabulous wealth. Those early breakfasts, while Aunt Maria and the children were asleep, and uncle bustled cheerfully about with the confidence of a seer in the future, have been treasured in my memory.

At half-past six I would leave the house, with a tin bucket containing bread and butter and a little cold meat to support me until nine at night. Thousands in similar condition were then trudging through the streets to their various tasks, bright, happy, and regular as clock-work. To all appearance they took pride in their daily toils, and I felt something of it, too, though the heavy shutters, which I took down and put up, made me wince when I remembered them. I think most of us would have preferred the work with the wages to the wages without the work. The mornings were generally sunless, the buildings very grimy, the atmosphere was laden with soot, and everything was dingy; but few of us thought of them as we moved in long and lively procession of men and boys, women and girls, with complexions blooming like peaches, and lips and ears reddened with rich blood.

As it drew near half-past nine at night, I would return home with different views. My back ached, I was hungry and tired, and a supper of cockles and shrimps, or bloater, was not at all stimulating. At half-past ten I would be abed, weary with excessive weariness.

So long as my fresh country strength endured, my habits were regular, but after two months the weight of the shutters conquered me, and sent me to bed for a week to recuperate. Meantime, the haberdasher had engaged a strong boy of eighteen in my place. Then followed a month of tramping about the streets again, seeking fresh work, during which I passed through the usual vicissitudes of hope and disappointment. The finances of the family fell exceedingly low. Nearly all my clothes departed to the house of the gilt balls, and their loss entailed a corresponding loss of the smartness expected in office or shop-boys.

Necessity drove me further afield, even as far as the Docks. It was then, while in search of any honest work, that I came across the bold sailor-boys, young middies, gorgeous in brass buttons, whose jaunty air of hardihood took my admiration captive. In the windows of the marine slop-shops were exposed gaudy kerchiefs stamped with the figures of the Royal Princes in nautical costume, which ennobled the sailor's profession, though, strange to say, I had deemed it ignoble, hitherto. This elevation of it seduced me to enter the Docks, and to inspect more closely the vessels. It was then that I marvelled at their lines and size, and read with feelings verging on awe the names 'Red Jacket,' 'Blue Jacket,' 'Chimborazo,' 'Pocahontas,' 'Sovereign of the Seas,' 'William Tapscott,' etc. There was romance in their very names. And what magnificent ships they were! Such broad and long-reaching extent of decks, such girth of hulk and dizzy height of masts! What an atmosphere of distant regions, suggestive of spicy Ind, and Orient isles! The perfume of strange products hung about them. Out of their vast holds came coloured grain, bales of silks hooped with iron, hogsheads, barrels, boxes, and sacks, continuously, until the piles of them rose up as high as the shed-roof.

I began to feel interested in the loud turmoil of commerce. The running of the patent tackles was like music to me. I enjoyed the clang and boom of metal and wood on the granite floors, and it was grand to see the gathered freight from all parts of the world under English roofs.

On boards slung to the rigging were notices of the sailing of the ships, and their destinations. Some were bound for New York, New Orleans, Demerara, and West Indies, others were for Bombay, Calcutta, Shanghai, the Cape, Melbourne, Sydney, etc. What kind of places were those cities? How did these monstrous vessels ever leave the still pools walled round with granite? I burned to ask these and similar questions.

There were real Liverpool boys about me, who were not unwilling to impart the desired information. They pointed out to me certain stern-faced men, with masterful eyes, as the captains, whose commands none could dispute at sea; men of unlimited energy and potent voices as the mates, or officers, who saw to the carrying out of their superior's commands; and the jerseyed workmen in the rigging — some of whom sported gold earrings, and expectorated with superb indifference — as the sailors who worked the ships from port to port. Each of these seamen bore on his face an expression which I interpreted to mean strength, daring, and defiance.

Before I parted from these boys, who were prodigies of practical wisdom, and profound in all nautical matters, I had learned by comparing the 'Red Jacket' and 'Dreadnought' with the 'American Congress' and 'Winfield Scott,' the difference between a first-class clipper and an ordinary emigrant packet, and why some ships were 'Black-Ballers' and others 'Red-Crossers,' and how to distinguish between a vessel built in Boston and one of British build.

One day, in my wanderings in search of work, I rambled up a by-street close to the Brambley Moor Dock, and saw over a butcher's stall a notice, 'Boy wanted.' I applied for the vacancy, and Mr. Goff, the proprietor, a pleasant-faced, prosperous-looking man, engaged me instantly and turned me over to his foreman. This man, a hard, sinister-faced Scotsman, for his fixed scowl, and implacable irascibility, was a twin brother of Spleen. There never was such a constant fault-finder, and, for general cantankerousness, I have never met his like. The necessity of finding some work to do, and of never leaving it, except for a change of work, called forth my utmost efforts to please; but the perpetual scolding and cross tantrums, in which he seemed to take delight, effectually baffled my simple arts. This man's eyes peculiarly affected me. They were of the colour of mud, and their pinpoint pupils sparkled with the cruel malignity of a snake's. When, in after years, I first looked into the visual orbs of the African crocodile, my first thought was of the eyes of Goff's foreman. Heaven forbid that after such a long period I should malign him, but I cannot resist the conviction that when he died, those who had known him must have breathed freer!

Wretched as was my fortnight's stay at the butcher's under the inhumanly-malicious foreman, it was the means of my becoming more intimately acquainted with the stern lords of the sea, and their stately ships; for my work consisted in carrying baskets of fresh provisions to the vessels in the docks; and Time and Fate had so ordered it that through this acquaintance I should be shunted into another line of life.

During the last few weeks domestic matters at Roscommon Street had not been at all pleasant. The finances of the family had fallen very low, and it had been evident that here, also, as at Ffynnon Beuno, there was a wide distinction between children who had parents and those who were orphaned. For if ever a discussion rose between my cousin and myself, my uncle and aunt were invariably partial to their own, when called to arbitrate between us. It was obvious that I was the least aggressive and troublesome, the most respectful and sympathetic, of the younger members of the family, but these merits were as naught when weighed in the scales of affection. Teddy's temper, made arrogant by the conceit that he was his father's son, required to be curbed sometimes; but if I asserted myself, and promised him a thrashing, the maternal bosom was a sure refuge; and, as each mother thinks her son more perfect than any other boy, a certain defeat awaited me. Just as I had submitted to the humours of David at Ffynnon Beuno, I was forced to submit to those of Teddy. If aunt's censures of me were not sufficient to ensure immunity to the nagging boy, there was the old man's rough tongue to encounter.

Slowly the thought was formed that if I were not to be permitted to resent Teddy's infirmities of temper, nor to obtain the protection of his over-indulgent parents, my condition could not be worse if I exchanged the growing intolerance of the evil for some other, where, at least, I should enjoy the liberty of kicking occasionally. On striking a balance between the gains of living with Teddy's family and the crosses received through Teddy's insolence, it appeared to my imperfect mind that my humiliation was in excess. I had not obtained the clerkship for which I had left Wales, my gold sovereign was gone, all my clothes were in the pawnshop. I had fallen so low as to become a butcher's errand boy, under a brute. At home, there was as little peace at night, as there was, during the day, with the foreman. Exposed to the unruly spitefulness of Teddy, the frowns of aunt, the hasty anger of uncle, and the unholy fury of the Scotsman, I was in a fair way of being ground very fine.

At this juncture, and while in an indifferent mood, Fate caused a little incident to occur which settled my course for me. I was sent to the packet-ship 'Windermere' with a basket of provisions, and a note to Captain David Hardinge. While the great man read his note, I gazed admiringly at the rich furniture of the cabin, the gilded mirrors, and glittering cornices, and speculated as to the intrinsic value of this gilding, but, suddenly, I became conscious that I was being scrutinised.

'I see,' said the captain, in a strong and rich voice, 'that you admire my cabin. How would you like to live in it?'

'Sir?' I answered, astonished.

'I say, how would you like to sail in this ship?'

'But I know nothing of the sea, sir.'

'Sho! You will soon learn all that you have to do; and, in time, you may become a captain of as fine a ship. We skippers have all been boys, you know. Come, what do you say to going with me as cabin-boy? I will give you five dollars a month, and an outfit. In three days we start for New Orleans, to the land of the free and the home of the brave.'

All my discontent gathered into a head in a moment, and inspired the answer: 'I will go with you, sir, if you think I will suit.'

'That's all right. Steward!' he cried; and, when the man came, the captain gave him his instructions about me. As he spoke, I realised somewhat more clearly what a great step I had taken, and that it was beyond my power to withdraw from it, even if I should wish to do so.

There was no difficulty in obtaining Goff's consent to quit his service; and the fiendish foreman only gave a sardonic smile which might mean anything. As I strode towards home, my feelings varied from spasms of regret to gushes of joy, as I mentally analysed the coming change. Larded bread, and a sordid life with its pawnshops and family bickerings, were to be exchanged for full rations and independence. Constant suppression from those who usurped the right to control my actions, words, and thoughts, was to be exchanged for the liberty enjoyed by the rest of the world's toilers. These were the thoughts which pleased me; but when I regarded the other side, a haunting sense of insecurity and foreboding sobered me, and made me unhappy. Then there was a certain feeling of affection for my native land and family. Oh! if my discontent had not been so great, if Uncle Tom had been only more just, I had clung to them like a limpet to a rock! It needed all the force of reason, and the memories of many unhappinesses and innumerable spites, to sever all connection with my humble love, and accept this offer of freedom and release from slavery. The magnitude of the change, and the inevitable sundering of all earthly ties at such short notice, troubled me greatly; but they had no effect in altering my decision.

When the old man reached home and heard the news, he appeared quite staggered. 'What! Going to America!' he exclaimed. 'Shipped as a cabin-boy! Come now, tell me what put that idea into your head? Has anything happened here that I do not know? Eh, wife, how is this?'

His sincere regret made it harder than ever to part. It was in my nature to hate parting. Aunt joined her arguments to those of Uncle Tom to dissuade me. But there rose up before me a great bulk of wretchedness, my slavish dependence on relatives who could scarcely support themselves, my unfortunate employment, Teddy's exasperating insolence, family recriminations, my beggar's wardrobe, and daily diet of contumely; and I looked up from the introspection, and, with fixed resolve, said: —

'It is no use, uncle. I must go. There is no chance of doing anything in Liverpool'; and, though he was not of a yielding disposition, uncle consented at last.

In strict justice, however, to his character, I must admit that, had circumstances been equal to his deserving, his nephew would never have been permitted to leave England with his consent; for, according to him, there was no place in all the world like England.

On the third day the 'Windermere' was warped out of dock, and then a steam-tug towed her out into mid-river. Shortly after, a tug brought the crew alongside. Sail was loosened, and our ship was drawn towards the ocean, and, as she headed for the sea, the sailors, with rousing choruses, hoisted topsails, and sheeted them home.

CHAPTER III

AT SEA

WHEN the 'Windermere' was deserted by the tug, and she rose and fell to the waves, I became troubled with a strange lightness of the head, and presently I seemed to stand in the centre of a great circle around which sea, and sky, and ship revolved at great speed. Then for three days I lay oblivious, helpless, and grieving; but, at the deck-washing on the fourth morning, I was quickened into sudden life and activity by hearing a hoarse, rasping voice, whose owner seemed in a violent passion, bawling down the scuttle: 'Now then, come out of that, you — young Britisher! Step up here in a brace of shakes, or I'll come down and skin your — — carcase alive!'

The furious peremptoriness of the voice was enough to rouse the dead, and the fear of the ogre's threats drove all feelings of sickly wretchedness away, and drew me on deck immediately. My nerves tingled, and my senses seemed to swim, as I cast a look at the unsteady sea and uneasy ship; but the strong penetrating breeze was certainly a powerful tonic, though not such a reviver as the sight of the ireful fellow who came on at a tearing pace towards me and hissed: 'Seize that scrubbing-broom, you — joskin! Lay hold of it, I say, and scrub, you — son of a sea-cook! Scrub like —! Scrub until you drop! Sweat, you — swab! Dig into the deck you — — white-livered lime-juicer!'

I stole the briefest possible glance at his inflamed face, to catch some idea of the man who could work himself into such an intense rage, for he was a kind of creature never dreamed of before by me. Seeing me bend to my task without argument or delay, he darted to another boy on the lee side, and with extreme irony and retracted lips, stooped, with hands on knees, and said to him: 'Now, Harry, my lad, I am sure you don't want the toe of my boot to touch ungently those crescents of yours. Do you now?'

'No, sir,' said the boy promptly.

'All right, then, my sweet son of a gun. Lay your weight on that broom, and let her rip, d' ye hear?'

'Aye, aye, sir.'

Nelson, for that was his name, straightened himself, and cruelly smiling, observed the sailors, who were scrubbing and holy-stoning with exemplary industry, and then moved towards them discharging salvoes of blasphemies on their heads, of varying force and character. I wondered, as between the tremendous oaths I heard the sigh of the sea and the moan of the wind, how long the Almighty would restrain His hand. I scrubbed away until I became heated, but my thoughts were far from my work. I was trying to unravel vague ideas about the oddness of things in this world. It seemed to me surprising that, while so many people on land feared to take the name of God in vain, men on the great sea, surrounded by perils and wonders, could shout aloud their defiance of heaven and hell. There was not a soul on board with whom I could exchange my inner thoughts, and, from this period, I contracted a habit of communing with myself.

At eight bells I was told I belonged to Nelson, the second mate's watch, and that my berth was with Harry, in the apprentice cabin on the main deck. There was no mention of the cabin-boy appointment. When the watch was relieved, Harry and I had a talk. This boy had already made one voyage on the 'Windermere,' and, though he despised greenhorns, among whom he classed me, he was pleased to be good-natured with me, probably because I showed such deference to his spirit and experience. He graciously promised to coach me, or, rather, put me 'up to the ropes,' that I might avoid a few of the punishments mates are so quick to bestow on dull ship-boys.

When I told him that I had been engaged as cabin-boy, he was uncommonly amused, and said that the skipper was at his 'old game.' 'On the last voyage we had two boys who had been induced to join in the same way, but, as soon as we were out to sea, Nelson got a hint from the "cappen" and fell on them like a thousand of bricks, and chased them forrard pretty quick, I tell ye. They were bully-ragged all the way to New Orleans, and at the pier they sloped, leaving their sea-duds to me. We made a good thing out of the young duffers. The skipper must have cleared twenty-five dollars in wages from the pair of them, the mates had their fun out of them, and I had their toggery.

'What you 've got to do is to mind your eye. Look out for Nelson, and be lively. That man ain't no softy, I tell ye. If he comes down on you, you 'll get it hot, and no mistake. When he sings out, jump, as though you were bitten, and answer, "Aye, aye, sir." Never forget to "sir" him. Whether it 's scrubbing, or brass-cleaning, or hauling, stick to your job like — and "sharp" 's the word every time. The second mate is bad enough, but Waters, the chief mate, is the very devil. With him the blow goes before the word, while Nelson roars like a true sea-dog before he strikes. Good Lord, I've seen some sights aboard this packet, I have.'

'But how did the captain make twenty-five dollars by the boys on the last voyage?'

'How? Well you *are* a goose! Why, they left their wages, over two months due, in his hands, when they ran away from the ship for fear of worse treatment going home. Aye, that 's the ticket, and the size of it, my little matey. Haze and bully the young lubbers well at sea, and they scoot ashore the first chance they get.'

'Were the mates not hard on you?'

'Oh, Waters took me into his watch, and showed a liking for me, for, you see, I was not quite a greeny. My father saw me properly shipped, and I signed articles. They did n't, but came aboard with the cappen's permission, and so did you. The skipper has to account for me when he gets to port; but you, you may be blown overboard, and no one would be the wiser. I am now as good as an ordinary seaman, though too young for the forecastle. I can furl royals as spry as any bucco sailor on board, and know every rope on the ship, while you don't know stem from stern.'

These glib nautical phrases, most of which were but vaguely understood by me, his assurance, his daring, his want of feeling, made me admire and wonder at him. He was a typical sea-boy, with a glitter in his eyes and bloom in his smooth cheeks that told of superabundant health and *hardiesse*. But for one thing, a prince might have been proud of him as a son.

Satan, I thought, had already adopted him. His absolute ignorance of religion, his awful coarseness of speech, removed him miles away from me, as though he were a brave young savage of another nation and language, nd utterly incomprehensible to me. He was not to be imitated in any way, and yet he obtained my admiration, bec use he had been to America, had manfully endured the tortures of sea-life, and bore himself indomitably.

Long Hart, the cook, was another kind of hero to me. He stood over six feet high in his galley felts, and his saffron complexion and creased neck spoke of foreign suns, maritime romance, and many voyages. The gold earrings he wore I suspected belonged to his dead wives. His nethers consisted of black doe-skin, his body was cased in a dark blue jersey, and a blue Phrygian cap covered his head. He disdained the use of sailors' colloquialisms, and spoke like a school-master in very grand words. My rustic innocence appeared to have an attraction for him; on the second evening after my recovery, he offered the freedom of his galley to me, and, when I brought the apprentice kids, he was generous in his helpings of soft-tack, scouse, and duff. During the dog-watches he spun long yarns about his experiences in deep-sea ships, and voyages to Callao, California, West Coast of Africa, and elsewhere, many of which were horrible on account of the cruelty practised on sailors. I heard of poor sailors hoisted up to the yard-arm, and ducked by the run in the sea until they were nearly drowned; of men being keel-hauled, tied stark-naked to the windlass, and subjected to the most horrible indignities, put over the ship's side to scrub the ship's coppers in the roasting hot sun, and much else which made me thankful that the captains of the day were not so cruel as those twenty years back. His condescension to a young lubber like myself, and his generosity, won from me such deference and civility that he assumed a kind of protectorship over me, and assisted in the enlightenment of my understanding about many things.

The crew consisted mainly of Anglo-Irish, Dutchmen, one or two English, and as many Yankees. They were undisciplined spirits, who found the wild sea-life congenial to their half-savage natures, and had formed the odd notion that to be sailors was to be of nobler stuff than shoremen, and accordingly swaggered magnificently whenever they could do it safely. For some reason they had conceived their nobility to lie in the fact that they had voluntarily adopted a more perilous profession than any practised by landsmen. They were adored by the girls in port, and enjoyed the privilege of gloriously swearing whenever they chose, and the pleasure of this conceit gave them happiness. Shoremen seldom swore, except the dockmen, who aped sailors' manners and gait. They went to church, feared the constables, seldom got drunk or went on a spree, sported gloves, and seemed afraid of work.

When they catch these shore-lubbers at sea, the sailors' contempt for them is very manifest. They are delighted when they are sea-sick, oaths and blows are freely dealt to them, they take pleasure in provoking their aversion to slush and tar, and secretly enjoy their cruel treatment by the mates. As they made me feel my inferiority to Harry, I have since witnessed many another treated in the same way. Poor brutes! considering the slave life they lead, it would be a pity to deprive them of this miserable consolation.

The discipline of the 'Windermere' was well begun by the time I regained health. It was the pride of the officers that, though the 'Windermere' was not a 'Black-Ball' packet, she was big and smart enough to be one, and they were resolved that the customs of the Black-Baller should prevail on board, and that the discipline should be of the same quality. Whether it came up to the regulation standard I do not know, but just as Francis flogged, beat, and pummelled the infants under his charge, so the ruffian mates stormed, swore, and struck or booted the full-grown wretches on board the 'Windermere.' The captain was too high and mighty to interfere, or he may have issued his orders to that purpose, and was satisfied with the zealous service of his mates: at any rate, I scarcely heard his voice except during gales of wind, and then it was stern and strident.

Strange to say, the majority of the sailors preferred the American ships, with all their brutality, to the English, with their daily doses of lime-juice. Harry, Long Hart, and the forecastle arguments which we had perforce to hear, as our den adjoined that of the sailors, sufficiently informed me of the fact that the soft-tack, plum-duff, good mess of beef of the

Yankees, were preferred to the weevilly-biscuit, horse-beef, and gill of lime-juice of the British. 'Give me,' said a forecastle orator, 'a Yankee ship, and not a lousy lime-juicer. Even on the worst Yankee ship afloat no bucco sailor need fear the mates. If a man knows his duty and won't shirk, he is safe against the devil himself, I say. Watch Bully Waters himself. He never drops on a real shell-back, but on some infernal land-lubber who has shipped as an A. B., when he is not fit to carry guts to a bear. It is the loutish Dutchmen and Swedes who have spoiled these packet-ships. You can't expect mates, in a squall of wind that may whip the masts off, to stand still until their orders enter the stupid head of a Dutchman who does n't know a word of English. Well, what must they do? The ship is their first duty, and they fly at the Dutchman, and if the Dutchman don't understand that he must skip — he must stand and be skinned. There's my sentiments.'

I heard such defence scores of times, which proves that the worst side has something to say for itself.

It may have been the shell-back's boast or Harry's criticism which induced me, when on deck, to observe more closely that professional superiority which made the 'bucco sailor' so fearless. It seemed to me that though the 'old hands' knew their work well, they took precious care to do as little as possible; and, had anyone asked me, after I had got safely ashore, what I thought of them, I should have said that they did more 'dusting round' than real work.

It is true the 'old salts' were loudest in their responses to the mate's commands, that they led the bowline song and the halliard chant, were cheerier with their 'Aye, ayes,' 'Belays,' 'Vast hauling,' and chorus; that they strove whose hands should be uppermost at the halliards and nearest to the tackles; but all this did not impress me so much as they might think it did. When the officers thundered out, 'All hands shorten sail,' 'Furl top-gallant sails,' or 'Reef topsail,' the shell-backs appeared to delay under various shifty pretexts to climb up the rigging, in order that being last they might occupy the safe position at the bunt of the sails; and when it was only a four-man job, the way in which they noisily passed the word along, without offering to move, was most artful. At serving, splicing, and steering, the skill of the old hands counted greatly, no doubt; but in work aloft they were nowhere, compared to those Dutchmen and Norwegians they so much derided. They were, in fact, strategists in the arts of shirking.

Sometimes the 'sojering,' as it was called, was a little too conspicuous; and then Bully Waters, with awful energy and frantic malice, drew blood from 'old salt' and 'joskin' indiscriminately, with iron belaying-pins, and kicked, and pounded, until I sickened at the sound of the deadly thuds, and the faces streaming with blood; but I was compelled to admit that for some days after there would be a more spontaneous briskness to obey orders, and old and young regarded the fiery mate from the corners of their eyes.

Five days from Liverpool there suddenly appeared on deck three stowaways, — two Irish boys of about fourteen and fifteen, and an Irishman, — ragged, haggard, and spiritless from hunger, sickness, and confinement. Of course they had to undergo the ordeal of inspection by the stern captain, who contemptuously dismissed them as though they were too vile to look at; but Nelson chivied the three unfortunates from the poop to the bow to 'warm their cockles,' as he phrased it. The cries of the youngest boy were shrillest and loudest, but, when he afterwards emerged to beg food, we guessed by his roguish smile that he had been least hurt. Harry expressed his opinion that he was a 'Liverpool rat,' who would certainly end his days in the State's prison.

Curiously enough, the presence of these two young stowaways acted as a buffer between me and a considerable amount of inglorious mauling, which Nelson, for practice' sake, would have inflicted on my 'Royal Bengal, British person,' as, with playful devilry, he admitted. But the rogues did not appear to be very sensitive about the indignity to which they were subjected. The younger Paddy disturbed the ship with shrill screams if Nelson but raised his hand, and thus his rat's wit saved him often. O'Flynn, the eldest boy, would run and dodge his tormentor, until Nelson, who seemed to love the fun of licking them, through cunning caught them, and then the cries of the innocents would be heart-rending.

Before many days had passed, I had discovered that Nelson

had also his arts. Though I had never been in a theatre, and could not understand, at first, why one man should assume so many poses, I should have been blind not to perceive that the real self of Nelson was kept in reserve, and that he amused himself by behaving differently to each on board. He had one way with the captain, another with his colleague, and various were the styles he assumed before the sailors. From profound deference to Captain Hardinge, and respectful fellowship with Waters, he gradually rose in his own estimation as he addressed himself to the lower grades, until to me he was arrogance personified, and to the stowaways a 'born-hellian.' With Harry he indulged in broad irony, to the more stodgy of the crew he was a champion prize-fighter, to others he spoke with a dangerous smoothness, with lips retracted; but behind every character he adopted stood the real Nelson, a ferocious and short-tempered brute, ready to blaze up into bloody violence.

Until we were abreast of Biscay Bay we experienced no bad weather, but rolled along comfortably under moderate breezes, with a spiteful gust or two. I was gradually becoming seasoned, and indifferent to the swing-swang of the sea. As Nelson said, with a condescending but evil smile, I was 'fresh as a daisy.' The gales and tempests about which Harry and Long Hart loved to talk were so long a-coming that I doubted whether the sea was really so very dreadful, or that the canvas towers would ever need to be taken in. From sunrise down to the decline of day our mast-heads drew apparently the same regular lines and curves against a clear sky. But now the blue disappeared under depths of clouds which intensified into blackness very rapidly, and the whistling whispers in the shrouds changed their note. The sea abandoned its mechanical heave, and languid upshoot of scattered crests. Whether the sky had signalled the change and the sea obeyed, or whether the elements were acting simultaneously, I knew not, but, just as the cloudiness had deepened, a shadow passed over the ocean, until it was almost black in colour; and then, to windward, I could see battalion after battalion of white-caps rushing gaily, exultingly, towards us. The watches were mustered: captain and mates appeared with oil-skins ready, and when the wind began to sing in louder notes, and the great packet surged over on her side, and the water shot through the scuppers, the captain shook his head disparagingly and cried, 'Shorten sail, Mr. Waters; in with royals and top-gallant sails, down with the flying jib,' etc., etc.

This was the period when I thought Mr. Waters was at his grandest. His trumpet-like voice was heard in 'larum tones, as though the existence of a fleet was at stake; and every 'man-jack' seemed electrified and flew to his duty with all ardour. Nor was Nelson behind Waters in energy. The warning sounds of the wind had announced that intensity of action was expected from every soul. The waves leaped over the high foreboard, and the ship was pressed over until the deck was as steep as the roof of a church, and a foaming cataract impended over us. Then it was the mates bawled out aloud, and sailors clambered up the shrouds in a frenzy of briskness, and the deck-hands bawled and sang after a fashion I had not heard before, while blocks tam-tammed recklessly, great sail-sheets danced wildly in the air, and every now and then a thunder sound, from bursting canvas, added to the general excitement. Though somewhat bewildered by the windy blasts, the uproar of rushing waters, and the fury of captain and crew, I could not help being fascinated by the scene, and admiring the passionate energy of officers and crew. A gale at sea is as stimulating as a battle.

When the area of sail had been reduced to the limit of safety, we had a clearer view fore and aft, and I had more leisure to listen to the wind-music in the shrouds, to observe the graver aspect of the sea, and to be influenced by unspeakable impressions. What a power this invisible element, which had stirred the sea to madness, was! If I raised my head above the bulwarks, it filled my eyes with tears, tore at my hair, drove up my nostrils with such force as to make me gasp. It flew up our trousers, and under our oilskin jackets, and inflated us until we resembled the plumpest effigies conceivable.

In the height of the turmoil, while trying to control my ideas, I was startled by the penetrating voice of Waters singing in my ear.

'Now, my young pudding-faced joker, why are you standing here with your mouth wide open? Get a swab, you monkey, and swab up this poop, or I'll jump down your — throat. Look alive now, you sweet-scented son of a sea-cook!'

That first voyage of mine was certainly a remarkable one, were it only for the new-fangled vocabulary I was constantly hearing. Every sentence contained some new word or phrase, coined extempore, and accentuated by a rope's end, or ungentle back-hander, with gutter adjectives and explosive epithets. Every order appeared to require the force of a gathered passion, as though obedience was impossible without it.

From this date began, I think, the noting of a strange coincidence, which has since been so common with me that I accept it as a rule. When I pray for a man, it happens that at that moment he is cursing me; when I praise, I am slandered; if I commend, I am reviled; if I feel affectionate or sympathetic towards one, it is my fate to be detested or scorned by him. I first noticed this curious coincidence on board the 'Windermere.' I bore no grudge, and thought no evil of any person, but prayed for all, morning and evening, extolled the courage, strength, and energy of my ship-mates, likened them to sea-lions, and felt it an honour to be in the company of such brave men; but, invariably, they damned my eyes, my face, my heart, my soul, my person, my nationality; I was damned aft, and damned forward. I was wholly obnoxious to everyone aboard, and the only service they asked of God towards me was that He should damn me to all eternity. It was a new idea that came across my mind. My memory clung to it as a novelty, and at every instance of the coincidence I became more and more confirmed that it was a rule, as applied to me; but, until it was established, I continued to bless those who persecuted me with their hideous curses. I am glad to think that I was sustained by a belief that I was doing right; for, without it, I should have given scope to a ferocious and blasphemous resentment. It cheered me with a hope that, by and by, their curses would be blessings; and, in the meantime, my mind was becoming as impervious to such troubles as a swan's back to a shower of rain.

Harry, on the contrary, made a distinction. He allowed no one to curse him, except the officers. When a sailor ventured to swear at him, he returned the swearing with interest, and clenched his fist ready for the violent sequel. He had long ago overcome the young boy's squeamishness at an oath. If anything, he was rather prone to take the boy's advantage over a man, and dare him to prove himself a coward by striking one younger and weaker. It is a cunning method of fence, which I have since found is frequently practised by those who, without loss of manliness, can resort to screaming. When I confided to him that the crew of the 'Windermere' were a very wicked set, he said the 'Windermere' was Heaven compared to a Black-Ball packet-ship. I believe that he would have liked to see more belaying-pins and marline-spikes thrown at the men by the mates, more knuckle-dusting, and sling-shot violence. According to him, brutal sailors should be commanded by brutal mates. 'Lime-juicers' were too soft altogether for his kidney.

From the day we reached the region of the Trades, we enjoyed blue skies and dry decks, speeding along under square yards, with studding-sails below and aloft. Our work, however, was not a whit easier. The mates hated to see idleness, and found endless jobs of scrubbing paint-work, brass-cleaning, painting, oiling, slushing, and tarring, not to mention sennet-making, and serving shrouds and stays. Sundays, however, — weather permitting, — were restful. The sailors occupied themselves with overhauling their kits, shaving, hair-cutting, and clothes-mending. In the afternoon, after gorging themselves on duff, they were more given to smoke, and to spinning such sanguinary yarns of sea-life that I wondered they could find pleasure in following such a gory profession. When sea and sky were equally sympathetic, and Waters and Nelson gave a rest to their vocal machines, there might have been worse places than the deck of the 'Windermere' on a Sunday; and, to us boys, the Sunday feed of plum-duff, with its 'Nantucket raisins,' soft-tack, and molasses, or gingerbread, contributed to render it delightful.

We were on the verge of the Gulf of Mexico, when one night, just after eight bells were struck, and the watch was turning out, Waters, who was ever on the alert for a drop on someone, hurled an iron belaying-pin at a group of sailors on the main deck, and felled a Norwegian senseless. Then, as though excited at the effect, he bounded over the poop-railing to the main deck, amongst the half-sleepy men, and struck right and left with a hand-spike, and created such a panic that old salts and joskins began to leap over each other in their wild hurry to escape from the demon. Four men lay on the deck still as death for a while, but, fortunately, they recovered in a short time, though the Norwegian was disabled for a week.

The next day, Nelson tried to distinguish himself. While washing decks, he caught the youngest Paddy fairly, and availed himself of the opportunity to avenge former failures so effectually that the boy had not a joke left in him. His fellow-stowaway was next made to regret ever having chosen the 'Windermere' to escape from the miseries inseparable from Liverpool poverty. Before many minutes Nelson was dancing about me, and wounding me in many a vulnerable point; and then, aspiring for bigger game, he affected to feel outraged at the conduct of the man at the wheel, and proceeded to relieve himself by clouting and kicking the poor fellow, until the bright day must have appeared like a starry sky to him.

Labouring under the notion that Liverpool sailors needed the most ferocious discipline, our two mates seldom omitted a chance to prove to them that they were resolved to follow every detail of the code, and to promote their efficiency; but, when about four days from the mouth of the Mississippi, they suddenly abstained from physical violence, and except by intermittent fits of mild swearing, and mordant sarcasm, they discontinued all efforts at the improvement of the men. The day before we arrived at the Balize, the mates astonished me by their extravagant praise of those they had so cruelly mauled and beaten. They called them 'Jolly Tars,' 'Yankee Boys' (a very high compliment), 'Ocean heroes,' etc., etc. Bully Waters exhibited his brilliantly white teeth in broad smiles, and Nelson gushed, and was jovially ebullient. I heard one sailor remark upon this sudden change of demeanour in them, that the mates knew when to ''bout face' and sing a new tune; and that old hands could tell how near they were to the levee by the way Yankee mates behaved, and that there was no place so unwholesome for bullies as the

New Orleans levee. Another sailor was of the opinion that the mates were more afraid of being hauled up before the court; he had often seen their like, — 'hellians at sea, and sweet as molasses near port.'

On the fifty-second day from Liverpool, the 'Windermere' anchored off one of the four mouths of the Mississippi River, in twenty-seven feet of water. The shore is called the Balize. Early next morning a small tug took our ship, and another of similar size, in tow, and proceeded up the river with us. We were kept very busy preparing the vessel for port, but I had abundant opportunities to note the strange shores, and the appearance of the greatest of American rivers. After several hours' steaming, we passed 'English turn,' which Harry described as the place where the English were 'licked' by the Americans on the 8th of January, 1815 — a story that was then incredible to me. After an ascent of about one hundred miles up the river, we came in view of the chief port of the Mississippi Valley, and, in due time, our vessel became one of three lying at a pier-head, pointing up among a seemingly countless number of ships and river-steamers, ranged below and above our berth. The boarding-house touts poured aboard and took possession of the sailors; and, before many minutes, Harry and I alone remained of the crew that had brought the big 'Windermere' across the sea to New Orleans.

Though about thirty-five years have elapsed since I first stood upon the levee of the Crescent City, scarcely one of all my tumultuous sensations of pleasure, wonder, and curiosity, has been forgotten by me. The levee sloped down with a noble breadth to the river, and stretched for miles up and down in front of the city, and was crowded with the cargoes of the hundreds of vessels which lay broadside to it. In some places the freights lay in mountainous heaps, but the barrels, and hogsheads, and cotton bales, covered immense spaces, though arranged in precise order; and, with the multitudes of men, — white, red, black, yellow, — horses, mules, and drays and wagons, the effect of such a scene, with its fierce activity and new atmosphere, upon a raw boy from St. Asaph, may be better imagined than described.

During my fifty-two days of ship-life there had filtered

into my mind curious ideas respecting the new land of America and the character of the people. In a large measure they were more complimentary than otherwise; but the levee of New Orleans carried with its name a reputation for sling-shots, doctored liquor, Shanghai-ing, and wharf-ratting, which made it a dubious place for me. When Harry directed my attention to the numerous liquor saloons fronting the river-side, all the scandalous stories I had heard of knifing, fighting, and manslaughter, recurred at once to my mind, and made me very shy of these haunts of villainy and devilry. As he could not forego the pleasure of introducing me to a city which he had constantly praised, he insisted that I should accompany him for a walk that first night up Tchapitoulas Street, and to some 'diggins' where he had acquaintances. I accepted his invitation without any misgiving, or any other thought than of satisfying a natural curiosity.

I think it is one of the most vivid recollections I possess. The details of my first impressions, and an analysis of my thoughts, would fill many pages. Of the thousands of British boys who have landed in this city, I fancy none was so utterly unsophisticated as myself — for reasons which have already been related.

Directly the sun was set we were relieved from duty, and were allowed liberty to go ashore. We flew over the planking laid across the ships, light as young fawns; and, when I felt the shore under my feet, I had to relieve myself by an ecstatic whirl or two about Harry, crying out, 'At last! At last! New Orleans! It is too good to be true!' I was nearly overwhelmed with blissful feeling that rises from emancipation. I was free! — and I was happy, yes, actually happy, for I was free — at last the boy was free!

We raced across the levee, for joy begets activity, and activity is infectious. What was a vivid joy to me, was the delight of gratified pride to Harry. 'I told you,' he said, beaming, 'what New Orleans was. Is it not grand?' But 'grand' did not convey its character, as it appeared to my fresh young eyes. Some other word was wanted to express the whole of what I felt. The soft, balmy air, with its strange scents of fermenting molasses, semi-baked sugar, green coffee, pitch, Stockholm tar, brine of mess-beef, rum, and whiskey drippings, contributed a great deal towards imparting the charm of romance to everything I saw. The people I passed appeared to me to be nobler than any I had seen. They had a swing of the body wholly un-English, and their facial expressions differed from those I had been accustomed to. I strove hard to give a name to what was so unusual. Now, of course, I know that it was the sense of equality and independence that made each face so different from what I had seen in Liverpool. These people knew no master, and had no more awe of their employers than they had of their fellow-employees.

We reached the top of Tchapitoulas Street, the main commercial artery of the city. The people were thronging home from the business quarters, to the more residential part. They passed by in many hundreds, with their lunch-buckets, and, though soiled by their labours, they were not wearied or depressed. In the vicinity of Poydras Street, we halted before a boarding-house, where Harry was welcomed with the warmth which is the due of the returned voyager. He ordered dinner, and, with appetites sharpened by youth and ocean airs, we sat down to a spread of viands which were as excellent as they were novel. Okra soup, grits, sweet potatoes, brinjalls, corn scones, mush-pudding, and 'fixings' — every article but the bread was strange and toothsome. Harry appropriated my praise of the meal to himself, paid for it with the air of one whose purse was deep beyond soundings, and then invested a silver piece in cigars; for American boys always smoked cigars, and, when in New Orleans, English boys loved to imitate them.

Now, when I stepped on the levee, frisky as a lamb, I was about as good as a religious observance of the Commandments can make one. To me those were the principal boundary-stones that separated the region of right from that of wrong. Between the greater landmarks, there were many well-known minor indexes; but there were some which were almost undiscoverable to one so young and untravelled as I was. Only the angelically-immaculate could tread along the limits of right and wrong without a misstep.

After dinner we sauntered through a few streets, in a state of sweet content, and, by and by, entered another house, the proprietress of which was extremely gracious. Harry whispered something to her, and we were shown to a room called a parlour. Presently, there bounced in four gay young ladies, in such scant clothing that I was speechless with amazement. My ignorance of their profession was profound, and I was willing enough to be enlightened; but, when they proceeded to take liberties with my person, they seemed to me to be so appallingly wicked that I shook them off and fled out of the house. Harry followed me, and, with all the arts he could use, tried to induce me to return; but I would as soon have jumped into the gruel-coloured Mississippi as have looked into the eyes of those giggling wantons again. My disgust was so great that I never, in after years, could overcome my repugnance to females of that character.

Then Harry persuaded me to enter a bar-room, and called for liquor, but here, again, I was obstinate. 'Drink yourself, if you like,' said I, 'but I belong to the Band of Hope and have signed the pledge, so I must not.'

'Well smoke then, do something like other fellows,' he said, offering me my choice.

As I had never heard that smoking was a moral offence, and had a desire to appear manly, I weakly yielded, and, putting a great cigar between my lips, puffed proudly and with vigour. But alas! my punishment was swift. My head seemed to swim, and my limbs were seized with a trembling; and, while vainly trying to control myself, a surge of nausea quite overpowered me, and I tried to steal back to the ship, as abjectly contrite as ever repentant wretch could well be. Thus ended my first night at New Orleans.

Harry's story of the two English boys, who had been compelled to abscond from the 'Windermere' the voyage before, recurred to me more than once after Nelson's greeting next morning. 'Hello! you here still! I thought you had vamoosed like the Irish stowaways. Not enough physic, eh? Well, sonny, we must see what we can do for you.'

I was put to cleaning brass-work — a mechanical occupation that breeds thought. If, attracted by a lively levee scene, I lifted my eyes, one or other of the mates bawled out, 'Now, you scalawag, or, you little sweep, what in — are you doing? Get on with that work, you putty-faced son of a —!' and so on! Ever some roaring blasphemy, some hideous epithet, with a kick or a clout, until, on the fifth day, conviction stole upon every sense that it was to a set purpose; and my small remnant of self-respect kindled into a revolt. I understand now that it was the pitiful sum of money due to me they wished to save for the ship-owners or captain, that prevented them from saying right out, 'You may go, and be — to you.' Such a dismissal entailed a settlement. Just as Moses Owen lacked the moral courage to despatch me from his presence, these men were at the same game of nagging; and it succeeded in inspiring indifference as to what would become of me. I could say, at last, 'Better to rot on this foreign strand than endure this slave's life longer.'

That evening I declined to go ashore with Harry, and sat pondering in the loneliness of my cabin, and prayer, somewhat fallen into disuse of late, was remembered; and I rose from my knees primed for the venture. Habit of association, as usual with me, had knit some bonds of attachment between me and the ship. She connected me with England; by her I came, and by her I could return. Now that was impossible; I must follow the stowaways, and leave the floating hell for ever.

I lit the swinging pewter lamp, emptied my sea-bag on the floor, and out of its contents picked my best shore clothes, and the Bishop's Bible. I dressed myself with care, and, blowing out the lamp, lay down. By and by, Harry reeled in, half-stupefied with his excesses, rolled into his bunk above me; and, when he was unconscious, I rose and glided out. Five minutes later, I was hurrying rapidly along the river-side of the levee; and, when about half a mile from the ship, I plunged into the shadows caused by a pile of cotton bales, and lay down to await day-break.

CHAPTER IV

AT WORK

SOON after sunrise I came out of my nest, and after dusting myself, strode towards Tchapitoulas Street.

> 'The world was all before me where to choose,
> And Providence my guide.'

The absolutely penniless has a choice of two things, work or starve. No boy of my age and vitality could deliberately choose starvation. The other alternative remained to me, and for work, work of any kind, I was most ready; with a strong belief that it was the only way to achieve that beautiful independence which sat so well on those who had succeeded. I was quite of the opinion of my Aunt Mary, that 'rolling stones gathered no moss,' and I wanted permanent work, wherein I could approve myself steady, and zealously industrious. Hitherto, I had been most unfortunate in the search. Respectful civility, prompt obedience, and painstaking zeal, had been at a discount; but, such is the buoyancy of healthy youth, I still retained my faith that decent employment was within reach of the diligent, and it was this that I was now bent upon.

Hastening across the levee, I entered the great commercial street of the city, at a point not far from St. Thomas Street, and, after a little inward debate, continued down Tchapitoulas Street, along the sidewalk, with all my senses wide-awake. I read every sign reflectively. The store-owners' names were mostly foreign, and suggestive of Teutonic and Hibernian origin; but the larger buildings were of undeniable Anglo-Saxon. At the outset, lager-beer saloons were frequent; then followed more shanties, with rusty tin roofs; but, beyond these, the stores were more massive and uniform, and over the doors were the inscriptions, 'Produce and Commission Merchants,' etc.

As I proceeded, looking keenly about for the favourable

chance, the doors were flung open one by one, and I obtained a view of the interior. Negroes commenced to sweep the long alleys between the goods piles, and to propel the dust and rubbish of the previous day's traffic towards the open gutter. Then flour, whiskey, and rum barrels, marked and branded, were rolled out, and arranged near the kerbstone. Hogsheads and tierces were set on end, cases were built up, sacks were laid in orderly layers, awaiting removal by the drays, which, at a later hour, would convey them to the river-steamers.

Soon after seven, I had arrived near the end of the long street; and I could see the colossal Custom-House, and its immense scaffolding. So far, I had not addressed myself to a single soul, and I was thinking I should have to search in another street; when, just at this time, I saw a gentleman of middle age seated in front of No. 3 store, reading a morning newspaper. From his sober dark alpaca suit and tall hat, I took him to be the proprietor of the building, over the door of which was the sign, 'Speake and McCreary, Wholesale and Commission Merchants.' He sat tilted back against what appeared to be the solid granite frame of the door, with a leisured ease which was a contrast to the activity I had previously noticed. After a second look at the respectable figure and genial face, I ventured to ask, —

'Do you want a boy, sir?'

'Eh?' he demanded with a start; 'what did you say?'

'I want some work, sir; I asked if you wanted a boy.'

'A boy,' he replied slowly, and fixedly regarding me. 'No, I do not think I want one. What should I want a boy for? Where do you hail from? You are not an American.'

'I came from Liverpool, sir, less than a week ago, by a packet-ship. I shipped as cabin-boy; but, when we got to sea, I was sent forward, and, until last night, I was abused the whole voyage. At last, I became convinced that I was not wanted, and left. As you are the first gentleman I have seen, I thought I would apply to you for work, or ask you for advice as to how to get it.'

'So,' he ejaculated, tilting his chair back again. 'You are friendless in a strange land, eh, and want work to begin making your fortune, eh? Well, what work can you do? Can you read? What book is that in your pocket?'

'It is my Bible, a present from our Bishop. Oh, yes, sir, I can read,' I replied proudly.

He held out his hand and said, 'Let me see your Bible.'

He opened it at the fly-leaves, and smiled, as he read the inscription, 'Presented to John Rowlands by the Right Revd. Thomas Vowler Short, D. D., Lord Bishop of St. Asaph, for diligent application to his studies, and general good conduct. January 5th, 1855."

Returning it to me, he pointed to an article in his newspaper, and said, 'Read that.' It was something about a legislative assembly, which I delivered, as he said, 'very correctly, but with an un-American accent.'

'Can you write well?' he next asked.

'Yes, sir, a good round-hand, as I have been told.'

'Then let me see you mark that coffee-sack, with the same address you see on the one near it. There is the marking-pot and brush."

In a few seconds, I had traced '⟨S⟩MEMPHIS, TENN.,' and looked up.

'Neatly done,' he said; 'now proceed and mark the other sacks in the same way.'

There were about twenty of them, and in a few minutes they were all addressed.

'Excellent!' he cried; 'even better than I could do it myself. There is no chance of my coffee getting lost *this* time! Well, I must see what can be done for you. Dan,' he cried to a darkie indoors, 'when is Mr. Speake likely to be in?'

''Bout nine, sah, mebbe a leetle aftah.'

'Oh, well,' said he, looking at his watch, 'we have ample time before us. As I don't suppose you have breakfasted yet, you had better come along with me. Take the paper, Dan.'

We turned down the next street, and as we went along he said first impressions were very important in this world, and he feared that if his friend James Speake had seen cotton fluff and dust on my jacket, and my uncombed hair, he might not be tempted to look at me twice, or care to trust me among his groceries; but, after a breakfast, a hair-cut, and a good clean-up, he thought I would have a better chance of being employed.

I was taken to a restaurant, where I was provided with

superb coffee, sugared waffles, and doughnuts, after which we adjourned to a basement distinguished by a pole with red, white, and blue paint.

Everyone who has been operated upon by an American barber will understand the delight I felt, as I lay submissive in the luxurious chair, to be beautified by a demi-semi-gentleman, with ambrosial curls! The mere fact that such as he condescended to practise his art upon one who but yesterday was only thought worthy of a kick, gave an increased value to my person, and provoked my conceit. When my dark hair had been artistically shortened, my head and neck shampooed, and my face glowed with the scouring, I looked into the mirror and my vanity was prodigious. A negro boy completed my toilet with an efficient brushing and a boot-polish, and my friend was pleased to say that I looked first-rate.

By the time we returned to Speake and McCreary's store, Mr. James Speake had put in an appearance. After a cordial greeting, my benefactor led Mr. Speake away by the arm and held a few minutes' earnest conversation with him. Presently I was beckoned to advance, and Mr. Speake said with a smile to me, —

'Well, young man, this gentleman tells me you want a place. Is that so?'

'Yes, sir.'

'That is all right. I am willing to give you a week's trial at five dollars, and if we then find we suit each other, the place will be permanent. Are you agreeable?'

There could be no doubt of that fact, and Mr. Speake turned round to two young gentlemen, one of whom he called Mr. Kennicy, and the other Mr. Richardson, and acquainted them with my engagement as a help to Mr. Richardson in the shipping business. The generosity of my unknown friend had been so great that, before addressing myself to any employment, I endeavoured to express my gratitude; but my strong emotions were not favourable to spontaneous fluency. The gentleman seemed to divine what I wished to say, and said, —

'There, that will do. I know what is in your heart. Shake hands. I am going up-river with my consignments, but I shall return shortly and hope to hear the best accounts of you.'

For the first half-hour my heart was too full, and my eyes

too much blurred, to be particularly bright. The gentleman's benevolence had been immense, and as yet I knew not even his name, his business, or what connection he had with the store of Speake and McCreary. I was in the midst of strangers, and, so far, my experience of them had not been of that quality to inspire confidence. In a short time, however, Mr. Richardson's frankness and geniality made me more cheerful. He appeared to take pride in inducting me into my duties, and I responded with alacrity. He had an extremely pleasant manner, the candour of Harry, without his vulgarity. Before an hour had passed, I was looking up to him as to a big brother, and was asking him all sorts of questions respecting the gentleman who had taken me out of the street and started me so pleasantly in life.

From Mr. Richardson I learned that he was a kind of broker who dealt between planters up-river and merchants in New Orleans, and traded through a brother with Havana and other West Indian ports. He had a desk in the store, which he made use of when in town, and did a good deal of safe business in produce both with Mr. Speake and other wholesale merchants. He travelled much up and down the river, taking large consignments with him for back settlements up the Arkansas, Washita, and Saline, and other rivers, and returning often with cotton and other articles. *His name was* MR. STANLEY. His wife lived in St. Charles Street, in a first-class boarding-house, and, from the style Mr. and Mrs. Stanley kept up, he thought they must be pretty well off. This was the extent of the information Mr. Richardson could give me, which was most gratifying, and assured me that I had at least one friend in the strange city.

There have been several memorable occasions in my life; but, among them, this first initial stage towards dignity and independence must ever be prominent. What a proud, glad holiday-spirit moved me then! I soon became sensible of a kindling elation of feeling, for the speech of all to me was as though everyone recognised that I had entered into the great human fraternity. The abruptness of the transition, from the slave of yesterday into the free-man of to-day, endowed with a sacred inviolability of person, astonished me. Only a few hours ago, I was as one whose skull might be smashed at the impulse of a moment; and now, in an instant, as it were, I was free of the severe thraldom, and elevated to the rank of man.

Messrs. Kennicy and Richardson were good types of free-spoken young America. They were both touchy in the extreme, and, on points of personal honour, highly intolerant. America breeds such people by thousands, who appear to live eternally on the edge of resentment, and to be as inflammable as tinder. It is dangerous to deal with them in badinage, irony, sarcasm, or what we call 'chaff.' Before the expiration of the first day, I had noted that their high spirits scarcely brooked a reproof, or contradiction, the slightest approach to anything of the kind exciting them to a strange heat. When I saw that they became undisguisedly angry because Mr. Speake happened to ask them why some order for goods had not been completed, I really could not help feeling a little contempt for them. Otherwise, they were both estimable young men, clean as new pins, exquisitely dressed, and eminently cordial — especially Richardson, whom I warmly admired.

My first day's employment consisted in assisting Dan and Samuel, the two negroes, in taking groceries on trucks from the depths of the long store to the sidewalk, or rolling liquor or flour-barrels on the edges of thin boards, — an art I acquired very soon, — and in marking sundry lots for shipment to Mississippi ports with strange names, such as Bayou Placquemine, Attakapas, Opelousas, etc., etc. Richardson was, in the meantime, busy in making out bills of lading, and arranging with the pursers of the steamers for their transportation. The drays clattered to the door, and removed the goods as fast as we could get them ready. Every moment of the day added to my rapture. The three lofts above the ground-floor contained piles upon piles of articles such as could be comprised under the term groceries, besides rare wines and brandies, liqueurs and syrups. The ground-floor was piled up to the ceiling almost with sacks of coffee-berries, grains, and cases of miscellanea, barrels of flour, tierces of bacon, hams, etc., etc. It was informing even to read the titles on the neatly-branded cases, which contained bottled fruit, tinned jams, berries of all kinds, scented soaps, candles, vermicelli, macaroni, and other strange things. If I but stepped on the sidewalk, I saw something new and unheard-of before. The endless drays thundering by the door, and the multitudes of human beings, not one of whom was like the other in head-gear or dress, had a fascination for me; and, with every sound and sight, I was learning something new.

While influenced by all these things, I sprang upon work of any kind with an avid desire to have it completed; but the negroes did their utmost to suppress my boisterous exuberance of spirit by saying, 'Take it easy, little boss, don't kill yourself. Plenty of time. Leave something for to-morrow.' Had the mates of the 'Windermere' but looked in upon us, they might have learned that a happy crew had more work in them, than when driven by belaying-pins and rope's ends.

Towards evening we swept up; and, when we had tidied the store, it came to my mind that I knew no lodging-house. In consulting with Dan, he said he knew a Mrs. Williams, who kept a nice, cheap boarding-house on St. Thomas Street, where I could be most comfortable. It was arranged that he should introduce me, and I walked up Tchapitoulas Street, with the two slaves, whose tin lunch-buckets swung heavily, I thought, as they moved homeward.

Mrs. Williams, a young and black beauty, with intelligent features, was most affable, and agreed to board me at a rate which would leave me a respectable margin at the end of the week, and to give me a large attic room for myself. Her house was of wood, with a garden in front, and a spacious tree-shaded yard at the rear. The maternal solicitude she showed in providing for my comfort greatly charmed me, though I was forced to smile at her peculiar English and drawling accent. But when, just as I was about to retire to my bedroom, she, in the most matter-of-fact way, assisted me to undress, and took possession of my shirt and collar, saying they would be washed and ironed by morning, that I might look more 'spruce,' my estimation of her rose very high indeed, and affected me to such a degree that I revolved all the kindnesses I had experienced during the day, and was reminded to give thanks to Him, Who, 'like as a father, pitieth His children and them that fear Him.'

The next morning, by half-past six, I was at the door of Speake and McCreary's store, fit for any amount of work, and glorying in my condition. By eight o'clock the store, which was about one hundred feet long, was sweet and clean, the sidewalk was swept, and the earlier instalments of goods duly arranged on it for shipment. Then the book-keeper and shipping-clerk entered, fresh and scented as for courtship, took off their street coats, and donning their linen 'dusters,' resumed business. About nine, Mr. James Speake — McCreary was dead — appeared with the mien of gracious masterhood, which to me was a sign of goodness, and stimulative of noble efforts in his service.[1]

My activity and fresh memory were soon appreciated. Half-a-dozen times a day my ready answers saved time. My hearing seemed to them to be phenomenal; and my accuracy in remembering the numbers of kegs, cases, and sacks remaining in store, caused me, before the end of the week, to be regarded as a kind of walking inventory. I could tell where each article was located, and the contents of the various lofts had also been committed to my memory. Unlike the young gentlemen, I never argued, or contradicted, or took advantage of a pettish ebullition to aggravate temper; and, what was a great relief to persons with responsibilities in a warm climate, I was always at hand, near the glass-door of the office, awaiting orders. Previous to my arrival, Dan and Samuel had always found something to do at a distance, either upstairs or in the back-yard; they pretended not to hear; and it had been a fatiguing task to call them, and trying to the patience to wait for them; but now I was within easy hail, and my promptitude was commended. Thereupon my week's trial ended satisfactorily, even more so than I had anticipated, for I was permanently engaged at twenty-five dollars a month. Such a sum left me with fifteen dollars a month, net, after payment of board and lodging, and was quite a fortune in

[1] Early in 1891, I visited New Orleans, with my husband. He tried to find the houses and places he had known as a boy. The following remarks are from his note-book: —

'We walked up Canal Street, and took the cars at Tchapitoulas Street, as far as Annunciation Street. Looked at No. 1659, which resembles the house I sought; continued down to No. 1323 — above Thalis Street; this also resembled the house, but it is now occupied by two families; in former days, the house had but one occupant. I seemed to recognize it by its attics. The houses no doubt have been re-numbered. We then returned to Tchapitoulas Street, and thence into St. Peter's Street, which formerly was, I think, Commerce Street. Speake's house was between Common and Canal Street — No. 3. Here, also, there has been a change; No. 3 is now No. 5. The numbers of the next houses are now in the hundreds.' — D. S.

my eyes. Mr. Speake, moreover, advanced a month's pay, that I might procure an outfit. Mr. Richardson, who boarded in the more fashionable Rampart Street, undertook to assist in my purchases, and presented me with a grand, brass-bound trunk of his own, which, besides having a tray for shirts, and a partition for neck-ties and collars, was adorned on the lid with the picture of a lovely maiden. Truly, a boy is easily pleased! I had more joy in contemplating that first trunk of mine, and imprisoning my treasures under lock and key, than I have had in any property since!

My rating was now a junior clerk. Our next-door neighbours, Messrs. Hall and Kemp, employed two junior clerks, whose pay was four hundred dollars a year. They were happy, careless lads, who dressed well, and whose hardest toil was with the marking-pot. I was now as presentable as they, but I own to be proud that I had no fear of soiling my hands or clothes with work, and I never allowed a leaky sack of coffee, or barrel of flour, to leave our store for want of a little sewing or coopering — tasks which they felt it to be beneath them to do!

Long before the 'Windermere' had sailed back for Liverpool with her cotton cargo, a great change had come over me. Up to my arrival in New Orleans, no indulgence had been shown me. I was scarcely an hour away from the supervision of someone. From my nurse's maternal care, I had passed under the strict régime of the Orphan's Academy — the Workhouse; thence I had been transferred to the no-less-strict guardianship of Aunt Mary, and the severe Moses, thence into that of Uncle Tom; and, afterwards, had tasted of the terrible discipline of an American packet-ship. Draconian rules had been prescribed; the birch hung ever in view in one place, censure and menace at another. At Uncle Tom's there was no alternative but obedience or the street; and the packet-ship was furnished with rope's ends and belaying-pins. But, within a few weeks of arriving in America, I had become different in temper and spirit. That which was natural in me, though so long repressed, had sprung out very quickly under the peculiar influence of my surroundings. The childish fear of authority had fled — for authority no longer wore its stern, relentless aspect, but was sweetly reasonable. Those who exercised it were gentle and sociable, and I repaid them with respect and gratitude. To them I owed my happiness; and my new feeling of dignity made me stretch myself to my full height, and revel luxuriously in fond ideas. I possessed properties in my person which I instinctively valued, and felt bound to cultivate. The two-feet square of the street I occupied were mine for the time being, and no living man could budge me except at his peril. The view of the sky was as freely mine as another's. These American rights did not depend on depth of pocket, or stature of a man, but every baby had as much claim to them as the proudest merchant. Neither poverty nor youth was degrading, nor was it liable to abuse from wealth or age. Besides my youth, activity, and intelligence, of which I had been taught the value, I had become conscious of the fact that I possessed privileges of free speech, free opinions, immunity from insult, oppression, and the contempt of class; and that, throughout America, my treatment from men would solely depend upon my individual character, without regard of family or pedigree. These were proud thoughts. I respired more freely, my shoulders rose considerably, my back straightened, my strides became longer, as my mind comprehended this new feeling of independence. To the extent of so much I could not be indebted to any man living; but for the respectability of the covering and comfort of the body, and the extension of my rights to more ground than I could occupy standing, I must work.

Inspired of these thoughts, I was becoming as un-English in disposition as though I had been forty years in the land, and, as old Sir Thomas Browne puts it, 'of a constitution so general that it consorted and sympathised' with things American. My British antipathies and proclivities were dropping from me as rapidly as the littlenesses of my servile life were replaced by the felicities of freedom. I shared in the citizens' pride in their splendid port, the length and stability of their levee, their unparalleled lines of shipping, their magnificent array of steamers, and their majestic river. I believed, with them, that their Custom-House, when completed, would be a matchless edifice, that Canal Street was unequalled for its breadth, that Tchapitoulas Street was, beyond compare, the busiest street in the world, that no markets equalled those of

New Orleans for their variety of produce, and that no city, not even Liverpool, could exhibit such mercantile enterprise, or such a smart go-ahead spirit, as old and young manifested in the chief city of the South. I am not sure that I have lost all that lively admiration yet, though I have since seen dozens of cities more populous, more cultivated, and more opulent. Many years of travel have not extinguished my early faith, but it would require ages to eradicate my affection for the city which first taught me that a boy may become a *man*.

Had the joylessness of boyhood endured a few years longer, it is probable that the power of joyousness would have dried up; but, fortunately, though I had seen fifteen summers, I was a mere child in experience. It was only eighteen months since I had left St. Asaph, and but two months and a half since I had entered the world outside my family. Since I became a man, I have often wondered what would have become of me had my melting mood that last night at Roscommon Street lasted a little longer. It was the turning-point of my life, I am disposed to think, and it was good for me to have had the courage to say 'No,' at that critical moment. A trifle more perseverance, on the part of Uncle Tom, would have overcome my inclination for departure from England, and made me a fixture within his own class. On that occasion my weakly, half-hearted negative served me to good purpose; but I should have been spared many trials had I been educated to utter my 'Noes' more often, more loudly, and more firmly than I have; and I suppose most men have had cause to condemn that unsatisfactory education which sent them into the world so imperfectly equipped for moral resistance. In my opinion, the courage to deliver a proper 'No' ought to be cultivated as soon as a child's intelligence is sufficiently advanced. The few times I have been able to say it have been productive of immense benefit to me, though to my shame, be it said, I yearned to say 'Yes.'

That soft habit of becoming fondly attached to associations, which made me weep on leaving St. Asaph, Ffynnon Beuno, Brynford, Liverpool, and even the 'Windermere,' made me cling to my attic room in the house of Mrs. Williams. My increase of pay enabled me to secure a larger and more comfortable room; but, detesting change, I remained its occupant. My self-denial was compensated, however, by a fine surplus of dollars, with which I satisfied a growing desire for books.

So far, all the story-books I had read, beyond the fragments found in School-readers, consisted of that thrilling romance about Enoch and his brothers, a novelette called 'First Footsteps in Evil,' 'Kaloolah,' by Dr. Mayo, which I had found at Ffynnon Beuno, and 'Ivanhoe,' in three volumes, at which I had furtively glanced as it lay open in my cousin's study at Brynford.

Through the influence of cheap copies of standard books, millions of readers in America have been educated, at slight cost, in the best productions of English authors; and when these have been delegated to the second-hand bookstalls, it is wonderful what a library one can possess at a trifling expense. There was such a stall existing conveniently near St. Thomas Street, which I daily passed; and I could never resist fingering the books, and snatching brief delights from their pages. As soon as my wardrobe was established, I invested my surplus in purchases of this description, and the bookseller, seeing a promising customer in me, allowed me some latitude in my selection, and even catered to my tastes. The state of the binding mattered little; it was the contents that fascinated me. My first prize that I took home was Gibbon's 'Decline and Fall,' in four volumes, because it was associated with Brynford lessons. I devoured it now for its own sake. Little by little, I acquired Spenser's 'Faery Queen,' Tasso's 'Jerusalem Delivered,' Pope's 'Iliad,' Dryden's 'Odyssey,' 'Paradise Lost,' Plutarch's 'Lives,' Simplicius on Epictetus, a big 'History of the United States,' the last of which I sadly needed, because of my utter ignorance of the country I was in.

Mrs. Williams gave me a few empty cases, out of which, with the loan of a saw, hammer, and nails, I constructed a creditable book-case; and, when it was put up, I do believe my senses contained as much delight as they were able to endure, without making me extravagant in behaviour. My attic became my world now, and a very great expansible world, full of kings, emperors, knights, warriors, heroes, and angels. Without, it might have been better, less sordid; within, it was glorious for great deeds and splendid pageantry.

It affected my dreams, for I dreamed of the things that I had read. I was transported into Trojan Fields, and Odyssean Isles, and Roman Palaces; and my saturated brain revolved prose as stately as Gibbon's, and couplets that might have been a credit to Pope, only, if I chanced to remember at daybreak what I had been busy upon throughout the night, the metre and rhyme were shameful!

My self-indulgence in midnight readings was hurtful to my eyes, but they certainly interposed between me and other harms. The passion of study was so absorbing that it effectually prevented the intrusion of other passions, while it did not conflict with day-work at the store. Hall and Kemp's young gentlemen sometimes awoke in me a languid interest in Ben de Bar's Theatrical troupe, or in some great actor; but, on reaching home, my little library attracted my attention, and a dip into a page soon effaced all desire for other pleasure. What I am I owe to example, nature, school-education, reading, travel, observation, and reflection. An infinitesimal amount of the mannerisms observed clung to me, no doubt. The housewifely orderliness of Aunt Mary, the serious propriety of Cousin Moses, — then, when I went to sea, the stern voice of the captain, the ripping, explosive manner of the mates, the reckless abandon of the sailors, — after that, the conscientious yielding of myself to details of business, — all this left indelible impressions on me.

About the fourth week Mr. Stanley returned, with a new batch of orders. He warmly congratulated me upon my improved appearance, and confidentially whispered to me that Mr. Speake was thoroughly satisfied with my devotion to business. He gave me his card, and said that on the following Sunday he would be glad to see me at breakfast.

When the day arrived, I went to St. Charles Street, a quarter greatly superior to St. Thomas Street. The houses were aristocratic, being of classic design, with pillared porticoes, and wide, cool verandahs, looking out upon garden-shrubbery and flowering magnolias. Mr. Stanley was in an easy-chair, awaiting me. But for that, I should have hesitated at mounting the wide steps, so imposing the establishment appeared. He took me by the hand to an ample room luxuriously furnished, and introduced me to a fragile little lady, who was the picture of refinement. My reception was of such a character that it led me to believe she was as tender and mild as her quiet and subdued looks; and the books on the centre table made me think her pious. Nothing could have been better calculated to conquer my shyness than the gracious welcome she accorded me. We took our respective places at once, she as a motherly patroness, and I as a devotedly-grateful protégé, fully sensible of what was due to her as the wife of my benefactor. Her husband stood towering over me with his hand on my head, and an encouraging smile on his face, that I might speak out without fear; and he watched the impression I made on his wife. The ordeal of presentation was made easy through her natural goodness, and the gentle art she possessed of winning my confidence. She placed me on a divan near her, and I was soon prattling away with a glibness that a few minutes before would have been deemed impossible to such a stocky boy.

To confine within a sentence my impressions of the first lady I ever conversed with, is entirely beyond my power. There was an atmosphere about her, in the first place, which was wholly new. The elaborateness and richness of dress, the purity and delicacy of her face, the exquisite modulations of her voice, the distinctness of her enunciation, and the sweet courtesy of her manner, I will not say awed me, but it kindled as much of reverence as ever I felt in my life. If I were to combine this with a feeling that the being beside me might command me to endure practically any torture, or dare any danger, for her sake, it will perhaps sum up the effect which this gentlewoman made on my raw mind. It was at this hour I made the discovery of the immense distance between a lady and a mere woman; and, while I gazed at her clear, lustrous eyes, and noted the charms which played about her features, I was thinking that, if a lady could be so superior to an ordinary housewife, with her careless manner of speech, and matter-of-fact ways, what a beautiful thing an angel must be!

When we adjourned to the breakfast-table, I found more material to reflect upon. There were about a dozen people, of about the age and rank of Mr. and Mrs. Stanley, at the table; and it struck me that there was an almost impassable gulf between me and them. Their conversation was beyond my understanding, mostly, though I could spell and interpret each word; but the subjects of their talk left me in the clouds. Their remarks upon literature, politics, and social life, seemed to me most appropriate to books; but it surprised me to think that people could exchange so much learning across a table with the fluency of boys discussing the quality of pudding. Their soothing manner of address, the mutual respect, and deferent temper, greatly elevated them above my coarse-grained acquaintances; and, though they must have guessed, by my manner and age, that I did not belong to their sphere, they paid me the honour of including me in their courteous circle, until, unconsciously, I was straining to acquit myself worthily. Altogether, it was a memorable breakfast; and, when I reached home, it seemed to me that fortune was about to spoil me; otherwise, why this glow and pride that I felt?

After this Sunday, my acquaintance with Mr. Stanley rapidly ripened into something exceeding common gratitude. His bearing towards me was different from that which anybody else showed to me. Many were kind and approving; but, nevertheless, no one stooped to court my notice with that warm, genial manner which distinguished Mr. Stanley. I felt frequently flattered by the encomiums of Mr. Speake, and the friendship of Richardson; but still, there was something of reserve between us, which kept me somewhat tongue-tied in their presence. They never inquired about my welfare or health, or how I liked my boarding-house, or what I thought of anything, or made any suggestion which would stimulate confidence. Their talks with me were all about the business appertaining to the store, or some hap-hazard remark about the weather, or some scene in the street; but Mr. Stanley's way was as though it specially concerned him to know everything about me personally, which had the quality of drawing me out, and making me garrulous, to the verge of familiarity. So, little by little, I came to regard him as an elderly associate, with such a charming, infectious frankness, that I could only, for want of a comparison, remember my affection for my old grandfather, as corresponding with the mixed feelings of regard and awe I had towards him. Besides, to be in his company, even for a brief time, was an education for one so ignorant as myself. Information about somebody or something dropped from his lips with every remark he made. I felt myself becoming intelligent, informed about the geography and history of the city and state that I was in, and learned in the ways and customs of the people. The great merchants and institutions assumed a greater interest for me. They were something more than strange names for repetition; they had associations which revealed personalities of worth, colossal munificence, remunerative enterprise, etc., etc.

Every Sunday morning I spent with the Stanleys, and the instantaneous impression I had received of their goodness was more than confirmed. Mrs. Stanley seemed to become at each visit more tender and caressingly kind, in the same manner as he manifested a more paternal cordiality. I yielded myself wholly to their influence, so that my conduct when out of their sight was governed by the desire to retain their good opinions. Without them, probably, my love of books would have proved sufficient safe-guard against the baser kind of temptations; but, with them, I was rendered almost impregnable to vice. They took me to church, each Sabbath; and, in other ways, manifested a protective care. I resumed the custom of morning and evening prayer, my industry at the store was of a more thoughtful kind, my comings and goings were of more exemplary punctuality. The orderly, industrious life I was following not only ensured me the friendship of the Stanleys, but won me favour from Mr. Speake, who, though wearing often a somewhat anxious expression, restrained himself whenever he had an occasion to communicate with me.

In the third month there was a change at the store. Mr. Speake had some words with Mr. Kennicy, the book-keeper, who, being, as I said, touchy, resigned on the spot. A Mr. J. D. Kitchen was employed in his stead, and Mr. Speake saw fit to increase my salary to thirty dollars a month, giving for his reason the fact that the store had never been in such admirable order as it had been since I had entered it. I was immensely proud, of course, at this acknowledgement; but it was only natural that, being so susceptible and impressionable, it should stimulate me to greater efforts to deserve his approbation. Enlightening me, as it did, in duties expected of me, it might be said to have increased my interest in the condition of the store, until it partook of that which a fond proprietor might feel in it. Envious, or ill-natured, people might have said it was fussy, or officious. At any rate, this disposition to have everything clean, to keep the stacks in orderly arrangement, to be on hand when wanted, to keep my notes of shipment methodically, to be studiously bent upon perfection in my duties, led to the following incident.

We were ordered to take stock, and, while counting cases, and sacks, and barrels, etc., I had now and then to rearrange the stacks, because, in the hurry of business, a box of pickles or jams had become mixed with biscuits or candle-boxes; and, in handling these articles, it struck me that several of them were uncommonly light. I mentioned this, but it did not attract much attention. It was discovered, also, that the coffee-sacks were much slacker than they ought to be; but, though the rents through which the contents must have escaped appeared as if made by rats, as the quantity of berries on the ground was inadequate to the loss, I knew no other way in which to account for it. However, when, on going to the lofts, we gauged the contents of the wine-puncheons and syrup-barrels, and found them to be half-emptied, matters began to look serious. The leakage on the floor was not sufficient to explain the loss of so many gallons; and the discussion between the book-keeper and shipping-clerk suggested trouble when the 'old man' would be informed. From what I gathered, the former book-keeper, Mr. Kennicy, was supposed to be in fault. We were short of several boxes of biscuits, sardines, and other articles; and it seemed obvious that Mr. Kennicy must have omitted to enter sales on his book, and thus caused this unexpected discrepancy.

Mr. Speake, as had been anticipated, exhibited much vexation, though, in the presence of Mr. Kitchen and Mr. Richardson, he could only ask, querulously, 'How could such articles disappear in such a disproportionate manner? We do not sell by retail. If we sold wine, or syrup, at all, we would sell by the cask, or barrel, and not by the gallon. The barrels seem to tally, but the contents are diminished in some mysterious manner. Then there are the emptied cases, of which this boy has spoken: how can we account for bottles taken from one, and tins from another? The invoices were checked when the goods came in, and no deficiency was reported to me. There is gross carelessness somewhere, and it must be looked into,' etc., etc.

Both Mr. Kitchen and Mr. Richardson, under this argument, laboured under the sense of reproach, and I was not wholly free from a feeling of remissness. I strove hard to remember whether in conveying the cases to their respective piles, or hoisting the barrels to the lofts, a suspicion of light weight had entered my mind; and while filled with a sense of doubt and misgiving, I proceeded to hunt for a broom to sweep up, before closing. I found one in the corner of the back-yard; but, on drawing it to me, a tin lunch-bucket was disclosed, the sight of which in such an unexpected place suggested that the broom had been placed to screen it from view. On taking hold of it, I was amazed at its weight; but, on lifting the lid, I no longer wondered, for it was three-fourths full of golden syrup. It flashed across my mind that here was the solution of the mystery that troubled us, and that, if one bucket was made the means of surreptitiously conveying golden syrup, a second might be used for the same purpose. On searching for the other negro's bucket, I found it placed high above my reach, on a peg, and under his outdoor coat. Seizing a board, I struck it underneath, and a few drops of a dark aromatic liquor trickled down the sides. As, now, there could be no reason to doubt that the culprits had been discovered, I hastened to the office to give my information.

By great good-luck, Mr. Stanley appeared at that moment, and I at once acquainted him with what I had found. Mr. Richardson joined us, and, when he had heard it, he became hotly indignant, and cried, 'I see it all now. Come on, let us inform Mr. Speake, and have this affair cleared up at once!'

Mr. Speake and Mr. Kitchen were in the office turning over ledger, journal, and day-book, comparing entries, when we burst upon them with the discovery. Mr. Speake was astonished and exclaimed, 'There now, who would have thought of these fellows? A systematic robbery has been going on for goodness knows how long!'

While breathlessly discussing the matter, we suddenly

remembered various strange proceedings of the negroes, and our suspicions were excited that there must be certain secret nests of stores somewhere in the building; and Richardson and I were sent off to explore. The same idea seemed to be in our minds, for we first searched the dark alleys between the goods-piles, and, in a short time, we had lit upon the secret hoards. Hams, sardines, and tins of biscuits, packages of candles, etc., etc., were found between the hogsheads and tierces; and, when we had carried them to the office, the indignation of everyone was very high.

Dan and Samuel had been all this time in the upper lofts, and were now called down. When questioned as to their opinions about the disappearance of certain articles, they both denied all knowledge, and affected the ignorance of innocence; but, when they were sharply told to lead us to their tin buckets, their features underwent a remarkable change, and assumed a strange grey colour. Dan pretended to forget where he had placed his bucket; but, when Mr. Speake took him by the collar and led him to the broom that hid it, he fell on his knees, and begged his master's pardon. Mr. Speake was, however, too angry to listen to him, and, snatching the lid off, revealed to us half a gallon of the best golden syrup, which the wretch had intended to have taken home. When Sam's useful utensil was examined, it was found that its owner had a preference for sweet Malmsey wine!

A constable was called in, and Dan and Samuel were marched off to the watch-house, to receive on the next day such a flogging as only practised State-officials know how to administer. Dan, a few days later, was reinstated at the store; but Samuel was disposed of to a planter, for field-work.

The last Sunday morning Mr. Stanley was in the city, on this occasion, was marked with a visit he paid to me at my humble boarding-house. He was pleased to express his great surprise that, at that early hour, my attic was arranged as though for inspection. He scrutinised my book-case, and remarked that I had a pretty broad taste, and suggested that I should procure various books which he mentioned. In self-defence, I was obliged to plead poverty, and explained that my books were only such as I could obtain at a second-hand book-stall. He finally condescended to breakfast with me, and made himself especially agreeable to Mrs. Williams and her guests; after which, we went to church, and thence he took me to dine with him. In the afternoon, we drove in a carriage down Levee Street, past the French Market, and I was shown many of the public buildings, banks, and squares; and, later, we took a short railway trip to Lake Ponchartrain, which is a fair piece of water, and is a great resort for bathers. When we returned to the city, late in the evening, I was fairly instructed in the topography of the city and neighbourhood, and had passed a most agreeable and eventful day.

On the next evening, I found a parcel addressed to me, which, when opened, disclosed a dozen new books in splendid green and blue covers, bearing the names of Shakespeare, Byron, Irving, Goldsmith, Ben Jonson, Cowper, etc. They were a gift from Mr. Stanley, and in each book was his autograph.

The summer of 1859, according to Mr. Richardson, was extremely unhealthy. Yellow fever and dysentery were raging. What a sickly season meant I could not guess; for, in those days, I never read a newspaper, and the city traffic, to all appearance, was much as usual. On Mr. Speake's face, however, I noticed lines of suffering; and one day he was so ill that he could not attend to business. Three or four days later, he was dead; and a message came from the widow that I should visit her, at her home, at the corner of Girod and Carondelet Streets. She was now in a state of terrible distress, and, clad in heavy mourning, she impressed me with very sombre thoughts. It comforted her to hear how sensible we all were of her loss; and then she communicated to me her reasons for desiring my presence. Through her husband she had been made aware of my personal history, and, on account of the interest it had excited in her, she had often induced her husband to tell her every incident at the store. She proceeded to reveal to me the flattering opinion he had formed of me, in terms that augmented my grief; and, as a mark of special favour, I was invited to stay in the house until after the funeral.

That night, I was asked to watch the dead, a duty of which I was wholly unaware before. The body rested in a splendid open coffin, covered with muslin, but the ghastliness of death was somewhat relieved by the Sunday costume in which the defunct merchant was clothed. When the traffic of the streets had ceased, and the silence of the night had fallen on the city, the shadows in the ill-lit room grew mysterious. About midnight, I dozed a little, but suddenly woke up with an instinctive feeling that the muslin had moved! I sprang to my feet, and memories of spectral tales were revived. Was it an illusion, begotten of fear? Was Mr. Speake really dead? There was, at that moment, another movement, and I prepared to give the alarm; but a sacrilegious 'meow' betrayed the character of the ghost! A second later, it was felled by a bolster; and, in its haste to escape, the cat entangled its claws in the muslin, and tore and spat in a frenzy; but this was the means of saving me from the necessity of chasing the wretched animal along the corridors, for, as it was rushing through the door, I caught the veil.

The next day, a long procession wound through the streets towards the cemetery.[1] The place of interment was surrounded by a high wall, which contained several square tablets, commemorative, as I supposed, of the dead lying in the earth; but I was much shocked when I learned that, behind each tablet, was a long narrow cell wherein bodies were corrupting. One of these cells had just been opened, and was destined for the body of my late employer; but, unfortunately for my feelings, not far off lay, huddled in a corner, the relics of mortality which had occupied it previously, and which had been ruthlessly displaced.

Within a short time, the store, with all its contents, was disposed of by auction, to Messrs. Ellison and McMillan. Messrs. Kitchen and Richardson departed elsewhere, but I was retained by the new firm. Mrs. Cornelia Speake and her two children removed to Louisville, and I never saw either of them again.

About this time there came to Mrs. Williams's boarding-house a blue-eyed and fair-haired lad, of about my own age, seeking lodgings. As the house was full, the landlady insisted

[1] From Note-Book: —

'In the morning, hired hack, visited Saint Roch's, or Campo Santo, St. Louis — 1, 2, 3, & 4, Cemeteries — drove to Girod's Cemetery — examined book, and found that James Speake died October 26th, and was buried October 27th, 1859, aged 47.'

on accommodating him in my room, and bedding him with me; and, on finding that the boy was English, and just arrived from Liverpool, I assented to her arrangement.

My intended bed-fellow called himself Dick Heaton, and described himself as having left Liverpool in the ship 'Pocahontas,' as a cabin-boy. He also had been a victim to the hellish brutality of Americans at sea, the steward apparently having been as callous and cruel as Nelson of the 'Windermere'; and, no sooner had his ship touched the pier, than the boy fled, as from a fury. Scarcely anything could have been better calculated to win my sympathy than the recital of experiences similar to my own, by one of my own age, and hailing from the same port that I had come from.

Dick was clever and intelligent, though not well educated; but, to make up for his deficiency in learning, he was gifted with a remarkable fluency, and had one of the cheeriest laughs, and a prettiness of manner which made up for all defects.

Our bed was a spacious four-poster, and four slim lads like us might have been easily accommodated in it. I observed, however, with silent surprise, that he was so modest he would not retire by candle-light, and that when he got into bed he lay on the verge of it, far removed from contact with me. When I rose in the morning, I found that he was not undressed, which he explained by saying that he had turned in thus from the habit of holding himself ready for a call. On beginning his voyage he had been so severely thrashed for a delay caused by dressing, that he had scarcely dared to take off his boots during the whole voyage. He also told me that, when he had discovered how almost impossible it was to avoid a beating from the steward and cook, he had resorted to the expedient of padding the seat of his trousers with cotton, and wearing a pad of the same material along the spine, but to avert suspicion that he was thus cunningly fortified against the blows, he had always continued to howl as freely as before. The naïveté of the revelation was most amusing, though I was surprised at the shameless way in which he disclosed his tricks and cowardly fears. However, it did not deter me from responding to his friendly advances, and in two days I came to regard him as a very charming companion. The third morning, being Sunday, we chatted longer abed; but, when rising together, I cast a glance at his hips, and remarked that he need have no fear of being thrashed at New Orleans. He appeared a little confused at first, but, suddenly remembering, he said that on the Monday he would have to purchase a new pair of trousers and seek work. A little later, it struck me that there was an unusual forward inclination of the body, and a singular leanness of the shoulders, compared with the fulness below the waist in him; and I remarked that he walked more like a girl than a boy. 'So do you,' he retorted, with a liberty natural to our age, at which I only laughed.

I proposed to him that we should breakfast at the French Market that morning, to which he willingly agreed. We walked down Levee Street, down to the foot of Canal Street, where we saw fifty or sixty river steamers assembled, which, massed together, made a most imposing sight. Turning to take a view of the scene up-river, with its miles upon miles of shipping, its levee choked with cotton, and other cargoes, he said that it was a finer sight than even the docks of Liverpool. After a cup of coffee and some sugared waffles, we proceeded on a tour through the old quarter of the city, and wandered past the Cathedral of St. Louis, and through Royal, Chartres, Burgundy, and Toulouse Streets, and, coming home by Rampart Street, entered Canal Street, and continued our weary way, through Carondelet and St. Charles Streets, home, where we arrived heated and hungry. Dick had shown himself very observant, and professed to be astonished at the remarkable variety of complexions and appearance of the population. So long as we were in the neighbourhood of the levee he had been rather shy, and had cast anxious glances about him, fearing recognition from some of the crew of the 'Pocahontas'; but, after we had gone into some of the back streets, he had been more at ease, and his remarks upon the types of people we met showed much shrewdness.

Monday morning I woke at an early hour, to prepare myself for the week's labour; and, on looking towards Dick, who was still sound asleep, was amazed to see what I took to be two tumours on his breast. My ejaculation and start woke my companion. He asked what was the matter? Pointing to his open breast, I anxiously inquired if those were not painful?

He reddened, and, in an irritable manner, told me that I had better mind my own business! Huffed at his ungraciousness, I turned resentfully away. Almost immediately after, I reminded myself of his confusion, his strange manner of entering a clean bed with his clothes on, his jealous avoidance of the light, his affectation of modesty, his peculiar suppleness and mincing gait, and the odd style of his figure. These things shaped themselves rapidly into proofs that Dick was not what he represented himself to be. True, he had a boy's name, he wore boy's clothes, he had been a cabin-boy; but such a strange boy I had never seen. He talked far too much and too fluently, he was too tricky, too nimble, somehow. No, I was convinced he could *not* be a boy! I sat up triumphantly, and cried out with the delight of a discoverer: —

'I know! I know! Dick, you are a girl!'

Nevertheless, when he faced me, and unblushingly admitted the accusation, it frightened me; and I sprang out of bed as though I had been scorched!

'What,' I exclaimed, 'do you mean to say you are a girl?'

'Yes, I am,' said she, turning pale, as she became infected with my excitement.

Perplexed at this astounding confirmation of what, after all, had been only a surmise of playful malice, I stammeringly demanded, —

'Well, what *is* your name, then? It cannot be Dick, for that belongs to a boy.'

'I am Alice Heaton. There, now, you have my whole secret!' she said with asperity.

'Alice Heaton!' I echoed, quite confounded at the feminine name; and I reproachfully asked, 'If you are a girl, say, what do you mean by coming into my bed, and passing yourself off as a boy?'

She had kept up bravely so far, but she now answered me with tears and sobs, and every doubt of her sex vanished, while I was in such a medley of emotions that I stood like one utterly bereft of sense, not knowing what to do. Presently, she said, 'Come, let us dress, and I will tell you all about it.'

I lost no time in doing what she advised; and, after taking a turn or two in the yard, returned to find her ready for me.

Now that her sex was revealed, I wondered that I had been so blind as not to perceive it before, for, in every movement, there was unmistakeable femininity. Alice made me sit down, and the substance of the story she now told me was as follows:

She had been born at Everton, Liverpool, and, since she had begun to walk, she had lived with a severe old grandmother, who grew more cross as she aged. From childhood, she had known nothing but ill-treatment; she was scolded and slapped perpetually. When she was twelve years of age, she began to struggle with her granny, and, in a short time, she proved that her strength was too great to be beaten by an infirm old woman; little by little, her grandmother desisted from the attempt, but substituted, instead, the nagging system. As she approached her fourteenth year, her grandmother developed a parsimony which made her positively hateful. Every crust she ate at the house was begrudged to her, though, so far as she knew, there was no cause for this pinching and starving. Her home contained evidences of respectability. The furniture was abundant and of good quality, and the many curios in the glass cases in the parlour showed that her parents had been in comfortable circumstances. How her grandmother obtained her means of living, Alice did not know; but, judging from her dress and condition, her poverty was not so distressing as to be the cause of such extreme penuriousness.

During the last five or six months, as she was getting on to fifteen, Alice had been acquainted with girlish neighbours, and through them, with some young middies who had just returned from their voyages. These had delighted to tell her friends of the wonders of foreign lands, and of the genial welcome they had met with from their foreign friends. The stories of their sea-life, and the pictures of America which they gave, fascinated her; and she secretly resolved that, upon the first violent outbreak of her grandmother's temper, she would try her fortune as a cabin-boy. With this view, every penny she could scrape, or steal, from her grandmother she hoarded, until, at last, she had enough to purchase from a slop-shop all she needed for a disguise. When her grandmother finally broke out into a bad fit of temper, and, provoked by her defiance, ordered her out of the house, she was ready for her venture. She went to a barber's shop and had her hair cut close; returning home, she dressed herself in boy's costume, and, with a sailor's bag on her back, entered a boarding-house near the docks. A few days later, she had the good luck to be engaged as a cabin-boy by the captain of the 'Pocahontas,' and, by careful conduct, escaped detection during the voyage, though nothing would avail her to avoid the rope's ending and cuffing of the steward and his fellow-officers.

By the time she had concluded her narrative, it was full time for me to depart to my work. We hurriedly agreed to consult together about future plans upon my return in the evening, and I left her with an assurance that all my means and help were at her service. All that day her extraordinary story occupied my mind, and, though she was undoubtedly an artful and bold character, her uncommon spirit compelled my admiration, while her condition was such as to compel my sympathy.

At the closing hour I sped homeward, but, on arriving at Mrs. Williams's, I was told Alice had not been seen since the early morning. I waited many hours, but waited in vain. She was never seen, or heard of, by me again; but I have hoped ever since that Fate was as propitious to her, as I think it was wise, in separating two young and simple creatures, who might have been led, through excess of sentiment, into folly.

The next Sabbath after the disappearance of Alice, I paid my usual visit to Mrs. Stanley, and was shocked and grieved to hear, from her maid, Margaret, that she was seriously ill, and under medical treatment. A glass of ice-water which she had taken on Friday had been speedily followed by alarming symptoms of illness. She was now so prostrated by disease that she required constant attendance. Margaret's face betrayed so much fatigue and anxiety that I tendered my services, and even begged her to employ me in any way. After a little hesitation, she said I might be useful in enabling her to take a little rest, if I would sit at the door, and, upon any movement or sound within the sick chamber, call her. I kept my post all through the day and night, and, though there were frequent calls on Margaret, her snatches of rest served to maintain her strength. As I went off to my labour, I promised to solicit a few days' leave from Mr. Ellison, and to return to her within the hour.

Mr. Ellison, however, to whom I preferred my request for a few days' liberty, affected to regard me as though I had uttered something very outrageous, and curtly told me I 'might go to the D——, if I liked, and stay with him for good.' Such an offensive reply, a few months earlier, would have made me shrink into myself; but the New Orleans atmosphere ripens one's sense of independence and personal dignity, and I replied with something of the spirit that I had admired in Mr. Kennicy and Mr. Richardson, and said: —

'Very well, sir. You may discharge me at once!' Of course, to a person of Mr. Ellison's sanguinary hair and complexion, the answer was sufficient to ensure my furious dismissal on the instant.

Margaret was greatly vexed at my action when she heard of it, but consoled me by saying that a few days' liberty would do me no harm. My whole time was now placed at her disposal, and I had reason to know that my humble services were a considerable relief and assistance to her at this trying time. Meanwhile, poor Mrs. Stanley was becoming steadily worse; and, on Wednesday night, her case was reported to be desperate by the physician. There was no more sleep for any of us until the issue should be decided. Near midnight, Margaret, with a solemn and ghastly face, beckoned me into the sick lady's room. With my heart throbbing painfully, and expecting I know not what, I entered on tiptoe. I saw a broad bed, curtained with white muslin, whereon lay the fragile figure of the patient, so frail and delicate that, in my rude health, it seemed insolence in me to be near her. It had been easy for me to speak of illness when I knew so little of what it meant; but, on regarding its ravages, and observing the operation of death, I stood as one petrified.

Margaret pushed me gently to the bedside, and I saw by the dim light how awfully solemn a human face can be when in saintly peace. Slowly, I understood how even the most timid woman could smilingly welcome Death, and willingly yield herself to its cold embrace. I had hitherto a stony belief that those who died had only been conquered through a sheer want of will on their part ('All men think all men mortal but themselves' [1]), and that the monster, with its horrors of cold, damp earth, and worms, needed only to be defied to be defeated of its prey. While listening at the door, I had wished that, in some way, I could transfuse a portion of my fulness of spirit into her, that she might have the force to resist the foe; for, surely, with a little more courage, she would not abandon husband, friends, and admirers, for the still company in the Churchyard. But the advance of Death was not like that of a blustering tyrant. It was imperceptible, and inconceivably subtle, beginning with a little ache — like one of many known before. Before it had declared its presence, it had narcotized the faculties, eased the beats of the heart, lessened the flow of blood, weakened the pulse; it had sent its messenger, Peace, before it, to dispel all anxieties and regrets, and to elevate the soul with the hope of Heaven; and then it closed the valves.

She opened her mild eyes, and spoke words as from afar: 'Be a good boy. God bless you!' And, while I strained my hearing for more, there was an indistinct murmur, the eyes opened wide and became fixed, and a beautiful tranquillity settled over the features. How strangely serene! When I turned to look into Margaret's eyes, I knew Death had come.

By a curious coincidence, Captain Stanley, her brother-in-law, arrived from Havana the next day, in a brig. He knew nothing of me. There was no reason he should be tender to my feelings, and he intimated to me, with the frankness of a ship's captain, that he would take charge of everything. Even Margaret subsided before this strong man; and, being very miserable, and with a feeling of irretrievable loss, I withdrew, after a silent clasp of the hands.

About three days later I received a letter from Margaret, saying that the body had been embalmed, and the casket had been put in lead; and that, according to a telegram received from Mr. Stanley, she was going up the river to St. Louis with it, by the steamer 'Natchez.'

For a period, I was too forlorn to heed anything greatly. I either stayed at home, reading, or brooding over the last scene in Mrs. Stanley's chamber, or I wandered aimlessly about the levee, or crossed over to Algiers, where I sat on the hulks, and

[1] Young.

watched the river flowing, with a feeling as of a nightmare on me.

My unhappy experiences at Liverpool had not been without their lessons of prudence. My only extravagances so far had been in the purchase of books; and, even then, a vague presentiment of want had urged me to be careful, and hurry to raise a shield against the afflictions of the destitute. Though at liberty, there was no fear that I should abuse it.

By and by, the cloud lifted from my mind; and I set about seeking for work. Fortune, however, was not so kind this time. The Mr. Stanleys of the world are not numerous. After two weeks' diligent search, there was not a vacancy to be found. Then I lowered my expectations, and sought for work of any kind. I descended to odd jobs, such as the sawing of wood, and building wood-piles for private families. The quality of the work mattered little.

One day there came a mate to our boarding-house, who told me that his captain was ill, and required an attendant. I offered myself, and was accepted.

The vessel was the 'Dido,' a full-sized brig. The captain suffered from a bilious fever, aggravated by dysentery, from drinking Mississippi water, it was thought. He was haggard, and yellow as saffron. I received my instructions from the doctor, and committed them to paper to prevent mistakes.

My duties were light and agreeable. During the remission of fever, the captain proved to be a kindly and pious soul; and his long grey beard gave him a patriarchal appearance, and harmonized with his patient temper. For three weeks we had an anxious time over him, but, during the fourth, he showed signs of mending, and took the air on the poop. He became quite communicative with me, and had extracted from me mostly all that was worth relating of my short history.

At the end of a month I was relieved from my duties; and as I had no desire to resume sea-life, even with so good a man, I was paid off most handsomely, with a small sum as a 'token of regard.' As I was about to depart, he said some words which, uttered with all solemnity, were impressive. 'Don't be down-hearted at this break in the beginning of your life. If you will only have patience, and continue in well-doing, your future will be better than you dream of. You have uncommon faculties, and I feel certain that, barring accidents, you will some day be a rich man. If I were you, I would seek your friend at St. Louis, and what you cannot find in this city, you may find in that. You deserve something better than to be doing odd jobs. Good-bye, and take an old man's best wishes.'

The old captain's words were better than his gold, for they gave me a healthful stimulus. His gold was not to be despised, but his advice inspired me with hope, and I lifted my head, and fancied I saw clearer and further. All men must pass through the bondage of necessity before they emerge into life and liberty. The bondage to one's parents and guardians is succeeded by bondage to one's employers.

On the very next day I took a passage for St. Louis, by the steamer 'Tuscarora'; and, by the end of November, 1859, I reached that busy city. The voyage had proved to me wonderfully educative. The grand pictures of enterprise, activity, and growing cities presented by the river shores were likely to remain with me forever. The successive revelations of scenery and human life under many aspects impressed me with the extent of the world. Mental exclamations of 'What a river!' 'What a multitude of steamers!' 'What towns, and what a people!' greeted each new phase. The intensity of everything also surprised me, from the resistless and deep river, the driving force within the rushing boats, the galloping drays along the levees, to the hurried pace of everybody ashore. On our own steamer my nerves tingled incessantly with the sound of the fast-whirling wheels, the energy of the mates, and the clamour of the hands. A feverish desire to join in the bustle burned in my veins.

On inquiring at the Planters' Hotel, I extracted from the hotel clerk the news that Mr. Stanley had descended to New Orleans on business a week before! For about ten days I hunted for work along the levee, and up and down Broadway, and the principal streets, but without success; and, at last, with finances reduced to a very low ebb, the river, like a magnet, drew me towards it. I was by this time shrunk into a small compass, even to my own perception. Self-depreciation could scarcely have become lower.

Wearied and disheartened, I sat down near a number of flatboats and barges, several of which were loading, or loaded, with timber, boards, and staves; and the talk of the men,—rough-bearded fellows,—about me, was of oak, hickory, pine shingles, scantling, and lumber; and I heard the now familiar names of Cairo, Memphis, and New Orleans. At the last word, my attention was aroused, and I discovered that one of the flat-boats was just about to descend the river to that port. Its crew were seated on the lumber, yarning light-heartedly; and their apparent indifference to care was most attractive to an outcast. I stole nearer to them, found out the boss, and, after a while, offered to work my passage down the river. Something in me must have excited his rough sympathy, for he was much kinder than might have been expected from his rough exterior. I had long since learned that the ordinary American was a curious compound of gentleman and navvy. His garb and speech might be rough, his face and hands soiled, beard and hair unkempt, but the bearing was sure to be free, natural, and grand, and his sentiments becoming; the sense of manly dignity was never absent, and his manners corresponded with his situation. My services were accepted, not without receiving a hint that loafing could not be tolerated aboard a flat-boat. Being the youngest on board, I was to be a general helper, assist the cook, and fly about where wanted. But what a joy to the workless is occupation! Independence may be a desirable thing, but the brief taste I had had of it had, by this, completely sickened me.

We cast off at day-break, and committed our huge unwieldy boat to the current of the Mississippi, using our sweeps occasionally to keep her in the middle. For the most part it seemed to me a lazy life. The physical labours were almost nil, though, now and then, all hands were called to exert their full strength, and the shouting and swearing were terrific. When the excitement was passed, we subsided into quietude, smoking, sleeping, and yarning. A rude galley had been set up temporarily for the cook's convenience, and a sail was stretched over the middle of the boat as a shelter from the sun and rain. There were eleven of us altogether, including myself. My promiscuous duties kept me pretty busy. I had to peel potatoes, stir mush, carry water, wash tin pans, and scour the plates, and on occasions lend my strength at pulling one of the tremendously long oars.

No special incident occurred during the long and tedious voyage. Once we narrowly escaped being run down by the 'Empress' steamer, and we had a lively time of it, the angry men relieving themselves freely of threats and oaths. Steamers passed us every day. Sometimes a pair of them raced madly side by side, or along opposite banks, while their furnaces, fed by pitch-pine, discharged rolling volumes of thick smoke, which betrayed, for hours after they had disappeared from view, the course they had taken. The water would splash up the sides of our boat, and the yellow river would part into alarming gulfs on either hand. At large towns, such as Cairo, Memphis, Vicksburg, and Natchez, we made fast to the shore; and, while the caterer of the mess took me with him to make his purchases of fresh provisions, the crew sought congenial haunts by the river-side for a mild dissipation. By the end of the month, our voyage terminated at some stave and lumber-yards between Carrolltown and New Orleans.

On the whole, the flat-boatmen had been singularly decent in their behaviour. Their coarseness was not disproportionate to their circumstances, or what might be expected from wage-earners of their class; but what impressed me most was the vast amount of good feeling they exhibited. There had been a few exciting tussles, and some sharp exchanges of bellicose talk between the principals, but their bitterness vanished in a short time, while, towards myself, they were more like protectors than employers. Nevertheless, a few painful truths had been forced on my notice; I had also gained valuable experience of the humours of rivers. The fluvial moods had considerably interested me. The play of currents, eddies, and whirlpools afforded inexhaustible matter for observation. The varying aspects of the stream in calm and storm, when deep or shallow, in the neighbourhood of snags, sandbars, and spits, reflecting sunshine or leaden sky, were instructive, and the veteran flat-boatmen were not averse to satisfying my inquisitiveness. Being naturally studious and reflective, I carried away with me far more than I could rehearse of what was of practical value; but, boy-like, I relegated my impressions to memory, where, in process of time, they could be solidified into knowledge.

CHAPTER V

I FIND A FATHER

AFTER tying up, I was at liberty to renovate my person. My shore-clothes restored me to the semblance of my former self, and, with many a protest of good-will from my late companions, I walked towards the city. In a few hours I reached St. Charles Street, and, as though wearied with its persecution of me, Fortune brought me into the presence of Mr. Stanley. His reception of me was so paternal that the prodigal son could not have been more delighted. My absence from New Orleans had but intensified my affection for the only friend I seemed to possess in all America. Once out of his presence, I felt as a stranger among strangers; on re-entering it, I became changed outwardly and inwardly. Away from him, I was at once shy, silent, morosely severe; with him, I was exuberantly glad, and chatted freely, without fear of repulse. Since we had parted, I had met some thousands, and spoken with a few hundreds; but no one had kindled in me the least spark of personal interest. It may, then, be understood how my greeting expressed my sense of his preeminence and rarity.

Between the last sentence and what follows, there should be an interval represented by many * * * * * *. I do not know how it came about, but I was suddenly fixed immovably, for a period. Preoccupied with my bursting gladness, I had observed nothing but our mutual gratification; and then I had poured my tale of woes unchecked, except by an expression of sympathy, now and again, from him. But, presently, after some commonplaces, his words sounded a deeper note, and stirred my innermost being. A peculiar sensation — as though the wind of a strong breathing was flowing down my back, and ran up with a refluent motion to the head, blowing each hair apart — came over me, and held me spellbound and thrilled to the soul. *He was saying, with some* *emotion, that my future should be his charge!* He had been so powerfully affected by what Margaret had told him, with all the warmth of her Irish nature, of the last scene at the death-bed of his wife, that he had been unable to dissociate me from his thoughts of her; he had wondered what I was doing, what had become of me, imagined that I was starving, and, knowing how friendless and unsophisticated I was, each conjecture had been dismal and pitiful; and he had resolved, on reaching New Orleans, to make diligent search for me, and take me to himself. While he related his extraordinary intentions, it seemed to me as if my spirit was casting an interested regard upon my own image, and was glorying in the wonderful transformation that was taking place. To think that any man should be weaving such generous designs upon a person so unworthy and insignificant as myself, and plotting a felicitous future for me, nursed in contumely and misery, seemed to me to be too wonderful for belief! Then, again, there was a certain mysterious coincidence about it which awed me. In my earliest dreams and fancies, I had often imagined what kind of a boy I should be with a father or mother. What ecstasy it would be if my parent came to me, to offer a parent's love, as I had enviously seen it bestowed on other children. In my secret prayers, something of a wish of this kind had been behind the form of words; and now, as an answer from the Invisible, came this astounding revelation of His power! He had cast a little leaven of kindness into the heart of a good man. From the very first encounter, it had acted beneficially for me; and now it had leavened his whole nature, until it had become a fatherly affection, which would shield my youth from trial and temptation, and show me the best side of human nature!

Before I could quite grasp all that this declaration meant for me, he had risen, taken me by the hand, and folded me in a gentle embrace. My senses seemed to whirl about for a few half-minutes; and, finally, I broke down, sobbing from extreme emotion. It was the only tender action I had ever known, and, what no amount of cruelty could have forced from me, tears poured in a torrent under the influence of the simple embrace.

The golden period of my life began from that supreme

moment! As I glance back at it from the present time, it seems more like a dream, as unreal as a vision of the night. Compared with these matter-of-fact days, or the ruthless past, it was like a masquerade among goodly felicities and homely affections, and its happy experiences have been too precious and sacred for common chat, though they have lain near enough for the fitting occasion, moulded and ready for utterance. They have formed my best memories, and furnished me with an unfading store of reflections, and, probably, have had more influence than any other upon my conduct and manners. For, to be lifted out of the depths of friendlessness and destitution to a paternal refuge, and made the object of care and solicitude so suddenly, at a time, too, when I was most impressionable, without an effort on my own part, and without an advocate, bordered on the miraculous. Predisposed to inward communing, with a strong but secret faith in Providence, I regarded it as principally the result of a Divine interposition, the course of which was a mystery not to be lightly talked of, but to be remembered for its significance.

After a restful night, and when breakfast had been despatched, we adjourned to a room used as an office and sitting apartment, and there I was subjected to a sympathetic cross-examination. Every incident of my life, even to the fancies that had fled across the mind of callow boyhood, was elicited with the assistance of his searching questions, and then I was, as it were, turned completely inside out. Mr. Stanley said that what I had told him only bore out the conclusion he had long before arrived at concerning me. He had suspected that I was an orphan, or one who had been flatly disowned, and a waif exposed to every wind of Chance; and he was glad that it had deposited me in his keeping. He expressed amazement that helpless children were treated so unfeelingly in England, and marvelled that no one cared to claim them. Being a childless man, he and his wife had often prayed for the blessing of offspring, until they were wearied with desiring and expecting. Then they had gone to the Faubourg St. Mary, and had visited the Infant Asylum, with the view of adopting some unclaimed child; but they had made no choice, from over-fastidiousness. It much surprised him that none of my relations had discovered in me what had struck him and Speake. Had he searched New Orleans all through, he said, he could not have found one who would have shared his views respecting me with more sympathy than his friend; and, had Mr. Speake lived, he added, I should have been as good as established for life. Mr. Speake had written his estimates of my character often, and, in one letter, had predicted that I was cut out for a great merchant, who would eventually be an honour to the city. Mr. Kitchen, the book-keeper, had also professed to be impressed with my qualities; while young Richardson had said I was a prodigy of activity and quick grasp of business.

Then, at some length, he related the circumstances which had induced him to take a warmer interest in me. He had often thought of the start I had given him by the question, 'Do you want a boy, sir?' It seemed to voice his own life-long wish. But he thought I was too big for his purpose. For the sake, however, of the long-desired child, he determined to do the best he could for me, and had obtained my engagement with his friend Speake. When he had gone home, his wife had been much interested in the adventure with me, and had often asked how his 'protégé' was getting on? When she had, finally, seen me, she had said something to him which had given a new turn to his thoughts; but, as I was already established, and was likely to succeed, he had ceased thinking about it. On Margaret's arrival at St. Louis with his wife's remains, she had been so eloquent in all the details of what had occurred, that he inwardly resolved that his first object on reaching the city should be to seek me and undertake what God had pointed out to him; namely, to educate me for the business of life, and be to me what my father should have been. 'The long and the short of it is,' said he, 'as you are wholly unclaimed, without a parent, relation, or sponsor, I promise to take you for my son, and fit you for a mercantile career; and, in future, *you are to bear my name,* "*Henry Stanley*."' Having said which, he rose, and, dipping his hands in a basin of water, he made the sign of the cross on my forehead, and went seriously through the formula of baptism, ending with a brief exhortation to bear my new name worthily.

In answer, as it might seem, to the least shade of doubt on

my face, which he thought he observed, he gave me a brief summary of his own life, from which I learned that he had not always been a merchant. He told me that he had been educated for the ministry, and had been ordained, and for two years had preached in various places between Nashville and Savannah; but, finally, becoming lukewarm, he had lost his original enthusiasm for his profession, and had turned his attention to commerce. Intimacy with men of business, and social life, had led him by degrees to consider himself unfitted for a calling which seemed to confine his natural activities; but, though he had lost the desire to expound the Christian faith from the pulpit, he had not lost his principles. The greater gains of commerce had seemed to him to be more attractive than the work of persuading men and women to be devout. After one or two unsuccessful essays as a storekeeper, he had finally adopted a commission business, and had succeeded in several profitable ventures. He thought that, in a few years, he would return to the store business, and settle in 'one of the back-country places' for which he had a great hankering; but, at present, he could not make up his mind to terminate his city connections. Much else he related to me, for it was a day of revelations; but to me, personally, it mattered little — it was quite sufficient that he was he, my first, best friend, my benefactor, my father!

Only the close student of the previous pages could compass my feelings at finding the one secret wish of my heart gratified so unexpectedly. To have an unbreathed, unformed wish plucked out of the silence, and fashioned into a fact as real as though my dead father had been restored to life and claimed me, was a marvel so great that I seemed to be divided into two individuals — one strenuously denying that such a thing could be, and the other arraying all the proofs of the fact. It was even more of a wonder than that Dick the boy should be transformed into Alice the girl! But when hour after hour passed, and each brought its substantial evidence of the change, the disturbed faculties gradually returned to their normal level, though now more susceptible to happiness than when existence was one series of mortifications.

As we walked the streets together, many a citizen must have guessed by my glowing face and shining eyes that I was brimful of joy. I began to see a new beauty in everything. The men seemed pleasanter, the women more gracious, the atmosphere more balmy! It was only by severe suppression that I was able to restrain myself from immoderate behaviour, and breaking out into hysteric and unseemly ebullience. A gush of animal enjoyment in life, from this date, would sometimes overtake me, and send me through the streets at the rate of a professional pedestrian. I would open my mouth and drink the air, with deep disdain for all physical weakness. I had to restrain the electrical vitality, lest the mad humour for leaping over a dray or cart might awaken the suspicion of the policeman. On such days, and during such fits, it was indeed joy to be alive, — 'but to be young was very Heaven.'

Most of the day was spent in equipping me for the new position I was to assume. I was sumptuously furnished with stylish suits, new linen, collars, flannels, low-quarter shoes, and kip[1] boots: toilet articles to which I was an utter stranger, such as tooth- and nail-brushes, and long white shirts, resembling girls' frocks, for night-dresses. It had never entered my head, before, that teeth should be brushed, or that a nail-brush was indispensable, or that a night-dress contributed to health and comfort! When we returned to Mr. Stanley's boarding-house, we had a pleasant time in the arrangement of the piles of new garments and accessories, and in practising the first lessons in the art of personal decoration. In Wales the inhabitants considered it unbecoming in one who aspired to manliness to ape the finicky niceties of women, and to be too regardful of one's personal appearance; and had they heard my new father descant so learnedly on the uses of tooth- and nail-brushes, I feel sure they would have turned away with grimaces and shrugs of dissatisfaction. What would stern Aunt Mary have said, had she viewed this store of clothing and linen that was destined for the use of a boy whom, at one time, she had seriously meditated indenturing to a cobbler? But, previous to the assumption of my new habiliments, I was conducted to a long bath, set in a frame of dark wood, and, while looking at it, and wondering at its splendour, I heard so many virtues ascribed to its daily use that I contracted quite a love for it, and vowed to myself that since it

[1] A special kind of leather.

appeared to be a panacea for so many ills, all that scented soap and scrubbing could effect would be gladly tested by me.

I steeped myself that afternoon, as though I would wash out the stains ugly poverty and misery had impressed upon my person since infancy; and, when I emerged out of the bath, my self-esteem was as great as befitted the name and character I was hereafter to assume. But there was much to improve inwardly as well as outwardly. The odium attached to the old name, and its dolorous history, as it affected my sense of it, could not be removed by water, but by diligent application to a moral renovation, and making use of the new life, with the serious intent to hold the highest ideal I knew of, as my exemplar. To aid me in my endeavours, my new father was gentleness itself. At first, he made no great demand on me; but our intercourse was permitted to grow to that familiar intimacy which inspired perfect confidence. There was no fear that I could ever be contemptuous or disrespectful; but, had he not allowed a certain time for familiarising me with his presence and position towards me, I might not have been able to overcome a natural timidity which would have ill-suited our connection. When I had learned to touch him without warning, and yet receive a genial welcome, laugh in his presence unchecked, and even comb his beard with my fingers, then I came completely out of my shell; and, after that, development was rapid.

'Boys should be seen, and not heard,' had been so frequently uttered before me that I had grown abashed at the sound of an adult's voice. The rule was now agreeably reversed. I was encouraged to speak upon every occasion, and to utter my opinions regardless of age and sex. No incident occurred, and no subject was mentioned, that I was not invited to say what I thought of it.

Apart from commercial and cognate details, I think my ripening understanding was made more manifest in anything relating to human intercourse and human nature, owing, probably, to the greater efforts made by my father to assist me in recovering lost ground. Boys bred up at home pick up, instinctively, the ways and manners prevailing there. I had had no home, and therefore I was singularly deficient in the little graces of home life. Unconsciously to myself, from the moment I had stepped out of the bath-room in my new garments, I began that elementary education which was to render me fit to be seen by the side of a respectable man. I had to lose the fear of men and women, to know how to face them without bashfulness or awkwardness, to commune with them without slavish deference, to bear myself without restraint, and to carry myself with the freedom which I saw in others; in a word, I had to learn the art of assimilating the manner, feeling, and expression of those around me. Being attentive and intelligent, acute of hearing, quick of eye-sight, and with a good memory, I had gained immensely in my father's estimation, and he was, to me, a sufficient judge.

Our wanderings from city to city, steamer to steamer, and store to store, which the business of my father necessitated, I do not propose to dwell upon; in fact, it would be impossible to contain within a volume all that I remember of this, and subsequent periods. I am more concerned with the personal element, the cardinal incidents, and the tracing of my growth to maturity. Besides, the banks of the Mississippi and its lower tributaries have little to recommend them to a youngster after the first expressive Oh! of admiration. The planters' mansions, the settlements, and cities, are mainly of uniform colour and style of architecture. When we have seen one mansion, settlement, or city, we seem to have seen all. One river-bank is like the other. The houses are either of wood with a verandah, and painted, or of red brick; there is a church spire here, and, there, a mass of buildings; but presently, after a second view, there is as little of lasting interest as in the monotonous shores of the great river. I only record such incidents as affected me, and such as clearly stand out conspicuously in the retrospect, which have been not only a delight to memory, but which I am incapable of forgetting.

During nearly two years, we travelled several times between New Orleans, St. Louis, Cincinnati, and Louisville; but most of our time was spent on the lower Mississippi tributaries, and on the shores of the Washita, Saline, and Arkansas Rivers, as the more profitable commissions were gained in dealings with country merchants between Harrisonburg and Arkadelphia, and between Napoleon and Little Rock. From these business tours I acquired a better geographical knowledge than any amount of school-teaching would have given me; and at one time I was profound in the statistics relating to population, commerce, and navigation of the Southern and South-Western States. Just as Macaulay was said to be remarkable for being able to know a book from beginning to end by merely turning over its pages, I was considered a prodigy by my father and his intimate friends for the way names and faces clung to my memory. I could tell the name of every steamer we had passed, the characteristics of her structure, and every type of man we met. A thing viewed, or a subject discussed likely to be useful, became impressed indelibly on the mind. Probably this mental acquisitiveness was stimulated by the idea that it formed the equipment of a merchant, which I believed it was my ultimate destiny to be; and that every living man should be a living gazetteer, and possess facts and figures at his fingers' ends. Meantime, my memory was frequently of great use to my father as an auxiliary to his memorandum-book of shipments, purchases, and sales. Once having seen the page, I could repeat its record with confidence; and I was often rewarded by his admiring exclamation, 'Well, I never heard the like! It is perfectly astonishing how you remember details,' etc. But, though eyes and ears and technical memory were well exercised, it was some time before judgment was formed. Understanding was slow. It took long for me to perceive wherein lay the superiority of one sugar over another, or why one grade of flour fetched a higher price than another, or wherein Bourbon whiskey was superior to rye, and to distinguish the varying merits of coffees, teas, etc. What a man said, or how he looked, his dress, appearance, and so on, were ineffaceable; but the unwritten, or untold, regarding him was a blank to me; and when I heard comments from bystanders upon the nature of some person, I used to wonder how they formed their opinions. However, the effect of these criticisms upon men and their manners was to inspire me with a desire to penetrate beneath, and to school myself in comparing different people. I had abundance of opportunities, in the multitudes we met in the crowded steamers, and the many towns we visited; but that which would have given the key to the mystery was wanting, viz., personal intercourse. In the absence of direct conversation and dealings with people, it was difficult to discover the nature of a spirit lurking under a fair outside.

When we left New Orleans, at the end of 1859, we had brought with us a portmanteau packed with choice literature, and I was given to understand that the histories of Rome, Greece, and America, poetry and drama, were especially for my use, and that I was to pursue my studies as diligently as at a school. The practice of travel enabled my father to dispose himself comfortably for the indulgence of reading, within a very short time after reaching his cabin. He acted as one who had only changed his room, and was only concerned with his own business. With such a man, a river-voyage was no impediment to instruction. He set me an example of application to my book, which, added to my own love of study, enabled me to cultivate indifference to what was passing outside of our cabin. Our travelling library was constantly replenished at the large cities, with essays, memoirs, biographies, and general literature; but novels and romances were rigidly excluded.

He first taught me how a book should be read aloud, and, in a few seconds, had corrected a sing-song intonation which was annoying to him. He said that one could almost tell whether a reader understood his author by the tone of his delivery; and, taking up a Shakespeare, he illustrated it by reading, 'Who steals my purse steals trash,' etc.; and the various styles he adopted were well calculated to enforce his lesson. From the monotone I was unable to see any beauty or point in the quotation; but, when he assumed the tone of the moralist, the lines certainly set me thinking, and the truth of the sentiments appeared so clear that I was never able to forget the quotation.

Sometimes, also, when reading aloud a page of history, I would come to a dull paragraph, and my attention would flag; but he was quick to detect this, and would compel me to begin again, because he was sure that I knew not what I had been reading. I merely note this because during two years we read together a large number of books; and, as I had the benefit of his disquisitions and comments on my reading, it will be seen that with such a companion these river-voyages considerably advanced my education, as much so, indeed, as though I had been with a tutor. Nor, when we dropped our books, and promenaded the deck, was my mind left to stagnate in frivolity. He took advantage of every object worthy of notice to impress on me some useful, or moral lesson, — to warn me against errors of omission, or commission.

Whatever it may have been in my personal appearance that first attracted him to me, it is certain that the continued affection he always showed towards me was secured by my zealous efforts always to follow his slightest suggestion. I think it would have been difficult to have found a boy in the neighbourhood of the Mississippi who observed his parent's wishes with a more scrupulous exactitude than I did those of my adopted father. As I came to have an entire knowledge of him, I knew not which to admire most, the unvarying, affectionate interest he showed in my personal welfare, or his merits as a man and moral guardian. Being of original ideas, acute mind, and impressive in speech, the matter of his conversation glued itself into my memory, and stirred me to thought.

I remember well when, one day, he revealed something of the method he proposed to follow with me for the perfecting of my commercial education, I expressed a doubt as to whether, after all his trouble and care, I would ever come up to his expectations. I said that as to carrying out plain instructions with all good-will there need be no fear — I loved work, and the approbation given to fidelity and industry; but, when I contemplated being left to my own judgement, I felt strong misgivings. How admirably he interpreted my thoughts, explained my doubts! He infused me with such confidence that, had a store been given me there and then, I should have instantly accepted its management! 'But,' he said, 'I am not going to part with you yet. You have much to learn. You are a baby in some things yet, because you have been only a few months in the world. By the time I have wound up matters, you will have learned thousands of little trifles, and will be so grounded in solid knowledge that you may safely be trusted under another merchant to learn the minutiæ of business, and so get ready to keep store with me.'

I suggested to him that I laboured under disadvantages such as hampered very few other boys, which would act as a clog on the free exercise of my abilities, and that, even if other people refrained from alluding to my Parish breeding, the memory of it would always have a depressing effect on me. But such thoughts he met with something like angry contempt. 'I don't know,' said he, 'what the custom of the Welsh people may be, but *here* we regard personal character and worth, not pedigree. With us, people are advanced, not for what their parentage may have been, but for what they are themselves. All whom I meet in broadcloth have risen through their own efforts, and not because they were their father's children. President Buchanan was made our chief magistrate because he was himself, and not because of his father, or his ancestors, or because he was poorly or richly brought up. We put a premium on the proper exercise of every faculty, and guarantee to every man full freedom to better himself in any way he chooses, provided always he does not exercise it at the expense of the rights of other people. It is only those who refuse to avail themselves of their opportunities, and shamefully abuse them, that we condemn.'

At other times, the vehemence of youth would frequently betray itself; and, if I had not been checked, I should probably have developed undue loquacity. Being of sanguine temper by nature, I was led through gushes of healthy rapture into excesses of speech; but he would turn on me, and gravely say that he was not accustomed to carry magnifiers with him; that, owing to his own sense of proportion, my figures gave him no true idea of the fact I wished to state, that my free use of unnecessary ciphers only created confusion in his mind. Sometimes he would assume a comical look of incredulity, which brought me to my senses very quickly, and made me retract what I had said, and repeat the statement with a more sacred regard for accuracy. 'Just so,' he would say; 'if a thing is worth stating at all, it might as well be stated truly. A boy's fancy is very warm, I know; but, if once he acquires the habit of multiplying his figures, every fact will soon become no better than a fable.'

Being an early riser himself, he insisted on my cultivating the habit of rising at dawn, but he also sent me to bed at an early hour. He lost no occasion to urge me to apply the morning hours to study; and, really, his anxiety that I should snatch the flying minutes appeared to be so great, that I was often infected with it as though they were something tangible, but so elusive that only a firm grasp would avail. If he saw me idly gazing on the shores, he would recall me, to ask if I had finished some chapter we had been discussing, or if I had found a different answer to his question than I had last given; and, if he detected an inclination in me to listen to the talk of passengers round the bar, he would ask if there were no books in the cabin, that I must needs hanker for the conversation of idlers. 'All the babble of these topers, if boiled down,' he would say, 'would not give a drachm of useful knowledge. Greatness never sprang from such fruitless gossip. Those men were merely wasting time. From motives of selfishness, they, no doubt, would be glad to exchange trivial talk with anyone, big or little, who might come near them, but it was not to my interest to be in their company.'

He would put his arm in mine, and lead me away to deliver himself of his thoughts on the glory of youth, painting it in such bright colours that, before long, I would be seized with a new idea of its beauty and value. It appeared to be only a brief holiday, which ought to be employed for the strengthening of muscles, gathering the flowers of knowledge, and culling the riper fruits of wisdom. Youth was, really, only the period for gaining strength of bone, to endure the weight put on it by manhood, and for acquiring that largeness of mind necessary to understand the ventures I should hereafter be compelled to take. To squander it among such fellows as congregated around bar-rooms and liquor-counters was as foolish as to open my veins to let out my life-blood. 'Now is the time to prepare for the long voyage you are to take. You have seen the ships in the docks taking in their stores before leaving for the high sea where nothing can be bought. If the captains neglect their duties, the crews will starve. You are in the dock to-day; have you everything ready for your voyage? Are *all* your provisions aboard? If not, then, when you have hoisted your sails, it will be too late to think of them, and only good-luck can save you from misfortune'; and so on, until, through his forcible manner, earnestness, and copious similes, I returned to my studies with intense application.

The sight in the steamer saloons of crowds of excited gamblers was employed by him in exposition of his views on the various ways of acquiring wealth. Those piles of golden eagles that glittered on the table of the saloon would enrich none of the gamblers permanently. Money obtained by such methods always melted away. Wealth was made by industry and economy, and not by gambling or speculating. To know how to be frugal was the first step towards a fortune, the second was to practice frugality, and the third step was to know what to do with the money saved. It was every man's duty to put something aside each day, were it only a few cents. No man in America was paid such low wages that, if he were determined, he could not put away half of them. A man's best friend, after God, was himself; and, if he could not rely on himself, he could not rely on anybody else. His first duty was to himself, as he was bound to his own wants all his life, and must provide for them under every circumstance; if he neglected to provide for his own needs, he would always be unable to do anything towards the need of others. Then, as his custom was, he would proceed to apply these remarks to my case. I was to retain in my mind the possibility of being again homeless, and friendless, and adrift in the world, the world keeping itself to itself, and barring the door against me, as it did at Liverpool, New Orleans, and St. Louis, 'The poor man is hated, even by his own neighbour; but the rich man has many friends,' etc., etc.

An original method of instruction which he practised with me was to present me different circumstances, and ask me what I would do. These were generally difficult cases, wherein honesty, honour, and right-doing, were involved. No sooner had I answered, than he would press me with another view of it, wherein it appeared that his view was just as fair as the one I had; and he would so perplex me that I would feel quite foolish. For instance, a fellow-clerk of mine was secretly dishonest, but was attached to me in friendship. He made free with his employer's till, and one day was discovered by me alone. What would I do? I would dissuade him. But supposing, despite his promises to you, he was still continuing to abstract small sums: what then? I would accuse him of it, and say to him he was a thief. Supposing that, seeing you could give no positive proof of his theft, he denied it? Then he would be a liar, too, and there would be a quarrel. And what then? That is all. What of the employer? In what way? Is he not in question? does he not pay you for looking after his interests? But I do look after his interests, in trying to prevent the theft. And yet, with all your care of his interests, the pilfering goes on, and nobody knows it but you. You think, then, that I ought to tell on him, and ruin him? Well, when you engaged with your employer, did you not make something of a bargain with him, that, for a certain wage, you would make his interests your own, and keep him duly informed of all that was going on?

This is one example of the painstaking way in which he would stir up my reasoning powers. When we walked through the streets, he would call my attention to the faces of the passers-by, and would question me as to what professions or trades they belonged to; and, when I replied that I could not guess them, he would tell me that my eyes were the lamps to my feet, and the guides to my understanding, and would show me that though I might not guess accurately each time, in many instances I might arrive at the truth, and that, whether wrong or right, the attempt to do so was an exercise of the intellect, and would greatly tend, in time, to sharpen my wits.

Moral resistance was a favourite subject with him. He said the practice of it gave vigour to the will, which required it as much as the muscles. The will required to be strengthened to resist unholy desires and low passions, and was one of the best allies that conscience could have. Conscience was a good friend, and the more frequently I listened to it, the more ready it was with its good offices. Conscience was the sense of the soul; and, just as the senses of smell and taste guarded my body from harm or annoyance, it guarded the spirit from evil. It was very tender and alert now, because I was yet at school and the influence of the Scriptures was strong in me; but, when neglected, it became dull and insensitive. Those, however, who paid heed to it grew to feel the sensation of its protective presence, and, upon the least suspicion of evil, it strenuously summoned the will to its aid, and thus it was that temptations were resisted.

Whether afloat or ashore, his manners were so open and

genial, that one would think he courted acquaintance. Many people, led by this, were drawn to accost him; but no man knew better than he, how to relieve himself of undesirable people, and those who enjoyed his company were singularly like himself, in demeanour and conversation. It is from the character of his associates that I have obtained my most lasting impressions of Americans, and, whenever mentioned, these are the figures which always rise first in the mental view. 'Punch's' 'Jonathan' I have never had the fortune to meet, though one who has travelled through two-thirds of the Union could scarcely have failed to meet him, if he were a common type. Among his kind, my adopted father was no mean figure. I once heard a man speak of him as 'a man of a soft heart but a hard head,' which I fancied had a sound of depreciation; but, later, I acknowledged it as just.

It was some six months or so after my adoption that I ventured to broach a subject of more than ordinary interest to me. In fact, it was my only remaining secret from him. It had been often on the tip of my tongue, but I had been restrained from mentioning it through fear of scorn. My ideas respecting the Deity I suspected were too peculiar to trust them to speech; and yet, if someone did not enlighten me, I should remain long in ignorance of the Divine character. True, certain coincidences made me secretly believe that God heard me; nevertheless, I burned to know from an authoritative source whether I was the victim of illusions, or whether the Being of my conceptions bore any resemblance to that of the learned and old I had met. I imagined God as a personality with human features, set in the midst of celestial Glory in the Heaven of Heavens; and, whenever I prayed, it was to Him thus framed that I directed my supplications. My father did not ridicule this idea as I feared he would, and I was much relieved to hear him ask how I had come to form such a fancy. This was difficult to express in words, but, at last, I managed to explain that, probably, it was from the verse which said that God had made man after His own image, and because clergymen always looked upward when in church.

I cannot give his own words, but this is the substance of my first intelligible lesson on this subject.

'God is a spirit, as you have often read. A spirit is a thing that cannot be seen with human eyes, because it has no figure or form. A man consists of body and spirit, or, as we call it, soul. The material part of him we can see and feel; but that which animates him, and governs his every thought, is invisible. When a person dies, we say his spirit has fled, or that his soul has departed to its Maker. The body is then as insensible as clay, and will soon corrupt, and become absorbed by the earth.

'We cannot see the air we breathe, nor the strong wind which wrecks ships, and blows houses down, yet we cannot live without air, and the effects of the winds are not disputed. We cannot see the earth move, and yet it is perpetually whirling through space. We cannot see that which draws the compass-needle to the Pole; yet we trust our ships to its guidance. No one saw the cause of that fever which killed so many people in New Orleans last summer, but we know it was in the air around the city. If you take a pinch of gunpowder and examine it, you cannot see the terrible force that is in it. So it is with the soul of man. While it is in him, you witness his lively emotions, and wonder at his intelligence and energy; but, when it has fled, it leaves behind only an inert and perishable thing, which must be buried quickly.

'Well, then, try and imagine the Universe subject to the same invisible but potent Intelligence, in the same way that man is subject to his. It is impossible for your eyes to see the thing itself; but, if you cannot see its effects, you must be blind. Day after day, year after year, since the beginning, that active and wonderful Intelligence has been keeping light and darkness, sun, moon, stars, and earth, each to their course in perfect order. Every living being on the earth to-day is a witness to its existence. The Intelligence that conceived this order and decreed that it should endure, that still sustains it, and will outlast every atom of creation, we describe under the term of God. It is a short word, but it signifies the Being that fills the Universe, and a portion of Whom is in you and me.

'Now, what possible figure can you give of that Being that fills so large a space, and is everywhere? The sun is 95 millions of miles from us; imagine 95 millions of miles on the other side, yet the circle that would embrace those two points is but a small one compared to the whole of space. However far that space extends, the mighty Intelligence governs all. You are able to judge for yourself how inconceivable, for the mind of man, God is. The Bible says "As the Heavens are higher than the earth, so are His ways higher than our ways." God is simply indefinable, except as a spirit, but by that small fraction of Him which is in us, we are able to communicate with Him; for He so ordered it that we might be exalted the more we believe in Him.'

'But how, then, am I to pray?' I asked, as my little mind tried to grasp this enormous space, and recoiled, baffled and helpless. 'Must I only think, or utter the words, without regard to the object or way I direct them?'

'It seems to me our Saviour Himself has instructed us. He said, "But thou, when thou prayest, enter into thy closet, and when thou hast shut thy door, pray to thy Father which is in secret; and thy Father, which seeth in secret, shall reward thee openly. Your Father knoweth what things ye have need of before ye ask Him."

'Prayer is the expression of a wish of the heart, whether you speak aloud, or think it. You are a creature of God, destined to perform His design, be it great or little. Out of the limits of that design you cannot venture, therefore prayer will not avail you. Within the limits you will be wise to pray, in order that you may be guided aright. The understanding that He has seen fit to give you is equal to what you are destined to do. You may do it well, or ill; but that is left to your choice. How wide, or how narrow, those limits are, no one knows but Himself. Your existence may be compared to this: supposing I give you a sum of money which I know to be enough to take you to New Orleans and return here. If you spend that money faithfully and properly, it will suffice to bring you comfortably back; but, if you are foolish and waste it by the way, it may not even be enough to take you half-way on your journey. That is how I look upon our existence. God has furnished us with the necessary senses for the journey of life He has intended we should take. If we employ them wisely, they will take us safely to our journey's end; but if, through their perversion, we misuse them, it will be our own fault. By prayer our spirits communicate with God. We seek that wisdom, moral strength, courage, and patience to guide and sustain us on the way. The Father, Who has all the time observed us, grants our wish, and the manner of it is past finding out; but the effect is like a feeling of restored health, or a burst of gladness. It is not necessary to make long or loud prayers: the whisper of a child is heard as well as the shout of a nation. It is purity of life, and sincerity of heart, that are wanted when you approach the Creator to implore His assistance. We must first render the service due to Him by our perfect conduct, before we seek favours from Him.'

'But what does the verse "So God created him in His own image" mean, then?'

'If you still cling to the idea that the human form is a tiny likeness of the Almighty, you are more childish than I believed you to be. "Image," in the Bible sense, means simply a reflection. In our souls and intelligence we reflect, in a small way, God's own mightier spirit and intelligence, just as a small pocket mirror reflects the sun and the sky, or your eyes reflect the light.'

Having had my doubts satisfied upon these essential points, there was only one thing more which I craved to know, and that was in regard to the Scriptures. Were they the words of God? If not, what was the Bible?

According to him, the Bible was the standard of the Christian faith, a fountain whence we derived our inspiration of piety and goodness, a proof that God interfered in human affairs, and a guide to salvation. He read from Timothy, 'All scripture is given by inspiration of God, and is profitable for doctrine, for reproof, for correction, for instruction in righteousness: that the man of God may be perfect, thoroughly furnished unto all good works'; and from Paul he quoted that 'it was written for our learning, that we through patience and comfort might have hope.'

'You are not,' said he, 'to pay too much attention to the set phrases, but to the matter and spirit of what is written, which are for the promotion of virtue and happiness. Many of the books have been written by men like ourselves, who lived between two thousand and four thousand years ago, and they used words peculiar to their own time. The mere texts or form of the words they used are not the exact words of God, but are simply the means of conveying the messages breathed into their understandings; and, naturally, they delivered them in the style of their period, and according to their ability, with such simplicity as would enable the common people to comprehend them. If I had to convey to you the proclamation of the President of the United States, I should have to write it more simply, and in a form that you would understand: so these Divine proclamations have been given to us by His chosen messengers, more faithfully than literally.'

The above are a few of the intelligent ideas which I obtained from my father, and for which I have been as grateful as for his unusual goodness in other respects. Probably, many a sermon which I had heard had contained them in a diluted form; but they had not been adapted to my understanding, and his clear exposition of these subjects was an immense relief to me. It was a fortunate thing for me that my foggy beliefs, and vague notions, in regard to such high matters, could be laid open with all trust and confidence before one so qualified and tender, before they became too established in my mind, otherwise, as my own intelligence ripened, I might have drifted into atheistical indifference. The substance of my father's sayings, which I have always remembered, illustrate the bent of his mind. I carefully copied them into a beautiful memorandum-book of which he made me a present, New Year's Day, 1860, and which I was so proud of that, during the first few days, I had filled more than half of it with the best words of my father.

It must not be supposed that I was at all times deserving of his solicitude, or equal to his expectations. I was one who could not always do the right and proper thing, for I was often erring and perverse, and at various times must have tried him sorely. My temper was quick, which, with an excess of false pride, inspired me to the verge of rebellion. A sense of decency prevented me from any overt act of defiance, but the spirit was not less fierce because I imposed the needful restraint on it. Outwardly, I might be tranquil enough, but my smothered resentment was as wicked and unjustifiable as if I had openly defied him. A choleric disposition on his part would have been as a flame to my nature, and the result might have been guessed. Happily for me, he was consistently considerate, and declined to notice too closely the flushed face, and the angry sparkles of the eye, which betokened revolt. An occasional blood-letting might perhaps have been beneficial to me; but he had discovered other methods, just as efficacious, for reducing me to a state of reason, and never once had recourse to threats. My fits of sullenness had been probably provoked by an unexpected sharpness of tone, or a denial of some liberty, or graver censure than I thought I deserved. Constrained to silence by the magnitude and character of my obligations to him, I, of course, magnified my grievances; and, the longer reconciliation was deferred, the larger these seemed. Before this dangerous mood sought vent, some look, a word, some secret transmission of sympathy occurred, and, in an instant, the evil humour vanished; for weeks afterwards, I would endeavour to atone for my churlish behaviour by a contrite submissiveness which was capable of undergoing any penance.

'I do not punish you,' he said, 'because I want you to remember that you are a little man, and the only difference between us is that I am an older man. If I were in the habit of striking you, you would run away from me, or it would be noticeable in you by a slinking gait, or a sly eye, or a sullen disposition, or a defiant look, or you would become broken-spirited; all this I do not want you to be — I wish for your filial regard, and your respect, which I would not deserve if I terrified. Misery and suffering would wreck your temper, while kindness and reason will bring out the best qualities of your nature; for you, as well as every child that is born, possess something that is good, and it is the sunshine of tenderness that makes it grow.'

To one who considers that neither the closest ties of relationship, nor the highest claims of affection, are sufficient to preserve the rebellious spirit in an angelic temper for a long time, this boyish inconsistency and perverseness will be no surprise; but I was sensible that it was only owing to his patience that it did not receive the condign punishment it deserved. This, in itself, was an education; for I learned, after several experiences, not to disturb myself too seriously because of a temporary change in his manner or mood, and to accept it rather as being due to some cross in business, or physical condition, than to any offence in me, and so the customary cordiality was soon restored.

If I could only have made similar allowances earlier, and with other persons in later life, I should have had much less unhappiness to bewail; but, in his case, the necessity of doing so was impressed on me by my intimate knowledge of his fatherliness, and affectionate considerateness, and by the constant sense that I owed him unreserved submission.

CHAPTER VI

ADRIFT AGAIN

MY education did not consist solely of his discussions upon books, morality, and religion, but it embraced a countless variety of topics suggested by our travels. By his method of teaching, no passive reception of facts was possible, and the stimulus to intellect was given by being urged to observe, sift, and examine every article of conversation. I absorbed considerable practical knowledge during this period. His level-headedness, which I was prone to regard at that time as the height of worldly wisdom, and his intense realness, aided greatly to clarify my ideas upon many things, and was excellently adapted to form a sound judgment. He could be as genial as a glad boy on his summer holiday, lofty as a preacher, frank as a brother; but righteously austere, hilariously familiar and jocose, yet sublime, according to occasion. The candour and good faith with which he spoke, the expansive benevolence, and the large amount of sympathy he always showed when I sought his advice, or exposed my doubts or fears, were the very qualities which were best calculated to ensure my affection, extract my shy confidences, and cultivate in me a fearless openness. With the exception of those fits of sullen resentment to which I was now and then subject, like other human whelps, my life with him was one unbroken period of pleasantness, and, so far as I required and knew, every condition of a Paradise was present, in the unfretting, fair, and healthful existence which I led.

I sometimes imagine that he must have discerned something attractive in me, though I myself was unconscious of the cause. If I review my appearance at that time, I can find nothing to admire. I was naturally shy, silent, short of figure, poorly clad, uninteresting, and yet he chose me, from the first moment he saw me, to be an object of his charity. I endeavoured to be, as the phrase is, good and grateful; but,

HENRY M. STANLEY, AT 17

as I have reason to remember, I was by no means perfect in my endeavours. I think zeal, good-will, docility, were my only commendable traits; but they strike me now as being insufficient to account for my undeniable good fortune.

I can only remember one noticeable incident, outside of the common, in connection with this period, and that occurred in the middle of 1860. We were passengers on the steamer 'Little Rock,' as she was returning, laden with cotton, down the Washita. My father had been paid money due to him for goods by a merchant near Fairview, and, through neglect, or some other reason, had deferred entrusting it to the purser longer than he ought. We were approaching near Sicily Island, when, in the gloom caused by the mountain-pile of cotton bales, I observed a man lingering rather suspiciously near our cabin-door. At first, I took him for one of the stewards; but, on observing him more particularly, his conduct, I thought, suggested some nefarious design. My father had retired, and, according to custom, I ought to have been abed; but the unusual freight of cotton the boat carried had kept me in a state of suppressed excitement. Being light and active, I ensconced myself in a dark gap between two tiers of bales, and waited patiently. After a little time the man put his ear to our door, and presently opened it, and entered our cabin. In a few minutes, I heard my father's voice ask, 'Who is there?' and, immediately, sounds of a struggle were heard. Upon this I bounded in, and found the stranger wrestling with my father, and one of the two seemed to be choking. Upon seeing me, the intruder turned rapidly towards me. I saw the flash as of steel, and something struck me between my arm and left breast in my overcoat, and a piece of metal tinkled on the floor. Then, with a deep curse, I was flung aside, and the man fled along the guards. We instantly raised a cry of 'Thieves!' which brought crowds of stewards and passengers to us, carrying lights. These revealed an open portmanteau, with rumpled contents, and the half of a carving-knife blade on the floor. On examining my coat it was seen that it had a cut as far as the canvas stiffening. All these evidences tended to prove that a daring attempt at robbery had been made, and, it was suspected, by someone connected with the boat. The chief steward mustered the waiters, but they all answered to their names. He next counted the carving-knives, and, according to him, one was missing. The incident caused quite a commotion for the time, but the culprit was never discovered.

Beyond this incident, we were singularly free from mishaps, and exciting episodes, upon waters that had been the scene of many a calamity; and yet, when I chanced to find myself among a group of passengers, I frequently heard terrible recitals of experiences at boiler-explosions, and shipwrecks, and other events hazardous to life. We had often been fellow-passengers with gamblers, some of whom were wrought into fury by their losses at cards; but, whether it was owing to my good or evil fortune, I never happened to be present when the issue was left to the arbitrament of revolver and bowie-knife, as there were plenty of peace-makers always ready to interfere at the critical moment.

In September of 1860, we met a tall and spruce gentleman, of the name of Major Ingham, on board of a steamer bound to New Orleans. From what I gathered, he was a South Carolinian by birth, but, some few years since, had removed to Saline County, Arkansas, and had established a plantation not far from Warren. My father and he had an abundant amount of small-talk together relating to acquaintances and localities, which occupied their leisure during the voyage. The Major also ingratiated himself with me, and, through his description of the forests of pine and oak, and accounts of the wild animals, such as catamounts, bears, and deer, in his region, I became warmly attached to him. Before reaching New Orleans, we had become so intimate that he extended an invitation to me to spend a month with him on his Arkansas plantation; and, on referring him to father, I found that he was not so averse to the proposal as I feared he would be. The subject was deferred for further consideration in the city.

After about a fortnight's stay at the St. Charles Hotel, my father was made anxious by a letter from Havana from his brother, and he resolved to go and see him. He then disclosed to me that after much mental discussion he had concluded that Major Ingham's invitation had assisted greatly in smoothing matters. For some time he had been debating as to how it would be best to take the first step for establishing my future. He had been much struck with the opportunities for doing a good business in a country store, at some place below Pine Bluff on the Arkansas. There were a large number of planters settled there, and a general supply store such as he had fancied for their convenience could not fail to be a success. Major Ingham's plantation was situated about forty miles back of the Arkansas River, and, at Cypress Bend, there was a friend of his who, upon a letter from him, would take me in to teach me the details of a country merchant's business. Here was an opportunity of approaching his project in a methodical way without loss of time. His brother's illness at Havana had caused some confusion in his affairs, and it was necessary for him to cross the Gulf and set things in order. Meantime, I had a safe escort to within a day's drive of the merchant's store, to which, after being tired of the plantation, I was to go to be grounded in the minutiæ of a retail store; and in a few months he would have wound up his commission business, and be able to avail himself of my local knowledge, and proceed to choose the best locality.

I saw no objection to any of his arrangements, as they rather coincided with my secret ambitions, which had been fostered by many previous allusions to such a scheme as had been now explained. The suddenness of the parting was somewhat of a drawback to the beauty of the project; but, as accident was the cause, and his absence was to be only for a few months, during which we could often correspond, I became inclined, with the sanguineness of my nature, to anticipate much enjoyment from the novelty of the situation. In my highly-coloured fancy, I saw illimitable pine-woods, infested by Indians, and by wild-cats, and other savage felines; and the fact that I was about to prepare myself to be a dealer in merchandise, preliminary to a permanent establishment, appeared such an enchanting prospect that I felt no disposition to peer into sober realities. Could we have foreseen, however, that this parting, so calmly proposed and so trustfully accepted, was to be for ever, both of us would have shrunk from the thought of it; but, unknown to ourselves, we had arrived at the parting of the ways, and though we both sincerely hoped the ways would meet, we were gliding along steep planes which would presently precipitate us into the wide gulf of separation.

From the moment it was agreed to part for a while, my father lost no opportunity to fill me with practical counsel, which, had my memory been a knapsack, I could have extracted at will for consolation and guidance. Unfortunately, for some things my memory was like a sieve: it retained the larger rules, but dropped the lesser ones; it preserved certain principles that had an affinity with my nature, but the multitude of minor ones that he had attempted to graft on my nature fell away, one by one. I was to be industrious, orderly, honourable, and steady, patient, and obliging. But something of these I would naturally have shown under any circumstances; but contact with real life discovers that these virtues are insufficient to keep us serene and immaculate, that the spirit of youth requires its sensibilities to be disciplined in many ways before it endures with sweetness and patience the spurns, and gibes, and mocks, of a rude world. It frequently meets conditions wherein nothing will avail but force, of a most strenuous kind.

When the hour came for my father's departure, Major Ingham and I accompanied him on board the Havana steamer. The last parting occurred in the state-room. At that moment, there was a wild fluttering of the heart; and something like an ugly cloud of presentiments, vague shadows of unknown evils to come, which started strong doubts of the wisdom of parting, came over me all at once. But, as usual, when clear expression was most needed, I was too tongue-tied for much speech, so many ideas thronged for utterance, and I turned away as though stricken dumb. Half an hour later, the steamer was only discernible by its trail of smoke.

After he had gone, the flood-gates were opened, the feelings relieved themselves by torrents of words, and my loss and loneliness pressed hard upon the senses. Much as I had valued him, it needed this time of anguish to reveal fully what he had been to me. Then, pang after pang of poignant contrition pierced me through and through. I was dissatisfied with the sum of my conduct, with his own professions that I had been to him what he had hoped and wished. If he had but returned there and then, with the clear light that fell on my deficiencies now, how I should have striven to satisfy my own exact ideas of what was due to him! This little absence, with its unutterable remorse, had been more efficacious in showing me my own inwardness than all his unselfish generosity.

Nearly five and thirty years have passed since, and I have not experienced such wretchedness as I did that night following his departure. A very little more, and I think it would have exceeded the heart's power to bear. My emotions were much more distressing than anyone could have judged from my appearance. I caught a view of myself in a mirror, and my face struck me as exhibiting an astonishing contrast to the huge disorder beneath it. For the first time, I understood the sharpness of the pang which pierces the soul when a loved one lies with folded hands, icy cold, in the sleep of Death. I vexed myself with asking, Had my conduct been as perfect as I then wished it had been? Had I failed in aught? Had I esteemed him as he deserved? Then a craving wish to hear him speak but one word of consolation, to utter one word of blessing, made me address him as though he might hear; but no answer came, and I experienced a shiver of sadness and wished that I could die.

I have often looked back upon the boy who sat like a stone in his father's chair for hours, revolving with fixed eyes and unmoved face all that this parting seemed to him to mean. Up to a certain point he traced minutely all its details, went over every word and little act, and then a great blank wall met him, into which he strove and strove again to penetrate, and, being baffled, resumed his mental rehearsals.

Before Major Ingham turned his steps homeward, I received a letter from my father duly announcing his arrival at the island of Cuba. After describing the passage across the Gulf, he went on to say that the more he thought of his plans, the more he was inclined to regard the Major's invitation as a happy incident in his programme. He had often pondered over the best means of starting me in a business for which I had a decided bent, and he had been sounding several country merchants with a view of giving me a preliminary training, but he had constantly deferred a decision in the hope of finding something that more nearly suited his ideas. Now, however, it all seemed clear. He had always fancied the Arkansas River, as it had a richer back country than any other, and, by means of the steamers and its superior navigation, was in direct communication with the cities on the Mississippi. There were many professions and trades for which I was fit, but he thought that I was more partial to a mercantile career, and he was glad of it. He went on to say that I had made a wonderful advance during the last year with him, but it was on the next few years that my future depended. For tiding over them successfully, I had only to hold fast to my principles, and be fearless in all manly things; to persevere and win.

The letter seemed to be his very self, full of practical sense. I felt enriched by its possession. It was a novelty to have a letter of my own, sent from such a distance. I read it over and over, and found new meanings and greater solace each time. The signature attracted my attention with its peculiar whip, or flourish, below; and in my reply, which covered many pages, I annexed that whip and ended my first epistle with it; and, ever since, no signature of mine has been complete without it.

Soon after, Major Ingham started on his return home in a stern-wheeler bound for the Washita and Saline Rivers. The Washita, next to the Arkansas, is the most important river which passes through the state of Arkansas — pronounced 'Arkansa*w*.' The Saline is one of its feeders, and has a navigable course of only about one hundred and twenty-five miles. The Washita in its turn empties into the Red River, and the latter into the Mississippi.

On, or about, the seventh day from New Orleans, the steamer entered the Saline, and a few miles above Long View we landed on the right bank, and, mounting into a well-worn buggy, were driven a few miles inland to Ingham's plantation.

I am as unaware of the real status of my host among his neighbours, as I am of the size of his domain. It then appeared in my eyes immense, but was mostly a pine forest, in the midst of which some few score of black men had cleared a large space for planting. The house was of solid pine logs, roughly squared, and but slightly stained by weather, and neatly chinked without with plaster, and lined within with planed boards, new and unpainted — it had an air of domestic comfort.

My welcome from Mrs. Ingham left nothing to be desired. The slaves of the house thronged in her train, and curtsied and bobbed, with every token of genuine gladness, to the 'Massa,' as they called him, and then were good enough to include me in their bountiful joy. The supper which had been got ready was something of a banquet, for it was to celebrate the return of the planter, and was calculated to prove to him that, though New Orleans hotels might furnish more variety, home, after all, had its attractions in pure, clean, well-cooked viands. When the hearth-logs began to crackle, and the firelight danced joyfully on the family circle, I began to feel the influence of the charm, and was ready to view my stay in the western woods with interest and content.

But there was one person in the family that caused a doubt in my mind, and that was the overseer. He joined us after supper, and, almost immediately, I contracted a dislike for him. His vulgarity and coarseness revived recollections of levee men. His garb was offensive; the pantaloons stuffed into his boots, the big hat, the slouch of his carriage, his rough boisterousness, were all objectionable, and more than all his accents and the manner of his half-patronising familiarity. I set him down at once as one of those men who haunt liquor-saloons, and are proud to claim acquaintance with bar-tenders. Something in me, perhaps my offishness, may probably have struck him with equal repulsion. Under pretence of weariness I sought my bed, for the circle had lost its charm.

The next day the diet was not so sumptuous. The breakfast at seven, the dinner at noon, and the supper at six, consisted of pretty much the same kind of dishes, except that there was good coffee at the first meal, and plenty of good milk for the last. The rest mainly consisted of boiled, or fried, pork and beans, and corn scones. The pork had an excess of fat over the lean, and was followed by a plate full of mush and molasses. I was never very particular as to my diet, but as day after day followed, the want of variety caused it to pall on the palate. Provided other things had not tended to make me critical, I might have gratefully endured it, but what affected me principally were the encomiums lavished upon this style of cookery by the overseer, who, whether with the view of currying favour with Mrs. Ingham, or to exasperate my suppressed squeamishness, would bawl out, 'I guess you can't beat this, howsumdever you crack up New Or-lee-ans. Give me a raal western pot-luck, to your darned fixin's in them 'ar Mississippi towns.'

With such society and fare, I could not help feeling depressed, but the tall pine forest, with its mysterious lights and shades, had its compensations. As, in process of time, the planter intended to extend his clearing and raise more cotton, every tree felled assisted in widening the cultivable land. On learning this, I asked and obtained permission to cut down as many trees as I liked, and, like a ruthless youth with latent destructive propensities, I found an extraordinary pleasure in laying low with a keen axe the broad pines. I welcomed with a savage delight the apparent agony, the portentous shiver which ran from root to topmost plume, the thunderous fall, and the wild recoil of its neighbours, as it rebounded and quivered before it lay its still length. After about a score of the pine monarchs had been levelled, the negroes at work presented new features of interest. On the outskirts of the clearing they were chopping up timber into portable or rollable logs, some were 'toting' logs to the blazing piles, others rolled them hand over hand to the fires, and each gang chanted heartily as it toiled. As they appeared to enjoy it, I became infected with their spirit and assisted at the log-rolling, or lent a hand at the toting, and championed my side against the opposite. I waxed so enthusiastic over this manly work, which demanded the exertion of every ounce of muscle, that it is a marvel I did not suffer from the strain; its fierce joy was more to my taste than felling timber by myself. The atmosphere, laden with the scent of burning resin, the roaring fires, the dance of the lively flames, the excitement of the gangs while holding on, with grim resolve and in honour bound, to the bearing-spikes, had a real fascination for me. For a week, I rose with the darkies at the sound of the overseer's horn, greeted the revivifying sunrise with anticipating spirits, sat down to breakfast with a glow which made the Major and his wife cheerier, and then strode off to join in the war against the pines with a springy pace.

How long this toil would have retained its sportive aspect for me I know not, but I owed it to the overseer that I ceased to love it. He was a compound of a Legree[1] and Nelson, with an

[1] The cruel slave-driver, in *Uncle Tom's Cabin*, comparable with Nelson, bully of the 'Windermere.'

admixture of mannerism peculiarly his own. It was his duty to oversee all the gangs, the hoers, wood-cutters, fire-attendants, log-rollers, and toters. When he approached the gang with which I worked, the men became subdued, and stopped their innocent chaff and play. He had two favourite songs: one was about his 'deah Lucindah,' and the other about the 'chill winds of December,' which he hummed in a nasal tone when within speaking distance of me, while the cracks of his 'black snake' whip kept time. But, as he sauntered away to other parts, I felt he was often restive at my presence, for it imposed a certain restraint on his nature. One day, however, he was in a worse humour than usual. His face was longer, and malice gleamed in his eyes. When he reached us we missed the usual tunes. He cried out his commands with a more imperious note. A young fellow named Jim was the first victim of his ire, and, as he was carrying a heavy log with myself and others, he could not answer him so politely as he expected. He flicked at his naked shoulders with his whip, and the lash, flying unexpectedly near me, caused us both to drop our spikes. Unassisted by us, the weight of the log was too great for the others, and it fell to the ground crushing the foot of one of them. Meantime, furious at the indignity, I had engaged him in a wordy contest: hot words, even threats, were exchanged, and had it not been for the cries of the wounded man who was held fast by the log, we should probably have fought. The end of it was, I retired from the field, burning with indignation, and disgusted with his abominable brutality.

I sought Major Ingham, whom I found reclining his length in an easy-chair on the verandah. Not hearing the righteous condemnation I had hoped he would express, and surprised at his want of feeling, I hotly protested against the cruelty of the overseer in attacking a man while all his strength was needed to preserve others from peril, and declaimed against him for using a whip in proximity to my ears, which made the Major smile compassionately at my inexperience in such matters. This was too much for my patience, and I then and there announced my intention to seek the hospitality of Mr. Waring, his neighbour, as I could not be any longer the guest of a man who received my complaint so unsympathetically. On hearing me say this, Mrs. Ingham came out of the house, and expressed so much concern at this sudden rupture of our relations that I regretted having been so hasty, and the Major tried to explain how planters were compelled to leave field-work in charge of their overseer; but it was too late. Words had been uttered which left a blister in the mind, personal dignity had been grossly wounded, the Major had not the art of salving sores of this kind, and I doggedly clung to my first intentions. In another quarter of an hour I had left the plantation with a small bundle of letters and papers, and was trudging through the woods to Mr. Waring's plantation.

We have all our sudden likes and dislikes. The first view of the comfortable homeliness of Mr. Waring's house gave me an impression of family felicity, and when the old man with several smiling members of his family came to the door, it appeared to me as if it revived a picture I had seen somewhere in Wales, and all my heart went out to those who were in the house.

Strange to say, in proportion to the period spent at Major Ingham's, I possess a more vivid recollection of the night I passed at Mr. Waring's, and my thoughts have more often reverted to the more ancient house and its snugness and pleasant details, than to the other. As I did not mention anything about the causes of my departure from his neighbour's plantation, it was tacitly understood that I was only resting for the night, previous to resuming my journey next morning, and they did not press me to stay. I begged, however, Mr. Waring to do me the favour to send a buggy for my trunk the next morning. When it arrived, I repacked it; and, leaving it in his charge, I set off on a tramp across country to the Arkansas, rejecting many an offer of aid up to the last minute.

The road wound up and down pine-clothed hills, and, being a sandy loam, was dry and tolerably smooth. In the hollows I generally found a stream where I quenched my thirst, but I remember to have travelled a considerable distance for a young pedestrian without meeting any water, and to have reflected a little upon what the pains of dying from thirst would be like. I rested at a small farm-house that night; and, next morning, at an early hour, was once more footing it bravely, more elated, perhaps, than my condition justified. I regarded myself as being upon a fine adventure, the narration of which would surprise my father. My eyes travelled through far-reaching colonnades of tapering pine and flourishing oak, and for a great part of the time I lost consciousness of my circumstances, while my mind was absorbed in interminable imaginings of impossible discoveries and incidents. I saw myself the hero of many a thrilling surprise, and looked dreamily through the shades, as though in some places like them I would meet the preying beasts whom it would be my fortune to strike dead with my staff. But, invariably, on being brought to a proper sense of the scenes, and my real condition, I recognized how helpless I was against a snarling catamount, or couchant panther; I was devoutly thankful that Arkansas was so civilised that my courage was in no fear of being tested.

Just at dusk I reached the Arkansas River at Cypress Bend, having travelled about forty miles across country, without having met a single adventure.

Mr. Altschul's store, at which I was to devote myself to acquiring the arts and details of a country merchant's business, was situate about fifty miles S. E. of Little Rock, and halfway between Richmond and South Bend. I found no difficulty at all in entering the establishment, for I had no sooner introduced myself than I was accepted by his family with all cordiality. The store was, in reality, a country house of business. It stood isolated in a small clearing in the midst of Cypress Grove, and was removed from the dwelling-house of the family by a quarter of a mile. It was a long one-storied building of solid logs, divided into four apartments, three of which contained all manner of things that ironmongers, gunners, grocers, drapers, stationers, are supposed to sell; the fourth room, at the back, was used as an office during the day, and as a bedroom at night, by the clerks in charge. I commenced my duties in November, 1860, being warmly hailed as a fellow-clerk by Mr. Cronin, the salesman, and Mr. Waldron, the assistant-salesman.

Cronin was an Irishman from New York, about thirty years old; the assistant was the son of a small planter in the vicinity. The first was a character for whom I had a pitying fondness. One-half of him was excellent, all brightness, cleverness, and sociability, the other half, perhaps the worse, was steeped in whiskey. He was my Alphabet of the race of topers. I have never been able to be wrathful with his kind, they are such miracles of absurdity! Here and there one may meet a malignant, but they are mostly too stupid to be hated. Cronin knew his duties thoroughly. He was assiduous, obliging, and artful beyond anything with the ladies. He won their confidences, divined their preferences, and, with the most provoking assurance, laid the identical piece of goods they wanted before them, and made them buy it. It was a treat to observe the cordial, and yet deferent, air with which he listened to their wishes, the deft assistance he gave to their expression, his bland assents, the officious haste and zeal he exhibited in attending on them, and the ruthless way he piled the counters with goods for their inspection. Sometimes I suspected he was maliciously making work for me, for, being the junior, I had to refold the goods, and restore them to their places; but, in justice to him, I must say he nobly assisted in the re-arrangement. Cronin was a born salesman, and I have never met his equal since.

The poorer class of women he dazzled by his eloquent commendations, his elaborate courtesy, and the way he made them conceited with their own superior knowledge of what was genuine and rich. If the woman was a coloured person, he was benevolent and slightly familiar. His small grey eyes twinkled with humour, as he whispered friendly advice as to the quality of the goods, and besieged her with such attentions that the poor thing was compelled to buy.

With the planters, who were of varying moods, Mr. Cronin bore himself with such rare good-humour and tact, that one found a pleasure in watching the stern lips relax, and the benignant look coming to their gloomy eyes. He would go forward to meet them, as they stepped across the threshold, with hearty abandon and joviality, put fervour into his handshakes, sincerity into his greeting, and welcome into his every act. He anxiously enquired after their healths, condoled with them in their fevers, sympathised with them in their troubles about their cotton-crops, and soon found excuse to draw them to the liquor apartment, where he made them taste Mr. Altschul's latest importations.

According to Mr. Cronin, the 'cobwebs' were cleared by the

preliminary drink, and it enabled both salesman and buyer to take a cheerier view of things, and to banish thoughts that would impede business. Naturally, the planters cared little for cotton-prints or jaconets, though they often carried daintily-pencilled commissions from the ladies at home, which Mr. Cronin satisfactorily executed at once, on the plea that ladies must be served first; but when these were disposed of, — always with reverent regard for the fair sex, — Mr. Cronin flung off his tenderness and became the genial salesman again. Had the gentleman seen the new Californian saddles, or the latest thing in rifles, shot-guns that would kill duck at ninety yards? Those who heard him expatiate upon the merits of fire-arms wondered at the earnestness he threw into his language, and at the minute knowledge he seemed to possess of the properties of each article. Or the subject was saddles. I heard with amazement about the comparative excellencies of the Californian, English, and cavalry article, and thought his remarks ought to be printed. In this way, with regard to rifles, I soon got to know all about the merits of the Ballard, Sharp, Jocelyn rifles, their special mechanisms, trajectory, penetration, and range. If I alluded to the revolvers, his face glowed with a child's rapture as he dilated upon the superiority of the Tranter over the Colt, or the old-fashioned 'pepper-box'; but, when he took up a beautiful Smith and Wesson, he became intoxicated with his own bewildering fluency, and his gestures were those of an oratorical expert. Then some other excuse would be found for adjourning to the liquor room, where he continued to hold forth with his charming persuasiveness, until he succeeded in effecting a sale of something.

Mr. Cronin was indeed an artist, but Mr. Altschul did not appreciate him as his genius deserved. The proprietor laid too much stress upon his propensity to drink, which was certainly incurable, and too little upon the profits accruing to him through his agency. He also suspected him of gross familiarities with female slaves, which, in Mr. Altschul's eyes, were unpardonable. Therefore, though he was invaluable to me as a model salesman, poor Cronin was obliged to leave after a while.

Waldron in a short time found counter-work too irksome

and frivolous for his nature, and he also left; then two young men, very proud and high-stomached, and not over-genial to customers, were engaged instead.

But by this time I had become sufficiently acquainted with the tone of the planter community to be able to do very well, with a few instructions from Mr. Altschul. I had learned that in the fat cypress lands there was a humanity which was very different from that complaisant kind dwelling in cities. It had been drawn from many States, especially from the South. The Douglasses were from Virginia, the Crawfords from 'Old Georgia,' the Joneses and Smiths from Tennessee, the Gorees from Alabama. The poorer sort were from the Carolinas, Mississippi, Missouri, and Tennessee, the professional men and white employers from a wider area — which included Europe. Several of the richer men owned domains of from six to ten square miles. They lived like princelings, were owners of hundreds of slaves over whom they were absolute except as to life or limb, and all their environments catered to their egotism. Though genially sociable to each other, to landless people like myself they conducted themselves as though they were under no obligations. Such manners as they exhibited were not so much due to neighbourly good-feeling as to their dislike of consequences which might result from a wanton offishness. When they emerged from their respective territories to the common view, their bearing seemed to say that they yielded to us every privilege belonging to free whites, but reserved to themselves the right to behave as they deemed fitting to their state, and of airing any peculiarity unquestioned, and unremarked by the commonalty. They were as exclusive as the proud county families of Wales.

It may easily be seen, then, what a sight our store presented when about a dozen magnates of this kind, fresh from their cotton principalities, and armed, cap-à-pie, each in his own peculiar dress, assembled in it. In time, of course, I became used to it; and, considering their anxieties, the malarial climate, and the irritating 'ague-cake,' they behaved well, on the whole. Their general attitude was, however, stiff and constrained. Each slightly raised his hat as he came in, and their 'Sirs' were more formal and punctilious than, as neighbours or fellow-citizens, they ought to have been.

My proud fellow-clerks were disposed to think it was the dread of the pistol which made them so guarded in speech and action, but I thought that it was the fear of compromising the personal dignity by a disgraceful squabble with men untaught in the forms of good society. Arkansas is sometimes known as the Bear State, and many of its people at that time were singularly bearish and rude. The self-estimate of such men was sometimes colossal, and their vanities as sensitive as hair-triggers. None of them could boast of the piety of saints, but nearly all had been influenced by the religion of their mothers — just as much as might enable them to be distinguished from barbarians. It is wonderful what trivial causes were sufficient to irritate them. A little preoccupation in one's own personal affairs, a monosyllabic word, a look of doubt, or a hesitating answer, made them flare up hotly. The true reason for this excessive sensitiveness was that they had lived too much within their own fences, and the taciturnity engendered by exclusiveness had affected their habits. However amiable they might originally have been, their isolation had promoted the growth of egotism and self-importance. This is the essence of 'Provincialism,' wherever it is met with, in country or in city life.

Few visited our store who did not bear some sign of the pernicious disease, which afflicted old and young in the bottom-lands of the Arkansas. I had not been a week at the store before I was delirious from the fever which accompanies ague, and, for the first time in my life, was dieted on calomel and quinine. The young physician of our neighbourhood, who boarded with Mr. Altschul, communicated to me many particulars regarding the nature of this plague. In the form termed by him 'congestive chills,' he had known many cases to terminate fatally within a few hours. Blacks as well as whites were subject to it. Nothing availed to prevent an attack. The most abstemious, temperate, prudent habits no more prevented it than selfish indulgence or intemperance. So, what with isolation on their wide estates, their life amongst obsequious slaves, indigestion, and inflamed livers, their surroundings were not well adapted to make our wealthy customers very amiable or sociable.

Though I had a bowing acquaintance with scores, only half-a-dozen or so people condescended to hold speech with me. The mention of these reminds me that one day one of my friends, named Newton Story, and myself were weighed in the scales, and while Story, a fine manly fellow, weighed one hundred and eighty-five pounds, I was only ninety-five pounds, — within three pounds of seven stone. The frequency of ague attacks had reduced me to skin and bone. It was a strange disease, preceded by a violent shaking, and a congealed feeling as though the blood was suddenly iced, during which I had to be half-smothered in blankets, and surrounded by hot-water bottles. After a couple of hours' shivering, a hot fit followed, accompanied by delirium, which, about the twelfth hour, was relieved by exhausting perspiration. When, about six hours later, I became cool and sane, my appetite was almost ravenous from quinine and emptiness. For three or four days afterwards, unless the fever was tertian, I went about my duties as before, when, suddenly, a fit of nausea would seize me, and again the violent malady overpowered me. Such was my experience of the agues of the Arkansas swamp-land; and, during the few months I remained at Cypress Bend, I suffered from them three times a month.

The population of the State in that year (1861) was about 440,000; and I find, to my astonishment, that now (1895) it is over a million and a quarter, of whom only about 10,000 are foreign-born. Neither the dreadful ague, which exceeds in virulence the African type, nor the Civil War, has been able to check the population. What a hope for much-scorned Africa there is in these figures!

But this is a digression due to my desire to be just to my bilious fellow-sufferers in the swamp-land. One of our new salesmen was famous as a violinist, and his favourite song and tune was about the 'Arkansas Traveller,' who, losing his way in one of the sloughy highways through the swamp, disappeared in the mud leaving his hat behind him to indicate the spot. Reflective people will see in this story another obstacle to social intercourse.

Every new immigrant soon became infected with the proud and sensitive spirit prevailing in Arkansas. The poor American settler, the Irish employee, the German-Jew storekeeper, in a brief time grew as liable to bursts of deadly passion, or fits of cold-blooded malignity, as the Virginian aristocrat. In New Orleans, and other great cities, the social rule was to give and take, to assert an opinion, and hear it contradicted without resort to lethal weapons, but, in Arkansas, to refute a statement was tantamount to giving the lie direct, and was likely to be followed by an instant appeal to the revolver or bowie. Sometimes, an '*if* you said so, then I said so,' staved off the bloody arbitrament, but such folk were probably late immigrants and not old citizens.

It struck even a youth like me as being ridiculous for a servile German-Jew pedlar to fancy himself insulted by a casual remark from some mean and ill-bred white, and to feel it necessary to face the tube of a backwoodsman, when he might have ignored him and his rudeness altogether. It was hard to understand why he should resent his honour being doubted, except from a mistaken sense of his importance, for the ill-opinion of the planter community he had trebly earned already, by being a trader, a foreigner, and a Jew; and the small portion of regard he aspired to win by an act of daring bluff was not worth a thought, least of all the peril of his life, or the smart of a wound. With regard to his 'honour,' it seemed to bear a different meaning on different banks of a river. On the eastern shore of the Mississippi, it meant probity in business; on the western shore, it signified popular esteem for the punishment of a traducer, and he who was most prompt in killing anyone who made a personal reflection obtained most honour, and therefore every pedlar or clerk in Arkansas hastened to prove his mettle.

At South Bend, about nine miles below us, there was a storekeeper who prided himself more upon the 'honour' he had won as a duellist than upon commercial integrity. It was the example of his neighbourhood which had fired this abnormal ambition, and, on my arrival at the Arkansas, his clerks had begun to imitate him. The neighbouring merchants, envious of his fame, essayed the perilous venture; and, at last, Mr. Altschul was smitten with the mania. There is no doubt that, had his courage been of a more compact quality, he would have competed with the man of South Bend for 'honour.' He selected, however, the choicest of his stock of Smith and Wesson's vest-pocket revolvers, and was lavishly extravagant with the ammunition. At the outset, he could not resist blinking at the flash of his own pea-shooter, but, by dint of practice, he succeeded in plugging a big tree at twenty paces. Then, in an evil moment, his mounting spirit was inspired to turn his pistolette on a motherly old sow which had strayed among his cabbages, and he mortally wounded her. The owner of the animal was cross old Mr. Hubbard, a small planter, who came on an ambling mule, presently, with a double-barrel shot-gun, charged with an awful number of buck-pellets, to interview Mr. Altschul. When he returned home, I inferred, from Hubbard's satisfied smile, that the interview had not been unsatisfactory to him. From that moment we noticed that Mr. Altschul abandoned pistol practice — for, naturally, the pistolette was not a fit weapon to cope with a shot-gun. One of my fellow-clerks remarked that it was a pity Mr. Hubbard had no excuse for calling upon the man at South Bend for damages.

If the craze for shooting had been communicated to such a respectable man as Mr. Altschul, it may be imagined what a fascination pistols had for us youths. We had hip-pockets made in our trousers, and the Smith and Wesson was regarded as an indispensable adjunct to manhood. Our leisure hours were devoted to target-practice, until my proficiency was so great that I could sever a pack-thread at twenty paces. Theoretically, we were already man-slaughterers, for our only object in practice was to be expert in killing some imaginary rowdy, or burglar. In our rude world such a person might present himself at any moment. The rowdy needed only a little liquor to develop himself, and the store, guarded only by a boy at night, offered a tempting inducement to a burglarious individual. Among our hundred and odd customers there were several who were not over-regardful of our susceptibilities; and as my colleagues were of their own kidney, and had an acute sense of their dignity, there was no saying when a crisis might arise. Personally, I was not yet wrought up to this fine susceptiveness, though, probably, I had as quick a spirit as any fire-eater in Arkansas County. What I might do if my patience was abused, or how much bullying would be required to urge me to adopt the style in vogue, was, however, as yet undetermined. Of the code of honour and usage I had heard enough, but whenever I supposed myself to be the object of rude aggression, the dire extreme made me shrink. The contingency was a daily topic, but, when I dwelt on the possibility of being involved, I inwardly held that liquory ebullience ought not to be noticed.

Among our customers was a man named Coleman, a large, loose-jointed young fellow, who owned a plantation and some twenty slaves. At regular intervals he came to make his purchase of cloth for his slaves, provisions, etc., and always departed with a bottle of whiskey in each saddle-bag. One day he and some chance acquaintance had commenced a bottle of Bourbon, and under the influence of the liquor he became objectionable, and hinted to one of the salesmen that it was 'rot-gut,' diluted with swamp-water. At the commencement it was taken to be the rough pleasantry of a drunken rustic; but, as Coleman reiterated the charge, the clerk's patience was exhausted, and he retorted that swamp-water was wholesome for drunkards such as he. After this, one savage retort provoked another, and Coleman drew his revolver; but, as he aimed it, I crooked his elbow, and the bullet pierced the roof. Almost immediately after, the clerk had flung himself against his opponent, and we all three came to the floor. Then, while I clung to his thumb, to prevent his raising the hammer, assistance came from the next store-room; and the one who most efficiently interfered was a strong and stalwart planter, named Francis Rush, for he wrenched the weapon from his hand. There followed a disagreeable quarter of an hour: both Coleman and the clerk were wild to get at each other, but in the end we forced a truce. Coleman's saddle-bags were put on his horse, and I held his stirrups while he mounted. He glared fiercely at me awhile, and then, after a warning that I had better avoid meddling with other people's quarrels, he rode away.

Coleman never returned to the store again. Some weeks after this event, I was despatched round the neighbourhood to collect debts, and his name was on my list. There was an ominous silence about his house as I rode up, but, on making my way to the negro quarter to make enquiries, I was told in a frightened whisper that their master had disappeared into parts unknown, after killing Francis Rush.

An evening came when the long-expected burglarious adventure occurred. Night had fallen by the time I returned to the store from supper at Mr. Altschul's, but there was a moonlight which made the dead timber in the Cypress Grove appear spectral. Near the main entrance to the store was a candle, which I proceeded to light after entering the building. Then, closing and dropping the strong bar across the door, I walked down the length of the store towards the office and my bedroom. Holding the candle well up, I noticed as I passed the fire-place a pile of soot on the hearth-stone. As it had been swept clean after the day's business, the sight of it instantly suggested a burglar being in the chimney. Without halting, I passed on to the office, cast a quick look at the back door and windows, and, snatching my little revolver from under the pillow, retraced my steps to the fire-place. Pointing the weapon up the chimney, I cried out, 'Look out, I am about to fire. After the word "three" I shall shoot. One! two! — ' A cloud of soot poured down on my arm, the rumble of a hasty scramble was heard, and I fired into the brick to hasten his departure. I then flew into the office, set my candle upon a chair, opened the back door, and darted out in time to see a negro's head and shoulders above the chimney-top. By means of threats, and a sufficient demonstration with the fire-arm, he was made to descend, and marched to Mr. Altschul's house, where he surrendered to the proprietor. Except that he was severely bound, his treatment was respectful, for he represented over a thousand dollars, and to injure him was to injure Dr. Goree, his owner, and one of our most respected customers.

Mr. Altschul was an Israelite and kept open store on Sunday, for the benefit of the negroes around. The clerks, being Christians, were, of course, exempted from labour that day; but, on one special Sunday, one of our party had volunteered to take Mr. Altschul's place at the counter. In the afternoon, he was attending a clamouring crowd of about thirty negroes, with his counter littered with goods. As I came in, I observed that he was not so alertly watchful as he ought to have been, with such a number of men, and so many exposed articles. I sat down and closely watched, and saw that, each time his back was turned, two men abstracted stockings, thread-spools, and ribands, stuffing them into their capacious pockets. After considering the best method of compelling restoration, I withdrew and called Simon, Mr. Altschul's burly slave, and instructed him how to assist me.

A few seconds after re-entering the store, the two halves of the front door were suddenly flung to, and barred, and a cry of 'Thieves' was raised. There was a violent movement towards me, but Simon flourished a big knife above his head, and swore he would use it, if they did not stand still and be searched. Those who were conscious of their innocence sided with us; and through their help we turned out a pretty assortment of small goods, which the clerk, by referring to his sales-book, found had not been sold.

I went out to shoot turtle-doves one holiday, and aimed at one on a branch about thirty feet above the road, and overhanging it. Almost immediately after, old Hubbard, the planter, emerged into view from round the corner, in a tearing rage, and presented his shot-gun at me. Seeing no one else near, and assuming that he was under some great mistake, I asked what the matter was, upon which he boldly accused me of shooting at him, and he put his hand to his face to show the wound. As there was not the slightest trace of even a bruise, I laughed at him, as it seemed to me that only an overdose of whiskey could account for such a paroxysm of passion.

Since my arrival at Auburn I had received three letters from my father from Havana, within a period of about nine weeks. Then, month after month of absolute silence followed. The last letter had stated that his brother was convalescent, and that, in about a month, he intended to return to New Orleans, and would then pay me a visit. Until well into March, 1861, I was in daily expectation of hearing from him, or seeing him in person. But we were destined never to meet again. He died suddenly in 1861 — I only heard of his death long after. In the mean time, wholly unheeded by me, astounding national events had occurred. Several of the Southern States had openly defied the United States Government. Forts, arsenals, and ships of war had been seized by the revolted States, and, what was of more importance to me, the forts below New Orleans had been taken by the Louisiana troops.

These events were known to readers of newspapers in Arkansas, but the only newspaper taken at the Auburn store was a Pine Bluff weekly, which, as I seldom saw it, I never imagined would contain any news of personal interest to me.

It was not until March that I began dimly to comprehend that something was transpiring which would involve every individual. Dr. Goree, our neighbour planter, happened to meet Mr. W. H. Crawford, an ex-Representative of Georgia, at our store, and began discussing politics. Their determined accents and resolute gestures roused my curiosity, and I heard them say that the States of Alabama, Georgia, Louisiana, and others, had already formed a separate government, and that one called Jeff Davis had been proclaimed President of the new government; and they wondered why Arkansas was so slow to join the Confederates, etc., etc. This was news to me, and when they unfolded their respective newspapers and read extracts from them, it dawned upon me that if I wished to post myself upon the grave national affairs, I should have to read those stupid sheets which hitherto I had regarded as being only fit for merchants and bearded men.

Thus stimulated to think that the events of the time affected the people of Arkansas County, even youths like myself, I began to read the Pine Bluff paper, and to be more inquisitive; and it was not long before I had a vague conception that the country was in a terribly disturbed state, and that there would be war. Notwithstanding the information gleaned from persons who gave themselves little trouble to satisfy a strange boy, it was not until young Dan Goree returned from Nashville College that I could assimilate properly all that I had heard. Young Dan was a boy of about my own age, and being the son of such a politician as Dr. Goree, was naturally much more advanced in political matters than I. He it was who, in friendly converse, acted as my Mentor, and gave me the first intelligent exposition of how affairs stood between the two sections of the Union. It was from him I learned that the election of Abe Lincoln, in the November previous, had created a hostile feeling in the South, because this man had declared himself opposed to slavery; and as soon as he became President, in March, he would do all in his power to free all the slaves. Of course, said he, in that event all slaveholders would be ruined. His father owned about one hundred and twenty slaves, worth from $500 to $1200 a head, and to deprive him of property that he had bought with cash was pure robbery. That was the reason that all the people of the South were rising against the Northern people, and they would fight, to the last man. When the State of Arkansas 'seceded,' then every man and boy would have to proceed to the war and drive those wretched Abolitionists back to their homes, which would be an easy task, as one Southerner was better than ten of those Northern fellows, many of whom had never seen a gun! Dan thought that the boys of the South, armed with whips, would be quite sufficient to lick the thieving hounds!

I need not pursue the theme, but it was from such a source that I obtained my elementary lessons in American Politics. From the time when, in December, 1857, I had read some leaderette about the Louisiana Legislative Assembly, politics had been repulsively dry to me, and newspapers were only useful for their shipping and trade details.

Specially interesting to me, however, was it to know that Missouri and its metropolis, St. Louis, would assuredly join the South; though I was saddened to learn that Cincinnati and Louisville were enemies. What curious emotions that word 'enemies' caused in me! People I knew well, with whom I had worshipped, boys with whom I had contracted delightful friendships at Newport and Covington, to be enemies! Then I wondered how we were to obtain our goods in future. Consignments of arms, medicine, dry-goods, and ironware, had come to us from St. Louis, Cincinnati, and even Chicago. The conditions of trade would be altogether altered!

It was not, however, until I had propounded the question as to how the seizure of the Mississippi forts affected people who were abroad, and wished to return home, that I understood how deeply involved I was by this rupture of relations between the North and South. I was told that all communication was stopped, that ships coming in from sea would be turned back, or else, if they were permitted to come in by the cruisers outside, would certainly not be permitted to leave; that every ship insisting on going to New Orleans would be searched, and, if anything likely to assist the enemy was found, she would be detained, and perhaps confiscated; and that, as no vessel was permitted to enter the river, so none would have the privilege of leaving. Here was something wholly unexpected! My father was shut out, and I was shut in! He could not come to me, nor could I join him. In some mysterious way somebody had built an impassable wall round about us, and the South was like a jail, and its inhabitants had been deprived of the liberty of leaving. From the moment that I fully realised this fact, everything bore a different aspect to what it had before. I was a strange boy in a strange land, in the same condition of friendlessness as when I fled from the 'Windermere.' I had prepared myself to convince my father that the valley of the Arkansas was not a fit place to live in. My staring bones and hollow eyes should speak for me, and we would try the Washita Valley, or ascend the Arkansas, towards Little Rock, where the country was healthier, but anywhere rather than in such a pestilential place as the swamp-land of Arkansas. But my intentions had come to naught, my cherished hopes must be abandoned. I was stranded effectually, and I had no option but to remain with Mr. Altschul.

It was an evil hour to meditate any design of a personal nature, for the sentiment of the period was averse from it. The same unperceivable power that had imprisoned me in the fever-and-ague region of Arkansas was rapidly becoming formidable. Man after man unresistingly succumbed to its influence. Even the women and children cried for war. There was no Fiery Cross, but the wire flashed the news into every country-place and town, and, wherever two met, the talk was all about war. Most of the cotton States had already seceded, and as our State was their sister in sentiment, habit, and blood, Arkansas was bound to join her sisters, and hasten with her sons to the battle-field, to conquer or die. Early in May, the State Representatives met at Little Rock, and adopted the ordinance of secession; whereupon the fighting spirit of the people rose in frenzy. Heroic sayings, uttered by ancient Greek and Roman heroes, were mouthed by every stripling. The rich planters forgot their pride and exclusiveness, and went out and orated among the common folk. They flourished their hats and canes, and cried, 'Give us Liberty, or give us

Death!' The young men joined hands and shouted, 'Is there a man with soul so dead, Who never to himself hath said — This is my own, my native land?' 'An honourable death is better than a base life,' etc., etc. In the strident tones of passion, they said they would welcome a bloody grave rather than survive to see the proud foe violating their altars and their hearths, and desecrating the sacred soil of the South with their unholy feet. But, inflamed as the men and youths were, the warlike fire that burned within their breasts was as nothing to the intense heat that glowed within the bosoms of the women. No suggestion of compromise was possible in their presence. If every man did not hasten to the battle, they vowed they would themselves rush out and meet the Yankee vandals. In a land where women are worshipped by the men, such language made them war-mad.

Then one day I heard that enlistment was going on. Men were actually enrolling themselves as soldiers! A Captain Smith, owner of a plantation a few miles above Auburn, was raising a Company to be called the 'Dixie Greys.' A Mr. Penny Mason, living on a plantation below us, was to be the First-lieutenant, and Mr. Lee, nephew of the great General Lee, was to be Second-lieutenant. The youth of the neighbourhood were flocking to them and registering their names. Our Doctor, — Weston Jones, — Mr. Newton Story, and the brothers Varner, had enlisted. Then the boy Dan Goree prevailed upon his father to permit him to join the gallant braves. Little Rich, of Richmond Store, gave in his name. Henry Parker, the boy nephew of one of the richest planters in the vicinity, volunteered, until it seemed as if Arkansas County was to be emptied of all the youth and men I had known.

About this time, I received a parcel which I half-suspected, as the address was written in a feminine hand, to be a token of some lady's regard; but, on opening it, I discovered it to be a chemise and petticoat, such as a negro lady's-maid might wear. I hastily hid it from view, and retired to the back room, that my burning cheeks might not betray me to some onlooker. In the afternoon, Dr. Goree called, and was excessively cordial and kind. He asked me if I did not intend to join the valiant children of Arkansas to fight? and I answered 'Yes.'

At my present age, the whole thing appears to be a very laughable affair altogether; but, at that time, it was far from being a laughing matter. He praised my courage, and my *patriotism*, and said I should win undying glory, and then he added, in a lower voice, 'We shall see what we can do for you when you come back.'

What *did* he mean? Did he suspect my secret love for that sweet child who sometimes came shopping with her mother? From that confidential promise I believed he did, and was, accordingly, ready to go anywhere for her sake.

About the beginning of July we embarked on the steamer 'Frederick Notrebe.' At various landings, as we ascended the river, the volunteers crowded aboard; and the jubilation of so many youths was intoxicating. Near Pine Bluff, while we were making merry, singing, 'I wish I was in Dixie,' the steamer struck a snag which pierced her hull, and we sank down until the water was up to the furnace-doors. We remained fixed for several hours, but, fortunately, the 'Rose Douglas' came up, and took us and our baggage safely up to Little Rock.

We were marched to the Arsenal, and, in a short time, the Dixie Greys were sworn by Adjutant-General Burgevine into the service of the Confederate States of America for twelve months. We were served with heavy flint-lock muskets, knapsacks, and accoutrements, and were attached to the 6th Arkansas Regiment of Volunteers, Colonel Lyons commanding, and A. T. Hawthorn, Lieutenant-colonel.

General Burgevine was, in later years, Commander of the Mercenaries, in the Imperial Chinese army against the Taipings, and an ally of General (Chinese) Gordon, at one time. Dismissed by the Imperialists, he sought the service of the Taipings. Wearied of his new masters, he conceived a project of dethroning the Emperor, and reigning in his stead; he went so far as to try and tempt Gordon to be his accomplice!

HENRY M. STANLEY, AT 20

CHAPTER VII

SOLDIERING

I AM now about to begin a period lasting about six years, which, were it possible, I should gladly like to re-live, not with a view of repeating its woes and errors, pains and inconsistencies, but of rectifying the mistakes I made. So far, I had made none of any importance; but enlisting in the Confederate service, because I received a packet of female clothes, was certainly a grave blunder. But who is able to withstand his fate or thwart the designs of Providence? It may have been time for me, getting close on to eighteen, to lose some of the soft illusions of boyhood, and to undergo the toughening process in the trail of war. Looking backward upon the various incidents of these six years, though they appear disjointed enough, I can dimly see a connection, and how one incident led to the other, until the curious and somewhat involved design of my life, and its purpose, was consummated. But this enlistment was, as I conceive it, the first of many blunders; and it precipitated me into a veritable furnace, from which my mind would have quickly recoiled, had I but known what the process of hardening was to be.

Just as the fine edge of boyish sensitiveness was blunted, somewhat, by the daring blasphemy of the 'Windermere' officers, so modesty and tenderness were to be shocked, by intercourse with men who cast off sweet manners with their civilian clothes, and abandoned themselves to the rude style of military life. A host of influences were at work sapping moral scruples. The busy days, the painful events, the excitement of the camp, the general irreligiousness, the disregard of religious practice, the contempt for piety, the licentious humours of the soldiers, the reckless and lavish destruction of life, the gluttonous desire to kill, the devices and stratagems of war, the weekly preaching in defence of it, the example of my elders and superiors, the enthusiasm of beautiful women for strife — finally, all that was weak, vain, and unfixed in my own nature, all conspired to make me as indifferent as any of my fellows to all sacred duties.

I had to learn that that which was unlawful to a civilian was lawful to the soldier. The 'Thou shalt not' of the Decalogue, was now translated 'Thou shalt.' Thou shalt kill, lie, steal, blaspheme, covet, and hate; for, by whatever fine names they were disguised, everyone practised these acts, from the President down to the private in the rear rank. The prohibition to do these things was removed, and indulgence in licence and excess was permissible. My only consolation, during this curious 'volte-face' in morality, was, that I was an instrument in the strong, forceful grip of circumstance, and could no more free myself than I could fly.

Heaven knows if any among the Dixie Greys can look at the acts of the war with my eyes. Not having been educated as I had been, nor become experienced afterwards in the ways of many lands, it is not likely any of them would. Many of them went to the war as passionate patriots in the spirit of religious duty, blessed by their families; others with an appetite for glory, the desire of applause, a fondness for military excitement, or because they were infected with the general craze, or to avoid tedious toil, or from the wildness of youth, etc. It was passionate patriotism that was the rule, and brought to its standard all sorts and conditions of men; and it was this burning passion that governed all conduct, and moulded public life to its will.

Now all men who knew our brigade commander will concede that, whatever virtues he may have had, ambition was his distinguishing characteristic. It was commonly said that he was a man of genius, could command a Department, or be a first-class Minister of War; but, from what I can recollect of him, he aimed at the highest office in the land, and was sufficiently unscrupulous to establish himself as a dictator. Colonel Lyons was purely and simply a soldier: Lieutenant-colonel A. T. Hawthorn was too vain of military distinction, and the trappings of official rank, to have stooped to be a patriot in the ranks; but Captain S. G. Smith was a patriot of the purest dye, of the most patrician appearance, one of the finest and noblest types of men I have ever met: a man of stubborn honour and high principles, brave, and invariably gentle in demeanour and address. Our First-lieutenant was a Mr. Penny Mason, a Virginian, bright, soldierly, zealous, and able, and connected with the oldest families of his State. He rose, as his military merits deserved, to the rank of Adjutant-general. Our Second-lieutenant was a nephew of General Lee, who in the soldiers' parlance was a 'good fellow.' He also became distinguished during the war. Our Third-lieutenant was a 'dandy,' who took immense trouble with his appearance, and was always as neat as a military tailor and the laundry could make him. Our Orderly-sergeant was an old soldier of the name of Armstrong, an honest and worthy fellow, who did his duty with more good-humour and good-nature than would have been expected under the circumstances.

The privates were, many of them, young men of fortune, sons, or close relations, of rich Arkansas planters of independent means; others were of more moderate estate, overseers of plantations, small cotton-growers, professional men, clerks, a few merchants, and a rustic lout or two. As compared with many others, the company was a choice one, the leaven of gentlehood was strong, and served to make it rather more select than the average. Still, we were only a tenth of a regiment, and, though a fifth of the regiment might be self-respecting, gentlemanly fellows, daily contact in camp with a majority of rough and untaught soldiers is apt to be perverting in time.

We were not subjected to the indignity of being stripped and examined like cattle, but were accepted into the military service upon our own assurance of being in fit condition; and, after being sworn in, we shed our civil costumes, and donned the light grey uniforms. Having been duly organized, we next formed ourselves into messes. My mess consisted of Jim Armstrong, the Orderly-sergeant; Newton Story, the Colour-sergeant, who had been overseer of Dr. Goree's plantation; Dan Goree, a boy, the son and heir of Dr. Goree; Tom Malone, a genial fellow, but up to every gambling trick, a proficient in 'High-low-jack,' Euchre, Poker, and Old Sledge, and, when angered, given to deliver himself in very energetic language; old Slate, knowing as any, anecdotive, and pleasant. Tomasson, a boisterous fellow, who acted frequently like a bull in a china-shop, was admitted by Armstrong to the mess because he was a neighbour, and full of jests. A Sibley tent, an improvement on the bell-tent, contained the whole of us comfortably.

Dan Goree had brought his slave Mose, a faithful blackie, to wait upon him. The mess annexed his services as cook and tin-washer, and, in return, treated Dan with high consideration. Mose was remarkable for a cow-like propensity to kick backward, if we but pointed our fingers at him. Armstrong contributed to the general comfort a stylish canteen and the favour of his company; and the rest of us gave our services and means to make the social circle as pleasant as possible, which, as we were 'bright, smart, and alive,' meant a great deal; for, if there were any fowls, butter, milk, honey, or other accessories to diet in our neighbourhood, they were sure to be obtained by some indefatigable member of the mess. I was too 'green' in the forager's arts, at the beginning of the campaign, but I was apt; and, with such ancient campaigners as Armstrong and old Slate, — both of whom had been in the Mexican War of 1847, — I did not lack tuition by suggestion.

When clothed in our uniforms, each of us presented a somewhat attenuated appearance; we seemed to have lost in dignity, but gained in height. As I looked at Newton Story's form, I could scarcely believe my eyes. Instead of the noble portliness for which he had been distinguished, he was lean as a shorn sheep. Sleek Dan Goree was girlishly slender, while I had a waspish waist, which measured a trifle more than two hands. Dr. Jones was like a tall, over-grown lad; and, as for the Varner brothers, they were elegant to the verge of effeminacy.

With military clothes, we instinctively assumed the military pose: our heads rose stiff and erect above our shoulders, our chests bulged out, and our shoulder-blades were drawn in. We found ourselves cunningly peeping from the corners of our eyes, to observe if any admired our martial style. The Little Rock 'gals,' crowding about the Arsenal grounds, were largely responsible for the impressive airs we took. The prettiest among them drew into her circle a score or more of heroic admirers, whose looks pictured their admiration; and how envied were they who obtained a smile from the fair! And how they strutted, with their eyeballs humid with love! If, when we promenaded the streets, with equal step and arm-in-arm, we detected the presence of cambric frocks on a 'stoep,' or in some classic porch, we became as ridiculous as peacocks from excess of vanity. Indeed, in those early days, we were all over-troubled with patriotic thrills, sanguinary ardour, and bursts of 'bulliness.' The fever of military enthusiasm was at its height, in man, woman, and child; and we, who were to represent them in the war, received far more adulation than was good for us. The popular praise turned our young heads giddy, and anyone who doubted that we were the sanest, bravest, and most gallant boys in the world, would have been in personal danger! Unlike the Spartans, there was no modesty in the estimate of our own valour. After a few drills, we could not even go to draw rations without the practice of the martial step, and crying out 'Guide centre,' or 'Right wheel,' or some other order we had learned. At our messes, we talked of tactics, and discussed Beauregard's and Lee's merits, glorified Southern chivalry, and depreciated the Yankees, became fluent in the jargon of patriotism, and vehement in our hatred of the enemy. Few of us had ever smelled the fumes of battle, but that did not deter us from vividly painting scenes of carnage when the blood rolled in torrents, and the favoured 'Dixie Greys' led the van to victory.

Our martial souls were duly primed for the field by every adjunct of military system. The fife, drum, and trumpet sounded many times a day. A fine brass band thrilled us, morning and evening, with stirring music. The drum and fife preceded us to the drilling-ground, and inspired us to sprightliness, campward. We burnished brass buttons, arms, and accoutrements, until they shone like new gold. We bought long Colt's revolvers, and long-bladed bowie-knives; we had our images taken on tin-types in our war-paint and most ferocious aspects, revolver in one hand, bowie-knife in the other, and a most portentous scowl between the eyebrows. We sharpened the points of our bayonets, and gave a razor-edge to our bowies, that the extermination we intended should be sudden and complete.

After a few weeks we made our last march through the Arkansan capital. The steamer was at the river-side, to take us across. The streets were gay with flags and ladies' dresses.

The people shouted, and we, raw and unthinking, responded with cheers. We raised the song, 'We 'll live and die for Dixie,' and the emotional girls waved their handkerchiefs and wept. What an imposing column we made! The regiment was in full strength. The facets of light on our shining muskets and bayonets were blinding. Banners of regiments and companies rustled and waved to the breeze. We strode down to the levee with 'eyes front,' after the manner of Romans when reviewed by their tribunes!

Once across the river, that August day, we strapped our knapsacks, slung our haversacks and water-canteens, and felt more like veterans. All being ready, our physically-noble Colonel Hawthorn, prancing on his charger, drew his bright sword, and, after he had given us a sufficiently stern glance, rode to the head of the regiment; the brass band struck up a lively tune, and we swung gaily in column of four along the pike, towards the interior. Our officers and orderly walked parallel with us. The August sun was extremely hot, the pike was hard, dry, and dusty. At first, the officers' voices had a peremptory and sharp ring in them as they sang out, 'Keep step, there! Left shoulder, shift arms! Dress up!' but after a while, as the heat began to force a copious perspiration, and the limy dust from the metalled highway parched our throats, they sobered down, and allowed us to march at ease.

Within an hour the sweat had darkly stained our grey coats about the arm-pits and shoulders, and it rolled in streams down our limbs into our boots, where, mingling with the dust and minute gravel, it formed a gritty mud which distressed our feet. Our shoulders ached with the growing weight and hardness of the muskets, our trousers galled us sorely, the straps and belts became painfully constrictive, and impeded respiration, but, through fear of shame, we endured all, without complaint. At the end of the hour we were halted for five minutes' rest, and then resumed the march.

Like all new recruits, we carried a number of things that veterans dispense with: for instance, keepsakes, and personal treasures; mine were a daguerreotype of my adopted father, and a lock of his grey hair, — very trivial and valueless to others, but my own peculiar treasures, carried in my knapsack to be looked at every Sunday morning when we smartened up. With these, toilet articles, soap, changes of underclothing, camp-shoes, etc., besides extra uniform, and blankets, made up our luggage, which, with heavy musket, bayonet-accoutrements, and canteen of water, weighed about sixty pounds, and more, in some cases. For growing and lean youths this was a tremendous weight; and, during the second hour, the sense of oppression and soreness rapidly increased; but, excepting more frequent changes of the musket from shoulder to shoulder, we bated nothing of our resolve to endure.

After the second halt we were sensibly lamer. The gravel created blisters, and the warm mud acted like a poultice on the feet. The military erectness gave way to a weary droop, and we leaned forward more. We were painfully scalded, restlessly shifted our weapons, and tried scores of little experiments, hustled our cartridge-pouches, inch by inch, then from back to front, from right to left; tugged at our breast-straps, eased our belts, drank copious draughts of water; and still the perspiration rolled in a shower down our half-blinded faces, and the symptoms of collapse became more and more pronounced.

Finally, the acutest point of endurance was reached, and nature revolted. Our feet were blistered, our agonies were unendurable, and, despite official warning and menace, we hopped to the road-side, whipped off our boots to relieve our burning feet; after a little rest, we rose and limped after the company. But the column had stretched out to a tremendous length with its long wagon-train, and to overtake our friends seemed hopeless. As we limped along, the still untired soldiers mocked and jeered at us, and this was very hard to endure. But, by and by, the stragglers became more numerous; the starch appeared to be taken out of the strongest, and, the longer the march continued, the greater was the multitude of the weary, who crawled painfully in the rear of the column.

Had the Little Rock ladies witnessed our arrival at camp late at night, we should have been shamed for ever. But, fortunately, they knew nothing of this; and blessing the night which hid our roasted faces and sorry appearance, we had no sooner reached the precincts of the camp than we embraced the ground, pains and aches darting through every tortured limb, feet blistered and bleeding, our backs scorched, and our shoulders inflamed. No bed that I had ever rested on gave me a tithe of the pleasure afforded me now by the cold, damp pasture-land.

The next day was a halt. Many of us were more fitted for hospital at day-break than for marching, but, after a bathe in the stream, a change of linen, and salving our wounds, we were in better mood. Then Armstrong, the old orderly, suggested that we should shed our knapsacks of all 'rubbish,' and assisted his friends by his advice as to what was indispensable and what was superfluous. The camp-fires consumed what we had rejected, and, when we noted the lightened weight of our knapsacks after this ruthless ransackment, we felt fitter for the march than on the day we departed from the Arkansas River.

Our surroundings at camp were novel for inexperienced youths. We were tented along the road-side, having taken down the fences of a field, and encroached on farm-lands, without asking permission. The rails were also freely used by us as firewood. A town of canvas had risen as if by magic, with broad, short streets, between the company tents; and in the rear were located the wagons carrying provisions, ammunition, and extra equipments.

In a few days we were camped in the neighbourhood of Searcy, about sixty miles from Little Rock. The aspect of the country was lovely, but there was something fatal to young recruits in its atmosphere. Within two weeks an epidemic carried off about fifty, and quite as many more lay in hospital. Whether it was the usual camp typhus, or malarious fever, aggravated by fatigue and wretched rations, I was too young to know or to concern myself about; but, in the third week, it seemed to threaten us all, and I remember how the soldiers resorted to the prayer-meetings in each company, and how solemn they were at service on Sunday. The pressure of an impending calamity lay heavy upon us all while in camp, but, as soon as we left it, we recovered our spirits.

It was at this camp I acquired the art of diving. At swimming I was a proficient a long time before, but the acquisition of this last accomplishment soon enabled me to astonish my comrades by the distance I could traverse under water.

The brigade of General Hindman was at last complete in its

organisation, and consisted of four regiments, some cavalry, and a battery of artillery. About the middle of September we moved across the State towards Hickman on the Mississippi, crossing the Little Red, White, Big Black, and St. Francis Rivers, by the way. Once across the Mississippi, we marched up the river, and, in the beginning of November, halted at what was then called 'the Gibraltar of the Mississippi.'

On the 7th of November, we witnessed our first battle, — that of Belmont, — in which, however, we were not participants. We were held in readiness on the high bluffs of Columbus, from whence we had a commanding view of the elbow of land nearly opposite, whereon the battle took place. The metaphor 'Gibraltar' might, with good reason, be applied to Columbus, for General Polk had made notable exertions to make it formidable. About one hundred and forty cannon, of large and small calibre, had been planted on the edge of the steep and tall bluffs opposite Belmont, to prevent the descent of the river by the enemy.

A fleet of vessels was discerned descending, a few miles above Belmont, and two gun-boats saucily bore down and engaged our batteries. The big guns, some of them 128-pound Parrott-rifled, replied with such a storm of shell that they were soon obliged to retreat again; but we novices were delighted to hear the sound of so many cannon. We received a few shots in return, but they were too harmless to do more than add to the charm of excitement. The battle began at between ten and eleven in the morning, the sky then being bright, and the day gloriously sunny; and it continued until near sunset. Except by the volleying, and thick haze which settled over the woods, we could not guess what was occurring. The results were, on our side, under General Polk, 641 killed, wounded, and missing. On the Federal side, under General Grant, the loss was 610 killed, wounded, and missing. To add to our casualties, a 128-pound rifled-gun burst at our battery, by which seven of the gunners were killed, and General Polk and many of his officers were wounded.

A youth requires to be educated in many ways before his manhood is developed. We have seen what a process the physical training is, by the brief description of the first day's march. It takes some time to bring the body to a suitable state for ungrudging acceptance of the hard conditions of campaigning, so that it can find comfort on a pike, or in a graveyard, with a stone for a pillow, and ease on clods, despite drenching rain and chilling dew. Then the stomach has to get accustomed to the soldier's diet of fried, or raw, bacon and horse-beans. The nerves have to be inured to bear, without shrinking, the repeated shocks and alarms of the camp. The spirit has to be taught how to subject itself to the spurns and contumely of superior and senior, without show of resentment; and the mind must endure the blunting and deadening of its sensibilities by the hot iron of experience.

During the long march from Little Rock to Columbus we became somewhat seasoned, and campaigning grew less and less unpleasant. Our ordinary march was now more in the nature of an agreeable relief from monotonous camp-duties. We were not so captious and ready to take offence as at first, and some things that were once most disagreeable were now regarded as diversions.

I now fully accepted it as a rule that a soldier must submit to military law; but many, like myself, had lost a great deal of that early enthusiasm for a soldier's life by the time we had reached Columbus. It had struck us when at picket-duty alone, in the dark, that we had been great fools to place ourselves voluntarily in a position whence we could not retreat without forfeit of life; and that, by a monosyllable, we had made our comrades our possible enemies upon a single breach of our oath. We had condemned ourselves to a servitude more slavish than that of the black plantation-hands, about whose condition North and South had declared war to the death. We could not be sold, but our liberties and lives were at the disposal of a Congress about which I, at least, knew nothing, except that, somewhere, it had assembled to make such laws as it pleased. Neither to Captain Smith, nor to Lieutenant Mason, nor even to my messmate Armstrong, could I speak with freedom. Any of them might strike me, and I should have to submit. They could make me march where they pleased, stand sentry throughout the night, do fatigue-duty until I dropped, load my back as they would a mule, ride me on a rail, make a target of me if I took a quiet nap at my post; and there was no possible way out of it.

To say the truth, I had not even a desire to shirk the duties I had undertaken. I was quite prepared and ready to do all that was required; for I loved the South because I loved my Southern friends, and had absorbed their spirit into every pore. Nevertheless, when far removed from the hubbub of camp, at my isolated post, my reason could not be prevented from taking a cynical view of my folly in devoting myself to be food for powder, when I might have been free as a bird, to the extent of my means. And if, among my vague fancies, I had thought that, by gallantry, I might win promotion such as would be some compensation for the sacrifice of my liberty, that idea had been exploded as soon as I had measured myself by hundreds of cleverer, abler, and braver men, and saw that they, even, had no chance of anything but to fill a nameless grave. The poetry of the military profession had departed under the stress of many pains, the wear and tear, and the certainty that soldiering was to consist of commonplace marches, and squalid camp-life.

The punishment inflicted on such as were remiss in their duties during the march had opened my eyes to the consequences of any misdemeanour, or an untimely ebullience of youthful spirits. I had seen unfortunate culprits horsed on triangular fence-rails, and jerked up by vicious bearers, to increase their pains; others, straddled ignominiously on poles; or fettered with ball and chain; or subjected to head-shaving; or tied up with the painful buck and gag; or hoisted up by the thumbs; while no one was free of fatigue-duty, or exempt from fagging to someone or other, the livelong day.

Those who were innocent of all breaches of 'good order and discipline' had reason to lament having sacrificed their independence, for our brigade-commander, and regimental officers, were eaten up with military zeal, and were resolved upon training us to the perfection of soldierly efficiency, and, like Bully Waters of the 'Windermere,' seemed to think that it was incumbent on them to get the full value of our keep and pay out of us. They clung to the antiquated notion that soldiers were appointed as much to drudge for their personal service as for the purposes of war. Besides the morning and evening musters, the nine o'clock dress-parade, the drill from that hour to noon, the cleaning of arms and accoutrements, the frequent interruptions of rest by the 'long roll' heard in the dead of night, the guard-duty, or picket, we had to cook our provisions, put up the officers' tents, make their beds soft as straw and hay or grass could make them, collect fuel for their fires, dig ditches around their tents, and fag for them in numberless ways. These made a mighty list of harassments, which, on account of the miserably hard fare, and insufficient preparation of it, weighed on our spirits like lead, tended to diminish our number by disease, and sent hundreds to the hospital.

The Dixie Greys, for instance, consisted mostly of young men and lads who were as ignorant of the art of converting their ration of raw beef and salt pork, field beans, and flour, into digestible food, as they were of laundry work; yet they were daily served with rations, which they might eat raw, or treat as they liked. Of course, they learnt how to cook in time; but, meanwhile, they made sorry messes of it, and suffered accordingly. Those with good constitutions survived their apprenticeship, and youth, open air, and exercise, enabled them to bear it a long time; but when, with improper food, the elements chilled and heated us with abrupt change, and arbitrary officialism employed its wits to keep us perpetually on the move, it becomes evident, now, why only the hardiest were enabled to bear the drudgery and vexation imposed upon them, and why disease slew more than two-thirds of the whole number of soldiers who perished during the war.

The fault of the American generalship was that it devoted itself solely to strategy and fighting, and providing commissariat supplies; but seldom, or never, to the kindly science of health-preservation. The officers knew how to keep their horses in good condition; but I do not remember ever to have seen an officer who examined the state of our messes, or stooped to show that, though he was our military superior, he could take a friendly and neighbourly interest in our well-being, and that his rank had not estranged his sympathies. If, at the muster, a soldier was ill, he was put on the sick-list; but it never seems to have struck any officer, from General Lee down to the Third-lieutenant of an infantry company, that it might be possible to reduce the number of invalids by paying attention to the soldiers' joys and comforts. The raw provisions were excellent and abundant, and they only needed to be properly prepared to have made us robust and strong.

Just as the regimental physician and his assistants were requisite for the *cure* of illness, a regimental 'chef,' as superior of the company's cooks, would have been useful for the *prevention* of it, in fifty per cent of the cases; but the age was not advanced enough to recognise this.

Although I am apt to assign causes for things in my old age, it must not be supposed that I, as a boy, could then know much about such matters. I was, fortunately, blessed with the power of endurance, and was of so elastic a disposition that I could act my part without cavil or criticism. At that time, I felt that I had no other business in the world than to eat, work, and use my eyes, wits, and powers as a soldier, and to be as happy as my circumstances would allow; and I do not think I made myself obnoxious to any living soul. Within our mess we were not without our disagreements, and I had to bear my share of banter from my elders; but none can say, 'This was he whom we had sometime in derision, and a proverb of reproach. We accounted his life madness, and his end to be without honour.'

The exigencies of war necessitated our removal by train from Columbus to Cave City, Kentucky, where we arrived about the 25th of November, 1861. We remained in this camp until about the middle of February, 1862. The force around Bowling Green and Cave City numbered 22,000. Our brigade was attached to the Division of General Hardee, author of 'Tactics.' During the time we remained there, no fighting occurred; but we made several midnight marches towards Green River, and posted ourselves in positions to surprise the enemy, expected to come from Munfordville.

During the winter in this camp I won the approval of the mess by an aptitude for lessening the inconveniences under which we suffered in mid-winter, and my success in foraging. Instead of a fire under the Sibley tripod, which, besides endangering our feet and bedding, smoked us, I suggested that we should sink a hearth and build a fire-place with a flue and regular chimney of mud outside; and, with the help of the veteran Slate, the work was executed so well that our tent was always warm and clear of smoke, while the edges of the hearth made comfortable seats by which we could toast our feet, and recline back luxuriously. Tomasson, our bawling mess-mate, was not worth his salt at any work except legitimate soldiering. He seemed to consider that, by dusting around like a clown at a pantomime, and giving us the honour of his company, he did enough for the general welfare. Armstrong and Story were sergeants; and, of course, their Mightinesses were exempt from doing more than stooping to praise! Dan, being in the leading-strings of Story, was not permitted to roam; therefore, when it came to a consideration of ways and means for improving our diet, it devolved upon Malone, Slate, and myself to exert ourselves for the mess.

The long halt at Cave City served to initiate me into the mysteries of foraging, which, in army-vocabulary, meant not only to steal from the enemy, but to exploit Secessionist sympathisers, and obtain for love and money some trifles to make life more enjoyable. Malone and Slate were very successful and clever in all sorts of ruses. I was envious of the praises given to them, and resolved to outdo them. What rackings of the brain I suffered, as I mentally revolved the methods to adopt! General Sidney Johnston gave not so much time to the study of inflicting defeat on the Yankees, as I gave to win glory from the mess by my exploits. Half-a-dozen times in December it had been my turn to forage, but, somehow, my return was not greeted with any rapturous applause. However, by Christmas Eve I had a fair knowledge of the country and the temper of the people about, and my mind was stored with information regarding Secessionists, Unionists, and lanes, and farms, to a radius of five miles around the camp. Just on the edge of my circle, there lay one fat farm towards Green River, the owner of which was a Yank, and his neighbour told me he corresponded with the enemy. For a foot-soldier, the distance was somewhat far, but for a horseman, it was nothing.

The day before Christmas, through the assistance of a man named Tate, I had the promise of a mule; and having obtained the countersign from Armstrong, I set out, as soon as it was dark, to levy a contribution on the Unionist farmer. It was about ten o'clock by the time I reached the place. Tying my mule in the angle of a fence, I climbed over, and explored the grounds. In crossing a field, I came to half-a-dozen low mounds, which I was certain contained stores of potatoes, or something of the kind. I burrowed into the side of one of them with my bayonet, and presently I smelled apples. These were even better than potatoes, for they would do splendidly for dumplings. I half-filled a sack with them. After burrowing into two or three others, I came to one which contained the winter store of potatoes, and I soon raked out enough to make a load. I hurried with my booty to my mule, and secured it on the mule.

Then, thinking that a goose, or even a duck or a fowl or two, would make our Christmas dinner complete, I was tempted to make a quest for them, anticipating, as I crept towards the farm, the glory I should receive from my mess. I reached the out-houses with every faculty strained, and I soon had the pleasure of wringing the neck of a goose, a duck, and two fowls.

I ought to have had the discretion to retire now, but the ambition to extinguish Malone and Slate, to see the grin of admiration on Armstrong's face, and Newton Story open his eyes, and Tomasson compelled to pay homage to worth, left me still dissatisfied; and just then scenting a hog-pen, I quietly moved towards it. By the light of a feeble moon I worked into the piggies' home, and there, cuddled about the hams of their mother, I saw the pinky forms of three or four plump shoats. Aye, a tender shoat, roasted brown and crisp, would be the crown of a Christmas dinner! I bounded lightly as a lean fox into the sty, snatched a young porkling up by the heels, creating a terrifying clamour by the act. We were all alarmed, the mother hoarsely grunted, the piggies squealed in a frightful chorus, the innocent rent the midnight air with his cries; but, determined not to lose my prize, I scrambled over, ended its fears and struggles by one fierce slash, dumped the carcase into the sack, and then hastened away. Lights were visible in the farm-house, doors slammed, and by a broad beam of light I saw a man in the doorway with a gun in his hand. A second later a shower of pellets whistled about me, fortunately without harm, which sent me tearing madly towards my mule. In a few minutes, bathed in perspiration, I was astride of my mule, with my sack of dead meat in front of me, and potatoes and apples thumping the sides of my animal as I rode away towards camp.

Long before dawn, I made my triumphant appearance in front of my tent, and was rewarded by every member of the mess with the most grateful acknowledgements. The Christmas dinner was a splendid success, and over twenty invited guests sat down to it, and praises were on every lip; but without the apple dumplings and fritters it would not have been complete to us youngsters. Secretly, I was persuaded that it was as wrong to rob a poor Unionist as a Secessionist; but the word 'foraging,' which, by general consent, was bestowed on such deeds, mollified my scruples. Foragers were sent out by the authorities every other day, and even authorised to seize supplies by force; and, according to the military education I was receiving, I did not appear to be so very wicked as my conscience was inclined to make me out to be.

When I set out foraging in the daytime I was amply furnished with funds, and sought some fraternal 'Secesh.' Towards Green River, beyond the pickets, an old Secessionist lady and I became great friends, trusting one another without reservation. I would give her ten dollars at a time to invest in eggs, butter, and fowls; and she would trust me with bowls, tins, and linen, to take the articles to camp. The old lady was wont to bless my 'honest face' and to be emotional, as I told her of the sufferings of my fellow-'Dixies' at camp, out in the snow and wintry gale. Her large faith in me, and her good heart, made me so scrupulous that I ran many risks to restore her property to her. Her features and widowed condition, the sight of her dairy utensils, clean, and smelling of laitage, cream, and cheese, revived pleasing recollections of kine and their night-stalls, and led on to Aunt Mary and her chimney-side; from that moment, I was her most devoted admirer. Through her favouritism for me, our mess was often able to lend a pound of fresh butter and a dozen eggs to the officers' mess.

One of the most singular characteristics of my comrades was their readiness to take offence at any reflection on their veracity or personal honour, and the most certain provocation of fury was to give anyone the lie. They could stand the most vulgar horse-play, sarcastic badinage, and cutting jokes, with good-humour; but, if that unhappy word escaped one in heat, or playful malice, it acted on their nerves as a red rag is said to do on a mad bull. The glory of a native Southerner consists in being reputed brave, truth-telling, and reverent towards women. On such subjects, no joking was permissible. He who ventured to cast a doubt upon either was liable to be called upon at an instant to withdraw it; and, if an angry tone made the doubter writhe, and indisposed to submit, there was sure to be a scene. To withdraw a word at an imperious command was to confess oneself inferior in courage to him who challenged; and, as all prided themselves on being of equal rank, and similarly endowed with the best qualities of manhood, I never met one who was morally brave enough to confess his fault and apologise, unless he was compelled by overwhelming odds.

During that winter I absorbed so many of these 'chivalrous' ideas that I was in a fair way of becoming as great a 'fire-eater' as any son of the South. Had it not been for Newton Story and Armstrong, who knew intuitively when to interpose their authority, Tomasson's rudeness, which flared me up many a time, would, I am sure, have been followed by deplorable consequences. There was young Dan also; he was often in a wrangling mood, and by his over-insistent glorifications of Southern chivalry brought us within a hair's breadth of triggers.

The tedium of camp-life at Cave City was relieved by outbreaks of this kind, for, when we were not required to exhibit our courage against the common foe, the spirit of mischief found it an easy task to influence our susceptiveness when discussing such dear and near matters as valour, chastity, honour, and chivalry, the four chiefest virtues of the South. It is not an easy task to identify myself in the sunken hearth of the tent at Cave City, talking grandly upon such themes; but several scenes recur to the mind, and compel me to the humiliating confession that it *was* I.

This life did not tend to awaken spiritual thoughts, or religious observations. When, after a long lapse from piety, I strove to correct my erring disposition with the aid of prayer, how very faint-hearted I felt! I shrank from the least allusion to any goody-goodiness manifested; I became shame-faced if I was accused of being pious; the Bible was only opened by stealth; and I was as ready to deny that I prayed, as Peter was to deny Christ. A word or act of my neighbour became as perilous to my spiritual feelings as a gust of east wind is to a sufferer from Influenza. Every hour brought its obstacle; but I came, by degrees, to realise that, just as one must concentrate his reasoning faculties for the solution of a problem, I must, if I hoped to win in the great fight, summon every good thought to my assistance, and resolutely banish all false pride.

But these were not my worst faults. Tomasson's mad humour was as infectious as Dan's dissertations upon Southern chivalry. Indoors he was jestive, amusing, vulgarly-entertaining; outdoors, he made us all join him in uproarious laughter. The prank of a mule, the sight of a tall hat, the apparition of a black coat, a child, a woman, a duel between two cocks, a culprit undergoing penance, it mattered not what, tickled his humorous nerve, and instigated him to bawl, and yell, and break out into explosions of laughter; and whether we laughed at him, or at that which had caught his fancy, in a second we had joined in the yelling, the company became smitten with it, then the regiment, and, finally, the army, was convulsed in idiotic cachinnations. I really blushed at the follies that people like Tomasson often led us into; but, after all, these occasional bursts of jolly imbecility were only a way these free-born natures took to express their animal discontent and mild melancholy, under the humiliating circumstances of that crude period. It was really pathetic, after a mild paroxysm of this kind, to hear them sigh, and turn to each other and ask, 'Who would sell a farm to become a soldier?'

From the day when personal decoration was not expected from the private soldiers, and we learned that endurance was more esteemed than comeliness, a steady deterioration in our appearance took place. We allowed weeks to pass by without a bath; our hair was mown, not cut, making a comb unnecessary; a bottle of water sufficed for ablution, a pocket-handkerchief, or the sleeve of our jacket, served for a towel; a dab of bacon-fat was all that was needed for our boots; our dingy grey uniforms required no brushing. Soldiering, as practised in time of war, was most demoralising in many ways; for the conflict against hunger, fatigue, cold, and exposure, exhausted the energies and strength of each individual.

By February, 1862, we had learned the trade of war tolerably well, and were rich in 'wrinkles'; for no teacher is so thorough as necessity. We were no longer harrowed by the scarcity of comforts, and the climate, with its fickleness and inclemency, we proudly disregarded. Whether it rained, sleeted, or snowed, or the keen frost bit through to the marrow, mattered as little to us as it did to the military geniuses who expected raw soldiers to thrive on this Spartan training. To perfect content with our lot we could not hope to attain, so long as we retained each our spiritual individualities, and remembered what we had enjoyed in times gone-by; but, after a course of due seasoning, the worst ills only provoked a temporary ill-humour; while our susceptibility to fun so sweetened our life that there was scarcely anything in our lives but conduced to a laugh and prompted a jest.

The fall of Forts Henry and Donelson, on the 6th and 16th February, 1862, required our instant evacuation of Cave City and Bowling Green, to Nashville, lest we should be cut off by the Union advance up the Cumberland and Tennessee Rivers, behind us. We were therefore obliged to march through the snow to the rear of Bowling Green, where we were packed into the cars and speedily taken to Nashville, arriving there on the 20th February. Thence, after a couple of days, we were marched towards the South, viâ Murfreesboro, Tullahoma, Athens, and Decatur, a march of two hundred and fifty miles. At the latter place we took the cars again, and were transported to Corinth, where we arrived on the 25th March. Here it leaked out that a surprise was intended against our army, by the conqueror of Donelson, who had landed from the Tennessee River near Shiloh, some twenty-four miles away from us. Brigades and regiments were daily arriving, belonging to the divisions of Generals Clark, Cheatham, Bragg, Withers, and Breckenridge, which were finally formed into three army corps, under the inspection commands of Polk, Braxton, Bragg, and Hardee, and were now united under the commands of Generals Albert Sidney Johnston, and P. G. T. Beauregard.

CHAPTER VIII

SHILOH

ON April 2, 1862, we received orders to prepare three days' cooked rations. Through some misunderstanding, we did not set out until the 4th; and, on the morning of that day, the 6th Arkansas Regiment of Hindman's brigade, Hardee's corps, marched from Corinth to take part in one of the bloodiest battles of the West. We left our knapsacks and tents behind us. After two days of marching, and two nights of bivouacking and living on cold rations, our spirits were not so buoyant at dawn of Sunday, the 6th April, as they ought to have been for the serious task before us. Many wished, like myself, that we had not been required to undergo this discomfort before being precipitated into the midst of a great battle.

Military science, with all due respect to our generals, was not at that time what it is now. Our military leaders were well acquainted with the science of war, and, in the gross fashion prevailing, paid proper attention to the commissariat. Every soldier had his lawful allowance of raw provender dealt out to him; but, as to its uses and effects, no one seemed to be concerned. Future commanding generals will doubtless remedy this, and when they meditate staking their cause and reputation on a battle, they will, like the woodman about to do a good day's work at cutting timber, see that their instruments are in the best possible state for their purpose.

Generals Johnston and Beauregard proposed to hurl into the Tennessee River an army of nearly 50,000 rested and well-fed troops, by means of 40,000 soldiers, who, for two days, had subsisted on sodden biscuit and raw bacon, who had been exposed for two nights to rain and dew, and had marched twenty-three miles! Considering that at least a fourth of our force were lads under twenty, and that such a strenuous task was before them, it suggests itself to me that the omission to take the physical powers of those youths into their calculation had as much to do with the failure of the project as the obstinate courage of General Grant's troops. According to authority, the actual number of the forces about to be opposed to each other was 39,630 Confederates against 49,232 Federals. Our generals expected the arrival of General Van Dorn, with 20,000 troops, who failed to make their appearance; but, close at hand to Grant, was General Buell's force of 20,000, who, opportunely for Grant, arrived just at the close of the day's battle.

At four o'clock in the morning, we rose from our damp bivouac, and, after a hasty refreshment, were formed into line. We stood in rank for half an hour or so, while the military dispositions were being completed along the three-mile front. Our brigade formed the centre; Cleburne's and Gladden's brigades were on our respective flanks.

Day broke with every promise of a fine day. Next to me, on my right, was a boy of seventeen, Henry Parker. I remember it because, while we stood-at-ease, he drew my attention to some violets at his feet, and said, 'It would be a good idea to put a few into my cap. Perhaps the Yanks won't shoot me if they see me wearing such flowers, for they are a sign of peace.' 'Capital,' said I, 'I will do the same.' We plucked a bunch, and arranged the violets in our caps. The men in the ranks laughed at our proceedings, and had not the enemy been so near, their merry mood might have been communicated to the army.

We loaded our muskets, and arranged our cartridge-pouches ready for use. Our weapons were the obsolete flint-locks,[1] and the ammunition was rolled in cartridge-paper, which contained powder, a round ball, and three buckshot. When we loaded we had to tear the paper with our teeth, empty a little powder into the pan, lock it, empty the rest of the powder into the barrel, press paper and ball into the muzzle, and ram home. Then the Orderly-sergeant called the roll, and we knew that the Dixie Greys were present to a man. Soon after, there was a commotion, and we dressed up smartly. A young Aide galloped along our front, gave some instructions

[1] Beauregard (*Military Operations*, vol. i, p. 300), writing of the battle-field of Shiloh, says, "One cheering feature, however, was the strewing of old flint-locks and double-barrelled shot-guns, exchanged for the Enfield and Minie rifles abandoned by the enemy." — D. S.

to the Brigadier Hindman, who confided the same to his Colonels, and presently we swayed forward in line, with shouldered arms. Newton Story, big, broad, and straight, bore our company-banner of gay silk, at which the ladies of our neighbourhood had laboured.

As we tramped solemnly and silently through the thin forest, and over its grass, still in its withered and wintry hue, I noticed that the sun was not far from appearing, that our regiment was keeping its formation admirably, that the woods would have been a grand place for a picnic; and I thought it strange that a Sunday should have been chosen to disturb the holy calm of those woods.

Before we had gone five hundred paces, our serenity was disturbed by some desultory firing in front. It was then a quarter-past five. 'They are at it already,' we whispered to each other. 'Stand by, gentlemen,'—for we were all gentlemen volunteers at this time,—said our Captain, L. G. Smith. Our steps became unconsciously brisker, and alertness was noticeable in everybody. The firing continued at intervals, deliberate and scattered, as at target-practice. We drew nearer to the firing, and soon a sharper rattling of musketry was heard. 'That is the enemy waking up,' we said. Within a few minutes, there was another explosive burst of musketry, the air was pierced by many missiles, which hummed and pinged sharply by our ears, pattered through the tree-tops, and brought twigs and leaves down on us. 'Those are bullets,' Henry whispered with awe.

At two hundred yards further, a dreadful roar of musketry broke out from a regiment adjoining ours. It was followed by another further off, and the sound had scarcely died away when regiment after regiment blazed away and made a continuous roll of sound. 'We are in for it now,' said Henry; but as yet we had seen nothing, though our ears were tingling under the animated volleys.

'Forward, gentlemen, make ready!' urged Captain Smith. In response, we surged forward, for the first time marring the alignment. We trampled recklessly over the grass and young sprouts. Beams of sunlight stole athwart our course. The sun was up above the horizon. Just then we came to a bit of packland, and overtook our skirmishers, who had been engaged in exploring our front. We passed beyond them. Nothing now stood between us and the enemy.

'There they are!' was no sooner uttered, than we cracked into them with levelled muskets. 'Aim low, men!' commanded Captain Smith. I tried hard to see some living thing to shoot at, for it appeared absurd to be blazing away at shadows. But, still advancing, firing as we moved, I, at last, saw a row of little globes of pearly smoke streaked with crimson, breaking-out, with spurtive quickness, from a long line of bluey figures in front; and, simultaneously, there broke upon our ears an appalling crash of sound, the series of fusillades following one another with startling suddenness, which suggested to my somewhat moidered sense a mountain upheaved, with huge rocks tumbling and thundering down a slope, and the echoes rumbling and receding through space. Again and again, these loud and quick explosions were repeated, seemingly with increased violence, until they rose to the highest pitch of fury, and in unbroken continuity. All the world seemed involved in one tremendous ruin!

This was how the conflict was ushered in — as it affected me. I looked around to see the effect on others, or whether I was singular in my emotions, and was glad to notice that each was possessed with his own thoughts. All were pale, solemn, and absorbed; but, beyond that, it was impossible for me to discover what they thought of it; but, by transmission of sympathy, I felt that they would gladly prefer to be elsewhere, though the law of the inevitable kept them in line to meet their destiny. It might be mentioned, however, that at no time were we more instinctively inclined to obey the voice of command. We had no individuality at this moment, but all motions and thoughts were surrendered to the unseen influence which directed our movements. Probably few bothered their minds with self-questionings as to the issue to themselves. That properly belongs to other moments, to the night, to the interval between waking and sleeping, to the first moments of the dawn — not when every nerve is tense, and the spirit is at the highest pitch of action.

Though one's senses were preternaturally acute, and engaged with their impressions, we plied our arms, loaded, and fired, with such nervous haste as though it depended on each of us how soon this fiendish uproar would be hushed. My nerves tingled, my pulses beat double-quick, my heart throbbed loudly, and almost painfully; but, amid all the excitement, my thoughts, swift as the flash of lightning, took all sound, and sight, and self, into their purview. I listened to the battle raging far away on the flanks, to the thunder in front, to the various sounds made by the leaden storm. I was angry with my rear rank, because he made my eyes smart with the powder of his musket; and I felt like cuffing him for deafening my ears! I knew how Captain Smith and Lieutenant Mason looked, how bravely the Dixie Greys' banner ruffled over Newton Story's head, and that all hands were behaving as though they knew how long all this would last. Back to myself my thoughts came, and, with the whirring bullet, they fled to the blue-bloused ranks afront. They dwelt on their movements, and read their temper, as I should read time by a clock. Through the lurid haze the contours of their pink faces could not be seen, but their gappy, hesitating, incoherent, and sensitive line revealed their mood clearly.

We continued advancing, step by step, loading and firing as we went. To every forward step, they took a backward move, loading and firing as they slowly withdrew. Twenty thousand muskets were being fired at this stage, but, though accuracy of aim was impossible, owing to our labouring hearts, and the jarring and excitement, many bullets found their destined billets on both sides.

After a steady exchange of musketry, which lasted some time, we heard the order: 'Fix Bayonets! On the double-quick!' in tones that thrilled us. There was a simultaneous bound forward, each soul doing his best for the emergency. The Federals appeared inclined to await us; but, at this juncture, our men raised a yell, thousands responded to it, and burst out into the wildest yelling it has ever been my lot to hear. It drove all sanity and order from among us. It served the double purpose of relieving pent-up feelings, and transmitting encouragement along the attacking line. I rejoiced in the shouting like the rest. It reminded me that there were about four hundred companies like the Dixie Greys, who shared our feelings. Most of us, engrossed with the musket-work, had forgotten the fact; but the wave after wave of human voices, louder than all other battle-sounds together, penetrated to every sense, and stimulated our energies to the utmost.

'They fly!' was echoed from lip to lip. It accelerated our pace, and filled us with a noble rage. Then I knew what the Berserker passion was! It deluged us with rapture, and transfigured each Southerner into an exulting victor. At such a moment, nothing could have halted us.

Those savage yells, and the sight of thousands of racing figures coming towards them, discomfited the blue-coats; and when we arrived upon the place where they had stood, they had vanished. Then we caught sight of their beautiful array of tents, before which they had made their stand, after being roused from their Sunday-morning sleep, and huddled into line, at hearing their pickets challenge our skirmishers. The half-dressed dead and wounded showed what a surprise our attack had been. We drew up in the enemy's camp, panting and breathing hard. Some precious minutes were thus lost in recovering our breaths, indulging our curiosity, and re-forming our line. Signs of a hasty rouse to the battle were abundant. Military equipments, uniform-coats, half-packed knapsacks, bedding, of a new and superior quality, littered the company streets.

Meantime, a series of other camps lay behind the first array of tents. The resistance we had met, though comparatively brief, enabled the brigades in rear of the advance camp to recover from the shock of the surprise; but our delay had not been long enough to give them time to form in proper order of battle. There were wide gaps between their divisions, into which the quick-flowing tide of elated Southerners entered, and compelled them to fall back lest they should be surrounded. Prentiss's brigade, despite their most desperate efforts, were thus hemmed in on all sides, and were made prisoners.

I had a momentary impression that, with the capture of the first camp, the battle was well-nigh over; but, in fact, it was only a brief prologue of the long and exhaustive series of struggles which took place that day.

Continuing our advance, we came in view of the tops of another mass of white tents, and, almost at the same time, were met by a furious storm of bullets, poured on us from a long line of blue-coats, whose attitude of assurance proved to us that we should have tough work here. But we were so much heartened by our first success that it would have required a good deal to have halted our advance for long. Their opportunity for making a full impression on us came with terrific suddenness. The world seemed bursting into fragments. Cannon and musket, shell and bullet, lent their several intensities to the distracting uproar. If I had not a fraction of an ear, and an eye inclined towards my Captain and Company, I had been spell-bound by the energies now opposed to us. I likened the cannon, with their deep bass, to the roaring of a great herd of lions; the ripping, cracking musketry, to the incessant yapping of terriers; the windy whisk of shells, and zipping of minie bullets, to the swoop of eagles, and the buzz of angry wasps. All the opposing armies of Grey and Blue fiercely blazed at each other.

After being exposed for a few seconds to this fearful downpour, we heard the order to 'Lie down, men, and continue your firing!' Before me was a prostrate tree, about fifteen inches in diameter, with a narrow strip of light between it and the ground. Behind this shelter a dozen of us flung ourselves. The security it appeared to offer restored me to my individuality. We could fight, and think, and observe, better than out in the open. But it was a terrible period! How the cannon bellowed, and their shells plunged and bounded, and flew with screeching hisses over us! Their sharp rending explosions and hurtling fragments made us shrink and cower, despite our utmost efforts to be cool and collected. I marvelled, as I heard the unintermitting patter, snip, thud, and hum of the bullets, how anyone could live under this raining death. I could hear the balls beating a merciless tattoo on the outer surface of the log, pinging vivaciously as they flew off at a tangent from it, and thudding into something or other, at the rate of a hundred a second. One, here and there, found its way under the log, and buried itself in a comrade's body. One man raised his chest, as if to yawn, and jostled me. I turned to him, and saw that a bullet had gored his whole face, and penetrated into his chest. Another ball struck a man a deadly rap on the head, and he turned on his back and showed his ghastly white face to the sky.

'It is getting too warm, boys!' cried a soldier, and he uttered a vehement curse upon keeping soldiers hugging the ground until every ounce of courage was chilled. He lifted his head a little too high, and a bullet skimmed over the top of the log and hit him fairly in the centre of his forehead, and he fell heavily on his face. But his thought had been instantaneously general; and the officers, with one voice, ordered the charge; and cries of 'Forward, forward!' raised us, as with a spring, to our feet, and changed the complexion of our feelings. The pulse of action beat feverishly once more; and, though overhead was crowded with peril, we were unable to give it so much attention as when we lay stretched on the ground.

Just as we bent our bodies for the onset, a boy's voice cried out, 'Oh, stop, *please* stop a bit, I have been hurt, and can't move!' I turned to look, and saw Henry Parker, standing on one leg, and dolefully regarding his smashed foot. In another second, we were striding impetuously towards the enemy, vigorously plying our muskets, stopping only to prime the pan and ram the load down, when, with a spring or two, we would fetch up with the front, aim, and fire.

Our progress was not so continuously rapid as we desired, for the blues were obdurate; but at this moment we were gladdened at the sight of a battery galloping to our assistance. It was time for the nerve-shaking cannon to speak. After two rounds of shell and canister, we felt the pressure on us slightly relaxed; but we were still somewhat sluggish in disposition, though the officers' voices rang out imperiously. Newton Story at this juncture strode forward rapidly with the Dixies' banner, until he was quite sixty yards ahead of the foremost. Finding himself alone, he halted; and turning to us smilingly, said, 'Why don't you come on, boys?' You see there is no danger!' His smile and words acted on us like magic. We raised the yell, and sprang lightly and hopefully towards him. 'Let's give them hell, boys!' said one. 'Plug them plum-centre, every time!'

It was all very encouraging, for the yelling and shouting were taken up by thousands. "Forward, forward; don't give them breathing time!' was cried. We instinctively obeyed, and soon came in clear view of the blue-coats, who were scornfully unconcerned at first; but, seeing the leaping tide of men coming on at a tremendous pace, their front dissolved, and they fled in double-quick retreat. Again we felt the 'glorious joy of heroes.' It carried us on exultantly, rejoicing in the spirit which recognises nothing but the prey. We were no longer an army of soldiers, but so many school-boys racing, in which length of legs, wind, and condition tell.

We gained the second line of camps, continued the rush through them, and clean beyond. It was now about ten o'clock. My physical powers were quite exhausted, and, to add to my discomfiture, something struck me on my belt-clasp, and tumbled me headlong to the ground.

I could not have been many minutes prostrated before I recovered from the shock of the blow and fall, to find my clasp deeply dented and cracked. My company was not in sight. I was grateful for the rest, and crawled feebly to a tree, and plunging my hand into my haversack, ate ravenously. Within half an hour, feeling renovated, I struck north in the direction which my regiment had taken, over a ground strewn with bodies and the débris of war.

The desperate character of this day's battle was now brought home to my mind in all its awful reality. While in the tumultuous advance, and occupied with a myriad of exciting incidents, it was only at brief intervals that I was conscious of wounds being given and received; but now, in the trail of pursuers and pursued, the ghastly relics appalled every sense. I felt curious as to who the fallen Greys were, and moved to one stretched straight out. It was the body of a stout English Sergeant of a neighbouring company, the members of which hailed principally from the Washita Valley. At the crossing of the Arkansas River this plump, ruddy-faced man had been conspicuous for his complexion, jovial features, and good-humour, and had been nicknamed 'John Bull.' He was now lifeless, and lay with his eyes wide open, regardless of the scorching sun, and the tempestuous cannonade which sounded through the forest, and the musketry that crackled incessantly along the front.

Close by him was a young Lieutenant, who, judging by the new gloss on his uniform, must have been some father's darling. A clean bullet-hole through the centre of his forehead had instantly ended his career. A little further were some twenty bodies, lying in various postures, each by its own pool of viscous blood, which emitted a peculiar scent, which was new to me, but which I have since learned is inseparable from a battle-field. Beyond these, a still larger group lay, body overlying body, knees crooked, arms erect, or wide-stretched and rigid, according as the last spasm overtook them. The company opposed to them must have shot straight.

Other details of that ghastly trail formed a mass of horrors that will always be remembered at the mention of Shiloh. I can never forget the impression those wide-open dead eyes made on me. Each seemed to be starting out of its socket, with a look similar to the fixed wondering gaze of an infant, as though the dying had viewed something appalling at the last moment. 'Can it be,' I asked myself, 'that at the last glance they saw their own retreating souls, and wondered why their caskets were left behind, like offal?' My surprise was that the form we made so much of, and that nothing was too good for, should now be mutilated, hacked, and outraged; and that the life, hitherto guarded as a sacred thing, and protected by the Constitution, Law, Ministers of Justice, Police, should, of a sudden, — at least, before I can realise it, — be given up to death!

An object once seen, if it has affected my imagination, remains indelibly fixed in my memory; and, among many other scenes with which it is now crowded, I cannot forget that half-mile square of woodland, lighted brightly by the sun, and littered by the forms of about a thousand dead and wounded men, and by horses, and military equipments. It formed a picture that may always be reproduced with an almost absolute fidelity. For it was the first Field of Glory I had seen in my May of life, and the first time that Glory sickened me with its repulsive aspect, and made me suspect it was all a glittering lie. In my imagination, I saw more than it was my fate to see with my eyes, for, under a flag of truce, I saw the bearers pick up the dead from the field, and lay them in long rows beside a wide trench; I saw them laid, one by one, close together at the bottom, — thankless victims of a perished cause, and all their individual hopes, pride, honour, names, buried under oblivious earth.

My thoughts reverted to the time when these festering bodies were idolized objects of their mothers' passionate love, their fathers standing by, half-fearing to touch the fragile little things, and the wings of civil law out-spread to protect parents and children in their family loves, their coming and going followed with pride and praise, and the blessing of the Almighty over-shadowing all. Then, as they were nearing manhood, through some strange warp of Society, men in authority summoned them from school and shop, field and farm, to meet in the woods on a Sunday morning for mutual butchery with the deadliest instruments yet invented, Civil Law, Religion, and Morality complaisantly standing aside, while 90,000 young men, who had been preached and moralized to, for years, were let loose to engage in the carnival of slaughter.

Only yesterday, they professed to shudder at the word 'Murder.' To-day, by a strange twist in human nature, they lusted to kill, and were hounded on in the work of destruction by their pastors, elders, mothers, and sisters. Oh, for once, I was beginning to know the real truth! Man was born for slaughter! All the pains taken to soothe his savage heart were unavailing! Holy words and heavenly hopes had no lasting effect on his bestial nature, for, when once provoked, how swiftly he flung aside the sweet hope of Heaven, and the dread of Hell, with which he amused himself in time of ease!

As I moved, horror-stricken, through the fearful shambles, where the dead lay as thick as the sleepers in a London park on a Bank Holiday, I was unable to resist the belief that my education had been in abstract things, which had no relation to our animal existence. For, if human life is so disparaged, what has it to do with such high subjects as God, Heaven, and Immortality? And to think how devotional men and women pretended to be, on a Sunday! Oh, cunning, cruel man! He knew that the sum of all real knowledge and effort was to know how to kill and mangle his brothers, as we were doing to-day! Reflecting on my own emotions, I wondered if other youths would feel that they had been deluded like myself with man's fine polemics and names of things, which vanished with the reality.

A multitude of angry thoughts surged through me, which

I cannot describe in detail, but they amounted to this, that a cruel deception had been practised on my blank ignorance, that my atom of imagination and feeling had been darkened, and that man was a portentous creature from which I recoiled with terror and pity. He was certainly terrible and hard, but he was no more to me now than a two-legged beast; he was cunning beyond finding out, but his morality was only a mask for his wolfish heart! Thus, scoffing and railing at my infatuation for moral excellence as practised by humanity, I sought to join my company and regiment.

The battle-field maintained the same character of undulated woodland, being, in general, low ridges separated by broad depressions, which sunk occasionally into ravines of respectable depth. At various places, wide clearings had been made; and I came across a damp bottom or two covered with shrubs. For a defensive force there were several positions that were admirable as rallying-points, and it is perhaps owing to these, and the undoubted courage exhibited by the Federal troops, that the battle was so protracted. Though our attack had been a surprise, it was certain that they fought as though they were resolved to deny it; and, as the ground to be won from the enemy was nearly five miles in depth, and every half mile or so they stood and obstinately contested it, all the honours of the day were not to be with us.

I overtook my regiment about one o'clock, and found that it was engaged in one of these occasional spurts of fury. The enemy resolutely maintained their ground, and our side was preparing for another assault. The firing was alternately brisk and slack. We lay down, and availed ourselves of trees, logs, and hollows, and annoyed their upstanding ranks; battery pounded battery, and, meanwhile, we hugged our resting-places closely. Of a sudden, we rose and raced towards the position, and took it by sheer weight and impetuosity, as we had done before. About three o'clock, the battle grew very hot. The enemy appeared to be more concentrated, and immovably sullen. Both sides fired better as they grew more accustomed to the din; but, with assistance from the reserves, we were continually pressing them towards the river Tennessee, without ever retreating an inch.

About this time, the enemy were assisted by the gun-boats,

which hurled their enormous projectiles far beyond us; but, though they made great havoc among the trees, and created terror, they did comparatively little damage to those in close touch with the enemy.

The screaming of the big shells, when they first began to sail over our heads, had the effect of reducing our fire; for they were as fascinating as they were distracting. But we became used to them, and our attention was being claimed more in front. Our officers were more urgent; and, when we saw the growing dyke of white cloud that signalled the bullet-storm, we could not be indifferent to the more immediate danger. Dead bodies, wounded men writhing in agony, and assuming every distressful attitude, were frequent sights; but what made us heart-sick was to see, now and then, the well-groomed charger of an officer, with fine saddle, and scarlet and yellow-edged cloth, and brass-tipped holsters, or a stray cavalry or artillery horse, galloping between the lines, snorting with terror, while his entrails, soiled with dust, trailed behind him.

Our officers had continued to show the same alertness and vigour throughout the day; but, as it drew near four o'clock, though they strove to encourage and urge us on, they began to abate somewhat in their energy; and it was evident that the pluckiest of the men lacked the spontaneity and springing ardour which had distinguished them earlier in the day. Several of our company lagged wearily behind, and the remainder showed, by their drawn faces, the effects of their efforts. Yet, after a short rest, they were able to make splendid spurts. As for myself, I had only one wish, and that was for repose. The long-continued excitement, the successive tautening and relaxing of the nerves, the quenchless thirst, made more intense by the fumes of sulphurous powder, and the caking grime on the lips, caused by tearing the paper cartridges, and a ravening hunger, all combined, had reduced me to a walking automaton, and I earnestly wished that night would come, and stop all further effort.

Finally, about five o'clock, we assaulted and captured a large camp; after driving the enemy well away from it, the front line was as thin as that of a skirmishing body, and we were ordered to retire to the tents. There we hungrily sought after provisions, and I was lucky in finding a supply of biscuits and a canteen of excellent molasses, which gave great comfort to myself and friends. The plunder in the camp was abundant. There were bedding, clothing, and accoutrements without stint; but people were so exhausted they could do no more than idly turn the things over. Night soon fell, and only a few stray shots could now be heard, to remind us of the thrilling and horrid din of the day, excepting the huge bombs from the gun-boats, which, as we were not far from the blue-coats, discomforted only those in the rear. By eight o'clock, I was repeating my experiences in the region of dreams, indifferent to columbiads and mortars, and the torrential rain which, at midnight, increased the miseries of the wounded and tentless.

An hour before dawn, I awoke from a refreshing sleep; and, after a hearty replenishment of my vitals with biscuit and molasses, I conceived myself to be fresher than on Sunday morning. While awaiting day-break, I gathered from other early risers their ideas in regard to the events of yesterday. They were under the impression that we had gained a great victory, though we had not, as we had anticipated, reached the Tennessee River. Van Dorn, with his expected reinforcements for us, was not likely to make his appearance for many days yet; and, if General Buell, with his 20,000 troops, had joined the enemy during the night, we had a bad day's work before us. We were short of provisions and ammunition, General Sidney Johnston, our chief Commander, had been killed; but Beauregard was safe and unhurt, and, if Buell was absent, we would win the day.

At daylight, I fell in with my Company, but there were only about fifty of the Dixies present. Almost immediately after, symptoms of the coming battle were manifest. Regiments were hurried into line, but, even to my inexperienced eyes, the troops were in ill-condition for repeating the efforts of Sunday. However, in brief time, in consequence of our pickets being driven in on us, we were moved forward in skirmishing order. With my musket on the trail I found myself in active motion, more active than otherwise I would have been, perhaps, because Captain Smith had said, 'Now, Mr. Stanley, if you please, step briskly forward!' This singling-out of me wounded my *amour-propre*, and sent me forward like a rocket. In a short time, we met our opponents in the same formation as ourselves, and advancing most resolutely. We threw ourselves behind such trees as were near us, fired, loaded, and darted forward to another shelter. Presently, I found myself in an open, grassy space, with no convenient tree or stump near; but, seeing a shallow hollow some twenty paces ahead, I made a dash for it, and plied my musket with haste. I became so absorbed with some blue figures in front of me, that I did not pay sufficient heed to my companion greys; the open space was too dangerous, perhaps, for their advance; for, had they emerged, I should have known they were pressing forward. Seeing my blues in about the same proportion, I assumed that the greys were keeping their position, and never once thought of retreat. However, as, despite our firing, the blues were coming uncomfortably near, I rose from my hollow; but, to my speechless amazement, I found myself a solitary grey, in a line of blue skirmishers! My companions had retreated! The next I heard was, 'Down with that gun, Secesh, or I'll drill a hole through you! Drop it, quick!'

Half a dozen of the enemy were covering me at the same instant, and I dropped my weapon, incontinently. Two men sprang at my collar, and marched me, unresisting, into the ranks of the terrible Yankees. *I was a prisoner!*

When the senses have been concentrated upon a specific object with the intensity which a battle compels, and are forcibly and suddenly veered about by another will, the immediate result is, at first, stupefying. Before my consciousness had returned to me, I was being propelled vigorously from behind, and I was in view of a long, swaying line of soldiers, who were marching to meet us with all the precision of drill, and with such a close front that a rabbit would have found it difficult to break through. This sight restored me to all my faculties, and I remembered I was a Confederate, in misfortune, and that it behoved me to have some regard for my Uniform. I heard bursts of vituperation from several hoarse throats, which straightened my back and made me defiant.

'Where are you taking that fellow to? Drive a bayonet into the —— ——! Let him drop where he is!' they cried by the dozen, with a German accent. They grew more excited as we drew nearer, and more men joined in the opprobrious chorus. Then a few dashed from the ranks, with levelled bayonets, to execute what appeared to be the general wish.

I looked into their faces, deformed with fear and fury, and I felt intolerable loathing for the wild-eyed brutes! Their eyes, projected and distended, appeared like spots of pale blue ink, in faces of dough! Reason had fled altogether from their features, and, to appeal for mercy to such blind, ferocious animalism would have been the height of absurdity, but I was absolutely indifferent as to what they might do with me now. Could I have multiplied myself into a thousand, such unintellectual-looking louts might have been brushed out of existence with ease — despite their numbers. They were apparently new troops, from such back-lands as were favoured by German immigrants; and, though of sturdy build, another such mass of savagery and stupidity could not have been found within the four corners of North America. How I wished I could return to the Confederates, and tell them what kind of people were opposing them!

Before their bayonets reached me, my two guards, who were ruddy-faced Ohioans, flung themselves before me, and, presenting their rifles, cried, 'Here! stop that, you fellows! He is our prisoner!' A couple of officers were almost as quick as they, and flourished their swords; and, amid an expenditure of profanity, drove them quickly back into their ranks, cursing and blackguarding me in a manner truly American. A company opened its lines as we passed to the rear. Once through, I was comparatively safe from the Union troops, but not from the Confederate missiles, which were dropping about, and striking men, right and left.

Quickening our pace, we soon were beyond danger from my friends; after which, I looked about with interest at the forces that were marching to retrieve their shame of yesterday. The troops we saw belonged to Buell, who had crossed the Tennessee, and was now joined by Grant. They presented a brave, even imposing, sight; and, in their new uniforms, with glossy knapsacks, rubbers undimmed, brasses resplendent, they approached nearer to my idea of soldiers than our dingy grey troops. Much of this fine show and seeming steadiness was due to their newer equipments, and, as yet, unshaken nerves; but, though their movements were firm, they were languid, and lacked the élan, the bold confidence, of the Southerners. Given twenty-four hours' rest, and the enjoyment of cooked rations, I felt that the Confederates would have crumpled up the handsome Unionists within a brief time.

Though my eyes had abundant matter of interest within their range, my mind continually harked back to the miserable hollow which had disgraced me, and I kept wondering how it was that my fellow-skirmishers had so quickly disappeared. I was inclined to blame Captain Smith for urging me on, when, within a few minutes after, he must have withdrawn his men. But it was useless to trouble my mind with conjectures. I was a prisoner! Shameful position! What would become of my knapsack, and my little treasures, — letters, and souvenirs of my father? They were lost beyond recovery!

On the way, my guards and I had a discussion about our respective causes, and, though I could not admit it, there was much reason in what they said, and I marvelled that they could put their case so well. For, until now, I was under the impression that they were robbers who only sought to desolate the South, and steal the slaves; but, according to them, had we not been so impatient and flown to arms, the influence of Abe Lincoln and his fellow-abolitionists would not have affected the Southerners pecuniarily; for it might have been possible for Congress to compensate slave-owners, that is, by buying up all slaves, and afterwards setting them free. But when the Southerners, who were not averse to selling their slaves in the open market, refused to consider anything relating to them, and began to seize upon government property, forts, arsenals, and war-ships, and to set about establishing a separate system in the country, then the North resolved that this should not be, and that was the true reason of the war. The Northern people cared nothing for the 'niggers,' — the slavery question could have been settled in another and quieter way, — but they cared all their lives were worth for their country.

At the river-side there was tremendous activity. There were seven or eight steamers tied to the bank, discharging troops and stores. The commissariat stores and forage lay in mountainous heaps. In one place on the slope was a corral of prisoners, about four hundred and fifty in number, who had been captured the day before. I was delivered to the charge of the officer in command of the guards, and, in a few minutes, was left to my own reflections amid the unfortunates.

The loss of the Union troops in the two days' fight was 1754 killed, 8408 wounded, and 2885 captured; total, 13,047. That of the Confederates was 1728 killed, 8012 wounded, and 959 missing; total, 10,699.

The loss of Hindman's Brigade was 109 killed, 546 wounded, 38 missing; total, 693, — about a fifth of the number that went, on the Sunday morning, into action.

Referring to these totals, 1754+1728=3482, killed, General Grant, however, says, in his article on Shiloh: 'This estimate of the Confederate loss must be incorrect. We buried, by actual count, more of the enemy's dead in front of the divisions of McClernand and Sherman alone than here reported; and 4000 was the estimate of the burial parties for the whole field.'[1]

Nine days after the battle of Shiloh, a conscript law was passed by the Confederate Congress which annulled all previous contracts made with volunteers, and all men between eighteen and thirty-five were to be soldiers during the continuance of the war. General T. C. Hindman, our brigade

[1] Stanley, now having become a prisoner, is not able to conclude his personal account of this historical contest. It may be of interest to the reader if I briefly summarise the final result.

On Sunday, April 6, 1862, was fought the greatest battle of the war. As General D. C. Buell says in a magazine article: 'The battle of Shiloh was the most famous, and, to both sides, the most interesting of the war.' The Confederate army advanced upon the Federal army, penetrated its disconnected lines, assaulted its camps in front and flank, and drove it from position to position, towards the Tennessee River.

At the close of the day, when the retreating army was driven to take refuge in the midst of its magazines, a re-enforcing army was marching to its assistance, and an advance division, on the opposite bank of the river, checked the attacking force.

At dawn, the next morning, Monday, April 7, General Buell heading the re-enforcing army, and with a fresh division of the defeated force, drove the Confederates from the field and recaptured the camps, after ten hours' desperate fighting.

Whereupon General Beauregard, seeing the hopelessness of prolonging the contest, withdrew his army, in perfect order, and unmolested, to Corinth. There was no pursuit; and this was afterwards much commented on. But both armies appear to have been utterly spent, the Federal troops being as much outdone as the Confederates. General Grant stated that, though desirous of pursuing the retreating army, he 'had not the heart to order it to men who had fought desperately for two days, lying in the mud and rain, whenever not fighting.' — D. S.

commander, was appointed, fifty days after Shiloh, commanding general of Arkansas, and enforced the conscript law remorselessly. He collected an army of 20,000 under this law, and such as deserted were shot by scores, until he made himself odious to all by his ruthlessness, violence, and tyranny.

While at Atlanta, Georgia, in March, 1891, I received the following letter (which is copied verbatim) from 'old Slate,' as we used to call him, owing to a certain quaint, old-mannish humour which characterised him.

BLUE RIDGE, GA.
March 28th, 1891.

DEAR SIR, — I am anxious to know if you enlisted in Company E., Dixie Greys, 6th Arkansas Regiment, Col. Lyon commanding, Lieut.-Col. Hawthorn, Capt. Smith commanding Dixie Greys, Co. E. Col. Lyons was accidently killed on the Tennessee River, by riding off Bluff and horse falling on him.

On the 6th April, 1862, the Confederates attacked the Yankees at Shiloh. Early in the morning I was wounded, and I never saw our boyish-looking Stanley no more, but understood he was captured, and sent North. I have read everything in newspapers, and your Histories, believing you are the same Great Boy. We all loved you, and regretted the results of that eventful day. This is enough for you to say, in reply, that you are the identical Boyish Soldier. You have wrote many letters for me. Please answer by return mail.

Very truly yours,

JAMES M. SLATE.

Address:
J. M. SLATE, BLUE RIDGE.

CHAPTER IX

PRISONER OF WAR

ON the 8th of April we were embarked on a steamer, and despatched to St. Louis. We were a sad lot of men. I feel convinced that most of them felt, with myself, that we were ill-starred wretches, and special objects of an unkind Fate. We made no advances to acquaintanceship, for what was the value of any beggarly individual amongst us? All he possessed in the world was a thin, dingy suit of grey, and every man's thoughts were of his own misfortune, which was as much as he could bear, without being bothered with that of another.

On the third day, I think, we reached St. Louis, and were marched through the streets, in column of fours, to a Ladies' College, or some such building. On the way, we were not a little consoled to find that we had sympathisers, especially among the ladies, in the city. They crowded the sidewalks, and smiled kindly, and sometimes cheered, and waved dainty white handkerchiefs at us. How beautiful and clean they appeared, as compared with our filthy selves! While at the college, they besieged the building, and threw fruit and cakes at the struggling crowds in the windows, and in many ways assisted to lighten the gloom on our spirits.

Four days later, we were embarked on railroad cars, and taken across the State of Illinois to Camp Douglas, on the outskirts of Chicago. Our prison-pen was a square and spacious enclosure, like a bleak cattle-yard, walled high with planking, on the top of which, at every sixty yards or so, were sentry-boxes. About fifty feet from its base, and running parallel with it, was a line of lime-wash. That was the 'dead-line,' and any prisoner who crossed it was liable to be shot.

One end of the enclosure contained the offices of the authorities. Colonel James A. Milligan, one of the Irish Brigade (killed at Winchester, July 24th, 1864) commanded the camp. Mr. Shipman, a citizen of Chicago, acted as chief commissary.

At the other end, at quite three hundred yards distance, were the buildings allotted to the prisoners, huge, barn-like structures of planking, each about two hundred and fifty feet by forty, and capable of accommodating between two hundred and three hundred men. There may have been about twenty of these structures, about thirty feet apart, and standing in two rows; and I estimated that there were enough prisoners within it to have formed a strong brigade — say about three thousand men — when we arrived. I remember, by the regimental badges which they wore on their caps and hats, that they belonged to the three arms of the service, and that almost every Southern State was represented. They were clad in home-made butternut and grey.

To whatever it was due, the appearance of the prisoners startled me. The Southerners' uniforms were never pretty, but when rotten, and ragged, and swarming with vermin, they heightened the disreputability of their wearers; and, if anything was needed to increase our dejection after taking sweeping glances at the arid mud-soil of the great yard, the butternut and grey clothes, the sight of ash-coloured faces, and of the sickly and emaciated condition of our unhappy friends, were well calculated to do so.

We were led to one of the great wooden barns, where we found a six-foot wide platform on each side, raised about four feet above the flooring. These platforms formed continuous bunks for about sixty men, allowing thirty inches to each man. On the floor, two more rows of men could be accommodated. Several bales of hay were brought, out of which we helped ourselves for bedding. Blankets were also distributed, one to each man. I, fortunately, found a berth on the right-hand platform, not far from the doorway, and my mate was a young sprig of Mississippi nobility named W. H. Wilkes (a nephew of Admiral C. Wilkes, U. S. Navy, the navigator, and captor of Mason and Slidell, Confederate Commissioners).

Mr. Shipman soon after visited us, and, after inspection, suggested that we should form ourselves into companies, and elect officers for drawing rations and superintending of quarters. I was elected captain of the right-hand platform and berths below it. Blank books were served out to each captain, and I took the names of my company, which numbered over one hundred. By showing my book at the commissariat, and bringing a detail with me, rations of soft bread, fresh beef, coffee, tea, potatoes, and salt, were handed to me by the gross, which I had afterwards to distribute to the chiefs of messes.

On the next day (April 16th), after the morning duties had been performed, the rations divided, the cooks had departed contented, and the quarters swept, I proceeded to my nest and reclined alongside of my friend Wilkes, in a posture that gave me a command of one-half of the building. I made some remarks to him upon the card-playing groups opposite, when, suddenly, I felt a gentle stroke on the back of my neck, and, in an instant, I was unconscious. The next moment I had a vivid view of the village of Tremeirchion, and the grassy slopes of the hills of Hiraddog, and I seemed to be hovering over the rook woods of Brynbella. I glided to the bedchamber of my Aunt Mary. My aunt was in bed, and seemed sick unto death. I took a position by the side of the bed, and saw myself, with head bent down, listening to her parting words, which sounded regretful, as though conscience smote her for not having been so kind as she might have been, or had wished to be. I heard the boy say, 'I believe you, aunt. It is neither your fault, nor mine. You were good and kind to me, and I knew you wished to be kinder; but things were so ordered that you had to be what you were. I also dearly wished to love you, but I was afraid to speak of it, lest you would check me, or say something that would offend me. I feel our parting was in this spirit. There is no need of regrets. You have done your duty to me, and you had children of your own, who required all your care. What has happened to me since, was decreed should happen. Farewell.'

I put forth my hand and felt the clasp of the long, thin hands of the sore-sick woman, I heard a murmur of farewell, and immediately I woke.

It appeared to me that I had but closed my eyes. I was still in the same reclining attitude, the groups opposite were still engaged in their card games, Wilkes was in the same position. Nothing had changed.

I asked, 'What *has* happened?'

'What could happen?' said he. 'What makes you ask? It is but a moment ago you were speaking to me.'

'Oh, I thought I had been asleep a long time.'

On the next day, the 17th April, 1862, my Aunt Mary died at Fynnon Beuno!

I believe that the soul of every human being has its attendant spirit, — a nimble and delicate essence, whose method of action is by a subtle suggestion which it contrives to insinuate into the mind, whether asleep or awake. We are too gross to be capable of understanding the signification of the dream, the vision, or the sudden presage, or of divining the source of the premonition, or its purport. We admit that we are liable to receive a fleeting picture of an act, or a figure, at any moment; but, except being struck by certain strange coincidences which happen to most of us, we seldom make an effort to unravel the mystery. The swift, darting messenger stamps an image on the mind, and displays a vision to the sleeper; and if, as sometimes follows, among tricks and twists of an errant mind, or reflex acts of the memory, it happens to be a true representation of what is to happen, or has happened, thousands of miles away, we are left to grope hopelessly as to the manner and meaning of it, for there is nothing tangible to lay hold of.

There are many things relating to my existence which are inexplicable to me, and probably it is best so; this death-bed scene, projected on my mind's screen, across four thousand five hundred miles of space, is one of these mysteries.

After Wilkes and I had thoroughly acquainted ourselves with all the evil and the good to be found at Camp Douglas, neither of us saw any reason at first why we could not wait with patience for the exchange of prisoners. But, as time passed, we found it to be a dreary task to endure the unchanging variety of misery surrounding us. I was often tempted with an impulse to challenge a malignant sentry's bullet, by crossing that ghastly 'dead-line,' which I saw every day I came out. A more unlovely sight than a sick Secessionist, in a bilious butternut, it is scarcely possible to conceive. Though he had been naked and soiled by his own filth, there would still have remained some elements of attractiveness in him; but that dirty, ill-made, nut-coloured homespun aggravated every sense, and made the poor, sickly wretch unutterably ugly.

In our treatment, I think there was a purpose. If so, it may have been from a belief that we should the sooner recover our senses by experiencing as much misery, pain, privation, and sorrow as could be contained within a prison; and, therefore, the authorities rigidly excluded every medical, pious, musical, or literary charity that might have alleviated our sufferings. It was a barbarous age, it is true; but there were sufficient Christian families in Chicago, who, I am convinced, only needed a suggestion, to have formed societies for the relief of the prisoners. And what an opportunity there was for such, to strengthen piety, to promote cheerfulness, soothe political ferocity, and subdue the brutal and vicious passions which possessed those thousands of unhappy youths immured within the horrible pen!

Left to ourselves, with absolutely nothing to do but to brood over our positions, bewail our lots, catch the taint of disease from each other, and passively abide in our prison-pen, we were soon in a fair state of rotting, while yet alive. The reaction from the excitement of the battle-field, and the cheerful presence of exulting thousands, was suspended for a few days by travel up the Mississippi, the generosity of lady-sympathisers in St. Louis, and the trip across Illinois; but, after a few days, it set in strong upon us, when once within the bleak camp at Chicago. Everything we saw and touched added its pernicious influence — the melancholy faces of those who were already wearied with their confinement, the numbers of the sick, the premature agedness of the emaciated, the distressing degeneration of manhood, the plaints of suffering wretches, the increasing bodily discomfort from ever-multiplying vermin, which infested every square inch.

Within a week, our new draft commenced to succumb under the maleficent influences of our surroundings. Our buildings swarmed with vermin, the dust-sweepings were alive with them. The men began to suffer from bilious disorders; dysentery and typhus began to rage. Day after day my company steadily diminished; and every morning I had to see them carried in their blankets to the hospital, whence none ever returned. Those not yet delirious, or too weak to move unaided, we kept with us; but the dysentery — however they contracted it — was of a peculiarly epidemical character, and its victims were perpetually passing us, trembling with weakness, or writhing with pain, exasperating our senses to such a degree that only the strong-minded could forego some expression of their disgust.

The latrines were all at the rear of our plank barracks, and each time imperious nature compelled us to resort to them, we lost a little of that respect and consideration we owed our fellow-creatures. For, on the way thither, we saw crowds of sick men, who had fallen, prostrate from weakness, and given themselves wholly to despair; and, while they crawled or wallowed in their filth, they cursed and blasphemed as often as they groaned. In the edge of the gaping ditches, which provoked the gorge to look at, there were many of the sick people, who, unable to leave, rested there for hours, and made their condition hopeless by breathing the stenchful atmosphere. Exhumed corpses could not have presented anything more hideous than dozens of these dead-and-alive men, who, oblivious to the weather, hung over the latrines, or lay extended along the open sewer, with only a few gasps intervening between them and death. Such as were not too far gone prayed for death, saying, 'Good God, let me die! Let me go, O Lord!' and one insanely damned his vitals and his constitution, because his agonies were so protracted. No self-respecting being could return from their vicinity without feeling bewildered by the infinite suffering, his existence degraded, and religion and sentiment blasted.

Yet, indoors, what did we see? Over two hundred unwashed, unkempt, uncombed men, in the dismalest attitudes, occupied in relieving themselves from hosts of vermin, or sunk in gloomy introspection, staring blankly, with heads between their knees, at nothing; weighed down by a surfeit of misery, internal pains furrowing their faces, breathing in a fine cloud of human scurf, and dust of offensive hay, dead to everything but the flitting fancies of the hopeless!

One intelligent and humane supervisor would have wrought wonders at this period with us, and arrested that swift demoralization with which we were threatened. None of us were conspicuously wise out of our own sphere; and of sanitary laws we were all probably as ignorant as of the etiology of sclerosis of the nerve-centres. In our colossal ignorance, we were perhaps doing something half-a-dozen times a day, as dangerous as eating poison, and constantly swallowing a few of the bacilli of typhus. Even had we possessed the necessary science at our finger-tips, we could not have done much, unaided by the authorities; but when the authorities were as ignorant as ourselves, — I cannot believe their neglect of us was intentional, — we were simply doomed!

Every morning, the wagons came to the hospital and dead-house, to take away the bodies; and I saw the corpses rolled in their blankets, taken to the vehicles, and piled one upon another, as the New Zealand frozen-mutton carcases are carted from the docks!

The statistics of Andersonville are believed to show that the South was even more callous towards their prisoners than the authorities of Camp Douglas were. I admit that we were better fed than the Union prisoners were, and against Colonel Milligan and Mr. Shipman I have not a single accusation to make. It was the age that was brutally senseless, and heedlessly cruel. It was lavish and wasteful of life, and had not the least idea of what civilised warfare ought to be, except in strategy. It was at the end of the flint-lock age, a stupid and heartless age, which believed that the application of every variety of torture was better for discipline than kindness, and was guilty, during the war, of enormities that would tax the most saintly to forgive.

Just as the thirties were stupider and crueller than the fifties, and the fifties were more bloody than the seventies, in the mercantile marine service, so a war in the nineties will be much more civilized than the Civil War of the sixties. Those who have survived that war, and have seen brotherly love re-established, and reconciliation completed, when they think of Andersonville, Libby, Camp Douglas, and other prisons, and of the blood shed in 2261 battles and skirmishes, must in this present peaceful year needs think that a moral epidemic raged, to have made them so intensely hate then what they profess to love now. Though a democratic government like the American will always be more despotic and arbitrary than that of a constitutional monarchy, even its army will have its Red Cross societies, and Prisoners' Aid Society; and the sights we saw at Camp Douglas will never be seen in America again.

Were Colonel Milligan living now, he would admit that a better system of latrines, a ration of soap, some travelling arrangements for lavatories, a commissioned superintendent over each barrack, a brass band, the loan of a few second-hand books, magazines, and the best-class newspapers (with all war-news cut out), would have been the salvation of two-thirds of those who died at Camp Douglas; and, by showing how superior the United States Government was to the Confederate States, would have sent the exchanged prisoners back to their homes in a spirit more reconciled than they were. Those in authority to-day also know that, though when in battle it is necessary to fight with all the venom of fiends for victory, once the rifle is laid down, and a man becomes a prisoner, a gracious treatment is more efficacious than the most revolting cruelty. Still, the civilized world is densely ignorant. It has improved immensely in thirty years, but from what I have seen in my travels in many lands, it is less disposed to be kind to man than to any other creatures; and yet, none of all God's creatures is more sadly in need of protection than he!

The only official connected with Camp Douglas whom I remember with pleasure is Mr. Shipman, the commissary. He was gentlemanly and white-haired, which, added to his unvarying benevolence and politeness, caused him to be regarded by me as something of an agreeable wonder in that pestful yard. After some two days' acquaintance, while drawing the rations, he sounded me as to my intentions. I scarcely comprehended him at the outset, for Camp Douglas was not a place to foster intentions. He explained that, if I were tired of being a prisoner, I could be released by enrolling myself as a Unionist, that is, becoming a Union soldier. My eyes opened very wide at this, and I shook my head, and said, 'Oh, no, I could not do that.' Nothing could have been more unlikely; I had not even dreamed that such an act was possible.

A few days later, I said to Mr. Shipman, 'They have taken two wagon-loads of dead men away this morning.' He gave a sympathetic shrug, as if to say, 'It was all very sad, but what can we do?' He then held forth upon the superiority of the North, the certainty of defeat for the South, the pity it was to see young men throw their lives away for such a cause as slavery, and so on; in short, all that a genuinely kind man, but fervidly Northern, could say. His love embraced Northerners and Southerners alike, for he saw no distinction between them, except that the younger brother had risen to smite the elder, and must be punished until he repented.

But it was useless to try and influence me by political reasons. In the first place, I was too ignorant in politics, and too slow of comprehension, to follow his reasonings; in the second place, every American friend of mine was a Southerner, and my adopted father was a Southerner, and I was blind through my gratitude; and, in the third place, I had a secret scorn for people who could kill one another for the sake of African slaves. There were no blackies in Wales, and why a sooty-faced nigger from a distant land should be an element of disturbance between white brothers, was a puzzle to me. I should have to read a great deal about him, ascertain his wrongs and his rights, and wherein his enslavement was unjust and his liberty was desirable, before I could venture upon giving an opinion adverse to 20,000,000 Southerners. As I had seen him in the South, he was a half-savage, who had been exported by his own countrymen, and sold in open market, agreeable to time-honoured custom. Had the Southerners invaded Africa and made captives of the blacks, I might have seen some justice in decent and pious people exclaiming against the barbarity. But, so far as I knew of the matter, it was only the accident of a presidential election which had involved the North and South in a civil war, and I could not take it upon me to do anything more than stand by my friends.

But, in the course of six weeks, more powerful influences than Mr. Shipman's gentle reasoning were undermining my resolve to remain as a prisoner. These were the increase in sickness, the horrors of the prison, the oily atmosphere, the ignominious cartage of the dead, the useless flight of time, the fear of being incarcerated for years, which so affected my spirits that I felt a few more days of these scenes would drive me mad. Finally, I was persuaded to accept with several other prisoners the terms of release, and enrolled myself in the U. S. Artillery Service, and, on the 4th June, was once more free to inhale the fresh air.

But, after two or three days' service, the germs of the prison-disease, which had swept so many scores of fine young fellows to untimely graves, broke out with virulence in my system. I disguised my complaint as much as was possible, for, having been a prisoner, I felt myself liable to be suspected; but, on the day of our arrival at Harper's Ferry, dysentery and low fever laid me prostrate. I was conveyed to the hospital, and remained there until the 22nd June, when I was discharged out of the service, a wreck.

My condition at this time was as low as it would be possible to reduce a human being to, outside of an American prison. I had not a penny in my pocket; a pair of blue military trousers clothed my nethers, a dark serge coat covered my back, and a mongrel hat my head. I knew not where to go: the seeds of disease were still in me, and I could not walk three hundred yards without stopping to gasp for breath. As, like a log, I lay at night under the stars, heated by fever, and bleeding internally, I thought I ought to die, according to what I had seen of those who yielded to death. As my strength departed, death advanced; and there was no power or wish to resist left in me. But with each dawn there would come a tiny bit of hope, which made me forget all about death, and think only of food, and of the necessity of finding a shelter. Hagerstown is but twenty-four miles from Harper's Ferry; but it took me a week to reach a farm-house not quite half-way. I begged permission to occupy an out-house, which may have been used to store corn, and the farmer consented. My lips were scaled with the fever, eyes swimming, face flushed red, under the layer of a week's dirt — the wretchedest object alive, possibly, as I felt I was, by the manner the good fellow tried to hide his disgust. What of it? He spread some hay in the out-house, and I dropped on it without the smallest wish to leave again. It was several days before I woke to consciousness, to find a mattress under me, and different clothes on me. I had a clean cotton shirt, and my face and hands were without a stain. A man named Humphreys was attending to me, and he was the deputy of the farmer in his absence.

By dint of assiduous kindness, and a diet of milk, I gained strength slowly, until I was able to sit in the orchard, when, with open air, exercise, and more generous food, I rapidly mended. In the early part of July, I was able to assist in the last part of the harvest, and to join in the harvest supper.

The farm-house where my Good Samaritan lived is situated close to the Hagerstown pike — a few miles beyond Sharpsburg. My friend's name is one of the few that has escaped my memory. I stayed with him until the middle of August, well-fed and cared for, and when I left him he insisted on driving me to Hagerstown, and paying my railway fare to Baltimore, viâ Harrisburg.[1]

[1] Stanley remembered, afterwards, that the farm-house belonged to a Mr. Baker, and that, in June, 1862, he had walked there from Harper's Ferry — three miles from Sharpsburg, and nine miles from Hagerstown. Mr. Baker's house seemed to have been near the cross-roads — near the extreme left flank of McClellan's army. — D. S.

PART II

THE LIFE, FROM STANLEY'S JOURNALS, NOTES, ETC.

CHAPTER X

JOURNALISM

UP to this point Stanley has told his own story. The chapter which follows is almost wholly a weaving together of material which he left.

That material consists, first, of an occasional and very brief diary, which he kept from 1862; then, at irregular intervals through many years, entries in a fuller journal, and occasional comments and retrospects in his note-books, during the last peaceful years of life.

He was discharged from Harper's Ferry, June 22, 1862. Then he seems to have turned his hand to one resource and another, to support himself; we find him 'harvesting in Maryland,' and, later, on an oyster-schooner, getting upon his feet, and out of the whirlpool of war into which he had naturally been drawn by mere propinquity, so to speak; now his heart turned with longing to his own kin, and the belated affection which he trusted he might find.

November, 1862. I arrived, in the ship 'E. Sherman,' at Liverpool. I was very poor, in bad health, and my clothes were shabby. I made my way to Denbigh, to my mother's house. With what pride I knocked at the door, buoyed up by a hope of being able to show what manliness I had acquired, not unwilling, perhaps, to magnify what I meant to *become;* though what I was, the excellence of my present position, was not so obvious to myself! Like a bride arraying herself in her best for her lover, I had arranged my story to please one who would, at last, I hoped, prove an affectionate mother! But I found no affection, and I never again sought for, or expected, what I discovered had never existed.

I was told that 'I was a disgrace to them in the eyes of their neighbours, and they desired me to leave as speedily as possible.'

This experience sank so deep, and, together with the life in earlier years, had so marked an effect on Stanley's character, that it seemed best to give it to the reader just as he noted it down as he mused over his life, near its close. When fame and prosperity came to him, he was just to the claims of blood, and gave practical help; but the tenderness which lay deep in his nature, and the repeated and hopeless rebuffs it encountered, produced, in the reaction, an habitual, strong self-suppression. The tenderness was there, through all the stirring years of action and achievement; but it was guarded against such shocks as had earlier wounded it, by an habitual reserve, and an austere self-command.

He returned to America, and, with a sort of rebound towards the world of vigorous action, threw himself, for a time, into the life of the sea. The motive, apparently, was partly as a ready means of livelihood, and partly a relish for adventure; and adventure he certainly found. Through 1863, and the early months of 1864, he was in one ship and another, in the merchant service; sailing to the West Indies, Spain, and Italy.

He condenses a ship-wreck into a two-line entry: 'Wrecked off Barcelona. Crew lost, in the night. Stripped naked, and swam to shore. Barrack of Carbineers . . . demanded my papers!'

The end of 1863 finds him in Brooklyn, New York, where we have another brief chronicle: —

> Boarding with Judge X——. Judge drunk; tried to kill his wife with hatchet; attempted three times. — I held him down all night. Next morning, exhausted; lighted cigar in parlour; wife came down — insulted and raved at me for smoking in her house!

In August, 1864, he enlisted in the United States Navy, on the receiving ship 'North Carolina,' and was then assigned to the 'Minnesota,' and afterwards to the 'Moses H. Stuyvesant,' where he served in the capacity of ship's writer. Nothing shows that he was impelled by any special motive of sympathy with the national cause. It has been told how he went into the Confederate service, as a boy naturally goes, carried along with the crowd. At this later time he may have caught something of the enthusiasm for the Union that filled the community about him; or, very probably, he may have gone on a fighting ship simply as more exciting to his adventurous spirit than a peaceful merchantman. In any case, he embarked on what proved to be the beginning of his true occupation and career, as the observer and reporter of stirring events; later, he was to play his part as a maker of events.

There is nothing to show just how or why he became a newspaper correspondent, but we know *the where;* and no ambitious reporter could ask a better chance for his first story than Stanley had when he witnessed the first and second attacks of the Federal forces on Fort Fisher, North Carolina. Those attacks are part of the history of the great war; how, in December, 1864, General Butler assailed the port from the sea, the explosion under its walls of a vessel charged with powder being a performance as dramatic as many of Butler's military exploits; how, a year later, a carefully-planned expedition under General Terry, attacked the fort; how, after a two days' bombardment by the fleet, two thousand sailors and marines were landed, under instructions to 'board the fort in a seaman-like manner'; how they were repelled by a murderous fire, while a force of soldiers assaulting from another side drove the defenders back, in a series of hand-to-hand contests, till the fort was won.

On both those occasions, it fell to Stanley to watch the fight, to tell the story of it in his own lucid and vigorous style, and to have his letters welcomed by the newspapers, and given to the world.

Three months later, in April, 1865, the war was ended, and Stanley left the Navy. Then, for a twelve-month, his diary gives only such glimpses of him as an occasional name of a place with date. 'St. Joseph, Missouri, — across the Plains, — Indians, — Salt Lake City, — Denver, — Black Hawk, — Omaha.' Apparently through this time, he was impelled by an overflowing youthful energy, and an innate love of novelty and adventure.

In his later years, he told how, in his early days, his exuberant vigour was such, that when a horse stood across his path his impulse was, not to go round, but to jump over it! And he had a keen relish for the sights and novelties, the many-coloured life of the West. So he went light-heartedly on his way, —

> 'For to admire and for to see,
> For to behold the world so wide.'

Through this period he seems to have done more or less newspaper correspondence, and to have tended towards that as a profession. Here belongs an episode which is told in one of the autobiographic fragments; the reckless frolic of boys recounted with the sobriety of age.

Being connected with the press, my acquaintance was sought by some theatrical people in Omaha; at which, being young and foolish, I was much gratified. After a benefit performance, which I was principally the means of getting up for them, I supped with them, and for the first time, I drank so much wine that I tasted the joys and miseries of intoxication. My impression will not be forgotten, for though the faculty of self-restraint was helpless, the brain was not so clouded that I did not know what I was about. I was conscious of an irrepressible hilarity, which provoked me to fling decorum to the winds, and of being overwhelmingly affectionate to my boon companions.

The women of the party appeared more beautiful than houris, especially one for whom I felt ecstatic tenderness.

When we had supped and drank and exhausted our best stories, about two o'clock in the morning we agreed to separate, the ladies to their own homes, but we men to a frolic, or lark, in the open. The effect of wine was at its highest. We sallied out, singing, 'We won't go home till morning.' I was soon conscious that my tread was different, that the sidewalk reminded me of the deck of a ship in a gale, the lamp-posts were not perpendicular, and leaned perilously over, which made me babble about the singular waywardness and want of uprightness in houses and lamp-posts and awning columns, and the curious elasticity of the usually firm earth. I wished to halt and meditate about this sudden change of things in general. Scraps of marine songs about the 'briny ocean,' 'brave sailor boys,' and 'good ships be on her waters,' were suggested to me by the rocking ground, and burst in fluent song from my lips; a noisier set than we became, it is scarcely possible to imagine.

I wonder now we were not shot at, for the Omaha people were not very remarkable for forbearance when angered, and a charge of small shot would have been no more than we each of us well deserved. But someone suggested that vengeful men were after us, and that was enough to send us scampering, each to his home, at four o'clock in the morning. I reached my place without accident, and without meeting a single constable; and, plunging into bed, I fell into a deep sleep. My first waking made me aware of a racking headache, and a deep conviction that I had behaved disgracefully.

I was enriched, however, by an experience that has lasted all my life, for I then vowed that this should be the last time I would have to condemn myself for a scandalous act of the kind. 'What an egregious fool I have been! Hang N—— and all his gang!' was my thought for many a day.

Like David Copperfield's first supper-party, one such lesson was enough for a man who was to do a man's part; he never again fell under Circe's spell. But the hunger for robust exploit was there, and he had found a companion of kindred tastes. With W. H. Cook, in May, 1866, he started for Denver. 'We bought some planking and tools, and, in a few hours, constructed a flat-bottomed boat. Having furnished it with provisions and arms against the Indians, towards evening we floated down the Platte River. After twice upsetting, and many adventures and narrow escapes, we reached the

Missouri River.' From Omaha they travelled to Boston, where in July, 1866, they took a sailing-ship for Smyrna.

They had planned to go far into Asia. The precise nature of their plan is not recounted; but there is little doubt that Stanley was acting partly as a newspaper-correspondent. What was the base of supplies, or how ambitious were their hopes, is not told; but they went on their own resources, and were well provided with money. Stanley seems from the first to have commanded good prices for his newspaper work, and he notes that he early took warning from the extravagance and dissipation which brought many a bright young fellow in the profession to grief.

'I practiced a rigid economy, punished my appetites, and, little by little, the sums acquired through this abstinence began to impart a sense of security, and gave an independence to my bearing which, however I might strive to conceal it, betrayed that I was delivered from the dependent state.' Thus, presumably, he had saved the sinews of war for this expedition. The opening stage, from the approach to the Asian shore, was crowded with interest. Stanley records with enthusiasm the appeal of classic and biblical association, the strangeness and fascination of Oriental scenery, the aspects of country and people. On leaving Smyrna, they plunged into the interior. It was his first draught of the wonder-world of the Orient, and he drank eagerly.

But a speedy change fell on the travellers. First, the American lad whom they had brought with them as an attendant, out of sheer mischief set a fire ablaze, which spread, and threatened wide destruction, bringing upon them a crowd of infuriated villagers, whom they had great difficulty in appeasing. Then, when they had penetrated into wilder regions, they fell in with a treacherous guide, who brought upon them a horde of Turkomans. They were severely beaten, and robbed of all their money, — twelve hundred dollars, — their letter of credit, and all their personal equipment; then dragged to a village, and arraigned as malefactors; then hustled from place to place for five days, with indignity and abuse, to escape imminent death only by the intervention of a benevolent old man.

The semi-civilized prison to which they were at last consigned proved a haven of refuge, for there appeared on the scene a Mr. Peloso, Agent of the Imperial Ottoman Bank at Constantinople, who bestirred himself in the friendliest manner on their behalf. Setting the facts of the case before the Turkish Governor, he completely turned the tables on the ruffianly accusers by getting them put in prison to await their trial, while Stanley and his companions moved on their way to Constantinople. There, again, they received most effective friendship at the hands of Mr. Edward Joy Morris, the American Minister, and Mr. J. H. Goodenow, the American Consul-general. Warm hospitality was shewn them; Mr. Morris advanced £150 for their needs, their assailants were tried, found guilty, and punished; ultimately the Turkish Government made good the money stolen.

That was the end of the Stanley-Cook exploration of Asia. The explorer's first quest had met a staggering set-back. But, 'repulse is interpreted according to the man's nature,' as Morley puts it; 'one of the differences between the first-rate man and the fifth-rate lies in the vigour with which the first-rate man recovers from this reaction, and crushes it down, and again flings himself once more upon the breach.'

CHAPTER XI

WEST AND EAST

INDIAN WARS OF THE WEST.—ABYSSINIAN CAMPAIGN, ETC.

STANLEY writes: 'My first entry into journalistic life as a selected "special" was at St. Louis after my return from Asia Minor. Hitherto, I had only been an attaché, or supernumerary, as it were, whose communications had been accepted and most handsomely rewarded, when, as during the two bombardments of Fort Fisher, they described events of great public interest. I was now instructed to "write-up" North-western Missouri, and Kansas, and Nebraska. In 1867, I was delegated to join General Hancock's expedition against the Kiowas and Comanches, and, soon after the termination of a bloodless campaign, was asked to accompany the Peace Commission to the Indians.'

These two expeditions he reported in a series of letters to the 'Missouri Democrat,' which, in 1895, he made into the first of two volumes, 'My Early Travels and Adventures.' It is the graphic story of a significant and momentous contact of civilization with savagery. Two years after the close of the Civil War, the tide of settlers was swiftly advancing over the great prairies of the West. The Union Pacific Railroad was being pushed forward at the rate of four miles a day. The Powder River military road was being constructed to Montana, and forts erected along its line, through the best and most reliable hunting-grounds of the Sioux, and without their consent. The Indians throughout a wide region were thrown into a ferment, and there were outbreaks against the white settlers. In March, a force was sent out under General Hancock, which Stanley accompanied, with the general expectation of severe fighting. But General Hancock soon imparted to Stanley his views and purposes, which were to feel the temper of the Indians, to see who were guilty, and who were not; to learn which tribes were friendly-disposed; to separate them from the tribes bent on war; to make treaties wherever practicable; and to post more troops on certain roads.

In a march of four hundred and fifty miles, he practically accomplished this plan. The hostile Sioux and Cheyennes were detached from their allies, the Kiowas, Arapahoes, and Comanches; and when the hostiles stole away from the conference, and began outrages on the settlers, they were punished by the destruction of their villages. But after Hancock's return, the plains still seethed with menace and occasional outbreaks, and a general Indian war seemed imminent.

In July, Congress met the emergency by the appointment and despatch of a Peace Commission. At its head was General Sherman, with a group of distinguished officers, two chief Indian Commissioners, and Senator Henderson, of Missouri. Sherman, after some very effective speeches to the Indians, left the further work to the other Peace Commissioners, who travelled far and wide over the Plains, for two thousand miles. They met the principal tribes in council, and made a series of treaties, which, with the distribution of presents, and the general view impressed upon the Indians in addresses, frank, friendly, and truthful, brought about a general pacification.

In Stanley's picturesque story of all this, perhaps the most striking feature is the speeches of the Indian chiefs as they set forth the feelings and wishes of their people. Said old Santanta; 'I love the land and the buffalo, and will not part with them. I don't want any of those medicine houses built in the country; I want the papooses brought up exactly as I am. I have word that you intend to settle us on a Reservation near the mountains. I don't want to settle there. I love to roam over the wide prairie, and, when I do it, I feel free and happy; but, when we settle down, we grow pale and die.'

'Few,' writes Stanley, 'can read the speeches of the Indian chiefs without feeling deep sympathy for them; they move us by their pathos and mournful dignity. But they were asking the impossible. The half of a continent could not be kept as a buffalo pasture and hunting-ground.' Reviewing the situation many years later, he pronounces that the decline and disappearance of the Indians has been primarily due, not to the wrongs by the whites, but to their innate savagery, their mutual slaughter, the ravages of disease, stimulated by unsanitary conditions; and, especially, the increased destructiveness of their inter-tribal wars, after they had obtained fire-arms from the whites. His account of the complaints laid before the Commissioners shows that there were real and many wrongs on the part of the whites. To one story of a wanton murder, and the comment, 'Those things I tell you to show you that the pale-faces have done wrong as well as the Indians,' that stout old veteran of the Plains, General Harney, replied: 'That 's so, the Indians are a great deal better than we are.' But of the broad purpose of the Government, and the spirit in which the Commission acted, Stanley writes: 'These letters describe the great efforts made by the United States Government to save the unfortunate Indians from the consequences of their own rash acts. The speeches of General Hancock and General Sherman and the Peace Commissioners faithfully reflect the sentiments of the most cultivated Americans towards them, and are genuine exhortations to the Indians to stand aside from the overwhelming wave of white humanity which is resistlessly rolling towards the Pacific, and to take refuge on the Reservations, where they will be fed, clothed, protected, and educated in the arts of industry and Christian and civilised principles.' The replies of the Indian chiefs no less faithfully reflect their proud contempt of danger, and betray, in many instances, a consciousness of the sad destiny awaiting them.

In all this, Stanley was unconsciously acquiring a preliminary lesson in dealing with savage races. The tone in which Sherman, Henderson, and Commissioner Taylor, spoke to the Indians, now as to warriors, now as to children, gave hints which, later, Stanley put to good use. And the experience of the Indians suggests a parallel with that of the Congo natives as each met the whites. The wise and generous purposes of men like Sherman and Taylor, as afterwards of Stanley, were woefully impeded in their execution by the less fine temper of their subordinates.

And now, from the West, Stanley goes to the East. The point of departure is given in the Journal.

January 1st, 1868. Last year was mainly spent by me in the western Territories, as a special correspondent of the 'Missouri Democrat,' and a contributor to several journals, such as the 'New York Herald,' 'Tribune,' 'Times,' 'Chicago Republican,' 'Cincinnati Commercial,' and others. From the 'Democrat' I received fifteen dollars per week, and expenses of travel; but, by my contributions to the other journals, I have been able to make on an average ninety dollars per week, as my correspondence was of public interest, being the records of the various expeditions against the warlike Indians of the plains. By economy and hard work, though now and then foolishly impulsive, I have been able to save three thousand dollars, that is, six hundred pounds. Hearing of the British expedition to Abyssinia, and as the Indian troubles have ceased, I ventured at the beginning of December last to throw up my engagement with the 'Democrat,' proceeded to Cincinnati and Chicago, and collected my dues, which were promptly paid to me; and in two cases, especially the 'Chicago Republican,' most handsomely.

I then came over to New York, and the 'Tribune' and 'Times' likewise paid me well. John Russell Young, the Editor of the New York 'Tribune,' was pleased to be very complimentary, and said he was sorry he knew of nothing else in which he could avail himself of the services of 'such an indefatigable correspondent.' Bowing my thanks, I left the 'Tribune,' and proceeded to the 'Herald' office; by a spasm of courage, I asked for Mr. Bennett. By good luck, my card attracted his attention, and I was invited to his presence. I found myself before a tall, fierce-eyed, and imperious-looking young man, who said, 'Oh, you are the correspondent who has been following Hancock and Sherman lately. Well, I must say your letters and telegrams have kept us very well informed. I wish I could offer you something permanent, for we want active men like you.'

'You are very kind to say so, and I am emboldened to ask you if I could not offer myself to you for the Abyssinian expedition.'

'I do not think this Abyssinian expedition is of sufficient interest to Americans, but on what terms would you go?'

'Either as a special at a moderate salary, or by letter. Of course, if you pay me by the letter, I should reserve the liberty to write occasional letters to other papers.'

'We do not like to share our news that way; but we would be willing to pay well for exclusive intelligence. Have you ever been abroad before?'

'Oh, yes. I have travelled in the East, and been to Europe several times.'

'Well, how would you like to do this on trial? Pay your own expenses to Abyssinia, and if your letters are up to the standard, and your intelligence is early and exclusive, you shall be well paid by the letter, or at the rate by which we engage our European specials, and you will be placed on the permanent list.'

'Very well, Sir. I am at your service, any way you like.'

'When do you intend to start?'

'On the 22nd, by the steamer "Hecla."'

'That is the day after to-morrow. Well, consider it arranged. Just wait a moment while I write to our agent in London.'

In a few minutes he had placed in my hands a letter to 'Colonel Finlay Anderson, Agent of the "New York Herald," The Queen's Hotel, St. Martin's Le Grand, London'; and thus I became what had been an object of my ambition, a regular, I hope, correspondent of the 'New York Herald.'

On the 22nd, in the morning, I received letters of introduction from Generals Grant and Sherman, which I telegraphed for, and they probably will be of some assistance among the military officers on the English expedition. A few hours later, the mail steamer left. I had taken a draft on London for three hundred pounds, and had left the remainder in the bank.

The letters to the 'New York Herald,' narrating the Abyssinian campaign, were afterwards elaborated into permanent form, the last half of Stanley's book, 'Coomassie and Magdala.' The campaign has become a chapter of history; the detention of Consul Cameron by the tyrannical King Theodore, of Abyssinia, continued for years; the imprisonment and abuse of other officers and missionaries, to the number of sixty; the fruitless negotiations for their release; the despatch from India of a little army of English and Punjabis, under Sir Robert Napier, afterwards Lord Napier, of Magdala; the marching columns of six thousand men, with as many more to hold the sea-coast, and the line of communication; the slow advance for months through country growing more wild and mountainous, up to a height of ten thousand feet; Napier's patient diplomacy with chiefs and tribes already chafing against Theodore's cruelties; the arrival before the stronghold; the sudden impetuous charge of the King's force; the quick repulse of men armed with spears and match-locks before troops handling rocket-guns, Sniders, and Enfields; the surrender of the captives, and their appearance among their deliverers; the spectacle of three hundred bodies of lately-massacred prisoners; the next day's assault and capture of the town; Theodore shot by his own hand; the return to the coast: all this Stanley shared and told.

His telling, in its final form,[1] has for setting an account of antecedent events, the early success and valour of Theodore, his degeneracy, the queer interchange of courtesies and mutual puzzlements between Downing Street and Magdala, and the organisation of the rescue force. These historical prefaces were characteristic of Stanley's books; the story of what he saw had an illuminating background of what had gone before, worked out by assiduous study. The record of the campaign is told with plentiful illustration of grand and novel landscape, of barbaric ways, of traits in his companions. There is a pervading tone of high spirits and abounding vitality. At first looked at a little askance, as an American, by the other correspondents, he soon got on very good terms with them. 'Their mess,' he writes, 'was the most sociable in the army, as well as the most loveable and good-tempered'; and he names the London correspondents, individually, as his personal friends. Lord Napier was courteous, and gave him the same privileges as his English col-

[1] See Stanley's *Coomassie and Magdala.*

leagues. With the officers, too, he got on well. There is occasional humorous mention in the book, and more fully in the Journal, of a certain captain whose tent he shared for a while, and whom he names 'Smelfungus,' after Sterne; he might have been dubbed 'Tartarin de Tarascon,' for he was a braggadocio, sportsman, and warrior, whose romances first puzzled, and then amused, Stanley, until he learned that a severe wound, and a sun-stroke, had produced these obscurations in a sensible and gallant fellow.

As a correspondent he scored a marked success, for which he had good fortune, as well as his own pains, to thank. On his way out, he had made private arrangements with the chief of the telegraph office, at Suez, about transmitting his despatches. 'My telegrams,' he notes in the Journal, 'are to be addressed to him, and he will undertake that there shall be no delay in sending them to London, for which services I am to pay handsomely if, on my return, I hear that there had been no delay.' This foresight was peculiarly characteristic of Stanley. On the return march, he could not get permission to send an advance courier with his despatches; these had to go in the same bag which carried the official and the other press bulletins. In the Red Sea, the steamer stuck aground for four days; and, under the broiling heat, an exchange of chaff between a colonel and captain generated wrath and a prospective duel; Stanley's mediation was accepted; reconciliation, champagne, and — Suez at last; but only to face five days of quarantine! Stanley manages to get a long despatch ashore, to his friend in the telegraph office. It is before all the others, and is hurried off; then the cable between Alexandria and Malta breaks, and for weeks not another word can pass! Stanley's despatch brings to London the only news of Theodore's overthrow. Surprise, incredulity, denunciations of the 'Herald' and its 'imposture,' — then conviction, and acceptance! Stanley had won his place in the world's front rank of correspondents! He notes in his Journal, 'Alexandria, June 28th, 1868. I am now a permanent employee of the "Herald," and must keep a sharp look-out that my second "coup" shall be as much of a success as the first. I wonder where I shall be sent to next.'

He was sent to examine the Suez Canal, which he found giving promise of completion within a year. Then, on to Crete, to describe the insurrection; and here he found no startling public news, but met with a personal experience which may be given in full.

The Island of Syra, Greece, August 20th, 1868. Christo Evangelides seems desirous of cultivating my acquaintance. He has volunteered to be my conductor through Hermopolis. As he speaks English, and is a genial soul, and my happiness is to investigate, I have cordially accepted his services. He first took me on a visit of call to Mrs. Julia Ward Howe, of Boston, and then to the Greek seminary, where I saw some young Greeks with features not unworthy of the praise commonly ascribed to Greek beauty. On the way to the Square, Evangelides, observing my favourable impressions, took advantage of my frank admiration and suggested that I should marry a Greek girl. Up to this moment it never had entered my mind that it must be some day my fate to select a wife. Rapidly my mind revolved this question. To marry requires means, larger means than I have. My twelve hundred pounds would soon be spent; and on four hundred pounds a year, and that depending on the will of one man, it would be rash to venture with an extravagant woman. Yet the suggestion was delicious from other points of view. A wife! My wife! How grand the proprietorship of a fair woman appeared! To be loved with heart and soul above all else, for ever united in thought and sympathy with a fair and virtuous being, whose very touch gave strength and courage and confidence! Oh dear! how my warm imagination glows at the strange idea!

Evangelides meanwhile observes me, and cunningly touches the colours of my lively fancy, becomes eloquent upon Greek beauty, the virtues, and the constant affections of Greek women. 'But, how is it possible for a wanderer like myself to have the opportunity of meeting such a creature as you describe? I have no resting-place, and no home; I am here to-day, and off to-morrow. It is not likely that a man can become so infatuated with a woman at a glance, or that she would follow a stranger to the church, and risk her happiness at a nod. Why will you distract a poor fellow with your raptures upon the joy of marriage?' And much else, with breathless haste, I retorted.

I looked at Evangelides and saw his age to be great, beard white as snow, though his face was unwrinkled. Swiftly, I tried to dive beneath that fair exterior, and, somehow, I compared him to a Homer, or some other great classic, who loved to be the cicerone of youth, and took no note of his own years. The charm of Hellas fell upon me, and I yielded a patient hearing to the fervid words, and all discretion fled, despite inward admonitions to beware of rashness.

He said he would be my proxy, and would choose a damsel worthy of every praise for beauty and for character. Like one who hoped and yet doubted, believed and yet suspected, I said: 'Very well, if you can show me such a girl as you describe, I will use my best judgement, and tell you later what I think of her.' And so it was agreed.

In the evening I walked in the Square with Evangelides, who suddenly asked me what I thought of his own daughter, Calliope. Though sorely tempted to laugh, I did not, but said gravely that I thought she was too old for me. The fact is, Calliope is not a beauty; and though she is only nineteen according to her father, yet she is not one to thaw my reserve.

August 21st. This morning Evangelides proposed his daughter in sober, serious earnest, and it required, in order not to offend, very guarded language to dispel any such strange illusion. Upon my soul, this is getting amusing! It is scarcely credible that a father would be so indifferent to his daughter's happiness as to cast her upon the first stranger he meets. What is there in me that urges him to choose me for a son-in-law? Though he claims to be a rich man, I do not think he has sufficient hundreds to induce me to entertain the offer. My liberty is more precious than any conceivable amount of gold.

August 22nd. Rode out during the morning into the country beyond Hermopolis, and crossed the mountains to the village of Analion. I was delighted with all I saw, the evidences of rural industry, the manifest signs of continuous and thoughtful care of property, the necessity for strictest economy, and unceasing toil, to make both ends meet, the beauty of the stainless sky, and the wide view of dark blue sea, which lay before me on every side. If it was calculated on the part of Evangelides, he could scarcely have done anything better than propose this ride; for what I saw during the ride, by recalling all I had read of Greece, made Greek things particularly dear to me. When I returned to the town, I quite understood Byron's passion for Hellas.

In the evening Evangelides walked with me on a visit to a family which lived on another side of the Square. We were received by a very respectable old gentleman in sober black, and a stout lady who, in appearance, dress, and surroundings, showed that she studied comfort. Evangelides seemed to be on good terms with them, and they all bandied small change of gossip in a delightfully frank and easy manner. Presently, into the sitting-room glided a young lady who came as near as possible to the realisation of the ideal which my fancy had portrayed, after the visions of marriage had been excited by Evangelides's frolicsome talk. She, after a formal introduction, subsided on a couch, demure, and wrapped in virgin modesty.

Her name was Virginia, and well it befitted her. Where had I seen her face, or whom did she recall? My memory fled over scores of faces and pictures, and instantly I bethought me of the Empress Eugénie when she was the Countess Montijo. A marvellous likeness in profile and style! She is about sixteen, and, if she can speak English, who knows? Simultaneously with the drift of my thoughts, Evangelides in the easiest manner led the conversation with the seniors to marriage of young people. He was so pointed that I became uneasy. My face began to burn as I felt the allusions getting personal. Jove! what a direct people these Greeks are! Not a particle of reserve! No shilly-shallying, or beating about the bush, but, 'I say, is your daughter ripe for marriage? If so, here is a fine young fellow quite ready.'

Evangelides was nearly as plain as this. Then the mother turned to me, and asked, 'Are you married?'

'Heaven forbid!' said I.

'Why?' she said, smiling, with proud consciousness of superior knowledge on her face. 'Is marriage so dreadful?'

'I am sure I don't know, but I have not thought of the subject.'

'Oh, well, I hope you will think of it now; there are many fair women in Greece; and Greek women make the best wives.'

'I am quite ready to believe you, and if I met a young Greek lady who thought as much of me as I of her, I might be tempted to sacrifice my independence,' I answered, more with a view to avoid an awkward silence than with a desire to keep up such a terribly personal conversation with strangers.

'I am sure,' said the lady, 'if you look around, you will find a young lady after your heart.'

I bowed, but my face was aflame.

With astonishing effrontery Evangelides maintained the pointed conversation until I saw my own uneasiness reflected in Virginia's face, who grew alternately crimson and pale. Both colours agreed with her, and I pitied her distress, and frowned on Evangelides, who, however, was incorrigible. Then I began to ask myself, was this really Greek custom, or was it merely a frantic zeal on Evangelides's part? Was this the Sirens' Isle, wherein the famed Ulysses was so bewitched, or was the atmosphere of the Cyclades fatal to bachelorhood? It would never do to tell in detail all I thought, or give all my self-questionings; but, ever and anon in my speculations, I stole a glance at Virginia's face, and each glance started other queries. 'Is this to be a farcical adventure, or shall it be serious"? I felt that only the mute maiden could answer such a question. Susceptible and romantic I know I am, but it requires more than a pretty face to rouse passionate love.

We rose to go, each protesting that we had passed a pleasant evening. The lady of the house promises, half-seriously, to find a nice wife for me. 'Do,' say I, 'and I will be eternally grateful. Good-bye, Miss Virginia.'

'Good-bye,' she says timidly, blushing painfully.

I note she has a French accent. I find she only knows a few words of English, but she is fluent in French. Here then comes another obstacle. I could make no love in French, without exploding at my own ignorance of it. But there is no doubt that, so far as beauty goes, Virginia is sufficient.

September 9th. After a short absence, I have returned. Evangelides welcomed me effusively. Passed the evening with Virginia's family. There were two brothers of Virginia's, fine young fellows, present, and a sister. It was clear that my letter had been a subject of family discussion, for every eye was marked by a more discerning glance than would have been noticeable otherwise. Even on the little girl's face I read, 'I wonder if he will suit me as a brother-in-law.' I wished I could say to her, 'So far as you and Virginia are concerned, I do not think you will have cause for regret.' On the whole, the ordeal was not unsatisfactory. I was conscious that Virginia was favourable. No decision has been arrived at yet, but I feel that where there are so many heads in council, father, mother, brothers, relatives, friends, and Evangelides, there must be a deal to debate.

September 10th. A friend of the family came into my room

this afternoon, and was, in features, voice, and conduct, infectiously congratulatory. He told me that the marriage was as good as concluded, that I had only to name the day. I gasped, and with good reason. Here was an event which I had always considered as sacred, mysterious, requiring peculiar influences and circumstances to bring within range of possibilities, so imminent, that it depended only on my own wish. Incredulous, I asked, 'But are you certain?'

'As certain as I am alive. I have only just left them, and came expressly to enquire your wishes in the matter.'

Feeling that retreat was as undesirable as it would be offensive, I replied, 'Then, of course, as my business admits of no delay, I should like the marriage to take place next Sunday.'

'All right,' he said, 'next Sunday will suit us perfectly.' And he left me quivering, almost, and certainly agitated.

In the evening I visited the house. I was allowed to see Virginia, and, in a short time, whatever misgivings I may have had as to the wisdom of my act were banished by the touch of her hand, and the trust visible in her eyes. There was no doubt as to her ultimate responsiveness to the height and depth of love. As yet, naturally, there was no love; but it was budding, and, if allowed to expand, there would be no flaw in the bloom. If I know myself at all, I think that my condition was much the same. All that I knew of her I admired; and, if she were as constant in goodness as she was beautiful, there would be no reason to regret having been so precipitate.

From these rapid reflections I was recalled by the mother's remarks, which in a short time satisfied me that the marriage was not so positively determined upon as I had been led to believe that afternoon. As she went on I perceived it was not settled at all. The same fear I had felt, of committing an imprudence, was swaying her. She said that I was quite a stranger, of whose antecedents everyone in Syra was quite ignorant, and she was therefore obliged to ask me to have patience until all reasonable assurances had been given that I was what I represented myself to be.

The wisdom of this act I could not but applaud. The mother was just and prudent, and my respect for her increased.

Still, it was tantalising. My decision to marry, though so quickly arrived at, cost me a struggle and some grief. My independence I valued greatly. Freedom was so precious to me. To be able to wander where I liked, at a moment's thought, with only a portmanteau to look after, I should not have bartered for a fortune. But now, after looking into the face of such a sweet girl as Virginia, and seeing her readiness to be my companion, for better, or for worse, and believing that she would not hinder my movements, the disagreeability of being wedded had been removed, and I had been brought to look upon the event as rather desirable.

'Well, so be it,' I said; 'though I am sorry, and perhaps you may be sorry, but I cannot deny that you are just and wise.'

September 11th. I gave a dinner to the family at the Hôtel d'Amérique. Virginia was present, lovelier than ever. It is well that I go away shortly, for I feel that she is a treasure; and my admiration, if encouraged, would soon be converted into love, and if once I love, I am lost! However, the possibility of losing her serves to restrain me.

September 12th. Dined with Virginia's family. I had the honour of being seated near her. We exchanged regards, but we both felt more than we spoke. We are convinced that we could be happy together, if it is our destiny to be united. Toasts were drunk, etc., etc. Afterwards, Virginia exhibited her proficiency on the piano, and sang French and Greek sentimental songs. She is an accomplished musician, beautiful and amiable. She is in every way worthy.

September 13th. Left Syra for Smyrna by the 'Menzaleh.' Virginia was quite affectionate, and, though I am outwardly calm, my regrets are keener at parting than I expected. However, what must be, must be.

September 26th. Received answer from London that I am to go to Barcelona, viâ Marseilles, and wire for instructions on reaching France.

September 27th. Wrote a letter to Evangelides and Virginia's mother, that they must not expect my return to Syra unless they all came to a positive decision, and expressly invited me, as it would be an obvious inconvenience, and likely to be resented at headquarters.

CHAPTER XII

A ROVING COMMISSION

SO the fair Greek disappears; and Stanley, free and heart-whole, is whirled away again by the 'Herald's' swift and changing summons: to Athens, to witness a Royal Baptism, and describe the temples and ruins, with which he was enraptured; to Smyrna, Rhodes, Beyrout, and Alexandria; thence to Spain, where great events seemed impending. But he has barely interviewed General Prim, when he is ordered to London; there the 'Herald's' agent, Colonel Finlay Anderson, gives him a surprising commission.

It is vaguely reported that Dr. Livingstone is on his way homeward from Africa. On the chance of meeting him, and getting the first intelligence, Stanley is to go to Aden, and use his discretion as to going to Zanzibar. It looks like a wild-goose chase, but his, 'not to make reply; his, not to reason why'; and he is off to Aden, which he reaches November 21, 1868. Not a word can he learn of Livingstone. He writes enquiries to Consul Webb at Zanzibar, and, in the wretched and sun-scorched little town, sets himself to wait; but not in idleness. He works the Magdala campaign into book-form, designing in some indefinite future to publish it. (It came out five years later.) Then he falls upon 'a pile of good books which my interesting visit to Greece and Asia Minor induced me to purchase—Josephus, Herodotus, Plutarch, Derby's "Iliad," Dryden's "Virgil," some few select classics of Bohn's Library, Wilkinson's and Lane's books on "Egypt," hand-books to Greece, the Levant, and India, Kilpert's maps of Asia Minor, etc. Worse heat, worse dust, and still no word of Livingstone!'

New Year's Day, 1869. Many people have greeted me, and expressed their wish that it should be a happy one, and that I should see many more such days. They were no doubt sincere, but what avail their wishes, and what is happiness? What a curious custom it is, to take this day, above all others, to speak of happiness, when inwardly each must think in his soul that it admonishes him of the lapse of time, and what enormous arrears there still remain to make up the sum of his happiness!

As for me, I know not what I lack to make me happy. I

have health, youth, and a free spirit; but, what to-morrow may bring forth, I cannot tell. Therefore, take care to keep that health. The knowledge that every moment makes me older, the fluctuations to which the spirit is subject, hour by hour, for ever remind me that happiness is not to be secured in this world, except for brief periods; and, for a houseless, friendless fellow like myself, those periods when we cast off all thought which tends to vex the mind cannot, by any possibility, be frequent. But, if to be happy is to be without sorrow, fear, anxiety, doubt, I have been happy; and, if I could find an island in mid-ocean, remote from the presence or reach of man, with a few necessaries sufficient to sustain life, I might be happy yet; for then I could forget what reminds me of unhappiness, and, when death came, I should accept it as a long sleep and rest.

But, as this wish of mine cannot be gratified, I turn to what many will do to-day; meditate; think with regret of all the things left undone that ought to have been done; of words said that ought not to have been uttered; of vile thoughts that stained the mind; and resolve, with God's help, to be better, nobler, purer. May Heaven assist all who wish the same, and fill their hearts with goodness!

January 7th, 1869. Six days of this New Year are already gone, and one of the resolutions which I made on the first day I have been compelled to break. I had mentally resolved to smoke no more, from a belief that it was a vice, and that it was my duty to suppress it. For six days I strove against the hankering, though the desire surged up strongly. To-day I have yielded to it, as the effort to suppress it absorbed too much of my time, and now I promise myself that I shall be moderate, in order to soothe the resentment of my monitor.

Still no news of Livingstone, and scant hope of any! Stanley critically examines Aden; notes its unfortified condition, its importance when once the Suez Canal is finished; and sketches its future possibilities as a great distributing centre, and the case of a cheap railway into the heart of Arabia.

After ten weeks at Aden, February 1st, 'I am relieved, at last!' And so he turns his back on Livingstone, who is still deep in the wilds of Africa. As he mixes with civilised men in his travels, he is sometimes struck by their triviality, sometimes by their malicious gossip.

February 9th, 1869. At Alexandria. Dined with G. D. and his wife. Among the guests was one named J——. This young man is a frequent diner here, and the gossips of Alexandria tell strange things. Truly the English, with all their Christianity, and morals, and good taste, and all that sort of thing, are to be dreaded for their propensity to gossip, for it is always malicious and vile. Oh, how I should like to discover my island, and be free of them!

Apropos of this, it reminds me of my journey to Suez last November. Two handsome young fellows, perhaps a year or so younger than myself, were fellow-passengers in the same coupé. They were inexperienced and shy. I was neither the one, nor, with the pride of age, was I the other. I had provided myself with a basket of oranges and a capacious cooler. They had not; and when we came abreast of the dazzling sands, and to the warm, smothering mirage, and the fine sand came flying stinging hot against the face, they were obliged to unbutton and mop their faces, and they looked exceedingly uncomfortable. Then it was that I conquered my reserve, and spoke, and offered oranges, water, sandwiches, etc.

Their shyness vanished, they ate and laughed and enjoyed themselves, and I with them. The pipes and cigars came next, and, being entertainer, as it were, I did my best for the sake of good fellowship, and I talked of Goshen, Pithom,[1] and Rameses, Moses' Wells, and what not. We came at last to Suez, and, being known at the hotel, I was at once served with a room. While I was washing, I heard voices. I looked up; my room was separated from the next by an eight-foot partition. In the next room were my young friends of the journey, and they were speaking of me! Old is the saying that 'listeners hear no good of themselves'; but, had I been a leper or a pariah, I could not have been more foully and slanderously abused.

This is the third time within fourteen months that I have known Englishmen, who, after being polite to my face, had slandered me behind my back. Yes, this soulless gossip is to be dreaded! I have learned that if they entertain me with gossip about someone else, they are likely enough to convey to somebody else similar tales about me.

[1] A city of Egypt mentioned in Exodus i, 11, along with Rameses.

In the enforced leisure of a Mediterranean trip comes a piece of self-observation.

February 20th, 1869. At sea, under a divine heaven! There is a period which marks the transition from boy to man, when the boy discards his errors and his awkwardness, and puts on the man's mask, and adopts his ways. The duration of the period depends upon circumstances, and not upon any defined time. With me, it lasted some months; and, though I feel in ideas more manly than when I left the States, I am often reminded that I am still a boy in many things. In impulse I am boy-like, but in reflection a man; and then I condemn the boy-like action, and make a new resolve. How many of these resolutions will be required before they are capable of restraining, not only the impulse, but the desire, when every action will be the outcome of deliberation? I am still a boy when I obey my first thought; the man takes that thought and views it from many sides before action. I have not come to that yet; but after many a struggle I hope to succeed. 'Days should speak, and a multitude of years should teach wisdom.'

It is well for me that I am not so rich as the young man I met at Cairo who has money enough to indulge every caprice. I thank Heaven for it, for if he be half as hot-blooded and impulsive as I am, surely his life will be short; but necessity has ordained that my strength and youth should be directed by others, and in a different sphere; and the more tasks I receive, the happier is my life. I want work, close, absorbing, and congenial work, only so that there will be no time for regrets, and vain desires, and morbid thoughts. In the interval, books come handy. I have picked up Helvetius and Zimmerman, in Alexandria, and, though there is much wisdom in them, they are ill-suited to young men with a craze for action.

And now he is back at headquarters in London, and gets his orders for Spain; and there he spends six months, March to September, 1869, describing various scenes of the revolution, and the general aspect of the country, in a graphic record. These letters are among the best of his descriptive writings. The Spanish scenery and people; the stirring events; the barricades and street-fighting; the leaders and the typical characters; the large issues at stake — all make a great and varied theme.

On arriving in Spain, Stanley commenced studying Spanish, with such success, that, by June, he was able to make a speech in Spanish, and became occasional correspondent to a Spanish newspaper.

The insurrection of September, 1868, which drove Isabella from the Throne, led to a provisional Government under a Regency, General Prim acting as Minister of War.

On June 15, 1869, Stanley was present in the Plaza de Los Cortes when the Constitution was read to twenty thousand people, who roared their 'vivas.'

Stanley was in the prime of his powers, and these powers were not, as afterwards in Africa, taxed by heavy responsibilities, and ceaseless executive work, but given solely to a faithful and vivid chronicle of what he saw. 'I went to Spain,' he wrote, 'the young man going to take possession of the boy's heritage, those dear dreams of wild romance, stolen from school-hours.'

When a Carlist rising threatened, hundreds of miles away, Stanley immediately hastened off to the scene. On one occasion, he hurried from Madrid in search of the rebellious Carlists, who were said to have risen at Santa Cruz de Campescu. 'As soon as I reached the old town of Vittoria, I took my seat in the diligence for Santa Cruz de Campescu; our road lay westward towards the Atlantic through the valley of Zadora. If you have read Napier's "Battles of the Peninsula," you can well imagine how interesting each spot, each foot of ground, was to me. This valley was a battle-field, where the armed legions of Portugal, Spain, and England, matched themselves against Joseph Buonaparte's French Army.'

At Santa Cruz, Stanley found the insurrectionists had fled to the mountains, leaving forty prisoners; he returned to Madrid, to join General Sickles and his suite, on a visit to the Palace of La Granja, called the 'Cloud Palace of the King of Spain.'

He hears in Madrid, one evening, that several battalions and regiments had been despatched towards Saragossa. 'Naturally I wanted to know what was going on there. What did the departure of all these troops to Saragossa mean? So one hour later, at 8.30 P. M., I took the train, and arrived at Saragossa the next morning at 6 A. M.'

And here Stanley witnessed a rising of the people, 'proud and passionate, the Berber and Moorish blood coursing through their veins.' They resisted the order to give up Arms. 'Then, with their bayonets, they prise up the granite blocks, and, with the swiftness of magic, erect a barricade, formidable, wide, a granite and cobblestone fortification, breast-high. One, two, three, four, and five, aye, ten barricades are thrown up, almost as fast as tongue can count them. 'My eye,' says Stanley, 'finds enough to note; impossible to note the whole, for there are a hundred things and a thousand things taking place. Carts are thrown on the summit of the barricades; cabs caught unawares are launched on high, sofas and bureaux and the strangest kind of obstructions are piled above all.'

Stanley himself was on a balcony, not within the barricade, but half a block outside. He saw a battery of mounted trained Artillery halt five hundred yards from where he stood. He watched them dismount the guns and prepare for action; and was present at the bursting and rending of shells and the ceaseless firing of musketry from the barricades.

'As the bullets flattened themselves with a dull thud against the balcony where I stood, I sought the shelter of the roof, and behind a friendly cornice, I observed the desperate fighting.'

Though the firing had been incessant for an hour, little damage had been done to the barricade. The soldiers, advancing at short range, were shot down; again the Artillery thundered, and, when the smoke dispersed, Stanley saw the soldiers had approached nearer. 'The scene was one of desperation against courage allied with a certain cold enthusiasm; as fast as one soldier fell, another took his place. I witnessed personal instances of ferocity and courage which made me hold my breath. To me — who was, I really believe, the sole disinterested witness of that terrible battle — they appeared like characters suddenly called out to perform in some awful tragedy; and, so fascinated was I by the strange and dreadful spectacle, I could not look away.'

Night fell, and the bugles sounded retreat; the soldiers had lost heart after three hours' persistent fighting, with nothing gained. The dead lay piled at the barricades. Stanley remained on the roof until he was chilled and exhausted; he had been awake thirty-nine hours. 'I retired for a couple of hours' rest, completely fatigued, yet with the determination to be up before daylight; and, by five in the morning, I was at my post of observation on the roof.'

Stanley graphically described the scene behind the barricade, before the battle recommenced. Fresh troops now arrived, former failure was to be avenged. Again they hurl themselves on the barricades; 'but they are thrust back by protruding bayonets, they are beaten down by clubbed muskets, they are laid low by hundreds of deadly bullets, which are poured on them; but, with fearless audacity, the Regulars climb over their own dead and wounded, and throw themselves over the barricades into the smoke of battle, to be hewed to death for their temerity.'

This completed the fourth defeat the Government troops experienced, and in the greatest disorder they ran towards the Corso; while the 'Vivas' to the Republic were deafening. 'The Artillery re-open fire with grape, shell, and solid shot, and once more the old city of Saragossa quivers to its foundations. Another battalion has been added, and nearly six hundred men are found before the breast-works.'

The rear ranks were impelled electrically forward, and bodily heaved over the front ranks, quite into the barricades; others crowded on, a multitude bounded over, as if swept on by a hurricane, and the first barricade was taken, the insurgents threw down their arms, fell down on their knees, and cried for 'quarter.' Thus was Saragossa quelled and a thousand prisoners taken. 'The valour and heroism of the insurgents, will, I fancy, have been chronicled solely by me, because the Government won the day, as they were bound to do.'

Stanley now hastened to Valencia, 'from whence came reports of fierce cannonading; it was not in my nature to sit with folded arms, and let an important event, like that, pass without personal investigation.'

He was told he could not go, the trains did not run, miles of railway had been destroyed. 'Can I telegraph? — No — Why? — No telegrams are allowed to pass by order of the Minister of War. — Heigh-ho! to Alicante, then! — Thence by sea to Valencia. I 'll circumnavigate Spain! but I *shall* get to Valencia! I exclude all words like "fail," "can't," from my vocabulary.'

Stanley had great difficulty, and many adventures, before he got, by sea, into Valencia, and found himself amid the roar of guns and the whiz of bullets.

He wandered from street to street, always confronted by soldiers with fixed bayonets, until, at last, he saw a chance of getting into an hotel; but he had to run the gauntlet of twenty feet of murderous firing. Officers remonstrated against the folly. 'But twenty feet! Count three and jump! I jumped, took one peep at the barricade in my mid-air flight, and was in the hotel portico, safe, with a chorus of "bravos" in my rear, and a welcome in front.'

But how can I give samples of Stanley's vivid word-painting; it is like snipping off a corner of a great historical picture. The foregoing passages, however, will suffice to show how Stanley's whole being throbbed with energy, and with the desire to excel.

Sometimes he rides all night, in order to reach betimes a remote place, where fighting is reported; he watches the stirring scenes all day, and reports his observations before taking rest.

Extracts from one or two private letters are given here. One was written to a friend who pressed him to take a holiday.

MADRID, June 27, 1869.

You know my peculiar position, you know who, what, and where I am; you know that I am not master of my own actions, that I am at the beck and call of a chief whose will is imperious law. The slightest inattention to business, the slightest forgetfulness of duty, the slightest laggardness, is punished severely; that is, you are sent about your business. But I do not mean to be sent about my business. I do not mean to be discharged from my position. I mean by attention to my business, by self-denial, by indefatigable energy, to become, by this very business, my own master, and that of others. Hitherto, so well have I performed my duty, surpassing all my contemporaries, that the greatest confidence is placed in me.

I have *carte blanche* at the bankers'; I can go to any part of Spain I please, that I think best; I can employ a man in my absence. This I have done in the short space of eighteen months, when others have languished on at their business for fifteen years, and got no higher than the step where they entered upon duty. How have I done this? By intense application to duty, by self-denial, which means I have denied myself all pleasures, so that I might do my duty thoroughly, and exceed it. Such has been my ambition. I am fulfilling it. Pleasure cannot blind me, it cannot lead me astray from the path I have chalked out. I am so much my own master, that I am master over my own passions. It is also my interest to do my duty well. It is my interest not to throw up my position. My whole life hangs upon it — my future would be almost blank, if I threw up my place. You do not — cannot suppose that I have accepted this position merely for money. I can make plenty of money anywhere — it is that my future promotion to distinction hangs upon it. Even now, if I applied for it, I could get a consulship, but I do not want a consulship — I look further up, beyond a consulship.

My whole future is risked. Stern duty commands me to stay. It is only by railway celerity that I can live. Away from work, my conscience accuses me of forgetting duty, of wasting time, of forgetting my God. I cannot help that feeling. It makes me feel as though the world were sliding from under my feet. Even if I had a month's holiday, I could not take it; I would be restless, dissatisfied, gloomy, morose. To the —— with a vacation! I don't want it.

. . . .

I have nothing to fall back upon but energy, and much hopefulness. But so long as my life lasts, I feel myself so much master of my own future, that I can well understand Cæsar's saying to the sailors, 'Nay, be not afraid, for you carry Cæsar and his fortunes!' I could say the same: 'My body carries Stanley and his fortunes.' With God's help, I shall succeed!

A telegram called him to Paris, to meet Mr. Bennett in person; and there, October 16, 1869, he received a commission of startling proportions. He was to search for Livingstone in earnest, — not for an interview, but to discover, and, if necessary, extricate him, wherever he might be in the heart of Africa. But this was to be only the climax of a series of preliminary expeditions. Briefly, these consisted of a report of the opening of the Suez Canal; some observations of Upper Egypt, and Baker's expedition; the underground explorations in Jerusalem; Syrian politics; Turkish politics at Stamboul; archæological explorations in the Crimea; politics and progress in the Caucasus; projects of Russia in that region; Trans-Caspian affairs; Persian politics, geography, and present conditions; a glance at India; and, finally, — a search for Livingstone in Equatorial Africa!

Into this many-branched search for knowledge Stanley now threw himself. He carried out the whole programme, up to its last article, within the next twelve-month, with as much thoroughness as circumstances permitted in each case. The record, as put into final shape twenty-five years later, makes a book of 400 pages, the second volume of 'My Early Travels and Adventures.' It is impossible even to epitomise briefly here the crowded and stirring narrative. The observer saw the brilliant pageant of the great flotilla moving for the first time in history from the Mediterranean Sea, through the Suez Canal, to the Indian Ocean.

Stanley was present at the ceremony of blessing the Suez Canal. On the following day, the 17th November, 1869, he was to see 'a new route to commerce opened.' The Empress Eugénie, the Emperor of Austria, the Crown Prince of Prussia, and many notabilities had arrived.

'A beautiful morning ushered in the greatest drama ever witnessed or enacted in Egypt. It is the greatest and last, so far, of all the magnificent periods which Egypt has witnessed.'

At eight o'clock in the morning, the Empress's yacht led the procession through the Canal, and Stanley followed, in the steamer 'Europe.'

He next went up the Nile, to Upper Egypt, as one of a party of seventy invited guests of the Khedive; 'twenty-three days of most exquisite pleasure, unmarred by a single adverse incident.'

The next part of his programme was to visit Jerusalem, where he saw the unearthing of her antique grandeurs, sixty feet underground.

Stanley proceeded thence to Constantinople, where he wrote a long letter for the 'New York Herald,' on the Crimea; and here he met, once more, his kind friend, the American Minister, Mr. Joy Morris, who presented him with a beautiful Winchester rifle, and gave him letters of introduction to General Ignatieff, General Stoletoff, and various Governors and Ministers in Persia.

Stanley now travelled through the Caucasus, where he found unexpected civilisation. He rated highly the advantages which Russia's much-censured conquest of the Caucasus had brought in its train: warring tribes brought to peace, feuds and mutual slaughter stopped, local religions and customs respected, and an end put to barbarism and feudality, 'which terms are almost synonymous, as witness the mountain towers and fortresses, once the terror of the country, now silent and crumbling.'

Tiflis affords as much amusement and comfort as any second-rate town or city in Europe. From his Journal are here given one or two passages, to illustrate how Stanley observed and judged the individuals of his own race and civilisation.

February 5th, 1870. Reached the Dardanelles at noon. One of my fellow-voyagers is the Rev. Dr. Harman, of Maryland, an elderly and large man, who is a marvel of theological erudition, a mixture of Jonathan Edwards and the Vicar of Wakefield. Most of the morning we had passed classic ground, and, as he is a Greek scholar of some repute, his delight was so infectious that we soon became warm friends. He also has been to Jerusalem, Damascus, and Ephesus, and many other places of biblical and classical interest; and, in a short time, with a face shining with enthusiasm, he communicated to me many of his impressions and thoughts upon what he had seen, as my sympathy was so evident. St. Paul is his favourite; the Seven Churches of Asia, and the inwardness of the Revelations, are topics dear to him; and, perceiving that I was a good listener, the dear old gentleman simply 'let himself go,' uttering deep and weighty things with a warmth that was unexpected.

His exact words I have already forgotten; but the picture that he made, as he sat clad in sober black on his deck-chair, the skirts of his frock-coat touching the deck, his spectacled eyes thoughtfully fixed on the distant horizon, while his lips expressed the learned lore he had gathered from reading and reflection, will be ineffaceable. If I were rich enough, this is the type of man whom I should choose for my mentor, until the unfixedness of youth had become set in a firm mould. On two points only was he inclined to be severe. His Presbyterianism could not endure the Pope; and, had he the power, he would like to drive the Padishah and his Turks far away into inner Asia, where they belonged. Otherwise, he is one of the largest-hearted Christians I have ever met.

Many-sided in his sensitiveness to the attractions and charms of life, there were some aspects against which he was proof. At Odessa he fell in with highly congenial English society, and, at the close of his visit, he touches on one aspect that repelled, and one that attracted him; the twofold attitude is not unrelated to the state of mind the final sentence portrays.

March 6th. The Carnival was a novel sight to me. It is the first I have ever seen, and I thank my stars that it is not my fate to see many more such. The mad jollity and abandon wherein both sexes seemed agreed to think of nothing but their youth and opportunities, positively abashed me! To decline being drawn within the whirl of dissipation, and to discountenance fair gauzy nymphs who insidiously tempt one to relax austere virtue, is not easy; but the shame of it, more than any morality, prevented me from availing myself of the licence.

At the Cathedral I heard the most glorious vocal music it has ever been my lot to hear. There was one voice — a priest's — that rang like a clarion through the building, so flawless in its rich tones that every heart, I should fancy, was filled with admiration; and when the choir joined in the anthem, and filled the entire concave with their burst of harmony, and the organ rolled its streams of tremulous sound in unison, I became weak as a child, with pure rapture and unstrung nerve! That half-hour in the Cathedral is unforgettable. Whether it is due to the air of Odessa, the perfect health I enjoyed, the warm hospitality I received, or what, I am inclined to think that for once I have known a brief period of ideal pleasure, unmarred by a single hour of unhappiness.

Stanley now travelled along the Russian, Persian, and Turkestan coasts, observing the people and noting manners, customs, and events. Towards the end of May, 1870, he reached Teheran; his description of the Palaces and Bazaars, the Shah and his people, are wonderful reading. From Teheran he rode to Ispahan.

My friends among the English colony at Teheran gave me several wise admonitions, among which were, that I was never to travel during the day on account of the heat, but to start just at sunset, by which I might make two stations before I halted; I was also to look out for myself, as there were numerous brigands on the road, who would not scruple to strip me of everything I possessed.

I followed their advice for the first few stages; but, as the rocks retain the heat, I think the discomfort of night-travel is greater than that of day. Besides, the drowsiness was overpowering, and I was constantly in danger of falling from my horse. The landscape had no interest; the mountains appeared but shapeless masses, and the plains were vague and oppressively silent. I reached the salt desert of Persia, after a ride over country which steadily became more sterile and waterless.

The fervour of that tract was intense. My thermometer indicated 129° Fahr. Yet this terrible tract, with its fervid glow and its expanse of pale yellow sand almost at white heat, was far more bearable by day than a night ride through it would have been — for, though I could distinguish nothing but a quivering vapour, the strange forms of the mirage were more agreeable than the monotonous darkness.

Then follows a graphic picture of Ispahan, where he spent a week, and then onwards, ever onwards, riding through oven heat.

At Kûmishah, I invited myself to pass the night in the telegraph station, for there was nobody at home.

When evening came, I made my bed on the house-top, whence I had a good view of the town and of the myriad of mud towers, of acres of tomb-stones, and lion sphynxes. And there I dropped to sleep with the clear heaven for my canopy.

At Yezdikhast I had to spend the day; there were no horses, but, at 4 A. M., the relay arrived and away I sped, to the ruins of Pasargadæ. Inclining a little towards the right, I came to a group of low and greyish hills, on the most southward of which I caught a glimpse of a whitish stone wall. Riding up to it, I found it to be a marble platform, or, rather, a marble wall, which encased the hill.

The natives call it Solomon's Throne, and on it once stood the Castle of Pasargadæ. To commemorate the overthrow of the Babylonian Empire, Cyrus the Great, in the year 557 B. C., caused to be erected on it a fort, or castle, containing a Holy Place, whither he went to worship, and where his successors were wont to be inaugurated as Kings of Persia.

From Pasargadæ Stanley rides to Persepolis, and here he lingers amid the ruins, for he loves to dream of and reconstruct the mighty Past.

I slept in the first portal of Persepolis, all night. The only food I could get was wafer bread and plenty of milk.

Early the next morning, July 1st, Stanley rode away, after cutting his name deep on the Temple. Away, away to Shiraz, where he visits the graves of Saadi, Hafiz, and one of the many graves given to Bathsheba!

At last Stanley reaches Bushire, where he took steamer and entered the Persian Gulf; he visits Bunder-Abbas, and then continues his journey to Muscat, Arabia; thence to Kurrachi, arriving at Bombay, on August 1, 1870, his long programme carried through, up to the verge of its last supreme undertaking, the search for Livingstone. First, he brings his story up to date, for the 'Herald,' writing seventeen long letters about the Caucasus and Persian experiences; then he plunges deep into books on African Geography, 'for I feel very ignorant about most things concerning Africa.'

And here on the verge of the great venture, we may see how he reviewed and estimated the long preparatory stage, reckoning it not as a twelve-month, but as six years, when he looked back on it, toward the end.

As may be imagined, these six years formed a most important period of my life; I had seen about fifteen fair battles with the military service, and three naval bombardments. Twice I had been shipwrecked, and I had been spectator of mighty events; I had seen many sovereign-monarchs, princes, ministers, and generals; I had explored many large cities, and rubbed against thousands of men of vast nations; and, having been compelled to write of what I had seen in a daily paper, it can be understood how invaluable such a career and such a training, with its compulsory lessons, was to me, preparing me for the great work which awaited me. To this training I owed increasing powers of observation, and judgment; the long railway journeys taught me, while watching and meditating upon the characters I met, how to observe most keenly and guide myself; by which I was enabled, I think, to achieve a certain mastery of those infirmities which, I was only too conscious, had cropped up since I had entered the Army [*i. e.*, during the Civil War].

And now, at last, — for Africa and Livingstone! Zanzibar is to be his starting-point; there is no direct communication from Bombay: so he must creep and zig-zag, by irregular sailing-ship. He starts, October 12, 1870, in the barque 'Polly,' a six weeks' voyage to Mauritius. Off again, in the brigantine 'Romp'; and, in seventeen days, to St. Anne's Island, Seychelles group. Thence, in the little brigantine whaler, 'Falcon,' to creep along for nineteen days more.

Still at sea, light breezes every day. Oh! how I suffer from ennui! Oh, torment of an impatient soul! What is the use of a sailing-boat in the tropics? My back aches with pain, my mind becomes old, and all because of these dispiriting calms.

December 31st, 1870. Eighty days from Bombay, and Zanzibar, at last!

But to find what? No letters from Bennett, nor his agent; so, of course, no money. No news of Livingstone since his departure, years before; and of him, then, this cheerful gossip: —

'—— gave me a very bad opinion of Livingstone; he says that he is hard to get along with; is cross and narrow-minded; that Livingstone ought to come home, and allow a younger man to take his place; that he takes no notes nor keeps his Journal methodically; and that he would run away, if he heard any traveller was going to him.'

This was the man, to find whom Stanley is to plunge into an unknown tropical Continent; he, who in all his travellings has had either a beaten road, or guides who knew the country; who has no experience with Africans, nor in organising and leading an expedition; who can find funds for his search only from a friendly loan of Captain F. R. Webb, and who is thrown on his own resources, almost as if he were entering a new world! But — forward!

CHAPTER XIII

THE FINDING OF LIVINGSTONE

IN his book, 'How I Found Livingstone,' Stanley has told that story at length. What here follows is arranged from material hitherto unpublished, and is designed to give the main thread of events, to supply some fuller illustration of his intercourse with Livingstone, and his final estimate of him, and, especially, both in this, and in his later explorations, to show from his private Journal something of the workings of his own heart and mind, in the solitude of Africa.

Though fifteen months had elapsed since I had received my commission, no news of Livingstone had been heard by any mortal at Zanzibar. According to one, he was dead; and, according to another, he was lost; while still another hazarded the conviction that he had attached himself to an African princess, and had, in fact, settled down. There was no letter for me from Mr. Bennett, confirming his verbal order to go and search for the traveller; and no one at Zanzibar was prepared to advance thousands of dollars to one whom nobody knew; in my pocket I had about eighty dollars in gold left, after my fifteen months' journey!

Many people since have professed to disbelieve that I discovered the lost traveller in Africa! Had they known the circumstances of my arrival at Zanzibar, they would have had greater reason for their unbelief than they had. To me it looked for a time as though it would be an impossibility for me even to put foot on the mainland, though it was only twenty-five miles off. But, thanks to Captain Webb, the American consul, I succeeded in raising a sum of money amply sufficient, for the time being, for my purpose.

The 'sinews of war' having been obtained, the formation of the expedition was proceeded with. On the 21st of March, 1871, it stood a compact little force of three whites, thirty-one armed freemen of Zanzibar, as escort, one hundred and fifty-three porters, and twenty-seven pack-animals, for a transport corps, besides two riding-horses, on the outskirts of the coast-town of Bagamoyo; equipped with every needful article for a long journey that the experience of many Arabs had suggested, and that my own ideas of necessaries for comfort or convenience, in illness or health, had provided. Its very composition betrayed its character. There was nothing aggressive in it. Its many bales of cloth, and loads of beads and wire, with its assorted packages of provisions and medicine, indicated a peaceful caravan about to penetrate among African tribes accustomed to barter and chaffer; while its few guns showed a sufficient defensive power against bands of native banditti, though offensive measures were utterly out of the question.

I passed my apprenticeship in African travel while traversing the maritime region — a bitter school — amid rank jungles, fetid swamps, and fly-infested grass-lands, during which I encountered nothing that appeared to favour my journey. My pack and riding-animals died, my porters deserted, sickness of a very grievous nature thinned my numbers; but, despite the severe loss I sustained, I struggled through my troubles.

Into the narrative of external events is here inserted what he recorded of an interior experience at this time.

In the matter of religion, I doubt whether I had much improved (during the preceding years of trial and adventure). Had this stirring life amongst exciting events continued, it is probable that I should have drifted further away from the thoughts of religion.

Years of indifference and excitement have an unconscious hardening power, and I might have lapsed altogether; but my training in the world of politics, of selfish hustling, of fierce competition, stopped in time; for, on commencing the work of my life, my first journey into Africa, I came face to face with Nature, and Nature was the means, through my complete isolation, of recalling me to what I had lost by long contact with the world.

I had taken with me my Bible, and the American consul had given me, to pack up bottles of medicine with, a great many 'New York Heralds,' and other American newspapers. Strange connection! But yet strangest of all was the change wrought in me by the reading of the Bible and these newspapers in melancholy Africa.

My sicknesses were frequent, and, during my first attacks of African fever, I took up the Bible to while away the tedious, feverish hours in bed. Though incapacitated from the march, my temperature being constantly at 105° Fahr., it did not prevent me from reading, when not light-headed. I read Job, and then the Psalms; and when I recovered and was once more in marching state, I occupied my mind in camp in glancing at the newspaper intelligence; and then, somehow or another, my views towards newspapers were entirely recast; not as regards my own profession, which I still esteemed very highly, perhaps too highly, but as to the use and abuse of newspapers.

Solitude taught me many things, and showed newspapers in quite a new light. There were several subjects treated in a manner that wild nature seemed to scorn. It appeared to me that the reading of anything in the newspapers, except that for which they were intended, namely news, was a waste of time; and deteriorative of native force, and worth, and personality. The Bible, however, with its noble and simple language, I continued to read with a higher and truer understanding than I had ever before conceived. Its powerful verses had a different meaning, a more penetrative influence, in the silence of the wilds. I came to feel a strange glow while absorbed in its pages, and a charm peculiarly appropriate to the deep melancholy of African scenery.

When I laid down the book, the mind commenced to feed upon what memory suggested. Then rose the ghosts of bygone yearnings, haunting every cranny of the brain with numbers of baffled hopes and unfulfilled aspirations. Here was I, only a poor journalist, with no friends, and yet possessed by a feeling of power to achieve! How could it ever be? Then verses of Scripture rang iteratingly through my mind as applicable to my own being, sometimes full of promise, often of solemn warning.

Alone in my tent, unseen of men, my mind laboured and worked upon itself, and nothing was so soothing and sustaining as when I remembered the long-neglected comfort and support of lonely childhood and boyhood. I flung myself on my knees, and poured out my soul utterly in secret prayer to Him from whom I had been so long estranged, to Him who had led me here mysteriously into Africa, there to reveal Himself, and His will. I became then inspired with fresh desire to serve Him to the utmost, that same desire which in early days in New Orleans filled me each morning, and sent me joyfully skipping to my work.

As seen in my loneliness, there was this difference between the Bible and the newspapers. The one reminded me that, apart from God, my life was but a bubble of air, and it bade me remember my Creator; the other fostered arrogance and worldliness. When that vast upheaved sky, and mighty circumference of tree-clad earth, or sere downland, marked so emphatically my personal littleness, I felt often so subdued that my black followers might have discerned, had they been capable of reflection, that Africa was changing me.

It may be taken for granted that some of the newspaper issues which I took up, one after another, when examined under this new light, were uncommonly poor specimens of journalism. Though all contained some facts appertaining to the progress of the world's affairs, in which every intelligent man ought to be concerned, these were so few and meagre that they were overwhelmed by the vast space devoted to stupid personalities, which were either offensively flattering or carpingly derogatory; and there came columns of crime records, and mere gutter-matter.

It was during these days I learned that, as teeth were given to chew our bread, and taste to direct our sense of its quality, so knowledge and experience were capable of directing the judgment; and from that period to this, I have never allowed another to govern my decisions upon the character of any person, or to pervert my own ideas as to the rights and wrongs of a matter. I find, if one wishes to be other than a mere number, he must learn to exercise his own discretion. I have practised these rules ever since, and I remember my delight when I first found that this method had so trained and expanded my judgment that my views upon things affecting other people, or affairs in which I had no personal concern, were in harmony with those expressed by the best leading journals.

A multitude of records of African travel have been read by me during twenty-four years; but I do not remember to have come across anything which would reveal the inward transition, in the traveller's own feelings, from those which move him among his own kindred, to those he feels when he discovers himself to be a solitary white man in the new world of savage Africa, and all the pageantry of civilisation, its blessings, its protection, its politics, its energy and power, — all have become a mere memory. I was but a few days in the wilderness, on the other side of the Kingani River, when it dawned upon me with a most sobering effect. The sable native regarded me with as much curiosity as I should have regarded a stranger from Mars. He saw that I was outwardly human, but his desire to know whether my faculties and usages were human as well was very evident, and until it was gratified by the putting of my hand into his and speaking to him, his doubt was manifest.

My mission to find Livingstone was very simple, and was a clear and definite aim. All I had to do was to free my mind from all else, and relieve it of every earthly desire but the finding of the man whom I was sent to seek. To think of self, friends, banking-account, life-insurance, or any worldly interest but the one sole purpose of reaching the spot where Livingstone might happen to rest, could only tend to weaken resolution. Intense application to my task assisted me to forget all I had left behind, and all that might lie ahead in the future.

In some ways, it produced a delightful tranquillity which was foreign to me while in Europe. To be indifferent to the obituaries the papers may publish to-morrow, that never even a thought should glance across the mind of law-courts, jails, tombstones; not to care what may disturb a Parliament, or a Congress, or the state of the Funds, or the nerves excited about earthquakes, floods, wars, and other national evils, is a felicity few educated men in Britain know; and it compensated me in a great measure for the distress from heat, meagreness of diet, malaria, and other ills, to which I became subject soon after entering Africa.

Every day added something to my experience. I saw that

exciting adventures could not happen so often as I had anticipated, that the fevers in Africa were less frequent than in some parts of the Mississippi Valley, that game was not visible on every acre, and that the ambushed savage was rare. There were quite as many bright pictures to be met with as there were dark. Troubles taught patience, and with the exercise of patience came greater self-control and experience. My ideas respecting my Zanzibari and Unyamwezi followers were modified after a few weeks' observation and trials of them. Certain vices and follies, which clung to their uneducated natures, were the source of great trouble; though there were brave virtues in most of them, which atoned for much that appeared incorrigible.

Wellington is reported to have said that he never knew a good-tempered man in India; and Sydney Smith thought that sweetness of temper was impossible in a very cold or a very hot climate. With such authorities it is somewhat bold, perhaps, to disagree; but after experiences of Livingstone, Pocock, Swinburne, Surgeon Parke, and other white men, one must not take these remarks too literally. As for my black followers, no quality was so conspicuous and unvarying as good-temper; and I think that, since I had more occasion to praise my black followers than blame them, even I must surely take credit for being more often good-tempered than bad; and besides, I felt great compassion for them. How often the verse in the Psalms recurred to me: 'Like as a father pitieth his own children'!

It was on my first expedition that I felt I was ripening. Hitherto, my faculties had been too busy in receiving impressions; but, like the young corn which greedily absorbs the rain and cool dews, and, on approaching maturity, begins to yellow under summer suns, so I began to feel the benefit of the myriad impressions, and I grew to govern myself with more circumspection.

On the 8th May, 1871, we began to ascend the Usagara range, and, in eight marches, we arrived on the verge of the dry, rolling, and mostly wooded plateau, which continues, almost without change, for nearly six hundred miles westward. We soon after entered Ugogo, inhabited by a bumptious, full-chested, square-shouldered people, who exact heavy tribute from all caravans. Nine marches took us through their country; and, when we finally shook the dust of its red soil off our feet, we were rich in the experience of native manners and arrogance, but considerably poorer in means.

Beyond Ugogo undulated the Land of the Moon, or Unyamwezi, inhabited by a turbulent and combative race, who are as ready to work for those who can afford to pay as they are ready to fight those they consider unduly aggressive. Towards the middle of this land, we came to a colony of Arab settlers and traders. Some of these had built excellent and spacious houses of sun-dried brick, and cultivated extensive gardens. The Arabs located here were great travellers. Every region round about the colony had been diligently searched by them for ivory. If Livingstone was anywhere within reach, some of these people ought surely to have known. But, although I questioned eagerly all whom I became acquainted with, no one could give me definite information of the missing man.

I was preparing to leave the Arab colony in Unyanyembe when war broke out between the settlers and a native chief, named Mirambo, and a series of sanguinary contests followed. In the hope that, by adding my force to that of the Arabs, a route west might be opened, I, foolishly enough, joined them. I did not succeed in my enterprise, however, and a disastrous retreat followed. The country became more and more disturbed; bandits infested every road leading from the colony; cruel massacres, destruction of villages, raids by predatory Watuta, were daily reported to me; until it seemed to me that there was neither means for advance nor retreat left.

As my expedition had become thoroughly disorganized during my flight with the Arabs from the fatal campaign against Mirambo, I turned my attention to form another, which, whether I should continue my search for the lost traveller, or abandon it, and turn my face homeward, would be equally necessary; and, as during such an unquiet period it would be a task requiring much time and patience, I meanwhile consulted my charts, and the best informed natives, as to the possibility of evading the hostile bands of Mirambo by taking a circuitous route round the disturbed territory.

Finally, on the 20th of September, 1871, I set out from the

Arab settlement at Kwihara to resume the journey so long interrupted. I had been detained three months at Unyanyembe by an event totally unlooked-for when the expedition left the sea. Almost every day of this interval had witnessed trouble. Some troubles had attained the magnitude of public and private calamities. Many Arab friends had been massacred; many of my own people either had been slain in battle or had perished from disease. Over forty had deserted. One of my white companions was dead; the other had become a mere burden. All the transport animals but two had died; days of illness from fever had alternated with days of apparent good health. My joys had been few indeed, but my miseries many; yet this day, the third expedition that I had organised, through great good fortune numbered nearly sixty picked men, almost all of whom were well armed, and loaded with every necessary that was portable, bound to demonstrate if somewhere in the wild western lands the lost traveller lived, or was dead.

The conclusion I had arrived at was, that, though Mirambo and his hordes effectually closed the usual road to Lake Tanganyika, a flank march might be made, sufficiently distant from the disturbed territory and sufficiently long to enable me to strike west, and make another attempt to reach the Arab colony on Lake Tanganyika. I calculated that from two hundred to three hundred miles extra marching would enable me to reach Ujiji safely.

Agreeably to this determination, for twenty-two days we travelled in a south-westerly direction, during which I estimated we had performed a journey of two hundred and forty miles. At a place called Mpokwa, Mirambo's capital lying due north ten days distant, I turned westward, and after thirty-five miles, gradually turned a little to the westward of north. At the 105th mile of this northerly journey we came to the ferry of the Malagarazi River, Mirambo being, at that point, eight days' march direct east of us, from whence I took a north-westerly course, straight for the port of the Arab colony on the great Lake. With the exception of a mutiny among my own people, which was soon forcibly crushed, and considerable suffering from famine, I had met with no adventures which detained me, or interrupted my rapid advance on the Lake.

At the river just mentioned, however, a rumour reached me, by a native caravan, of a white man having reached Ujiji from Manyuema, a country situated a few hundred miles west of the lake, which startled us all greatly. The caravan did not stay long. The ferriage of the river is always exciting. The people were natives of West Tanganyika. The evidence, such as it was, — brief, and given in a language few of my people could understand, — was conclusive that the stranger was elderly, grey-bearded, white, and that he was a man wearing clothes somewhat of the pattern of those I wore; that he had been at Ujiji before, but had been years absent in the western country; and that he had only arrived either the same day they had left Ujiji with their caravan, or the day before.

To my mind, startling as it was to me, it appeared that he could be no other than Livingstone. True, Sir Samuel Baker was known to be in Central Africa in the neighbourhood of the Nile lakes — but he was not grey-bearded; a traveller might have arrived from the West Coast, — he might be a Portuguese, a German, or a Frenchman, — but then none of these had ever been heard of in the neighbourhood of Ujiji. Therefore, as fast as doubts arose as to his personality, arguments were as quickly found to dissipate them. Quickened by the hope that was inspired in my mind by this vague rumour, I crossed the Malagarazi River, and soon after entered the country of the factious and warlike Wahha.

A series of misfortunes commenced at the first village we came to in Uhha. I was summoned to halt, and to pay such a tribute as would have beggared me had I yielded. To reduce it, however, was a severe task and strain on my patience. I had received no previous warning that I should be subjected to such extortionate demands, which made the matter worse. The inevitable can always be endured, if due notice is given; but the suddenness of a mishap or an evil rouses the combative instincts in man. Before paying, or even submitting to the thought of payment, my power of resistance was carefully weighed, but I became inclined to moderation upon being assured by all concerned that this would be the only instance of what must be endured unless we chose to fight. After long hours of haggling over the amount, I paid my forfeit, and was permitted to proceed.

The next day I was again halted, and summoned to pay. The present demand was for two bales of cloth. This led to half-formed resolutions to resist to the death, then anxious conjectures as to what would be the end of this rapacity. The manner of the Wahha was confident and supercilious. This could only arise from the knowledge that, whether their demands were agreeable or not to the white man, the refusal to pay could but result in gain to them. After hours of attempts to reduce the sum total, I submitted to pay one bale and a quarter. Again I was assured this would be the last.

The next day I rose at dawn to resume the march; but, four hours later, we were halted again, and forfeited another half-bale, notwithstanding the most protracted and patient haggling on my part. And for the third time I was assured we were safe from further demands. The natives and my own people combined to comfort me with this assurance. I heard, however, shortly after, that Uhha extended for two long marches yet, further west. Knowing this, I declined to believe them, and began to form plans to escape from Uhha.

I purchased four days' rations as a provision for the wilderness, and at midnight I roused the caravan. Having noiselessly packed the goods, the people silently stole away from the sleeping village in small groups, and the guides were directed, as soon as we should be a little distance off, to abandon the road and march to the southward over the grassy plain. After eighteen hours' marching through an unpeopled wilderness, we were safe beyond Uhha and the power of any chief to exact tribute, or to lay down the arbitrary law, 'Fight, or pay.' A small stream now crossed was the boundary line between hateful Uhha and peaceful Ukaranga.

That evening we slept at a chief's village in Ukaranga, with only one more march of six hours, it was said, intervening between us and the Arab settlement of Ujiji, in which native rumour located an old, grey-bearded, white man, who had but newly arrived from a distant western country. It was now two hundred and thirty-five days since I had left the Indian Ocean, and fifty days since I had departed from Unyanyembe.

At cock-crow of the eventful day,[1] the day that was to end all doubt, we strengthened ourselves with a substantial meal,

[1] Friday, November 10, 1871.

and, as the sun rose in the east, we turned our backs to it, and the caravan was soon in full swing on the march. We were in a hilly country, thickly-wooded, towering trees nodding their heads far above, tall bush filling darkly the shade, the road winding like a serpent, narrow and sinuous, the hollows all musical with the murmur of living waters and their sibilant echoes, the air cool and fragrant with the smell of strange flowers and sweet gums. Then, my mind lightened with pleasant presentiments, and conscience complaisantly approving what I had done hitherto, you can imagine the vigour of our pace in that cool and charming twilight of the forest shades!

About eight o'clock we were climbing the side of a steep and wooded hill, and we presently stood on the very crest of it, and on the furthest edge looked out into a realm of light — wherein I saw, as in a painted picture, a vast lake in the distance below, with its face luminous as a mirror, set in a frame of dimly-blue mountains. On the further side they seemed to be of appalling height. On the hither side they rose from low hills lining the shore, in advancing lines, separated by valleys, until they terminated at the base of that tall mountain-brow whereon I stood, looking down from my proud height, with glad eyes and exultant feelings, upon the whole prospect.

On our admiring people, who pressed eagerly forward to gaze upon the scene, contentment diffused itself immediately, inspiring a boisterous good-humour; for it meant a crowning rest from their daily round of miles, and a holiday from the bearing of burdens, certainly an agreeable change from the early reveillé, and hard fare of the road.

With thoughts still gladder, if possible, than ever, the caravan was urged down the descent. The lake grew larger into view, and smiled a broad welcome to us, until we lost sight of it in the valley below. For hours I strode nervously on, tearing through the cane-brakes of the valleys, brushing past the bush on the hill-slopes and crests, flinging gay remarks to the wondering villagers, who looked on the almost flying column in mute surprise, until near noon, when, having crossed the last valley and climbed up to the summit of the last hill, lo! Lake Tanganyika was distant from us but half a mile!

Before such a scene I must halt once more. To me, a lover

of the sea, its rolling waves, its surge and its moan, the grand lake recalls my long-forgotten love! I look enraptured upon the magnificent expanse of fresh water, and the white-tipped billows of the inland sea. I see the sun and the clear white sky reflected a million million times upon the dancing waves. I hear the sounding surge on the pebbled shore, I see its crispy edge curling over, and creeping up the land, to return again to the watery hollows below. I see canoes, far away from the shore, lazily rocking on the undulating face of the lake, and at once the sight appeals to the memories of my men who had long ago handled the net and the paddle. Hard by the lake shore, embowered in palms, on this hot noon, the village of Ujiji broods drowsily. No living thing can be seen moving to break the stilly aspect of the outer lines of the town and its deep shades. The green-swarded hill on which I stood descended in a gentle slope to the town. The path was seen, of an ochreous-brown, curving down the face of the hill until it entered under the trees into the town.

I rested awhile, breathless from my exertions; and, as the stragglers were many, I halted to re-unite and re-form for an imposing entry. Meantime, my people improved their personal appearance; they clothed themselves in clean dresses, and snowy cloths were folded round their heads. When the laggards had all been gathered, the guns were loaded to rouse up the sleeping town. It is an immemorial custom, for a caravan creeps not up into a friendly town like a thief. Our braves knew the custom well; they therefore volleyed and thundered their salutes as they went marching down the hill slowly, and with much self-contained dignity.

Presently, there is a tumultuous stir visible on the outer edge of the town. Groups of men in white dresses, with arms in their hands, burst from the shades, and seem to hesitate a moment, as if in doubt; they then come rushing up to meet us, pursued by hundreds of people, who shout joyfully, while yet afar, their noisy welcomes.

The foremost, who come on bounding up, cry out: 'Why, we took you for Mirambo and his bandits, when we heard the booming of the guns. It is an age since a caravan has come to Ujiji. Which way did you come? Ah! you have got a white man with you! Is this his caravan?'

Being told it was a white man's caravan by the guides in front, the boisterous multitude pressed up to me, greeted me with salaams, and bowed their salutes. Hundreds of them jostled and trod on one another's heels as they each strove to catch a look at the master of the caravan; and I was about asking one of the nearest to me whether it was true that there was a white man in Ujiji, who was just come from the countries west of the Lake, when a tall black man, in long white shirt, burst impulsively through the crowd on my right, and bending low, said, —

'Good-morning, sir,' in clear, intelligent English.

'Hello!' I said, 'who in the mischief are you?'

'I am Susi, sir, the servant of Dr. Livingstone.'

'What! is Dr. Livingstone here in this town?'

'Yes, sir.'

'But, are you sure; sure that it is Dr. Livingstone?'

'Why, I leave him just now, sir.'

Before I could express my wonder, a similarly-dressed man elbowed his way briskly to me, and said, —

'Good-morning, sir.'

'Are you also a servant of Dr. Livingstone?' I asked.

'Yes, sir.'

'And what is your name?'

'It is Chuma.'

'Oh! the friend of Wekotani, from the Nassick School?'

'Yes, sir.'

'Well, now that we have met, one of you had better run ahead, and tell the Doctor of my coming.'

The same idea striking Susi's mind, he undertook in his impulsive manner to inform the Doctor, and I saw him racing headlong, with his white dress streaming behind him like a wind-whipped pennant.

The column continued on its way, beset on either flank by a vehemently-enthusiastic and noisily-rejoicing mob, which bawled a jangling chorus of 'Yambos' to every mother's son of us, and maintained an inharmonious orchestral music of drums and horns. I was indebted for this loud ovation to the cheerful relief the people felt that we were not Mirambo's bandits, and to their joy at the happy rupture of the long silence that had perforce existed between the two trading colonies of Unyanyembe and Ujiji, and because we brought news which concerned every householder and freeman of this lake port.

After a few minutes we came to a halt. The guides in the van had reached the market-place, which was the central point of interest. For there the great Arabs, chiefs, and respectabilities of Ujiji, had gathered in a group to await events; thither also they had brought with them the venerable European traveller who was at that time resting among them. The caravan pressed up to them, divided itself into two lines on either side of the road, and, as it did so, disclosed to me the prominent figure of an elderly white man clad in a red flannel blouse, grey trousers, and a blue cloth, gold-banded cap.

Up to this moment my mind had verged upon non-belief in his existence, and now a nagging doubt intruded itself into my mind that this white man could not be the object of my quest, or if he were, he would somehow contrive to disappear before my eyes would be satisfied with a view of him.

Consequently, though the expedition was organized for this supreme moment, and every movement of it had been confidently ordered with the view of discovering him, yet when the moment of discovery came, and the man himself stood revealed before me, this constantly recurring doubt contributed not a little to make me unprepared for it. 'It may not be Livingstone after all,' doubt suggested. If this is he, what shall I say to him? My imagination had not taken this question into consideration before. All around me was the immense crowd, hushed and expectant, and wondering how the scene would develop itself.

Under all these circumstances I could do no more than exercise some restraint and reserve, so I walked up to him, and, doffing my helmet, bowed and said in an inquiring tone,—

'Dr. Livingstone, I presume?'

Smiling cordially, he lifted his cap, and answered briefly, 'Yes.'

This ending all scepticism on my part, my face betrayed the earnestness of my satisfaction as I extended my hand and added, —

HENRY M. STANLEY, 1872

'I thank God, Doctor, that I have been permitted to see you.'[1]

In the warm grasp he gave my hand, and the heartiness of his voice, I felt that he also was sincere and earnest as he replied, —

'I feel most thankful that I am here to welcome you.'

The principal Arabs now advanced, and I was presented by the Doctor to Sayed bin Majid, a relative of the Prince of Zanzibar; to Mahommed bin Sali, the Governor of Ujiji; to Abed bin Suliman, a rich merchant; to Mahommed bin Gharib, a constant good friend; and to many other notable friends and neighbours.

Then, remarking that the sun was very hot, the Doctor led the way to the verandah of his house, which was close by and fronted the market-place. The vast crowd moved with us.

After the Arab chiefs had been told the latest news of the war of their friends with Mirambo, with salaams, greetings, and warm hand-shakings, and comforting words to their old friend David (Livingstone), they retired from the verandah, and a large portion of the crowd followed them.

Then Livingstone caught sight of my people still standing in the hot sunshine by their packs, and extending his hand, said to me, —

'I am afraid I have been very remiss, too. Let me ask you now to share my house with me. It is not a very fine house, but it is rain-proof and cool, and there are enough spare rooms to lodge you and your goods. Indeed, one room is far too large for my use.'

I expressed my gratification at his kind offer in suitable terms, and accordingly gave directions to the chiefs of the caravan about the storing of the goods and the purchase of rations; and Livingstone charged his three servants, Susi, Chuma, and Hamoyda, to assist them. Relieved thus happily and comfortably from all further trouble about my men, I introduced the subject of breakfast, and asked permission of the Doctor to give a few directions to my cook.

The Doctor became all at once anxious on that score. Was

[1] In his book *How I Found Livingstone*, Stanley recognised the guiding hand of an over-ruling and kindly Providence in the following words: —

'Had I gone direct from Paris on the search, I might have lost him; had I been enabled to have gone direct to Ujiji from Unyanyembe, I might have lost him.'

my cook a good one? Could he prepare a really satisfactory breakfast? If not, he had a gem of a female cook — and here he laughed, and continued, 'She is the oddest, most eccentric woman I have ever seen. She is quite a character, but I must give her due credit for her skill in cooking. She is exceedingly faithful, clean, and deft at all sorts of cooking fit for a toothless old man like myself. But, perhaps, the two combined would be still better able to satisfy you?'

Halima, a stout, buxom woman of thirty, was brought at once to our presence, grinning, but evidently nervous and shy. She was not uninteresting by any means, and as she opened her capacious mouth, two complete and perfect rows of teeth were revealed.

'Halima,' began Livingstone, in kind, grave tones, 'my young brother has travelled far, and is hungry. Do you think you and Ferajji, his cook, can manage to give us something nice to eat? What have you?'

'I can have some dampers, and kid kabobs, and tea or coffee ready immediately, master, if you like; and by sending to the market for something, we can do better.'

'Well, Halima, we will leave it to you and Ferajji; only do your best, for this is a great day for us all in Ujiji.'

'Yes, master. Sure to do that.'

I now thought of Livingstone's letters, and calling Kaif-Halek, the bearer of them, I delivered into the Doctor's hands a long-delayed letter-bag that I had discovered at Unyanyembe, the cover of which was dated November 1st, 1870.

A gleam of joy lighted up his face, but he made no remark, as he stepped on to the verandah and resumed his seat. Resting the letter-bag on his knees, he presently, after a minute's abstraction in thought, lifted his face to me and said, 'Now sit down by my side, and tell me the news.'

'But what about your letters, Doctor? You will find the news, I dare say, in them. I am sure you must be impatient to read your letters after such a long silence.'

'Ah!' he replied, with a sigh, 'I have waited years for letters; and the lesson of patience I have well learned! — I can surely wait a few hours longer! I would rather hear the general news, so pray tell me how the old world outside of Africa is getting along.'

Consenting, I sat down, and began to give a résumé of the exciting events that had transpired since he had disappeared in Africa, in March, 1866.

When I had ended the story of triumphs and reverses which had taken place between 1866 and 1871, my tent-boys advanced to spread a crimson table-cloth, and arrange the dishes and smoking platters heaped up profusely with hot dampers, white rice, maize porridge, kid kabobs, fricasseed chicken, and stewed goat-meat. There were also a number of things giving variety to the meal, such as honey from Ukawendi, forest plums, and wild-fruit jam, besides sweet milk and clabber, and then a silver tea-pot full of 'best tea,' and beautiful china cups and saucers to drink it from. Before we could commence this already magnificent breakfast, the servants of Sayed bin Majid, Mohammed bin Sali, and Muini Kheri brought three great trays loaded with cakes, curries, hashes, and stews, and three separate hillocks of white rice, and we looked at one another with a smile of wonder at this Ujiji banquet.

We drew near to it, and the Doctor uttered the grace: 'For what we are going to receive, make us, O Lord, sincerely thankful.'

I need not linger over a description of Livingstone. All this may be found in books, in mine among the number; but I will note some other discoveries relating to him which I made, which may not be found in books. At various times I have remarked that the question most frequently given to me has been: 'Why did not Livingstone return of his own accord when he found his energies waning, age creeping on him and fettering him in its strong bonds, his means so reduced that he was unable to accomplish anything, even if youth could have been restored to him?'

Briefly, I will answer that his return to home and kindred was prevented by an over-scrupulous fidelity to a promise that he had made to his friend Sir R. Murchison — that he would set the matter of that watershed north of the Tanganyika at rest. But, strive as he might, misfortune dogged him; dauntlessly he urged his steps forward over the high plateaus between Nyasa and Tanganyika, but, steadily, evil, in various disguises, haunted him. First, his transport animals died, his

Indian escort malingered, and halted, faint-hearted, on the road, until they were dismissed; then his Johanna escort played the same trick and deserted him, after which his porters under various pretences absconded; the natives took advantage of his weakness, and tyrannised over him at every opportunity. A canoe capsized on Lake Bangweolo, which accident deprived him of his medicine-chest; then, malarial diseases, finding the body now vulnerable and open to attack, assailed him, poisoned his blood, and ravished his strength. Malignant ulcers flourished on the muscles of his limbs, dysentery robbed him of the vital constituent of his body. Still, after a time, he rose from his sick-bed, and pressed on unfalteringly.

The watershed, when he reached it, grew to be a tougher problem than he had conceived it to be. On the northern slope, a countless multitude of streams poured northward, into an enormously wide valley. At its lowest depression, they were met by others, rushing to meet them from the north and east. United, they formed a river of such volume and current that he paused in wonder. So remote from all known rivers — Nile, Niger, Congo — and yet so large! Heedless of his beggared state, forgetful of his past miseries, unconscious of his weakness, his fidelity to his promise drives him on with the zeal of an honourable fanatic. He *must* fulfil his promise, or die in the attempt!

We, lapped as we are in luxury, feeding on the daintiest diet, affecting an epicurean cynicism, with the noble virtues of our youth and earlier life blunted from too close contact with animal pleasures, can only smile contemptuously, compassionating these morbid ideas of honour! This man, however, verging upon old age, is so beset by these severely-rigid scruples of his that he *must* go on.

He traces that voluminous river until it enters a shallow lake called Bangweolo, which spreads out on either hand beyond sight, like a sea. He attempts to navigate it; his intention is frustrated by a calamity — the last of his medicines are lost, his instruments are damaged. He determines to go by land, reaches Cazembe, and by the natives he is told of other lakes and rivers without end, all trending northward. He directs his steps north and west to gather the clues to the riverine labyrinth, until he is, perforce, halted by utter exhaustion of his means. He meets an Arab, begs a loan for mere subsistence; and, on that account, must needs march whither the Arab goes.

Hearing of a caravan bound coastward, he writes a letter to Zanzibar in 1867, and directs that goods should be sent to him at Ujiji; and, bidding his soul possess itself with patience, he wanders with the Arab merchant for a whole year, and, in 1869, arrives at Ujiji. There is nothing there for him; but a draft on Zanzibar suffices to purchase, at an extortionate charge, a few bags of beads and a few bales of cloth, with which he proposes to march due west to strike that great river discovered two years before so far south. This is loyalty to a friend with a vengeance!

The friend to whom he had given his promise, had he but known to what desperate straits the old man was reduced, would long ago have absolved him. Livingstone was now in his fifty-seventh year, toothless, ill-clad, a constant victim to disease, meagre and gaunt from famine: but Livingstone's word was not a thing to be obliterated by forgetfulness — he had made it his creed, and resolved to be true to it.

Well, this insatiable zeal for his word demands that he proceed due west, to find this river. He travels until within a hundred miles of it, when he is stricken down by African ulcers of a peculiarly virulent type, which confine him to his bed for months. During this forced rest, his few followers become utterly demoralised; they refuse to stay with a man who seems bent on self-destruction, and so blind, they say, that he will not see he is marching to his doom. The ninth month brings relief — his body is cured, a small re-enforcement of men appear before him, in answer to the letter he had sent in 1867.

The new men inform him they have only come to convey him back to the coast. He repudiates the insinuation their words convey with indignant warmth. He buys their submission by liberal largesse, and resumes his interrupted journey westward. In a few days, he arrives at the banks of the Lualaba, which is now two thousand yards wide, deep, and flowing strong still northward, at a point thirteen hundred miles from its source. The natives as well as the Arab traders unite in the statement that, as far as their acquaintance with it is, its course is northward. The problem becomes more and more difficult, and its resolution is ever elusive. His instruments make it only two thousand feet above the sea — the Nile, six hundred miles northward, is also two thousand feet! How can this river be the Nile, then? Yet its course is northward and Nileward, — has been northward and Nileward ever since it left Bangweolo Lake, seven hundred miles south of where he stands, — and, for many weeks' travel along its banks, all reports prove that it continues its northerly flow.

To settle this exasperating puzzle, he endeavours to purchase canoes for its navigation; but his men become rebellious and frantic in their opposition, and Livingstone finds that every attempt he makes is thwarted. While hesitating what to do, he receives a letter, which informs him that another caravan has arrived for him at Ujiji. He resolves to journey back to Lake Tanganyika, and dismiss these obstinate and mutinous followers of his; and, with new men, carefully chosen, return to this interesting field, and explore it until he discovers the bourn of that immense river.

He arrives at Ujiji about the 1st of November, 1871, only to find that his caravan has been disbanded, and the goods sold by its chief; in other words, that his present state is worse than ever!

He is now in his fifty-ninth year, far away from the scene of his premeditated labours; the sea, where he might have rest and relief from these continually-repeating misfortunes, though only nine hundred miles off, is as inaccessible as the moon to him, because Mirambo and his bandits are carrying on a ravaging and desolating war throughout all the region east of Ujiji. The Arabs of the colony have no comfort to impart to him, for they, too, feel the doom of isolation impending over them. Over and over again, they have despatched scouts eastward, and each time these have returned with the authentic news that all routes to the sea are closed by sanguinary brigandage. Not knowing how long this period may last, the Arabs practise the strictest economy; they have neither cloth nor bead currency to lend, however large may be the interest offered for the loan. But, as the position of the old man has become desperate, and he and his few followers may die of starvation, if no relief be given, Sayed bin Majid and Mohammed bin Gharib advance a few dozen cloths to him, which, with miserly economy, may suffice to purchase food for a month.

And then? Ah! then the prospect will be blank indeed! However, 'Thy will be done. Elijah was fed by a raven; a mere dove brought hope to Noah; unto the hungering Christ, angels ministered. To God, the All-bountiful, all things are possible!'

To keep his mind from brooding over the hopeless prospect, he turns to his Journal, occupies himself with writing down at large, and with method, the brief jottings of his lengthy journeys, that nothing may be obscure of his history in the African wilds to those who may hereafter act as the executors and administrators of his literary estate. When fatigued by his constrained position on the clay floor in that east-facing verandah, he would lift his heavy Journal from his lap, and, with hand to chin, sit for hours in his brooding moods, thinking, ever thinking — mind ever revolving the prayer, 'How long, O Lord, must Thy servant bear all this?'

At noon, on the tenth day after his arrival at Ujiji from the west, — while he was in one of these brooding fits on the verandah, — looking up to the edge of that mountain-plateau, whence we, a few hours before, had gazed in rapture on the Tanganyika, several volleys of musketry suddenly startled him and his drowsy neighbours. The town was wakened from its *siesta* by the alarming sound of firing. The inhabitants hurriedly issued out of their homes somewhat frightened, asking one another if it were Mirambo and his bandits. The general suspicion that the strangers could be no other than the ubiquitous African chief and his wild men caused all to lay their hands on their arms and prepare for the conflict. The boldest, creeping cautiously out of the town, see a caravan descending slowly towards Ujiji, bearing the Zanzibar and American flags in front, and rush back shouting out the news that the strangers are friends from Zanzibar.

In a few minutes the news becomes more definite: people say that it is a white man's caravan. Looking out upon the market-place from his verandah, Livingstone is, from the first, aware of the excitement which the sudden firing is causing;

but if it be Mirambo, as all suspect it to be, it does not matter much to him, for he is above the miserable fear of death; violent as it may be, it will be but a happy release from the afflictions of life. Soon, however, men cried out to him, 'Joy, old master, it is a white man's caravan; it may belong to a friend of thine.' This Livingstone contemptuously declines to believe. It is then that Susi appears, rushing up to me with his impulsive 'Good-morning.' None knew better than Susi what a change in the circumstances of his old master and himself the arrival of an English-speaking white man foreshadowed. With even more energy of movement he returned to Livingstone, crying, 'It is true, sir, it is a white man, he speaks English; and he has got an American flag with him.' More than ever perplexed by this news, he asks, 'But are you sure of what you say? Have you seen him?'

At this moment the Arab chiefs came in a group to him, and said, 'Come, arise, friend David. Let us go and meet this white stranger. He may be a relative of thine. Please God, he is sure to be a friend. The praise be to God for His goodness!'

They had barely reached the centre of the market-place, when the head of the caravan appeared, and a few seconds later the two white men — Livingstone and myself — met, as already described.

Our meeting took place on the 10th November, 1871. It found him reduced to the lowest ebb in fortune by his endless quest of the solution to the problem of that mighty river Lualaba, which, at a distance of three hundred miles from Lake Tanganyika, flowed parallel with the lake, northward. In body, he was, as he himself expressed it, 'a mere ruckle of bones.'

The effect of the meeting was a rapid restoration to health; he was also placed above want, for he had now stores in abundance sufficient to have kept him in comfort in Ujiji for years, or to equip an expedition capable of solving within a few months even that tough problem of the Lualaba. There was only one thing wanting to complete the old man's happiness — that was an obedient and tractable escort. Could I have furnished this to him there and then, no doubt Livingstone would have been alive to-day,[1] because, after a few days' rest at Ujiji,

[1] This was written in 1885. — D. S.

we should have parted — he to return to the Lualaba, and trace the river, perhaps, down to the sea, or until he found sufficient proofs that it was the Congo, which would be about seven hundred miles north-west of Nyangwe; I journeying to the East Coast.

As my people, however, had only been engaged for two years, no bribe would have been sufficient to have made them tractable for a greater period. But, inasmuch as Livingstone would not relinquish his unfinished task, and no men of the kind he needed were procurable at Ujiji, it was necessary that he should return with me to Unyanyembe, and rest there until I could provide him with the force he needed. To this, the last of many propositions made to him, he agreed. After exploring together the north end of Lake Tanganyika, and disproving the theory that the Lake had any connection with the Albert Nyanza, we set out from Ujiji, on the 27th December, 1871, and arrived at Unyanyembe on the 18th February, 1872.

January 3, 1872. Had some modest sport among some zebras, and secured a quantity of meat, which will be useful. Livingstone, this afternoon, got upon his favourite topics, the Zambesi Mission, the Portuguese and Arab slave-trade, and these subjects invariably bring him to relate incidents about what he has witnessed of African nature and aptitudes. I conclude, from the importance he attaches to these, that he is more interested in ethnology than in topographical geography. Though the Nile problem and the central line of drainage are frequently on his lips, they are second to the humanities observed on his wanderings, which, whether at the morning coffee, tiffin, or dinner, occupy him throughout the meal.

The Manyuema women must have attracted him by their beauty, from which I gather that they must be superior to the average female native. He speaks of their large eyes, their intelligent looks, and pretty, expressive, arch ways. Then he refers to the customs at Cazembe's Court, and the kindness received from the women there.

In a little while, I am listening to the atrocities of Tagamoyo, the half-caste Arab, who surrounded a Manyuema market, and, with his long-shirted followers, fired most murderous volleys on the natives as they were innocently chaffering about their wares. Then there is real passion in his language, and I fancy from the angry glitter in his eyes that, were it in his power, Tagamoyo and his gang should have a quick taste of the terror he has inspired among the simple peoples of Manyuema. He is truly pathetic when he describes the poor enchained slaves, and the unhappy beings whose necks he has seen galled by the tree-forks, lumbering and tottering along the paths, watched by the steady, cruel eyes of their drivers, etc., etc.

The topics change so abruptly that I find it almost impossible to remember a tithe of them; and they refer to things about which I know so little that it will be hard to make a summary of what I am told at each meal. One cannot always have his note-book handy, for we drop upon a subject so suddenly, and often, in my interest, I forget what I ought to do. I must trust largely to the fact that I am becoming steeped in Livingstonian ideas upon everything that is African, from pity for the big-stomached picaninny, clinging to the waist-strings of its mother, to the missionary bishop, and the great explorers, Burton, Speke, and Baker.

He is a strong man in every way, with an individual tenacity of character. His memory is retentive. How he can remember Whittier's poems, couplets out of which I hear frequently, as well as from Longfellow, I cannot make out. I do not think he has any of these books with him. But he recites them as though he had read them yesterday.

March 3. Livingstone reverted again to his charges against the missionaries on the Zambesi, and some of his naval officers on the expedition.

I have had some intrusive suspicions, thoughts that he was not of such an angelic temper as I believed him to be during my first month with him; but, for the last month, I have been driving them steadily from my mind, or perhaps to be fair, he by his conversations, by his prayers, his actions, and a more careful weighing and a wider knowledge of all the circumstances, assists me to extinguish them. Livingstone, with all his frankness, does not unfold himself at once; and what he leaves untold may be just as vital to a righteous understanding of these disputes as what he has said. Some reparation I owe him for having been on the verge of prejudice before I even saw him. I expected, and was prepared, to meet a crusty misanthrope, and I was on my guard that the first offence should not come from me; but I met a sweet opposite, and, by leaps and bounds, my admiration grew in consequence. When, however, he reiterated his complaints against this man and the other, I felt the faintest fear that his strong nature was opposed to forgiveness, and that he was not so perfect as at the first blush of friendship I thought him. I grew shy of the recurrent theme, lest I should find my fear confirmed. Had I left him at Ujiji, I should have lost the chance of viewing him on the march, and obtaining that more detailed knowledge I have, by which I am able to put myself into his place, and, feeling something of his feelings, to understand the position better.

It was an ungrateful task to have to reproach the missionaries for their over-zeal against the slave-traders, though he quite shared their hatred of the trade, and all connected with it; but to be himself charged, as he was, with having been the cause of their militant behaviour, to be blamed for their neglect of their special duties, and for their follies, by the very men whom he has assisted and advised, was too much.

But, in thinking that it was rather a weakness to dwell on these bitter memories, I forgot that he was speaking to me, who had reminded him of his experiences, and who pestered him with questions about this year and another, upon this topic and that; and I thought that it was not fair to retaliate with inward accusations that he was making too much of these things, when it was my own fault. Then I thought of his loneliness, and that to speak of African geography to a man who was himself in Africa, was not only not entertaining, but unnecessary; and that to refuse to speak of personal events would, from the nature of a man, be imputed to him as reserve, and, perhaps, something worse. These things I revolved, caused by observations on his daily method of life, his pious habits, in the boat, the tent, and the house.

At Kwikuru, just before the day we got our letters from Europe, I went to the cook Ulimengo, who was acting in Ferajji's place; and, being half-mad with the huge doses of quinine I had taken, and distressingly weak, I sharply scolded him for not cleaning his coffee-pots, and said that I tasted the verdigris in every article of food, and I violently asked if he meant to poison us. I showed him the kettles and the pots, and the loathsome green on the rims. He turned to me with astounding insolence, and sneeringly asked if I was any better than the 'big master,' and said that what was good for him was good for me — the 'little master.'

I clouted him at once, not only for his insolent question, but because I recognised a disposition to fight. Ulimengo stood up and laid hold of me. On freeing myself, I searched for some handy instrument; but, at this juncture, Livingstone came out of the tent, and cried out to Ulimengo, 'Poli-poli-hapo' [Gently there]! What is the matter, Mr. Stanley?' Almost breathless between passion and quinine, I spluttered out my explanations. Then, lifting his right hand with the curved forefinger, he said, 'I will settle this.' I stood quieted; but, what with unsatisfied rage and shameful weakness, the tears rolled down as copiously as when a child.

I heard him say, 'Now, Ulimengo, you are a big fool: a big, thick-headed fellow. I believe you are a very wicked man. Your head is full of lying ideas. Understand me now, and open your ears. I am a Mgeni [guest] and only a Mgeni, and have nothing to do with this caravan. Everything in the camp is my friend's. The food I eat, the clothes on my back, the shirt I wear, all are his. All the bales and beads are his. What you put in that belly of yours comes from him, not from me. He pays your wages. The tent and the bed-clothes belong to him. He came only to help me, as you would help your brother or your father. I am only the "big master" because I am older; but when we march, or stop, must be as *he* likes, not me. Try and get all that into that thick skull of yours, Ulimengo. Don't you see that he is very ill, you rascal? Now, go and ask his pardon, Go on.'

And Ulimengo said he was very sorry, and wanted to kiss my feet; but I would not let him.

Then Livingstone took me by the arm to the tent, saying, 'Come now, you must not mind him. He is only a half-savage, and does not know any better. He is probably a Banyan slave. Why should you care what he says? They are all alike, unfeeling and hard!'

Little by little, I softened down; and, before night, I had shaken hands with Ulimengo. It is the memory of several small events, which, though not worth recounting singly, muster in evidence and strike a lasting impression.

'You bad fellow. You very wicked fellow. You blockhead. You fool of a man,' were the strongest terms he employed, where others would have clubbed, or clouted, or banned, and blasted. His manner was that of a cool, wise, old man, who felt offended, and looked grave.

March 4, Sunday. Service at 9 A. M. Referring to his address to his men, after the Sunday service was over, he asked me what conclusions I had come to in regard to the African's power of receiving the gospel?

'Well, really, to tell you the truth, I have not thought much of it. The Africans appear to me very dense, and I suppose it will take some time before any headway will be made. It is a slow affair, I think, altogether. You do not seem to me to go about it in the right way — I do not mean you personally, but missionaries. I cannot see how one or two men can hope to make an impression on the minds of so many millions, when all around them is the whole world continuing in its own humdrum fashion, absorbed in its avocations, and utterly regardless of the tiny village, or obscure district, where the missionaries preach the gospel.'

'How would you go about it?' he asked.

'I would certainly have more than one or two missionaries. I would have a thousand, scattered not all over the continent, but among some great tribe or cluster of tribes, organised systematically, one or two for each village, so that though the outskirts of the tribe or area where the gospel was at work might be disturbed somewhat by the evil example of those outside, all within the area might be safely and uninterruptedly progressing. Then, with the pupils who would be turned out from each village, there would be new forces to start elsewhere outside the area.'

'In a way, that is just my opinion; but someone must begin the work. Christ was the beginner of the Christianity that is now spread over a large part of the world, then came the Twelve Apostles, and then the Disciples. I feel, sometimes, as if I were the beginner for attacking Central Africa, and that others will shortly come; and, after those, there will come the thousand workers that you speak of. It is very dark and dreary, but the promise is, "Commit thy way to the Lord, trust in Him, and He shall bring it to pass." I may fall by the way, being unworthy to see the dawning. I thought I had seen it when the Zambezi mission came out, but the darkness has settled again, darker than ever. It will come, though, it *must* come, and I do not despair of the day, one bit. The earth, that is the whole earth, shall be filled with the knowledge of the Lord, as the waters cover the sea.

'Loneliness is a terrible thing, especially when I think of my children. I have lost a great deal of happiness, I know, by these wanderings. It is as if I had been born to exile; but it is God's doing, and He will do what seemeth good in His own eyes. But when my children and home are not in my mind, I feel as though appointed to this work and no other. I am away from the perpetual hurry of civilisation, and I think I see far and clear into what is to come; and then I seem to understand why I was led away, here and there, and crossed and baffled over and over again, to wear out my years and strength. Why was it but to be a witness of the full horror of this slave-trade, which, in the language of Burns, is sending these pitiless half-castes

> "Like bloodhounds from the slip,
> With woe and murder o'er the land!"

'My business is to publish what I see, to rouse up those who have the power to stop it, once and for all. That is the beginning; but, in the end, they will also send proper teachers of the gospel, some here, and some there, and what you think ought to be done will be done in the Lord's good time.

> "See, yonder, poor, o'er-laboured wight,
> So abject, mean, and vile!
> Who begs a brother of the earth
> To give him leave to toil!"

I have often quoted those lines of Burns to myself, on my travels in Manyuema, when I saw the trembling natives just on the run, when they suspected that we were Arabs about to take them from their homes and compel them to carry their stolen ivory. Oh, well, there is a good God above who takes note of these things, and will, at the proper moment, see that justice will be measured out to these monsters.'

March 13, 1872. This is the last day of my stay with dear old Livingstone; the last night we shall be together is present, and I cannot evade the morrow. I feel as though I should like to rebel against the necessity of departure. The minutes beat fast, and grow into hours. Our door to-night is closed, and we both think our own thoughts. What his are, I know not — mine are sad. My days seem to have been spent far too happily, for, now that the last day is almost gone, I bitterly regret the approach of the parting hour. I now forget the successive fevers, and their agonies, and the semi-madness into which they often plunged me. The regret I feel now is greater than any pains I have endured. But I cannot resist the sure advance of time, which is flying to-night far too fast. What must be, must be! I have often parted with friends before, and remember how I lingered and wished to put it off, but the inevitable was not to be prevented. Fate came, and, at the appointed hour, stood between us. To-night I feel the same aching pain, but in a greater degree; and the farewell I fear may be for ever. For ever? and 'For ever' echo the reverberations of a woeful whisper!

I have received the thanks that he had repressed all these months in the secrecy of his heart, uttered with no mincing phrases, but poured out, as it were, at the last moment, until I was so affected that I sobbed, as one only can in uncommon grief. The hour of night and the crisis, — and oh! as some dreadful doubts suggested the eternal parting, — his sudden outburst of gratitude, with that kind of praise that steals into one and touches the softer parts of the ever-veiled nature, — all had their influence; and, for a time, I was as a sensitive child of eight or so, and yielded to such bursts of tears that only such a scene as this could have forced.

I think it only needed this softening to secure me as his obedient and devoted servitor in the future, should there ever be an occasion where I could prove my zeal.

On the 14th March, my expedition left Unyanyembe, he accompanying me for a few miles. We reached the slope of a ridge overlooking the valley, in the middle of which our house where we had lived together looked very small in the distance. I then turned to him and said, —

'My dear Doctor, you must go no further. You have come far enough. See, our house is a good distance now, and the sun is very hot. Let me beg of you to turn back.'

'Well,' he replied, 'I will say this to you: you have done what few men could do. And for what you have done for me, I am most grateful. God guide you safe home and bless you, my friend!'

'And may God bring you safe back to us all, my dear friend! Farewell!'

'Farewell!' he repeated.

We wrung each other's hands, our faces flushed with emotion, tears rushing up, and blinding the eyes. We turned resolutely away from each other; but his faithful followers, by rushing up to give their parting words, protracted the painful scene.

'Good-bye, all! Good-bye, Doctor, dear friend!'

'Good-bye!'

At the moment of parting, the old man's noble face slightly paled, which I knew to be from suppressed emotion, while, when I looked into his eyes, I saw there a kind of warning, to look well at him as a friend looks for the last time; but the effort well-nigh unmanned me, — a little longer, and I should have utterly collapsed. We both, however, preferred dry eyes, and outward calm.

From the crest of the ridge I turned to take a last long look at him, to impress his form on my mind; then, waving a last parting signal, we descended the opposite slope on the home road.

On the fifty-fourth day after leaving Dr. Livingstone, I arrived at Zanzibar. Two weeks later, that is on the 20th May, fifty-seven men, chosen people of good character, sailed from Zanzibar for the mainland, as the expeditionary force which was to accompany Livingstone for a period of two years for the completion of his task of exploration. They arrived at Unyanyembe on the 11th August, 1872, having been eighty-two days on the road.

Fourteen days later, Livingstone, amply equipped and furnished with men, means, medicines, and instruments, and a small herd of cattle, set out for the scene of his explorations. Eight months later, the heroic life came to its heroic end.

From an unpublished Memorial to Livingstone by Stanley, the following passages are taken.

He preached no sermon, by word of mouth, while I was in company with him; but each day of my companionship with him witnessed a sermon acted. The Divine instructions, given of old on the Sacred Mount, were closely followed, day by day, whether he rested in the jungle-camp, or bided in the traders' town, or savage hamlet. Lowly of spirit, meek in speech, merciful of heart, pure in mind, and peaceful in act, suspected by the Arabs to be an informer, and therefore calumniated, often offended at evils committed by his own servants, but ever forgiving, often robbed and thwarted, yet bearing no ill-will, cursed by the marauders, yet physicking their infirmities, most despitefully used, yet praying daily for all manner and condition of men! Narrow, indeed, was the way of eternal life that he elected to follow, and few are those who choose it.

Though friends became indifferent to his fate, associates neglectful, and his servants mocked and betrayed him, though suitable substance was denied to him, and though the rain descended in torrents on him in his wanderings, and the tropic tempests beat him sore, and sickened him with their rigours, he toiled on, and laboured ever in the Divine service he had chosen, unyielding and unresting, for the Christian man's faith was firm that 'all would come right at last.'

Had my soul been of brass, and my heart of spelter, the powers of my head had surely compelled me to recognise, with due honour, the Spirit of Goodness which manifested itself in him. Had there been anything of the Pharisee or the hypocrite in him, or had I but traced a grain of meanness or guile in him, I had surely turned away a sceptic. But my every-day study of him, during health or sickness, deepened my reverence and increased my esteem. He was, in short, consistently noble, upright, pious, and manly, all the days of my companionship with him.

He professed to be a Liberal Presbyterian. Presbyterianism I have heard of, and have read much about it; but Liberal Presbyterianism, — whence is it? What special country throughout the British Isles is its birthplace? Are there any more disciples of that particular creed, or was Livingstone the last? Read by the light of this good man's conduct and single-mindedness, its tenets would seem to be a compound of religious and practical precepts.

'Whatever thy right hand findeth to do, do it with all thy might.'

'By the sweat of thy brow thou shalt eat bread.'

'For every idle word thou shalt be held accountable.'

'Thou shalt worship the Lord thy God, and Him only shalt thou serve.'

'Thou shalt not kill.'

'Swear not at all.'

'Be not slothful in business, but be fervent in spirit, and serve the Lord.'

'Mind not high things, but condescend to men of low estate.'

'Live peaceably with all men.'

'We count those happy who endure.'

'Remember them that are in bonds, and them which suffer adversity.'

'Watch thou, in all things; endure afflictions; do the work of an evangelist; make full proof of thy ministry.'

'Whatsoever ye do, do it heartily.'

'Set your affections on things above, not on things of the earth.'

'Be kind to one another, tender-hearted, and forgiving.'

'Preach the gospel in the regions beyond you, and boast not in another man's line, of things made ready to your hand.'

I never discovered that there was any printed code of religious laws or moral precepts issued by his church, wherein these were specially alluded to; but it grew evident during our acquaintance that he erred not against any of them. Greater might he could not have shown in this interminable exploration set him by Sir Roderick Murchison, because the work performed by him was beyond all proportion to his means and physical strength. What bread he ate was insufficient for his bodily nourishment, after the appalling fatigues of a march in a tropical land.

His conversation was serious, his demeanour grave and earnest. Morn and eve he worshipped, and, at the end of every march, he thanked the Lord for His watchful Providence. On Sundays he conducted Divine Service, and praised the glory of the Creator, the True God, to his dark followers. His hand was

DOCTOR LIVINGSTONE

clear of the stain of blood-guiltiness. Profanity was an abomination to him. He was not indolent either in his Master's service, or in the cause to which he was sacrificing himself. His life was an evidence that he served God with all his heart.

Nothing in the scale of humanity can be conceived lower than the tribes of Manyuema with whom he daily conversed as a friend. Regardless of such honours as his country generally pays to exceeding merit, he continued his journeyings, bearing messages of peace wherever he went; and when he rested, chief and peasant among the long-neglected tribes ministered to his limited wants. Contented with performing his duty according as he was enabled to, such happiness as can be derived from righteous doings, pure thoughts, and a clear conscience, was undoubtedly his. His earnest labours for the sake of those in bonds, and the unhappy people who were a prey to the Arab kidnapper and land pirate, few will forget. The number of his appeals, the constant recurrence to the dismal topic, and the long lines of his travels, may be accepted as proofs of his heartiness and industry.

He was the first to penetrate to those lands in the Chambezi and the Lualaba valleys; his was the first voice heard speaking in the hamlets of Eastern Sunda of the beauties of the Christian religion; and he was the first preacher who dared denounce the red-handed Arab for his wickedly aggressive acts. In regions beyond ken of the most learned geographers of Europe, he imitated the humility of the Founder of his religion, and spoke in fervent strains of the Heavenly message of peace and good-will.

Should I ever return to the scenes that we knew together, my mind would instantaneously revert to the good man whom I shall never see more. Be it a rock he sat upon, a tree upon which he rested, ground that he walked upon, or a house that he dwelt in, my first thought would naturally be that it was associated with him. But my belief is that they would flush my mind with the goodness and nobleness of his expression, appealing to me, though so silently, to remember, and consider, and strive.

I remember well when I gazed at Ujiji, five years later, from the same hill as where I had announced the coming of my caravan: I had not been thinking much of him until that moment, when, all at once, above the palm grove of Ujiji, and the long broad stretch of blue water of the lake beyond, loomed the form of Livingstone, in the well-remembered blue-grey coat of his marching costume, and the blue naval cap, gold-banded, regarding me with eyes so trustful, and face so grave and sad.

It is the expression of him that so follows and clings to me, and, indeed, is ever present when I think of him, though it is difficult to communicate to others the expression that I first studied and that most attracted me. There was an earnest gravity in it; life long ago shorn of much of its beauty — I may say of all its vulgar beauty and coarser pleasures, a mind long abstracted from petty discontents, by preference feeding on itself, almost glorifying in itself as all-sufficient to produce content; therefore a composure settled, calm, and trustful.

Even my presence was impotent to break him from his habit of abstraction. I might have taken a book to read, and was silent. If I looked up a few minutes later, I discovered him deeply involved in his own meditations, right forefinger bent, timing his thoughts, his eyes gazing far away into indefinite distance, brows puckered closely — face set, and resolute, now and then lips moving, silently framing words.

'What can he be thinking about?' I used to wonder, and once I ventured to break the silence with, —

'A penny for your thoughts, Doctor.'

'They are not worth it, my young friend, and let me suggest that, if I had any, possibly, I should wish to keep them!'

After which I invariably let him alone when in this mood. Sometimes these thoughts were humorous, and, his face wearing a smile, he would impart the reason with some comic story or adventure.

I have met few so quickly responsive to gaiety and the lighter moods, none who was more sociable, genial, tolerant, and humorous. You must think of him as a contented soul, who had yielded himself with an entire and loving submission, and who laboured to the best of his means and ability, awakening to the toil of the day, and resigning himself, without the least misgiving, to the rest of the night; believing that the effect of his self-renunciation would not be altogether barren.

If you can comprehend such a character, you will understand Livingstone's motive principle.

CHAPTER XIV

ENGLAND AND COOMASSIE

IT is not unadvisedly that the last chapter has been devoted almost as much to Livingstone as to Stanley. The main story of Stanley's quest he has told effectively elsewhere;[1] and in his interior life, which is the central theme of the present book, his intercourse with Livingstone was no small factor. The way he knew and loved Livingstone reveals Stanley. But to give the whole story of those sixteen months its true perspective, the reader should either turn to the full narrative, or should, at least, give some little play to his own imagination.

The few lines given to the contest with Mirambo represent months of struggle with a bandit-chief, and with slippery allies.

The three-line mention of the joint exploration of Lake Tanganyika stands for four weeks of adventurous voyaging, geographical discovery, and encounters with hostile or thievish natives. Through the whole period Stanley carried an immense and varied responsibility. He was not only commander, and chief of staff, but the whole staff. The discipline, commissariat, and medical care, of a force often numbering two hundred and more, all fell on him. For his followers he had to take the part of doctor, and occasionally of nurse, sometimes including the most menial offices. Often he was prostrated by fever, and once, before finding Livingstone, he lay unconscious for a week.

Problems of war and diplomacy confronted him. Shall he pay tribute, or resist? Shall he join forces with the friendly tribes, and fight the fierce and powerful Mirambo who blocks the way to Ujiji? He fights, and his allies fail him at the pinch; so then he resorts to a long flanking march through unknown country, and literally circumvents his foes. So, for over a year, every faculty is kept at the highest tension.

Along with the developing effect of the experience, comes the solitary communing with Nature, which brings a spiritual exaltation. Then follows the companionship with Livingstone, a man of heroic and ideal traits, uniquely educated by the African wilds; these two learn to know each other by the searching test of hourly companionship, amid savages, perils, perplexities, days of adventure, nights of intimate converse; Stanley's deepest feelings finding worthy object and full response in the man he had rescued, and suggestions of spiritual and material resources in the unknown continent,

[1] In *How I Found Livingstone.*

destined to germinate and bear fruit; — all this his first African exploration brought to Stanley.

His return to civilisation was not altogether a genial home-coming. In a way, he had been more at home in Africa than he found himself in England. There his companionship had been with Nature, with Livingstone, with his own spirit; the difficulties and dangers confronting him had been a challenge to which his full powers made response; and 'the free hand,' so dear to a strong man, had been his. Now he was plunged into a highly-artificial society; its trappings and paraphernalia, its formal dinners, and ceremonies, were distasteful to him; above all, he was thrust into a prominence which brought far more pain than pleasure.

A flood of importunate, or inquisitive, letters from strangers poured in on him; he notes that in one morning he has received twenty-eight. Relatives and acquaintances of his early years became suddenly affectionate and acquisitive; greedy claims were made on his purse, which he would not wholly reject. Worst of all, with the acclamations of the public which greeted him, were mingled expressions of doubt or disbelief, innuendoes, sneers! Men, and journals, of high standing, were among the sceptics.

Sir Henry Rawlinson, President of the Royal Geographical Society, wrote to the 'Times' that it was not true that Stanley had discovered Livingstone, but that Livingstone had discovered Stanley! The silly quip had currency long after Sir Henry Rawlinson had changed his tone, and the Society had passed a vote of thanks to Stanley. The 'Standard,' in oracular tones, called for the sifting of the discoverer's story by experts; it 'could not resist some suspicions and misgivings'; it found 'something inexplicable and mysterious' in the business! There were those who publicly questioned the authenticity of letters which, at Stanley's suggestion, Livingstone had written to the 'Herald.'

Geographical pundits mixed their theoretic speculations with slighting personal remarks. Perhaps no great and eminent body of scholars escapes a touch of the Mutual-Admiration Society; there are shibboleths of nationality, of social class, of clan and coterie; and when an outsider steps on the stage, there is solemn wrinkling of official foreheads, and lifting of distinguished eyebrows. So from the 'Royal Geographical' some chill whiffs blew towards this 'American,' who brought strange tidings from Africa. To Stanley, sensitive, high-strung, conscious of hard work, loyally done and faithfully reported, not hungry for fame, but solicitous of trust and confidence, all this was intensely bitter.

There was a field-day at Brighton at the meeting of the Geographical Section of the British Association, under the presidency of Mr. (now, Sir) Francis Galton. Stanley was the central figure of the occasion. He spoke to an audience of three thousand, with a group of great geographers, and Eminences of high degree, including the ex-Emperor and Empress of the French. The 'Telegraph's' report describes him as speaking with entire self-possession, with composure, with a natural and effective oratory, and 'with the evident purpose to speak his mind to everybody, without the slightest deference, or hesitation.'

But, in his Journal, he records that his stage-fright was so extreme he could only begin after three trials. At the request of the 'Royal Geographical,' he had prepared a brief paper, dealing only with the exploration of the north end of Lake Tanganyika. But, unexpectedly, he was called on to give some account of his whole expedition.

He told his story, and read his paper. A general discussion followed, turning mainly on certain geographical questions; and, at the end, Stanley was called on for some final words, and 'winged words' they were, of passionate ardour and directness. On some of the geographical opinions, there was criticism; and a special attack was made on the theory to which Livingstone inclined, that the river Lualaba was the source of the Nile. Stanley had grave doubts of that theory, which he was destined ultimately to disperse; but, for Livingstone's sake, he wanted it treated at least with *respect*.

In the discussion there were allusions to himself, perhaps tactless rather than intentional; as when Mr. (now, Sir) Francis Galton remarked that they were not met to listen to sensational stories, but to *serious facts!* Whether malicious, or only maladroit, such allusions were weighted by what had gone before in the Press.

Stanley summed up with a fervent eulogy of Livingstone, and a biting comparison of the arm-chair geographer, waking from his nap, to dogmatise about the Nile, with the gallant old man seeking the reality for years, amid savage and elemental foes.

One cannot doubt that his own essential veracity and manliness stamped themselves on the minds of his audience; and, in truth, the great preponderance of intelligent opinion seems to have been, from the first, wholly in his favour. The 'Times,' the 'Daily News,' the 'Daily Telegraph,' and 'Punch,' were among his champions. Livingstone's own family gratefully acknowledged his really immense services, and confirmed beyond question the genuineness of Livingstone's letters brought home by Stanley, so confounding those who had charged him with forgery. Lord Granville, at the Foreign Office, handed him, on the Queen's behalf, a note of congratulation, and a gold snuff-box set with diamonds; and, in a word, the world at large accepted him, then and thenceforward, as a true man and a hero.

But Stanley suffered so keenly and so long, not only at the time, but afterwards, from the misrepresentation and calumny he encountered, that a word more should be given to the subject. The hostility had various sources. In America, the 'New York Herald,' always an aggressive, self-assertive, and successful newspaper, had plenty of journalistic foes.

A former employee of Stanley's, whose behaviour had caused serious trouble, and brought proper punishment on him, gained the ear of a prominent editor, who gave circulation to the grossest falsehoods. In later years, other subordinates, whom Stanley's just and necessary discipline had offended, became his persistent calumniators. The wild scenes of his explorations, and the stimulus their wonders gave to the imagination, acted sometimes like a tropical swamp, whence springs fetid and poisonous vegetation. Stories of cruelty and horror seemed to germinate spontaneously. Stanley himself laid stress on the propensity in average human nature to noxious gossip, and the pandering to this taste by a part of the Press.

It is to be remembered, too, that the circumstances of his early life heightened his sensitiveness to gossiping curiosity and crude misrepresentation. And, finally, he had in his nature much of the woman, the *Ewigweibliche;* he craved fame far less than love and confidence.

Renown, as it came, he accepted, not with indifference, — he was too human for that, — but with tempered satisfaction. He met praise in the fine phrase Morley quotes from Gladstone, 'as one meets a cooling breeze, enjoyed, but not detained.' The pain which slander brought he turned to account, setting it as a lesson to himself not to misjudge others. His thoughts upon his own experience may be sufficiently shewn by an extract from one of his Note-books.

The vulgar, even hideous, nonsense, the number and variety of untruths published about me, from this time forth taught me, from pure sympathy, reflection, and conviction, to modify my judgment about others.

When anyone is about to become an object of popular, *i. e.*, newspaper censure, I have been taught to see how the scavenger-beetles of the Press contrive to pick up an infinitesimal grain of fact, like the African mud-rolling beetle, until it becomes so monstrously exaggerated that it is absolutely a mass of filth.

The pity of it is that most of the writers forget for whom they write. We are not all club-loungers, or drawing-room gossips; nor are we all infected with the prevailing madness of believing everything we see in the newspapers. We do not all belong to that large herd of unthinking souls who say, 'Surely, where there is so much smoke, there must be a fire'; those stupid souls who never knew that, as likely as not, the fire was harmless enough, and that the alarming cloud of smoke was owing to the reporter's briarwood!

Therefore I say, the instant I perceive, whether in the Press, or in Society, a charge levelled at some person, countryman, or foreigner, I put on the brake of reason, to prevent my being swept along by the general rage for scandal and abuse, and hold myself unconscious of the charge until it is justified by conviction.

All the actions of my life, and I may say all my thoughts, since 1872, have been strongly coloured by the storm of abuse and the wholly unjustifiable reports circulated about me then. So numerous were my enemies, that my friends became dumb, and I had to resort to silence, as a protection against outrage.

It is the one good extracted from my persecution that, ever since, I have been able to restrain myself from undertaking to pass sentence on another whom I do not know. No man who addresses himself to me is permitted to launch judgment out in that rash, impetuous newspaper way, without being made to reflect that he knew less about the matter than he had assumed he did.

This change in me was not immediate. The vice of reckless, unthinking utterance was not to be suddenly extirpated. Often, as I opened my mouth in obedience to the impulse, I was arrested by the self-accusation, 'Ah! there you go, silly and uncharitable as ever!' It was slow unlearning, but the old habit was at last supplanted by the new.

Stanley bore himself in the spirit of the words which F. W. H. Myers[1] applies to Wordsworth:—

'He who thus is arrogantly censured should remember both the dignity and the frailty of man, . . . and go on his way with no bitter broodings, but yet . . . "with a melancholy in the soul, a sinking inward into ourselves from thought to thought, a steady remonstrance, and a high resolve."'

In the months following his return to England, alternating with indignant protests against misrepresentation, his Journal records many public and private hospitalities, and meetings with eminent and interesting people, on some of whom he makes shrewd and appreciative comment. One portraiture cannot be omitted, — his impressions of Queen Victoria. The first occasion on which he was received by Her Majesty was at Dunrobin Castle, when he visited the Duke of Sutherland, in company with Sir Henry Rawlinson, who did his best to make amends for his early doubts.

Monday, 10th September, 1872. About noon, we had got ready for our reception by the Queen. Sir Henry had been

[1] *Wordsworth*, by F. W. H. Myers; in the 'English Men of Letters' series.

careful in instructing me how to behave in the Presence, that I had to kneel and kiss hands, and, above all, I was not to talk, or write, about what I should see or hear. I almost laughed in his face when he charged me with the last, for I doubt whether the Queen's daughter would be less apt for gossip about such things than I. As for kneeling, I was pleased to forget it. We stood for a while in a gay salon, and presently Her Majesty, followed by Princess Beatrice, entered. We all bowed most profoundly, and the Queen advancing, Sir Henry introduced me in a short sentence. I regarded her with many feelings, first as the greatest lady in the land, the mistress of a great Empire, the head of brave soldiers and sailors whom I had seen in various lands and seas, the central figure to which Englishmen everywhere looked with eyes of love and reverence; and, lastly, as that mysterious personage whom I had always heard spoken of, ever since I could understand anything, as '*The Queen*.' And poor, blind Sir Henry, to think that I would venture to speak or write about this lady, whom in my heart of hearts, next to God, I worshipped! Besides, only of late, she has honoured me with a memorial, which is the more priceless that it was given when so few believed me.

The word 'Majesty' does not rightly describe her bearing. I have often seen more majestic creatures, but there was an atmosphere of conscious potency about her which would have marked her in any assemblage, even without the trappings of Royalty. The word 'Royal' aptly describes another characteristic which clung to her. Short in stature as she is, and not majestic, the very carriage of her person bespeaks the fact of her being aware of her own inviolability and unapproachableness. It was far from being haughty, and yet it was commanding, and serenely proud.

The conversation, which was principally about Livingstone and Africa, though it did not last more than ten minutes, gave me abundant matter to think about, from having had such good opportunities to look into her eyes, and absorb as it were my impressions, such as they were.

What I admired most was the sense of power the eyes revealed, and a quiet, but unmistakeable, kindly condescension; and an inimitable calmness and self-possession. I was glad to have seen her, not only for the honour, and all that, but also, I think, because I have carried something away to muse over at leisure. I am richer in the understanding of power and dominion, sitting enthroned on human features.

He began in England his career as a public lecturer, and in pursuance of it went, in November, 1872, to America. He was received with high honours by the public, and with great cordiality by his old friends; was given a warm welcome by 'the boys,' the sub-editors of the 'Herald,' and was banqueted by the Union League Club, and the St. Andrew's Society, etc., etc. Then he spent several months in travelling and lecturing.

Returning to England, before the clear summons came to his next great exploration, he once more, as correspondent of the 'Herald,' accompanied and reported the British campaign against the Ashantees, in 1873–74. That warlike and savage people, under King Coffee, had been harrying the Fantees, who had lately come under the British Protectorate, as occupying the 'hinterland' of Elmina on the Gold Coast, which England had taken over from the Dutch.

At intervals for half a century there had been harassing and futile collisions with the Ashantees, and it was now determined to strike hard. 'In 1823, Sir Charles McCarthy and six hundred gallant fellows perished before the furious onset of the Ashantees, and that brave soldier's skull, gold-rimmed and highly venerated, was said still to be at Coomassie, used as a drinking-cup by King Coffee.

'In 1863–64, the English suffered severe loss. Couran marched to the Prah, eighty miles from here, and marched back again, being obliged to bury or destroy his cannon, and hurriedly retreat to the Cape Coast.'

Stanley gave permanent form to his record in the first half of his book, 'Coomassie and Magdala' (1874). This campaign on the West Coast, under Sir Garnet Wolseley, was like, and yet unlike, the Abyssinian expedition on the East Coast, under Sir Robert Napier. The march inland was only one hundred and forty miles, but, instead of the grand and lofty mountains of Abyssinia, the British soldiers and sailors had to cut their way through unbroken jungle. Stanley's book is the spirited story of a well-conducted expedition, told with a firm grasp of the historical and political situation, with graphic sketches of the English officers, some of an heroic type, and with descriptions of a repulsive type of savagery.

Writing of the march, Stanley says: —

What languishing heaviness of soul fills a man, as he, a mere mite in comparison, travels through the lofty and fearful forest aisle. If alone, there is an almost palpable silence, and his own heart-pulsations seem noisy. A night darkness envelops him, and, from above, but the faintest gleams of daylight can be seen. A brooding melancholy seems to rest on the face of nature, and the traveller, be he ever so prosaic, is filled with a vague indefinable sense of foreboding.

The enemy lay hiding in wait, in the middle of a thorny jungle, so dense in some places that one wonders how naked men can risk their unprotected bodies. This vast jungle literally chokes the earth with its density and luxuriance. It admits every kind of shrub, plant, and flower, into a close companionship, where they intermingle each other's luxuriant stalks, where they twine and twine each other's long slender arms about one another, and defy the utmost power of the sun to penetrate the leafy tangle they have reared ten and fifteen feet above the dank earth. This is the bush into which the Ashantee warriors creep on all fours, and lie in wait in the gloomy recesses for the enemy. It was in such localities Sir Garnet found the Ashantees, and where he suffered such loss in his Staff and officers. Until the sonorous sounds of Danish musketry [1] suddenly awoke the echoes, few of us suspected the foe so near; until they betrayed their presence, the English might have searched in vain for the hidden enemy. Secure as they were in their unapproachable coverts, our volleys, which their loud-mouthed challenge evoked, searched many a sinister-looking bush, and in a couple of hours effectually silenced their fire.

The fighting, when it came, was stubborn. King Theodore's warriors had shewn no such mettle as did the Ashantees, who, for five continuous days, waged fierce fight. On the first day, with the 42nd Highlanders, the Black Watch, bearing the brunt, and the whole force engaged, the battle of Amoaful was won; then three days of straggling fighting; finally, on the fifth day, with the Rifle Brigade taking its turn at the post of honour, and Lord Gifford's Scouts always in front, the decisive battle of Ordahsu was won, and Coomassie was taken. In the Capital were found ghastly relics of wholesale slaughters, incidents of fetish-worship, which far outdid the horrors of King Theodore's court.

We are unable to realise, or are liable to forget, what Africa was before the advent of Explorers and Expeditions. The Fall of Coomassie, though attended with great loss of life, put an end to indescribable horrors and atrocities.

Stanley writes:—

[1] The natives used old Danish muskets.

Each village had placed its human sacrifice in the middle of the path, for the purpose of affrighting the conquerors. The sacrifice was of either sex, sometimes a young man, sometimes a woman. The head, severed from the body, was turned to meet the advancing army, the body was evenly laid out with the feet towards Coomassie. This meant, no doubt, 'Regard this face, white man, ye whose feet are hurrying on to our capital, and learn the fate awaiting you.'

Coomassie is a town insulated by a deadly swamp. A thick jungly forest — so dense that the sun seldom pierced the foliage; so sickly that the strongest fell victims to the malaria it cherished — surrounded it to a depth of about one hundred and forty miles seaward, and one hundred miles to the north; many hundred miles east and west.

Through this forest and swamp, unrelieved by any novelty or a single pretty landscape, the British Army had to march one hundred and forty miles, leaving numbers stricken down by fever and dysentery — the terrible allies of the Ashantee King with his one hundred thousand warriors.

Stanley, speaking of Coomassie, writes: —

The grove, which was but a continuation of the tall forest we had travelled through, penetrated as far as the great market-place. A narrow foot-path led into this grove, where the foul smells became suffocating. After some thirty paces we arrived before the dreadful scene, but it was almost impossible to stop longer than to take a general view of the great Golgotha. We saw some thirty or forty decapitated bodies in the last stages of corruption, and countless skulls, which lay piled in heaps, and scattered over a wide extent. The stoutest heart and the most stoical mind might have been appalled.

At the rate of a thousand victims a year, it would be no exaggeration to say, that over one hundred and twenty thousand people must have been slain for 'custom,' since Ashantee became a kingdom.

Lord Wolseley wrote: 'Their capital was a charnel-house; their religion a combination of cruelty and treachery; their policy the natural outcome of their religion.'

Terms of submission were imposed on King Coffee, and the force returned to the coast.

Stanley writes of Lord Wolseley: —

> He has done his best, and his best has been a mixture of untiring energy and determination; youthful ardour, toned down by the sense of his grave responsibilities, excellent good-nature, which nothing seems to damp; excessive amiability, by which we are all benefitted; wise forethought, which, assisted by his devotion to work, proves that the trust reposed in him by the British Government will not be betrayed.

Stanley occasionally criticises with freedom, both the Government, for not taking a larger view of the whole situation, and Sir Garnet Wolseley, for a somewhat hasty settlement of the business, after the fighting was over.

Stanley's political foresight and desire for the promotion of civilisation and commerce, even in such a benighted part of West Africa, is well exemplified by the following passage:—

> If we are wise, we will deprive our present enemy of their king, attach to ourselves these brave and formidable warriors, and through them open the whole of Central Africa to trade and commerce and the beneficent influences of civilisation. The Romans would have been delighted at such an opportunity of extending their power, for the benefit of themselves and the world at large.

Nothing in Stanley's book indicates that he took any personal share in the fighting. But in Lord Wolseley's 'Story of a Soldier's Life,' volume ii, p. 342, occurs this passage: 'Not twenty yards off were several newspaper correspondents. One was Mr. Winwood Reid, a very cool and daring man, who had gone forward with the fighting-line. Of the others, one soon attracted my attention by his remarkable coolness. It was Sir Henry Stanley, the famous traveller. A thoroughly good man, no noise, no danger ruffled his nerve, and he looked as cool and self-possessed as if he had been at target practice. Time after time, as I turned in his direction, I saw him go down to a kneeling position to steady his rifle, as he plied the most daring of the enemy with a never-failing aim. It is nearly thirty years ago, and I can still see before me the close-shut lips, and determined expression of his manly face, which, when he looked in my direction, told plainly I had near me an Englishman in plain clothes, whom no danger could appall. Had I felt inclined to run away, the cool, unflinching manliness of that face would have given me fresh courage. I had been previously somewhat prejudiced against him, but all such feelings were slain and buried at Amoaful. Ever since, I have been proud to reckon him amongst the bravest of my brave comrades; and I hope he may not be offended if I add him amongst my best friends also.'

It was on his way home from the Ashantee War that the tidings met Stanley, which he accepted and acted upon as a summons to his real life's work.

25th February, 1874. Arrived at the Island of St. Vincent, per 'Dromedary,' I was shocked to hear, on getting ashore, of the death of Livingstone at Ilala, near Lake Bangweolo, on May 4th, 1873. His body is on its way to England, on board the 'Malwa,'[1] from Aden. Dear Livingstone! another sacrifice to Africa! His mission, however, must not be allowed to cease; others must go forward and fill the gap. 'Close up, boys! close up! Death must find us everywhere.'

May I be selected to succeed him in opening up Africa to the shining light of Christianity! My methods, however, will not be Livingstone's. Each man has his own way. His, I think, had its defects, though the old man, personally, has been almost Christ-like for goodness, patience, and self-sacrifice. The selfish and wooden-headed world requires mastering, as well as loving charity; for man is a composite of the spiritual and earthly. May Livingstone's God be with me, as He was with Livingstone in all his loneliness. May God direct me as He wills. I can only vow to be obedient, and not to slacken.

[1] The 'Malwa' arrived at Southampton on April 16, 1874.

CHAPTER XV

THROUGH THE DARK CONTINENT

IN a camp in the heart of Africa, not far from Lake Bangweolo, David Livingstone, the traveller-evangelist, lay dead. His followers, numbering about three-score negroes of Zanzibar, deliberated upon their future movements. To return to the coast ruled by their Sultan, without their great white master, would provoke grave suspicion. They resolved to prepare the remains so as to be fit for transportation across a breadth of tropical region which extended to the Indian Ocean, fifteen hundred miles. After many weary months of travel, they arrived at the sea-coast with the body. In charge of two of the faithful band, it was placed on board a homeward-bound steamer, to be finally deposited [1] in a vault in Westminster Abbey.

At the same period when the steamer coasted along the shores of Eastern Africa, I was returning to England along the coast of Western Africa, from the Ashantee campaign.

At St. Vincent, on February 25th, 1874, cable news of the death of Livingstone, substantiated beyond doubt, was put into my hands.

'At Lake Bangweolo the death occurred,' said the cablegram. Just one thousand miles south of Nyangwe! The great river remains, then, a mystery still, for poor Livingstone's work is unfinished!

Fatal Africa! One after another, travellers drop away. It is such a huge continent, and each of its secrets is environed by so many difficulties, — the torrid heat, the miasma exhaled from the soil, the noisome vapours enveloping every path, the giant cane-grass suffocating the wayfarer, the rabid fury of the native guarding every entry and exit, the unspeakable misery of the life within the wild continent, the utter absence of every comfort, the bitterness which each day heaps upon the poor white man's head, in that land of blackness, the som-

[1] On Saturday, April 18, 1874.

brous solemnity pervading every feature of it, and the little — too little — promise of success which one feels on entering it.

But, never mind, I will try it! Indeed, I have a spur to goad me on. My tale of the discovery of Livingstone has been doubted. What I have already endured in that accursed Africa amounts to nothing, in men's estimation. Here, then, is an opportunity for me to prove my veracity, and the genuineness of my narrative!

Let me see: Livingstone died in endeavouring to solve the problem of the Lualaba River. John Hanning Speke died by a gun-shot wound during a discussion as to whether Lake Victoria was one lake, as he maintained it to be; or whether, as asserted by Captain Burton, James McQueen, and other theorists, it consisted of a cluster of lakes.

Lake Tanganyika, being a sweet-water lake, must naturally possess an outlet somewhere. It has not been circumnavigated and is therefore unexplored. I will settle that problem also.

Then I may be able to throw some light on Lake Albert. Sir Samuel Baker voyaged along some sixty miles of its north-eastern shore, but he said it was illimitable to the south-west. To know the extent of that lake would be worth some trouble. Surely, if I can resolve any of these, which such travellers as Dr. Livingstone, Captains Burton, Speke, and Grant, and Sir Samuel Baker left unsettled, people must needs believe that I discovered Livingstone!

A little while after the burial[1] of Livingstone at Westminster, I strolled over to the office of the 'Daily Telegraph,' and pointed out to the proprietors how much remained shrouded in mystery in Dark Africa.

The proprietor asked, 'But do you think you can settle all these interesting geographical problems?'

'Nay, Mr. Lawson,[2] that is not a fair question. I mean to say I can do my level best, that nothing on my part shall be lacking to make a systematic exploration which shall embrace all the regions containing these secrets; but Africa includes so many dangers from man, beast, and climate, that it would be the height of immeasurable conceit to say I shall be successful.

[1] For a full account of the funeral obsequies, see the Memoir prefacing Stanley's book, *How I Found Livingstone*.

[2] Now Lord Burnham.

My promise that I will endeavour to be even with my word, must be accepted by you as sufficient.'

'Well, well! I will cable over to Bennett of the New York "Herald," and ask if he is willing to join in this expedition of yours.'

Deep under the Atlantic, the question was flashed. Gordon Bennett tore open the telegram in New York City, and, after a moment's thought, snatched a blank form and wrote, 'Yes! Bennett.'

This was the answer put into my hand the same day at 135, Fleet Street. You may imagine my feelings, as I read the simple monosyllable which was my commission: bales, packages, boxes, trunks, bills, letters, flowing in a continuous stream; the writing, telegraphing, and nervous hurry and flurry of each day's work, until we sailed! Follow me in thought to the deck of the steam-ferry across the English Channel; fancy that you hear my plucky fisher-boys from the Medway,[1] saying to the white cliffs of Dover, 'Good-bye, dear England! and if for ever, then for ever good-bye, O England!' Think of us a few weeks later, arrived at Zanzibar, where we make our final preparations for the long journey we are about to make.

Zanzibar is an island, as I suppose you know, situate three hundred and sixty-nine miles south of the Equator, and about twenty miles from the eastern mainland.

Its ruler is Prince Barghash, son of Sayed. His subjects are very mixed, and represent the rasping and guttural Arab, the soft-tongued and languid Balooch, the fiery-eyed and black-bearded Omanee, the flowing-locked and tall-hatted Persian, the lithe, slim-waisted Somali, and at least a hundred specimens of the African tribes.

It was in the bazaars and shops of the principal city that we bought the cottons, the various beads, the coils of brass wire, the tools, cordage, ammunition, and guns. It was in a house at Zanzibar that we rolled these cloths into seventy-pound bales, sacked the beads in similar weights, packed the wire, and boxed the ammunition and tools. Meantime we enlisted three hundred and fifty-six chosen fellows. They left

[1] Francis and Edward Pocock, who, with Frederick Barker, were his only white companions in the expedition. All three did gallant work, and not one returned. — D. S.

their porter-work, gossiping in the bazaar, the care of their fields and gardens without the town, to become sworn followers of the Anglo-American expedition, to carry its loads at so much per month, in any direction on the mainland I should wish; to stand by the master in times of trouble, to die with him, if necessary. I also, on my part, swore to treat them kindly; to medicate them, if sick or bilious; to judge honestly and impartially between man and man in their little camp squabbles; to prevent ill-treatment of the weak by the strong; to be a father and a mother, brother and sister, to each; and to resist, to the utmost of my ability, any murderous natives who, encouraged by the general forbearance of the white man, would feel disposed to do them harm.

We call upon the One, and Compassionate, and Just God, to witness our mutual pledges.

On the 11th of November, 1874, we sail away from our friends, who are gathered on the beach at sunset, to witness our departure. The evening breeze sweeps us across the Zangian Channel. The shadows of the night fall over the mainland and the silent sea, as we glide on to the destiny that may be awaiting us in the Dark Continent.

The next morning we debarked, and, a few days later, took the native path which led to the west. I will not trouble you with a description of the journeys made each day. That native path, only a foot wide, leading westward, presently entered a jungle, then traversed a plain, on which the sun shone dazzling, and pitilessly hot. We came to a river: it swarmed with hippopotami and crocodiles. On the western bank the road began again; it pierced a scrubby forest, ascended the face of a rising land, dipped down again into a plain; it then curved over a wooded hill, tracks of game becoming numerous; and so on it went, over plain, hill, valley, through forest and jungle, cultivated fields of manioc, maize, and millet, traversing several countries, such as Udoe, Uruguru, Useguhha, Usagara. By the time we had gone through Ugogo, we were rich in experience of African troubles, native arrogance, and unbridled temper.

But, as yet, we had suffered no signal misfortune. A few of our men had deserted, one or two bales had been lost. On leaving Ugogo, we turned north-westward, and entered an enormous bush-field. No charts could aid me to lay out the route, no man with me had ever been in this region, guides proved faithless as soon as they were engaged. I always endeavoured to secure three days' provisions, at least, before venturing anywhere unknown to the guides. But three days passed away, and the bush-field spread out on either side, silent and immense. We had followed the compass course north-west, staggering on blindly under our heavy loads, hoping, hourly, that we should see something in the shape of game, or signs of cultivation. The fourth day passed; our provisions were exhausted, and we began to be anxious. We had already travelled eighty miles through the straggling jungle. The fifth day we took the road at sunrise and travelled briskly on, myself leading the way, compass in hand, my white assistants, the brothers Pocock and Barker, with a dozen select men, as rear-guard. You may rest assured that my eyes travelled around and in front, unceasingly, in search of game. At noon, we halted at a small pond, and drank its filthy nitrous water.

About two, we started again through the wilderness of thorny bush and rank-smelling acacia; the fifth day ended with nothing but our hopes to feed upon. The sixth, seventh, and eighth days passed in like manner, hoping, ever hoping! Five people perished from absolute starvation during the eighth day. On the ninth, we came to a small village; but there was not a grain to be bought for money, or obtained through fear, or love, of us. We obtained news, however, that there was a large village a long day's journey off, north-westerly. I despatched forty of the stoutest men with cloth and beads to purchase provisions. Though pinched with hunger they reached the place at night, and the next day the gallant fellows returned with eight hundred pounds of grain. Meantime, those that remained had wandered about in search of game, and had found the putrid carcase of an elephant, and two lion whelps, which they brought to me. Finding that the pain of hunger was becoming intolerable, we emptied a sheet-iron trunk, filled it three-quarters with water, into which we put ten pounds of oatmeal, four pounds of lentil flour, four pounds of tapioca, half a pound of salt, out of which we made a gruel. Each man and woman within an hour was served with a cupful of gruel. This was a great drain on our medical stores, when we might say only a twentieth part of the journey had been performed; but the expedition was saved.

The effect of that terrible jungle experience was felt for many a day afterwards. Four more died within two days, over a score were on the sick list, consequently, the riding asses were loaded with bales, and all of us whites were obliged to walk.

Twenty-eight miles under a hot sun prostrated one of the brothers Pocock. To carry him in a hammock, we had to throw some loads into the bush, to relieve the heavily-burdened caravan. In this condition we entered Ituru — a land of naked people, whose hills drain into a marsh, whence issue the southernmost waters of the Nile.[1]

A presentiment of evil depressed all of us, as the long column of wearied and sick people entered Ituru. My people hurried their women away out of sight, the boys drove the herds away from our foreground in order that, if the looming trouble ruptured, the cattle might not be hurt. By dint of diplomatic suavity, we postponed the conflict for many days. We gave presents freely, the slightest service was royally rewarded. Though our hearts were heavy at the gloomy prescience of our minds, we smiled engagingly; but I could see that it was of no use. However, it deferred the evil. Finally, Edward Pocock died; we buried him in the midst of our fenced camp, and the poor fisher-boy lay at rest for ever.

Four days later, we arrived at the village of Vinyata. We had been ten days in the land of Ituru, and, as yet, the black cloud had not lifted, nor had it burst. But, as we entered Vinyata, a sick man suffering from asthma lingered behind, unknown to the rear-guard. The fell savages pounced on him, hacked him to little pieces, and scattered them along the road. It was the evening of the 21st of January, 1875. The muster-roll as usual was read. We discovered his absence, sent a body of men back along the road; they found his remains, and came back bearing bloody evidences of the murder.

'Well, what can I do, my friends?'

'But, master, if we don't avenge his death, we shall have to

[1] It was here, on this watershed, that Stanley discovered the southernmost source of the Nile. — D. S.

mourn for a few more, shortly. These savages need a lesson. For ten days we have borne it, expecting every minute just what has happened.'

'It is I who suffer most. Don't you see the sick are so numerous that we can scarcely move? Now, you talk of my giving a lesson to these people. I did not come to Africa to give such lessons. No, my friends, we must bear it; not only this, but perhaps a few more, if we are not careful.'

We fenced the camp around with bush, set a guard, and rested. Up to this day twenty men had died, eighty-nine had deserted; there were two hundred and forty-seven left, out of whom thirty were on the sick-list. Ituru was populous, and the people warlike; two hundred and seventeen indifferent fighters against a nation could do nothing. We could only forbear.

We halted the next day, and took advantage of it to purchase the favour of the natives. At night we thought we had succeeded. But the next day two brothers went out into the bush to collect fuel: one was speared to death, the other rushed into camp, a lance quivering in his arm, his body gashed with the flying weapons, his face streaming with blood from the blow of a whirling knobstick. We were horrified. He cried out, 'It is war, the savages are coming through the bush all round the camp!'

'There, master!' said the chief men, as they rushed up to assist the wounded man, 'What said we? We are in for it, sure enough, this time!'

'Keep silence,' I said. 'Even for this, I will not fight. You know not what you say. Two lives are lost; but that is small loss compared with the loss of a hundred, or even fifty. You cannot fight a tribe like this without paying a heavy forfeit of life. I cannot afford to lose you. We have a thousand tribes to go through yet, and you talk of war now. Be patient, men, this will blow over.'

'Never!' cried the men.

While I was arguing for peace, the camp was being gradually surrounded. As the savages came into view, I sent men to talk with them. It staggered the natives. They seemed to ask one another, 'Have they not yet received cause enough to fight?' But as it took two sides to fight, and one was unwilling, it was influencing them; and the matter might have ended, had not a fresh force, remarkable for its bellicose activity, appeared upon the scene.

'Master, you had better prepare; there is no peace with these people.'

I gave the order to distribute twenty rounds of cartridges per man, and enjoined on all to retire quietly to their several places in the camp.

My interpreters still held on talking soothingly, while I watched, meanwhile, to note the slightest event.

Presently, the murderous band from the bush south of our camp appeared, and again the clamour for war rose loudly on our ears.

I disposed two companies of fifty each on either side of the gate, to resist the rush. There was a hostile movement, the interpreters came flying back, the savages shot a cloud of arrows. On all sides rose bodies of savages. A determined rush was made for the gate of the camp. A minute later, firing began, and the companies moved forward briskly, firing as they went. Then every axe-man was marched out, to cut the bush, and fortify the camp. The savages were driven back for an hour, and a recall was sounded. No enemy being in sight, we occupied ourselves in making the camp impregnable, constructed four towers, twenty feet high, to command all sides, and, filling them with marksmen, waited events.

The day, and the night, passed quietly. Our camp was unassailable. I had only lost two men so far. At nine o'clock, the enemy reappeared in good order, re-enforced in numbers, for the adjoining districts had responded to the war-cries we had heard pealing the day before. They advanced confidently, probably two thousand strong. The marksmen in the towers opened deliberately on them, and two companies were marched out of camp, and deployed. A deadly fire was kept up for a few minutes, before which the enemy fell back. A rush was made upon them, the natives fled.

I called back my people, and then formed out of these companies five detachments of twenties, each under a chosen man. Instructions were given to drive the natives back rapidly, as far as possible, a company of fifty to follow, and secure cattle, grain, fowls, and food. Those remaining behind cleared the bush further, so that we might have an open view two hundred yards all around. Until late in the afternoon the fighting was kept up, messengers keeping me in contact with my people. At 4 P. M., the enemy having collected on the summit of a hill several miles away, my men retired upon our camp. Our losses amounted to twenty-two killed, and three wounded. My effective force now numbered two hundred and eight. The camp was full of cattle, goats, fowls, milk, and grain. I could stand a siege for months, if necessary.

The third morning came. We waited within the camp; but, at 9 A. M., the natives advanced as before, more numerous than ever. Despite the losses they had experienced, they must have been heartened by what we had suffered. This explains their pertinacity. If we lost twenty each day, ten days would end us all. It was thus they argued. I, on the other hand, to prevent this constant drain, was resolved to finish the war on this day. Accordingly, when they appeared, we advanced upon them with one hundred and fifty rifles; and, leaving only fifty in the camp, delivered several volleys, and pursued them from village to village, setting fire to each as soon as captured. In close order, we made the circuit of the entire district of Vinyata, until we arrived at the stronghold of the tribe, on the summit of the hill. We halted a short time to breathe, and then assailed it by a rush. The enemy fled precipitately, and we returned to camp, having lost but two killed throughout the arduous day.

There only remained for me to re-arrange the caravan. January, 1875, had been a disastrous month to us! Altogether, nine had perished from hunger in the wilderness of Uveriveri; in Ituru, twenty-six had been speared in battle; five had died by disease, the consequence of the misery of the period; on my hands I had four wounded, and twenty-five feeble wretches scarcely able to walk. I had thus lost a fourth of my effective force, with nearly seven thousand miles of a journey still before me!

Suppressing my grief as much as possible, I set about reducing the baggage, and burnt every possible superfluous article. I clung to my boat and every stick of it, though sorely tempted. The boat required thirty of the strongest men for its carriage. Personal baggage, luxuries, books, cloth, beads, wire, extra tents, were freely sacrificed.

At day-break, on the 26th of January, we departed, every riding ass, and all chiefs and supernumeraries, being employed as porters. We entered a forest, and emerged from it three days later, in the friendly and hospitable land of Usukuma. Our booty in bullocks and goats sufficed to enlist over a hundred fresh carriers. After a halt, to recover from our wounds and fatigues, I turned northward through a gracious land, whence issued the smell of cattle and sweet grass, a land abounding with milk and plenty, where we enjoyed perfect immunity from trouble of any kind. Each day saw us winding up and down its grassy vales and gentle hills, escorted by hundreds of amiable natives. Everywhere we were received with a smiling welcome by the villagers, who saw us departing with regret. 'Come yet again,' said they; 'come, always assured of welcome.'

With scarcely one drawback to our pleasure, we arrived on the shores of the Victoria Nyanza, on the one hundred and fourth day from the sea, after a journey of seven hundred and twenty miles.

Sixteen years and seven months previous to our arrival at the lake, Captain Speke had viewed it from a point just twelve miles west of my camp. Reflecting on the vast expanse of water before him, Speke said, 'I no longer felt any doubt that the lake at my feet gave birth to that interesting river, the source of which has been the subject of so much speculation, and the object of so many explorers.' This bold hypothesis was warmly disputed by many, principally by his fellow-explorer, Captain Burton. This led to Speke making a second expedition, with Captain Grant for a companion, during which he saw a great deal of its western, and half of its northern shores, from prominent points as he travelled overland. Captain Burton and his brother theorists declined to be satisfied; consequently, it was interesting to know, by actual survey, what was the character of this Victoria Nyanza. Was it really one lake, or a cluster of shallow lakes or marshes?

I had thought there could be no better way of settling, once and for ever, the vexed question, than by the circumnavigation of the lake, or lakes. For that purpose I had brought with

X

me from England, in sections, a cedar boat, forty feet long, and six feet beam.

Of course, all my people knew the object of the boat, but when I asked for volunteers to man it for the voyage, they all assumed a look of wonder, as though the matter had dawned on their minds for the first time!

'Where are the brave fellows who are to be my companions?' I asked.

There was a dead silence; the men gazed at one another and stupidly scratched their hips.

'You know, I cannot go alone!'

Their eyes travelled over one another's faces; they had suddenly become blank-faced mutes.

'You see the beautiful boat, made in England, safe as a ship, swift as a sea-bird. We shall stow plenty of chop; we will lie lazily down on the thwarts; the winds will bear us gaily along. Let my braves step out; those men who will dare accompany their master round this sea.'

Up, and down, their eyes traversed each other's forms, and, finally, became fixed on their feet.

'Come, come; this will not do. Will you join me?'

'Ah, master, I cannot row. I am a land-lubber. My back is as strong as a camel's. There is no one like me for the road; but the sea!—Uh! uh! the water is only fit for fishes, and I am a son of the firm earth!'

'Will you join me, my boy?'

'Dear master, you know I am your slave, and you are my prince; but, master, look at the great waves!—Boo! boo! all the time!—Please, master, excuse me this time. I will never do it again.'

'Will you go with me, to live a pleasant month on the sea?'

'Ha! ha! good master, you are joking! Who? I? I, who am the son of Abdallah, who was the son of Nasib! Surely, my master, my hamal's back was made to carry loads! I am a donkey for that, but you cannot make a sailor of a donkey!'

'Will you come with me? I have had my eye on you for a long time?'

'Where to, master?' he asked innocently.

'Why, round this sea, of course, in my boat!'

'Ah, sir, put your hand on my breast. You feel the thumping of the heart. A mere look at the sea always sends it bounding that way. Pray don't kill me, master, that sea would be my grave!'

'So! you are donkeys, eh? camels? land-lubbers? hamals only, eh? Well, we will try another plan! Here, you sir, I like you, a fine, handsome, light weight! Step into that boat; and you, you look like a born sailor, follow him; and you — heavens! what a back and muscles! You shall try them on the oars! And you, a very lion in the fight at Ituru! I love lions, and you shall roar with me to the wild waves of the Nyanza! And you, the springing antelope, ha! ha! you shall spring with me over the foaming surge!' I selected eleven. 'Oh, you young fellows, I will make sailors of you, never fear! Get ready, we must be off within an hour.'

We set sail on the 8th of March. The sky was gloomy. The lake reflected its gloom, and was of the colour of ashy-grey. The shores were stern and rugged. My crew sighed dolorously, and rowed like men bound to certain death, often casting wistful looks at me, as though I shared their doubts, and would order a return, and confess that the preparations were only an elaborate joke. Five miles beyond our port we halted for the night at a fishing-village. A native — shock-headed, ugly, loutish, and ungainly in movement — agreed, for a consideration, to accompany us as pilot and interpreter of lake dialects. The next day, steering eastward, we sailed at early dawn. At 11 A. M., a gale blew, and the lake became wild beyond description. We scudded before the tempest, while it sang in our ears and deafened us with its tumult. The waves hissed as we tore along; leaping seas churned white, racing with us and clashing their tops with loud, engulfing sounds. The crew collapsed, and crouched with staring eyes into the bottom of the boat, and expected each upward heave, and sudden fall into the troughs, to be the end of the wild venture; but the boat, though almost drowned by the spray and foam, dashed gaily along, until, about three o'clock, we swept round to the lee of an island, and floated into a baylet, still as a pond. We coasted around the indented shores of Speke Gulf, and touched at Ukerewe, where our guide had many friends, who told us, for the exceeding comfort of my crew, that it would take years to sail around their sea; and who, at that time, would be left alive to tell the tale? On its shores dwelt a people with long tails; there was a tribe which trained big dogs for purposes of war; there were people, also, who preferred to feed on human beings, rather than on cattle or goats. My young sailors were exceedingly credulous. Our mop-headed guide and pilot grunted his terror, and sought every opportunity to escape the doom which we were hurrying to meet.

From Ukerewe we sailed by the picturesque shores of Wye; thence along the coast of populous Ururi, whence the fishermen, hailed by us as we glided by, bawled out to us that we should be eight years on the voyage. We were frequently chased by hippopotami; crocodiles suddenly rose alongside, and floated for a moment side by side, as though to take the measure of our boat's length. As we sailed by the coast of Irirui, large herds of cattle were seen browsing on green herbage; the natives of Utiri fell into convulsions of laughter as they looked on the novel method of rowing adopted by us. When we hoisted the sail, they ceased mocking us and ran away in terror. Then we laughed at them!

Beyond Utiri loomed the dark mountainous mass of Ugeyeya; to the west of it, grim and lofty, frowned the island of Uguigo. Grey rocky islets studded the coast. By swelling and uneven lines of hills, gentle slopes all agreen with young grass, on which many herds and flocks industriously fed, past many a dark headland, and cliffy walls of rock, and lovely bays, edged by verdure and forest, and cosy lake-ports, the boat sailed day after day, some curious adventure marking each day's voyage, until the boat's head was turned westward.

While close to the shore of Ugamba, a war-canoe manned by forty paddlers drew near to us. When within fifty yards, most of them dropped their paddles and flourished tufted lances and shields. We sat still; they wheeled round us, defyingly shaking their spears; they edged nearer, and ranged their canoe alongside. Lamb-like, we gazed on them; they bullied us, and laid their hands on everything within reach. We smiled placidly, for resentment we had none. We even permitted them to handle our persons freely. Tired with that, they seized their slings and tried to terrify us with the whiz of the stones, which flew by our heads dangerously near.

They then chanted a war-song, and one, cheered by the sound, became bolder, and whirled a rock at my head. I fired a revolver into the water, and the warriors at once sprang into the lake and dived, as though in search of the bullet. Not finding it, I suppose, they swam away, and left the fine canoe in our hands!

We were delighted, of course, at the fun; we begged them to come back. After much coaxing, they returned and got into their canoe. We spoke — oh, so blandly! — to them. They were respectful, but laughed as they thought of the boom, boom, boom, of the pistol. They gave me a bunch of bananas, and we mutually admired one another. At last we parted.

Another gale visited us at Usuguru, blowing as though from above. Its force seemed to compress the water; repelled by the weightier element, it brushed its face into millions of tiny ripples. Suddenly, the temperature fell 20°; hailstones as large as filberts pelted us; and, for fully ten minutes, we cowered under the icy shower. Then such tropical torrents of rain poured, that every utensil was employed to bale the boat to prevent foundering. The deluge lasted for hours, but near night we uncovered, baled the boat dry, and crept for refuge, through the twilight, into a wild arbour on an island, there to sleep.

A few days later, we coasted by the island of Wavuma. Five piratical craft came up, and we behaving, as we always did, in that lackadaisical, so fatally-encouraging manner, they became rude, insolent, and, finally, belligerent. Of course, it resulted in a violent rupture; there was an explosion, one of their canoes sank, and then we had peace, and sailed away. We were on the Equator now. We cut across the Napoleon Channel, through which the superfluous waters of the lake flow. At the northern end they abruptly fall about eight feet, and then rush northward as the Victoria Nile.

On the western side of the channel is Uganda, dominated by a prince, entitled Kabaka, or Emperor. He is supreme over about three millions of people, not quite so degraded or barbarous as those we had hitherto viewed. He soon heard of the presence of my boat on the lake, and despatched a flotilla to meet me. Strangely enough, the Emperor's mother had dreamed the night before that she had seen a boat sailing, sailing, like a fish-eagle, over the Nyanza. In the stern of the boat was a white man gazing wistfully towards Uganda.

The dream of the Imperial lady is no sooner told, than a breathless messenger appears at the palace gate and informs the astonished Court that he had seen a boat, with white wings like those of the fish-eagle, skimming along the shores, and at the after-end of the boat there was a white man, scrutinizing the land!

Such a man as this, who sends visions to warn an Empress of his approach, must needs be great! Let worthy preparations be made at once, and send a flotilla to greet him!

Hence, the commodore of the flotilla, on meeting with me, uses words which astonish me by their courtly sound; and, following in the wake of the canoes, we sail towards Usavara, where, I am told, the Emperor of Uganda awaits me.

We see thousands of people arranging themselves in order, as we come in view of the immense camp. The crews in the canoes fire volleys of musketry, which are answered by volleys from shore. Kettle and bass-drums thunder out a welcome, flags and banners are waved, and the people vent a great shout.

The boat's keel grided on the beach; I leapt out, to meet several deeply-bowing officials; they escorted me to a young man standing under an enormous crimson flag, and clad like an Arab gentleman, the Katekiro, or Prime Minister, Ah. I bowed profoundly; he imitated the bow, but added to it a courteous wave of the hand. Then the courtiers came forward and greeted me in the Zanzibar language. 'A welcome, a thousand welcomes to the Kabaka's guest!' was cried on all sides.

I was escorted to my quarters. Hosts of questions were fired off at me, about my health, journey, Zanzibar, Europe and its nations, the oceans, and the heavens, the sun, moon, and stars, angels, demons, doctors and priests, and craftsmen in general. I answered to the best of my power, and, in one hour and ten minutes, it was declared unanimously that I had passed!

In the afternoon, after receiving a present of fourteen oxen, sixteen goats and sheep, a hundred bunches of bananas, three dozen fowls, four jars of milk, four baskets of sweet potatoes, a basket of rice, twenty fresh eggs, and ten pots full of banana wine, — which you must admit was an imperial gift for a boat's crew and one white man, — and after I had bathed and brushed, I was introduced to the foremost man of Equatorial Africa. Preceded by pages in white cotton robes, I was ushered into the Imperial Presence through a multitude of chiefs, ranked in kneeling or seated lines, drummers, guards, executioners, and pages.

The tall, clean-faced, and large-lustrous-eyed Mtesa rose, advanced, and shook hands. I was invited to be seated; and then there followed a mutual inspection. We talked about many things, principally about Europe and Heaven. The inhabitants of the latter place he was very anxious about, and was specially interested in the nature of angels. Ideas of those celestial spirits, picked up from the Bible, Paradise Lost, Michael Angelo, and Gustave Doré, enabled me to describe them in bright and warm colours. Led away by my enthusiasm, I may have exaggerated somewhat! However, I was rewarded with earnest attention, and, I do believe, implicit faith!

Every day while I stayed, the 'barzah' was kept up with ceremony. One afternoon Mtesa said, 'Stamlee, I want you to show my women how white men can shoot.' (There were about nine hundred of them.)

We adjourned the barzah, and proceeded to the lake shore. The ladies formed a crescent line, Mtesa in the midst, and amused themselves by criticising my personal appearance — not unfavourably, I hope! It was, 'Stamlee is this,' and 'Stamlee is that,' from nine hundred pairs of lips. There was at first a buzz, then it grew into a rippling murmur; hundreds of lips covered and uncovered, alternately, dazzling white teeth; the Equatorial stars were not half so brilliant as the beautiful and lustrous jet-black eyes that reflected the merriness of the hearts. An admiral with a fleet of canoes searched for a crocodile, at which I might take aim. They discovered a small specimen, sleeping on a rock at the distance of a hundred yards.

To represent all the sons of Japhet was a great responsibility; but I am happy to say that my good luck did not desert me. The head of the young reptile was nearly severed from the body by a three-ounce ball, and this feat was accepted as a conclusive and undeniable proof that all white men were dead shots!

In person, Mtesa is slender and tall, probably six feet one inch in height. He has very intelligent and agreeable features, which remind me of some of the faces of the great stone images at Thebes, and of the statues in the Museum at Cairo. He has the same fulness of lips, but their grossness is relieved by the general expression of amiability, blended with dignity, that pervades his face, and the large, lustrous, lambent eyes that lend it a strange beauty, and are typical of the race from which I believe him to have sprung. His face is of a wonderfully smooth surface.

When not engaged in council, he throws off, unreservedly, the bearing that distinguishes him when on the throne, and gives rein to his humour, indulging in hearty peals of laughter. He seems to be interested in the discussion of the manners and customs of European courts, and to be enamoured of hearing of the wonders of civilisation. He is ambitious to imitate, as much as lies in his power, the ways of the European. When any piece of information is given him, he takes upon himself the task of translating it to his wives and chiefs, though many of the latter understand the language of the East Coast as well as he does himself.

Though at this period I only stayed with him about twelve days, as I was anxious about my camp at Kagehyi, yet the interest I conceived for the Emperor and his people at this early stage was very great. He himself was probably the main cause of this. The facility with which he comprehended what was alluded to in conversation, the eagerness of his manner, the enthusiasm he displayed when the wonders of civilisation were broached to him, tempted me to introduce the subject of Christianity, and I delayed my departure from Uganda much longer than prudence counselled, to impress the first rudimentary lessons on his mind.

I did not attempt to confuse him with any particular doctrine, nor did I broach abtruse theological subjects, which I knew would only perplex him. The simple story of the Creation as related by Moses, the revelation of God's power to the

Israelites, their delivery from the Egyptians, the wonderful miracles He wrought in behalf of the children of Abraham, the appearance of prophets at various times foretelling the coming of Christ; the humble birth of the Messiah, His wonderful life, woeful death, and the triumphant resurrection, — were themes so captivating to the intelligent pagan, that little public business was transacted, and the seat of justice was converted into an alcove where only the religious and moral law was discussed.

But I must leave my friend Mtesa, and his wonderful court, and the imperial capital, Rubaga, for other scenes.

Ten days after we left the genial court, I came upon the scene of a tragedy, which was commented upon in Parliament. We were coasting the eastern side of a large island, looking for a port where we could put in to purchase provisions. We had already been thirty-six hours without food, and though the people on the neighbouring main were churlish, I hoped the islanders would be more amenable to reason and kindly largesse of cloth. Herds of cattle grazed on the summit and slopes of the island hills; plantations of bananas, here and there, indicated abundance. As we rowed along the shore, a few figures emerged from the shades of the frondent groves. They saw us rowing, and raised the war-cry in long-drawn, melodious notes. It drew numbers out of the villages; they were seen gathering from summit, hollow, and slope. Besides the fierce shouting, their manner was not reassuring. But hungry as we were, and not knowing whither to turn to obtain supplies, this manifest hostility we thought would moderate after a closer acquaintance.

We pulled gently round a point to a baylet. The natives followed our movements, poising their spears, stringing their bows, picking out the best rocks for their slings. Observing them persistent in hostile preparations, we ceased rowing about fifty yards from the shore. The interpreter with the mop head was requested to speak to the natives. You can imagine how he pleaded, hunger inspiring his eloquence! The poised spears were lowered, the ready rocks were dropped, and they invited us by signs with open palms to advance without fear. We were thirteen souls, including myself; they between three and four hundred. Prudence advised retreat, hunger impelled us on; the islanders also invited us. Wisdom is a thing of exceedingly slow growth; had we been wise, we should have listened to the counsels of prudence.

'It is almost always the case, master,' said Safeni, the coxswain. 'These savages cry out and threaten, and talk big; but, you will see, these people will become fast friends with us. Besides, if we leave here without food, where shall we get any?' At the same time, without waiting for orders, four men nearest the bow dipped their oars into the water, and gently moved the boat nearer.

Seeing the boat advance, the natives urged us to be without fear. They smiled, entered the water up to their hips, held out inviting hands. They called us 'brothers,' 'friends,' 'good fellows.' This conquered our reluctance; the crew shot the boat towards the natives; their hands closed on her firmly; they ran with her to the shore; as many as could lay hold assisted, and dragged her high and dry about twenty yards from the lake.

Then ensued a scene of rampant wildness and hideous ferocity of action beyond description. The boat was surrounded by a forest of spears, over fifty bows were bent nearly double, with levelled arrows, over two hundred swart demons contended as to who should deliver the first blow. When this outbreak first took place, I had sprung up to kill and be killed, a revolver in each hand; but, as I rose to my feet, the utter hopelessness of our situation was revealed to me — a couple of mitrailleuses only could have quenched their ferocious fury. We resigned ourselves to the tempest of shrieking rage with apparent indifference. This demeanour was not without its effect; the delirious fury subsided. Our interpreter spoke, our coxswain pleaded with excellent pantomime, and, with Kiganda words, explained; but the arrival of fifty newcomers kindled anew the tumult; it increased to the perilous verge of murder. The coxswain was pushed headlong into the boat; Kirango's head received a sounding thwack from a lance-staff; a club came down heartily on the back of my mop-headed guide. I grinned fiendishly, I fear, because they deserved it for urging me to such a hell.

I had presently to grin another way, for a gang paid their attentions to me. They mistook my hair for a wig, and attempted to pull it off. They gave it a wrench until the scalp tingled. Unresisting, I submitted to their abuse. But, though I was silent, I thought a great deal, and blessed them in my heart.

After a little while they seized our oars — our legs, as they called them. The boat would lie helpless in their power, they thought. The natives took position on a small eminence about two hundred yards away, to hold a palaver. It was a slow affair. They lunched and drank wine. At 3 P. M., drums were beaten for muster. A long line of natives appeared in war costume. All had smeared their faces with black and white pigments. The most dull-witted amongst us knew what it portended!

A tall young fellow came bounding down the hill and pounced upon our Kiganda drum. It was only a curio we had picked up; we let them have it. Before going away he said, 'If you are men, prepare to fight.'

'Good,' I said; 'the sentence is given, suspense is over. Boys,' I said, 'if I try to save you, will you give me absolute submission, unwavering obedience? — no arguing or reasoning, but prompt, unhesitating compliance?'

'Yes, we will; we swear!'

'Do you think you can push this boat into the water?'

'Yes.'

'Just as she is, with all her goods in her, before those men can reach us?'

'Yes, certainly.'

'Stand by, then. Range yourselves on both sides of the boat, carelessly. Each of you find out exactly where you shall lay hold. I will load my guns. Safeni, take these cloths on your arm, walk up towards the men on the hill; open out the cloths one by one, you know, as though you were admiring the pattern. But keep your ears open. When I call out to you, throw the cloths away and fly to us, or your death will lie on your own head! Do you understand?'

'Perfectly, master.'

'Then go.'

Meantime, I loaded my guns, my elephant-rifle, double-barrelled shot-gun, Winchester repeater, and two or three Sniders belonging to the men.

'Lay hold firmly, boys; break the boat rather than stop. It is life or death.'

Safeni was about fifty yards off; the natives' eyes were fastened on him, wondering why he came.

'Now, boys, ready?'

'Ready! please God, master!'

'Push! push, Saramba, Kirango! Push, you villain, Baraka.'

'Aye, aye, sir! push it is.'

The boat moved, the crew drove her sternward, her keel ploughing through the gravel, and crunching through the stony beach. We were nearing the lake.

'Hurrah, boys! Push, you scoundrels! Ha! the natives see you! They are coming! Safeni! Safeni! Safeni! Push, boys, the natives are on you!'

Safeni heard, and came racing towards us. The boat glided into the water, and carried the crew with her far out with the impetus with which she was launched. 'Swim away with her, boys, don't stop!'

Alas for Safeni!

A tall native who bounds over the ground like a springbok, poises his spear for a cast. The balanced spear was about to fly — I could not lose my man — I fired. The bullet perforated him, and flew through a second man.

'Jump, Safeni, head first into the lake!' The bowmen came to the lake, and drew their bows; the Winchester repeater dropped them steadily. The arrows pierced the boat and mast, and quivered in the stern behind me. One only drew blood from me. When we had got one hundred yards from the shore, the arrows were harmless. I lifted a man into the boat, he assisted the rest. We stopped for Safeni, and drew him safely in.

The natives manned four canoes. My crew were told to tear the bottom-boards of the boat up for paddles. The canoes advancing fiercely on us, we desisted from paddling. I loaded my elephant-rifle with explosive bullets, and when the foremost canoe was about eighty yards off, took deliberate aim at a spot in it between wind and water. The shell struck, and tore a large fragment from the brittle wood. The canoe sank. Another canoe soon after met the same fate; the others returned. We were saved!

After being seventy-six hours without food, we reached Refuge Island. We shot some ducks, and discovered some wild fruit. Delicious evening, — how we enjoyed it! The next day we made new oars; and, finally, after fifty-seven days' absence from our camp, relieved our anxious people.

'But where is Barker?' I asked Frank Pocock.

'He died twelve days ago, sir, and lies there,' pointing to a new mound of earth near the landing-place.

I must pass briefly over many months, replete with adventures, sorrow, suffering, perils by flood and field. Within a few weeks, the King of Ukerewe having furnished me with canoes, I transported the expedition across the lake from its south-eastern to its north-western extremity, with a view to explore Lake Albert. In passing by the pirate island of Bumbireh, the natives again challenged us to pass by them without their permission; and as that permission would not be given, I attacked the island, capturing the King and two of the principal chiefs, and passed on to Uganda.

Before I could obtain any assistance from Mtesa, I had to visit him once again. Being at war with the Wavuma, he detained me several months.

The good work I had commenced was resumed. I translated for him sufficient out of the Bible to form an abridged sacred history, wherein the Gospel of St. Luke was given entire.

When my work of translation was complete, Mtesa mustered all his principal chiefs and officers, and after a long discourse, in which he explained his state of mind prior to my arrival, he said: —

'Now I want you, my chiefs and soldiers, to tell me what we shall do. Shall we believe in Jesus, or in Mohammed?'

One chief said, 'Let us take that which is the best.' The Prime Minister, with a doubtful manner, replied, 'We know not which is the best. The Arabs say their book is the best, while the white man claims that his book is the best. How can we know which speaks the truth?' The courtly steward of the palace said, 'When Mtesa became a son of Islam, he taught me, and I became one. If my master says he taught me wrong, now, having more knowledge, he can teach me right.'

Mtesa then proceeded to unfold his reasons for his belief that the white man's book must be the true book, basing them principally upon the difference of conduct he had observed between the Arabs and the whites. The comparisons he so eloquently drew for them were in all points so favourable to the whites, that the chiefs unanimously gave their promise to accept the Christians' Bible, and to conform, as they were taught, to the Christian religion.

To establish them in the new faith which they had embraced, it only rested with me to release Darlington, my young assistant-translator, from my service, that he might keep the words of the Holy Book green in their hearts, until the arrival of a Christian mission from England. Seldom was an appeal of this nature so promptly acceded to, as Mtesa's appeal that pastors and teachers should be sent to his country; for £14,000 was subscribed in a short time for the equipment of a Missionary expedition, under the auspices of the Church Missionary Society. Three months before we reached the Atlantic Ocean, the missionaries for Uganda arrived at Zanzibar, the island we had left nineteen months previously.[1]

On the conclusion of peace, Mtesa gave me two thousand three hundred men for an escort. With these we travelled west from the north-west corner of Lake Victoria and discovered the giant mountain Gordon Bennett, in the country of Gambaragara, and halted near Lake Muta-Nzige. But as the Wanyoro gathered in such numbers as to make it impossible to resist them, we retreated back to Lake Victoria. We then bade adieu to the Waganda, and travelled south until we came to Lake Tanganyika. We launched our boat on that lake, and, circumnavigating it, discovered that there was only a periodical outlet to it. It is, at this present time, steadily flowing out by the Lukuga River, westward to the Lualaba, until, at some other period of drought, the Tanganyika shall again be reduced, and the Lukuga bed be filled with vegetation.

Thus, by the circumnavigation of the two lakes, two of the

[1] This Uganda Mission encountered tragic as well as heroic experiences, including an aggressive rivalry by the Roman Catholics, fierce persecution by the Mohammedans, and many martyrdoms. Ultimately, it prospered and grew, and the *Guardian*, November 25, 1908, speaks of it as 'the most successful of modern missions.'—D. S.

geographical problems I had undertaken to solve were settled. The Victoria Nyanza I found to be one lake, covering a superficial area of 21,500 square miles. The Tanganyika had no connection with the Albert Nyanza; and, at present, it had no outlet. Should it continue to rise, as there was sufficient evidence to prove that for at least thirty years it had been steadily doing, its surplus waters would be discharged by the Lukuga River into the Lualaba.

There now remained the grandest task of all, in attempting to settle which Livingstone had sacrificed himself. Is the Lualaba, which he had traced along a course of nearly thirteen hundred miles, the Nile, the Niger, or the Congo? He himself believed it to be the Nile, though a suspicion would sometimes intrude itself that it was the Congo. But he resisted the idea. 'Anything for the Nile,' he said, 'but I will not be made black man's meat for the Congo!'

I crossed Lake Tanganyika with my expedition, lifted once more my gallant boat on our shoulders, and after a march of nearly two hundred and twenty miles arrived at the superb river on the banks of which Livingstone had died.

Where I first sighted it, the Lualaba was fourteen hundred yards wide — a noble breadth, pale grey in colour, winding slowly from south and by east. In the centre rose two or three small islets, green with the foliage of trees and the verdure of sedge. It was my duty to follow it to the ocean, whatever might hap during the venture.

We pressed on along the river to the Arab colony of Mwana-Mamba, the chief of which was Tippu-Tib, a rich Arab, who possessed hundreds of armed slaves. He had given considerable assistance to Cameron. A heavy fee, I thought, would bribe him to escort me some distance, until the seductions of Nyangwe would be left far behind.

'I suppose, Tippu-Tib, you would have no objections to help me, for a good sum?'

'I don't know about that,' he said, with a smile; 'I have not many men with me now. Many are at Imbarri, others are trading in Manyuema.'

'How many men have you?'

'Perhaps three hundred, — say two hundred and fifty.'

'They are enough.'

'Yes, added to your people, but not enough to return alone after you would leave me, through such a country as lies beyond Nyangwe.'

'But, my friend, think how it would be with me, with half a continent before me.'

'Ah, well, if you white people are fools enough to throw away your lives, that is no reason why Arabs should! We travel little by little, to get ivory and slaves, and are years about it. It is now nine years since I left Zanzibar.'

After a while, he called a man named Abed, son of Friday, who had penetrated further than any man, westward and northward.

'Speak, Abed; tell us what you know of this river.'

'Yes, I know all about the river. Praise be to God!'

'In which direction does it flow, my friend?'

'It flows north.'

'And then?'

'It flows north.'

'And then?'

'Still north. I tell you, sir, it flows north, and north, and north, and there is no end to it. I think it reaches the Salt Sea; at least, my friends say that it must.'

'Well, point out in which direction this Salt Sea is.'

'God only knows.'

'What kind of a country is it to the north, along the river?'

'Monstrous bad! There are fearfully large boa-constrictors, in the forest of Uregga, suspended by their tails, waiting to gobble up travellers and stray animals. The ants in that forest are not to be despised. You cannot travel without being covered by them, and they sting like wasps. There are leopards in countless numbers. Every native wears a leopard-skin cap. Gorillas haunt the woods in legions, and woe befall the man or woman they meet; they run and fasten their fangs in the hands, and bite off the fingers one by one, and spit them out one after another. The people are man-eaters. It is nothing but constant fighting. A party of three hundred guns started for Uregga; only sixty returned. If we go by river, there are falls after falls. Ah, sir, the country is bad, and we have given up trying to trade in that direction.'

But, despite the terrible news of Abed, the son of Friday,

Tippu-Tib was not averse to earning a decent fee. Pending his definite acceptance of a proffered sum of a thousand pounds, I consulted my remaining companion, Frank Pocock.

While my little ebon page Mabruki poured out the evening's coffee, I described the difficulty we were in. I said, 'These Arabs have told such frightful tales about the lands north of here, that unless Tippu-Tib accepts my offer, the expedition will be broken up, for our men are demoralized through fear of cannibals and pythons, leopards and gorillas, and all sorts of horrible things. Canoes we cannot get; both Livingstone and Cameron failed. Now, what do you say, Frank, shall we go south to Lake Lincoln, Lake Kamalondo, Lake Bemba, and down to the Zambezi?'

'Ah, that's a fine trip, sir.'

'Or shall we explore north-east of here until we strike the Muta Nzige, then strike across to Uganda, and back to Zanzibar?'

'Ah, that would be a fine job, sir, if we could do it.'

'Or shall we follow this great river, which for all these thousands of years has been flowing northward through hundreds, possibly thousands of miles, of which no one has ever heard a word? Fancy, by and by, after building or buying canoes, floating down the river, day by day, to the Nile, or to some vast lake in the far north, or to the Congo and the Atlantic Ocean! Think of steamers from the mouth of the Congo to Lake Bemba!'

'I say, sir, let us toss up, best two out of three to decide it!'

'Toss away, Frank; here is a rupee. Heads for the north and the Lualaba; tails for the south and Katanga.'

Frank, with beaming face, tossed the coin high up. It showed tails!

He tossed again, and tails won six times running! But despite the omen of the coin, and the long and short straws, I resolved to cling to the north and to the Lualaba.

Frank replied, 'Sir, have no fear of me! I shall stand by you. The last words of my dear old father were, "Stick by your master," and there is my hand, sir; you shall never have cause to doubt me.' And poor Frank kept his word like a true man.

Tippu-Tib eventually agreed, and signed a contract, and I gave him a promissory note for one thousand pounds.

On the 5th of November, 1876, a force of about seven hundred people, consisting of Tippu-Tib's slaves and my expedition, departed from the town of Nyangwe and entered the dismal forest-land north. A straight line from this point to the Atlantic Ocean would measure one thousand and seventy miles; another to the Indian Ocean would measure only nine hundred and twenty miles; we had not reached the centre of the continent by seventy-five miles.

Outside the woods blazed a blinding sunshine; underneath that immense and everlasting roof-foliage were a solemn twilight and the humid warmth of a Turkish bath. The trees shed continual showers of tropic dew. Down the boles and branches, massive creepers and slender vegetable cords, the warm moisture trickled and fell in great globes. The wet earth exhaled the moisture back in vapour, which, touching the cold, damp foliage overhung high above our heads, became distilled into showers. As we struggled on through the mud, the perspiration exuded from every pore. Our clothes were soon wet and heavy, with sweat and the fine vapoury rain. Every few minutes we crossed ditches filled with water, overhung by depths of leafage. Our usual orderly line was therefore soon broken; the column was miles in length. Every man required room to sprawl, and crawl, and scramble as he best could, and every fibre and muscle was required for that purpose.

Sometimes prostrate forest-giants barred the road with a mountain of twigs and branches. The pioneers had to carve a passage through for the caravan and the boat sections. If I was so fortunate as to gain the summit of a hill, I inhaled long draughts of the pure air, and looked out over a sea of foliage stretching to all points of the compass. I had certainly seen forests before, but all others, compared to this, were mere faggots. It appalled the stoutest heart; it disgusted me with its slush and reek, its gloom and monotony.

For ten days we endured it; then the Arabs declared they could go no further. As they were obstinate in this determination, I had recourse to another arrangement. I promised them five hundred pounds if they would escort us twenty marches only. It was accepted. I proposed to strike for the river. On our way to it, we came to a village, whose sole street was adorned with one hundred and eighty-six skulls, laid in two parallel lines. The natives declared them to be the skulls of gorillas, but Professor Huxley, to whom I showed specimens, pronounced them to be human.

Seventeen days from Nyangwe, we saw again the great river. Remembering the toil of the forest-march, and viewing the stately breadth and calm flow of the mighty stream, I here resolved to launch my boat for the last time.

While we screwed the sections together, a small canoe, with two Bagenya fishermen, appeared in front of our camp by the river.

'Brothers!' we hailed them, 'we wish to cross the river. Bring your canoes and ferry us across. We will pay you well with cowries and bright beads.'

'Who are you?'

'We are from Nyangwe.'

'Ah! you are Wasambye!'

'No, we have a white man as chief.'

'If he fills my canoe with shells, I will go and tell my people you wish to go over.'

'We will give you ten shells for the passage of every man.'

'We want a thousand for each man.'

'That is too much; come, we will give you twenty shells for every man.'

'Not for ten thousand, my brother. We do not want you to cross the river. Go back, Wasambye; you are bad. Wasambye are bad, bad, bad!'

They departed, singing the wildest, weirdest note I ever heard. I subsequently discovered it to be a kind of savage-telegraphy, which I came to dread, as it always preceded trouble.

About noon, the boat was launched for her final work. When we rowed across the river, the mere sight of her long oars, striking the water with uniform movement, alarmed the unsophisticated aborigines. They yielded at last, and the double caravan was transported to the left bank. We passed our first night in the Wenya land in quietness; but, in the morning, the natives had disappeared. Placing thirty-six of the people in the boat, we floated down the river with the current, close to the left bank, along which the land-party marched. But the river bore us down much faster than the land-party was able to proceed. The two divisions lost touch of one another for three days.

Nothing could be more pacific than the solitary boat gliding down on the face of the stream, without a movement of oar or paddle; but its appearance, nevertheless, was hailed by the weird war-cries of the Wenya. The villages below heard the notes, shivered with terror, and echoed the warning cry 'to beware of strangers afloat.'

We came to the confluence of the Ruiki with the Lualaba. I formed a camp at the point to await our friends. I rowed up the Ruiki to search for them. Returning two hours later, I found the camp was being attacked by hosts of savages.

On the third day the land-column appeared, weary, haggard, sick, and low-spirited. Nevertheless, nothing was to be gained by a halt. We were in search of friendly savages, if such could be found, where we might rest. But, as day after day passed on, we found the natives increasing rather than abating in wild rancour, and unreasonable hate of strangers. At every curve and bend they 'telephoned' along the river the warning signals; the forests on either bank flung hither and thither the strange echoes; their huge wooden drums sounded the muster for fierce resistance; reed arrows, tipped with poison, were shot at us from the jungle as we glided by. To add to our distress, the small-pox attacked the caravan, and old and young victims of the pest were flung daily into the river. What a terrible land! Both banks, shrouded in tall, primeval forests, were filled with invisible, savage enemies; out of every bush glared eyes flaming with hate; in the stream lurked the crocodiles to feed upon the unfortunates; the air seemed impregnated with the seeds of death!

On the 18th of December, our miseries culminated in a grand effort of the savages to annihilate us. The cannibals had manned the topmost branches of the trees above the village of Vinya Njara; they lay like pards crouching amidst the garden-plants, or coiled like pythons in clumps of sugar-cane. Maddened by wounds, we became deadly in our aim; the rifle seldom failed. But, while we skirmished in the woods, the opposite bank of the river belched flotillas, which recalled us to the front, and the river-bank. For three days, with scarcely any rest, the desperate fighting lasted. Finally, Tippu-Tib appeared. His men cleared the woods; and by night I led a party across the river, and captured thirty-six canoes belonging to those who had annoyed us on the right bank. Then peace was made. I purchased twenty-three canoes, and surrendered the others.

Beyond Vinya Njara, the Arabs would not proceed, and I did not need them. We were far enough from Nyangwe. Its seductive life could no longer tempt my people. Accordingly, we prepared to part.

I embarked my followers in the canoes and boat. Tippu-Tib ranged his people along the bank. His Wanyamuezi chanted the mournful farewell. We surrendered ourselves to the strong flood, which bore us along to whatever Fate reserved in store for us.

Dense woods covered both banks and islands. Though populous settlements met our eyes frequently, our intercourse with the aborigines was of a fitfully fierce character. With an audacity sprung from ignorance, and cannibal greed, they attacked us with ever fresh relays. A few weak villages allowed our flotilla to glide by unmolested, but the majority despatched their bravest warriors, who assailed us with blind fury. Important tributaries, such as the Uruidi, the Loweva, the Leopold, and the Lufu, opened wide gaps in the dark banks, and lazy creeks oozed from amid low flats and swamps.

Armies of parrots screamed overhead as they flew across the river; aquatic birds whirred by us to less disturbed districts; legions of monkeys sported in the branchy depths; howling baboons alarmed the solitudes; crocodiles haunted the sandy points and islets; herds of hippopotami grunted thunderously at our approach; elephants bathed their sides by the margin of the river; there was unceasing vibration from millions of insects throughout the livelong day. The sky was an azure dome, out of which the sun shone large and warm; the river was calm, and broad, and brown. While we floated past the wilderness, we were cheered by its calm and restful aspect, but the haunts of the wild men became positively hateful.

Such were my experiences until I arrived at what is now known as the Stanley Falls. The savages gathered about us on the river, and lined the shore to witness the catastrophe, but I faced the left bank, drove the natives away, and landed. For twenty-two days I toiled to get past the seven cataracts — my left flank attacked by the ruthless and untiring natives, my right protected by the boiling and raging flood. On the 28th of January, my boats were safe below the Falls.

I was just twenty miles north of the Equator. Since I first sighted the mysterious Lualaba, I had only made about sixty miles of westing in a journey of nearly four hundred miles. Therefore its course had been mainly northward and Nileward, almost parallel with the trend of the Tanganyika.

I myself was still in doubt as to what river-system it belonged to. But below the Falls, the Lualaba, nearly a mile wide, curved northwest. 'Ha! it is the Niger, or the Congo,' I said. I had not much time to speculate, however. Every hour was replete with incidents. The varied animal life on the shores, the effervescing face of the turbid flood, the subtle rising and sinking of the greedy crocodile, the rampant plunge and trumpet snort of the hippos, the unearthly, flesh-curdling cry of the relentless cannibal — had it not been for these, which gave tone to our life, there was every disposition to brood, and dream, and glide on insensibly to eternal forgetfulness. Looked I ahead, I viewed the stern river streaming away — far away into a tremulous, vaporous ocean. If you followed that broad band of living waters, quick and alert as the senses might be at first, you soon became conscious that you were subsiding into drowsiness as the eyes rested on the trembling vapours exhaled by river and forest, which covered the distance as with silver gauze; then the unknown lands loomed up in the imagination, with most fantastic features, the fancy roamed through pleasing medleys, —

> 'And balmy dreams calmed all our pains,
> And softly hushed our woes.'

But see! we have arrived at the confluence of the Lualaba with a river which rivals it in breadth. Down the latter, a frantic host of feathered warriors urge a fleet of monstrous canoes. They lift their voices in a vengeful chorus, the dense forest repeats it, until it flies pealing from bank to bank. The war-horns are blown with deafening blasts, the great drums boom out a sound which fills our ears and deafens our sense of hearing. For a moment, we are aghast at the terrific view! The instinct of most of our party is to fly. Fly from that infuriate rush! Impossible! The rifles of our boat are directed against the fugitives. They are bidden to return, to form a line, to drop anchor. The shields which have been our booty from many a fight are lifted to bulwark the non-combatants, the women and the children; and every rifleman takes aim, waiting for the word. It is 'neck or nothing'! I have no time to pray, or take sentimental looks around, or to breathe a savage farewell to the savage world!

There are fifty-four canoes. The foremost is a Leviathan among native craft. It has eighty paddlers, standing in two rows, with spears poised for stabbing, their paddles knobbed with ivory, and the blades carved. There are eight steersmen at the stern, a group of prime young warriors at the bow, capering gleefully, with shield and spear; every arm is ringed with broad ivory bracelets, their heads gay with parrot-feathers.

The Leviathan bears down on us with racing speed, its consorts on either flank spurting up the water into foam, and shooting up jets with their sharp prows; a thrilling chant from two thousand throats rises louder and louder on our hearing.

Presently, the poised spears are launched, and a second later my rifles respond with a ripping, crackling explosion, and the dark bodies of the canoes and paddlers rush past us. For a short time, the savages are paralyzed; but they soon recover. They find there is death in those flaming tubes in the hands of the strangers, and, with possibly greater energy than they advanced, they retreat, the pursued becoming the pursuers in hot chase.

My blood is up. It is a murderous world, and I have begun to hate the filthy, vulturous shoals who inhabit it. I pursue them up-stream, up to their villages; I skirmish in their streets, drive them pell-mell into the woods beyond, and level their ivory temples; with frantic haste I fire the huts, and end the scene by towing the canoes into mid-stream and setting them adrift!

Now, suspecting everything with the semblance of man, like hard-pressed stags, wearied with fighting, our nerves had become unstrung. We were still only in the middle of the continent, and yet we were being weeded out of existence, day by day, by twos and threes. The hour of utter exhaustion was near, when we should lie down like lambs, and offer our throats to the cannibal butchers.

But relief and rest were near. The last great affluent had expanded the breadth of the Lualaba to four miles. A series of islands were formed in mid-river, lengthy and narrow, lapping one another; and between each series there were broad channels. I sheered off the mainland, entered these channels, and was shut out from view.

'Allah,' as I cried out to my despairing people, 'has provided these liquid solitudes for us. Bismillah, men, and forward.'

But, every two or three days, the channels, flowing diagonally, floated us in view of the wild men of the mainland. With drumming and horn-blowing, these ruthless people came on, ignoring the fact that their intended victims might hold their lives dear, might fight strenuously for their existence. The silly charms and absurd fetishes inspired the credulous natives with a belief in their invulnerability. They advanced with a bearing which, by implication, I understood to mean, 'It is useless to struggle, you know. You cannot evade the fate in store for you! Ha, ha; meat, meat, we shall have meat to-day!' and they dashed forward with the blind fury of crocodiles in sight of their prey, and the ferocious valour of savages who believe themselves invincible.

What then? Why, I answered them with the energy of despair, and tore through them with blazing rifles, leaving them wondering and lamenting.

I sought the mid-channel again, and wandered on with the current, flanked by untenanted islets, which were buried in tropical shade by clustered palms and the vivid leafage of paradise. Ostracised by savage humanity, the wilds embraced us, and gave us peace and rest. In the voiceless depths of the watery wilderness we encountered neither treachery nor guile. Therefore we clung to them as long as we could, and floated down, down, hundreds of miles.

The river curved westward, then south-westward. Ah, straight for the mouth of the Congo! It widened daily; the channels became numerous. Sometimes in crossing from one to another there was an open view of water from side to side. It might have been a sea for all we knew, excepting that there was a current, and the islands glided by us.

After forty days, I saw hills; the river contracted, gathered its channels one by one, until at last we floated down a united and powerful river, banked by mountains. Four days later we emerged out of this on a circular expanse. The white cliffs of Albion were duplicated by white sand-cliffs on our right, at the entrance, capped by grassy downs. Cheered at the sight, Frank Pocock cried out, 'Why, here are the cliffs of Dover, and this singular expanse we shall call Stanley Pool!'

The stretch of uninterrupted navigation I had just descended measured one thousand and seventy statute miles. At the lower end of Stanley Pool, the river contracted again, and presently launched itself down a terraced steep, in a series of furious rapids.

Resolved to cling to the river, we dragged our canoes by land past the rapids, lowered them again into the river, paddled down a few miles with great rock-precipices on either hand. We encountered another rapid, and again we drew our canoes overland. It grew to be a protracted and fatal task. At Kalulu Falls six of my men were drowned. Accidents occurred almost every day. Casualties became frequent. Twice myself and crew were precipitated down the rapids. Frank Pocock, unwarned by the almost every-day calamity, insisted that his crew should shoot the Massassa Falls. The whirlpool below sucked all down to the soundless depths, out of which Frank and two young Zanzibaris never emerged alive.

But still resolute to persevere, I continued the desperate task, and toiled on and on, now in danger of cataracts, then besieged by famine, until, on the 31st of July, I arrived at a point on the Lower Congo, last seen by Captain Tuckey, an English Naval officer, in 1816. I knew then, beyond dispute of the most captious critic, that the Lualaba, whose mystery had wooed Livingstone to his death, was no other than the 'lucid, long-winding Zaire,' as sung by Camoens, or the mighty Congo.

Now, farewell, brave boat! seven thousand miles, up and down broad Africa, thou hast accompanied me! For over five thousand miles thou hast been my home! Now lift her up tenderly, boys, so tenderly, and let her rest!

Wayworn and feeble, we began our overland march, through a miserable country inhabited by a sordid people. They would not sell me food, unless for gin, they said. Gin! and from me! 'Why, men, two and a half years ago I left the Indian Sea, and can I have gin? Give us food that we may live, or beware of hungry men!' They gave us refuse of their huts, some pea-nuts, and stunted bananas. We tottered on our way to the Atlantic, a scattered column of long and lean bodies, dysentery, ulcers, and scurvy, fast absorbing the remnant of life left by famine.

I despatched couriers ahead. Two days from Boma, they returned with abundance. We revived, and, staggering, arrived at Boma on the 9th of August, 1877, and an international gathering of European merchants met me, and, smiling a warm welcome, told me kindly that I 'had done right well.'

Three days later, I gazed upon the Atlantic Ocean, and I saw the puissant river flowing into the bosom of that boundless, endless sea. But, grateful as I felt to Him who had enabled me to pierce the Dark Continent from east to west, my heart was charged with grief, and my eyes with tears, at the thought of the many comrades and friends I had lost.

The unparalleled fidelity of my people to me demanded that I should return them to their homes. Accordingly, I accompanied them round the Cape of Good Hope to Zanzibar, where, in good time, we arrived, to the great joy of their friends and relatives, when father embraced son, and brother brother, and mothers their daughters, and kinsmen hailed as heroes the men who had crossed the continent.

Only the inevitable limitations of space prevent a citation from the fuller account of this expedition in Stanley's book, 'Through the Dark Continent,' of some passages illustrating the loyal and tender relations between him and his black followers. Nothing in the story exceeds in human interest the final scene, his conveying of his surviving force, from the mouth of the Congo, around the Cape, to their homes in Zanzibar, so removing their depression arising from the fear that, having found again his own people, he may leave them; their gladness at the re-assurance he gives; the arrival at

HENRY M. STANLEY AND HIS MEN AT ZANZIBAR, 1877

Zanzibar, after three weeks' voyage; the astonishment and delight of the reunion with relatives and friends; the sorrowful parting with their master. When he went on board the steamer to sail for Europe, a deputation of the best followed him on board, to offer their help in reaching his home, if he needed it, and to declare that they would start for no new adventure on the continent until they heard that he had safely reached his own land.

The second pay-day was devoted to hearing the claims for wages due to the faithful dead. Poor, faithful souls! With an ardour and a fidelity unexpected, and an immeasurable confidence, they had followed me to the very death! True, negro nature had often asserted itself; but it was, after all, but human nature. They had never boasted that they were heroes, but they exhibited truly heroic stuff while coping with the varied terrors of the hitherto untrodden, and apparently endless, wilds of broad Africa.

They were sweet and sad moments, those of parting. What a long, long and true friendship was here sundered! Through what strange vicissitudes of life had they not followed me! What wild and varied scenes had we not seen together! What a noble fidelity these untutored souls had exhibited! The chiefs were those who had followed me to Ujiji in 1871: they had been witnesses of the joy of Livingstone at the sight of me; they were the men to whom I entrusted the safe-guard of Livingstone on his last and fatal journey; who had mourned by his corpse at Muilla, and borne the illustrious dead to the Indian Ocean.

In a flood of sudden recollection, all the stormy period, here ended, rushed in upon my mind; the whole panorama of danger and tempest through which these gallant fellows had so staunchly stood by me — these gallant fellows now parting from me! Rapidly, as in some apocalyptic trance, every vision, every scene of strife with Man and Nature, through which these poor men and women had borne me company, and solaced me by the simple sympathy of common suffering, came hurrying across my memory; for each face before me was associated with some adventure, or some peril; reminded me of some triumph, or of some loss.

What a wild, weird retrospect it was, that mind's flash over the troubled past! So like a troublous dream!

And for years and years to come, in many homes in Zanzibar, there will be told the great story of our journey, and the actors in it will be heroes among their kith and kin. For me, too, they are heroes, these poor ignorant children of Africa; for, from the first deadly struggle in savage Ituru, to the last struggling rush into Embomma, they had rallied to my voice like veterans; and in the hour of need they had never failed me. And thus, aided by their willing hands and by their loyal hearts, the expedition had been successful, and the three great problems of the Dark Continent's geography had been fairly solved. LAUS DEO.

CHAPTER XVI

FOUNDING THE CONGO STATE

THE first work, exploration, was done. Now for the harder task, civilisation. That was henceforth the main purpose and passion of Stanley's life. For him, the quest of wider knowledge meant a stage towards the betterment of mankind. He had laid open a tract comparable in extent and resources to the basin of the Amazon, or the Mississippi. What his vision saw, what his supreme effort was given to, was the transformation of its millions of people from barbarism, oppressed by all the ills of ignorance, superstition, and cruelty, into happy and virtuous men and women. His aim was as pure and high as Livingstone's. But, as a means, he looked not alone to the efforts of isolated missionaries, but to the influx of great tides of beneficent activities.

He sought to pour the civilisation of Europe into the barbarism of Africa, and the prime force to which he looked was the natural, legitimate desire for gain, by ways of traffic; the African and the European both eager for the exchanges which should be for the good of both. With this, he counted on the scientific curiosity, and the philanthropic zeal, of the civilised world to assist the work.

The curse of interior Africa had been its isolation. Its only contact with the outer world had been through the ferocious slave-trade, carried on by Europeans on its western shore through four centuries, until suppressed under English leadership, but still maintained by Arabs, working wholesale ruin from the east.

A natural channel, and an invitation to legitimate and wholesome commerce, was the vast waterway of the Upper Congo, which Stanley had just discovered. The obstacle which had prevented its employment was a strip of two hundred miles next the sea, where a succession of cataracts and rapids, through rough and sterile hills, made navigation impossible. This strip must be pierced, first by a wagon-road, later by a railroad. Its human obstacles, principally the rapacious African traders, or 'middle-men,' shrewd, greedy, and jealous of the white man's intrusion, must be propitiated. Then, from mouth to source of the river, stations must be established as centres of trade and of friendly intercourse.

That was Stanley's plan; and for fit and adequate support he looked first to the English people and the English Government.

Before he touched English soil, on his return at the end of 1877, his letters in the 'Telegraph' had hinted at the vast and inviting political possibilities which the new country offered to England.

With scarcely a breathing-space, he threw himself into the work of persuading, preaching, imploring, the ruling powers in English Commerce and in public affairs to seize this grand opportunity.

He spoke in all the commercial centres, especially in Manchester and Liverpool, setting forth the immense advantages to trade of such an enterprise. He had audience with such public men as would listen, or seem to listen. But the Government and the people of England turned a deaf ear.

Stanley was, by some, called 'Quixotic'; by others, an 'adventurer,' or 'a buccaneer.' Others professed to be shocked, and said he put Commerce before Religion!! So he received no help or encouragement from Britain.

But, in Belgium, King Leopold was already keenly interested in African possibilities. In the summer of 1877, he had convened a company of geographers and scientific men, who had organised the 'International African Association' for exploration, and, perhaps, something further. Their first essays were mostly on the eastern coast.

On Stanley's return, at the end of 1877, he was met at Marseilles by messengers of King Leopold, to urge him to come to Brussels for a conference, and for the initiation of further African enterprise.

He excused himself on the plea of physical exhaustion and unfitness for further undertakings. But he had other reasons, in his strong preference for England as his supporting power. After half a year of ill-success in that quarter, in August, he met King Leopold's Commissioners in Paris. In the discussion there, the vague purpose to do something scientific or commercial in the basin of the Congo crystallised into Stanley's plan as given above. There was close study, analysis, and detail; the papers were transmitted to the King, and Stanley kept in touch with the project. *But again he urged upon England that she should take the lead; and, again, in vain.*

Thereupon, he accepted an invitation to the Royal Palace at Brussels in November, and there met 'various persons of more or less note in the commercial and monetary world, from England, Germany, France, Belgium, and Holland.' An organisation was made, under the name, 'Comité d'Étude du Haut Congo' (which afterward became practically identified with the 'International'). Plans were adopted on a modest scale; the sum of twenty thousand pounds was subscribed for immediate use; and Stanley was put in charge of the work. Colonel Strauch, of the Belgian Army, was chosen President of the Society; and he, and his associates, selected Stanley's European assistants, and acted as his base of supplies during the five and a half years — January, 1879, to June, 1884 — which he spent in the work.

The story of that work is told at large in Stanley's book, 'The Congo, and the Founding of its Free State.' Less full of adventure and wonder than his preceding and following works, it is rich in material for whoever studies the relations, actual and possible, between civilised and savage men. The merest outline of it is given here, with quotations chosen mainly to illustrate the character of its leader. For the nucleus of his working force, he went back to Zanzibar, and chose seventy men, forty of whom had before gone with him through Africa, and who, as a body, now served him with a like fidelity and devotion. He took them around the continent, by Suez and Gibraltar, and reached the mouth of the Congo in August, 1879.

August 15, 1879. Arrived off the mouth of the Congo. Two years have passed since I was here before, after my descent of the great River, in 1877. Now, having been the first to explore it, I am to be the first who shall prove its utility to the world. I now debark my seventy Zanzibaris and Somalis for the purpose of beginning to civilise the Congo Basin.

With a force recruited up to two hundred and ten negroes, and fourteen Europeans, and with four tiny steamers, he set out for the mastery of the river. A few miles' steaming away from the trading establishments at the mouth, up to the head of navigation, and the first station, Vivi, is planted; wooden huts brought from England are set up, and wagon-roads are made. Then, a Labour of Hercules, transport must be found for steamers and goods through a long stretch of rugged hills. After exploration, the route must be chosen; then the stubborn, dogged labour of road-building, over mountains and along precipices; the Chief, hammer and drill in hand, showing his men how to use their tools; endless marching and hauling; and, at last, a whole year's work (1880) is done; forward and backward, they had travelled two thousand five hundred and thirty-two miles, and, as a result, they had won a practicable way of fifty-two miles — 'not a holiday affair,' this! Strenuous toil, a diet of beans, goat's meat, and sodden bananas; the muggy atmosphere of the Congo Cañon, with fierce heat from the rocks, and bleak winds through the gorges! Six European and twenty-two native lives, and thirteen whites invalided and retired, were part of the price.

Now, a second station, Isangila, is built; here, as at Vivi, a treaty is made with the natives, and land for the station fairly bought.

Next, we have eighty-eight miles of waterway, and, then, another station at Manyanga. Here came a plague of fever, and the force was further weakened by garrisons left for the three stations. Stanley was desperately ill; after ten days' fight with the fever, the end seemed at hand; he prescribed for himself sixty grains of quinine, and a few minims of hydrobromic acid, in an ounce of Madeira wine; under this overpowering dose his senses reeled; he summoned his European comrades for a farewell, while Death loomed before him, and a vision of a lonely grave. Grasping the hand of his faithful Albert, he struggled long and vainly to speak the words of a parting charge; and when, at last, he uttered an intelligible sentence, — that success brought a rush of relief, and he cried, 'I am saved!' Then came unconsciousness for twenty-four hours; and, afterwards, just life enough to feel hungry; and thus he reached convalescence and recovery.

A push of eight days further, to Stanley Pool, where begins the uninterrupted navigation of the Upper Congo. Here he finds that M. de Brazza, in the pay of France, though *aided by funds from the Comité International of Belgium*, having heard of Stanley's doings, has raced across from the sea, and bargained with the natives for a great strip on the north bank of the river. So, for this region, Stanley secured the south bank. At last, greatly to his encouragement and help, came a re-enforcement of the good Zanzibaris.

Early in 1882, he planted a fine station, named Leopoldville, in honour of the monarch whom Stanley heartily admired, and relied on. On this settlement, when he had finished it to his mind, Stanley looked with special pride and complacency: the block-house, impregnable against fire or musketry; the broad-streeted village for his natives; their gardens of young bananas and vegetables; the plentiful water and fuel; the smooth promenade, where he imagined his Europeans strolling on Sundays, to survey the noble prospect of river, cataract, forests, and mountain.

Stanley, however, saw more than met the eye. He dwelt on the possible future of that magnificent country, with its well-watered soil, now neglected, but richer than any in the whole Mississippi Valley. 'It is like looking at the intelligent face of a promising child: though we find nought in it but innocence, we fondly imagine that we see the germs of a future great genius, — perhaps a legislator, a savant, warrior, or a poet.'

Soon after, a violent fever so disabled him that he was obliged to return to Europe, in 1882. He made his report to the Comité de l'Association Internationale du Congo, which had assumed the authority and duties of the Comité d'Étude. He showed them that he had accomplished all, and more than all, his original commission aimed at, and urged them to complete the work by building a railroad along the lower river, extending the chain of stations, and obtaining concessions of authority from the chiefs along the whole course of the Congo.

To all this the Committee assented, but they were urgent that Stanley should return to take charge. He consented, in spite of impaired health, and started back, after only six weeks in Europe; making condition only, and that with all the persuasiveness at his command, that they should send him able assistants, instead of the irresponsible, flighty-headed youngsters on whom he had been obliged so largely to rely. He dreaded what they might have done, or undone, in his absence. His fears were justified; his journey up the river lay through a mournful succession of neglected and blighted stations; and Leopoldville, of which he had hoped so much, was a grass-grown hungry waste! He did his best to repair the mis-

HENRY M. STANLEY, 1882

chief, and pushed on up the river, the one dominating idea being to establish a succession of stations for a thousand miles along the Upper Congo, as far as Stanley Falls.

Briefly, his route from the ocean covered 110 miles of steaming; then a land march of 235 miles to Stanley Pool, whence the Upper Congo gives clear navigation, for 1070 miles, to Stanley Falls. Numerous tributaries multiply the navigable waterways to about 6000 miles. The district thus watered Stanley estimated as a square of 757 miles either way, a superficies of 57,400 square miles, nearly the dimensions of the future Free State. He found the Lower Congo region unproductive, yielding at first only ground-nuts, palm-oil, and feed-cake for cattle, and, further up-stream, some production of rubber, gum-copal, and ivory. But the Upper Congo was rich in valuable forests and in fertile soil; woods for building, for furniture, and dyes; gums, ivory of elephant and hippopotamus; india-rubber, coffee, gum-copal, and much besides. All this potentiality of 'wealth, beyond the dreams of avarice,' could only be actualised through the perfection of communication: already Stanley was eagerly planning for a railway that should link the Upper Congo with the sea.

Now, for a year and a half, his principal care was to negotiate treaties with the chiefs, which should give political jurisdiction over the territory. Throughout the enterprise, amiable relations with the natives were most successfully cultivated; friction was overcome by patience and tact; firmness, combined with gentleness, in almost every instance averted actual strife. The chiefs were willing enough to cede their political sovereignty, receiving in each case some substantial recompense; foreign intrusion was barred; and the private rights and property of the natives were respected.

Over four hundred chiefs were thus dealt with, and so the foundations of the Free State were established. On his journey up the river he was constantly meeting tribes who were his old acquaintances of six years before. Old *friends* they could scarcely be called, but new friends they readily became. A halo of wonder hung round his first advent; the curiosity born of that memory was heightened by the marvel of the steamboats; the offer of barter was always welcome, and the bales of cloth, the brass rods, the trinkets, — first as a present, then in trade, — were the beginnings of familiar intercourse. Stanley's diplomacies, his peace-makings between hostile tribes, his winning of good-will and enforcement of respect, make a story that should be studied in his full narrative.

The summer of 1884 found the work of founding the State virtually finished, and Stanley nearly finished, too. There had been difficulties of all kinds, in which almost the entire responsibility had rested on his shoulders, and he had reached the limit of his strength; could he but hand over his work to a fit successor! He writes: —

There was a man at that time in retreat, near Mount Carmel. If he but emerged from his seclusion, he had all the elements in him of the man that was needed: indefatigable industry; that magnetism which commands affection, obedience, and perfect trust; that power of reconciling men, no matter of what colour, to their duties; that cheerful promise that in him lay security and peace; that loving solicitude which betokens the kindly chief. That man was General Gordon. For six months I waited his coming; finally, letters came announcing his departure for the Soudan; and, soon after, arrived Lieutenant-colonel Sir Francis de Winton, of the Royal Artillery, in his place.

General Gordon had arranged to take the Governorship of the Lower Congo, under Stanley, who was to govern the Upper Congo; and, together, they were to destroy the slave-trade at its roots. General Gordon wrote a letter to Stanley in which he said that he should be happy to serve under him, and work according to Stanley's ideas. When Sir Francis de Winton went out, Stanley transferred to him the Government of the Congo, and returned to England.

This same year, 1884, saw the recognition of the new State by the civilised powers. England's contribution was mainly indirect. She had previously made a treaty with Portugal, allowing her a strip of African coast, as the result of which she could now have excluded everyone else from the Congo. Manchester, Liverpool, and Glasgow, through their Chambers of Commerce, had remonstrated in vain.

The United States, meanwhile, had been the first to recognise the new State of the Congo. Spurred by General Sandford, formerly Minister to Belgium, who appealed, on the one hand, to American interest in Livingstone and Stanley, and, on the other hand, to commercial possibilities, the American Senate, on April 10, 1884, authorised President Arthur to recognise the International African Association as a governing power on the Congo River. This action, says Stanley, was the birth to new life of the Association.

In view of the menace to the world's trade by the Anglo-Portuguese treaty, Bismarck's strong personality now came to the front, somewhat prompted by King Leopold. Stanley admired the straightforward vigor of the German as much as he admired the philanthropy of the Belgian rule. Bismarck summoned a Conference at Berlin, to which the leading European powers sent delegates. There were also delegates from the United States, and with these Stanley was present as their 'technical adviser,' and, naturally, had a good hearing.

The Conference was mainly interested to secure the commercial freedom of the Niger and the Congo. It gave definite recognition to the Congo Free State. It did map-making with a free hand, marking out European dominions in Africa, with especial profit to France and Portugal, through the adroitness of the French Ambassador, says Stanley, and with the concurrence of Prince Bismarck. Also, quite incidentally, so to speak, the Conference proceeded to lay down the formalities by which a European power was to establish itself on virgin African soil, which consisted, virtually, in putting up a sign-board 'to whom it may concern.' By this simple process, and with no trouble of exploration, purchase, or settlement, Bismarck then calmly proceeded to appropriate a large slice of Eastern Africa, which had been opened up by the British.

The future course of African affairs, including the vesting of the Congo sovereignty in King Leopold, has no place in this story. In this whole chapter of Stanley's work, perhaps the most significant feature, as to his character, and, also, as a lesson in the art of civilisation, is his manner of dealing with the natives. As a concrete instance may be given the story of Ngalyema and the fetish.

Ngalyema, chief of Stanley Pool district, had demanded and received four thousand five hundred dollars' worth of cotton, silk, and velvet goods for granting me the privilege of establishing a station in a wilderness of a place at the commencement of up-river navigation. Owing to this, I had advanced with my wagons to within ten miles of the Pool. I had toiled at this work the best part of two years, and whenever I cast a retrospective glance at what the task had cost me, I felt that it was no joke, and such that no money would bribe me to do over again. Such a long time had elapsed since Ngalyema had received his supplies, that he affected to forget that he had received any; and, as I still continued to advance towards him after the warnings of his messengers, he collected a band of doughty warriors, painted their bodies with diagonal stripes of ochre, soot, chalk, and yellow, and issued fiercely to meet me.

Meantime, the true owners of the soil had enlightened me respecting Ngalyema's antecedents. He was only an enterprising native trader in ivory and slaves, who had fled from the north bank; but, though he had obtained so much money from me by pretences, I was not so indignant at this as at the audacity with which he chose to forget the transaction, and the impudent demand for another supply which underlay this. Ngalyema, having failed to draw any promise by sending messengers, thought he could extort it by appearing with a warlike company. Meantime, duly warned, I had prepared a surprise for him.

I had hung a great Chinese gong conspicuously near the principal tent. Ngalyema's curiosity would be roused. All my men were hidden, some in the steamboat on top of the wagon, and in its shadow was a cool place where the warriors would gladly rest after a ten-mile march; other of my men lay still as death under tarpaulins, under bundles of grass, and in the bush round about the camp. By the time the drum-taps and horns announced Ngalyema's arrival, the camp seemed abandoned except by myself and a few small boys. I was indolently seated in a chair, reading a book, and appeared too lazy to notice anyone; but, suddenly looking up, and seeing my 'brother Ngalyema,' and his warriors, scowlingly regarding me, I sprang up, and seized his hands, and affectionately bade him welcome, in the name of sacred fraternity, and offered him my own chair.

He was strangely cold, and apparently disgruntled, and said:—

'Has not my brother forgotten his road? What does he mean by coming to this country?'

'Nay, it is Ngalyema who has forgotten the blood-bond which exists between us. It is Ngalyema who has forgotten the mountains of goods which I paid him. What words are these of my brother?'

'Be warned, Rock-Breaker. Go back before it is too late. My elders and people all cry out against allowing the white man to come into our country. Therefore, go back before it be too late. Go back, I say, the way you came.'

Speech and counter-speech followed. Ngalyema had exhausted his arguments; but it was not easy to break faith and be uncivil, without plausible excuse. His eyes were reaching round seeking to discover an excuse to fight, when they rested on the round, burnished face of the Chinese gong.

'What is that?' he said.

'Ah, that — that is a fetish.'

'A fetish! A fetish for what?'

'It is a war-fetish, Ngalyema. The slightest sound of that would fill this empty camp with hundreds of angry warriors; they would drop from above, they would spring up from the ground, from the forest about, from everywhere.'

'Sho! Tell that story to the old women, and not to a chief

like Ngalyema. My boy tells me it is a kind of a bell. Strike it and let me hear it.'

'Oh, Ngalyema, my brother, the consequences would be too dreadful! Do not think of such a thing!'

'Strike it, I say.'

'Well, to oblige my dear brother Ngalyema, I will.'

And I struck hard and fast, and the clangorous roll rang out like thunder in the stillness. Only for a few seconds, however, for a tempest of human voices was heard bursting into frightful discords, and from above, right upon the heads of the astonished warriors, leaped yelling men; and from the tents, the huts, the forest round about, they came by sixes, dozens, and scores, yelling like madmen, and seemingly animated with uncontrollable rage. The painted warriors became panic-stricken; they flung their guns and powder-kegs away, forgot their chief, and all thoughts of loyalty, and fled on the instant, fear lifting their heels high in the air; or, tugging at their eyeballs, and kneading the senses confusedly, they saw, heard, and suspected nothing, save that the limbo of fetishes had suddenly broken loose!

But Ngalyema and his son did not fly. They caught the tails of my coat, and we began to dance from side to side, a loving triplet, myself being foremost, to ward off the blow savagely aimed at my 'brothers,' and cheerfully crying out, 'Hold fast to me, my brothers. I will defend you to the last drop of my blood. Come one, come all,' etc.

Presently the order was given, 'Fall in!' and quickly the leaping forms became rigid, and the men stood in two long lines in beautiful order, with eyes front, as though 'at attention.' Then Ngalyema relaxed his hold of my coat-tails, and crept from behind, breathing more freely; and, lifting his hand to his mouth, exclaimed, in genuine surprise 'Eh, Mamma! where did all these people come from?'

'Ah, Ngalyema, did I not tell you that thing was a powerful fetish? Let me strike it again, and show you what else it can do.'

'No! no! no!' he shrieked. 'I have seen enough!'

The day ended peacefully. I was invited to hasten on to Stanley Pool. The natives engaged themselves by the score to assist me in hauling the wagons. My progress was thenceforward steady and uninterrupted, and in due time the wagons and goods-columns arrived at their destination.

But this was only one incident in what may be called the 'education of Ngalyema.' Seldom has teacher had a more unpromising pupil. He was a braggart, a liar, greedy, capricious, abjectly superstitious, mischief-making. Stanley's diary shows how he handled him during three months of neighbourhood. For instance, Ngalyema begged certain articles as presents; Stanley coupled the gift with the stipulation that his followers were not to bring their arms into the camp. The promise was persistently broken; finally, at the head of his armed warriors, Ngalyema was suddenly confronted by Stanley's rifle, and fell at his feet, in abject panic, to be soothed, petted, and brought into a healthy state of mind. 'I am bound to teach this intractable "brother" of mine,' is the comment in the diary.

Again and again he makes trouble; and, always, he is met by the same firm, gentle hand. Slowly he improves, and at last is allowed once more to make 'blood-brotherhood,' with crossing of arms, incisions, and solemn pronouncement by the great fetish-man of the tribe, in token of renewed fraternity and fidelity. Ngalyema might fairly be pronounced a reformed character, and the friendship between him and Stanley became life-long.

Some of you may, perhaps, wonder at the quiet inoffensiveness of the natives, who, on a former expedition, had worried my soul by their ferocity and wanton attacks, night and day; but a very simple explanation of it may be found in Livingstone's Last Journals, dated 28th October, 1870. He says: 'Muini Mukata, who has travelled further than most Arabs, said to me, "If a man goes with a good-natured, civil tongue, he may pass through the worst people in Africa unharmed." This is true, but time also is required; one must not run through a country, but give the people time to become acquainted with you, and let their worst fears subside.'

Now, on the expedition across Africa I had no time to give, either to myself or to them. The river bore my heavy canoes downward; my goods would never have endured the dawdling required by this system of teaching every tribe I met who I was. To save myself and my men from certain starvation, I had to rush on and on, right through. But on this expedition, the very necessity of making roads to haul my enormous six-ton wagons gave time for my reputation to travel ahead of me. My name, purpose, and liberal rewards for native help, naturally exaggerated, prepared a welcome for me, and transformed my enemies of the old time into workmen, friendly allies, strong porters, and firm friends. I was greatly forbearing also; but, when a fight was inevitable, through open violence, it was sharp and decisive. Consequently, the natives rapidly learned that though everything was to be gained by friendship with me, wars brought nothing but ruin.

So it was that he went among these fierce savages as a messenger of good tidings, and they welcomed him. He put his superiority over them to use in making bridges across the gulf between their minds and his. He studied not only their languages, but their ceremonials, and adapted himself to their forms of justice and ways of settling disputes, as in the rite of blood-brotherhood. He brought them not only personal good-will and kind treatment, but the practical advantages of civilisation.

Everywhere he found eagerness to trade, and the possibility of commercial interchange that should be profitable to both sides. Many of them accepted training in labour, and recruited his road-making force. In his treaties with the chiefs, he did not hesitate to purchase full political sovereignty, usually in exchange for goods; for such sovereignty was worthless or harmful to these tribes, compared with the beneficent rule of a superior intelligence. But neither in the formal treaties, nor in the actual practice, was there the least trace of spoliation of land and goods which was practised later, when Stanley had left the Congo. 'It is agreed,' says one of his typical treaties, 'that the term "cession of territory" does not mean the purchase of the soil by the Association, but the purchase of the suzerainty by the Association.'

Stanley's whole treatment of the natives was as simple in its principle as the Golden Rule; it was applied with infinite skill and patience; and in a spirit of heartiest human good-will, dashed, often, with boyish humour that went home to the savage heart. He tells with gusto of the welcome given to frolicking races, and the gambols indulged in by his good Danish follower, Albert: —

The dark faces light up with friendly gleams, and a budding of good-will may perhaps date from this trivial scene. To such an impressionable being as an African native, the self-involved European, with his frigid, imperious manner, pallid white face, and dead, lustreless eyes, is a sealed book.

The most tragic pages in the history relate his coming upon a series of villages just ravaged by a ferocious slave-raid of the Arabs, and afterwards finding a herd of the wretched captives chained and guarded. It is a terrible picture. Over a hundred villages had been devastated, and the five thousand carried away as slaves stood for six times as many slain, or dying by the way-side.[1] The hot impulse rose to strike a blow for their liberation; but it would have been hopeless and useless. On his return journey, Stanley borrowed from the slave-traders several of their number as his companions down the river, to give them an object-lesson as to the impending check on their excursions. To extirpate this slave-trade was among the prime objects of his enterprise, and whatever else failed, this succeeded.

The furthest point he then reached was Stanley Falls, where he planted his station in charge of a solitary white man, the plucky little Scotch engineer, Binnie. Stanley, on his return down the river, reflects on the influences he has planted to extend his work.

We had sown seeds of good-will at every place we had touched, and each tribe would spread diffusively the report of the value and beauty of our labours. Pure benevolence contains within itself grateful virtues. Over natural people nothing has greater charm or such expansible power; its influence grows without effort; its subtlety exercises itself on all who come within hearing of it. Coming in such innocent guise, it offends not; there is nought in it to provoke resentment. Provided patience and good temper guides the chief of Stanley Falls station, by the period of the return of the steamers, the influence of the seedling just planted there will have been extended from tribe to tribe far inland, and amid the persecuted fugitives from the slave-traders.

Among the brightest pages of the story are the occasional returns to some station where a faithful and efficient subordinate, left in charge, has made the wilderness to blossom as a rose. Such is the picture of Equatorville, to which he returned, after a hundred days' absence, to find that the good-will and zeal of two young Army lieutenants had transformed the station from a jungle of waterless scrub; had built and furnished a commodious, tasteful, 'hotel'; had drawn up a code of laws for the moral government of the station, and the amelioration of the wild Bakuti; and planned sanitary improvements worthy of a competent Board of Public Works.

[1] The Rt. Hon. Joseph Chamberlain, presiding at a banquet, in connection with the London School of Tropical Medicine, on May 11, 1905, said: 'Compare the total number killed in the whole series of our expeditions and campaigns in Africa, and you will find they do not approach a fraction of the native population destroyed every year before our advent. My friend, Sir Henry M. Stanley, once told me that, at the time of his early expeditions, he estimated that more than a million natives were slain every year in the Continent of Africa, in inter-tribal warfare and slave-raiding. Where the British flag is planted, there must be British peace; and barbarous methods must be abolished, and law and order substituted for anarchy.'

But too frequent is the opposite story; the subordinates' indolence, neglect, perhaps desertion; and the decadence of the station. The painful element in the story, and ominous of future consequences, is the failures among the men sent out from Europe as his assistants. There were many and honourable exceptions, and these he praises warmly in the book.[1] Such were the Scotch engineer, Binnie, who so stoutly held his solitary post at Stanley Falls; the efficient and fine-spirited Danish sailor, Albert Christopherson; the Scandinavian seaman, Captain Anderson, with his genius for inspiring everyone near him to work; the Englishman, A. B. Swinburne, with a genius for gardening and home-making, and for winning the affection of both whites and blacks; the Italian mechanician, François Flamini, who charmed the steam-engines into docility. But the book tells often of the failures, and the private note-books detail the story more plainly, and tell, too, something of his difficulties with his native helpers.

All the officers, before I sent them to their posts, were instructed by me, orally and in writing, in the very minutiæ of their duties, especially in the mode of conduct to be adopted towards the natives.

The ridiculous inadequacy of our force as opposed to the native population required that each officer should be more prudent than brave, more tactful than zealous. Such conduct invariably made the native pleasantly disposed to us. If some characters among them presumed to think that forbearance sprang from cowardice, and were inclined to be aggressive, the same prudence which they had practised previously would teach them how to deal with such.

It was mainly impressed on the officers that they were to hold their posts more by wit than by force, for the latter was out of the question, except after forethought, and in combination with headquarters. This was due to the fact that the young officers were as ignorant of diplomacy as children. Their instincts were to be disciplinary and dictatorial. The cutting tone of command is offensive to savages, and terrifying to them as individuals.

Captain D. exceeded his instructions in assuming the responsibility of provoking the Arabs at Stanley Falls. He studied only his own fighting instincts, and British resentment against the slaver. At an early period he was too brusque;

[1] *The Congo, and the Founding of its Free State.*

this repelled confidence and roused resentment. While he was expected to represent civil law of the most paternal character, he regarded the thirty Houssas soldiers under his command as qualifying him for the rôle of a military dictator; and as soon as he appeared in that character, the Arabs became unanimous in asserting their independence. Before a man with thirty soldiers can adopt such a tone, he surely ought to have been prepared for the consequences. But he seems to have done nothing except challenge the Arabs. He knew he had so many rounds of ammunition, but his ammunition was damp, and he was not aware of it.[1]

I know that many of my Officers were inclined to regard me as 'hard.' I may now and then have deserved that character, but then it was only when nought *but* hardness availed. When I meet chronic stupidity, laziness, and utter indifference to duty, expostulation ceases, and coercion or hardness begins.

His associates had been the principal cause of the exhibition of this quality, and with some of them he had been very unfortunate.

To describe Bracconier's case, for example, would fill a good-sized book. Others were equally impenetrable to reason and persuasion.

Intuitively, I felt that Braconnier, though polite and agree-

[1] This note, from Stanley's pocket-book, refers to an officer in charge of the station of Stanley Falls. One of the concubines of an Arab chief fled for protection to Captain D., having been beaten by her master. The Arab demanded in civil terms that the woman be returned. Captain D. declared that the woman had sought his protection, and she should remain at his station. The chief insisted, Captain D. resisted. The Arab threatened, Captain D. scoffed at him, and dared him to do his worst. The Arabs thereupon came down, and shot everyone, with the exception of Captain D. and one or two others, who escaped in a terrible plight. The station was burnt, and everything utterly destroyed.

When I asked Stanley what *he* would have done, whether he would have returned the poor, beaten slave-wife to her cruel owner, Stanley replied, 'Certainly, rather than have my station wrecked, and the lives entrusted to me sacrificed; but it would never have come to that. I should have received the Arab with deference and much ceremony, and, after refreshment and compliments, I should have attempted some compromise, such as by offering to buy the woman for cloth and beads; or else I should have returned her, on receiving solemn assurance that she would be mercifully treated. I should explain that I was not free, that if I handed the woman back after she had sought my protection, my chief, hearing of it, would cut off my head, but I would give money for her. The Arab would have understood this kind of talk; he would have treated with me, all would have gone well, and we should have parted the best of friends. It is necessary to use your wit, and never to lose sight of the consequence of your acts.' — D. S.

able, was not to be entrusted with any practical work. His education and character had utterly unfitted him for work of any kind. He was asked to superintend a little road-making. He sought a nice, shady place, and fell asleep; and his men, of course, while they admired him for his easy disposition, did what was most agreeable to them, and dawdled over their work, by which we lost two days. When myself incapacitated by a sudden stroke of fever, I requested him to supervise the descent of the boiler-wagon down a hill; not ten minutes later the boiler and wagon were smashed, and he was brought to me, half-dead from his injuries! He was appointed chief of Leopoldville, but, in four months, the place resembled a ruin. Grass encroached everywhere, the houses were falling to pieces, the gardens choked with weeds, the steamers were lying corroding in the port, the natives were estranged, and he and his men were reduced to a state of siege.

He allowed a young Austrian lieutenant and six Zanzibaris to enter a small unsuitable canoe and attempt to ascend the Congo. Within fifteen minutes of their departure, they were all drowned!

There is always another side to these accusations, and those inclined to believe Bracconier's ridiculous charge of my 'hardness' should try, first, how they would like to endure three years of indolence and incapacity, before they finally dismissed the fellow; let those who criticised me ascertain whether this man distinguished himself in other fields and other missions; though I have no doubt that in a Brussels drawing-room he would be found to be an agreeable companion; but not in Africa, where work has to be done, and progress made.

Then, as regards the coloured people, good as the majority of Zanzibaris were, some of them were indescribably, and for me most unfortunately, dense. One man, who from his personal appearance might have been judged to be among the most intelligent, was, after thirty months' experience with his musket, unable to understand how it was to be loaded! He never could remember whether he ought to drop the powder, or the bullet, into the musket first! Another time he was sent with a man to transport a company of men over a river to camp. After waiting an hour, I strode to the bank of the river and found them paddling in opposite directions, each blaming the other for his stupidity, and, being in a passion of excitement, unable to hear the advice of the men across the river, who were bawling out to them how to manage their canoe.

Another man was so ludicrously stupid that he generally was saved from punishment because his mistakes were so absurd. We were one day floating down the Congo, and, it being near camping time, I bade him, as he happened to be bowman on the occasion, to stand by and seize the grass on the bank to arrest the boat, when I should call out. In a little while we came to a fit place, and I cried, 'Hold hard, Kirango!'—'Please God, Master,' he replied, and forthwith sprang on shore and seized the grass with both hands, while *we*, of course, were rapidly swept down-river, leaving him alone and solitary on the bank! The boat's crew roared at the ridiculous sight; but, nevertheless, his stupidity cost the tired men a hard pull to ascend again, for not every place was available for a camp. He it was, also, who, on an occasion when we required the branch of a species of arbutus which overhung the river to be cut away, to allow the canoes to be brought nearer to the bank for safety, actually went astride of the branch, and chopped away until he fell into the water with the branch, and lost our axe. He had seated himself on the *outer* end of the branch!

The coloured men accepted the reproaches they deserved with such good-nature that, however stupid they were, I could not help forgiving and forgetting. But it was not so with the officers. Their *amour-propre* was so much offended that, if I ventured on a rebuke, it was remembered with so much bitterness, that an officer who was continually erring was also constantly in a resentful mood. I could not discharge a man for a blunder, or even a few blunders; but, if disobeying and making unfortunate mistakes was his chronic state, and he always resented instruction, it can easily be imagined that life with such a one was not pleasant. There were periods when careless acts resulted fatally to others; or when great vexation, or pecuniary loss, went on for months consecutively; until I really became afraid to ask any officer to undertake any duty.

HENRY M. STANLEY, 1885

Who would suppose that out of five intelligent Belgian officers bidding a sixth *bon voyage* not one could perceive by the size of the canoe, the number of people in it, and the manner the departing friend was standing in the little cockle-shell, that the voyage must end disastrously? and yet not one had the least suspicion that the young man was going to his doom, and about to take six fellows with him! Who would have imagined that those five horror-struck gentlemen would have permitted two of their companions to venture upon attempting the same hazardous voyage the very next day? And yet they did, without so much as a protest; and, though the two unhappy voyagers saved their lives by springing on shore, their boat and all their effects were swept over a cataract.

Not long after, another of these officers, who belonged to a boat-club on a Belgian river, thought he would establish one of his own on the Upper Congo. As a first step he purchased an elegant canoe, paying heavily for it. He attached a keel-piece to it, made a mast and a sail, and one day he went sailing smoothly towards the middle of the river where it was four miles wide. Presently, having got beyond view of his station, the wind died away, and he was carried down by the mighty flood. He began to cry out for aid, as he had forgotten his paddles; but his cries could not be heard, he was alone on the wide waters! Towards midnight, his men, getting anxious, set out in search of him, and, after many hours, found him nearly distracted with terror, and brought him to camp, vowing he would never again trust himself alone on the Congo!

A short time after this, another officer and a French missionary were devoured by cannibals, with eleven Zanzibaris who accompanied them. The details of the story went to prove that, in this case again, the military officer proved his inaptitude to learn, though in other ways the young man was exemplary. Still, the disposition to blunder seemed so prevalent that he who was responsible for the good management of their affairs might well be pardoned, if, in his anxiety for the welfare of those under him, he should exact obedience in a more peremptory tone than formerly.

Another officer had his station burned twice, with all the property stored in it. He was relieved of his charge, and appointed to an honourable mission; but, after setting out, he suddenly decided to abandon his people; leaving them to find their own way, whilst he slipped off to the coast, 'to buy a pair of boots,' as he said. No one could have appeared more astonished than he was when, after the third glaring offence, he was told that he was no longer needed.

Another officer was supplied with a small company of choice men, and I instructed him to build a station with a friendly tribe, which had desired it for the opening of trade. Within a few days he began shooting promiscuously at the natives with a revolver; and, on one of his men expostulating with him, he turned the weapon upon his faithful servant and shot him in the head; upon which, the remainder of the men flung themselves upon him, and, having disarmed him, carried him, bound hand and foot, to me. The officer was escorted to the coast; I charged him with being a dangerous lunatic, though no one would have supposed, from his appearance and language, that he was thus afflicted.

I could go on with pages of these extraordinary misadventures, all of which I had to endure with some of the officers who were sent out to me. I but cite these few instances, taken at random, to prove that there is another view to be taken when the responsible head of an expedition, or enterprise of this kind, is charged with being 'hard.' One is not likely to be hard with persons who perform their duties; but it is difficult to be mild, or amiable, with people who are absolutely incapable, and who will not listen to admonition without bristling with resentment.

The only power I possessed with officers of this kind was that of dismissal, which I forbore to use too frequently because, in doing so, I punished the Association. It was only in extreme cases that the power was exercised. In Europe, of course, there would be no necessity for many words or sore feelings; but in Africa, I could not lose eighty pounds for a solitary evidence of incapacity. I practised forbearance, I tried to instruct, to expostulate, to admonish, —once, twice, thrice; I made every effort to teach and train; but, at last, when nothing availed, I was forced to have recourse to dismissal. Being of an open temper and frank disposition, and always willing to hear what my officers or men had to say, though as a leader of men I could not hob-nob with my officers, they ought to have found no difficulty in understanding me. The black man certainly was never at a loss to do so.

No man is free from imperfections; but when one is genially disposed, and evinces good-will, a man who fastens upon *one* imperfection, and constantly harps upon that, shows his own narrow-mindedness and incapacity.

I have had no friend on any expedition, no one who could possibly be my companion, on an equal footing, except while with Livingstone.

How could any young men, fresh from their school-rooms, look with my eyes upon any person or thing within notice? A mathematician might as well expect sympathy from an infant busy at the alphabet, as the much-travelled may expect to find responsive feelings in youths fresh from home or college. How can he who has witnessed many wars hope to be understood by one whose most shocking sight has been a nose-bleed?

I was still in that fierce period of life when a man feels himself sufficient for himself, when he abounds in self-confidence, glories in a blazing defiance of danger and obstacles, is most proud and masterful, and least disposed to be angelic.

It is strange that no novelist, to my knowledge, has alluded to this strong virility of purpose which, at a certain stage, is all-powerful in men's characters.

Though altogether solitary, I was never less conscious of solitude; though as liable to be prostrated by fever as the youngest, I was never more indifferent to its sharpest attacks, or less concerned for its results. My only comfort was my work. To it I ever turned as to a friend. It occupied my days, and I dwelt fondly on it at night. I rose in the morning, welcoming the dawn, only because it assisted me to my labour; and only those who regarded it from a similar temperament could I consider as my friends. Though this may be poorly expressed, neverthless, those who can comprehend what I mean will understand the main grounds.

The founding of the Congo Free State was the greatest single enterprise of Stanley's life. Perhaps nothing else so called out and displayed his essential qualities. Its ultimate fruit cannot be so clearly measured as the search for Livingstone, or the first exploration of the Congo. Of those enterprises he was himself the Alpha and the Omega; each was a task for a single man, and the achievement was measured by the man's personality. But the founding of the Free State was a multiple task, involving a host of workers. He had not made the selection of his helpers, except the rank and file, and the rank and file did not fail him. It was his lieutenants, selected by others, among whom the perilous defect was found. Further, his undertaking, in its essential nature, involved dangers which it was doubtless well he did not wholly foresee, for they might have daunted even *his* spirit.

He broke down the wall between a savage and a civilised people, and the tides rushed together, as at the piercing of Suez. On either side were both lifting and lowering forces. The faults and weakness of the savage were plain to see; his merit and his promise not so easy of discernment. But the 'civilised' influences, too, were extremely mixed. There was the infectious energy of the able trader, and his material contributions; there were the distinctly missionary workers; and there were sentiments of humanity and justice, often obscured or perplexed, but, when educated, powerful to compel Governments to ways of righteousness. With these higher powers mingled blind and selfish lust of gain; the degeneracy of philanthropy in its partnership with profit; the selfish feuds of race and nationality, each for itself, alone; lastly, the easy, deadly contempt of the white man for the 'nigger.' To cast a prosperous horoscope for the evolution of the African race, one must hold strongly to the higher power we call Providence.

The instrument of that power was the man who brought Europe and America into touch with Darkest Africa. His example and his ideal shine like a star above the continent he opened to the world's knowledge. When the observant savages watched him, as the rough ground of Vivi was subdued; when, later, they saw him, as the fifty-mile roadway was bridging the hills and chasms, and with drill and hammer he taught and led his followers, they gave him the name BULA MATARI, 'Breaker of Rocks.' By hit, or by wit, they struck his central quality — concentrated energy, victoriously battling with the hardest that earth could offer, all to make earth goodly and accessible to man. A Maker of Roads, a Breaker of Rocks, was he all his life long — *Bula Matari !*

CHAPTER XVII

THE RESCUE OF EMIN

PART I. THE RELIEF

MY fifth expedition was due to the overwhelming catastrophe which occurred at Khartoum, on January 26th, 1885. On that date the heroic defender of the city, General Charles George Gordon, of Chinese and African fame, and his Egyptian garrison were massacred, the population reduced to slavery, and all the vast Soudan submerged by barbarism. The only Egyptian force in the Soudan which escaped from the disaster was that which, led by Emin Pasha, had sought refuge among the savage tribes in the neighbourhood of Wadelai on the left bank of the Nile, about 25° north of the Albert Nyanza. Fearing that he would be unable to offer continued resistance, Emin began writing letters to the Egyptian Government, Mr. Mackay, the Missionary, the Anti-slavery Society, and Sir John Kirk, imploring assistance before he should be overwhelmed. Through the influence of Sir William Mackinnon, a relief-fund was collected in this country, Egypt promised an equal sum, and the Emin Relief Expedition was the consequence. When men hear a person crying out for help, few stay to ascertain whether he merits it; but they forthwith proceed to render what assistance is needed. It was rather harrowing to read, day by day, in the British Press that one of Gordon's officers, at the head of a little army, was in danger of perishing and sharing the remorseless fate which had overtaken the self-sacrificing chief and his garrison at Khartoum. It is to Dr. R. W. Felkin, of Edinburgh, who, as a casual traveller, had enjoyed Emin's hospitality between July and September, 1879, that I am indebted for that beautiful and inspiring picture of a Governor at bay in the far Soudan, defying the victorious Mahdists, and fighting bravely, inch by inch, for the land which he had been appointed to rule by General Gordon.

This Governor was described by him as a tall, military figure, of severe aspect, of rigid morals, inflexible will, scientific attainments — and his name was Emin. The picture became impressed on our imaginations.

The 'Mackinnon Clan,' as we fondly termed Sir William Mackinnon and his personal friends, were among the foremost to come forward. They offered to give ten thousand pounds if the Egyptian Government would advance a similar amount. The proposal received Egypt's prompt assent, and as the British Press and people strongly sympathised with the movement, the Government, also, cordially favoured it.

My old friend Sir William had asked me, before he had appealed to his friends, if, in the event of a fund being raised, I would lead the expedition. I replied that I would do so gratuitously; or, if the Relief Committee preferred another leader, as was very probable, I would put my name down for Five hundred pounds. Without waiting the issue of his appeal to his friends, I sailed for America to commence a lecturing-tour. Thirteen days after my arrival in America, I was recalled by cable; and on Christmas Eve, 1886, I was back in England.

Forthwith came appeals to me from the brave and adventurous and young, that I would be pleased to associate them with me in the enterprise of relief. They vowed strictest fidelity, obedience to any terms, and utmost devotion; and from among the host of applicants, Major Barttelot, of the 7th Fusiliers, Mr. Jameson, a rich young civilian, Lieutenant Stairs, of the Royal Engineers, Captain Nelson, of Methuen's Horse, Surgeon Parke, of the Army Medical Department, Mr. Jephson, and two or three others, were enrolled as members of the expedition to relieve Emin Pasha, Governor of Equatoria. Had our means only been equal to our opportunities, we might have emptied the barracks, the colleges, the public schools, — I might almost say the nurseries, — so great was the number of applications to join in the adventurous quest!

The route resolved upon was that from Zanzibar westward, viâ the south end of Lake Victoria, through Karagwe and Ankori and South-west Unyoro, to Lake Albert; but, about thirteen days before we sailed, the King of the Belgians, through his generous offers of assistance, induced us to change our plans. The advantages of the Congo route were about five hundred miles shorter land-journey, and less opportunities for desertion of the porters, who are quite unable to withstand the temptation of deserting. It also quieted the fears of the French and Germans that, behind this professedly humanitarian quest, we might have annexation projects.

A native force was recruited in Zanzibar, and the expedition travelled by sea to the mouth of the Congo, and went up the river, arriving March 21, 1887, at Stanley Pool. As far as that everything prospered. We had started from England with the good wishes of all concerned; and even the French Press, with one accord, were, for once, cordial and wished us *bon voyage*. But, on reaching the Pool, the steam flotilla was found to be only capable of carrying four-fifths of the expedition.

Fourteen hundred miles from the Atlantic, we reached the limit of Congo navigation, and found camp at Yambuya, a large village, situated on the edge of an unknown territory which extended as far as the Albert Nyanza. A steamer was at once sent down-river to bring the remainder of the force and stores left behind.

It should be remembered, that the last news from Emin was an urgent appeal for help. The last solemn injunction to us was to hurry forward, lest we be too late. Hitherto, we had been dependent on the fortunes of the sea, the skill of ship captains, and safe navigation by ocean and river. German and French jealousies had been dissipated; between our professional deserters and their island, Zanzibar, was half a continent, and much of it unknown. Now was the time, if ever, to prove that our zeal had not cooled. Six weeks, probably two months, would pass before the entire force could be collected at Yambuya. If Emin was in such desperate straits as he had described, his total ruin might be effected in that time, and the disaster would be attributed to that delay — just as Gordon's death had been attributed to Sir Charles Wilson's delay at Metemmeh. To avoid that charge, I had no option but to form an Advance Column, whose duty would be to represent the steady progress of the expedition towards its goal, while a second Column, under five experienced officers, would convey after us, a few weeks later, the reserve stores and baggage. If Tippu-Tib was faithful to his promise to supply the second Column with six hundred carriers, the work of the reserve Column would be comparatively easy. If the Arab chief was faithless, then the officers were to do the best they could with their own men; to follow after me, in that case, was obviously their best course.

On the thirteenth day after arrival at Yambuya, the advance, consisting of five Europeans and three hundred and eighty-four natives, entered the great Equatorial Forest. The unknown country which lay between Yambuya and the Albert Nyanza, on whose shores we hoped to meet the 'beleaguered' Governor, was five hundred and forty geographical miles in length, by about three hundred and thirty in width. We were absolutely ignorant of the character of any portion embraced within this area. The advance force was divided into four Companies, commanded by Stairs, Nelson, Jephson, and Parke. The pioneers consisted of select men who were to use the bill-hook, cutlass, and axe, for clearing a passage through the entangling underwood, without which it would have been impossible to advance at all. They had also to resist attack from the front, to scout, to search for fords, or to bridge the deeper creeks.

The daily routine began about six o'clock. After roll-calls, the pioneers filed out, followed, after a little headway had been gained, by each Company in succession. At this hour the Forest would be buried in a cheerless twilight, the morning mist making every tree shadowy and indistinct. After hacking, hewing, and tunnelling, and creeping slowly for five hours, we would halt for refreshment. At one o'clock, the journey would be resumed; and about four, we would prepare our camp for the night.

Soon after sunset the thick darkness would cover the limitless world of trees around; but, within our circle of green huts and sheds, a cheery light would shine from a hundred campfires. By nine o'clock the men, overcome by fatigue, would be asleep; silence ensued, broken only by sputtering fire-logs, flights of night-jars, hoarse notes from great bats, croakings of frogs, cricket-cheeps, falling of trees or branches, a shriek from some prowling chimpanzee, a howl from a peevish monkey, and the continual gasping cry of the lemur. But during many nights, we would sit shivering under ceaseless torrents of rain, watching the forky flames of the lightning, and listening to the stunning and repeated roars of the thunder-cannonade, as it rolled through the woody vaults.

During the first month not a man fell away from his duty; the behaviour of both officers and men was noble and faultless. Regularly as clock-work, each morning they took to the road, and paced as fast as the entanglements and obstacles of underwood, swamp, and oozy creeks allowed. Each day the Forest presented the same unbroken continuity of patriarchal woods, the same ghostly twilight at morning, the same dismal shade at noon. Foliage, from forty to a hundred feet thick, above us, a chaos of undergrowth around us, soft black humus, and dark soil, rich as compost, under our feet.

At intervals of ten, fifteen, or twenty miles, we came across small clearings, but their wild owners had fled, or stood skulking on our flanks unseen. As no possible chance of intercourse was offered to us, we helped ourselves to their manioc, plucked the bananas, and passed on.

At the end of the first month, there came a change. Our men had gradually lost their splendid courage. The hard work and scanty fare were exhausting. The absence of sunshine, and other gloomy environments, were morally depressing. Physically and morally, they had deteriorated; and a long rest was imperatively needed. But we could find no settlement that could assure the necessary provisions. Now that the blood was impoverished, too, the smallest abrasion from a thorn, a puncture from a mosquito, or a skewer in the path, developed rapidly into a devouring ulcer. The sick-list grew alarmingly large, and our boats and canoes were crowded with sufferers.

We, finally, entered upon a region that had been dispeopled and cruelly wasted by the Manyuema raiders, and it became a matter of life and death to get quickly through and beyond it. But, already famished and outworn, in body and spirit, by past struggles, our men were unable, and too dejected, to travel rapidly; and the tedious lagging involved still more penalties. Had they known how comparatively short was the distance that lay between them and supplies, they no doubt would have made heroic efforts to push on.

Then starvation commenced to claim its victims, and to strew the track with the dying and dead; and this quailed the stoutest hearts.

Ever before us rose the same solemn and foodless Forest the same jungle to impede and thwart our progress with ooze, frequently a cubit deep, the soil often as treacherous as ice to the barefooted carrier, creek-beds strewn with sharp-edged oyster-shells, streams choked with snags, chilling mist and icy rain, thunder-clatter and sleepless nights, and a score of other horrors. To add to our desperate state, several of our followers who had not sickened, lost heart, became mad with hunger and wild forebodings, tossed the baggage into the bush, and fled from us, as from a pest.

Although, when on the verge of hopelessness, our scouts would sometimes discover a plantation, whereat we could obtain a supply of plantains, past affliction taught them no prudence. They devoured their food without a thought of the want of the next day; and, in a few hours, the slow agony of hunger would be renewed.

Even the white man does not endure hunger patiently. It is a thing he never forgives. The loss of one meal obliterates the memories of a hundred feasts. When hunger begins to gnaw at his stomach, the nature of the animal comes out, as a tortoise-head, projected from the shell, discloses the animal within. Despite education and breeding, the white man is seldom more than twenty-four hours ahead of his black brother, and barely one hundred hours in advance of the cannibal; and ten thousand years hence he will be just the same. He will never be so civilised as to be independent of his stomach; so it must be understood that we also exhibited our weakness during that trying period; but, supported by little trifles of food, more prudent in economizing it, subjected to less physical strain, we forced ourselves to preserve the austerity and dignity of superiors.

On the hundred and thirty-seventh day from Yambuya we reached the first native settlement that had been untouched by the accursed raiders to whom we owed our miseries. It abounded with Indian corn, beans, vegetables, bananas, and plantains, upon which the famished survivors flung themselves, regardless of consequences. Our prolonged fast was at an end, but during the last seventy days of it I had lost one hundred and eighty men, through death and desertion. The place was called Ibwiri, since known as Fort Bodo; as our sufferings had been so intense, we halted here, and feasted for thirteen days.

The recuperation was rapid, strength had returned during the feasting, and there rose a general demand that we should continue the journey, in order that we might delight our eyes by the grass-land of which we now began to hear the first rumours. On the twelfth day after quitting Ibwiri, we emerged from the sombre twilight of the Forest into the unclouded light of a tropic sky. A feeling of exultation immediately possessed me, as if I had been released from Purgatory, to disport myself in the meads of Heaven. The very air was greedily sniffed.

The first smell of it that came to my open nostrils seemed as if, in the direction of the wind, there somewhere lay a great dairy and cattle-pen; and, almost at once, I sighted startled game, in close consult on the knolls and mounds, stamping and snorting in the first energy of alarm. The first view of the green rolling plain was as of a grassy Eden, which had been newly fashioned with a beautiful shapeliness, with a new sun, and a brand-new sky of intense blue. It transfigured every face in an instant, and the homeliest features were lit up by sincere emotions of gratitude, as though some dream of bliss had been realised. By one impulse we started to run; our exhilarated blood seemed foaming champagne, and sent us leaping over the soft sward; and the limbs, which had previously strained heavily through the forest thickets, danced as freely as those of bounding kids!

On the 13th December, one hundred and sixty-nine days from Yambuya, the expedition stood on the edge of the grassy plateau and looked down upon the Albert Nyanza, whose waters, as reported by Emin, were constantly navigated by his steamers, the 'Khedive' and 'Nyanza.'

After sufficiently enjoying the prospect, we commenced the steep descent of two thousand seven hundred feet, to the lake, and, early next morning, reached the shore which had been our goal. On inquiring from the natives as to the whereabouts of the 'white man with the smoke-boat,' they declared most positively that they had not seen any white man or steamer since Colonel Mason's visit, ten years before.

Our position was a cruel one. The Foreign Office had furnished me with copies of all Emin's letters, and from their tone, character, and numbers of statements, I had formed, what probably every one else had, an opinion of a Military Governor, who, with two steamers and steel boats, had been in the habit of visiting the various lake ports.

I asked again and again if a white man had been seen, and I received an answer always in the negative. I had left my steel boat at Ipoto, because of our depleted numbers. No food was obtainable on the alkalised plains bordering the lake. The native canoes were only suitable for inshore fishing and calm weather; and there was not a tree visible out of which a sizeable canoe could be made!

After consulting with the officers, I found that they also were surprised at the inexplicable absence of news of Emin, and a great many guesses wide of the truth, as it appeared later, were made. But no amount of guessing would feed two hundred hungry men, stranded on a naked lake shore. I therefore resolved, after three days' halt, to retrace our steps to Ibwiri, and there erect a small fort for the protection of the ammunition, and as a resting-place for my sick; after which we could return once more to the lake, and, launching my boat on its waters, sail in search of the missing Pasha.

Agreeably to this resolution, I turned my back on the lake on the 16th December, 1887, and, twenty-one days later, arrived at Ibwiri, the site of Fort Bodo. Without loss of time, I commenced building our fort. Meanwhile Lieutenant Stairs was sent, with a detachment, to collect the sick at Ipoto, under Surgeon Parke and Captain Nelson. On his return, he was sent with an escort of twenty carriers, who were to hunt for Major Barttelot's Column, which I expected was following us, and to collect all convalescents at Ugarrowas, below Ipoto.[1]

After the construction of the fort, its command was entrusted to Captain Nelson, and, accompanied by Jephson and Parke, I departed, a second time, to the Nyanza; but on this occasion I carried my steel boat, in sections.

[1] Mr. Stairs, not finding the Rear-Column, returned with the sick. — D. S.

One day's distance from the lake I heard that there was a packet awaiting me at Kavalli, from a white man called by the natives 'Malleju,' or the 'bearded man,' who, of course, was Emin Pasha. The packet contained a letter addressed to me by name, which showed, like the letter of November to Dr. Felkin, that he knew all about the objects of the expedition. It was dated March 25th, 1888, — it was now April 18th. Native rumour, according to Emin's letter, had stated that white men were at the south end of the lake, and he had embarked on one of his steamers to ascertain if the report were true. It was an extraordinary thing, that, after expecting us on the 15th December, he had required one hundred days to make up his mind to visit the south end of the lake!

Unless we chose to wait inactively for Emin to pay Kavalli a second visit, it was necessary to send the boat in search of him. Accordingly, Mr. Jephson, with a picked crew, was charged with this mission.

Towards sunset of the fifth day after his departure, those looking northward up the lake discovered a column of smoke. It rose from the funnel of the steamer 'Khedive.' At dusk she dropped anchor nearly abreast of our camp, and in a few moments our whale-boat, steered by Jephson, brought Emin Pasha, Captain Casati, and several Egyptian officers ashore. As may be imagined, our people were almost beside themselves with delight, because the object of our strenuous quest was at last amongst them.

We agreed to pitch our camps side by side. Emin and his guard of Soudanese to the right, and we to the left, on the edge of the lake.

For several days we luxuriated in our well-earned rest and good cheer. I was in a state of joyous ebullience; I acquiesced with all suggestions. Few men could have acted the part of hospitable and pleasant host so well as Emin. I quite understood now how Dr. Felkin had appreciated this side of Emin's character. He was cordial in manner, well-read, had seen much, and appeared to be most likeable.

Then also my anxieties respecting provisions for the people were at an end, for Emin had provided abundance of grain, and, as the main object of the expedition was now within view of being achieved, my feelings all round were those of unalloyed pleasure. Many a time afterwards, I looked back upon this period as upon a delightful holiday.

Until the 25th of May, our respective camps were close together; and we daily met and chatted about various things, during which, naturally, the topic as to whether he would stay in Equatoria, or accompany me to the coast, came up for discussion frequently. But, from the beginning to the end of our meetings, I was only conscious that I was profoundly ignorant of his intentions. On some days, after a friendly dinner the night previous, he held out hopes that he might accompany me; but the day following he would say, 'No, if my people go, I go; if they stay, I stay.' For ten days I assented to this; but it became impressed on my mind, that he had a personal objection to going to Egypt, from a fear that he might be shelved, and his life would become wasted in a Cairene or Stamboul coffee-house. The ideal Governor whom I had imagined, had been altogether replaced by a man who had other views than those of his Government. What those views were, I could never gather definitely, for, as has been observed, the impression of one day was displaced by that of the next; and his real opinions, upon any topic save an abstract question, were too transient to base a conclusion upon.

Altogether, I spent twenty-five days with Emin. I then retraced my steps to Fort Bodo. After carefully provisioning one hundred and seven men, and serving out twenty-five days' rations to each man, I commenced the search for the Rear-Column on the 16th June.

I have often been asked how I dared to face that terrible and hungry Forest alone, after such awful experiences. If I suggested admonitions of duty and conscience as being sufficient motives, I seldom failed to notice a furtive shrug. But, really, I fail to see what else could have been done. The Rear-Column was as much a part of the expedition as the Advance, and had there been only twenty blacks, it would have been as much my duty to seek them as to find what had become of two hundred and sixty Zanzibaris, with five white officers. As for sending any of my own officers to perform such an important mission, well, there is a saying which I believe in thoroughly, 'If you want a thing *done*, you must do it yourself.' Besides these motives, I was too nervously anxious about the long-absent Column, which had been instructed to follow us, and the suspense was intolerable.

It was also, principally, this nervous anxiety about these missing people that drove me through the Great Forest at such a rate, that what had taken us one hundred and twenty-nine days was now performed in sixty-two days. On August 17, 1888, the eighty-third day since quitting the Pasha, on Lake Albert, I came in view of the village of Banalya, ninety miles east of Yambuya.

Presently,[1] white dresses were seen, and quickly taking up my field-glass, I discovered a red flag hoisted. A suspicion of the truth crept into my mind. A light puff of wind unrolled the flag for an instant, and the white crescent and star was revealed. I sprang to my feet and cried out, 'The Major, boys! Pull away bravely!' A vociferous shouting and hurrahing followed, and every canoe shot forward at racing speed.

About two hundred yards from the village we stopped paddling, and as I saw a great number of strangers on the shore, I asked, 'Whose men are you?' —'We are Stanley's men,' was the answer, delivered in mainland Swahili. But assured by this, and still more so as I recognised a European near the gate, we paddled ashore. The European on a nearer view turned out to be William Bonny, who had been engaged as doctor's assistant to the expedition.

Pressing his hand, I said, —

'Well, Bonny, how are you? Where is the Major? Sick, I suppose?'

'The Major is dead, sir.'

'Dead? Good God! How dead? Fever?'

'No, sir, he was shot.'

'By whom?'

'By the Manyuema — Tippu-Tib's people.'

'Good heavens! Well, where is Jameson?'

'At Stanley Falls.'

'What is he doing there, in the name of goodness?'

'He went to obtain more carriers.'

'Well, where are the others?'

[1] Contrary to the rule hitherto observed, the following dramatic story of the discovery of the derelict Rear-Column is quoted from the account already published in *Darkest Africa*. — D. S.

'Gone home invalided, some months ago.'

These queries, rapidly put and answered as we stood by the gate at the water-side, prepared me to hear as deplorable a story as could be rendered of one of the most remarkable series of derangements that an organized body of men could possibly be plunged into.

If I were to record all that I saw at Banalya, in its deep intensity of unqualified misery, it would be like stripping the bandages off a vast sloughing ulcer, striated with bleeding arteries, to the public gaze, with no earthly purpose than to shock and disgust.

I put question after question to Bonny, to each of which I received only such answers as swelled the long list of misfortunes he gave me. The Column had met nothing but disaster.

The bald outline of Mr. Bonny's story was that Tippu-Tib had broken faith with me, and that the officers had kept on delaying to start after me, as agreed between Barttelot and myself. The Arab had fed them continually with false hopes of his coming; finally, after seven visits which Barttelot had paid him at Stanley Falls, and in the tenth month, he had brought to Yambuya four hundred men and boy carriers, and a more undisciplined and cantankerous rabble could not have been found in Africa. The Column had then departed, and been able to march ninety miles and reach Banalya, when, on July 19th, — or twenty-eight days before my arrival, — Barttelot left his house at dawn to stop some disorderly noises, and, a few minutes later, he was shot through the heart by a Manyuema head-man. Thus, on my arrival, Mr. Bonny was the only white man remaining. Out of two hundred and sixty coloured men who had originally formed the Column, only one hundred and two were alive, and forty-two of them were even then dying from the effects of eating poisonous manioc.

In a few days, I had re-organised a force of over five hundred men; and, hastily removing from Banalya, as from a pest-house, finished my preparations on an island in the Aruwimi, a few miles above. When all was ready, I started on my way to Fort Bodo, conveying all these people as best I could. The sick folk and the goods, I had carried in canoes, while the main body marched along my old track, parallel to the river, and kept time to the progress of the water-party. The people were now familiar with the route, and were no longer the funeral procession which had slowly dragged itself through the shades of the Forest, the year before. They knew that they were homeward-bound, and, fascinated by memories of the pastoral plains, and unencumbered with loads, they marched in high spirits.

About a month's march from Fort Bodo, I cast off the canoes and struck overland by a shorter way. Presently, I entered the land inhabited by pigmies. This race of dwarfs has dwelt in this section of the country since the remotest times, before history. The tallest male discovered by me did not exceed four feet, six inches; the average specimen was about four feet, two inches, in height, while many a child-bearing pigmy-woman did not exceed three feet high.

In the more easterly parts of the Forest there are several tribes of this primeval race of man. They range from the Ihuru River to the Awamba forest at the base of Ruwenzori. I found two distinct types; one a very degraded specimen, with ferrety eyes, close-set, and an excessive prognathy of jaw, more nearly approaching what one might call a cousin of the simian than was supposed to be possible, yet thoroughly human; the other was a very handsome type, with frank, open, innocent countenances, very prepossessing. I had considerable experience of both.[1] They were wonderfully quick with their weapons, and wounded to death several of my followers. The custom in the Forest is to shoot at sight, and their craft, quick sight, correct aim, and general expertness, added to the fatal character of the poison of their arrows, made them no despicable antagonists. The larger natives of the Forest, who form the clearings and plant immense groves of plantains, purchase their favour by submitting to their depredations.

I have seen some beautiful figures among the little people,

[1] The two different kinds of pigmies thus distinguished were the Batua, inhabiting the northern, and the Wambutti, the southern district of the territory traversed by Stanley, — the great Equatorial Forest, — which extends south of the Niam-Niam and Monbuttu countries. The correctness of Stanley's views regarding the pigmies has since been substantiated by Wolf, Wissman, and others. See Dr. Schlichter's paper, 'The Pigmy Tribes of Africa,' *Scottish Geographical Magazine*, 1892. — D. S.

as perfect from the knees upward as a sculptor would desire, but the lower limbs are almost invariably weak and badly-shaped.

They are quick and intelligent, capable of deep affection and gratitude; and those whom we trained showed remarkable industry and patience. One old woman, four feet, two inches in height, — possibly the ugliest little mortal that was ever in my camp, — exhibited a most wonderful endurance. She seemed to be always loaded like a camel, as she followed the caravan from camp to camp, and I often had to reduce a load that threatened to bury her under her hamper. Cooking-pots, stools, porridge-paddles, kettles, bananas, yams, flour, native rope, a treasure of ironware, cloth, what-not, everything was placed in her hamper, as if her strength was without limit. Towards the latter part of her acquaintance, I was able to make her smile, but it had been terribly hard work, as she was such an inveterate scold. By her action she seemed to say: 'You may beat me to pulp, you may load me until you smother me with your rubbish, you may work my fingers to the bone, you may starve me, but, thank Goodness, I can still scold, and scold I will, until I drop!'

I had a pigmy boy of eighteen, who worked with a zeal that I did not think possible to find out of civilisation. Time was too precious to him to waste in talk. On the march, he stoutly held his place near the van; and, on reaching camp, he literally rushed to collect fuel and make his master's fire. His mind seemed ever concentrated on his work. When I once stopped him to ask his name, his face seemed to say, 'Please don't stop me. I must finish my task'; and I never heard his voice while he was with me, though he was not dumb.

Another of my pigmy followers was a young woman, of whom I could honestly say that she was virtuous and modest, though nude. It was of no use for any stalwart young Zanzibari to be casting lover's eyes at her. She resolved that she had duties to perform, and she did them without deigning to notice the love-sick swains of our camp. Her master's tea or coffee was far too important to be neglected. His tent required her vigilant watchfulness, her master's comforts were unspeakably precious in her eyes, and the picture of the half-naked pigmy-girl, abjuring frivolities, and rendering due fidelity, and simple devotedness, because it was her nature to, will remain long in my mind as one of many pleasantnesses to be remembered.

I have often been asked whether I did not think the pigmies to be a degenerate stock of ordinary humanity. In my opinion, tribes and nations are subject to the same influences as families. If confined strictly to itself, even a nation must, in time, deteriorate.

Asia and Africa contain several isolated fragments of what were once powerful nations, and yet more numerous relics of once populous tribes. It is not difficult to judge of the effect on a race of three thousand years' isolation, intermarriage, and a precarious diet of fungi, wild fruit, lean fibrous meat of animals, and dried insects. The utter absence of sunshine, the want of gluten and saccharine bodies in their food, scarcely tend to promote increase of stature, or strength of limb; and, as it is said, 'where there is no progress, there must be decay,' I suppose that some deterioration must have occurred since the existence of the pigmies became known, as the result of their ancestors having captured the five Nassamonian explorers twenty-six centuries ago, as described by the Father of History. On every map since Hekateus's time, 500 years B. C., they have been located in the region of the Mountains of the Moon.

On the 20th of December, 1888, we burst out of the Great Forest, on the edge of the plantations of Fort Bodo; and, by 9 o'clock, the volleys of the rifles woke up the garrison at the fort to the fact that, after one hundred and eighty-eight days' absence, we had returned. What a difference there was between the admirable station, with its model farm-like appearance, and Banalya! But there was one mystery yet remaining. The Pasha and Jephson had promised to visit Fort Bodo within two months after my departure, say about the middle of August; it was now past the middle of December, and nothing had been heard of them. But the cure of all doubt, grief, misery, and mystery is action; and therefore I could not remain passive at Fort Bodo. I allowed myself three days' rest only, and then set out for Lake Albert for the third time.

On the 17th of January, 1889, when only one day's march

from the Albert Lake, a packet of letters was placed in my hands. They were from Emin Pasha and Mr. Jephson. There was a long account from Jephson, stating that he and the Pasha were prisoners to the revolted troops of the province since the 18th August, the very day after we had discovered the foundered Rear-Column at Banalya! There were some expressions in poor Mr. Jephson's letters which put a very relief-less aspect on his case. 'If I don't see you again, commend me to my friends!' The Pasha, also, seemed to think that nothing could be worse than the outlook, for he specially recommended his child to my care. Now, reading such words, a month after they were written, was not very assuring. However, I picked up a crumb of comfort in the fact that Mr. Jephson said he could come to me if he were informed of my arrival, which I decided was the best thing for him to do. Accordingly, an imperative message was sent to him, not to debate, but to act; and, like a faithful and obedient officer, he stepped into a canoe, and came.

After shaking hands, and congratulating him upon his narrow escape from being a footman to the Emperor of the Soudan, I said, 'Well, Jephson, speak. Is the Pasha decided by this what to do now?'

'To tell you the truth, I know no more what the Pasha intends doing now than I did nine months ago.'

'What, after nine months' intercourse with him?'

'Quite so, — not a bit.'

It was not long before the mystery that had struck me the year before was cleared up. The Pasha had been deceived by the fair-spoken, obsequious Egyptian and Soudanese officers; and, through his good-natured optimism, we, also, had been deceived. They had revolted three times, and had refused to obey any order he had given them. This was the fourth and final revolt. As early as 1879, Gessi Pasha had drawn General Gordon's attention to the state of affairs in Equatoria, and had reported that, immediately the communication with Khartoum had been suspended by the closing of the Upper Nile by the *Sudd*, the indiscipline had been such as to cause anxiety. In 1886, Emin Pasha had fled from the 1st Battalion, and, until his imprudent resolve to take Mr. Jephson among the rebels, had held no communication with them. The 2nd

Battalion, also, only performed just such service as pleased them when he condescended to use coaxing, while the Irregulars, of course, would follow the majority of the Regulars. This much was clear from the narrative, written and oral, of Mr. Jephson.

I resolved to try once more, and ascertain what measures agreeable to him I should take. Did he wish an armed rescue, or was it possible for him to do anything, such as seizing a steamer and following Jephson, or marching out of Tunguru, where he was a prisoner, to meet me outside of the fort? or had he quite made up his mind to remain a prisoner at Tunguru, until the rebels would dispose of him? Anyway, and every way, if he could only express a definite wish, we vowed we should help him to the uttermost. I wrote to him a ceremoniously-polite letter to that effect, for I was warned that the Pasha was extremely sensitive.

While my letter was on the lake being conveyed to Tunguru, matters were settled in quite an inconceivable fashion at Tunguru station. The rebel officers had sent a deputation to the Pasha to ask his pardon, and to offer to re-instate him in his Governorship. The pardon was readily given, but he declined yet awhile to accept the Governorship. They asked him if he would be good enough to accompany them to pay me a visit, and introduce them to me. The Pasha consented, embarked on board the steamer, the refugees likewise crowded on board the 'Khedive' and 'Nyanza,' and, on the 13th February, the two steamers approached our camp; two days later, the Pasha and rebel officers entered our camp.

According to the Pasha, the Mahdist invasion, the capture of four stations, and the massacre of many of their numbers, had cowed the rebels, and they were now truly penitent for their insane conduct to him; and every soul was willing to depart, out of the Equatorial Province, at least, if not to Egypt. The officers now only came to beg for time to assemble their families. Agreeably to the Pasha's request, a reasonable time was granted, and they departed. The Governor thought that twenty days would be sufficient; we granted a month. At the end of thirty days the Pasha requested another extension; we allowed fourteen days more. Finally, at the end of forty-four days, not one officer of the rebel party having made his appearance, we broke camp, and commenced our journey homeward with five hundred and seventy refugees, consisting of a few Egyptian officers, clerks, and their families; but, on the second day, an illness prostrated me, which permitted them twenty-eight days more, and yet, after seventy-two days' halt, only one person had availed himself of my offer.

On the seventy-third day since my meeting with the rebel officers, four soldiers brought a message stating that the rebels had formed themselves into two parties, under Fadle Mulla Bey, and Selim Bey, and the party of the first-named had seized all the ammunition from the other party, and had fled to Makraka. Selim Bey, unable to muster resolution to follow us, preferred to remain to curse Fadle Mulla Bey and his folly; and what the end of these misguided and unprincipled men may be, no person knows, outside of that unhappy region!

On the 8th May I resumed the march[1] for the Indian Ocean. The fifth day's march brought us to the edge of highlands, whence we looked down into a deep valley, two thousand six hundred feet below us. In width, it varied from six to twenty miles. To the north, we could see a bit of the south end of Lake Albert. Southward, seventy miles off, was another lake, to which I have given the name of Albert Edward; and the surplus waters of the southernmost lake meandered through this valley down into the northernmost, or Albert Lake.

Opposite to the place whence I looked upon the Semliki Valley, rose an enormous range of mountains, whose summits and slopes, for about three thousand feet, were covered with perpetual snow. As the snow-line near the Equator is found at a little over fifteen thousand feet, I may then safely estimate the height of these mountains to be between eighteen thousand and nineteen thousand feet above the level of the sea. The singular thing about these mountains is that so many white travellers — Sir Samuel and Lady Baker, Gessi Pasha, Mason Bey, Emin Pasha, and Captain Casati — should have been within observing distance and never had an opportunity to view them.

[1] Emin's people, alone, succoured and convoyed to the Coast by Stanley, numbered about a thousand. — D. S.

There were also a thousand of our expedition who were for seventy-two days, or thereabouts, within easy visual distance of the phenomenon, but not one man saw it until suddenly it issued out from the obscurity, its great peaks islanded in an atmosphere of beautiful translucence. And, for three days in succession, the wonderful mountains stood aloft in glorious majesty, with an indefinable depth of opaline sky above, beyond, and around them, the marvel of the curious and delighted multitude! For three days I saw them, spell-bound and wondering.

The natives generally called them the Ruwenzori Mountains. Scheabeddin, an Arab geographer, writing about Anno Domini 1400, says, 'In the midst of the Isle of Mogreb, which is Africa, are the deserts of the Negroes, which separate the country of the Negroes from that of Berbers. In this isle is also the source of that great river which has not its equal upon the earth. It comes from the Mountains of the Moon, which lie beyond the Equator. Many sources come from these mountains, and unite in a great lake. From this lake comes the Nile, the greatest, and most beautiful of the rivers of all the earth.' This is only one of the many early authorities which I have quoted in my book, 'Darkest Africa,' to prove that the Ruwenzori range forms the long-lost Mountains of the Moon.[1]

Still another discovery was that of the Albert Edward Nyanza — called in ancient times the Sea of Darkness, whose waters were said to be sweeter than honey, and more fragrant than musk. I cannot endorse this Oriental estimation of their excellence; to many, the waters of the muddy Missouri would be preferable!

Quitting the head-waters of the Nile, I ascended some three thousand feet into a higher altitude, and began a journey over a rich pastoral land, which extends to the south end of the

[1] These mountains make a chapter in the romance of historical geography. It was Stanley's discovery that brought them out of the realm of legend. Not long before his death, he expressed to the Royal Geographical Society his 'dear wish' that the range might be thoroughly explored. Their ascent was attempted by many, beginning with Captain Stairs in 1889, and the work was at last thoroughly and scientifically done by H. R. H., the Duke of the Abruzzi, in June, 1906, and he named the highest range, Mount Stanley, and the two highest points, Margherita Peak (16,815 feet) and Queen Alexandra Peak (16,749). — D. S.

Victoria Nyanza. In consideration of having driven Kabba Rega's raiders from the shores of the Albert Edward, and freed the salt lakes from their presence, I received hearty ovations and free rations from the various kings along a march of five hundred miles.

At the south end of Lake Victoria, I found reserve stores, which had been deposited there eighteen months before, awaiting us. Then, greatly strengthened by a good rest and food, on the 16th September I left that lake, having discovered an extension to it of six thousand square miles.

Four days from the sea, two American newspaper-correspondents arrived at my camp. One of them, a representative of the 'New York Herald,' delivered to me a supply of clothes, and other very necessary articles, besides a judicious supply of good wine, which cheered us greatly. A little later, we met a large caravan sent by Sir William Mackinnon, freighted with provisions and clothes for our people.

On the morning of the 4th December, 1889, Emin Pasha, Captain Casati, and myself were escorted by Major Wissmann to Bagamoyo, the port opposite Zanzibar; and, in the afternoon, the porters of the expedition filed in, to lay their weary burdens of sick and moaning fellow-creatures down for the last time. Our journey of six thousand and thirty-two miles from the Western Ocean to the Indian Sea was now at an end.

That night the German Imperial Commissary gave a banquet to thirty-four persons, consisting of our travellers, German, British, and Italian civil and military officers, and after a style that even New York could scarcely excel. The utmost cordiality prevailed, and laudatory and grateful speeches were delivered, and not the least graceful and finished was that of the Pasha. But within ten minutes afterwards, while the guests were most animated, the Pasha wandered away from the banqueting-hall out into the balcony; and, presently, in some unaccountable manner, fell over the low wall into the street, some eighteen feet below. Had not a zinc shed, five feet below the balcony which shaded the sidewalk, broken the fall, the accident would no doubt have been fatal. As it was, he received severe contusions, and a sharp concussion of the base of the brain. A German officer had him conveyed to the hospital, while three doctors hastened to his assistance. In less than a month he was sufficiently recovered to begin arranging his entomological collections.

Up to the time of his fall, it had been a pleasant enough intercourse since leaving Mtsora, in the middle of June. There had been no grievance or dispute between him and any of our party. The most kindly messages were interchanged daily; presents and choice gifts were exchanged; in fact, our intercourse was thoroughly fraternal. But his fall suddenly put a barrier in some strange way between us. If the British Consul-general expressed a desire to pay a visit to him, some excuse of a relapse was given. If I wished to go over to Bagamoyo, his condition immediately became critical. Surgeon Parke, who attended to him for the first three weeks, found that things were not so pleasant for him as formerly. If I sent my black boy, Sali, to him with a note of condolence, and some suggestion, the boy was told he would be hanged if he went to the hospital again! To our officers, Dr. Parke and Mr. Jephson, he freely complained of the German officers. My friendly note, asking him to have some regard to his reputation, was at once shown by him to Major Wissmann. It was curious, too, how the Pasha, who thought at Equatoria that his people were so dear to him that he professed himself ready to sacrifice his future for them, dropped his dear people from his mind, and told them with a brutal frankness that he had nothing further to do with them. The muster and pay-roll of the rescued Egyptians was, therefore, not sent to Egypt; and the poor fellows waited months for the many years' pay due to them, inasmuch as no one knew anything of the accounts.

Finally, in March, the secret was out: the Pasha had engaged himself to the Germans on the 5th of February; and then it transpired that all these strange and wholly unnecessary acts were with a view to cut himself adrift from all connection with his old friends and employers, before committing himself to a new employment!

However benevolent and considerate Emin's English friends may have been disposed to be towards him, they were not above being affronted at their kind offices being rejected so churlishly, and from the offended tone which the Press now assumed, may be gathered the nature of my own feelings when I first became acquainted with his uncertain disposition, and his capricious and eccentric nature. But, in its furious disappointment, a large portion of the Press was unable to discriminate between Emin and me. Day after day it lavished the foulest accusations and the most violent abuse against me. It was stated by the newspapers that I had captured Emin by force; that I had been tyrannical and overbearing; that the 'Rescue,' always printed with quotation-marks, had been a farce; that I had destroyed the 'civilised edifice' which Emin had so laboriously built, etc., etc.; and some even hinted that it was I who had pushed Emin over the balcony-wall. But why proceed?

As has been seen, Emin came to my camp of his own will; I had treated him with almost superhuman patience; my appearance at Kavalli was the means of saving his life; as for the 'civilised edifice,' Heaven save the mark! Emin's departure from that region broke up organised slave-bands, which, since Gordon's death, had, under the mask of government, committed as much devastation, robbery, and slave-raiding, as even the Manyuema had been guilty of.

Before many months had passed, the Germans in their turn began to be enlightened as to the true character of their eccentric countryman; and the German Commissioner, who had toiled so hard to secure Emin from the British, affected to be seriously pained and aggrieved by his pranks. After a few weeks' work, establishing three military stations, he appears to have become involved in a most unfortunate incident. The story goes that he came across a large caravan belonging to four Arabs, whose goods he wished to purchase at his own price. The traders were reluctant to forfeit their hopes of gain, which had induced the venture, and declined Emin's terms; whereupon, it is alleged, a charge of slave-trading was trumped up against them, their goods were seized, and they themselves were drowned in Lake Victoria.

News of this had no sooner reached the coast, than the Commissioner, after communicating with Berlin, received orders to recall him. Before this order could reach him, Emin had thrown up his appointment, taken German soldiers, in Government employ, and entered British territory with the idea of accomplishing some project hostile to English interests. With this view he continued his journey to Kavalli, where he met his old rebellious officers from the Equatorial Province. They were implored to enlist under his banner; but, with the exception of a few slaves, who soon after deserted him, the rebels turned a deaf ear to his appeals.

Baffled by what he called their 'ingratitude and perverseness,' he headed West, dismissed his only white companion, and soon after plunged into the Great Forest, where he came across an old acquaintance, Ismaili, who, in 1887, had almost made an end of Nelson and Parke. This man he succeeded in securing as guide towards the Congo. Four days' march from Kibongi, above Stanley Falls, Emin had the ill-luck to meet Said-bin-Abed, a kinsman of one of the Arabs alleged to have been drowned in the Lake. The Arab turned upon his slave Ismaili, and upbraided him savagely for guiding such an enemy into the Arab country, and ordered Ismaili immediately to kill him; whereupon Emin was seized, thrown upon the ground, and, while his assistants held him fast by the arms and legs, Ismaili drew his sword, and smote his head off. What a strange, eventful history, for this commonplace epoch of ours!

The unselfish joy which caused each man, black and white, to raise that shout of exultation when we first beheld Lake Albert, and knew that the goal was won, and that the long train of sad memories had been left behind, deserved that I should have been able to pay Emin Pasha the uttermost honour; but it was simply—impossible.

I console myself, however, that through this mission, I have been supplied with a store of remarkable reminiscences; that I have explored the heart of the great, primeval Forest; that I have had unique experiences with its pigmies and cannibals; that I have discovered the long-lost, snowy Mountains of the Moon, the sources of the Albertine Nile, also Lake Albert Edward, besides an important extension of the Victoria Nyanza; and that finally, through my instrumentality, four European Governments (British, French, German, and Portuguese) have been induced to agree what their several spheres of influence shall be in the future, in the Dark Continent, with a view to exercising their beneficent powers for its redemption from the state of darkness and woe in which it has too long remained.

In England there arose bitter controversies over stories of misdoings by some of the Rear-Column. There is no occasion to reopen these controversies; but Stanley in a letter, cabled from America to the 'Times,' dealt with the imputations that cruelty to the natives was an ordinary incident of English advance in Africa, and this expression of his sentiments deserves permanent record.

To THE EDITOR OF THE 'TIMES.'

SIR: — Now that the storm of controversy as to the rear-guard of the Emin Relief Expedition has somewhat cleared away, and, as an appendix, if I may so call it, to my letter of December 3, I will ask you to allow me a few more words, final words, on my part, as I hope, and dealing mainly with the most serious aspect of the affair — the impression produced upon other nations by the disclosure of certain acts done by Englishmen in Africa.

It is hardly yet time for me to express the sorrow I truly feel at the pain these inevitable disclosures have brought upon men and women innocent of any fault; but no one is likely to question the earnestness of my regret at a result so directly counter to the wishes close to my heart. As it is, this is an opportunity given to competing nations to cast a slur upon British enterprise in Africa. Beyond and above any personal question whatever stands the honour of the English name. I wish, therefore, to say, with whatever weight my long experience may give my words, that I believe that conduct such as that above alluded to is entirely unusual and exceptional among Englishmen engaged in pioneering work in Africa.

I believe no nation has surpassed the English in tone, temper, and principle, in dealing with the Negro races; on the other hand, there have been many English explorers, from my revered master, David Livingstone, down to my own comrades in the Advance Guard of this last expedition, who have united, in quite a singular degree, gentleness with valour.

For myself, I lay no claim to any exceptional fineness of nature; but I say, beginning life as a rough, ill-educated, impatient man, I have found my schooling in these very African experiences which are now said by some to be in themselves detrimental to European character. I have learnt by actual stress of imminent danger, in the first place, that self-control is more indispensable than gunpowder, and, in the second place, that persistent self-control under the provocation of African travel is impossible without real, heartfelt sympathy for the natives with whom one has to deal. If one regards these natives as mere brutes, then the annoyances that their follies and vices inflict are indeed intolerable.

In order to rule them, and to keep one's life amongst them, it is needful resolutely to regard them as children, who require, indeed, different methods of rule from English or American citizens, but who must be ruled in precisely the same spirit, with the same absence of caprice and anger, the same essential respect to our fellow-men.

In proof of the fact that British explorers, as a whole, have learnt these lessons, I would point simply to the actual state of British influence in Africa. That influence, believe me, could neither have been acquired, nor maintained, by physical force alone.

So long as Englishmen in Africa continue in the future the conduct which has, on the whole, distinguished them in the past, I fear for them no rivalry in the great work of tropical civilisation, a work which cannot be successfully carried out in the commercial, and, still less in the military, spirit alone.

It is only by shewing ourselves superior to the savages, not only in the power of inflicting death, but in the whole manner of regarding life, that we can attain that control over them which, in their present stage, is necessary to their own welfare, even more than to ours.

Africa is inhabited not by timid Hindoos, or puny Australian aborigines, but by millions of robust, courageous men. It is no cant or sentimentalism, it is an obvious dictate of ordinary prudence, to say that, if we are to hold these men in such control as shall make Africa equal to any continent in serviceableness to mankind at large, it is by moral superiority, first of all, that control must be won, and must be maintained, as far as any white man can hope to maintain it.

Yours truly,

HENRY MORTON STANLEY.

WASHINGTON, Dec. 8th, 1890.

In judging of human achievement, we may take Browning's view,

'Life 's just the stuff
To test the soul on.'

Never was there an experience which more displayed and developed the grandest qualities of manhood, than did this march through Darkest Africa, in chief, lieutenants, and followers.

The outward results should not be under-estimated, and the net outcome is well given in a letter of Sir George Grey, written three years afterwards, when he was fresh from reading, not Stanley's story, but Parke's.

AUCKLAND, February 24th, 1892.

MY DEAR STANLEY,

I have been reading the Journal of your surgeon, Mr. Parke. From it I understood for the first time what you had accomplished. I had looked at the whole expedition more as a matter of exploration than anything else, and thought that scant justice had been done you. Now, I regard what you accomplished as an heroic feat.

Let me put it to you from my point of view. Great Britain, in pursuit of a great object, had, through the proper authorities, sent an officer to rule a great province. He was accompanied by an Egyptian force, acting under his orders, that is, under those of British authorities; and the forces and civil officers were accompanied by wives, children, servants, and followers of every kind. They formed an offshoot from Khartoum, but very remote from it.

Disturbances arose in the country, Khartoum and its dependencies were cut off from intercourse with the external world. Great Britain determined to rescue her officers, and undertook to do so by the only route used by civilised man, that is, by the line of communication which led from the northward. She failed; Gordon fell; the attempt was abandoned. Emin Pasha, his provinces, his forces, his civil servants, and adherents, with all their women and children, were abandoned to their fate; but held out. Emin Pasha naturally strove to communicate with Europe, imploring to be extricated from his difficulties. His strong appeals roused sympathy, and shame at his abandonment.

It was determined to rescue him. How was this to be done? The only route by which this could be done was by reaching him from the southward. But what a task was this — an almost hopeless one!

What a journey from the East Coast, or West Coast, before one could turn northward and reach him! What difficult regions, in many parts unknown, to traverse! What wilds and forests to traverse! What barbarous tribes to confront! By what means were the requisite arms, ammunition, and supplies, to be carried, which would enable Emin to continue to hold his own, if he chose to remain; or enable you all to force, if necessary, your way to some port where you could embark?

Undaunted by these evident difficulties, you undertook this task. After truly severe exertions, you reach him. He joins you, emerges from his difficulties with all his followers. You have saved, at great sacrifices, portions of the arms and ammunition on which the safety of all depends. You now find that nearly a thousand human beings,

(Fac simile)

2, RICHMOND TERRACE,
WHITEHALL, S. W.

April 23. 1902.

At an early age I was impressed with the applicability of the verse "Whatever thy hand findeth to do, do it with thy might." All thy might, to myself. It seemed to fit my unconscious heart, for whether it was conning a lesson, laying leap frog, or tending sheep, my best power was exerted, not for the sake of praise or reward, but to satisfy a desire to excel. When I arrived to mature years I found only a small percentage of my fellow creatures striving to do anything in brain or hand work worthy of their strength or power. I never ceased wondering at this until I discovered that it was due to a difference of vitality & spirit. However ~~to~~ those whom I could influence I have always quoted my favorite text about work, for it is the indifference to work of any kind that leads to poverty & premature physical decay.

Henry M. Stanley

men, women, and children, are committed to your care. These you are to conduct by a long perilous route to a port, where they embark for Egypt. The whole native population along a great part of the route is hostile, or alarmed at this great body of armed men and their families invading their territories. They can little understand that they are returning to their homes. If so, why do they not return by the same way by which they left them? Naturally they view with suspicion and alarm this worn, diseased multitude, which they are often ill able to supply with sufficient food to save them from starvation.

Yet this body of human beings you have to supply with rations, with arms, with medicines; without horses or carriages of any kind, the sick and wounded had to be moved; little children and famishing mothers had to be got along somehow; through long and exhausting marches, water had to be found, wild beasts kept off, who, notwithstanding all precautions, carried off several little ones in the night. You had quarrels and animosities to compose, discipline to preserve amongst men of various races and languages, and a multitude of other cases to meet; yet you were in ill-health yourself, worn by great toils in previous years, and in an unhealthy climate, which rendered men fretful, sullen, and careless of life. Nevertheless, you accomplished your task, and led your people — but a residue of them, indeed — to a port of safety, without reward and without promotion, or recognition from your country.

I have thought over all history, but I cannot call to mind a greater task than you have performed. It is not an exploration, alone, you have accomplished; it is also a great military movement, by which those who were in the British service were rescued from a position of great peril.

Most truly yours,

George Grey.[1]

[1] The Rt. Hon. Sir George Grey, K. C. B., 'Soldier, Explorer, Administrator, Statesman, Thinker, and Dreamer,' to quote James Milne, was born in 1812, and died in 1898. He was buried in St. Paul's Cathedral, being accorded a public funeral.

Governor of South Australia, when twenty-nine, he was subsequently twice Governor, and, later, Premier, of New Zealand; appointed as the first Governor of Cape Colony, 1854–59, Sir George Grey, by a daring assumption of personal responsibility, 'probably saved India,' as Lord Malmesbury said, by diverting to India British troops meant for China, and also despatching re-enforcements from the Cape — the first to reach India — on the outbreak of the Mutiny.

He was active in English public life in 1868–70, and in Australian affairs in 1870–94 (Milne's *Romance of a Proconsul*).

Referring to Sir George Grey's masterly despatches, with their singularly clear and definite analysis of the conditions of South Africa, Basil Worsfold (*History of South Africa*, in Dent's Temple Series) says, 'In so far as any one cause can be assigned for the subsequent disasters, both military and administrative, of the British Government in South Africa, it is to be found in the unwillingness of the "man in Downing Street" to listen to the man at Cape Town.'

---

* At a very late stage of passing the 'Autobiography' through the Press, a controversy relating to this famous statement has been raised, the result of which, so far, seems to demand its qualification, to some extent. — *Vide* The Times, Aug. 27th, 1909, *et seq.*

PART II. PRIVATE REFLECTIONS

The foregoing pages are compiled partly from unpublished papers of Stanley's, and partly from his private Journals. Some further passages may here be given from private note-books, written in his leisure. The writing was evidently prompted by an impulse of self-defence; partly, with regard to Emin, whose real name was Edouard Schnitzer, and, partly, as the result of strictures on his own character as a commander, in the published Journals of some of his lieutenants. The perspective of events changes rapidly with time, and Emin has so fallen into the background of history, that it seems unnecessary to cite the many instances of his baffling behaviour and egregious weaknesses through his devious career.

STANLEY ON THE PERSONNEL AND TRIALS OF THE EXPEDITION

As to his lieutenants, the limitations of space forbid a full quotation of Stanley's frank and dramatic account of the difficulties in the early part of the march. There was a sharp difference before leaving the Congo. The Zanzibaris preferred formal complaint against two officers, for beating them, and taking away their food; the officers, each in turn, being summoned to the scene, made a hot defence, in such language and manner that Stanley dismissed them from the expedition on the spot. One of their brother officers interceded, and was told that the lieutenants' disrespect was evidently the culmination of secret disaffection and grumbling. Stanley said to them:—

'Never a sailing-ship sailed from a port but some of the crew have taken the first opportunity to "try it on" with the captain. In every group, or band, of men, it appears to be a rule that there must be a struggle for mastery, and an attempt to take the leader's measure, before they can settle down to their proper position. I hope you who remain will understand that there can be only one chief in command in this expedition, and I am that chief, and in all matters of duty I expect implicit obedience and respect.'

Thus Stanley addressed his officers; the two who had offended made manly apologies, which were accepted, and they were restored to their places. With the handshake of reconciliation the incident terminated, so far as Stanley was concerned. But what he calls 'stupid personalities,' in certain published Diaries, moved him to write out his own full and private statement of this, and some later fictions, which there seems no occasion now to reproduce.

But we are indebted to it for some portraitures, as well as for an exposition of the social and individual experiences, generated in the African wilds, which may well be given here.

For one so young, Stairs's abilities and sterling sense were remarkable; and, in military pliancy at the word of command, he was a born soldier. This is a merit which is inestimable in a tropical country, where duty has to be done. A leader in a climate like that of Africa, cannot sugar-coat his orders, and a certain directness of speech must be expected; under such fretting conditions as we were in, it was a source of joy to feel that in Stairs I had a man, who, when a thing had to be done, could face about, and proceed to do it, as effectively as I could do it in person. In the way of duty he was without reproach.

Surgeon Parke's temper was the best-fitted for Africa. With his unsophisticated simplicity, and amusing naïveté, it was impossible to bear a grudge against him. Outside of his profession, he was not so experienced as Stairs. When placed in charge of a company, his muster-book soon fell into confusion; but by the erasures, and re-arrangements, it was evident that he did his best. Such men may blunder over and over again, and receive absolution. He possessed a fund of genuine wit and humour; and the innocent pleasure he showed when he brought smiles to our faces, endeared him to me. This childlike naïveté, which distinguished him in Africa, as in London society, had a great deal to do with the affectionateness with which everyone regarded him. But he was super-excellent among the sick and suffering; then his every action became precise, firm, and masterful. There was no shade of doubt on his face, not a quiver of his nerves; his eyes grew luminous with his concentrated mind. Few people at home know what an African ulcer is like. It grows as large as the biggest mushroom; it destroys the flesh, discloses the arteries and sinews, and having penetrated to the bone, consumes it, and then eats its way round the limb. The sight is awful, the stench is horrible; yet Parke washed and dressed from twenty to fifty of such hideous sores daily, and never winced. The young man's heart was of pure gold. At such times, I could take off my cap, out of pure reverence to his heroism, skill, and enduring patience. When Stairs was wounded with a poisoned arrow, he deliberately sucked it, though, had the poison been fresh, it might have been a highly dangerous proceeding. All the whites passed through his hands; and, if they do not owe their lives to him, they owed him a great debt of gratitude for relief, ease, and encouragement, as well as incomparable nursing.

Personally, I was twice attacked by gastritis, and how he managed to create out of nothing, as it were, palatable food for an inflamed stomach, for such prolonged periods, and to maintain his tenderness of interest in his fractious patient, was a constant marvel to me. When consciousness returned to me, out of many delirious fits, his presence seemed to lighten that sense of approaching calamity that often pressed on me. Could the wounded and sick Zanzibaris have spoken their opinion of him, they would have said, 'He was not a man, but an angel'; for the attributes he showed to the suffering were so unusually noble and exquisitely tender, that poor, wayward human nature wore, for once, a divine aspect to them.

And Jephson, so honourable, and high-minded: though of a vehement character at first, one of his intelligence and heart is not long in adapting himself to circumstances. He developed quickly, taking the rough work of a pioneer with the indifference of a veteran. He was endowed with a greater stock of physical energy than any of the others, and exhibited most remarkable endurance. At first, I feared that he was inclined to be too rough on his company; but this was before he mastered the colloquial expressions, which, with old travellers, serve the same purpose as the stick.

When a young Englishman, replete with animal vigour, and braced for serious work, has to lead a hundred or so raw natives, who cannot understand a word he says, a good deal of ungentle hustling must be expected; but, as soon as he is able to express himself in the vernacular, both commander and natives soon lose that morbid fault-finding to which they were formerly disposed, and the stick becomes a mere badge of authority. Chaff, or a little mild malice, spiced with humour, is often more powerful than the rod with Africans. By the time we issued from the forest, Jephson had become a most valuable officer, with his strong, brave, and resolute nature, capable for any work. If I were to sum up the character of

Jephson in one word, I should say it was one of fine manliness, and courage.

Nelson, also, was a fine fellow, with whom I do not remember to have had a single misunderstanding. Considering that we were a thousand and thirty days together in Africa, and in the gloomiest part of it, for most of that time, it appears to me wonderful that we 'pulled together' so well.

India is a very old land, and provides countless aids to comfort, which are a great balm for trouble. Yet, as the Congo climate is more trying than that of India, and is quite barren of the 'comforts' which are supposed to sweeten an Englishman's temper, it ought not to be expected that five Englishmen should have been able to pierce through darkest Africa without a tiff or two.

As the preceding chapter[1] records all the misunderstandings that occurred between us, I felt justified on reaching the sea in saying, 'Well done' to each of them. Not even a saint is proof against a congested liver, and a miserable diet of horse-food and animal provender; and, yet, during their severe experiences of the Forest, the officers were in better temper than when, ascending the Congo, they enjoyed regular meals. The toughest human patience may be stretched to breaking when fever is rioting in the veins, when the head is filled with hot blood, and the poor victim of malaria is ready to sink with his burden of responsibilities, when black servants take advantage of their master's helplessness, and a thoughtless companion chooses that inopportune moment to air his grievances, or provoke a discussion. When one is recovering from a fever, his senses racked, his ears in a tumult with quinine, his loins aching with inflamed vitals, it is too much to expect a sufferer, at this stage, to smile like a full-fed dreamer at home.

One of my precautions against these intermittent periods of gloom and bitterness, when the temper is tindery, was to mess separately. Years ago, the unwisdom of being too much together had been forcibly impressed on me; I discovered that my remarks formed too much 'copy' for note-books, and that my friends were in the habit of indiscriminately setting down every word, too often in a perverted sense, and continually taking snap-shots at me, without the usual formula of the

[1] This refers to an unpublished private Journal, from which this is an extract.—D. S.

photographer, 'Look pleasant, please!' On the Congo, it is too hot to stand on an open-air pedestal for long! One *must* be in 'undress,' occasionally; and during such times he is not supposed to be posing for the benefit of Fleet Street! Then, upon the strength of table acquaintance, I found that the young men were apt to become overweening, familiar, and oblivious of etiquette and discipline. From that date, I took to living alone, by which my judgment of my subordinates was in no danger of being biassed by their convivial discourse; and I was preserved from the contempt which too often proceeds from familiarity.

No doubt, I was debarred by this isolation from much that was entertaining and innocent, as well as deprived of that instruction, which simple youngsters of the jolly, and silly, age are prone to impart to their seniors; but that was my loss, not theirs. On the other hand, my opinions of them were not likely to be tinctured by malicious gossip, which is generally outspoken at a dining-table, or in a camp; and I certainly discountenanced grumblers and cavillers. On an African expedition, there often arises a necessity for sudden orders, which must be followed by prompt obedience, and the stern voice and peremptory manner at such times are apt to jar on the nerves of a subaltern, whose jokes were lately received with laughter, unless he be one whose temper is controlled by his judgment.

When a young white officer quits England for the first time, to lead blacks, he has got to learn and unlearn a great deal. All that he knows is his mother-tongue, and the arts of reading, writing, and criticising. In Africa, he finds himself face to face with a new people, of different manners and customs, with whom he cannot exchange a word. He can do nothing for himself; there is no service that he can do with his arms; he cannot even cook his food, or set up his tent, or carry his bed. He has to depend on the black men for everything; but if he has a patient temper and self-control, he can take instruction from those who know the natives, and in many little ways he can make himself useful. If he is fault-finding, proud, and touchy, it will be months before he is worth his salt. In these early days he must undeceive himself as to his merits, and learn that, if he is humoured and petted more than the blacks, it is not because of his white skin, but because of his childish helplessness, and in the hope that when his eighteen months' apprenticehip is over, he will begin to show that his keep was to some purpose.

We *must* have white men in Africa; but the raw white is as great a nuisance there during the first year, as a military recruit who never saw a gun till he enlisted. In the second year, he begins to mend; during the third year, if his nature permits it, he has developed into a superior man, whose intelligence may be of transcendent utility for directing masses of inferior men.

I speak from a wide experience of white men whom I have had under me in Africa. One cannot be always expostulating with them, or courting their affection, and soothing their *amour-propre;* but their excessive susceptibility, while their bodies are being harrowed by the stern process of acclimatization, requires great forbearance. It took the officers some months to learn that, when they stood at the head of their companies, and I repeated for the benefit of the natives in their own language the orders already given to them in English, I was not speaking about themselves! By and by, as they picked up a word or two of the native language, they became less suspicious, and were able to distinguish between directness of speech and an affront. I, of course, knew that their followers, whom they had regarded as merely 'naked niggers,' were faithful, willing, hard-working creatures, who only wanted fair treatment and good food to make them loveable.

At this early period my officers were possessed with the notion that my manner was 'hard,' because I had not many compliments for them. That is a kind of pap which we may offer women and boys, but it is not necessary for soldiers and men, unless it is deserved. It is true that, in the Forest, their demeanour was heroic; but I preferred to wait until we were out of it, before telling them my opinion, just as wages are paid after the work is finished, and an epitaph is best written at the close of life. Besides, I thought they were superior natures, and required none of that encouragement, which the more childish blacks almost daily received.

In thinking of my own conduct I am at a disadvantage,

as there is no likelihood that I should appear to others as I appeared to myself. I may have been in the habit of giving unmeasured offence each day by my exclusiveness; but I was simply carrying out what African experience had taught me was best. My companions had more to learn from me than I had to learn from them.

For the first eighteen months they messed together; but during the latter half of the journey, they also lived apart, experience having taught them the same lesson as I had learned.

To some, my solitary life might present a cheerless aspect. But it was not so in reality. The physical exercise of the day induced a pleasant sense of fatigue, and my endless occupations were too absorbing and interesting to allow room for baser thoughts. There was a strange poverty about our existence, which could not well be matched anywhere. The climate gave warmth, and so we needed no fuel save for cooking. Our clothing could only be called presentable among naked people! There was water in abundance and to spare, but soap was priceless. Our food consisted of maize meal and bananas, but an English beggar would have disdained to touch it. Our salt was nothing better than pulverised mud.

I was not likely to suffer from colds, catarrh, and pneumonia; but the ague with its differing intensities was always with me. My bedding consisted of a rubber sheet and rug over a pile of leaves or grass. I possessed certain rights of manhood, but only so long as I had the nerve to cause them to be respected. My literature was limited to the Bible, Shakespeare, and a few choice authors, but my mind was not wrung by envy, scandal, disparagement, and unfairness; and my own thoughts and hopes were a perpetual solace.

It is difficult for anyone who has not undergone experiences similar to ours to understand the amount of self-control each had to exercise, for fifteen hours every day, amid such surroundings as ours. The contest between human dispositions, tempers, prejudices, habits, natures, and the necessity for self-command, were very disturbing. The extremest forms of repulsiveness were around us, and dogged us day by day; the everlasting shade was a continued sermon upon decay and mortality; it reeked with the effluvia as of a grave; insects pursued our every movement, with their worries of stings and bites, which frequently ended, because of our anæmic condition, in pimples, sores, and ulcers. Nelson was crippled with twenty-two obstinate ulcers, Jephson's legs will always bear the blue scars of many a terrible ulcer; and I was seldom free from nausea.

It would be impossible within a limited space to enumerate the annoyances caused by the presence of hundreds of diseased individuals with whom we travelled. Something or other ailed them by scores, daily. Animate and inanimate nature seemed arrayed against us, to test our qualities to the utmost. For my protection against despair and madness, I had to resort to self-forgetfulness; to the interest which my task brought; to the content which I felt that every ounce of energy, and every atom of self had been already given to my duty, and that, no matter what followed, nothing more could be extracted from me. I had my reward in knowing that my comrades were all the time conscious that I did my best, and that I was bound to them by a common sympathy and aims. This encouraged me to give myself up to all neighbourly offices, and was morally fortifying.

The anxieties of providing for the morrow lay heavy on me; for, in the savagest part of Africa, which, unknown to us, had been devastated by Manyuema hordes, we were not sure of being able to obtain anything that was eatable. Then again, the follies and imprudences of my black men were a constant source of anxiety to me, for raw levies of black men are not wiser than raw levies of white men; it requires a calamity to teach both how to live. Not a day passed but the people received instruction, but in an hour it was forgotten. If all had been prudent with their food, we should not have suffered so heavily; but the mutinous hunger of the moment obliterated every thought of the morrow's wants. How extremely foolish men can be, was exemplified by the series of losses attending ten months of camp-life at Yambuya.[1]

The Advance Column consisted of picked men, sound in health. In a month, however, many had been crippled by skewers in the path, placed there by the aborigines; these perforated their naked feet, some suffering from abrasions, or accidental cuts; others had their feet gashed by the sharp edges

[1] This refers to the Rear-Column. — D. S.

of oyster-shells as they waded through the creeks; the effect of rain, dew, damp, fatigue, and scant food, all combined to impoverish the blood and render them more liable to disease. The negligence and heedlessness of some of the men was astonishing: they lost their equipment, rifles, tools, and clothing, as though they were so many somnambulists, and not accountable beings. The officers were unceasing in their exertions, but it would have required an officer for every ten men, and each officer well-fed and in perfect health, to have overseered them properly. The history of the journey proves what stratagems and arts we resorted to each day to check the frightful demoralisation. It was in the aid and assistance given to me at this trying period that my officers so greatly distinguished themselves.

I have frequently been asked as to whether I never despaired during the time when the men were dropping away so fast, and death by starvation seemed so imminent. No, I did not despair; but, as I was not wholly free from morbid thoughts, I may be said to have been on the edge of it, for quite two months. 'How will all this end?' was a question that I was compelled to ask myself over and over again; and then my mind would speculate upon our slim chances, and proceed to trace elaborately the process of ruin and death. 'So many have died to-day, it will be the turn of a few more to-morrow, and a few others the next day, and so on. We shall continue moving on, searching for berries, fungi, wild beans, and edible roots, while the scouts strike far inland to right and left; but, by and by, if we fail to find substantial food, even the scouts must cease their search and will presently pass away. Then the white men, no longer supplied by the share of their pickings, which the brave fellows laid at their tent-doors, must begin the quest of food for themselves; and each will ask, as he picks a berry here and a mushroom there, how it will all end, and when. And while he repeats this dumb self-questioning, little side-shows of familiar scenes will be glanced at. One moment, a friend's face, pink and contented, will loom before him; or a well known house, or a street astir with busy life, or a church with its congregation, or a theatre and its bright-faced audience; a tea-table will be remembered, or a drawing-room animate with beauty and happiness, — at least something, out of the full life beyond the distant sea. After a while, exhausted nature will compel him to seek a leafy alcove where he may rest, and where many a vision will come to him of things that have been, until a profound darkness will settle on his senses. Before he is cold, a 'scout' will come, then two, then a score, and, finally, myriads of fierce yellow-bodied scavengers, their heads clad in shining horn-mail; and, in a few days, there will only remain a flat layer of rags, at one end of which will be a glistening, white skull. Upon this will fall leaves and twigs, and a rain of powder from the bores in the red wood above, and the tornado will wrench a branch down and shower more leaves, and the gusty blasts will sweep fine humus over it, and there that curious compost begun of the earthly in me will lie to all eternity'!

As I thought of this end, the chief feeling, I think, was one of pity that so much unselfish effort should finish in a heap of nothingness. I should not venture to say that my comrades shared in such thoughts. I could see that they were anxious, and that they would prefer a good loaf of bread to the best sermon; but their faces betrayed no melancholy gravity such as follows morbid speculations. Probably, the four brave young hearts together managed to be more cheerful than I, who was solitary; and thus they were able to cheat their minds out of any disposition to brood.

While, however, one part of my nature dwelt upon stern possibilities, and analysed with painful minuteness the sensations of those who daily perished from hunger, another part of me was excessively defiant, active in invention, fertile in expedients, to extricate the expedition from its impending fate, and was often, for no known reason, exhilarant with prescience of ultimate triumph. One half of me felt quite ready to seek a recess in the woods, when the time would come; the other half was aggressive, and obstinately bent upon not yielding, and unceasingly alert, day and night, in seeking methods to rescue us all. There was no doubt that the time had come to pray and submit, but I still felt rebellious, and determined to try every stratagem to gain food for my people.

The darkest night, however, is followed by dawn; and, by dint of pressing on, we emerged once more, after two months of awful trials, into a land of plenty; but before we could say a final farewell to those Equatorial woods much more had to be endured. Jephson had to retrace his steps, to convey succour to Nelson, who had been left to guard a camp of dying men; and I know not which to admire most, the splendid energy with which Jephson hastened to the help of his poor comrade, along a track strewn with the ghastly relics of humanity, or the strong and patient endurance of Nelson, who, for weeks, was condemned to sit alone amid the dying (at 'Starvation Camp').

Then came the turn of Parke and Nelson together, to struggle for months against the worrying band of Manyuema, whose fitful tempers and greed would have made a saint rebel; and Stairs had to return two hundred miles, and escort, all unaided, a long line of convalescents through a country where one hundred and eighty of their fellows had left their bones. This was a feat second to none for the exhibition of the highest qualities that a man can possess.

The true story of those four would make a noble odyssey. While learning the alphabet of African travel, they were open to criticism, as all men must be when they begin a strange work. They winced at a word, and were offended by a glance, and, like restive colts, untried in harness, they lashed and kicked furiously at me and everyone else, at first; but when these men who had been lessoned repeatedly by affliction, and plied so often with distresses, finished their epical experiences of the Great Forest, and issued into the spacious daylight, I certainly was proud of them; for their worth and mettle had been well tried, their sinews were perfectly strong, their hearts beat as one, and their discipline was complete. Each had been compelled to leave behind something that had gathered, in the artificial life of England, over his true self, and he now walked free, and unencumbered, high-hearted, with the stamp of true manhood on him.

Nor was the change less conspicuous in our dark followers. The long marching line was now alive with cheerfulness. Even if one stood aside on a hummock to observe the falling and rising heads, one could see what a lively vigour animated the pace, and how they rose to the toes in their strides. The smallest signal was obeyed by hundreds with a pleasant and beautiful willingness. At the word 'Halt!' they came to a

HENRY M. STANLEY AND HIS OFFICERS, 1890

dead stop on the instant. At 'Stack loads!' each dropped his burden in order; at the morning call of 'Safari!' there was no skulking; at the midnight alarm, they leapt, as one man, to arms.

We began now to re-date our time. What happened in the Forest was an old, old story, not to be remembered; it was like the story of toddling childhood; it is what happened *after* the Forest days that they loved to be reminded of! 'Ah! master,' they would say, 'why recall the time when we were "wayingo" (fools, or raw youths)?'

What singular merits we saw in one another now! We could even venture upon a joke, and no one thought of being sullen. We could laugh at a man, and he would not be displeased! Each had set his life upon a cast, stood bravely the hazard of the die, and triumphed! All were at peace, one with another, and a feeling of brotherhood possessed us, which endured throughout the happy aftertime between the Forest and the sea.

CHAPTER XVIII

WORK IN REVIEW

THE close of the story of Stanley's African explorations may fitly be followed by a survey of the net result. Such an estimate is given in a paper by Mr. Sidney Low, in the 'Cornhill Magazine,' for July, 1904, together with a sketch of Stanley's personality, at once so just and so sympathetic that the entire article, with only slight omissions, is here given a place.

'The map of Africa is a monument to Stanley, *aere perennius*.[1] There lie before me various atlases, published during the past sixty years, which is less than the span of Stanley's lifetime. I turn to a magnificently proportioned volume, bearing the date of 1849, when John Rowlands was a boy at school at Denbigh. In this atlas, the African Continent is exhibited, for about a third of its area, as a mighty blank. The coast is well-defined, and the northern part, as far as ten degrees from the Equator, is pretty freely sprinkled with familiar names. We have Lake Tchad, Bornu, Darfur, Wadi-el-Bagharmi, Sennaar, Kordofan, and Khartoum, and so on. But at the southern line of "the Soudan, or Nigritia," knowledge suddenly ceases; and we enter upon the void that extends, right through and across Africa, down to the Tropic of Capricorn. "Unexplored" is printed, in bold letters, that stride over fifteen hundred miles of country, from the tropical circle to well beyond the Equator! The great lakes are marked only by a vague blob, somewhere in the interior, west of the Zanzibar territory. The estuary of the "Congo, or Zaire" is shown, and a few miles of the river inland. After that we are directed, by uncertain dots, along the supposed course of the stream northward, to where it is imagined to take its rise in the Montes Lunae, for which the map-maker can do no better for us than to refer, in brackets, to "Ptolemy" and "Abulfeda Edrisi."

'I pass to another atlas, dated 1871. Here there is considerable progress, especially as regards the eastern side of the Continent. The White Nile and the Bahr-el-Ghazal have been traced almost to their sources. The Zambesi is known, and the Victoria Falls are marked. Lakes Victoria Nyanza and Nyassa appear with solid boundaries. Tanganyika, however, is still uncertain, the Albert Nyanza with its broken lines testifies to the doubts of the geographer, and the Albert Edward does not appear at all; and beyond the line of the lakes, and north of the tenth degree of south latitude,

[1] 'Monumentum aere perennius,' says Horace, or, as we may put it, 'an Everlasting memorial.' — D. S.

the blank of the interior is still as conspicuous, and almost as unrelieved, as it was two-and-twenty years earlier.

'By 1882, there is a great change. The name of Stanley has begun to be written indelibly upon the surface of the Continent. The vague truncated "Congo, or Zaire" is the "Livingstone River," flowing in its bold horseshoe through the heart of the formerly unexplored region, with "Stanley Falls" just before the river takes its first great spring westward, and "Stanley Pool" a thousand miles lower down, where, after a long southerly course, the mighty stream makes its final plunge to the sea. Tributary rivers, hills, lakes, villages, tribal appellations, dot the waste. Uganda is marked, and Urua, and Unyanyembe.

'If we pass on to the present day, and look at any good recent map, the desert seems to have become — as, indeed, it is — quite populous. There is no stretch of unknown, and apparently unoccupied land, except in the Sahara, and between Somaliland and the White Nile. All the rest is neatly divided off, and most of it tinted with appropriate national colours; the British, red; the French, purple; the German, brown; the Portuguese, green. In the map I am looking at there is, right in the middle, a big irregular square or polygon, which is painted yellow. It is twelve hundred miles from north to south, a thousand from east to west. It is scored by the winding black lines of rivers, — not the Congo only, but the Aruwimi, the Lualaba, the Sankalla, the Ubangi. It is the Congo Free State, one of the recognised political units of the world, with its area of 800,000 square miles, and its population computed at fifteen millions. The great hollow spaces have been filled in. The Dark Continent is, geographically at any rate, dark no longer. The secret of the centuries has been solved!

'Geographical science has still its unfulfilled tasks to finish; but there can never again be another Stanley! He is the last of the discoverers, unless, indeed, we shall have to reserve the title for his friend and younger disciple, Sven Hedin. No other man, until the records of our civilisation perish, can lay bare a vast unknown tract of the earth's surface, for none such is left. The North Pole and the South Pole, it is true, are still inviolate; but we know enough to be aware how little those regions can offer to the brave adventurers who strive to pierce their mysteries. There is no Polar continent, nor open Antarctic Sea, only a dreary waste of lifeless ice, and unchanging snow. But the habitable and inhabited globe is mapped and charted; and none of the explorers, who laboured at the work during the past fifty years, did so much towards the consummation as Stanley. Many others helped to fill in the blank in the atlas of 1849, which has become the network of names in the atlas of 1904.

'A famous company of strong men gave the best of their energies to the opening of Africa during the nineteenth century. They were missionaries, like Moffat and Livingstone; scientific inquirers, like Barth, Rohlfs, Du Chaillu, Teleki, and Thomson; adventurous explorers, like Speke, Grant, Burton, Cameron, and Selous; and soldiers, statesmen, and organisers, such as Gordon, Rhodes, Samuel Baker, Emin Pasha, Johnston, Lugard, and Taubman Goldie — but there is no need to go through the list. Their discoveries were made often with a more slender equipment and scantier resources; as administrators, one or two at least could be counted his equals. But those of the distinguished band, who still survive, would freely acknowledge that it was Stanley who put the crown and coping-stone on the edifice of African exploration, and so completed the task, begun twenty-four centuries ago with the voyage of King Necho's Phœnician captains, and the Periplus of Hanno.

'It was Stanley who gathered up the threads, brought together the loose ends, and united the discoveries of his predecessors into one coherent and connected whole. He linked the results of Livingstone's explorations with those of Speke, and Grant, and Burton, and so enabled the great lacustrine and riverine system of Equatorial Africa to become intelligible. Without him, the work of his most illustrious predecessors might still have remained only a collection of splendid fragments. Stanley exhibited their true relation to one another, and showed what they meant. He is the great — we may say the final — systematiser of African geography, and his achievements in this respect can neither be superseded nor surpassed, if only because the opportunity exists no longer.

'As a fact, Stanley not only completed, but he also corrected, the chief of all Livingstone's discoveries. The missionary traveller was steadily convinced that the Nile took its rise in Lake Tanganyika; or, rather, that it passed right through that inland sea. Stanley, when he had found the Doctor, and restored the weary old man's spirit and confidence, induced him to join in an exploration trip round the north end of Tanganyika, which proved that there was no river flowing out of the lake, and therefore that no connection was possible with the Nile system. But Livingstone still believed that he was on the track of the great Egyptian stream. He persisted in regarding his Lualaba as one of the feeders of the Nile, and he was in search of the three fountains of Herodotus, in the neighbourhood of Lake Bangweolo, when he made his last journey. It was reserved for Stanley to clear up the mystery of the Lualaba, and to identify it with the mighty watercourse which, after crossing the Equator, empties itself, not into the Mediterranean, but into the South Atlantic.

'Stanley regarded himself, and rightly, as the geographical legatee and executor of Livingstone. From the Scottish missionary, during those four months spent in his company in the autumn of 1871, the young adventurer acquired the passion for exploration and the determination to clear up the unsolved enigmas of the Dark Continent. Before that, he does not seem to have been especially captivated by the geographical and scientific side of travel. He liked visiting strange countries, because he was a shrewd observer, with a lively journalistic style, which could be profitably employed in describing people and places. But the finding of Livingstone made Stanley an explorer; and his own nature made him, in a sense, a missionary, though not quite of the Livingstone kind. He was a man who was happiest when he had a mission to accomplish, some great work entrusted to him which had to be got through, despite of difficulties and dangers; and when the famous traveller laid down his tired bones in the wilderness, Stanley felt that it was decreed for him to carry on the work. So he has said himself in the opening passage of the book in which he described the voyage down the Congo. When he returned to England in 1874, after the Ashanti War, it was to learn that Livingstone was dead: —

'"The effect which this news had upon me, after the first shock had passed away, was to fire me with a resolution to complete his work, to be, if God willed it, the next martyr to geographical science, or, if my life was to be spared, to clear up not only the secrets of the great river throughout its course, but also all that remained still problematic and incomplete of the discoveries of Burton and Speke, and Speke and Grant.

'"The solemn day of the burial of the body of my great friend arrived. I was one of the pall-bearers in Westminster Abbey, and when I had seen the coffin lowered into the grave, and had heard the first handful of earth thrown over it, I walked away sorrowing over the fall of David Livingstone."

'There must have been some among those present at the Memorial Service in Westminster Abbey, on May 17, 1904, who recalled these simply impressive words, and they may have wondered *why* the great Englishman who uttered them was not to lie with the great dead of England at Livingstone's side.

'It is not merely on geographical science that Stanley has left a permanent impress, so that, while civilised records last, his name can no more be forgotten than those of Columbus and the Cabots, of Hudson and Bartolomeo Diaz. His life has had a lasting effect upon the course of international politics. The partitioning of Africa, and its definite division into formal areas of administration or influence, might have been delayed for many decades but for his sudden and startling revelation of the interior of the Continent. He initiated, unconsciously, no doubt, and involuntarily, the "scramble for Africa" in which Germany, France, Great Britain, Italy, Belgium, and Portugal have taken part. The opening up of the Congo region, by his two great expeditions of 1874 and 1879, precipitated a result which may have been ultimately inevitable, but would perhaps have been long delayed without his quickening touch. The political map of Africa, as it now appears, and is likely to appear for many generations to come, was not the work of Stanley; but without Stanley it would not have assumed its present shape. His place is among those who have set the landmarks of nations and moulded their destinies.

'When you conversed with him, at least in his later years, you easily discovered that he had a firm grasp of the general sequence of European and Oriental history, and a considerable insight into modern ethnological and archæological learning. He had formed independent and original ideas of his own on these subjects; and when he talked, as he sometimes would, of the Sabæans and the Phœnicians, and the early Arab voyagers, you saw that, to the rapid observation of the man of action, he had added much of the systematising and deductive faculty of the scholar. He possessed the instinct of arrangement, which is the foundation of all true scholarship, and perhaps of all great practical achievement as well.

'His intellectual power was, I think, seldom appreciated at its true value. Its full measure is not given in his books, in spite of their vigorous style, their dramatic method of narration, and their brilliant pictorial passages; but nearly everything he wrote was in the nature of rather hurried journalism, the main object of which was to explain what had happened, or to describe what had been seen. Not in these graphic volumes, but in the achievements which gave rise to them, is Stanley's mental capacity made manifest. He was not only a born commander, prompt, daring, undaunted, irresistible, but also a great administrator, a great practical thinker. He thought out his problems with slow, thorough patience, examined every aspect of them, and considered all the possible alternatives, so that when the time came for action he knew what to do, and had no need to hesitate. His fiery, sudden deeds were more often the result of a long process of thought than of a rapid inspiration. The New York correspondent of the "Times," who knew him well, tells an illustrative story: —

'"He and his whole party had embarked on Lake Tanganyika, knowing that the banks were peopled, some with friendly, some with hostile tribes. His canoes moved on at a respectful distance from the nearest shore. Sometimes the friendly people came off to sell their boat-loads of vegetables and fruit. "But suppose they were not friendly," said Stanley to himself, "then, what?" So one day there approached a fleet of canoes, with all the usual signs of friendly commerce. They were piled high with bananas. "I thought" (said Stanley) "they had a large supply, and the boats were deep in the water; still, there was nothing that looked really suspicious. There were just men enough to paddle the canoes; no more. I let them come close, but I kept my eye on them, and my hand on the trigger of my elephant gun. They were but a few yards off when I saw a heap of bananas stir. I fired instantly, and instantly the water was black with hundreds of armed black men who had been hidden beneath the banana-heaps. I do not think many of them got ashore. If I had stopped to think, they would have been aboard us, and it is we who should not have got ashore. But I had done my thinking before they came near."

'Similarly he spoke of Gordon's end. "If," he said, "I had been sent to get the Khartoum garrison away, I should have thought of that and nothing else; I should have calculated the chances, made out exactly what resistance I would have to encounter, and how it could be overcome, and laid all my plans with the single object of accomplishing my purpose." I believe, though he did not say so, that he thought the retreat could have been effected, or the town held, till the Relief Column arrived, if proper measures had been taken, and the one definite aim had been kept steadily in view all the time. That was his principle of action. When he had an object to fulfil, a commission to carry out, he could think of nothing else till the work was done. Difficulties, toil, hardships, sacrifices of all kinds, of time, of men, of money, were only incidents in the journey that led to a goal, to be reached if human endeavour could gain it. "No honour," he wrote, "no reward, however great, can be equal to the subtle satisfaction that a man feels when he can point to his work and say: "'See, now, the task I promised you to perform with all loyalty and honesty, with might and main, to the utmost of my ability is, to-day, finished.'" This was the prime article in Stanley's confession of faith — to do the work to which he had set his hand, and in doing it, like Tennyson's Ulysses, —

"To strive, to seek, to find, and not to yield."

'Both aspects of his character, the practical and the intellectual, were revealed in the two great expeditions of 1874 and 1879. The crossing of Africa, which began in the first year, was a marvellous performance in every way. Its results were immense, for it was the true opening of the Equatorial region, and added more to geographical knowledge than any enterprise of the kind in the nineteenth century, or perhaps in any century. Great conquerors at the head of an army — an Alexander, or a Genghis Khan — may have done as much; but no single individual revolutionised so large a tract of the earth's surface, with only a handful of armed men and a slender column of camp-followers and attendants. Wonderful, indeed, was the tour of the great lakes, the circumnavigation of the Victoria Nyanza, the conversion of King Mtesa of Uganda, the unveiling of the fertile, semi-civilised country, islanded for centuries in the ocean of African barbarism, which is now a British Protectorate, linked up with Charing Cross by rail and steamer. But the toilsome journey up from the East Coast was nothing to that which followed, when the party left Uganda and turned their faces to the Congo, resolved to follow the great river down to the sea. His gifts of leadership were at their highest in this memorable march, from the time that he left Nyangwe, in November, 1876, to his arrival at Boma, near the Congo estuary, in August, 1877. He had to be everything by turn in this space of ten eventful months — strategist, tactician, geographer, medical superintendent, trader, and diplomatist. There were impracticable native chiefs to be conciliated, the devious designs of that formidable Arab potentate, Tippu-Tib, to be penetrated and countered, inexorably hostile savages to be beaten off by hard fighting. The expedition arrived at Boma, a remnant of toil-worn men, weakened by disease, and very nearly at the point of starvation. Stanley's white companions had perished, and his native contingent had suffered heavily; but the allotted task was accomplished, and the silent pledge, registered by Livingstone's grave, had been fulfilled.

'It was this famous journey — the most remarkable, if judged by its results, in the whole history of African travel — which placed Stanley's reputation as a leader and discoverer on the highest pinnacle. It was not an unassailed reputation. Much was said about his high-handed methods, and many good people in England, those

> "Good people, who sit still in easy chairs,
> And damn the general world for standing up,"

chose to regard him as a sort of filibuster. They contrasted his methods with those of some of his predecessors and contemporaries, who had contrived to spend years in Africa without fighting and bloodshed; but they did not allow for the difference in the conditions. Most of the other travellers had been the sport of circumstances. They had wandered from place to place, turned from their course, again and again, by hostile tribes and churlish chiefs. They found out a great deal, but not, as a rule, that which they came to find. Their discoveries were largely accidental; even Livingstone was constantly deflected from his route, and was unable to pursue to its conclusion the plan of tracing the central watershed which he had set before himself. Stanley had a perfectly definite purpose, which he determined to carry out; and he succeeded. His scheme involved passing through an immense region, inhabited by a comparatively numerous population, of a higher type than those encountered nearer the coast, more energetic and more warlike. As a rule, he made his way among them by bargain and negotiation; but, sometimes, he had to fight or to turn back; and he accepted the sterner alternative. If he had refused to do so, he could not have reached his goal. The expedition might still have added enormously to the sum of scientific knowledge, but in the achievement of its ultimate and clearly-conceived object it would have been a failure. Stanley did not mean that it should fail; he was always ready to sacrifice himself, and when necessary he was prepared, as great men who do great deeds must be, to sacrifice others. But there was never the smallest justification for representing him as a ruthless, iron-handed kind of privateer on land, who used the scourge and the bullet with callous recklessness. There was nothing reckless about Stanley, except, at times, his speech. In action, he was swift and bold, but not careless.

'To inflict superfluous suffering, to shoot and slay without thinking of the consequences — this was *utterly alien* to his systematic, calculating methods. He would do it, if there seemed no other means of gaining the end, as a general would order a column to destruction to save his army and win a victory. But he was essentially a humane man, masterful and domineering, and yet, *au fond*, gentle and kindly, particularly to the weak and suffering. Opposition stiffened the obstinate will to resistance; he was not a safe person to thwart, even in small matters. He remembered a benefit, and he did not forget an injury. It was said that he was unforgiving, and, perhaps, there was something in the charge. In his intense, self-contained nature wounds rankled long; and he had little of that talent for oblivion which is so easily developed among comfortable people, whose emotions and experiences have never been poignant enough to disturb their peace of mind.

'One who knew Stanley well, and studied him with an eye at once penetrating and friendly, believed that through life he bore the characteristic traces of his Cymric origin. He had the Welsh peasant's quickness of temper, his warmth of affection, his resentfulness when wronged, his pugnacity, and his code of ethics, ultimately derived from John Calvin. Welsh Protestantism is based on a conscientious study of the biblical text. Stanley carried his Bible with him through life, and he read it constantly; but I should imagine that he was less affected by the New Testament than by the prophetic and historical books of the Hebraic scriptures. He believed profoundly in the Divine ordering of the world; but he was equally assured that the Lord's Will was not fulfilled by mystical dreams, or by weak acquiescence in any wrong-doing that could be evaded by energetic action. With Carlyle, he held that strength is based on righteousness, and that the strong should inherit the earth; and saw no reason why there should be any undue delay in claiming the inheritance. "The White Man's Burden" could not be shirked, and should, on the contrary, be promptly and cheerfully shouldered.

'"It is useless" (he wrote, having in view the American Indians) "to blame the white race for moving across the continent in a constantly-increasing tide. If we proceed in that manner, we shall presently find ourselves blaming Columbus for discovering America, and the Pilgrim Fathers for landing on Plymouth Rock! The whites have done no more than follow the law of their nature and being."

'He had his own idea about prayer. A man, he thought, ought to lay his supplications before the Throne of the Universe; and he attached great value to prayers for deliverance from danger and distress. But the answer was not to be expected by way of a miracle. The true response is in the effect on the suppliant himself, in the vigour and confidence it gives to his spirit, and the mental exaltation and clearness it produces. That was Stanley's opinion; and he had no great respect for the martyrs, who yielded to their fate with prayer, when they might have averted it by action.

'The crossing of Africa was Stanley's premier achievement as a leader of men. The founding of the Congo State revealed him as a great administrator and organiser. It was a wonderful piece of management, a triumph of energy, resource, and hard work. Here it was that Stanley earned the title which, I think, gave him more satisfaction than the belated G. C. B., conferred on him towards the end of his life. The natives called him "Bula Matari," which, being interpreted, means "the Breaker of Rocks"—an appellation bestowed upon him by the brown-skinned villagers as they watched the sturdy explorer toiling, bare-armed, under the fierce African sun, with axe or hammer in hand, showing his labourers, by example and precept, how to make the road from Vivi to Isangela, which bridged the cataracts of the Lower Congo, and opened the way to the upper reaches of the river.

'The founding of the Congo State can be compared with the achievements of the two other great enterprises of our own time, which have converted vast tracts of primitive African savagery into organised states under civilised administration. But Stanley's task was heavier than that of the pioneers of Rhodesia, and the creators of Nigeria. The sphere of his operations was longer; the native populations were more numerous and more utterly untouched by external influences other than those of the Arab slave-raiders; the climatic and physical obstacles were more severe; he had foreign opposition to contend with from without, and many difficulties with the pedantry, the obstinacy, and the greed of some of the officials sent out to him by his employers. Yet in the short space of five years the work was done! The Congo was policed, surveyed, placed under control. A chain of stations was drawn along its banks; systematic relations had been established with the more powerful native potentates; an elaborate political and commercial organisation had been established; the transport difficulties had been overcome, and the whole region thrown open to trade under the complicated and careful regulations which Stanley had devised. It was no fault of Stanley's if the work has been badly carried on by his successors, and if the Congo State, under a régime of Belgian officials, not always carefully selected, has not, so far, fulfilled the promise of its inception. So long as Stanley was in Africa, no disaster occurred; there was no plundering of the natives, and no savage reprisals. If he had been permitted to remain a few years longer, the advance of the Congo State might have been more rapid, particularly if he could have been seconded by subordinates with a higher inherited capacity for ruling inferior races than Belgians could be expected to possess. It was a cause of regret to him, I believe, that England did not take a larger share in this international enterprise.

'But England for long ignored or belittled the work that Stanley did. It was not till public opinion, throughout the Anglo-Saxon and Latin world, had acclaimed him a hero, that the governing element recognised something of his greatness; and, *to the very last*, its recognition was guarded and grudging. One might have supposed that his services would have been enlisted for the Empire in 1884, when he came back from the Congo. He was in the prime of life, he was full of vigour, he had proved his capacity as a leader, a ruler, and a governor, who had few living equals. One thinks that employment worthy of his powers should have been pressed upon him. But the country which left Burton to eat out his fiery heart in a second-rate consulship, and never seemed to know what to do with Gordon, could not find a suitable post for Stanley! I do not imagine he sought anything of the kind; but it seems strange that it was not offered, and on such terms that he would have found it difficult to refuse.

'If he had been entrusted with some worthy imperial commission, he might have been saved from the fifth, and least fortunate, of his journeys into the interior of Africa. Nothing that Stanley ever did spoke more loudly for his courage, his resourcefulness, and his heroic endurance, than the expedition for the Relief of Emin Pasha. None but a man of his iron resolution could have carried through those awful marches and counter-marches in the tropical forest, and along the banks of the Aruwimi. But the suffering and privations were incurred for an inadequate object, and a cause not clearly understood. Many lives were lost, many brave men, white and black, perished tragically, to effect the rescue of a person who, it appeared, would, on the whole, have preferred not to be rescued!

'The journey from the Ocean to the Nile, and from the Nile to the East Coast, added much to geographical knowledge, and was the complement of Stanley's previous discoveries. But the cost was heavy, and the leader himself emerged with his health seriously impaired by the tremendous strain of those dark months. Most of his younger companions preceded him to the grave. Stanley survived Nelson, Stairs, and Parke, as well as Barttelot and Jameson; but the traces of the journey were upon him to the end, and no doubt they shortened his days.

'Those days — that is to say, the fourteen years that were left to him after he returned to England in the spring of 1890 — were, however, full of activity, and, one may hope, of content. No other great task of exploration and administration was tendered; and perhaps, if offered, it could not have been accepted. But Stanley found plenty of occupation. He wrote, he lectured, and he assisted the King of the Belgians with advice on the affairs of his Dependency. He was in Parliament for five years, and he took some part in the discussion of African questions. More than all, he was married, most happily and fortunately married, and watched over, and ministered to, with tactful and tender solicitude.

'The evening of that storm-tossed and strenuous life was calm and peaceful. Those who knew him only in these closing years saw him, I suppose, at his best, with something of the former nervous, self-assertive, vitality replaced by a mellow and matured wisdom. Whether there was much more than an external contrast between the Stanley of the earlier and him of the later period, I am unable to say; but one may suggest that the change was in the nature of a development.

'Does any man's character really alter, after the formative season of youth is over? Traits, half-hidden, or seldom-revealed in the fierce stress of active conflict and labour, may come to the surface when the battling days are done. I cannot think that the serene sagacity, the gentleness, and the magnanimity, which one noted in Stanley in his last decade, could have been merely the fruit of leisure and domestic happiness. No doubt the strands were always in his nature, though perhaps not easily detected by the casual eye, so long as "the wrestling thews that throw the world" had to be kept in constant exercise.

'In manner and appearance, and in other respects, he was the absolute antithesis of the type he sometimes represented to the general imagination. Short of stature, lean, and wiry, with a brown face, a strong chin, a square, Napoleonic head, and noticeable eyes, — round, lion-like eyes, watchful and kindly, that yet glowed with a hidden fire, — he was a striking and attractive personality; but there was nothing in him to recall the iron-handed, swash-buckling, melodramatic adventurer, such as the pioneers of new countries are often supposed to be. The bravest of the brave, a very Ney or Murat among travellers, one knew that he was; but his courage, one could see, was not of the unthinking, inconsequent variety, that would court danger for its own sake, without regard to life and suffering. What struck one most was that "high seriousness," which often belongs to men who have played a great part in great events, and have been long in close contact with the sterner reality of things. His temperament was intense rather than passionate, in spite of the outbursts of quick anger, which marked him, in his fighting period, when he was crossed or wronged. Much, far too much, was made of his "indiscretions" of language — as if strong men are not always indiscreet! It is only the weaklings who make no mistakes, who are for ever decorous and prudent.

'Much the same may be said of his early quarrel with the Royal Geographical Society. He did not find it easy to forgive that distinguished body, when it signified its desire to make amends for the coldness with which it had first treated him, and for the ungenerous aspersions, which some of its members had cast upon his fame. They gave him a dinner, and made flattering speeches about the man who had succeeded. It was thought to be ungracious of Stanley that he would not make up the quarrel, until he had vindicated his own part of it by a bitter recital of his grievances. But men who feel intensely, who have suffered deeply under unmerited injuries, and who have Stanley's defiant sense of justice, are not always so tactful and polite as the social amenitics require.

'As it was, the "indiscretions" for some years left a certain mark upon Stanley's reputation, and gave an easy handle to the cavillers and the hypercritical, and to the whole tribe of the purists, who are shocked because revolutions are not made with rose-water, or continents conquered in kid gloves. Even after his triumph was acknowledged, after he had been honoured by princes, and had won his way to the tardy recognition of the Royal Geographical Society, there were "superior persons" to repeat that he was egotistical and inhuman.

'To his friends, both charges must have seemed absurd. Of personal egotism, of mere vanity, he had singularly little. It needed a very obtuse observer to miss seeing that he was by nature simple, affectionate, and modest, with a wealth of kindness and generosity under his mantle of reserve. He had a sympathetic feeling for the helpless, and the unfortunate — for animals, for the poor, and for the children of all races. On the march from Ruwenzori, distressed mothers of Emin's motley contingent would bring their babies to Stanley's own tent, knowing that "Bula Matari" would have halted the caravan sooner than needlessly sacrifice one of these quaint brown scraps of humanity. He would tell the story himself; and afterwards, perhaps, he would describe how he made up the connubial differences of some jangling couple of half-clad aboriginals!

'His full and varied experiences were not easy to extract from him, for he disliked being "drawn," and preferred to talk on those larger, impersonal questions of politics, history, ethnology, and economics, in which he never ceased to be interested. But his friends were sometimes allowed to be entranced by some strange and stirring episode of African adventure, told with fine dramatic power, and relieved by touches of quiet humour. He was not a witty talker, but he had a fund of that amused tolerance which comes of comprehending, and condoning, the weaknesses of human nature. It is a trait which goes far to explain his success in dealing with native races.

'In the House of Commons he was not much at home. The atmosphere of the place, physical and intellectual, disagreed with him. The close air and the late hours did not suit his health. "I am a man," he once said to the present writer, "who cannot stand waste." The Commons' House of Parliament, with its desultory, irregular ways, its dawdling methods, and its interminable outpourings of verbose oratory, must have seemed to him a gigantic apparatus for frittering away energy and time. He was glad to escape from St. Stephen's to the Surrey country home, in which he found much of the happiness of his later years. Here he drained, and trenched, and built, and planted; doing everything with the same careful prevision, and economical adaptation of means to ends, which he had exhibited in greater enterprises. To go the round of his improvements with him was to gain some insight into the practical side of his character.

'It was not the only, nor perhaps the highest, side. There was another, not revealed to the world at large, or to many persons, and the time has scarcely come to dwell upon it. But those who caught glimpses into a temple somewhat jealously veiled and guarded, did not find it hard to understand why it was that Stanley had never failed to meet with devoted service and loyal attachment, through all the vicissitudes of the brilliant and adventurous career which has left its mark scored deep upon the history of our planet.

'SIDNEY LOW.'

A further testimony to the importance of Stanley's discoveries was given by Sir William Garstin, G. C. M. G., in a paper read on December 15, 1908, before the Royal Geographical Society, on the occasion of the Fiftieth Anniversary of the discovery of the Source of the White Nile by Captain John Speke.

'I now come,' said Sir William Garstin, 'to what is, perhaps, the most striking personality of all in the roll of the discoverers of the Nile, that of Henry Stanley.

'Stanley on his second expedition, starting for the interior, on November 17, 1874, circumnavigated Lake Victoria, and corrected the errors of Speke's map as to its shape and area.

'He visited the Nile outlet, and proved that the Nyanza was a single sheet of water, and not, as Burton had asserted, a series of small, separate lakes.

'On arriving at Mtesa's capital, Stanley's acute mind quickly grasped the possibilities of Uganda as a centre for missionary enterprise. He realised that, if he could succeed in interesting Great Britain in such a project, a most important departure would have been made in the direction of introducing European civilisation into Central Africa.

'First came his appeal by letter, followed later by Stanley himself, whose eloquence aroused enthusiasm in the English public. A great meeting held in Exeter Hall, resulted in funds being raised, and the first party of English missionaries started for Uganda in the spring of 1876.

'This, although not at the time realised, was in reality the first step towards the introduction of British rule in Equatorial Africa.

'Stanley's last voyage, and in some respects, his greatest expedition, was undertaken for the relief of Emin Pasha, at that time cut off from communication with the outer world. The Relief Expedition started in 1887, under Stanley's leadership. This time Stanley started from the Congo, and, travelling up that river, struck eastward into the Great Forest, which, covering many thousands of square miles, stretches across a portion of the Semliki Valley and up the western flank of Ruwenzori.

'On emerging from the Forest, Stanley reached the Valley of the Semliki, and, in May, 1888, he discovered the mountain chain of Ruwenzori.

'This discovery alone would have sufficed to have made his third journey famous. It was not all, however. After his meeting with Emin, he followed the Semliki Valley to the point where this river issues from the Albert Edward Nyanza.

'Stanley was the first traveller to trace its course, and to prove that it connects two lakes and, consequently, forms a portion of the Nile system.

'When skirting the north end of Lake Albert Edward, he recognised that he had really discovered this lake in his previous journey, although at the time unaware of this fact.

'Stanley has thus cleared up the last remaining mystery with respect to the Nile sources.

'It is impossible to exaggerate the importance of Stanley's work. The main facts regarding the sources of the Nile were finally revealed by him, and nothing was left for future explorers but to fill in the details. This was a magnificent achievement for one man to have compassed, and Stanley must always stand out as having done more than any other to clear up, and to correct, the errors in the geography of the Nile basin. Stanley not only completed thoroughly the work left unfinished by other explorers, but added largely to it by his own remarkable discoveries. To him also it was due that the first English Mission was despatched to Uganda.

'Stanley's glowing accounts of the fertility of the land of the Baganda encouraged British commercial enterprise, and originated the formation of the East African Chartered Company. As we now know, the inevitable sequence was the English occupation of the country.'

As to Stanley's African work, one or two features may here be specially noted. His master-passion was that, not of the discoverer, but of the civiliser. He had his own methods, but he was sympathetic and helpful toward other methods, and sometimes adopted them. To King Mtesa and his people, he took the part of a Christian missionary with rare efficiency. When the time for his departure came, Mtesa heard it with dismay, and asked: 'What is the use, then, of your coming to Uganda to disturb our minds, if, as soon as we are convinced that what you have said has right and reason in it, you go away before we are fully instructed?'

Stanley answered that every man has his own business and calling, that his business was that of a pioneer and not of a religious teacher, but if the king wanted real instructors, he would write to England and ask for them. The king said, 'Then write, Stamlee' (the native pronunciation of the name), 'and say to the white people that I am like a child sitting in darkness, and cannot see until I am taught the right way.' Thereupon followed the appeal to England, the prompt response, the planting of the mission, and the heroic story of the Uganda church triumphing over persecution and martyrdom. When Stanley wrote the story for the 'Cornhill Magazine,' January, 1901, the Uganda people had built for themselves three hundred and seventy-two churches, with nearly 100,000 communicants, who were not fair-weather Christians. A week or two after Stanley's death, the great cathedral of Uganda was solemnly consecrated, and opened for service.

Among these people whom Stanley visited, while taking Emin's refugees to safety in 1889, was the illustrious missionary A. M. Mackay, who had previously written, 'For a time the old gods of the land had to give way to the creed of Arabia, as the king saw something in that more likely to add prestige to his court than the charm-filled horns of the magic men, and frantic dance of the fore-tellers of fortune. Then came Stanley. Let his enemies scoff as they will, it is a fact indisputable that with his visit there commenced the dawn of a new era in the annals of the court of Uganda. The people themselves date from Stanley's day the commencement of leniency and law, in place of the previous reign of bloodshed and terror. "Since Stanley came," they say, "the king no more slaughters innocent people as he did before; he no more disowns and disinherits in a moment an old and powerful chief, and sets up a puppet of his own, who was before only a slave." Compared with the former daily changes and cruelties, as the natives describe them, one cannot but feel thankful to God for the mighty change.'

After the visit, Mackay writes: —

'I must say that I much enjoyed Mr. Stanley's company during the short stay here. He is a man of an iron will and sound judgment; and, besides, is most patient with the natives. He never allows any one of his followers to oppress, or even insult, a native. If he has had occasionally to use force in order to effect a passage, I am certain that he only resorted to arms when all other means failed.'

Stanley recognised and appreciated in Mackay a spirit akin to Livingstone. He judged that he had dangerously overtaxed his strength, and urged him to go away with him and secure a rest. But Mackay would not leave his post, and within half a year he succumbed to disease.[1]

Did space permit, a chapter might well be given to Stanley's labours for African civilisation by means of addresses to the English people, and his efforts, by lectures and personal interviews, to move the Government and the community to meet the successive calls for action. *Had England responded to his appeal to take over the Congo region*, the leadership, which was left to the Belgian sovereign, would have devolved on the British nation, and history would have had a different course.

After the founding of the Congo Free State, Stanley went over the length and breadth of England to address meetings, urging the English people to build the Congo Railway. *But again the deaf ear was turned to him.* Now, the wealth to shareholders in that railway is prodigious. He also did his utmost to spur and persuade a laggard and indifferent Government to plant and foster English civilisation in East Africa. He wanted not mere political control, but the efficient repression of the slave-trade, the advancement of material improvements, and especially the construction of railways to

[1] In *Darkest Africa*, Stanley notes that 'Mr. Mackay, the best missionary since Livingstone, died about the beginning of February, 1890.'

destroy the isolation which was ruinous to the interior. One lecture, entitled 'Uganda; a plea against its Evacuation,' is a masterpiece of large-minded wisdom, and true statesmanship. He spoke repeatedly before Anti-slavery Societies on the practical means of attaining the great end. His influence with King Leopold was always used to hasten and complete the extirpation of the Arab slave-trade. From that curse Equatorial Africa was freed, and in its deliverance Stanley was the leader.

Stanley constantly urged the vital importance of thoroughly training Medical Officers and Medical Missionaries in the knowledge of Tropical diseases, and the necessity of the proper medical equipment of expeditions and stations, and the considerate medical treatment of natives, as well as white men, for economic reasons, as well as on humanitarian grounds.

From his own terrible experiences Stanley realised to the full the barrier which Malaria and other dread Tropical diseases imposed against the progress of civilisation and commercial enterprise in Africa; and he followed with keen interest and hopefulness the discoveries of Sir Patrick Manson, and Major Ross, proving the mosquito to be the host and carrier of the malarial parasite, and also the successful devices of these scientists for checking and reducing the death-toll from this scourge.

He particularly applauded the great, far-seeing, Colonial Secretary, Joseph Chamberlain, for his practical measures, by which he had done more than any other Statesman to render the Tropical regions of the Empire habitable and healthy.

Stanley's last public appearance was at a dinner to Dr. Andrew Balfour, on his appointment as Director of the Wellcome Tropical Research Laboratories, Gordon Memorial College, Khartoum, and, in the course of a very moving speech on the development of Africa since his first expedition, Stanley said that, at one time, he thought the Equatorial regions possible for the habitation of natives only, except in limited highlands; but now, thanks to the work of the London and Liverpool Schools of Tropical Medicine, and these Research Laboratories in the heart of Africa, the deadly plagues that harassed mankind were being conquered, and the whole of that Dark Continent might yet become a white man's land.

One other trait of his African work may be mentioned. In a pecuniary sense, *it was absolutely disinterested*. He would never take the slightest personal advantage of the commercial opportunities incident to the opening of the new countries, on the Congo, or in Uganda. *I desire to emphasise the fact that such property as he had came almost entirely from his books and his lectures*. He gave his assistance to the establishment of the British East African Company because he believed in its influence for good, but *he declined any pecuniary interest*.

When the Congo Railway stock was paying very high dividends, he was asked why he did not take some of it, and he answered that 'he would not have even the appearance of personal profit out of Africa.' When princes and potentates made advantageous offers to him, they were quietly put aside. Once an English magnate in Africa, who had aggrandised England and enriched himself, asked playfully, 'Why don't *you* take some of the "corner lots" in Africa?' Stanley put the question by, and afterwards said: 'That way may be very well for him, but, for myself, I prefer my way.'

When the retention of Uganda was under discussion, Lord Salisbury said publicly: 'It is natural that Mr. Stanley should favour the retention, for we all know that he has interests in Africa.' Stanley took the earliest occasion to say publicly; 'It is true, but not in the sordid sense in which the imputation has been made; *my whole interest there is for Africa herself, and for humanity.*'

HENRY M. STANLEY, 1890, ON HIS RETURN FROM AFRICA

CHAPTER XIX

EUROPE AGAIN

THERE was a charm attached to the Great Forest that was only revealed to me after it had dropped beyond the horizon. I had found that a certain amount of determination was necessary to enter it.

The longer I hesitated, the blacker grew its towering walls, and its aspect more sinister. My imagination began to eat into my will and consume my resolution. But when all the virtue in me rose in hot indignation against such pusillanimity. I left the pleasant day, and we entered as into a tomb, I found it difficult to accustom myself to its gloom and its pallid solitude. I could find no comfort for the inner man, or solace for the spirit. It became impressed on me that it was wholly unfit for gregarious man, who loves to see something that appertains to humanity in his surroundings. A man can look into the face of the Sun and call him Father, the Moon can be compared to a mistress, the Stars to souls of the dear departed, and the Sky to our Heavenly Home; but when man is sunk in the depths of a cold tomb, how can he sing, or feel glad?

After I had got well out of it, however, and had been warmed through and through by the glowing sun, and was near being roasted by it, so that the skyey dome reminded me of a burning hot oven, and the more robustious savages of the open country pestered us with their darts, and hemmed us round about, day and night, then it dawned upon my mind that, in my haste, I had been too severe in my condemnation of the Forest. I began to regret its cool shade, its abundant streams, its solitude, and the large acquaintance I made with our own ever-friendly selves, with whom there was never any quarrelling, and not a trace of insincere affection.

I was reminded of this very forcibly when I descended from the Suez train, and entered Cairo. My pampered habits of solitary musing were outraged, my dreaming temper was shocked, my air-castles were ruthlessly demolished, and my illusions were rudely dispelled. The fashionables of Cairo, in staring at me every time I came out to take the air, made me uncommonly shy; they made me feel as if something was radically wrong about me, and I was too disconcerted to pair with any of them, all at once. They had been sunning without interruption in the full blaze of social life, and I was too fresh from my three years' meditations in the wilds.

If any of the hundreds I met chanced to think kindly of me at this period, it was certainly not because of any merit of my own, but because of their innate benevolence and ample considerateness. I am inclined to think, however, that I made more enemies than friends, for it could scarcely be otherwise with an irreflective world. To have escaped their censure, I ought to have worn a parchment band on my forehead, bearing the inscription: 'Ladies and gentlemen, I have been in Darkest Africa for three continuous years, living among savages, and I fear something of their spirit clings to me; so I pray you have mercy.'

Indeed, no African traveller ought to be judged during the first year of his return. He is too full of his own reflections; he is too utterly natural; he must speak the truth, if he dies for it; his opinions are too much his own. Then, again, his vitals are wholly disorganised. He may appear plump enough, but the plumpness is simply the effect of unhealthy digestion; his stomach, after three years' famishing, is contracted, and the successive feasts to which he is invited speedily become his bane. His nerves are not uniformly strung, and his mind harks back to the strange scenes he has just left, and cannot be on the instant focussed upon that which interests Society. To expect such a man to act like the unconscious man of the world, is as foolish as to expect a fashionable Londoner to win the confidence of naked Africans. We must give both time to recover themselves, or we shall be unjust.

To avoid the lounging critics that sat in judgment upon me at Shepheard's Hotel, I sought a retired spot, the Villa Victoria, surrounded by a garden, where, being out of sight, I might be out of mind. There was also an infectious sickness prevailing that season in London, and my friends thought it better that I should wait warmer weather. I reached Cairo in the middle of January, 1890, and, until the beginning of February, I toyed with my pen. I could not, immediately, dash off two consecutive sentences that were readable. A thousand scenes floated promiscuously through my head, but, when one came to my pen-point, it was a farrago of nonsense, incoherent, yet confusedly intense. Then the slightest message from the outside world led me astray, like a rambling butterfly. What to say first, and how to say it, was as disturbing as a pathless forest would be to a man who had never stirred from Whitechapel. My thoughts massed themselves into a huge organ like that at the Crystal Palace, from which a master-hand could evoke Handel's 'Messiah,' or Wagner's 'Walküre,' but which to me would only give deep discords.

The days went by, and I feared I should have to relegate my book to the uncertain future. At last I started on the 'Forest' chapter, the writing of which relieved me of the acuter feeling. Then I began the 'March from Yambuya'; and, presently, I warmed to the work, flung off page after page, and never halted until I had reached 'The Albert.' The stronger emotions being thus relieved, I essayed the beginning, and found by the after-reading that I was not over-fantastic, and had got into the swing of narrative. I continued writing from ten to fifty pages of manuscript during a day, from six in the morning until midnight; and, having re-written the former chapters with more method, was able on the eighty-fifth day to write 'Finis' to the record of the journey.

I think the title of it was a happy one — 'In Darkest Africa, or the Quest, Rescue, and Retreat of Emin Pasha.' It was the choice out of more than fifty taking titles on the same subject, but none of them was so aptly descriptive of the theme. Since then, some dozen or so book-titles have been founded on it, such as 'Darkest England,' 'Darkest London,' 'Darkest New York,' 'Darkest Russia,' etc., etc. It was the custom for Germans, Anglo-Germans, Philo-Germans, etc., etc., for some three or four years later, to print the word '*Rescue*' with quotation marks, which signified, of course, 'so-called'; but if the word is not absolutely truthful, I know not what is true.

Emin was rescued from being either sold to the Mahdists, or killed by Fadle Mullah, or perishing through some stupid act of his own; and, so long as he was in the British camp, he was safe. The very day he was kissed by his countrymen, he was doomed to fall, and he nearly cracked his poor head. When they placed power in his hands, they sent him to his death.

Though not secure from interruptions at the Villa Victoria, I could, at least, make my selection of the visitors who called. Might I have been as safe from the telegraph and mails, I should have been fairly comfortable; but my telegrams were numerous, and letters arrived sometimes by the hundred. The mere reading of the correspondence entailed a vast loss of time, the replies to them still more, and occupied the best efforts of three persons. What with a tedious sitting for my portrait, visits, interviews, dining-out, telegraphic and postal correspondence, calls of friends, instructions to the artist for the book, and revisions of my MS., it appears to me wonderful that I was able to endure the strain of writing half a million of words, and all else; but, thank Goodness! by the middle of April, the book was out of my hands, and I was alive and free.

From Cairo, I proceeded to Cannes, to consult with Sir William Mackinnon about East Africa, and explain about German aggressiveness in that region. Thence I moved to Paris; and, not many days later, I was in Brussels, where I was received with a tremendous demonstration of military and civilian honours. All the way to the royal palace, where I was to be lodged, the streets were lined with troops, and behind these was the populace shouting their 'vivas!' It appeared to me that a great change had come over Belgian public opinion about the value of the Congo. Before I departed for Africa, the Belgian journals were not in favour of Africa. But now, all was changed, and the King was recognised as 'the great benefactor of the nation.' While I was the guest of His Majesty, state, municipal, and geographical receptions followed fast upon one another; and at each of the assemblages I was impressed with the enthusiasm of the nation for the grand African domain secured to it by the munificence of their royal statesman and sovereign. Besides gold and silver medals from Brussels and Antwerp, the King graciously conferred on me the Grand Cross of the Order of Leopold, and the Grand Cross of the Congo.

Every morning, however, between 10.30 and 12, the King

led me into his private room, to discuss questions of absorbing interest to both of us. Since 1878, I had repeatedly endeavoured to impress on His Majesty the necessity of the railway, for the connection of the Lower with the Upper Congo, without which it was impossible to hope that the splendid sacrifices he proposed to make, or had made, would ever bear fruit. In 1885–86, I had been one of the principal agents in the promotion of an English Company for the construction of the Royal Congo Railway; but my efforts were in vain. Now, however, the King expressed his assurance that the time was ripe for the Belgian nation to construct the line, and he was pleased to say that it was my success which had produced this feeling, and that the welcome extended to me was a proof of it. I would have been better pleased if His Majesty had expressed his determination to economise in other directions, and devote his energies to the railway.

The next subject was the suppression of the slave-trade in the Congo. I proposed that troops should be pushed up the Congo, and that posts should be established at the mouths of the Aruwimi and Lumami, and that the garrisons should be increased month by month, until about two thousand troops had been collected, when an onward movement should be made against Stanley Falls, and the Arab power be summarily broken.

As this would be a signal of resolute action against all the Arabs above the Falls, about thirty steel boats should be provided, to enable the war to be carried up the Lualaba; for there would be no peace for the State, until every slaver in the Congo State had been extirpated or disarmed. I explained the project in great detail, and urged it vehemently, as after the treachery of Tippu-Tib in the Forest region, it was useless to hope that any other method would prevail. His Majesty promised cordial assent to the plan, and promised that the orders should be issued at once for the building of the boats.

The next subject debated was the better delimitation of the Congo State to the east. I proposed that instead of the vague and uncertain line of East longitude 30, the boundary between British territory and the Congo State should be the centre of the Albert Edward Nyanza and the course of the Semliki River, by which the parting of tribes would be avoided. The benefits to both England and the State would be that, while the whole of the snowy range of Ruwenzori, intact, would belong to England, the Congo State would be extended to the Albert Nyanza. In size, the exchanged territories would be about equal in area. His Majesty appeared pleased with the idea, and expressed his willingness to negotiate the exchange of territories with the East African Company.

The King introduced the third subject himself, by expressing his desire to know what point was the best to occupy as a central post along the Northern frontier between France and the Congo State. I unhesitatingly pointed out the confluence of the Mbornu with the Welle-Mubangi, but that to supply such a distant station would require a large number of steel whale-boats, such as Forrest & Son, of London, had made for me.

Then he wished to know how the North-eastern frontier could be defended. I replied that a clever officer would find no difficulty in establishing himself within easy reach of Makraka, and holding out inducements to the former Makraka soldiers of Emin, many of whom would be glad of a refuge against the Mahdists. At these private receptions His Majesty is accustomed to sit with his back to the window, on one side of a large marble-topped table, while his visitor sits on the other side. The table is well furnished with writing-paper, ink, pens, and pencils. Three years and a quarter had passed since I was in the room, where I had been fifty times before, probably; nothing had changed except ourselves. The King's beautiful brown beard had, in the interval, become grey from ear to ear; while my hair, which had been iron-grey, was now as white as Snowdon in winter.

I made a smiling reference to the changes Time had wrought in us since we had first met in June, 1878, and discussed the possibilities of introducing civilisation on the Congo.

The King began by saying that my visit to Brussels was sure to be followed by great results. He was very certain of being able to get the Congo Railway started now; for the Belgian people were thoroughly roused up, and were even enthusiastic. He said my letters from Africa and my present visit had caused this change. My description of the Forest had fired their imagination; and the people seemed to be about as eager to begin the railway as they were previously backward, indifferent, even hostile. The railway shares had been nearly all taken up, etc., etc.

'Now, Mr. Stanley,' said he, 'you have put me under still further obligations, by pointing out how slave-raiding can be stopped; you have also suggested how we could transform slave-raiders into policemen, which is a splendid idea; and, finally, you have indicated how we are to protect our frontiers and make use of Emin's troops, as soldiers in the service of the State.'

We now discussed the value of the country between the Congo and Lake Albert. He listened to what I said with the close attention of one who was receiving an account of a great estate that had just fallen to him, of which, previously, he had but a vague knowledge.

I said that from the mouth of the Aruwimi to within fifty miles of Lake Albert, the whole country, from 4° S., to about 3° N., was one dense tropical forest, and that its area was about equal to France and Spain put together.

'Does the Forest produce anything that is marketable in Europe?'

'Well, Sire, I suppose that when elephants have been exterminated in all other parts of Africa, there will still be some found in that Forest, so that the State will always be able to count upon some quantity of ivory, especially if the State has kindly set aside a reservation for them to retreat to, and forbidden the indiscriminate slaughter of these animals. Such a reservation will also be useful for the pigmies and other wild creatures of the forest. But the principal value of the Forest consists in the practically inexhaustible supply of valuable and useful timber which it will yield. You have a great source of revenue in this immense store of giant trees, when the Congo Railway enables timber merchants to build their saw-mills on the banks of the many tributaries and creeks which pierce it. The cotton-wood, though comparatively soft, will be adapted for cargo barges, because it is as unsinkable as cork, and will be useful for transporting down the Congo the mahogany, teak, greenheart, and the hard red and yellow woods.

'I think the timber-yards at Stanley Pool will be a sight to see, some few years hence. Then, for local purposes, the Forest will be valuable for furnishing materials for building all the houses in the Congo Valley, and for making wooden tram-lines across the portages of the many rivers. The Concessionaires will also find the rubber produce of the forest highly profitable. Almost every branchy tree has a rubber parasite clinging to it; as we carved our way through the Forest our clothes were spoiled by the rain of juice which fell on us. As there are so many rivers and creeks in the Forest, accessible by boats, and as along the Congo itself, for some hundreds of miles, the woods come down and overhang the water, a well-organised company will be able to collect several tons, annually, of rubber. When rubber is, even now, two shillings per pound,[1] you can estimate what the value of this product alone will be, when the industry has been properly developed.

'With every advance into the Forest, the gummy exudations will also be no mean gain. Every land-slip along the rivers discloses a quantity of precious fossil-gum, which floats down the streams in large cakes. Experience will teach the Concessionaires when and how to hunt for this valuable article of commerce. I am inclined to think, in fact, that the Great Forest will prove as lucrative to the State as any other section, however fertile the soil and rich its produce.

'No one can travel up the Congo without being struck by the need of the saw-mill, and how numerous and urgent are the uses of sawn timber for the various stations which are being erected everywhere.

'If you had saw-mills established now on the Aruwimi, they could not produce planking fast enough to satisfy all demands, and what a help for the railway hard-wood sleepers would be!'

I was then questioned as to the tribes of the Forest, and had to explain that as the experiences of these unsophisticated aborigines with strangers had been most cruel, it would not do to be too sanguine about their ability to supply labour at first demand. 'But,' I said, 'I came across no tribe, excepting the pigmies, which, after two years' acquaintance with the white man, could not be brought to a right sense of the value of their muscle. If a station were built in any part of the Forest, the

[1] The market-price of rubber is now (March, 1910) quoted at eight shillings and sixpence per pound.—D. S.

tribe in its neighbourhood might be induced by patient and fair treatment to become serviceable in a short time; but the other tribes would remain as aloof as ever, until they had the same opportunities of intimately knowing the white strangers. As the Forest is so dense, and so many miles of untrodden woods separate the tribes, it will be a long time before all the people will be tamed fit for employment. Good roads through the Forest, gentle treatment of the natives employed, and fair wages to them, will tend to hasten the white man's good influence; for rumour spreads rapidly; in a mysterious way good, as well as evil, news travels; and every month will show a perceptible increase in the numbers of those natives desirous of associating themselves with the white strangers.'

When the King asked me about the people of the grass-lands near the lakes, he was much interested at hearing, how, from enemies, formidable by their numbers and courage, they had become my allies, carriers, servants, and most faithful messengers. His Majesty was much impressed by this, and I told him how I had been affected by their amiability and good service; to any one listening to the warm praise I gave the Mazamboni and Kavallis, I might have appeared to exaggerate their good qualities; but His Majesty is so generous-minded that he could appreciate the frank way in which they had confessed their error in treating us as enemies, and the ready way in which they had atoned for it.

I showed the King that the grass-lands were not so distant from the Congo as my painful and long journey through the Forest had made them appear. 'Without any great cost it will be possible for the State to send expeditions to Lake Albert from the Congo within ten days. For, when saw-mills have been established at Yambuya, a wooden tram-line, topped by light steel bars, may be laid very easily along the Aruwimi, over which a small engine, drawing five trucks, could travel five miles an hour, or sixty miles a day. But before this tram-line will be possible, the railway to Stanley Pool must be finished, by which the resources of civilisation, saw-mills, tools, engines, boats, provisions, will be brought thirteen hundred miles nearer the lakes than they are now.'

After this, we adjourned to lunch, etc., etc.

A few weeks later, the King came over to London; and, after

a talk with Lord Salisbury and the principal Directors of the East African Company, whereby the boundaries between their respective territories were agreed to be the Albert, and Albert Edward, and the course of the river Semliki, from the centre of the southern shore of the Albert Edward to the northern head of the Tanganyika Lake, a strip of ten miles in width was secured to Great Britain for free transit,[1] with all powers of jurisdiction. Sir William Mackinnon and myself were the signatories duly empowered.[2] In my opinion, the advantages of this Treaty were on the side of the British, as there was now a free broad line of communications between Cape Town and British Equatoria, while my own secret hopes of the future of the Ruwenzori range were more likely to be gratified by its acquisition by the English, because, once the railway reached within a reasonable distance of the Snowy Mountains, a certain beautiful plateau — commanding a view of the snow-peaks, the plain of Usongora, the Lake Albert Edward, and the Semliki Valley — must become the site of the future Simla of Africa. On the other hand, the King was pleased with the extension of his territory to the Albert Nyanza, though the advantages are more sentimental than real. The narrow pasture-land between the Great Forest and the lake may become inhabited by whites, in which case the ninety-mile length of the Nyanza may be utilized for steamboat communication between the two ends of it.

As Monsieur Vankherchoven, King Leopold's agent, was by this time well on his way to the confluence of the headwaters of the Wellé-Mubangi, the conclusion of this Treaty necessitated a slight change in his instructions.

On arriving in England, April 26, 1890, I was met by a large number of friends at Dover, who escorted me on a special train to London. At Victoria Station a large crowd was assembled, who greeted me most warmly. The Baroness Burdett-Coutts and Mr. Burdett-Coutts had done me the honour of meeting me with their carriage, and in brief time I found

[1] The Cape-to-Cairo Route, on *all-British* territory, thus anticipated by Stanley, and rendered feasible by this Treaty, was lost to England owing to the weakness of the Liberal Government of the day, who were actually "bluffed" into cancelling the Treaty by German pressure.

[2] See *In Darkest Africa*, vol. ii.

myself in comfortable rooms at De Vere Gardens, which had been engaged and prepared for me by Sir Francis and Lady De Winton.

For the next three or four weeks, proof-reading and revising, banquets, preparing lectures, etc., absorbed far more time than was good for my health. Two of the most notable Receptions were by the Royal Geographical Society and the Emin Relief Committee; the first, at the Albert Hall, was by far the grandest Assembly I ever saw. About ten thousand people were present; Royalty, the Peerage, and all classes of Society were well represented. While Sir Mountstuart Grant-Duff, the President, was speaking, my eyes lighted on many a noble senator, chief of science, and prince in literature, whose presence made me realise the supreme honour accorded to me.

At the house of my dear wife-to-be, I met the ex-Premier, the Right Honourable Mr. W. E. Gladstone, who had come for a chat and a cup of tea, and to be instructed — as I had been duly warned — about one or two matters connected with the slave-trade. I had looked forward to the meeting with great interest, believing — deluded fool that I was! — that a great politician cares to be instructed about anything but the art of catching votes. I had brought with me the latest political map of East Africa, and, when the time had come, I spread it out conveniently on the table before the great man, at whose speaking face I gazed with the eyes of an African. 'Mr. Gladstone,' said I, intending to be brief and to the point, as he was an old man, 'this is Mombasa, the chief port of British East Africa. It is an old city. It is mentioned in the Lusiads, and, no doubt, has been visited by the Phœnicians. It is most remarkable for its twin harbours, in which the whole British Navy might lie safely, and —'

'Pardon me,' said Mr. Gladstone, 'did you say it was a harbour?'

'Yes, sir,' said I, 'so large that a thousand vessels could be easily berthed in it.'

'Oh, who made the harbour?' he asked, bending his imposing glance at me.

'It is a natural harbour,' I answered.

'You mean a port, or roadstead?'

'It is a port, certainly, but it is also a harbour, that, by straightening the bluffs, you —'

'But pardon me, a harbour is an artificial construction.'

'Excuse me, sir, a dock is an artificial construction, but a harbour may be both artificial and natural, and —'

'Well, I never heard the word applied in that sense.' And he continued, citing Malta and Alexandria, and so on.

This discussion occupied so much time that, fearing I should lose my opportunity of speaking about the slave-trade, I seized the first pause, and skipping about the region between Mombasa and Uganda, I landed him on the shores of the Nyanza, and begged him to look at the spacious inland sea, surrounded by populous countries, and I traced the circling lands. When I came to Ruwenzori, his eye caught a glimpse of two isolated peaks.

'Excuse me one minute,' said he; 'what are those two mountains called?'

'Those, sir,' I answered, 'are the Gordon Bennett and the Mackinnon peaks.'

'Who called them by those absurd names?' he asked, with the corrugation of a frown on his brow.

'I called them, sir.'

'By what right?' he asked.

'By the right of first discovery, and those two gentlemen were the patrons of the expedition.'

'How can you say that, when Herodotus spoke of them twenty-six hundred years ago, and called them Crophi and Mophi? It is intolerable that classic names like those should be displaced by modern names, and — '

'I humbly beg your pardon, Mr. Gladstone, but Crophi and Mophi, if they ever existed at all, were situated over a thousand miles to the northward. Herodotus simply wrote from hearsay, and — '

'Oh, I can't stand that.'

'Well, Mr. Gladstone,' said I, 'will you assist me in this project of a railway to Uganda, for the suppression of the slave-trade, if I can arrange that Crophi and Mophi shall be substituted in place of Gordon Bennett and Mackinnon?'

'Oh, that will not do; that is flat bribery and corruption':

and, smiling, he rose to his feet, buttoning his coat lest his virtue might yield to the temptation.

'Alas!' said I to myself, 'when England is ruled by old men and children! My slave-trade discourse must be deferred, I see.'

Turning now to the extraordinary charges made against me, on my return to Europe, that I deliberately employed slaves on my expedition, I would point out that every traveller, before setting out on his journey, took all precautions to avoid doing this. Each of my followers was obliged to prove that he was free — by personal declaration and two witnesses — before he could be enrolled. Four months' advance wages were paid to the men before they left Zanzibar, and, on their return, their full wages were delivered into their own hands. No doubt many who had been slaves had managed to get into the expedition, as I found to my cost, when well away in the interior; but, since they had been able to earn their own living, their slavery had been merely nominal, and all their earnings were their own to do what they liked with, and their owners never saw them except when, at the end of Ramadan, they called to pay their respects. To all intents and purposes, they were as much freemen as the free-born, inasmuch as they were relieved from all obligation to their masters.

To proceed on the lines that, because they were not free-born they must be slaves, one would have to clear out the Seedy-boy stokers from the British fleet in the Indian Ocean, and all the mail, passenger, and freight steamers which ship them at Aden and Bombay, Calcutta, Singapore, and Yokohama. All the British consulates on the East Coast — Zanzibar, Madagascar, etc.—would have to be charged with conniving at the slave-trade, as also all the British merchants in those places, because they employed house-servants, door and horse-boys, who were nominally slaves.

White men are not in the habit of proceeding to an Arab slave-owner, and agreeing with him as to the employment of his slaves. I employed English agents at Zanzibar to engage my people, and every precaution was taken that no one was enlisted who could not swear he was an Ingwaria, or freeman. I was only four days in Zanzibar, but, before these men were accepted, they had to re-swear their declarations before the British Consul-general that they were free.

The accusations made against me that I employed slaves were, therefore, most disgraceful. History will be compelled to acknowledge that I have some right to claim credit in the acts which have followed, one upon another, so rapidly of late, and which have tended to make slave-raiding impossible, and to reduce slave-trading to sly and secret exchanges of human chattels in isolated districts in the interior.

The book 'In Darkest Africa' was published in June by my usual publishers, Messrs. Sampson, Son & Co., and the Messrs. Scribners of New York brought it out in America. It was translated into French, German, Italian, Spanish, and Dutch, and in English it has had a sale of about one hundred and fifty thousand.

The month of May was mainly passed by me in stirring up the Chambers of Commerce and the Geographical Societies to unite in pressing upon the British Government the necessity of more vigorous action to prevent East Africa being wholly absorbed by Germany; and, on coming southward from Scotland, where I had been speaking, the news reached me that Lord Salisbury had secured for Great Britain, Zanzibar and the northern half of East Africa, but singularly curtailed of the extensive piece of pasture-land west of Kilimanjaro. This odd cutting off is due to a Permanent Official in the Foreign Office, whose hand can be traced in that oblique line running from the northern base of the Devil's Mountain to S. Lat. 10, on Lake Victoria. Had that gentleman been a member of an African expedition, he would never have had recourse to an oblique line when a straight line would have done better. However, while it remains a signal instance of his weakness, it is no less a remarkable proof of German magnanimity! For, though the Germans were fully aware that the official was one of the most squeezable creatures in office, they declined to extend the line to the Equator! Kilimanjaro, therefore, was handed over to Germany, '*because the German Emperor was so interested in the flora and fauna of that district!*' That, at any rate, was the reason given for the request!

DOROTHY STANLEY

CHAPTER XX

THE HAPPY HAVEN

ON Saturday, July 12, 1890, I was married to Stanley, at Westminster Abbey. He was very ill at the time, with gastritis and malaria, but his powerful will enabled him to go through with the ceremony.

We went straight to Melchet Court, lent to us for our honeymoon by Louisa, Lady Ashburton. Stanley's officer, Surgeon Parke, accompanied us, and together we nursed Stanley back to health.

Stanley's Journal contains the following passage: —

Saturday, 12th July, 1890.

Being very sick from a severe attack of gastritis, which came on last Thursday evening, I was too weak to experience anything save a calm delight at the fact that I was married, and that now I shall have a chance to rest. I feel as unimpressed as if I were a child taking its first view of the world, or as I did when, half-dead at Manyanga in 1881, I thought I had done with the world; it is all so very unreal. During my long bachelorhood, I have often wished that I had but one tiny child to love; but now, unexpectedly as it seems to me, I possess a wife; my own wife, — Dorothy Stanley now, Dorothy Tennant this morning, — daughter of the late Charles Tennant of Cadoxton Lodge, Vale of Neath, Glamorgan, and of 2, Richmond Terrace, Whitehall, London.

On the 8th August, after nearly a month at Melchet, we went to Maloja in the Engadine, where we spent a few quiet, happy weeks. Sir Richard Burton and his wife were there. Stanley had last seen him in 1886.

Had a visit from Sir Richard F. Burton, one of the discoverers of Lake Tanganyika. He seems much broken in health. Lady Burton, who copies Mary, Queen of Scotland, in her dress, was with him. In the evening, we met again. I proposed he should write his reminiscences. He said he could not do so, because he should have to write of so many people. 'Be charitable to them, and write only of their best qualities,'

I said.—'I don't care a fig for charity; if I write at all, I must write truthfully, all I know,' he replied.

He is now engaged in writing a book called 'Anthropology of Men and Women,' a title, he said, that does not describe its contents, but will suffice to induce me to read it. What a grand man! One of the real great ones of England he might have been, if he had not been cursed with cynicism. I have no idea to what his Anthropology refers, but I would lay great odds that it is only another means of relieving himself of a surcharge of spleen against the section of humanity who have excited his envy, dislike, or scorn. If he had a broad mind, he would curb these tendencies, and thus allow men to see more clearly his grander qualities.

From Maloja, we went to the Lake of Como, visited Milan, and spent a night at Captain Camperio's delightful house, 'La Santa,' near Monza. Stanley thus describes it:—

Camperio and Casati, the African travellers, were at the station to greet us. After twenty minutes' drive from Monza we reached Camperio's place; it was formerly a convent, and has been in possession of the family two hundred years. Captain Camperio has been the devoted friend and patron of Casati for many years, and was the cause of his going to Africa. It appears that Casati, far from being a champion of Emin, is now resentful towards him, because Emin, as usual with him, has been neglectful of his friend's susceptibilities. Casati has done very well with his Book.

Captain Camperio and his delightful family were soon fast friends with us. A few years later he died, and so La Santa became only a happy memory. We now turned homeward, going first to Geneva, then to Paris, and, finally, on the 3rd October, 1890, to Ostend, where we stayed at Hôtel Fontaine, as guests of the King. We dined at the Châlet Royal, and the next day Stanley took a long walk with the King. Thus we spent four days, Stanley walking daily with His Majesty. We dined every evening at the Châlet Royal. On the 8th, we left Ostend. State-cabins were given to us, and a Royal lunch served.

We now returned to London, and, on October 22nd, Stanley received his D. C. L., at Durham; on the 23rd, we went to Cambridge, where he received the LL. D., from the University. In June, Stanley had been made D. C. L., by Oxford, and, soon after, LL. D., by Edinburgh. The University of Halle had bestowed its Degree of Doctor of Philosophy in 1879.[1]

On the 29th October, we sailed for America. Stanley had undertaken a lecture tour, under the management of Major Pond. It was a tremendous experience; the welcome we received everywhere, and the kindness shown to us, were something very wonderful.

We remained over a week in New York, where Stanley lectured, and then we visited all the great Eastern cities.

Stanley, in his Journal, writes:—

> The untidiness and disorder of the streets of New York strike me as being terrible for so rich a city, and such an energetic population. The streets are cut up by rails in a disgraceful fashion. The noise of bells, and wheels, and horses' hoofs, dins the ears. Telegraph-posts, with numberless wires, obstruct the view, and suggest tall wire-fences; furlongs of posters meet the eye everywhere, and elevated railroads choke the view of the sky. The man who invented the hideous 'Elevated' deserves to be expelled from civilisation, and the people who permitted themselves to be thus tortured have certainly curious tastes. If they were of my mind, they would pull these structures down, and compel the shareholders to build it in such a manner that, while it might be more useful and safe, it would not be such an eyesore, nor so suggestive of insolence and tyranny on one side, and of slavish submission on the people's side.
>
> The view from our hotel-window shows me the street ploughed-up, square blocks of granite lying as far as the eye can see, besides planking, boarding, piles of earth, and stacks of bricks. I counted one hundred and seventy-four lines of wire in the air, rows of mast-like telegraph-poles, untrimmed and unpainted, in the centre of the American Metropolis! What taste!

We now travelled over the States and Canada, in a special Pullman-car, which had been named 'Henry M. Stanley.' It was palatial, for we had our own kitchen and cook, a dining-car, which, at night was converted into a dormitory, a drawing-room with piano, three state-bedrooms, and a bath-room.

After visiting all the Eastern cities, and Canada, we returned to New York. On Sunday, the 25th January, 1891, we dined with

[1] The mere list of Honorary Memberships of Geographical Societies, Addresses of Welcome, at home and abroad, and the Freedoms of all the leading cities in the United Kingdom, would occupy a large volume, and therefore cannot be more than alluded to here.—D. S.

Cyrus Field (who laid the first Atlantic Cable), at 123, Gramercy Park, and met General W. T. Sherman, David Dudley Field, Charles A. Dana, and others.

On the 31st, Stanley went to a Banquet given by the Press Club. The following is the entry in his Journal: —

Was dined by the Press Club. General Sherman was present, with a rubicund complexion, and in an exceedingly amiable mood. He and I exchanged pleasant compliments to each other in our after-dinner speeches.

On the 14th February, at Chicago, Stanley wrote in his Journal: —

The sad news reached us to-day of the death of General W. T. Sherman, the Leader of the Great March through Georgia, and the last of the Immortal Three — Grant, Sheridan, Sherman. His last public appearance was at the Press Club Banquet to me in New York. At the time of his death he was the most popular man in New York, and well deserved the popularity.

In his speech at the Press Club, I recognised an oratorical power few men not knowing him would have suspected. He had the bearing of one who could impress, also those easy gestures which fix the impression, and the pathos which charms the ear, and affects the feelings. When we remember what he was, and that we saw in him the last of that splendid trio who, by their native worth, proved themselves possessors of that old American patriotism of Revolutionary days, not genius, but fine military talents, directed by moderating single-mindedness to one common and dear object, — when we consider this, the effect of General Sherman's presence may be better understood than described.

Los Angeles, California, 21st March. A Fresno newspaper, in commenting on my personal appearance, said that I was only five feet, three inches, and quoted Cæsar and Napoleon as examples of what small men are capable of. The Los Angeles 'Herald' informed *its* readers this morning, that I am six feet, four inches! The truth is, I am five feet, five and a half inches in my socks.

Sunday, 29th March, 1891. Reached New Orleans after thirty-two years' absence. I left it in 1859, and return to it in 1891. I drove with D. to the French Market, down Tchapitoulas St., St. Andrew's St., Annunciation St., Charles Avenue, to St. Charles Hotel. Took a walk with D. to Tchapitoulas St., then to the Levee; gazed across the full view, and pointed to 'Algiers' opposite, where I had often sported.

Monday, 30th March. Rose at six-thirty and went with D. to French Market, to treat her to what I have often boasted of, 'a cup of the best coffee in the world.' The recipe appears to be two pounds of Java Coffee to one and a half gallons of water. Monsieur L. Morel owned the coffee-stand. He came from France in 1847. Very likely I must have drunk coffee, many a time, as a boy, at his stand!

We walked home by Charles Street, well known to me. New Orleans changes but slowly.

From New Orleans we visited Chattanooga. Went to the top of Lookout Mountain. People are very kind and attentive to us wherever we go, but I wish the lectures were over; I am very weary.

On Saturday, April 4th, we visited Nashville. Stanley's entry is simply 'Dear old Nashville!'

This tour was very exhausting. The constant travelling, lecturing, and social demands made upon us, taxed Stanley's strength severely. By nature shy and retiring, he shrank from ovations, and wished, above all things, to pass unnoticed. This letter written to me from our private car when I was in Colorado, where he joined me a few days later, will give an idea of his feelings: —

I spend most of my time in my own little cabin, writing or reading, enduring the breaks on my privacy because they are a necessity, each time invoking more patience, and beseeching Time to hurry on its lagging movement that I might once more taste of absolute freedom. Meanwhile, what pleasure I obtain is principally in reading, unless I come to a little town, and can slip, unobserved, out-of-doors for a walk. I often laugh at the ridiculous aspect of my feelings, as I am compelled to become shifty and cunning, to evade the eager citizens' advances. I feel like Cain, hurrying away with his uneasy conscience after despatching Abel, or a felonious cashier departing with his plunder! When I finally succeed in getting off without attracting anyone, you would be amused could you peep in underneath my waistcoat and observe the sudden lifting of the feelings, just like the sudden lighting of a waste of angry sea by the full sun, warm, bland, and full of promise. Then away I go against the keen, cold wind, but the feelings are rejoicing, laughing, babbling of fun and enjoyment; and the undertone of the great harmony is *Freedom!* I am free! Block after block is passed without a glance, until I get to the quieter parts, and then I straighten out, take a long breath, expressing by the act the indescribable relief I have of being away from the talking man, with his wayward moods, and exceeding sensitiveness.

I sometimes think with a shiver of what I shall have to endure in London: just because a person sends a polite invitation to dinner, or tea, or reception, one must note it down as a binding engagement for that evening or afternoon. One must not forget it; one must think of it, and cut out that period of existence from his short life, to eat and drink at the express hour! This is not freedom! To be free is to have no cares at all, no thought of the next hour, or the next day, or the next month; to be as we were at Melchet, — early breakfast, walk out, sit on chair or bench, walk in, or walk out, as though irresponsible beings. How I did enjoy Melchet! Afterwards came busy, exacting life, preparation for lectures, etc. All Europe and America were not so pleasant as lovely, dreamy Melchet.

There are butterflies and bees in the world; the butterflies like to play amid the flowers, I am content to belong to the bee class. The bees do not envy the butterflies, do not think at all about them, and that is the same with me. I might stand it for a week, perhaps a month; but the utter waste of life would begin to present itself, until, at last, my mind would conceive an accusing phantom, composed of lost days and weeks, with their hosts of lost opportunities ever reproaching me for my devotion to the inane and profitless. Ah, no, I must be doing *something;* no matter what it appears to others, if to me it satisfies the craving for doing or learning, that is enough.

On April 15, 1891, we sailed for Liverpool. Stanley ends the Journal of our American tour with the words: —

The greatest part of America is unequalled for its adaptability for the service of man, and her people are doing the utmost they can to utilize its productiveness. They have every right to be grateful for their land, and I think they are both grateful and proud of it.

The American farmer, of whom but little mention is made, is one of the finest natures in existence. Milton's description of Adam, 'the great Sire of all,' a little altered, would befit the typical American farmer. I never see one but I feel inclined to say to him, 'Good and honest man, all blessings attend thee!' His life is without reproach, his soul without fear, he has faith in God, he is affectionate, serene in demeanour; there is confidence in his gait, and he understands and loves the kindly earth. The typical American merchant is a sober and solid man, shrewd and practical, a pillar of the Commonwealth, and daringly enterprising on occasion.

We now returned to London, and from there Stanley went on a lecturing tour over England and Scotland. I did not accompany him throughout, but joined him at different places, so that I possess some delightful letters written to me when we were apart. In one he writes: —

Rest! Ah, my dear! we both need it — I more than you. Absolute stillness, somewhere in remote and inaccessible places, in an island, or in the air, only certain articles of food and comfort being indispensable. Then let me wake to strains of music, and I think I should rise to life again! Until then, existence is mere prolonged endurance.

Stanley all his life had a passion for reading, when he could not be 'doing.' He delighted in reading Cæsar, Thucydides, Xenophon, Polybius, and lighter books also did not come amiss. From Cheltenham, he wrote: —

I have begun again on Thucydides. Gladstone's 'Gleanings' are ended. They are all good. Strange! how I detect the church-going, God-fearing, conscientious Christian, in almost every paragraph. Julian Corbett's 'Drake' is fair; I am glad I read it, and refreshed myself with what I knew before of the famous sailor.

From the Bell Hotel, Gloucester, he wrote, June 3, 1891: —

I had a long walk into the country, which is simply buried under bushy green of grass and leaves.

I saw the largest river in England yesterday: it appears to be a little wider than what I could hop over with a pole in my best days. It was a dirty, rusty-coloured stream, but the meadows were fat. The country seems to perspire under its covering of leafy verdure. I always loved the English country, and my secret attachment for it seemed to me well confirmed to-day, as I thrilled with admiration and affection for all I saw.

June 4th. Took a walk along the heights of Clifton! What a picture of the Severn Gorge — woods, cliffs, villas, good roads, rosy-cheeked children, romping school-boys, fond mamas, and a score of other things — one can get from the Suspension Bridge!

His next letter was from Clifton: —

You press me to accept the invitation to preside at the Eisteddfod. I feel that we, the people of Wales generally, and I, are not in such close sympathy as to enable me to say anything sufficiently pleasing to their ears. How could it be otherwise? The Eisteddfod, as I understand it, is for the purpose of exciting interest in the Welsh nationality and language. My travels in the various continents have ill-prepared me for sympathising with such a cause. If I were to speak truly my mind, I should recommend Welshmen to turn their attention to a closer study of the English language, literature, and characteristics, for it is only by that training that they can hope to compete with their English brothers for glory, honour, and prosperity. There is no harm in understanding the Welsh language, but they should be told by sensible men that every hour they devote to it, occupies time that might be better employed in furthering their own particular interests. But who will dare tell men, so devoted to their own people and country as the Welsh, the real truth? *I* am not the man! There is no object to be gained save the good of the Welsh people themselves, who, unfortunately, fail to see it in that light, and would accordingly resent whatever was said to them. I am so ignorant of the blessings attending these *local studies*, that my speech would be barren and halting. If I could only feel a portion of what the fervid Welshman feels, I might carry through the day a bearing as though I enjoyed it all; but I fear I shall hang my head in self-abasement.

Now if it were a British community that met to celebrate British glories, what themes and subjects! But how can I shout for Cambria? What *is* Cambria, *alone?* What has she done, what hope for her, separate and distinct from her big sister Britannia, or rather Anglia? United, they are great; but divided, neither is aught. Now do you understand to what a hard shift I am put? I shall be hooted out of the country, because my stubborn tongue cannot frame agreeable fictions!

June 16, 1891, he wrote to me: —

You ought to have been with me at Camarvon, simply to be amazed at the excitement in North Wales, along the line, as I stepped from the train; the people, hard-featured, homely creatures, rushed up, the crowd being enormous. Yesterday I had a striking explanation of why and wherefore the woman in the Scriptures kissed the hem of the Master's garment: as I moved through the crowd, I felt hands touch my coat, then, getting bolder, they rubbed me on the back, stroked my hair, and, finally, thumped me hard, until I felt that the honours were getting so weighty I should die if they continued long. Verily, there were but few thumps between me and death! A flash of fierceness stole over me for a second, and I turned to the crowd; but they all smiled so broadly that, poor, dear, mad creatures, I forgave them, or, at least, resolved to submit. Well! until 11.45 P. M., from 5 P. M., I was either talking at the pitch of my voice to six thousand people, or being wrung by the hand by highly-strung, excited people. Were it not for the prayer, 'God bless you, Stanley! God prosper your work, Stanley! The Lord be praised for you, my man!' I could have done anything but feel grateful, the strain on my nerves was so exhausting. But I need prayers, and their blessings were precious.

The streets were full; eight excursion trains had brought the country folk; they blocked the way of the carriage, coming in, and going out. Dear sons of toil and their sisters, the grand stout-hearted mothers who bore them, and the grey-haired sires! My heart went out to them; for, underneath all, I felt a considerable admiration for them — indeed, I always had. I feel what all this means, just as I know what is passing in the African's heart, when I suddenly make him rich, instead of hurting him. There is a look, as of a lifting-up of the soul into the eyes, which explains as fully as words.

June 20th, 1891. I have nine more lectures to deliver, and then, God and man willing, I shall cast me down for rest.

I have just begun to read Walter Scott's 'Journal.' I like it immensely. The Life of Houghton is dull; his own letters are the best in it, but there is no observation, or judgment upon things; merely a series of letters upon town-talk; what he did, seldom, however, what he thought. Where you see his thought, it is worth reading twice.

It is a great relief at last to be able to 'speak my mind,' not to be chilled and have to shrink back. Between mother and child, *you* know the confidence and trust that exist; *I* never knew it; and now, by extreme favour of Providence, the last few years of my life shall be given to know this thoroughly. Towards you I begin trustfully to exhibit my thoughts and feelings; as one, unaccustomed to the security of a bank, places his hard-earned money in the care of a stranger, professing belief in its security, yet inwardly doubting, so I shyly revealed this and that, until now, when I give up all, undoubting, perfect in confidence.

June 29th. To-morrow, a lecture at Canterbury will finish my present course. And then I shall be at large to look at everything on earth with different eyes. Think of the novel liberty of lying in bed as long as I please, to take coffee in bed, the morning cigar and bath, without an inward monitor nagging persistently and urging to duty! By the way, apropos of that word, M. said yesterday she disliked the word 'duty.' I wonder if she has been reading Jeremy Bentham, who wrote to the same effect.

Duty, though an imperious, is a very necessary master; but I shall be very glad to pass a few weeks, at least, owing no duty but that which I shall owe to your pleasure and mine.

CANTERBURY, July 1st, 8.30 A. M. I have risen thus early to celebrate my emancipation from the thraldom imposed upon me by lecture agents and my own moral weakness, to write to you.

I have seen the time when I could have written gloriously about this singular old town; I love it no less now than I did years ago when I first saw it, but I am much busier with various things now than then.

The old Fountain Hotel is a typical English inn. I heard a little bit of vocal music from the Cathedral choir, and very much admired it. What a fine old Cathedral it is! But oh! how the religion that built it has faded! The worship of the Almighty Creator of Heaven and Earth, who, we were taught in our youth, sat in the Heaven of Heavens, has been so superseded by that degrading worship of gold and Society!

Apropos of this, I picked up at a book-stall yesterday a little brochure called 'Cæsar's Column,' a tale of the twentieth century, by Ignatius Donnelly. I read it through. It pretends to be a series of letters from a man named Gabriel, a visitor to New York from the State of Uganda, Central Africa. They are directed to one Heinreich, a resident of the village of Stanley! He describes the marvellous inventions of the age, especially the air-demons, which are air-warships loaded with bombs, charged with poisonous fumes, which, dropped from above in the streets, destroy a quarter of a million soldiers. The armed force of the State thus disposed of, the *canaille* proceed to exterminate the devotees of Society and the cold, selfish civilisation, or rather that methodical system founded upon spoliation and oppression of the poor which the wealthy have initiated by huge trusts, etc., wherein there is no thought of mercy, justice, or sweet charity.

The end of all is destruction and utter extermination of the wealthy classes over Europe and America, and the quick upheaval of everything resembling Order and Law by the Anarchist clan, and the two continents relapse, fast enough, into barbarism, in consequence. It is a powerful story — impossible, of course; but some of its readers will rise from reading it, thoughtful, and a small seedling of good may, or ought, to come from it.

At last, Stanley's holiday came, and we went to Switzerland at the end of July. The fine mountain air, the beauty of the scenery, long walks, peace and quiet, gave Stanley what he so needed — physical and mental rest. Of an evening, we read aloud, retiring very early, as Stanley had the African habit of rising at six.

I persuaded Stanley sometimes to play at cards, but he never much cared to do so; he not only thought cards a great waste of time, but he also thought playing for money discreditable; he wanted all the time he could get for reading, or planning something he meant to do, or write. He was, in fact, an inveterate worker.

We were returning to England at the end of August, when Stanley, in a damp mountain-meadow at Mürren, slipped and broke his left ankle. He suffered a good deal, the injury bringing on malaria; but the bone united without shortening the leg, and, in time, the lameness disappeared. This accident prevented his presiding at the Eisteddfod.

On the 2nd October, Stanley went to Ostend, by invitation of the King of the Belgians. Mr. Mounteney Jephson accompanied him. Stanley wrote to me: —

The King does not look greyer than I remember him during the last two years. He tells me he will be fifty-seven next April, and that he feels the approach of age, one sign of which is loss of memory. He cannot remember names. I told him that that fact did not strike me as suggestive of age, since the longer we lived the more names we had to remember, and there was a limit to one's power of remembering.

Stanley then wrote at length his conversation with the King; but I will not give it here.

After dinner, we adjourn to the King's private room to smoke. Baron Goffinet takes charge of Jephson, and shows him the Casino. The King tells me he walks twenty-five kilometres every day: his daily life begins at 5.30 A. M., when he takes a cup of tea; he breakfasts at 8.30. All his letters for his Ministers are written by himself between 6 A. M. and breakfast, and, at 10 o'clock, they are sent to the Ministers. He says he has been twenty-six years in active service.

After dinner, the King cautiously approached and sounded me on the possibility of my resuming my duties on the Congo.

I pointed to my broken leg, for I am still very lame.

'Oh,' he said, 'not now, but when you return from Australia, sound in health and limb.'

'We shall see, Your Majesty,' I said.

'I have a big task on hand for you, when you are ready,' were his last words.

In October, 1891, we left England for a visit to Australia, New Zealand, and Tasmania, travelling viâ Brindisi, some twelve miles from which our train came into collision with a goods train. Stanley thus describes the accident: —

At 3.45 P. M., we were rattling along at forty miles an hour, when the train jostled dangerously at the northern end of a siding. D. and I cast enquiring glances at each other, but, finding we were not derailed, resumed our composure. A second later there was an explosion like that of a rocket, and, the next second, there was a jar and a slight shock. 'Lift up your feet,' I cried to D.; and, at the words, my window burst into a shower of finely-powdered glass, which fell over me, and we stood stock-still. Rising on my crutch, I looked through the broken window and discovered four freight trucks, crumpled up into a pitiful wreck, just ahead of us, within about fifty yards of a levelled wall, and I then saw that our engine and van were lying on their side. Our escape was a narrow one, for our coupé compartment came next to the van. Fortunately, there was no loss of life.

I regret that space does not allow me to quote Stanley's descriptions of persons and places during his half-year in Australia. I give one or two personal passages from his Journal.

AUCKLAND, December 30th. Sir George Grey called on us in the afternoon, and took us out to show us the Public Library. There we saw valuable old Missals, with wonderful paintings of scroll-work and impossible leafage. In another room, he showed us private letters from Livingstone, received by him when Governor of Cape Colony. There were also some from Speke.

Livingstone's letters are marked '*Private.*' He must have recognised a kind of cousinship in Sir George, to have delivered himself so frankly. He wrote strongly and earnestly to one whom he rightly supposed would understand him.

Sir George, a traveller himself, and likewise a strong man, would appreciate him. It did me good to see his handwriting, and also to see letters of Speke.

I doubt whether Speke will ever be thoroughly known to the world, though there was much that was great and good in him; but Speke, unfortunately, could not express himself.

It was a keen pleasure to read these old letters, which breathed of work, loyalty of soul, human duties, imperial objects, and moral obligations, and then to look up at the face of the venerable statesman to whom they were addressed, and trace the benevolence, breadth of mind, and intelligence which elicited the spontaneous, free expression of their hopes from these travellers and pioneers. It is so elevating to see a man who is not tainted with meanness and pettiness, with whom one can talk as to a Father-confessor, without fear of being misunderstood, and without risk of finding it in the newspapers of the next day.

Sir George has a grand, quiet face, and a pair of round blue eyes beaming with kindness, and the light of wisdom. There are others like him in the world, no doubt, but it is only by a rare chance we meet them. Should I be asked what gave me the most pleasure in life, I would answer that it was the meeting with wise and good elders, who, while retaining a vivid interest in the affairs of life, could, from their height of knowledge and experience, approve what I had done, and bid me strive on, undaunted, undismayed.

I here give a letter from Sir George Grey, written a month later:

AUCKLAND, 29th Jan., 1892.

MY DEAR STANLEY, — This is the 52nd Anniversary of New Zealand, a public holiday.

I am left in perfect tranquillity, with full time for calm reflection, for all are gone on some party of pleasure. I have occupied my morning in following your sufferings and trials as recorded in Parke's 'Experiences in Equatorial Africa.' After reading, with the greatest pleasure, pages 512, 513, and 514, these have set me reflecting upon what you have done for the Empire by your services, and what has been the reward given publicly to you by the authorities of that Empire — well, neglect!

I am inclined to think it is best that the matter should stand thus.

All of danger, sorrow, suffering, trial of every kind that man could endure, you have undergone.

From all of these you have emerged unshaken, triumphant, every difficulty overcome, reverenced by those who served under you, Africa opened to the world, the unknown made manifest to all. So to have suffered, so to have succeeded, must have done much to form a truly great character, the remembrance of which will go down to posterity.

Yet one thing was wanting to render the great drama in which you have been the great actor complete. Could the man who had done all this, and supported such various trials, bear that — perhaps hardest of all — cold neglect, and the absence of national recognition and national reward for what he had accomplished? From this trial, as from all the others you have undergone, you have come out a conqueror — calm, unmoved, and uncomplaining. Your own character has been improved by this new trial, which will add an interest to your history in future times; and I sit here, not lamenting that you move amongst your fellow-men untitled, undecorated, but with a feeling that all has taken place for the best.

I had wished to write to you on several points. I was much struck by a statement in Parke's journal, that at one point it only took fifteen minutes to walk from the headwaters of the Nile to those of the Congo.[1] This distance could hardly be shown upon a small map, and probably caused an error in the old maps, or in verbal descriptions from which the old maps were made.

But I shall weary you with this long letter. I hope we shall meet again before long, but I fear some time may elapse before I can start for England. I feel that I owe duties to New Zealand, Australia, and the Cape, and, until I have at least partially fulfilled them, I hesitate to indulge my longing once more to revisit my early home, and my many relatives.

Will you give my regards to Mrs. Stanley, and tell her that the interesting photograph of yourself which you were good enough to send me has been handsomely framed and adorns the Public Library.

Yours truly,

G. GREY.

February 12th, TASMANIA. A curious thing happened this morning. I am obliged to rise at an early hour on account of habits contracted during more than twenty years of African travel, and to avail myself of the silent hours of the morning to procure an exercise-walk for the sake of health. At 5.30 I was shaving, and somehow my thoughts ran persistently on what Colonel J. A. Grant (the companion of Speke) said to me in the Jerusalem Chamber at Westminster, on my marriage day, July 12th, 1890. Said he, 'I must take this opportunity to say a long good-bye, for, after to-day, I don't suppose you will care to come to my symposium and talk about Africa.' — 'Why?' I asked. — 'Oh! well, you are married now, and marriage often parts the best of male friends.' — 'Oh, come!' I replied, 'I can't see how my marriage will affect our friendship; I will make it a point to disprove what you say.' Then Grant and I were separated. 'And it is quite true,' I reflected; 'we have not met since, somehow. But I will make it a point to visit Grant the first evening after I reach London.' And I shook my razor at the figure in the mirror, to confirm the mental vow. A short time afterwards, I went down; the hotel

[1] The Aruwimi branch of the Congo. — D. S.

was not yet opened. As I put my hand on the knob of the door to open it, the morning paper was thrust underneath the door by the newspaper-boy outside. Anxious to read the cablegrams from London, I seized the paper, and the first news to catch my attention was, — 'Death of Colonel J. A. Grant, the Nile Explorer.' What an odd coincidence!

This is the second time in my experience that a person thousands of miles away from me has been suddenly suggested to me a few moments preceding an announcement of this kind. From the day I parted with Grant, till this morning, his words had not once recurred to my mind.

On the other occasion, the message came as an apparition. I was in the centre of some hundreds of men,[1] and the vision of a woman lying on her bed, dying, appeared to me suddenly. I heard her voice plainly, every item of furniture in the room was visible to me; in fact, I had as vivid a picture of the room, and all within it, as though I stood there in broad daylight. The vision, clear as it was, passed away, and I awoke to the reality of things around me. I was bewildered to find that no one had witnessed any abstraction on my part, though one was so close, that he touched me. Yet, in spirit, I had been six thousand miles away, and saw my own figure at the bedside of the dying woman; months after, when I had actually arrived in Europe, I was told that she had died a few hours later.

[1] See page 207.

CHAPTER XXI

POLITICS AND FRIENDS

SOON after our marriage, I thought of Parliament for Stanley. It seemed to me that one so full of energy, with such administrative power and political foresight, would find in the House of Commons an outlet for his pent-up energy. I also felt he needed men's society. We had no country home then, and to be shut up in a London house was certainly no life for Stanley; also, at the back of my mind was the haunting fear of his returning to the Congo. I thought that, once in Parliament, he would be safely anchored.

At first, he would not hear of it, but his friend, Mr. Alexander Bruce,[1] of Edinburgh, joined me in persuading Stanley to become Liberal-Unionist candidate for North Lambeth. We went into the battle just ten days before the polling day. We were quite ignorant of electioneering, and I must say we had a dreadful ten days of it.

Stanley wrote in his Journal, Monday, 20th June, 1892:—

'Have consented to contest the constituency of North Lambeth against Alderman Coldwells, Radical. I accepted because D. is so eager for me to be employed, lest I fly away again to Africa.

On the 29th, Stanley held a great meeting at Hawkeston Hall, Lambeth, but he was howled down by an organised rabble imported for the purpose! The leader of these rowdies, stationed in the Gallery, from time to time waved a folded newspaper, which was the signal for fresh interruptions, and an incredible din. The platform was stormed, and we had to withdraw; when we tried to get into our brougham and drive away, the roughs held on to the door of the carriage and tore it off. Stanley was greatly disgusted: African savages, he thought, would have behaved better. He was not sorry to be beaten, though the majority against him was only one hundred and thirty.

But I persuaded him to remain the Liberal-Unionist candidate. He thought the election would not come for some years, and faint-heartedly consented, on condition that he would never be expected to call personally on voters — never visit from 'house-to-house.' He consented to speak at working-men's clubs and meetings, but '*never* will I degrade myself by asking a man for his vote,' and no man can boast that Stanley ever did so.

[1] See the second footnote on page 459.

I shall remember those meetings to my life's end. No one present could ever forget them. They took place at the local 'Constitutional Club' — in the York Road, Lambeth — and in various school-rooms. Here Stanley for some years, as Candidate, and then as Member, spoke on the great questions of the day.

He spoke to them of Empire, of Commerce, of what the Uganda railway could do — that railway which the Liberals had so hotly objected to constructing! He showed them what Home-Rule in Ireland really meant. He explained to them the Egyptian position; every subject he made clear. He did not harangue working-men on their wrongs, nor on their rights, but he spoke to them of their DUTY, and why they should give of their best and highest. He told them about our colonies, how they were made, not by loafers, but by men eager to carve out their own fortunes; and he told them what manner of man was required there now. He spoke with the greatest earnestness and simplicity, rising at times into a fiery eloquence which stirred the heart. I hardly ever failed to accompany him to those meetings.

Stanley took infinite trouble with these speeches, as with everything else he did. He wrote them out carefully, so as to impress the subject on his memory; but he did not read, nor repeat them by rote.

These lectures and addresses taught me a great deal, and further revealed to me the splendid power of Stanley.

I used to wish he had greater and better-educated audiences; but he never considered any such efforts too much trouble, if the humblest and poorest listened intelligently. I here give his first address to the Electors of North Lambeth, in 1892.

GENTLEMEN, I venture to offer myself as your representative in Parliament, in place of your esteemed Member who has just resigned.

The circumstances under which I place my services at your disposal, if somewhat unusual, are, I hope, such as may dispose you, at least, to believe in my earnest desire to serve you, and in serving you to serve my country.

Gentlemen, my one mastering desire is for the maintenance, the spread, the dignity, the usefulness of the British Empire. I believe that we Englishmen are working out the greatest destiny which any race has ever fulfilled, but we must go on, — or we shall go back. There must be firm and steady guidance in Downing Street, there must be an invincible fleet upon the seas, if trade is to expand, and emigrants to spread and settle, and the name of England still to be reverenced in every quarter of the globe. From which of the two great English parties

— I ask myself, and I ask you — may we expect the firmest, the steadiest guidance, the most unflinching effort to maintain our naval strength? The whole colonial and foreign policy of England under the last two administrations prompts to no doubtful reply. I have followed that policy, not as a partisan, but as a man deeply, vitally, concerned; a man who, at least, has based his opinions upon practical and personal conversance with great and difficult affairs. I say, unhesitatingly, that I believe that the continuance of Lord Salisbury's firm, temperate, wise foreign policy is worth to England millions of money, and again, far more important than money, though harder to measure in national power, national usefulness, and national honour.

First of all the merits of Lord Salisbury's Government, in my eyes, comes the enormous strengthening of the navy. Gentlemen, that is the essential thing. In this island, in this great city alone, is a treasure of life and wealth such as no nation ever had to guard before. It is no small achievement to have insured that wealth, those lives, by seventy new ships of war, while at the same time lightening taxation, and remitting especially those burdens which the poorest felt the most.

Gentlemen, I am, as you know, a man of the people. Whatever I have achieved in life has been achieved by my own hard work, with no help from privilege, or favour of any kind. My strongest sympathies are with the working-classes. And had the conflict of parties now been, as it once was, a conflict between a few aristocrats and many workers, between privilege and popular rights, I should have ranged myself, assuredly, on the workers' side. But I now see no such conflict. I see both sides following the people's mandate, honestly endeavouring to better the condition of the masses, and I see the Unionist party actually effecting those reforms of which Radicals are too often content to talk. Most of all do I see this in Ireland, — looking with a fresh eye, and with no party prepossessions, upon the Irish affairs, I cannot but perceive that while others may have declaimed eloquently, Mr. Balfour has governed wisely; that while others propose to throw all into the melting-pot, in the hope of some magical change which no one can define, Mr. Balfour and his colleagues are successfully employing all these methods, — steady and gentle rule, development of natural resources, administrative foresight and skill, which have, in times past, welded divided countries into unity, and lifted distressed and troubled communities into prosperity and peace.

I sympathise with all that the present Government has well done and wisely planned for the bettering of the lot of the people; to all such measures I will give the best thought that I can command. Yet I cannot but feel that the destiny of the English working-classes depends in the last resort on measures, on enterprises, of a larger scope. In the highlands of Africa, which skilful diplomacy has secured for England, those lands to which the Mombasa Railway will be the first practicable road, there is room and to spare for some twenty millions of happy and prosperous people. There is no need for the poorest among us to covet his neighbour's wealth, while nature still offers such immense, such inexhaustible boons. Only let England be united at home, wise abroad, and no man can assign a limit to the stability of our Empire, or to the prosperity of her sons.

In conclusion, the preservation of peace, with jealous care of the dignity and honour of the Empire, the wonderful economies effected during the past six years, the readiness to reform judiciously where reform was necessary, as manifested by Lord Salisbury's Government, are worthy of our best sympathies; and if you will do me the honour to return me to Parliament, I promise to be active and faithful in the discharge of my duties to my constituency.

I am,

Yours sincerely,

HENRY M. STANLEY.

2, RICHMOND TERRACE, WHITEHALL, LONDON,
June 21st, 1892.

After our defeat in 1892, I received the following letter from Sir George Grey, who was still in Auckland, New Zealand: —

October, 1893.

MY DEAR MRS. STANLEY, — I am only just recovered from a long and serious illness, and can as yet hardly hold my pen, but I am so ashamed of not having written to you, that I am determined to make an effort to do so, and to ask for your forgiveness. I was seriously sorry at Stanley losing his election, although we should have been on different sides in politics; but his profound judgment and knowledge of African affairs would have been of the greatest service in Parliament, and would, I believe, have prevented the Government from committing many errors. But the fact is, that Stanley's services to the empire have been too great and too *unusual*, and I ought to have known he would have to undergo many trials; perhaps he is lucky in having escaped being put in chains, as Columbus was! Men of this kind have no business to act in the unusual manner they generally do, throwing their contemporaries in the shade — this is never forgiven!

However, these truly great men can bear misfortunes in whatever guise they come, like heroes, and thus add greater lustre to their ultimate renown, and will make their history much more wonderful reading. Those who climb to heights must expect to meet with toils and many trials. Give my regards to Stanley, who, tried in so many, and such vast toils and dangers, whilst working for his fellow-men, will not falter now.

Truly yours,

G. GREY.

In January, 1893, Stanley wrote to me at Cambridge, where I was spending a week: —

Having announced my intention of standing again as Candidate for N. Lambeth, I propose doing so, of course, for your sake; but after my experience in North Lambeth you must not expect any enthusiasm, any of that perseverant energy, which I may have shewn elsewhere, and which I could still show in an honourable sphere.

But this political work involves lying, back-biting, morally-damaging your opponent in the eyes of the voters, giving and receiving wordy abuse, which reminds me of English village squabbles; and I cannot find the courage either to open my lips against my opponent, or to put myself in a position to receive from him and his mindless myrmidons that filthy abuse they are only too eager to give. That so many members of Parliament can do so, smiling, only shows difference of training as well as difference of character between us. I do not respect them less for the capacity of being indifferent to the vileness, but rather feel admiration that they can do something which I cannot do. If I were once in the House, possibly I should not feel so thin-skinned, and at the next fight, I should probably be able to face it better; but, not being in the House, and, finding the House moated around by the cess-pool of slander and calumny, I detest the prospect of wading in for so doubtful a satisfaction.

You remember that meeting in Lambeth. Well! I have been through some stiff scenes in my life, but I never fell so low in my own estimation as I fell that day; to stand there being slighted, insulted by venomous tongues every second, and yet to feel how hopeless, nay impossible, retort was! and to realise that I had voluntarily put myself in a position to be bespattered with as much foul reproaches as those ignorant fools chose to fling!

I will, nevertheless, stand again, but my forbearance must not be tested too far. I declare my strict resolve never to ask for a vote, never to do any silly personal canvassing in high streets or by-streets, never to address open-air meetings, cart or wagon work, or to put myself in any position where I can be baited like a bull in the ring. The honour of M. P. is not worth it.

If it is not possible to represent North Lambeth without putting my dignity under the Juggernaut of Demos, let Demos find someone else. I will visit committees, and would be pleased to receive them anywhere; I will speak at clubs and committee-rooms, or any halls, and pay the expenses, etc., but that is all. But this shall be my final effort. If I am beaten, I hope it will be by an overwhelming majority, which will for ever prove my incapacity as a candidate.

Six or seven years ago I was a different man altogether, but this last expedition has sapped my delight in the rude enjoyments of life, though never at any time could I have looked upon electioneering as enjoyable. The whole business seems to me degrading. I refuse to promise to the people that which I think harmful to the nation. I object to the abject attitude of politicians towards constituents. If I stand, it is as their leader, not their slave. I shall go to Parliament simply to work for some good end, and not for personal objects.

I now realised that since usage and custom demand that the Parliamentary candidate shall call on the voters, and that Stanley positively, and I think rightly, refused to do so, we were in danger of losing the Constituency.

I realised that whichever way the working-man means to vote, he likes to feel he has something you want, something he can give. He likes even to refuse you, and oblige you to listen to his views and his principles. So, if you do not choose to go and kow-tow before him, he puts you down as 'no good,' or, at any rate, 'not my sort.' After our defeat, therefore, in 1892, I resolved to 'nurse' North Lambeth, since that is the accepted term, and to do so in my own way.

It was hard work, undoubtedly, but very interesting and instructive; I had some unforgettable experiences, and on the whole I was very kindly and pleasantly received.

1893.—February 21st. General Beauregard died last night at New Orleans. He was my old General at the Battle of Shiloh, 1862. I remember, even now, how enthusiastic my fellow-soldiers were about him, and I, being but an inconsiderate boy, caught the fever of admiration and raved. Thank Heaven there were no reporters to record a boy's ravings! This is not to say that he was not worthy of the soldiers' respect. But his achievements were not those of a military genius, and genius alone deserves such unmeasured praise as we gave him.

The Civil War only developed two first-rank men, and those were Grant and Lee, but in the second rank there were many who might possibly, with opportunities, have rivalled the first two. I believe if it were put to the vote of the military class as to which was the greater of the two greatest captains of the war, the vote would be cast for Robert E. Lee. Nevertheless, there was something in Grant which, though not so showy as the strategy and dash of Lee, makes me cast my vote for Grant.

March 10th. Mrs. Annie Ingham died this day on the Congo, aged thirty-seven. She was the wife of Charles E. Ingham, ex-lifeguardsman, and missionary, mentioned in 'Darkest Africa.' She was a sweet, good woman. She is now safe in that heavenly home she laboured so hard to deserve. Such women as this one are the very salt of our race.

June 12th. Went to hear Lord Salisbury's speech at the Surrey Theatre. He just misses being an orator. Nature has given him a personality; a voice, education, experience, observation, and rank, have all contributed elements to the forming of an orator, and yet he lacks two things — imagination and fire. With those two qualities which he lacks, how he would have swayed that audience, how he would have straightened himself, and with the power of eye and voice, and the right word, he would have lifted everyone to a pitch of enthusiasm such as is almost unknown in England.

June 22nd, Thursday. My dear old friend Sir William Mackinnon, Bart., died this morning at 9.45, after a long illness contracted on his yacht 'Cornelia,' as the result of a cold, and deep depression of spirits created by a sense that his labours, great expenditure, and exercise of influence over his friends on behalf of British East Africa, were not appreciated as they deserved by Lord Rosebery and his colleagues in the Government. A lack of appreciation is indeed a mild term for the callous indifference shown by the Rosebery Government.

Sir William had for years (since 1878) been feeling his way towards this great achievement. By dint of generosity, long continued, he finally won the confidence of successive Sultans of Zanzibar, especially Syyed Barghash, and when once that confidence was established, he gradually developed his projects, by which he, as well as the Sultan, might greatly profit. Being already rich enough for gratifying his very simple wants, he wished to lead his friend the Sultan into the path of profitable enterprise. He was ably seconded by Sir John Kirk and Fred Holmwood, the Consul-general; and, though it was tedious work, he finally succeeded.

I claim to have assisted him considerably during my stay in 1887, and it was according to my advice that Barghash finally consented to sign the Concession, and Mackinnon hurried on the negotiation. A few weeks after I left, the Concession was signed, and Mackinnon's way to form a Company, and obtain a Charter from the British Government, was clear. Sir William subscribed fifty thousand pounds to the capital, and raised the remainder from among his own friends, for no friend of Mackinnon could possibly resist a request from him.

The object of the Company was mainly commercial, and, left alone by politicians, Mackinnon was the man to make it remunerative. But after the advent of Germany into the African field, with Bismarck at the helm, and the principles declared at the Berlin Conference behind them, it became necessary, in order to prevent collisions between Mackinnon's Company and the Germans, to give the East African Company a political status; hence, with the utmost good-will and promises of support, the Charter was given to it by the British Government, and the Company thereby incurred tremendous responsibilities.

Egged on, urged on, advised, spurred, encouraged by Her Majesty's Government, the Company had first of all quickly to gain other Concessions, for the Sultan's only covered the maritime region; and this meant the despatch of a series of costly expeditions into the interior, over a region that embraced hundreds of thousands of square miles; and as this region was almost unexplored, these expeditions meant the employment of some thousands of armed and equipped natives, led by English officers. Between 1887 and 1890, some thousands of pounds were squandered in these costly enterprises, and the capital that rightly was called for the development of the commerce of the maritime region, and would surely have been remunerative, was thus wasted on purely political work; which the national exchequer should have paid for.

In 1890, the Mackinnon Company entered Uganda, and, on account of the territories turned over to it *by me*, the government of the Company extended from Mombasa to the Albert Edward Nyanza, and North to the White Nile, and South of 1°S. The Company bravely and patriotically held on, however, and sustained the enormous expense of maintaining the communications open between Uganda and the sea; but it soon became evident to Mackinnon, who was always so hopeful and cheerful, that the responsibilities were becoming too great for his Company.

The transport of goods to Uganda to sustain the force required to occupy it, was very costly. Every ton cost three hundred pounds to carry to Uganda; that is, it required forty men to carry a ton, and as the distance was three months' travel from the coast, and little less than three months to return, and each man received one pound per month, two hundred and forty pounds was required for the pay of these forty men for six months, exclusive of their rations. The force in Uganda, the various garrisons maintained along the route, would naturally consume several hundred tons of goods each year, and every additional act of pressure from the Government increased this consumption and expense.

It is thus easily seen how, when the Government, always extravagant when they manage things themselves, dipped their hands into the coffers of a private Company, bankruptcy could not be far off. Though Mackinnon, through patriotism, held on much longer than his friends deemed prudent, he at last informed the Rosebery Government that the Company intended to abandon Uganda and the interior, and confine themselves to their own proper business, namely commerce, unless they were assisted by a subsidy.

I happened to be in Mackinnon's room at The Burlington a few minutes after he had sent the Foreign Office messenger with his answer to Lord Rosebery's question, what was the least sum the Company would accept per annum for five years to undertake, or rather to continue, the administration of Uganda, and I was told that Mackinnon's answer was fifty thousand pounds.

I remember when I heard the amount that I thought the matter was all over, for Rosebery, with Harcourt supervising the treasury, would never have the courage to allow such a sum. Why had he not asked for half that amount, twenty-five thousand pounds? 'But even fifty thousand pounds is insufficient,' cried Mackinnon. 'Certainly, after the style in which you have been administering during the last eighteen months; but it is clear by the nature of Rosebery's question, that "administering Uganda" means simply its occupation, and keeping things quiet in order to prevent its being abandoned to Germany, or reverting to the barbarous methods of Mwanga. Rosebery wants to stand well with the country, and at the same time to pacify Harcourt. And twenty-five thousand pounds a year he could easily persuade Harcourt to grant.'

We were still engaged in discussing this subject when the F. O. messenger returned with another letter. Mackinnon's hand trembled as he opened it, and when he had fully understood the letter, it was only by a great effort he was able to suppress his emotions. The letter contained but a few lines, to the effect that the sum demanded was impossible, and that there was no more to be said on the matter.

From that day my dear old friend became less cheerful; he was too great a soul to lay bare his feelings, but those who knew him were at no loss to find that the kind old face masked a good deal of inward suffering; had one questioned me about him, I should have said, 'I believe that as Mackinnon, since he made his fortune and was childless, devoted his ripest and wisest years and the greater part of his fortune to this idea, which, like the King of the Belgians, he had of making an African State valuable to his Government and people, he was struck to the heart by Rosebery's curt refusal to consider his offer and his determination to displace the Company by the Government. Had Rosebery said he was willing to allow twenty-five thousand pounds, Mackinnon would have accepted it rather than the world should say he had failed. East Africa had become Mackinnon's love, his pride, and the one important object of life. Mackinnon's soul was noble, his mind above all pettiness. His life was now bereft of its object, and the mainspring of effort had been removed, and so he visibly declined, and death came in kindness.

Sunday, 25th June. Called at the Burlington Hotel, and viewed the body. I found the Marquis of Lorne there, and both of us were much affected at seeing the small, still body on the bed. Was this the end of so many aspirations and struggles! I am glad I knew him, for he was in some things a model character, great of soul, though small of body. Too generous at times, and parsimonious where I would have been almost lavish; and yet I loved him for the very faults which I saw, because, without them, he would not have been just my dear Mackinnon, whose presence, somehow, was always a joy to me.

Tuesday, at 10 A. M., I left for Balinakill, Argyleshire, to attend the funeral of my friend Mackinnon. Arrived Wednesday. We walked from his house, after a simple service in the dining-room, which had witnessed such hospitable feasts, and kindly-hearted gatherings. The coffin was borne on the shoulders of relays of the Clachan villagers. In the parish grave-yard was an open grave, as for a peasant, into which the sumptuous oak coffin, enclosing a leaden one, was lowered. Two bundles of hay were spread over the coffin, and then the earth was shovelled in, and in a short time all that was mortal of a dearly-loved man lay beneath a common mound.

July 5th. Attended a Garden-party at Marlborough House. I generally dislike these mobs of people; but I met several interesting characters here, and, of course, the Prince and Princess of Wales were, as usual, charming.

July 13th. Glanced over Burton's Life—it is written by his wife. It is very interesting, but the real Burton is not to be found in this book; that is, as he was to a keen observer of his character and actions.

During the autumn, I received the following letters from Stanley:

CROMER, October 17th, 1893. Yesterday was a most enjoyable day for me. I feel its effects in an all-round completeness of health.

At 8.50 A. M., I was off by slow train, creeping, creeping west, within view of the sea for some time, then turning round a great horseshoe curve to east, as though the railway projectors had thought it necessary to show all that was really beautiful in these parts before taking the traveller towards the mouth of the Yare.

As I have been immensely pleased with the views so gained, I am grateful. All this part of East Anglia is wholly new to me, and not yet having you to talk to, my inward comments upon what I saw were more exclamatory than otherwise.

The beauty of this country is like the beauty of a fair Puritan; it is modest, and wholesome; no flashiness, nor regality, no proud uplift of majesty, no flaunting of wealth, or suggestion of worldliness; but quiet English homesteads, and little church-loving villages, tidy copses, lowly vales, and sweet, modest hills, breathed over by the sea-air, which the lungs inhale with grateful gasps.

By half-past eleven we rolled into Yarmouth, and, with only an umbrella in hand, I made my way to the sea, by a street which has some very nice houses of the modern Surrey-villa type. This was the reverse of what I had expected to see. Presently, I was on the parade, a straight two miles, flanked on one side by a long line of sea-side houses, and on the other by a broad, sandy strand, smoothly sloping to a greenish sea. Three or four piers running out from the drive caused me to think that the place must be crowded in the season. I can imagine the fine expanse of sands populous with children, nurses, and parents; music, in the air, from the band-stands, and a brisk circulation of human beings from all parts around; the famous Yarmouth yawls, doing a good business with the ambitious youths, who wish to boast of having sailed on the sea, when they return from their holidays; the seats comfortably filled with those who wish to fill the eye with the sights of the sea, and the ear with the sound of artificial music, blended with the countless whispers of the waves!

I strode down this parade, debating many things in my mind. I went past a military or naval hospital, a battery of old-fashioned, muzzle-loaders, which I fancy are not of much use except as means of drilling volunteers; then I came to a tall monument to Nelson — at a point of land given up to rubbish and net-drying, when I found that I had been travelling parallel with the Yare, and was now at its mouth. I crossed this point, and on coming to the river, walked up along the interesting quay. I was well rewarded, for as picturesque a sight as can be found in any sea-side town, in any country, met me.

The river is narrow, not quite the width of the Maritime Canal of Suez, I should say, but every inch of it seems serviceable to commerce. The useful stream is crowded with coast shipping, trawlers, luggers, small steamers, and inland barges, which lie mainly in a long line alongside this quay. It did my heart good to see the deep-bellied, strong, substantial vessels of the fisher-class, and still more entertainment I obtained in viewing the types of men who handled the fish, and the salt. The seed of the old vikings and Anglian invaders of Britain were all round me, as fond of the sea as their brave old ancestors!

I saw some splendid specimens of manhood among them, who were, I am certain, as proud of their avocation as the Rothschilds can be of banking. It was far better than going to a theatre to watch the healthy fellows swinging up their crates of salted herrings — the gusto of hoisting, hand-over-hand — the breezy, hearty lightsomeness of action — the faces as truly reflecting the gladness of the heart as the summer sea obeys the summer air.

I turned away deeply gratified by the sight, and sure that these fellows thought little of Home-Rule and other disturbing questions.

On reaching a bridge across the Yare, I found myself in 'Hall quay' with the Cromwell House, Star, Crown, and Anchor, and other old-fashioned houses. Then I turned into one of the rows, as the narrow alley-like streets are called, taking brief glances at the cheap wares for sale — boots, shod with iron, the nails recalling memories of early farm-life; mufflers of past days; 'two-penny-ha'-penny' wares in general, suitable for the slim purses of poor holiday-makers.

Then, after a long tour, I struck into a street running towards the sea, where the quieter people love to brood and dream away their summer. Finally, I came to the 'Queen's,' ordered my lunch, and afterwards took train to Norwich. As I was not yet too tired for sight-seeing, I drove to the Cathedral. It is like a long Parish-church within. The gateways are grim-looking objects, similar to many I have seen elsewhere, but quite ancient and venerable. The Cloisters, however, are grand, over one hundred and fifty feet square, and as good as we saw in Italy, to my mind. The Close has a remarkably ecclesiastical privacy and respectability about it, but had not enough greenery, green sward or foliage, to be perfect. Thence I wandered to the Castle, about which I had read so much in a lately-published romance.

What one sees is only a modern representation of the fine old keep, around which the writer had woven his story, and I suppose it is faithful to the original, without; but through the windows one sees a glass roof, and then it is evident that the building is only a shell, got up as for a Chicago Exhibition.

The mound on which it stands, and the deep, dry ditch around, are sufficiently ancient. As I walked around the Castle, old Norwich looked enchanting. I cannot tell whether the town is worth looking at, but I have seldom seen one which appeared to promise so much. The worst of these old towns is that their hotels are always so depressing. If the Grand Hotel of Cromer was at Yarmouth, it would totally change the character of the town, and so would a similar one for Norwich. On the Continent, they have just as interesting old towns to show the visitor, but they have also good hotels.

Yarmouth beach is equal to that of Cromer, but the hotels are deadly-dull places.

Well, after a good three hours' walk, I took the train for Cromer. It was a happy thought of mine coming here. I love to look at the sea, and hear the windows rattle, and the soughing of the waves; and between me and these delights, nothing human intervenes. For the sight of the sea is better than the sight of any human face just now. Whenever the nerves quiver with unrest, depend upon it, the ocean and the songs of the wind are more soothing than anything else; so when you arrive you will find me purified, and renovated somewhat, by this ogling with quiet nature.

CROMER, October, 1893. How I do begrudge the time spent on trifles, interminable waste of time, and prodigal waste of precious life as though our hours were exhaustless. When I think of it! Ah, but no more! That way madness lies! Oh! I am delighted with this Norfolk air, and this hotel, this rest, the tranquillizing effect — the deep inhalations, the pure God-blest air — the wonderful repose of the sea! When you join me here, how *we* shall enjoy ourselves!

Yesterday, while on my afternoon walk, I felt such a gust of joy, such a rapturous up-springing of joy to my very finger-tips, that I was all amazement at its suddenness. What was the cause? Only three miles of deserted sand-beach, a wide, illimitable sea, rolling from the east. Roll after roll of white-topped surge sounding on the shore, deep, solemn, continuous, as driven by a breeze, which penetrated into the farthest recesses of the lungs, and made them ache with fulness, and whipped the blood into a glow! Presently, I respond to the influence; I condescend to stoop, and whisk the round pebbles on the glorious floor of sand, smooth as asphalt. I burst out into song. Fancy! Years and years ago, I think I sang. The spirits were in an ecstasy, for the music of the waves, and the keen, salt wind, laden with scent of the sea, the absolute solitude, the immensity of my domain, caused me to sing for joy!

I knew there was something of my real old self, the lees, as it were, in me still; — but, such is civilised man, he enters a groove, and exit there is none, until solitariness discovers the boy, lying hidden under a thick husk of civilised custom! This solitude is so glorious, we must try and secure it for three months out of each year. Yes, this *is* glorious! No Africa for me, if I can get such solitude in England!!

There is a fox-terrier here, the duplicate of my old Randy in Africa, smooth-haired, the white like cream, the black on him deep sable, simply beautiful, a gentleman all over, understands every word, automatically obsequious; lies down with a thump, rises with a spring, makes faces like an actor! Say 'Rats!' — he wants to tear the room to pieces, he is sure he sees what is only in your own imagination! Why, his very tail is eloquent! I seem to understand every inclination or perpendicular of it! This dog is the embodiment of alertness and intelligence. The pity of it is, he is not for sale; no money would buy him. I would give twenty pounds for him, I should so like you to realise what a perfect dog can be!

Your patience may make something of our dog in time, but his nature is not gentle to begin with. *This* dog, as I said, is a gentleman — yet while gentle to friends, bold as a lion to all vermin — human and other.

He attracted my attention three days ago, as he was outside the hotel-door, beseeching to come in. He saw me take a step as though to go on my way, his eyes became more limpid, he whined; had he spoken English, I could not have understood him better!

November 15th, 1893. I left Manchester yesterday at noon, and arrived in London at 5 P. M., and found a mild kind of November fog and damp, cold weather here. After an anchorite's dinner, with a bottle of Apollinaris, I drove off to the Smoking-concert at the Lambeth. The programme consists of comic songs, ballads, and recitations, as usual; just when the smoke was amounting to asphyxiation, I was asked to 'say a few words.' I saw that my audience was more than usually mixed, very boyish young fellows, young girls, and many, not-very-intellectual-looking, men and women. The subjects chosen by me were the Matabele War, and the present Coal-war or Strike. In order to make the Matabele War comprehensible to the majority, I had to use the vernacular freely, and describe the state of things in South Africa, just as I would to a camp of soldiers.

In doing this, I made use of the illustration of an Englishman, living in a rented house, being interfered with in his domestic government by a burly landlord, who insisted on coming into his house at all hours of the day, and clubbing his servants; and who, on the pretence of searching for his lost dog and cat, in his tenant's house, marched away with the Englishman's dog and other trifles. You who know the Englishman, I went on, when in his house, after he has paid his rent and all just debts; you can best tell what his conduct would be! It strikes me, I said, that the average man would undoubtedly 'boot' the landlord, and land him in the street pretty quickly. Well, just what the Englishman in Lambeth would do, Cecil Rhodes did in South Africa with Lobengula. He paid his rent regularly, one thousand two hundred pounds a year or so, besides many hundreds of rifles, and ammunition to match, and other gifts, for the right to manage Mashonaland as he saw fit. Now in the concession to Rhodes, Lobengula had reserved no rights to meddle in the territory. Therefore, when, under the plea that his cattle had been stolen by Rhodes's servants, or subjects, the Mashonas, Lobengula marched into Rhodes's territory and slaughtered the Mashonas and took the white man's cattle, besides creating a general scare among the outlying farmers, and the isolated miners, — Jameson, who was acting as Rhodes's steward, sent the sub-agent Lendy upon the tracks of the high-handed Matabele, — hence the war.

This little exposition took amazingly, and there was not one dissentient voice.

About the Coal-war I was equally frank, and said, in conclusion, that, if I had any money to spare at the present time, it would not be given to men who were determined to be sulky, and who, to spite the coal-owners, preferred to starve, but to those poor, striving people, who, though they had nothing to do with the dispute between miners and coal-owners, had to bear the same misery which the miners were supposed to suffer from, and who were obliged to pinch and economise in food, in order not to be without coals. This drew a tremendous burst of cheers, and 'Aye, aye, that is true.'

Some very bad cigars and black coffee were thrust upon me, and I had to take a cigar, and a teaspoonful of the coffee; neither, you may rest assured, did me any good!

Yesterday, I read W. T. Stead's last brochure, '2 and 2

make 4.' — I think it is very good. Stead aims to be the 'universal provider' for such people as cannot so well provide for themselves. He is full of ideas, and I marvel how he manages to find time to write as he does; he has mortgaged his life for the benefit of the many sheep in London, who look to him as to a shepherd.

The 'Daily Paper,' of which I have a specimen, may be made very useful; and I hope he will succeed with it; but it does not touch the needs of the aristocratic, learned, and the upper-middle class. Some day, I hope some other type of Stead will think of *them*, and bring out a high-class journal which shall provide the best and truest news, affecting all political, commercial, monetary, manufacturing, and industrial questions at home and abroad; not forgetting the very best books published, not only in England, but in Europe, and America, and from which 'Sport' of all kinds will be banished.

It ought to be printed on good paper, and decent type; the editorials should be short; the paper should not be larger than the 'Spectator,' and the pages should be cut. I quite agree with Stead that it is about time we should get rid of the big sheets, and the paper-cutter. Wherefore I wish Stead all success, and that, some day, one may arise who will serve the higher intelligences in the country, with that same zeal, brightness, and inventiveness, which Stead devotes to the masses. Now I have faithfully said my say, and send you hearty greetings.

November 17th, 1893. I have been to Bedford, and am back. My inviter and entertainer was Mr. A. Talbot, a Master of the Grammar School at Bedford. This school was founded in 1552, by Sir William Harper, a Lord Mayor of London, who endowed it with land which, at the time, brought only one hundred and sixty pounds a year, but which has since grown to be sixteen thousand pounds a year. A new Grammar School was completed three years ago, at a cost of thirty thousand pounds, and is a magnificent structure of red brick with stone facings. Its Hall is superb, between forty and fifty feet high, and about one hundred feet, by forty feet. It was in this Hall I lectured to a very crowded audience.

The new lecture on 'Emin' was received in perfect silence until I finished, when the applause was long and most hearty.

But, to my astonishment, after all my pains to prune it down, it lasted one hour and fifty minutes in delivery. As I drew near the catastrophe, you could have heard a pin drop — and I really felt emotional, and was conscious that every soul sympathised with me when I came to the meeting of the avenger of blood and his victim, Emin.[1]

Strange! I read in a telegram in the 'Standard,' which came to the house before I left, that Said-bin-Abed, the avenger, had been caught by the Belgian officers at Kirundu (which I know well), was condemned to death, and shot. Thus retribution overtook him, too!

Few in this country know that I am the prime cause of this advance of the Belgians against the Arab slave-raiders. Indeed, people little realise how I have practically destroyed this terrible slave-trade, by cutting it down at its very roots. I have also been as fatal to Tippu-Tib, Rashid, his nephew, who captured Stanley Falls from Captain Deane, Tippu-Tib's son, Muini Mubala, and, lastly, Said-bin-Abed, — the son of my old host, 'Tanganyika,' as Abed-bin-Salim was called — as if I had led the avengers myself, which I was very much solicited to do.

It has all been part of the policy I chalked out for myself in Africa, and urged repeatedly on the King of the Belgians, at every interview I have had with him, with one paramount object in view, — the destruction of the slave-traffic.

At this very time, we have a great scheme which must not be disclosed, no! not even to you, yet! but which you may rest assured is for the ultimate benefit of that dark humanity in the Lualaba region.

Of course, military men, especially continentals, are rather more severe than I should have been; for, if I had caught Said-bin-Abed, I should have sent him to Belgium, even though he murdered Emin, or had murdered a friend. But the suppression of the Arabs had to be; and my prophecy to Charles Allen, of the Anti-slavery cause, that I made to him in June, 1890, has come to pass. I said that 'in the next five years, I should have done more for the Anti-slavery cause than all the Anti-slavery Societies in Europe could have done,' and it *is* done, in the complete conquest of those

[1] See page 375.

receivers and raiders, who have been so often mentioned in my lectures!

The king did not wish to proceed to extremes, but I drove home every argument I could think of, each time I met him, or wrote, to prove that it was essential. 'Yet,' I said, 'at the first sign of submission, remember mercy; but exercise it only when they have laid down their arms.' When the Belgians have reached Tanganyika Lake, and either drive the surviving Arabs across the lake, or into unconditional submission, the work may be considered over. The death of so many of my officers and men will then have been amply avenged; and an era of peace for the poor, persecuted natives will begin.

Mr. Phillpots, the Headmaster, I forgot to say, introduced me very nicely indeed by touching on the six journeys I have made to Africa, leaving me to speak upon the seventh. After the lecture, Mr. Phillpots, and all the Masters, supped at Mr. Talbot's, and I was in such a vein, that I kept them all up until it was a little after 1 A.M. I was horrified! and, soon after the departure of the guests, I jumped into bed, and was fast asleep within a few minutes.

I am at the Second Volume of Lowell, and time flies by so rapidly that I will not be able to read Lugard's book for a few days yet.

The First Volume of Lowell's Letters gives us a pretty clear idea of the man. I see in him the type of a literary character, whose nature I have often been made acquainted with in the past, though not in quite so cultured a form as in Lowell.

But, with all his culture, learning, and poetry, and though he is so kind-hearted, loving, sympathetic, ready to oblige, he is what I should call in England, 'provincial,' in every feeling. Though I never saw Lowell face to face, I feel as if I could make a presentment of every characteristic lineament, his walk, gesture, bearing, the smile on his face, the genial bluish-grey eye, even to his inches.

These Letters, however, only reveal the generous temper, humour, moods, and his fond weaknesses. We should know more about his inward thoughts, his best views of men, and matters political, literary, social, etc., etc., to get a complete knowledge of him. These letters only refer to Lowell and his immediate acquaintances, and there are very few things in them that a reader would care to hear twice. I could scarcely point to a dozen sentences, all told, that compel a pause.

How different this is from what one could show in Ruskin, the prose poet of England, or in Carlyle; or in Boswell's Johnson, or in De Quincey, even! Yet, I admit, it is unfair to judge Lowell by his Letters only, and that we should examine his prose and poetry before deciding. Twice, only, was I thrilled, just a little, and then from sympathy with the bereaved husband and father.

Had Lowell kept a journal like Sir Walter Scott, I feel the world would have had something worth reading. Sometimes I appear to look, as through a window, into the heart of the writer and his correspondent. There is something too frequent, also, in the phrase, 'I do not care what you think of my books, but I want you to like me!' I do not wish to pursue this theme, for fear you will get the impression that I do not like Lowell; but I do heartily like him; and, again, I think his journal would have been infinitely better.[1]

November 20th, 1893. This year has been fatal to my friends: Mackinnon, Parke, and now my best friend, Alexander Low Bruce.[2] He was one of the staunchest, wisest, trustiest men I ever knew. This England has some other men as worthy, as sensible, as good, as he, but it is not likely it will be my good fortune to meet again a man of this kind to whom I could expose all that is in my breast with full reliance on his sympathy and his honour. I always felt that Bruce was like a dear brother to me.

November 29th. This is the severest blow I have yet received. Bruce was more of my own age than either Mackinnon, or Parke, and it is perhaps owing in a measure to that fact, that his views of men and affairs were more congenial, or more in harmony with my own.

Mackinnon belonged to an older generation, and was the centre of many interests in which I had no concern. Parke again was of a younger generation, and with all his sweet, simple nature I found it difficult to maintain that level of ideas which belonged to his age. But, with Bruce, it was wholly

[1] A further reference to Lowell is given in the letter dated November 27, 1893. — D.S.

[2] A. L. Bruce married Livingstone's daughter Agnes, who survives him. The Livingstone family were always close and greatly-valued friends of Stanley. — D. S.

different. His judgment was formed, and he was in the free exercise of his developed faculties. He was originally of a stronger fibre than either Mackinnon or Parke, *i. e.*, from the common-sense point of view. He might not have the bold, business audacity of Mackinnon, nor his keen foresight for investments, but his level-headedness was more marked. One felt that Bruce's judgment could be trusted, not only in business matters, but in every concern included in practical life.

He was not a literary man, but truly imperial, and highly intelligent, endowed with such large sympathies, that nothing appertaining to British interests was too great or too small for him. In politics, he was simply indefatigable in behalf of the Union. Formerly a Liberal like myself, Gladstone's sudden '*volte-face*' was too much for him, which proves him to be more attached to principles than to whims.

The amount of correspondence entailed on him by the influence he exercised in South Scotland was something extraordinary; his bill for postage must have been unusual. His industry was incredible. His labours did not fray that kindly temper of his in the least, nor diminish the hearty, friendly glance of his eyes. I know no man living among my acquaintances who took life with such a delightful sense of enjoyment, and appeared so uniformly contented. Considering his remarkably penetrative discernment of character, this was the more to be wondered at. I really envied him for this. He could look into the face of a declared opponent, and, though I watched, I could not detect the slightest wavering of that honest, clear, straight look of kindness which was a recognised characteristic of Bruce. I could not do it: when I love, I love; and when I disagree, I cannot hide it!

I should say, though I do not pretend to that intimate knowledge of his boyhood that a relative or school-mate might have, his life must have been a happy one. It is nearly twenty years since I first knew him, and, during that time, there has been a steady growth of affection and esteem for him. I could have been contented on a desert island with Bruce, because contact with him made one feel stronger and nobler. Well, my dear, knowing and loving Bruce as you know I did, you can appreciate my present feelings.

These repeated blows make me less and less regardful of worldliness in every form. Indeed, I have done with the world, though there are a number of little things that I should do before quite surrendering myself to the inevitable. I wonder, indeed, that I am still here, — I, who, during thirty-five years, have been subjected to the evils of almost every climate, racked by over three hundred fevers, dosed with an inconceivable quantity of medicine, shaken through every nerve by awful experiences, yet here I am! and Bruce, and Parke, and Mackinnon, are gone; I write this to-day as sound, apparently, as when I started on my wanderings; but then a week hence, where shall I be?

November 27th, 1893.

MY DEAR D., — I finished Volume Two of Lowell's Letters yesterday. My former opinion needs slight modification, or rather expansion; it was incomplete, as any opinion of an unfinished career must be.

But, now that the career is ended, and the Life is closed, I am at liberty to amplify what I would willingly have said, at once, of any promising man who had continued in consistent goodness, that the expectations formed have been fulfilled. Soon after beginning the Second Volume the attention is not so often arrested by signs of youthful vanity. He has no sooner passed middle age, than one's love for the writer grows more and more complete. He is a '*littérateur*' above all things, to the last; but you also observe his growth from letter to letter into a noble-hearted, affectionate, upright old man.

He is not free, to the closing letter, of the Lowellian imperfections; but these do not detract from the esteem which I find to be increasing for him; like the weaknesses of some of one's personal friends, I rather like Lowell the better for them, for they lighten one's mood of severe respect towards him. After dipping into one or two specimens of poetry which the book contains, his letters do not reveal him wholly, in my opinion. There is one to 'Phœbe' which deeply moved me, and I feel convinced there must be gems of thought among his poetical productions. As I closed the books, Lowell's image, though I never saw him, came vividly before me as he sat in Elmwood library, listening to the leafy swirl without, the strange sounds made by winds in his ample chimney, and the shrill calls, 'wee-wee,' of the mice behind the white wainscoting!

May his covering of earth lie lightly, and his soul be in perfect communion with his loved dead!

December 12th, 1893. Sir Charles and Lady Euan-Smith, Mr. E. L. Berkley, of Zanzibar, and Mr. H. Babington Smith lunched with us.

January 1st, 1894. Sir Samuel White Baker died yesterday. Some years ago I had the photographs of the four greatest travellers of the period, Livingstone, Burton, Speke, and Baker, enlarged, and framed them all together. They are all dead now, Baker being the last to go!

Each was grand in his own way: Livingstone, as a missionary explorer, and the first of the four to begin the work of making known the unexplored heart of Africa, and he was deservedly the most famous; Burton, as a restless wanderer in foreign lands, and a remarkable and indefatigable writer; Speke, the hunter-explorer, with strong geographical instincts, was second to Livingstone for his explorations; Baker, as a hunter, carried his hunting into unknown parts, and distinguished himself by his discovery of the Albert Nyanza, and by his adventures.

The Prince of Wales became interested in him, and through the influence of the Prince, he was appointed Egyptian proconsul of the Upper Nile regions at a munificent salary. Baker was not an explorer in the sense that Livingstone and Speke were, and, consequently, beyond the discovery of the existence of the Albert Lake, he did little to make the Upper Nile region known. The record of his five years' rather violent administration of Equatoria is given in his book called 'Ismailia'; and it will be seen there that he left the region surrounding Ismailia almost as unknown, after his term of service was over, as when he reached it to begin his duties as Administrator.

Apart from this, however, he was a fine fellow — physically strong, masterful, and sensible; as a brave hunter, he was unmatched; as a writer of travels, he was a great success. He was a typical Conservative Englishman; he knew by intuition what

Englishmen like to hear of their countrymen's doings, which, added to his artistic style of writing, charmed his readers.

Another thing to his credit, be it said by me, who know whereof I am speaking, he was too great in mind, and too dignified in character, to belong to any geographical clique, and join in the partisan warfare which raged in Savile Row between 1860–80. He rather took the opposite way, and did not disdain to speak a good word for any explorer who happened to be an object of attack at the time.

November 28th. The death of another friend is to-day announced. This time it is Charles Edward Ingham, ex-guardsman and missionary, whom I employed, in 1887, for my transport service. He is reported as having been killed by an elephant. It is not long ago I recorded in these pages the death of his good and beautiful wife. This devoted couple were wonderful for their piety, and their devotion to the negroes of the Congo.

Early in 1894, Stanley caught cold, and had a succession of malarial attacks. Change of air was advised, and he went to the Isle of Wight, where I joined him a few days later. I here give extracts from his letter.

SHANKLIN, March 15th, 1894. I came here from Freshwater, because that place did not agree with me, and because the accommodation provided was wretched, and the rooms ill-ventilated. I wonder how many people died in the room I occupied? I fancied their spirits sailing about from corner to corner, trying to get out into the air, and at night settling around my head, disturbing my sleep in consequence! I have been reading Vasari's 'Machiavelli,' and, I am thankful to say, he has removed the disagreeable impression I had conceived of his principles from a book I read about him twenty-five years ago; or, perhaps my more mature age has enabled me to understand him better.

Vasari gives one chapter of comments, from various writers, on him; but the one that comes nearest the right judgment on him is Bacon, who said that gratitude was due to him, and to those like him, who study that which men do, instead of that which they ought to do. In fact, Machiavelli has written about contemporaneous Italy just as we speak privately, but dare not talk openly, of our political world.

When we described Gladstone, before his retirement, we called him by the euphonious term of the 'old Parliamentary hand.' What did we mean by that, we who are his opponents? We meant it in this strictly Machiavellian sense. This would once have shocked me, just as many of the Florentine's critics, especially Frederick the Great, affected to be; yet Frederick, and Napoleon, and almost every eminent English politician, except Balfour, were, and are, Machiavellian, and are bound to be!

The following passage is taken from the Journal: —

October 29th, 1894. D. and I left London for Dolaucothy, Llanwrda, S. Wales, to spend three days with Sir James and Lady Hills-Johnes.[1] Lord Roberts and his daughter Eileen were there. Sir James is a delightful host, a most kind, straightforward soldier. He is a V. C., because of dashing exploits in India. He has been Governor of Cabul.

Lord Roberts, Sir James, and myself were photographed by Lady Hills-Johnes. When the photograph came out, it was seen that we were all three of the same height, with a sort of brother-like resemblance.

Sir James is a very winning character, for he takes one's good-will and affection by storm. His heart is white and clean. As for Lady Hills-Johnes, her rare gifts of intellect and sympathy penetrate the heart, like welcome warmth.

I have been more talkative in this house than I have been in any house I can remember, except Newstead Abbey, where one was stimulated by that exceptional, most loveable being, Mrs. Webb.

I happened to be full of speech, and the Hills-Johnes had the gift of knowing how to make me talk. So, what with full freedom of speech, friendly faces, and genuine sympathy, I was very happy, and I fear I shall leave here with a reputation for loquacity. When I leave, I shall cork up again, and be my reserved self!

November 7th, Wednesday. Went to the Queen's Hall to hear Lord Salisbury speak. Again I was struck by the want of the proper spirit which makes the orator. His appearance,

[1] Lieutenant-general Sir James Hills-Johnes, G. C. B., V. C., who was dangerously wounded in the Indian Mutiny, where he won the V. C., for his extraordinary valour. — D. S.

especially his head, large brow, and sonorous voice, his diction, all befit the orator; but the kindling animation, that fire which warms an audience, is absent. The listener must needs follow a sage like the Marquis, with interest; but what an event it would be in the memory of those who haunt political gatherings of this kind, if, suddenly, he dropped his apparent listlessness, and were to speak like a man of genuine feeling, to feeling men! It would be a sight to see the effect on the warm-hearted audience!

Christmas, 1894, we spent on the Riviera, and here Stanley wrote part of his Autobiography, which he had commenced the year before.

MONTE CARLO. Have written a few pages of my Autobiography, but these spasmodic touches are naturally detrimental to style.

CHAPTER XXII

IN PARLIAMENT

IN June, 1895, Parliament was dissolved, and active electioneering commenced. On Monday, July 15, 1895, Stanley was elected M. P. for North Lambeth, with a majority of four hundred and five. Stanley had held many meetings, and I had worked very hard, so that when it came to polling-day, we were both extremely tired. At this contest, the Radical Press distinguished itself by virulent and abusive attacks. One leading Liberal journal, on the eve of the Election, wrote that 'Mr. Stanley's course through Africa had been like that of a red-hot poker drawn across a blanket,' and that 'he nightly slept on a pillow steeped in blood!!' I felt too nervous and unstrung to be present at the counting of votes. I therefore decided to remain at the little Club in the York Road, Lambeth, there to await Stanley. I crept upstairs, to a dark and empty attic, for I knew that between eleven and twelve o'clock I should see the signal: a red flash against the night sky, if we had won; a blue light, if our opponent, the Radical candidate, were returned.

As I knelt by the low window, looking out on the confused mass of roofs and chimneys, hardly distinguishable against the dark sky, I thought passionately of how I had worked and striven for this day; that because Stanley had consented to stand again, I had vowed (if it were possible, by personal effort, to help towards it) that he should be returned! I felt how great he was, and I prayed that he might not be defeated, and that I might thereby keep him from returning to Africa.

The hours passed slowly. The roar of London, as of a great loom, sounded in my ears, with the pounding of my arteries; and still my eyes were steadily fixed westward, where, about a half a mile away, the votes were being counted; and I kept thinking of Stanley. Suddenly, the sky flushed pink over the roofs; to the west, a rosy fog seemed gently to rise, and creep over the sky; and, soon, a distant, tumultuous roar came rolling like an incoming tide, and I went down to meet my Stanley!

When I reached the crudely-lighted Club-room, and stood by the door, the shout of multitudes was overwhelming. Men, in black masses, were surging up the street. They poured in, Stanley in their midst, looking white and very stern. He was seized, and swung up like a feather, on men's shoulders, and carried to a table at the further end of the Hall. As he passed me, I caught his hand; it was so cold, it seemed to freeze mine! He was called upon for a speech. 'Speak to us, Stanley,' was shouted. Stanley merely drew himself up, and, with a steady look, very characteristic, said quietly, 'Gentlemen, I thank you, and now, good-night!' In a few minutes, he and I were stepping into a hansom cab in a back street. During the drive we did not speak. In the hall of our home, I thought he would say something about the victory, but he only smiled at me, and said, 'I think we both need rest; and *now* for a pipe.' We both, as Stanley said, needed rest; I was tired out, and left London for the Engadine, whilst Stanley remained for the Opening of Parliament. He promised to keep a Journal of his first impressions of the House of Commons, and sent the pages to me day by day. I here give extracts from that 'Journal of one week in the House of Commons.'

August 12th, 1895. The architect of the House must have been very deficient in sense of proportion, it seems to me. I think, of all the Parliament Houses I ever saw, I am obliged to confess that any of the State Houses in America would offer superior accommodation to the Members. Where are the desks for the Members, the comfortable, independent chairs, the conveniences for making notes, and keeping papers? In contrast to what my mind recalls of other Chambers, this House is singularly unfurnished. Money has been lavished on walls and carved galleries, but nothing has been spent on conveniences. Then, again, the arrangements: the two Parties, opposed in feeling and principle, have here to confront one another, and present their sides to the Speaker, instead of their faces. Surely we ought to find something more congenial to look at than sour-looking opponents!

At ten minutes to two, I was back in the House. It was now crowded, every seat was occupied, Cross-benches, and under the Gallery, as well as both doorways. Then the House hushed, and in came an officer from the Lords, in old-fashioned costume of black, and a wig, gingerly carrying a gilded rod. He walked trippingly along the floor of the House to our table, at which sat three old-fashioned and be-gowned officers, and delivered a message in a not very clear voice. Whereupon the centre officer stood up, and advanced from behind the table towards him, the one with the gilded rod tripping mincingly backward. When they were both near the door, G. J. Goschen and a few other leaders strode after him; then, from either side of the House, Members poured and formed procession, until there were probably three hundred in it.

We marched through the passage in twos and threes, passing two great Halls crowded with visitors, many of whom were ladies. We halted at the Bar of the Lords. Then I knew we were in the 'gilded chamber,' which has been so often spoken about lately. This was my first view of it, and I looked about me curiously. To call it a 'gilded chamber' is a simple exaggeration. There was not enough gilding for it to merit that term. It was nearly empty, there being about sixteen Peers in their seats. Four scarlet-gowned, cock-hatted gentlemen sat in front of the Throne, and some twenty ladies occupied the settees on the right.

As soon as our 'Commons' officer, whom we had followed, had entered, the Clerk of the Lords, standing between him and the scarlet-gowned four, commenced reading from an elaborately-engraved parchment. He was well into his subject before I could get near enough to the Bar to hear his voice. I could not distinguish any word he said, but when he concluded, the Lord Chancellor — I suppose it was he — read in a much clearer voice some message to the effect that we could proceed to elect a Speaker. When he concluded, he and his three friends took off their hats; at which we retired, betaking ourselves to our own House through the long passage by which we had left.

I met many friends, but I have not been able to exchange twelve sensible words with any of them except Mr. Charles Darling, Q. C., M. P.,[1] and Colonel Denny, M. P. All the rest appear to be in a perfect fever. They no sooner grasp your hand and pour out congratulations than they turn away to another person, and, during their glib greetings, keep looking away to someone else.

I searched the faces on the Radical benches to see if I recognised John Burns and James J. O'Kelly. I would not be sure of O'Kelly, because he is so different from the slim young man I knew in Madrid in 1873 — twenty-three years ago.

It is too early yet to say whether I shall like the House or not. If there is much behaviour like that of Dr. Tanner in it, I shall not; but it is ominous to me that the man can be permitted to behave so badly.

William Allen, the Northumbrian, was a prominent figure among the Radicals, with his American felt hat, and loud grey

[1] Now Sir Charles Darling, Judge in the King's Bench Division.

suit. He is certainly a massive fellow; and I am half-inclined to think that he is rather vain, under all that Radical affectation of unkemptness. If true, it is a pity; for he must have a good heart, and plenty of good sense.

I have written this out on the spur of the moment, while all is fresh in my mind. Mayhap I will send you more of the hasty diary, the day after to-morrow.

Second day, 14th Parliament of Her Majesty's reign.

August 13th. I walked down to the House at 11 A. M. Members were just beginning to arrive. Secured my seat, this time on an upper bench, behind our leaders, that I might be away from the neighbourhood of that ill-mannered Dr. Tanner, and not *vis-à-vis* to the scowling Radicals.

I strode through the passages to the big ante-hall, where I found the Members had begun to gather. One came to me with level eyes, and was about to indulge in an ejaculation, when I said, 'I almost think I know you by your look. You can't be O'Kelly?' He softened, and answered 'Yes,'—upon which, of course, I expressed my surprise that this stout figure could be the slim young man I knew in Madrid, twenty-three years ago. At that time he had just been released from a Cuban prison, and had been sent to Spain by the Cuban authorities. Sickles, the American Minister, obtained his release on *parole*. Now, here he stood, transformed into an elderly legislator! I gently chaffed him that, knowing I had been in London so many years, he had never sought my acquaintance. 'Tell me, honestly,' I said, 'was it not because you had become such an important public man?' It confused him a little, but O'Kelly and I were always pretty direct with each other.

Just near me was the worthy Kimber, of Wandsworth. I turned to him, and said, 'Now come, have some tenderness for a stranger, and tell me something of someone. May we not sit together for this one time, and let me hear from you, who is who?'

'By all means, come,' he said, gaily; and, as it was drawing near noon, we entered the House, and we took our seats near old Sir John Mowbray. I was fairly placed for observation, and sufficiently distant from the Radicals.

'Who is that gentleman opposite to me, next to John Ellis, second in support of Speaker Gully yesterday?'—'That is

Farquharson, of Aberdeen. That light-haired young man is Allen, of Newcastle. The gentleman on the upper bench is Sir E. Gourley, of Sunderland; and the one opposite, on the other bench, is Herbert Gladstone.' But it is unnecessary to go further, you will understand his method. He pointed out quite two-score of people, with some distinctive remark about each.

It was two or three minutes past twelve. A hush fell on the House, the doors were thrown open, and in walked Black Rod, Captain Butler, straight to the Bar, but daintily, as though he were treading consecrated ground. He delivered his message to the Speaker, who sat bareheaded, out of courtesy to the stranger. Black Rod having backed a certain number of paces, the Speaker, William Court Gully, rose, stepped down to the floor, and marched resolutely forward. Members poured out in greater number than yesterday, as though to protect our gallant leader during the perils he was to encounter with the awful Lords. I looked up and down the procession, and, really, I think that not only the Speaker but the nation might have been proud of us. We made such a show! Of course, the halls were crowded with sight-seers.

By the time the Speaker was at the Bar, Kimber and I had got into the Gallery of the Peers' Chamber, and I now looked down upon the scene. The four big-wigs in scarlet and cocked hats were before the Throne. They looked so still that they reminded me of 'Kintu and his white-headed Elders.' [1] The Peers' House was much emptier even than yesterday; I counted five Peers only. The Speaker, backed by the faithful Commons, demanded freedom of debate, free exercise of their ancient privileges, access to Her Majesty's presence on occasion, etc., and when he had ended, the Lord Chancellor, immoveable as yesterday, read out that Her Majesty graciously approved his election as Speaker, and was pleased to grant that her faithful Commons should enjoy, etc., etc., etc.

It was over! Back we strode to our House, policemen bareheaded now. Our Speaker was full Speaker, if you please, and the First Commoner in the realm. We reached our House, the Speaker disappeared, and, when we had taken our seats again, he presently burst upon the scene. We all rose to our feet bareheaded. He was now in full heavy wig and robes.

[1] See 'The Legend of Kintu' in *My Dark Companions* (by Stanley).

He had a statelier pace. Irving could not have done it better on the Stage.

He rose to his chair, ampler, nobler, and sat down heavily; we all subsided, putting on our hats. Up rose the Speaker, and informed us that he had presented our petition to the Throne, and had been graciously received, and all the Commons' privileges had been confirmed. He took the opportunity, he said, while on his feet, of thanking us once more for the honour we had done him. He had not gone far with his speech before he said 'I graciously,' and then corrected himself, one or two Members near me grunting, 'Humph.' What will not nervousness make unhappy fellows say! He meant to say, 'I *sincerely*'!

We were now to prepare to take the Oath. He took it first, Sir Reginald Palgrave delivering it to him. He signed his name on the roll, after which the book was brought to the table, on which were five New Testaments, and five cards on which were these words: —

'I —— do solemnly swear to bear faithful and true allegiance to Her Majesty, Queen Victoria, her heirs and successors according to law. So help me God.'

Balfour, Goschen, Harcourt, Fowler, and another, stood up at the table, held the book up, repeated the oath, kissed the Testament, and each went to subscribe his name on the roll. What an Autograph-book, after all have signed it!

Another five Ministers came, took the Oath, and departed; another five, and then the Privy Councillors, and after them the ordinary Members. And now that stupid English habit of rushing occurred, just as they do everywhere, and on every occasion, at Queen's levées, at railway-stations, and steamer-gangways. An Englishman is a gregarious animal. He must rush, and crowd, and jostle, looking as stupidly-amiable as he can, but, nevertheless, very much bent on getting somewhere, along with the crowd. The table could not be seen for the fifty or more who formed a solid mass. I waited until 1.15 P.M. I then went; the mass was much reduced, but I was driven to the table with force. I looked behind. It was O'Kelly. 'Keep on,' he said; 'I follow the leader.' 'All right, I will pass the Testament to you next.' Two begged for it — Colonel Saunderson was one — but I was firm. 'Very sorry, Colonel, I have promised."

I repeated the Oath, kissed the Testament, and handed the book to O'Kelly, hoping he will be honest with his Oath, and 'bear faithful and true allegiance,' etc.!

I signed my name in the book,—'Henry M. Stanley, North Lambeth,'—was introduced to Mr. Speaker, who knows how to smile, and nod, and shake hands graciously,—passed through, and met the doorkeeper, who said, 'Mr. Stanley, I presume?' 'Yes.' 'Ah, I thought I recognised you. I heard you lecture once at Kensington,' etc., etc.

I was shown the way, got out into the street, took a hansom, and drove to Mr. (now, Sir Henry) Lucy's, at Ashley Gardens, for lunch, where we had an extremely pleasant party. Parted at 3.30, and I travelled home, where I looked over a pile of Blue-books, and wrote this long entry of the second day of Parliamentary life!

The 15th inst. was the beginning of work. I was at Prayers for the first time. Canon Farrar officiated. There was a short exhortation, when we turned our faces to the wall and repeated the Lord's Prayer after him; after which, we had three short prayers, and the 'Grace,' and it was over. I noticed the Members joined heartily on our side in the Lord's Prayer. It is at such times that Englishmen appear best to me. They yield themselves unreservedly to the customs of their forefathers, in utter defiance of the blatant atheism of the age. The ceremony was sweetly simple, yet it moved me; and, in my heart, I honoured every Member the more for it. I thought of Solomon's beautiful Prayer for Understanding, and the object of these supplications was for assistance in the right doing of the legislative work before the House.

The Speaker has grown sensibly, in my estimation, since the first day when he sat in the ranks, on the Radical benches. Then he appeared a clever, legal-looking member, of somewhat high colour, a veritable 'Pleydell' (Scott's 'Guy Mannering'). Though I have seen him in his process of transformation into the First Commoner, I was not quite prepared for this increased respect. I suppose the form and ceremony attending his coming and going, the ready obedience and respect of every Member and official, have somewhat to do with my conversion. I feel as if we were going to be proud of him.

The seconder of the Address was our friend Robertson, of

Hackney, who was in Court dress. He spoke well, but wandered discursively into matters that seemed to have no application to the Address. He referred slightly, by innuendo, to me, as being in the House, with a large knowledge of Africa. Dr. Tanner, contravening the usage of the House, cried out, 'That is Stanley!'

After Robertson, up rose Sir William Harcourt in a ponderous way, extremely old-fashioned and histrionic. I used, in my boyhood, to fancy this style was very grand; but, with more mature intelligence, I cannot say I admire it. It is so markedly stage-like, that I feel a resentful contempt for it. All the time I thought how much better his speech would sound if he left off that ponderous manner, and was more natural. He, no doubt, has the gift of speech; but the style is superfluous. It is slow and heavy, reminding one of the heavy gentlemen of a past age on the boards, playing The Justice; and, naturally, chaff came in freely; for it all seemed part of the comedy. Balfour called it 'easy badinage,' but that is his polite way.

I find that the art of speaking has not been cultivated. Each speaker, so far, has shewn that he possesses matter abundantly — words flow easily, which make readable speeches; but while I did not expect, where it was not needed, any oratorical vehemence or action, I did expect what I might call 'the oratorical deportment,' such as would fit the subject-matter. The speakers have words and intonations that ought, with improved manner, to elevate them in the mind of the listener. Their hands fidget about books and papers, their bodies sway in contrary attitude to the sentiment. I attribute this to want of composure, born of nervousness. Yet such veteran speakers by this time ought to be above being flurried by a sympathetic House.

Balfour came next, with a long speech, which was undoubtedly a relief.

Sir Charles Dilke jumped up after Balfour, and he seemed to me to come nearer to what I had been expecting to see. His voice is showy, but not so sweet as Balfour's. His manner is cool, composed, and more appropriate to the spirit of debate, as I conceive it. There is an absence of all affectation, so that he is vastly preferable to Harcourt. It is a cultivated style;

he seems to be sure of his facts, there is no deprecation, neither is there haughtiness. He is professionally courteous, and holds himself best of all. With the sweet voice of Balfour, his own composure and self-possession, I think Dilke would have been superior to all.

Mr. Seton-Karr was also excellent. Matter, style, bearing, most becoming; no hesitancy, doubt, or awkwardness, visible. Good-tempered, too. His subject was not such as to call for exertion of power; but he was decidedly agreeable.

Up rose Mr. Haldane, and gave us a lecture, extremely bantering in tone. His whole pose was so different from all his predecessors! The solemn ponderousness, and affected respect for the House, of Harcourt; the deprecating manner of Balfour; the professional gravity of Dilke, were so opposite to the gage-throwing style of Haldane. He is a combatant, and only bides his chance.

John Redmond followed, with a plain, matter-of-fact, but good speech. He does not aim at making impressions, but to deliver himself of a duty.

John Dillon was next. He, also, has a thin voice, and speaks well; but, while it would be impossible for him to excite excessive admiration, he wins our respect and friendly tolerance. There is no arrogance; but he impresses one as well-meaning, though blindly devoted to meaner glories for his country, and wholly unconscious of the grander glories that he might obtain for Ireland, if he had good sense.

After Dillon, followed Gerald Balfour, with his brother Arthur's voice and manner. He wins our regard for him personally, and we feel sure as he goes on that the speaker has a lofty idea of his duty, and that he will do it, too, though he die for it. There is not a single phrase that expresses anything of the kind; but the air is unmistakeable: neither bludgeons, nor knives, nor pistols held to his head would make him budge from the performance of duty! It is a noble pair of brothers — Arthur and he! We are all proud of them! They are fine personalities, 'out and out!'

The impossible Dr. Tanner, however, found that he could make objections to them. I was quite thirty-five feet away from him, and yet I heard him call him — Gerald — 'the Baby.' 'Baby does n't know. Oh, they are only snobs,' etc., etc.

There were sixty gentlemen on our side who heard Tanner, but all they said was 'Order! Order!' This, to me, is a wonderful instance of the courtesy to be found in the House. Sixty big, strapping gentlemen can sit still, and hear their chiefs insulted, and called 'snobs,' and only call 'Order! Order!'

'Tay-Pay' followed, which, if it had not been for the brogue, would have been equal to the best speech of the House. He might have been Curran, Shiel, O'Connell, and Burke combined, but the 'brogue' would have reduced his oratory to third-rate. Nevertheless, in the construction, copiousness, command of words, and easy, composed bearing, he deserves to rank with Dilke. But the sibilancy of his words distracts the ear, and that is a pity. He can be animated, though, and at the right time. He made good play with Gerald Balfour's expression of an 'unchanging, and an inflexible, opposition to Home-Rule.' I have always cared for 'Tay-Pay.'

At midnight, we rose and left the House. Before I had finished my pipe, and a chapter of Grote, it was 1 A. M. At 6 A. M. of the 17th, punctually, I was up again, made my own tea, and, at 7 A. M., I was at my desk writing this rapid sketch for my wife!

August 20th. Yesterday was one of the most wearying days I have experienced since leaving Africa. To secure a seat at all, one has to visit the House at an early hour to write his name, and then one had to be on hand for Prayers. The sitting began at 3 P. M., and ended this morning at 2.20 — eleven hours and forty minutes! We voted seven times, which occupied over three hours. We listened to the most dreary twaddle which it has ever been my lot to hear! Tim Healy was up from his seat oftener than any two men, and appeared to be maliciously bent on tiring us all out. He reminds me, when he speaks, of a gentle little zebra, trying to 'moo.' His round glasses, and the vast concave between his cheek-bones and eyebrows, give him this peculiar resemblance. When he turned to us, and said, 'I look across at the boasted Majority, and I cannot say I regard it with awe,' his likeness to a little zebra-cow was impressed on me by the way he brought out the words. It was a perfect, gentle 'moo,' in tone.

I have now learned to know all the most prominent among the Irish Members by sight. There is a marked difference in type between them and our Members. The Celtic, or Iberian, type affords such striking contrasts to the blonde, high-coloured Anglo-Saxon. There is the melancholy-looking John Dillon, who resembles a tall Italian or Spaniard; there is the sanguine Dalziell, like one of the Carlists of my youthful days; there is the quaint-faced Pickersgill, with the raven hair; 'Tay-Pay,' with hair dark as night, who, despite his London training, is still only a black-haired Celt; and many more singular types, strongly individualistic. While, on our side, Sir William Houldsworth best represents the florid-faced gentlemen who form the sturdy, long-suffering Majority.

The Obstructive tactics, about which I heard so much in the past, have been pursued for three days now, most skilfully. Like an unsophisticated new Member, I have sat watching curiously, speaker after speaker rising to his feet on the Opposition side, wondering why they showed so much greater energy than our people, and expecting to be rewarded with a great speech; but so far I have waited in vain. It dawned upon me, after a while, that they were all acting after a devised plan. There was absolutely nothing worth listening to in anything any one of them said, but it served admirably to waste time, and to exasperate, or, rather, fatigue one.

Towards midnight, the patience of the Government seemed worn out, and from that hour, until 2.20 A. M., we were kept marching to the lobbies, and being counted. Each count occupies from twenty minutes to half an hour. We went through the performance four times in succession, and our majorities were double the total number of the minority.

I was so tired, when I came home, that I felt as if I had undergone a long march. The close air of the House I feel is most deleterious to health, for the atmosphere of the small chamber after the confinement of about three hundred and fifty Members for eleven hours, must needs be vitiated.

We are herded in the lobbies like so many sheep in a fold; and, among my wonders, has been that such a number of eminent men could consent voluntarily to such a servitude, in which I cannot help seeing a great deal of degradation.

The criminal waste of precious time, devotion to antique customs, the silent endurance of evils, which, by a word, could be swept away, have afforded me much matter of wonder.

There are Irish M. P.'s who must feel amply rewarded, in knowing that, through sheer excess of impudence only, they can condemn so many hundreds of their betters to bend servilely to their behests! At many of the divisions, I have been almost smothered by Hicks-Beach, the Marquis of Lorne, Austin Chamberlain, Arthur Balfour, Tom Ellis, Arnold-Forster, Henry Chaplin, George Curzon, Lord Compton, Sydney Gedge, Lord Dalkeith, Coningsby Disraeli, and scores of great land-owners and others; temperature in the nineties. While, on the other side of our cage, stood Tim Healy in the cool hall, smiling inwardly at this servility on the part of so many noble and worthy men!

But, if I pity this dumb helplessness of our great Majority, and marvel at its meek submissiveness to the wholly unnecessary, I pity still more that solitary figure in the Speaker's Chair, who has been sitting, and standing, from 3 P. M. to 2.20 A. M. One said to me, 'What won't six thousand pounds a year do?' Well, I swear that I am above it, if the reward was double; because I should not survive it long, and hence would derive no benefit from the big pay. I pity him from my heart, and I hope sincerely that his constitution is strong enough to bear it. No mortal can sit eleven hours, on a rich diet, and long survive.

August 23rd. The vote in connection with the Foreign Office, on the 21st, formed a legitimate excuse for my rising to deliver a few remarks, in answer to Sir Charles Dilke. I see those remarks are called my Maiden Speech, but as I made no preparation — as I really did not suspect there would be any occasion for interposing in the debate — I do not think they deserve to be called a speech.

Sir Charles, in that professional manner I have already alluded to, began with drawing attention to Armenia and China, and, as though he was again about to set out on a tour through Greater Britain, soon entered upon the question of the evacuation of Egypt; and, then airily winging his way across the dark continent, lighted on West Africa and its affairs, dipped into the liquor traffic; then suddenly flew towards Uganda, and, after a short rest, continued his flight to Zanzibar and Pemba.

As an exhibition of the personal interest he took in matters abroad, in little-known countries, no fault could be found with his discursive flights; that is, if the Committee were sitting for the purpose of judging his proficiency and knowledge. But, as the House takes no interest in any one's personal qualifications, his speech was, I thought, superfluous.

It is not easy, however, to reply in the House, all at once. Half a score of Members are on the 'qui-vive' to discharge upon the submissive body their opinions. I perceive as each would-be speaker rises to attract the Chairman's attention that his thoughts are abundant; but, when he is permitted to speak, the thoughts do not flow so smoothly out of his lips as they may have coursed through his mind! If he is a new Member, he is a pitiable object at such a time. Even the old Members are not always happy.

Well, after Sir Charles Dilke sat down, our friend James Bryce rose, who, I must admit, speaks fluently, as well he might, with his great experience as a Lecturer, Member, and Minister. I do not think he is at all nervous; at least, I should not judge him to be so from his manner.

After him, rose Mr. McKenna to ask about Siam. I had made a little move, but I was too late, having not quite concluded in my own mind that I ought to speak.

When he finished, Commander Bethell had the floor. These old Members shoot to their feet with a sudden spring, like Jack-in-the-Box. He spoke upon Egypt and the new countries of Central Africa like one desirous of obtaining information upon matters which puzzled him.

Parker Smith, sitting beside me, was on his feet in an instant; but what he said seemed to me rather an indistinct echo of what his brother C. S. Smith (formerly Consul at Zanzibar) thinks of Zanzibar slavery.

I rose, a trifle after he finished; but the veteran, 'Tommy' Bowles, was ahead of me, and what he said was fatal to the repose, and concentration, of mind necessary for a speech. He speaks excellently, and delivers good, solid matter. My surprise at his power, and my interest in what he said, was so great, that I could not continue the silent evolution of thought in which I should have engaged, had he been less interesting and informing; and here I ought to say, that I do not join with some in their dislike of him. He is not a man to be despised.

As a public speaker, he comes very near in ability to Chamberlain, who is, without doubt, the best debater in the House. Given the fitting subject, suited to his manner, Mr. Bowles would certainly prove that my opinion of him as a Parliamentary debater is correct. He is quite cool, uses good language, and handles his arguments with skill. Then, again, there is no oddity or awkwardness of bearing, to neutralize the effect of his words. As I supposed he was drawing to a close, I resolutely collected my straying thoughts, and excluded what he was saying out of my mind; and, as he was sitting down, I stood up, and Mr. Lowther called out 'Mr. Stanley' in a firm, clear voice.

It is not a pleasant feeling to look down from the third row upon an intelligent and critical Opposition, who, you feel, are going to pay more attention to the manner than the matter of your speech. The reporters and editorial Members, in remarking upon how I spoke, gave free rein to their fancies. 'Tay-Pay,' as you must have seen in the pink 'Sun' I sent you, has excelled all the rest in his imaginative description of my deportment. You will wonder, perhaps, when I say that the picture of me, which he gives, is far from representing my inwardness. All my fellow-members have a remarkable gift of easy verbosity. There is a small kernel of fact in almost every sentence they deliver, but it is often indistinguishable, through the vast verbiage.

The veriest trifle of commonplace fact is folded round and round with tissue after tissue of superfluity. If a Member wished to say that he had seen a rat, he seems to be unable to declare the fact nakedly, but must hedge it about with so many deprecatory words that you are apt to lose sight of the substance. He says: 'I venture to say, with the permission of the House, that unless my visual organs deceive me, and the House will bear me out when I say that my powers of ocular perception are not of the most inferior kind, that,' etc., etc.

To nervous people, this verbiage serves as a shelter, until they can catch the idea they are groping for. I wanted some such shelter badly, for it requires a strong effort to marshal out your ideas and facts, so that there shall be no awkward break in the speech. Gladstone used to shelter to excess; he circumvented, to a weary length; and often required more than one sentence before he could muster courage to approach the fact.

Well! I have not got the art! First, I have not the patience; and, then, again, I disdain the use of the art, on principle. I want to say what I have to say, right out, and be done with it, — which does not tend to elegance.

Considering these, my Parliamentary imperfections, my facts rolled out without being over-detached. Some say I spoke rapidly. They are wrong. I spoke at the ordinary rate of public speech, and distinctly. By the kindness of the House, I was made to feel that I was not saying anything foolish or silly. That was the main point, and inspired me with just enough confidence to prevent an ignominious breakdown. I sat down with the feelings of one who had made a deep dive, and came up just in time to relieve the straining lungs. Members all said that I had done well. I was congratulated right and left. Well, honestly, I did not know whether I was doing well or ill! I had a few sentiments to utter, and I felt relieved that they were not botched.

In the afternoon, Parker Smith got up, and remarked that, in what I said, I had been 'trading on my reputation.' Fancy a young fellow, sitting next to you, getting up and saying such a thing, — and he a veteran Parliamentarian! I chose my time, and got up to say that I was wholly unaware of having uttered a word calling for such a remark; and I begged the honourable gentleman not to make any more such!

Yesterday, however, I did not make a brilliant figure. Ashmead-Bartlett, a truly busy bee, asked a question in regard to the hanging of Stokes, an English trader in East Africa. I, not wishing that the House should express too great an indignation, got up a question which, while it did justice to poor Stokes's merits, showed how rash and misguided he had been in consorting with Kibonge, the murderer of Emin Pasha, and supplying him with arms. But the question was too long, and the Speaker checked me when I was near the end of it.

I have not been clear of a headache all this week. The atmosphere in the House, during this great heat, is simply poisonous. I do not wonder, now, at the pasty, House-of-Commons complexion; four hundred people breathing for ten or eleven hours the air of one room must vitiate it. Then my late hours, 2 and 3 A. M., simply torture me. One night, I was relieved by Labouchere pairing with me; and so got home by midnight, and slept six hours. On all other nights, I have not been able to obtain more than four hours' sleep.

Yesterday, I paired with Labouchere, for the rest of the Session from to-night; so I shall lie in bed all day to-morrow, to rest; and, after finishing some private work, shall depart on my holiday.

Thus ends this Journal of Stanley's first week in Parliament.

CHAPTER XXIII

SOUTH AFRICA

JANUARY 1st, 1896. We have begun the New Year badly! The hurricane blast I predicted has burst out in the form of a denunciatory message from President Cleveland upon the subject of the Venezuela claims. Though it was very unstatesmanlike of Cleveland to word his message with such violence, we have given some provocation.

Time after time have various Secretaries of State written, urging us to come to some agreement with the Venezuelan Government, and offered their friendly arbitration, or mediation, as it was not conducive to good-will between us and the Americans, to have such long-standing grievances acting as an irritant between the Americans and the English people. Secretary Bayard's letter of appeal ought to have moved us to instant action, on account of its undoubtedly friendly sentiments, written with such earnestness and kindly feeling. The turning of a deaf ear to such a letter as this no doubt made the Americans believe that nothing but a thunder-clap, such as Cleveland has given, would rouse us to consider the matter seriously.

The English papers have been quite taken aback by it; and, here and there, some fools are talking of resistance! One man, who holds a high office in the State, talked to me last night of the manner we should fight the Americans! Poor old soul, he did not expect the contempt with which I extinguished his martial ardour. Why! if Venezuela and Guiana were both wiped out of the map, America and England would suffer from it far less than from recent speculative dishonesty. In addition to this shock from America, we are considerably disturbed by the Armenian atrocities, and what action we might be urged to take in behalf of the oppressed Armenians. The Radicals are very bellicose, and would applaud Lord Salisbury if he sent a fleet up the Dardanelles. To-day, we have news that Dr. Jameson has invaded the Transvaal, with a small force between four hundred and six hundred strong! The details are meagre, but the impression is that he is alone in this wild escapade. A 'Sun' interviewer has asked me my opinion in the matter, and I have said frankly that it is our duty to drive him back quicker than he went in. It is not so very long ago that I entertained both Jameson and Rhodes here. I never suspected that either of them would have been concerned in such a harum-scarum act as this!

July 7th, Tuesday. Dined with Mr. and Mrs. Yates Thompson. The Jameson Raid was very much discussed; and I found myself, in this instance, quite in accord with the Radicals whom I met there.

July 9th. Dined with Lord James of Hereford. I was surprised at his saying that there were extenuating circumstances for Jameson's act, but it is evident that his legal acumen is awry. Under no circumstances would we profit by this Raid, however successful it might have been.

Stanley greatly rejoiced at the arrival of our little boy, Denzil, and bought picture-books for him, and toys suited to a child of four! In 1896, during a long and serious illness, what best pleased Stanley was to have the baby placed beside him on the bed. One day, when the child was there, Stanley looked up at me and said, 'Ah, it is worth while now . . . to get well!'

It was these frequent attacks of gastralgia, or gastritis, complicated by malaria, which made me so dread his returning to Africa. After our marriage, I felt no security. He himself thought he would have to go back to the Congo, for a time, 'to put things right.' But I knew that he ought never to return there.

Stanley was constantly being attacked by fever and these internal pains, which came without any warning, and with such intensity, that breathing was impeded. The first attack was in the Forest of Central Africa, and he describes his illness in 'Darkest Africa,' an illness attributable, possibly, to the poor diet, and, afterwards, to starvation.

Two days before our marriage he was taken ill, in the same way, an illness that lasted many weeks.

During Stanley's malaria attacks, the shivering preceding the hot stage was so violent that the bed he lay on would shake, and the glasses on the table vibrate and ring. I might come in from a walk, and, not seeing Stanley in his library, run upstairs to his room, and find him in bed, covered with blankets, quilts, even great-coats; with chattering teeth, and hurried speech, he would bid me get hot-water bottles to pack round him. Then, when the cold fit had passed, and the heat had reached its maximum, he would speak to me re-assuringly, and tell me not to fear, that all would be well; that it was only 'Africa in me,' and I must get the quinine ready. The terrible sweating over, he would take twenty to twenty-five grains of quinine, and . . . wait! So I came to know exactly what to do; but I vowed, in my heart, that he should never return to the country which had taken so much of his splendid vitality; for Stanley had had three attacks of hæmaturic fever, in Africa, and more severe malaria fevers than he could number.

In June, 1896, we arranged to visit Spain, as he wanted to show me Madrid, Toledo, etc., etc.; but, in the train, four hours before we got to Madrid, he was seized with one of these mysterious gastric attacks, and when we arrived, soon after midnight, he was hardly conscious, from extreme pain.

I could not speak Spanish, and knew no one in Madrid. We went to the principal hotel, on the Puerta del Sol; and there I waited till morning, when a clever Austrian doctor came to my assistance, but there seemed little we could do. Day by day, Stanley grew weaker; and, at last, in desperation, I decided, ill as he was, to get him back to England. By the time we reached Paris, Stanley was rather better, and, for two days, he was free from the pain and intermittent fever. But it was only a short lull, for the spasms returned, with redoubled violence, and it was with the greatest difficulty that I succeeded in getting him back to our home in London.

There, I nursed him for three months, until he gradually recovered. Thus he would enjoy spaces of perfect health, with intervals of the old trouble. I think Stanley feared nothing in the world as he feared those first ominous stabs of pain; but when the spasms were steadily recurrent, and no doctor could give him any relief, Stanley accepted the pain and weakness, silently and stoically. Here, for instance, is an entry in his Journal, in 1897:—

> Pain has commenced — unable to take even milk without sickness; am resigned for a long illness — it is now inevitable; shall not be able to attend Parliament again this Session.

I knew by the sound of his voice, when he called me in the middle of the night, that the pain had come; sometimes it left quite suddenly, and we looked at each other, I, pale with fear, lest it should return. In 1897, the attack recorded above did not last, as he had feared, but, in 1898, at Cauterets, in the Pyrenees, he was again taken ill. He writes in his Journal, August 15th:—

> Felt the first severe symptoms of a recurring attack. Have had two attacks of fever, and now have steady pain since Sunday night, but rose to-day.
>
> August 17th, LUCHON. On arriving, went to bed at once, for my pains threatened to become unbearable.

September 11. BIARRITZ. All I know of Luchon is what I have gained during two short walks in the intervals of illness. On arriving here, I went straight to bed.

October 1st.—Left Biarritz for Paris; have been in bed the whole time.

October 10th.—Have been ill all the time in Paris; returned to London after the dreadful holidays.

When we returned to London, I felt very near despair, the starvation diet Stanley was kept on, had now reduced him to such a state of weakness he could not sit up in bed. Skilful massage, however, and an immediate, generous diet, restored Stanley, as by magic, to perfect health. I return now to the Journal for 1896.

December 21st, 1896. BRIGHTON. Warmest greetings to darling little Denzil, our own cherub! Possibly, I think too much of him. If I were not busy with work and other things, I should undoubtedly dwell too much on him, for, as I take my constitutional, I really am scarce conscious that I am in Brighton. For, look where I may, his beautiful features, lightened up with a sunny smile, come before my eyes all the time! I see him in your arms, and I marvel greatly at my great happiness in possessing you two! Believe it or not, as you like, but my heart is full of thankfulness that I have been so blessed.

Denzil is now inseparable from you — and you from him.—Together, you complete the once vague figure of what I wished; and now the secret of my inward thoughts is realised, a pre-natal vision, embodied in actual existence.

Now take up Denzil, look full into his angelic face, and deep down into those eyes so blue, as if two little orbs formed out of the bluest heaven were there, and bless him with your clean soul, untainted by any other thought than that which wishes him the best God can give him. At present, he is of such as are the beings of God's heaven, purity itself. — May he grow to noble manhood and serve God zealously!

Stanley left Southampton on October 9, 1897, per Union steamer 'Norman,' for South Africa, to assist in the opening of the Bulawayo Railway, by invitation of the citizens of Bulawayo.

October 13th, 1897, on Board. There are several wee things in arms on board, and I shake hands with them all in turns, every morning, as my 'devoir' to our Denzil. The white frocks remind me of him. A baby cries, — there is a child at home, with just such a voice, sometimes; and then he trots into memory's view, looks up brightly, and is gone. I can get a hundred views of him in a minute; it is, in fact, a mental kinematograph, and thus I see him continually floating in and out of my recollection. You are, alternately, recalled. My last thoughts on going to sleep are of you. I mutter a prayer; commit you to God, take another glance at the little baby-face, and am asleep.

S. S. NORMAN, October 25th, 1897. Ah — my dear! a little baby, nine months old, was buried yesterday morning at eight — she died from meningitis! She was perfectly well, until long after we passed Cape Verd. I had often encountered the father carrying his little girl, and dancing her gently up and down in his arms. He was a picture of happiness. Then the baby pined and sickened; for two days there was great anxiety; the third day there was but little hope left, and, in the night, the child died. The next morning the little body was consigned to the everlasting deep!

After visiting Rhodesia, Stanley took a short tour, through the Orange Free State, the Transvaal, and Natal. I can only give brief selections from his letters to me, giving, however, in full, his letter describing Krüger, which, for discernment of character, and political foresight, is certainly most remarkable, having been written to me two years before the war.

JOHANNESBURG, November 20th, 1897. Dined at the Club, where I learnt several lessons. In Bulawayo, Englishmen had rather an exalted feeling, as of men who had suddenly been made rich, and whose prospects were delightful. In Johannesburg, the feeling is different. I find them subdued, querulous, and recriminatory. They blame everybody but themselves. They recapitulate their failures to obtain justice, the indifference of the English colonial policy. They tell instances of Boer oppression, corruption, tyranny, and hypocrisy, with grinding teeth, and do not forget to allude to the mistakes of Jameson, the tactlessness, folly, and unhappy consequences of the Raid; but they are silent as regards their own conduct, and seem to think they are as hardly dealt with by the British Government, as by Krüger and his handful of oligarchs.

I wish I could repeat, word for word, what I have been told in very eloquent language; but, as I could not take my note-book out at the dinner-table, I can only say that I have been much impressed with all I have heard, and feel genuine sympathy for them, which makes me reluctant to wound them; but, the truth is, there are too many leaders, and each leader pulls a contrary way to his fellows; consequently, they have no concrete, well-considered policy. I quite agree with them that our Government is to blame for allowing the Convention to be broken so repeatedly; and that their action is not what that of the Germans would have been, for instance, had they so many subjects maltreated, and desired their Treaty rights.

But, though I would speak strongly of the weakness of England, I think that the Uitlanders are also to blame in not acting in concert, upon a well-arranged plan, compelling Krüger to come out of his shell, and force things quicker to an issue between England and the Transvaal.

I am assuming, of course, that the Johannesburgers feel all that they say, about oppression, tyranny, their feeling of desperation, etc., etc.; but all their pitiful tales of distresses endured, injuries inflicted on persons of property, audacious breaches of the Convention, and so on, will not induce England to wake up to her duty, nor move the Government to action. A Government, even that like the Salisbury-Chamberlain, at present in power, must have strong excuses to sanction an undertaking that may cost millions of money, and thousands of lives. It will certainly be no child's play to use compulsion on a man like Krüger. They would rather endure much than go to war; and yet, if the Uitlanders let the Unionists go out of office, without convincing them that they ought no longer to endure this state of things, they must try other things than mere telegraphic reports to the newspapers.

At the dinner-table, I told them all very frankly my opinion on the matter; and said, 'I was reminded of the words, "It is expedient that one man should die for many."' 'That is to say,' I explained, 'English people cannot be moved by these reports of breaches of the Convention. You must convince them that the sense of your injuries is so great you are willing to brave death rather than bear with what you consider intolerable.' 'But how can we do anything?' they asked.

'We are not allowed arms; not even a pistol is allowed to come to the Transvaal.'

'You do not want arms of any kind,' I said. 'I have seen enough to know that you could not do much with arms. You do not even want a pen-knife, as a weapon of offence. You simply want to prove to England your grievances are real, and your patience exhausted. Let England see that you dare to resist this iniquitous rule under which you suffer; and that you are defying the powers that be, risking liberty and property; and her opinion will be swiftly changed. Let every instance wherein you think you are wronged — which you can prove is against the Convention — be marked by resistance, not active, but passive. You called the Convention just now the charter of your rights: on the strength of these rights, let your resistance be based. The Boer officials will demand why such conduct; you will calmly say. They will pooh-pooh, and threaten you; you will refuse compliance. They will use compulsion of a kind; they will imprison or expel you. There will be ten, twenty, forty, a hundred examples of this punishment. The Uitlanders should continue the same resolute attitude of resistance, yielding not a jot.

'The Boers will soon perceive that this is serious; rather than expel a whole population, they must either come to terms, or try what violence can do. If the latter, some of you must become martyrs to your sense of what is right. Those martyrs will buy the freedom of the others, for England will be calling to arms. We all know that England ought to have acted as became her on the first breach of the Convention; but she resorted to discussion, and in discussion, at length, she has been beaten. Time, and time again, has the Convention been broken; and the answers England gave to all of them, are — a pile of Blue-books! The Boers can go on at that game for ever. The Boer head has become very big. The self-esteem of Krüger has grown intolerably large, to reduce which will require something more than reason. But you know, whether with an individual or a nation, how hard it is to suddenly change from courteous argument to the deadly arbitrament of force. Something is wanted to rouse the passions to that pitch. I know of nothing that will do it quicker than an act of violence by the Boers. When the Boers resort to violence, it will be all up with them. If I know anything of the English character, the first act of violence will not be committed by them,' etc., etc.

Colonel Saunderson, who was a fellow-guest, agreed with all I said.

As we walked to the Grand Central Hotel, it was the Colonel's opinion that the Uitlanders were not of that stuff from which martyrs are made. I agree, but, 'even worms will turn.'

November 23rd, 1897. Took train for Pretoria. I had a letter of introduction to Mr. Marks, of Lewis & Marks, who took me to a kind of bachelor house he keeps.

November 24th. Mr. Marks took me to President Krüger's house at 5.30 A. M. It is an unusually early time to visit, but the old man is an early riser, and is at his best in the morning.

He was sitting on the stoep, with two old Members of the Rand, taking his coffee, before leaving on an electioneering journey. When Marks told him of my desire for an interview, he motioned my conductor to take me to the reception saloon, which opened out on the stoep. A grandson of Krüger's showed me a chair. It happened to be directly in front of a full-length portrait of the President, so I was forced to look with wonder at the bad painting, and libellous likeness of the man I had come to see.

Presently Krüger came in, and seated himself under his portrait. Now, as he was the man who held the destinies of South Africa in his hand, I regarded him with interest, in order to divine what the future would be, from what I could gather of his character, by studying his features, gestures, and talk. In the past, I have often made fair guesses at the real man. As reporter, special correspondent in several campaigns, and in various cities, and as traveller over five continents, I have had opportunities enough; I found, when in the presence of African chiefs of whose language I was ignorant, that, long before the interpreter had spoken, I had rightly guessed what the chiefs had said, and I could often correct the interpreter. When two civilized men meet, both being strangers, absolutely independent, unconcerned, uninterested in each other further than mere civility requires, the little points that betray character, mood, or temper are not seen; and the disposition of human nature in general is to put the most civil construction possible upon one's fellow-creatures and their ways.

While the morning greetings were being interchanged, and my eyes kept glancing from Krüger's face to that of the portrait, the real man appeared loveable, compared with the portrait. His features, though terribly plain and worn, were amiable and human; and, if I had gone away after this, I would have carried with me the ordinary impression, which I have seen countless times in newspapers, that Krüger was not a bad kind of man; a little obstinate, perhaps, but, on the whole, well-meaning, and so on. But, in order to get a glimpse of the possible future of the relations between him and the Uitlanders, I began to praise Johannesburg, its growth, and the enterprise of the people, and I asked Mr. Krüger whether or not things were settling down more peacefully now. This was the beginning of an interview which, while it lasted, revealed Krüger, the man, sufficiently to me; so that if he were an African chief, and I had dealings with him, it would have taught me *exactly what to do,* and how to provide against every eventuality.

In short, I soon saw that he was a choleric and passionate old man, uncommonly obstinate, determined within himself that his view was the right one, and that no peaceful issue could be expected, unless his demands were complied with, and most implicit trust given to his word. Now, if the welfare of my expedition were at stake, and I thought my force was equal to his, or enough to enable me to inflict severe punishment upon him should he attempt to carry out his passionate words, I should not have parted from him without some better guarantee than trust in his mere word; and, if the guarantee would not be given, I should have gone away with the feeling that the old man meant mischief, and that it was incumbent on me to take every precaution against him.

Mr. Krüger's manner changed immediately I had mentioned Johannesburg and its people. His voice and its varying intonations, every line in his face, betrayed the strongest resentment; and, when I suggested that the smallest concessions to their demands would modify that attitude of hostility to him which angered him, he became the incarnation of fury, and his right hand went up and down like a sledge-hammer, and from his eyes, small and dull as they were, flashed forth the most implacable resolve that surrender must be on their side, not his!

When an old man like this, — he is seventy-four, — who, for the last sixteen years, at least, has had his own way, and been looked up to by Boer and Uitlander, as the 'man of the situation,' — when he has made up his mind upon having something, it is not likely that any other course than his own can he believe to be the right one. When we think of what has happened these last sixteen years — his visits to London, his negotiations in Pretoria and London concerning the Convention, the way everyone, Englishman and Boer, has yielded to him, the adulation paid to him for his success, one cannot wonder that he believes that in this matter of the Uitlander's rights, as in the things that went before, *his* methods, *his* style, and *his* way are the best and safest!

This has begotten in him an arrogance so large that, before he can be made sensible that he is wrong, his fierce pride must be humbled; his head has grown so big with this vain belief in his prowess in battle. His victories over Gladstone, Lord Salisbury, and others of the same calibre, the implicit trust of the Boers in him, and in his unconquerability, have been such, that, I am convinced, there is no room in that brain for one grain of common-sense to be injected into it.

His whole behaviour seems to say very clearly to the observer, 'What do I care for your Chamberlain, with his Milners and Greenes? They shall yield to me first. I don't care a snap of the finger for them; let them do their worst; better men than they have tried and failed, and they will fail too.' The unmitigated contempt for people who try conciliation has only to be seen in Krüger, for one to know that the old man is an impossible creature; and that he is only made implacable and fierce by beseeching and conciliating.

A recollection of the telegram asking 'How is Mrs. Krüger?' almost made me laugh aloud, in Krüger's presence. *Such* a telegram, to *this* kind of man!! Why! if a strong man, armed, and covered with impenetrable armour, were to suddenly rise in Krüger's sight, and boldly advance, and seize him by the scruff of the neck, and shake him, until a little of that wind of vanity, that has so inflated him, escaped, he would not have long to wait before Krüger would be amenable to reason and decent conversation! But the fellow must find himself faced by force!

An exchange of opinions is now impossible, as he flies directly into a passion at the mere suggestion that a different kind of treatment to the Uitlanders would secure to him the Presidency for life, and remove all fear of friction. For it is something connected with his own self-interest, probably a fear that the votes of the Uitlanders would upset him from the Chair he fills, drive him out of the house he occupies, diminish his importance and his affluent income,—all this is at the bottom of his extreme irascibility and stormy impatience when the Uitlanders are mentioned.

The interview did not last twenty-five minutes, but I had seen enough, and heard more than enough, to convince me that this was an extreme case, which only force could remedy.

You ask me to describe Krüger minutely. Well, he is very like his photographs; I should know him among ten thousand in the street; but to see and talk with him reveals scores of little things no photographs can give. You have seen lots of stout-bodied old Parisian concierges; and I dare say you have seen them in their seedy black clothes, when going out on a visit; put a little top-hat on one of them, give him stooping shoulders, with a heavy, lumbering, biggish body, and you will know Krüger at once! Well! let him sit *vis-à-vis* to you; put much obstinacy into a face that is unusually large, with an inch of forehead and two small eyes; let the figure sink in his chair, with an attitude of determination in every line, and give him a big briarwood pipe, which is held in his left hand, and there you have him!

Aged statesmen are liable, at a certain age, to develop symptoms of the refractoriness and arbitrariness of disposition which eventually makes them unsuitable for the requirements of the country, and impossible to their colleagues in the Cabinet. Well, 'that's what's the matter' with Krüger! He is quite past reasoning with. Neither Mr. Chamberlain, nor Sir Alfred Milner, nor Mr. Greene, will ever succeed with him; and I don't know any three men who so deserve to succeed as they. They are all capital fellows, brilliant, able, and deserving. Mr.

Chamberlain has a deal of perseverance and convictions of his own; but, ten minutes' talk with Krüger would give him the knowledge, at first-hand, that one should have to be able to deal effectively with a political opponent; and, as Sir Alfred Milner has not seen Krüger either, these two able men are really dealing haphazard with the President.

What amazes me is the extraordinary hopefulness of the men I meet. Many residents here have seen and known Krüger intimately; and yet, no sooner has one project for getting their rights been baffled, than they have some new scheme afoot. They have tried everything but the right thing, and will continue to do so. If Englishmen on the spot hardly realise the Boer cunning and determination, how impossible it is for the Englishman at home to do so!

Well! much talk with all kinds of South Africans and my talk with Krüger has opened my eyes to the perplexities of the situation. I heartily pity the Colonial Secretary, and I foresee that the Transvaal will continue to disturb his Office. The Boers of the Cape, the Boers of the Orange Free State, and the Boers of the Transvaal, will combine, if any inconsiderate step is taken by the Colonial Office.

What, then, is to be done? Keep still and be patient! Nothing more; for these people of South Africa, English and all, are exasperatingly contentious. The longer we are quiet, the more irascible they will get with each other; our cues must be obtained from South Africa, and if the Johannesburgers want us to help them, they must be braver, more united, and more convinced of the inutility of their unaided efforts; nay, were every Englishman and Afrikander in South Africa united, they could not alone, unaided, stand against the Boers.

Krüger will plod on his vindictive way, and he must, in time, wear out the Johannesburgers' patience. They will do something to rouse the Boer temper; there will be some attack by the Boers, — confiscation of property, of territory. We shall be asked if we are indifferent to our countrymen's distress, and so . . . the cup will be full, and the time will have come. That is the only way I see whereby the Transvaal is to be saved from King Krüger.

Mind you, this is Krüger's fourth term of office that he is seeking. Twenty years! Rule for so long a time makes for

Despotism; and, in an old man of his unbending nature, it makes for an accumulation of mistakes, caused by temper, arrogance, and conceit; it makes for the usual political calamity which precedes the salvation of a country or nation.

Marks and I left the house, and while Krüger hastened to get ready for his electioneering journey, I was being shewn the way to the Pretoria Club, where I was cordially received, and inducted into the opinions of other residents of the Boer capital.

I have met no one who can give me what I should call an intelligent idea of the outcome of this tension between the Boers and British. They all confine themselves to commonplace things and ideas. Krüger, Reitz, Joubert, whom I have seen to-day, are concerned only with what they want, and must have. Leyds, Kotze, Marks, are all afraid to engage in a discussion of any kind, and are really the most unlikely people to do so. The Club people, not knowing who may be listening, do not care to talk, and drop into monosyllables when politics are broached, though, with officious zeal, they allowed me to see, that, in their opinion, the Transvaal was ever so much better in many respects than England. Marks is a broker, who looks after certain interests of the President.

The population dwelling in the hollow below the dominating heights around, which are bristling with cannon, I presume have no thoughts worth anything, and are filled with content every time they look up at those defiant forts above their city.

I went to see Conyngham Greene, the English Political Resident here. He has a very nice house, situated in charming surroundings of green lawns and flowering shrubberies, and he is himself very agreeable and pleasant. He is too young to have any profound view into the meaning of things. I dare say he does his duty efficiently, which is to report, day after day, upon the state of affairs, as he believes it to be; but, though this may be satisfactory to his chief, the High Commissioner, Sir Alfred Milner, Mr. Greene's opinions appear to be far from being decided one way or the other. My impression is, that he thinks the present tension is not likely to last long, that it is a mere phase, consequent upon the sore feelings caused by the Jameson Raid; and, in short, that, though Krüger appears somewhat unappeasable and unrelenting, at present, he is sure to come round, by and by. It is so like what I have heard in England and at the Cape. 'Yes, Krüger is terribly obstinate, but he is a dear old fellow, you know, all the same; and he will be all right, give him time.'

But that is not *my* opinion. Krüger is not that sort of man at all! He must meet his master, and be *overcome*.

The week before I arrived at the Cape, that is to say, only a few weeks ago, Sir Alfred Milner made a speech in Cape Colony, wherein he is reported to have said that it was all 'humbug and nonsense for anyone to say that reconciliation was impossible, and that to expect good feeling between the two races was hopeless.' It may be supposed that he was only re-echoing what Mr. Conyngham Greene had written in his reports.

Mr. Chamberlain has spoken in the same spirit, in the House of Commons, because of Sir Alfred Milner's views as conveyed to him in despatches. I feel positive that if Sir Alfred Milner and Mr. Chamberlain were to see Krüger, face to face, they would drop that sanguine, optimistic tone, and quickly and resolutely prepare for a storm.

Despite all the wish that Chamberlain, Milner, and Greene may be right, the good-will I feel to all three of them, and the belief in their abilities, an *inner voice* tells me that they are all three wrong, that the Johannesburgers who share their views are living in a fool's paradise. Krüger will never, no never, give way to anything that is no harder than mere words! The man must be made to bow that inflexible spirit to a temper that is more hardened, a spirit that is more unyielding, and a force capable of carving its way, undeviatingly, to its object. Whence that force will come, it is impossible to say. I feel very much afraid that it will not come from England. England is losing her great characteristics, she is becoming too effeminate and soft from long inactivity, long enfeeblement of purpose, brought about by indolence and ease, distrust of her own powers, and shaken nerves. It is at such times that nations listen to false prophets, cranks, faddists, and weak sentimentalists.

It will take time, anyhow, to convince England that she ought to do anything; it will take her still longer to provide the means for doing her duty effectively; it will take longer still to understand the nature and bigness of the task which it is her bounden duty to undertake, and so be in a position to say with the necessary firmness of voice to Krüger, that he must come to terms, *immediately!*

People in England, for some reason, cannot be induced to believe in the reality of the Johannesburg grievances; they profess to regard them as a community of Jewish speculators in mines; and even the failure to assist Jameson in the Raid, etc., etc., has, unfortunately, rather deepened disbelief in their complaints, which they please to consider as nothing more than the usual methods resorted to by Stock-Exchange speculators to advertise their wares, and alarm investors, so that for their own ends they may make a 'grand coup!' But both Jew and Christian now are of the same mind as to the hopelessness of their condition, unless Krüger can be made to conform to the terms of the Convention of 1884.

Of course, it is possible that England may be roused to action sooner than expected, by some act of the Uitlanders. I believe that if the English people were to hear that the Uitlanders in their desperate state had resolved upon braving Krüger and his Boers to the death, and would show the necessary courage to bear martyrdom, conviction would come quicker to English minds than from years of futile despatch-writing. If the Uitlanders thus braved him, I feel sure that Krüger would deal with them in the harshest and most summary way, and, in doing so, he would be simply setting every instrument at work required to open the eyes and ears of Englishmen to his obdurate, implacable, and cruel nature; and, once they were convinced of this, Krüger's downfall would not be far off.

Now, of course, after the insight I have gained into the heart of the question, I confess I am not free from feeling a large contempt for my countrymen for being so slow-witted and deaf to the cries of the Uitlanders; and, yet, as I write this, I cannot see why I should feel such contempt for them, for certainly my own sympathies were but sluggish when first I accepted this opportunity of coming to South Africa.

To speak the truth, they were not so keen as to wish England might go to war with the Transvaal. But now I see things in a different light, and I shall carry away with me from the Transvaal, a firm conviction that the English people have been systematically misled about Krüger and his Boers. Gladstonianism, and that gushing, teary tone adopted by the sentimental Peace-at-any-price section of our nation, are solely responsible for the persecutions and insults to which our people have been subject, since 1884, in the Transvaal. If it should come to fighting, there will be much killing done, and *this will be entirely due to sentimentalists at home.*

The self-interest of men, who would be self-seekers even under the heel of the tyrant, has also largely contributed to mislead the people. Cowardice actuates those who would coax Krüger out of his sulks, and prefer to fawn on him instead of resenting his cruel treatment of his fellow-countrymen. They profess to believe in the piety of the Boers, and their love of peace; they dwell on Krüger's attachment to the Bible, and believe him to be a 'dear, good old fellow,' likely at any time to amaze the world by generous and just conduct.

Within a few hours, I believe I could carve a fair likeness of Krüger out of a piece of tough wood, because no Michael Angelo is needed to do justice to his rugged features and ungainly form, and I would be willing to guarantee that justice to the English would be sooner given by that wooden image than it will be by Mr. Krüger; on that I pin my faith in my perception of what is Krüger's true character.

Were either Russia, or Germany, in our position towards South Africa, things could not have come to this pass. Certainly the American Government would not have remained so long blind, not only to duty, but to the ordinary dictates of common-sense, as we have been.

A respectable third of the nation, I fancy, feel very much as I do upon the South African question; another third may be said to prefer letting Krüger do just what he pleases, on the ground that no South African question can be of sufficient importance to risk the danger of giving offence to the stubborn old fellow; and, if the question were put to them, point-blank, as to whether we should try and compel Krüger to abide by the terms of the Convention, or fight him, I feel sure they would say let South Africa go, rather than fight!

The remaining third comprises the nobodies, the people of the street, the mob, people who have no opinion on any subject except their own immediate and individual interest, who follow the Peace Party to-day, because the other Party, the Party for Compulsion, have not condescended to explain to them why they should do otherwise. Now, should it happen that the people of Johannesburg, either after my advice, or after their own methods, take a resolute front and dare to defy the tyrant, the Party for Compulsion would then have a text to preach upon; the ever-varying third might be influenced to side with it, and the Government might then find it the proper thing to declare war.

I believe, therefore, it may come to war. But, as war is a serious thing, even with such a small state as the Transvaal, (and who knows whether the Orange Free State may not join them?) I would not precipitately engage in it. I would prefer to give Krüger a good excuse to descend from that lofty and unalterable decision not to give way to anybody or anything. I would send a Peace Commission of half a dozen of the noblest, wisest, and most moderate men we have got, who could discuss all matters between the Dutch and ourselves, who would know when to yield on questions that do not affect the supremacy of England, or touch on her vital interests,—men who could be firm with courtesy.

This method, of course, is only to set ourselves right with the world, which is rather bitter against England just now, and give ourselves time to prepare, in case of the failure of the Peace Commission.

A few millions spent on equipping a complete Army Corps, ready to set out at an instant's notice, and another ready to support it, might morally effect a change in Krüger's disposition.

He is, I believe, ready on his side for any contingency, or thinks he is; otherwise, why those armed forts at Pretoria, and at Johannesburg, those ninety thousand Mauser rifles, and those batteries of artillery? Why, in fact, this attitude of irreconcileability on his part, were it not that he has been preparing for war?

My dear, I could go on for hours on this subject. I could tell you how I almost foresee war in this peaceful-looking country. The wise politicians at home would no doubt say, 'Ah, Stanley is all very well as an explorer, but in politics, statesmanship, etc., he is altogether out of his element.' But I can *read men*, and the signs of what shall come are written on Krüger's face. My business through life has been to *foresee*, and if possible *avert* calamity . . . but enough is enough! Time flies, and the day of departure from this land will soon arrive, and every day that passes brings me nearer to you and that dear, blessed, little child of ours, whom the gods sent to cheer our hungry hearts. My whole soul is in my pen as I write. God bless you and keep you both!

November 26th, 1897. In my hurry to go to bed last night, I omitted to say anything about my impressions of Ladysmith, the Aldershot of Africa. It was but a short view I had of Ladysmith, but it was sufficient to make me exclaim to my fellow-passengers that the officer who selected that spot for a military camp ought to be shot! Anyone who looks at the map of Natal may see that it would scarcely do to make a permanent military station too far in that point of land that penetrates between the Transvaal and the Orange Free State, unless it was resolved that the defences should be elaborate, and the provisions ample enough for a year at least.

Dreading what might some day be a trap for a British force, the military authorities have chosen a basin-like hollow, south of, and near, a river called the Tugela. When we came round a bend from Newcastle, the white tents of the English soldiers were seen, away down in the hollow, some hundreds of feet below us.

With Majuba ever on one's mind, with Krüger and his Boers so defiant and bold in their stubbornness, I cannot imagine what possesses the commander to undertake the responsibility of pretending to defend a camp, utterly indefensible according to my notions.

Of course, an officer, in time of peace, may camp anywhere in a loyal colony like Natal, on the condition that it is only temporary; but the danger of such a camp as this is, that stores of all kinds soon become enormously valuable as they gather day after day, and their removal is very serious work.

Even if a camp be but temporary, I am of the opinion that it should be the best site in the vicinity and the easiest defensible, were it only to keep alive that alertness and discipline which is necessary in war; but this Ladysmith lies at the mercy of a band of raiders, and if a body of Englishmen can be found in time of peace raiding into a country at peace with us, it is not beyond possibility that a body of Boers may try some day to imitate us, when we least expect it.

CHAPTER XXIV

FAREWELL TO PARLIAMENT

LONDON, Thursday, May 19th, 1898. Presided at Sir Alfred Lyall's lecture, on 'Chartered Companies and Colonization,' before the Society of Arts.

I have always a feeling, when observing an audience in England, that the people who appear to be listening are engaged upon their own particular thoughts. I have sometimes said to myself, 'Life with such people is not an earnest affair. They have come, out of sheer amiability, or to tide over an idle hour. They mechanically smile, and do not mind languidly applauding when someone warns them it is time to do so.'

In my remarks at the close of Sir Alfred Lyall's lecture, I took the opportunity of comparing the French doings at the end of the eighteenth century with those at the end of the nineteenth century, and predicted that when the French appeared on the White Nile, England would have to speak in no uncertain voice to France, or all our toils and expense, since 1882, in Egypt and the Soudan, would have to be considered wasted.

My earnest words roused our friends a little; then Lord Brassey, a typical Gladstonite, thinking I might lead them over to France, instanter, poured cold water upon the heat and said, 'You know it is only Mr. Stanley's way; he is always combative!'

Poor, dear old England! How she is bothered with sentimentalists and cranks! South Africa is almost lost, because no Englishman in office dares to say 'Stop! That is England's.' Yet, if Krüger eventually succeeds, our sea route to India, Australia, and the Isles of the Indian Ocean, will soon be closed.

If the French establish themselves on the White Nile, they will ally themselves with the Abyssinians, and soon find a way of re-arming the Mahdists; and it would not be long then before we should be driven out of Egypt, and clean away from the Suez Canal. Well, and then?

But what is the use? A cold water speech from Lord Brassey quenches, or appears to, any little patriotic ardour that our Society Englishmen confess to having felt. If these people were to be consulted, they would vote for making England as small as she was in the pre-Alfred days, on condition they were not to be agitated.

November 1st, 1898. Am gradually gaining strength after the illness which began in the South of France, August 15th.

The long weeks in bed have given me abundant time for thought, and I have decided that the time has come for me to seek my long-desired rest. It has become clearer to me, each day, that I am too old to change my open-air habits for the asphyxiating atmosphere of the House of Commons.

Consequent upon this Parliamentary life are the various petty businesses of the Constituency I represent; and a wearying correspondence with hundreds of people I am unacquainted with, but who insist on receiving replies. This correspondence, alone, entails a good three-hours' work each day. The demands of the Constituents consume, on an average, another two hours. The House opens at 3 P. M., and business continues to any hour between midnight and 3 A. M. It is therefore impossible to obtain air or exercise.

Long ago the House of Commons had lost its charm for me. It does not approach my conception of it. Its business is conducted in a shilly-shally manner, which makes one groan at the waste of life. It is said to begin at 3 P. M. Prayers are over at 3.10, but for the following twenty minutes we twiddle our fingers; and then commence Questions, which last over an hour. These questions are mainly from the Irish Party, and of no earthly interest to anyone except themselves; but even if they were, the Answers might be printed just as the Questions are; that would save an hour for the business of debate. A Member soon learns how wearying is debate. Out of six hundred and seventy members, some twenty of them have taken it upon themselves, with the encouragement and permission of the Speaker, to debate on every matter connected with the Empire, and after we have heard their voices some fifty times, however interesting their subjects may be, it naturally becomes very monotonous.

Chamberlain, however, is always interesting, because there is a method with him to get to his subject at once, and to deal with it in a lucid, straightforward manner, and have done with it. This is what we all feel, and therefore he is never tedious. Also, every speech Chamberlain delivers is different, and his manner varies; sometimes it is quite exciting, a mere steady look, suggestive of we know not what, gives the cue; sometimes it is only a false alarm; but often we have intense moments, when every word penetrates, and rouses general enlivenment.

Others on the Front Benches are not very interesting in speech or matter, excepting, occasionally, on army or naval questions.

I could name a dozen others who are too often allowed to afflict us on the Unionist side, but the speakers on the Opposition side are permitted even greater loquacity, and they really are terrible bores. Outside the House they are mostly all good fellows, but in the House they have no sense of proportion, and one and all take themselves too seriously. Some of them, I wish, could be sent to the Clock-Tower, where they could wrangle with Big Ben to their hearts' content. Others would be more esteemed if they were fettered to their seats and had their own lips locked, while a few are so bad that they should be sealed tight during the Session. At any rate, it is clearly no place for me.

The House was very full, four hundred and thirteen Members voted; and, of course, the war with the Transvaal was in every mind, and on every lip. All are agreed that Krüger's Ultimatum has been specially fortunate for the Government; for it has been easy to discover that, but for this hot-headed outburst of the Transvaal Government, the general distaste for violent and strong measures would have severely strained the loyalty of the Government's supporters, so much so, I think, that I doubt whether the majority would have been so great as to encourage the Government to formulate the demands which the necessity of the case required.

While listening to the remarks I heard on all sides of me in the Smoking-room, it appeared to me that the saying that 'those whom the gods wish to destroy, they first make mad,' was never so true as in this curious lapse of a Government that, suddenly, and for a trifle, throws all restraint aside, and becomes possessed of the most reckless fury. In his secret heart no Member, but thinks, after his own fashion, that it has been due to an interposition of Providence, Fate, Destiny, call it what name you like. I gather so much from the many ways the Members express their astonishment at Krüger throwing down the gauntlet, ending the discussion, and plunging into war.

It has been a long duel between the Colonial Office and Krügerism; successive Secretaries of State, since 1881, have tried their best to get the vantage over the old Dutchman, and have either failed miserably, or have just been able to save their faces; but Chamberlain, after four years of ups and downs, at one time almost in disgrace, being most unfairly suspected of abetting the Raid, and always verging on failure, comes out of the duel with flying colours, through the intractable old Dutchman tiring of the long, wordy contest.

The Irish have not been so violent as we expected they intended to be. We heard of a wish to be suspended; but, on the whole, they have been tame: though Willie Redmond did not spare Chamberlain.

Campbell-Bannerman spoke with two voices; in the first half of his speech he talked like an English patriot, in the latter half he seemed to have reminded himself that he was the Leader of the Opposition, and showed ill-nature. Harcourt spoke this afternoon, long but without much force. In fact, the strings of the Opposition have been rendered inutile by Krüger's Ultimatum to England, and the Boer invasion. The fact that we are at war checks everybody, and disarms them.

July 26th, 1900. To-day has been my last sitting in Parliament, for I have paired for the remainder of the Session, and Dissolution is very probable in September or October.

I would not stand again for much!

I have never been quite free, after I understood the Parliamentary machine, from a feeling that it degraded me somewhat to be in Parliament.

I have, as a Member, less influence than the man in the street. On questions concerning Africa, Dilke, or some other wholly unacquainted with Africa, would be called upon to speak before me. I have far less influence than any writer in a daily newspaper; for he can make his living presence in the world felt, and, possibly, have some influence for good: whereas I, in common with other respectable fellows, are like dumb dogs. Yet I have, nay we all have, had to pay heavily for the hustling we get in the House. The mention of our names in the Press draws upon us scores of begging letters, and impertinent door-to-door beggars, who, sometimes, by sheer impudence, effect an entrance into our houses. The correspondence postage alone is a heavy tax, and would make a handsome provision for a large family during the year. The expenses incident to Parliamentary candidature and Parliamentary life are very heavy, and, in my opinion, it is disgraceful that a Member should be called upon to subscribe to every church, chapel, sport, bazaar, sale, etc., in his Constituency. But, while I do not grieve so much for the stupid expense, I do begrudge the items which remind me of the annoying begging and the insolent importunity, that impressed me with the worthlessness of the honour of being a Parliamentary representative. Then, when I think of the uselessness of the expense, the labour of replying to the daily correspondence, the time wasted in it all, the late hours, the deadly air, the gradual deterioration of health, I wonder that anyone in his sober senses should consent to bother himself about a Parliamentary machine controlled as is this of ours. Any illusions that I may have had, illusions that I could serve the Empire, advance Africa's interests, benefit this country, were quickly dispelled. The Speaker's eye *could not* be caught; he would call on some glib talker, who really knew very little of his subject; and, in this respect, also, I felt there was some degradation for me, sitting there, to listen to such futilities.

Individually, I repeat, the Members are the best of good fellows in the Smoking-room; but Parliamentary procedure needs revising, and less opportunity should be given to those who talk only for talking's sake. Anyhow, I am glad at the prospect of retiring, and being quit of it all.

CHAPTER XXV

FURZE HILL

IN the autumn of 1898, Stanley decided to look for a house in the country. We had lived, since our marriage, at 2, Richmond Terrace, Whitehall, close to the Houses of Parliament and Westminster Abbey; but though we were near the Thames and St. James's Park, Stanley naturally felt the need of a more open-air life. We therefore decided to have a country retreat, as well as the home in town. In his Journal, November 1, 1898, he writes:—

To live at all, I must have open air, and to enjoy the open air, I must move briskly. I but wait to have a little more strength, when I can begin the search for a suitable house, with some land attached. It has long been my wish, and the mere thought of having come to a decision, that it is imperative to possess such a thing, before it is too late, tends towards the improvement of my health.

Whatever Stanley undertook was thoroughly done. He collected lists of most of the House and Estate-agents, cut out the advertisements of places likely to suit, sorted them according to localities, and then went to work visiting them systematically. In his Journal he writes:—

Between November 15th and 30th, I have seen twenty places, in Kent, Buckinghamshire, Berkshire, and Sussex, but found nothing suitable.

In the photographs and descriptions furnished me by the House-agents, several of them looked quite inviting; but often a mere glance was sufficient to turn me away disgusted. There was not a house which might be said to possess one decent-sized room; those D. saw, she utterly condemned.

December 16th. I have now visited fifty-seven places! Some few I reserved for a second visit with D. At last, I took her to see Furze Hill, Pirbright, Surrey, and, at the first glance, she said it was delightful, and could be made ideal. The more we examined it, the more we liked it; but there was much to improve and renovate. Therefore, as the place pleased me and my wife and her mother, I entered into serious negotiations for the purchase, and by Christmas, I had secured the refusal of it; but as it was let, possession was deferred to the 10th of June, 1899.

Furze Hill is not more than thirty miles from London, but it is in wild and lovely country, wild and lovely because kept so, by the War Department, for manœuvring grounds. The country around mostly consists of great stretches of furze and heather, which are golden and purple in summer, and rough pine woods. No one can buy land here, or build; and Furze Hill is planted in this beautiful wilderness, just a house, gardens, a few fields, a wood, and a quiet lake, fed by a little stream.

Furze Hill now became a great pleasure and occupation. The purchase of furniture occupied us all the spring and summer of 1899. Stanley's system and order was shewn in the smallest details. He kept lists and plans, with exact measurements of every room, passage, and cupboard.

On June 10th, he notes in his Journal: —

I have concluded the purchase and become the owner of Furze Hill; building operations have already begun for the purpose of adding a new wing to the house.

Stanley also commenced installing an electric lighting plant, and a very complete fire-engine. From the lake, which I called 'Stanley Pool,'[1] he pumped water to fill great tanks, the engine which drove the dynamo driving both pump and fire engine. On September 4th, he notes, 'went with D. to our House at Furze Hill. Slept for the first time at our country home.' He now took an ever-increasing delight in the place. He planned walks, threw bridges across streams, planted trees, built a little farm from his own designs, after reading every recent book on farm-building, and in a very short time transformed the place.

Everything Stanley planned and executed was to last, to be strong, and permanent. He replaced the wooden window-frames by stone; the fences were of the strongest and best description; even the ends of the gate and fence-posts, he had dipped in pitch, and not merely in tar, that the portion in the ground might resist decay. It was his pride and his joy that all should be well done. And so, at last, peace and enjoyment came to Stanley, and he was quietly happy, till the last great trial came. Those who knew him there, will never forget the Stanley who revealed himself in that happy intimacy,

[1] Our little wood I called the Aruwimi Forest. A stream was named the Congo. To the fields I gave such African names as 'Unyamwezi,' 'Mazamboni,' 'Katunzi,' 'Luwamberri,' etc. One side of Stanley Pool is 'Umfwa,' the other 'Kinchassa,' and 'Calino point.' Stanley was amused at my fancy, and adopted the names to designate the spots. — D. S.

those strolls through the woods and fields, those talks on the lawn, when we sat round the tea-table and listened to Stanley, till the dusk fell softly; those wonderful evenings, by the library fire, when he told us stories of Africa with such vivid force, that I never heard him without a racing heart, and quickened breath! No one who ever heard Stanley 'tell a story' could possibly forget it! Only the other day, Richard Harding Davis wrote to me, 'Never shall I forget one late afternoon when Stanley, in the gathering darkness, told us the story of Gordon!'

Stanley, however, was not always to be drawn; sometimes, therefore, I resorted to subterfuge, that I might lure him on. I would begin his stories all wrong, make many mistakes on purpose, knowing his love of accuracy, till he could bear it no longer, and, brushing my halting words aside, he would plunge in, and swing along with the splendid narrative to the end.

We were very happy now! Building, planting, sowing, reaping. We called Furze Hill the 'Bride,' and we competed in decking her, and making her gifts. Stanley gave the Bride a fine Broadwood piano, and a billiard table. I gave her a new orchard. Stanley gave her a bathing-house and canoes. I gave her roses.

One day Stanley told me that a case full of books had just arrived, which we could unpack together in the evening. The case was opened, and I greatly rejoiced at the prospect of book-shelves crammed with thrilling novels, and stories of adventure. Stanley carefully removed the layers of packing-paper, and then commenced handing out . . . translations of the Classics, Euripides, Xenophon again, Thucydides, Polybius, Herodotus, Cæsar, Homer; piles of books on architecture, on landscape gardening, on house decoration; books on ancient ships, on modern ship-building. 'Not a book for me!' I exclaimed dismally. Next week, another case arrived, and this time all the standard fiction, and many new books, were ranged on shelves awaiting them.

Stanley's appetite for work in one shape or another was insatiable, and the trouble he took was always a surprise, even to me. Nothing he undertook was done in a half-and-half way. I have now the sheets upon sheets of plans he drew, of the little farm at Furze Hill, every measurement carefully made to scale, and the cost of each item, recorded, on the margin.

And so he was happy, for his joy lay in the doing.

In this year, 1899, Stanley was created G. C. B.

How little any, but his few intimate friends, knew of Stanley! Others might guess, but they could not realise what of tenderness, gentleness, and emotion, lay behind that, seemingly, impenetrable reserve.

As an instance of the curious ignorance existing regarding the real Stanley, I will tell an anecdote, both laughable and pathetic.

A short time after my marriage, I went to tea with a dear old friend. After talking of many things, my friend suddenly put her hand impressively on mine and said, 'Would you mind my asking you a question, for, somehow, I cannot help feeling — well — just a little troubled? It may, in some mysterious way, have been deemed expedient; but why — oh, why — did your husband order a little black baby to be flung into the Congo!' The dear good lady had tears in her eyes, as she adjured me to explain! Indignation at first made me draw away from her, but then the ridiculous absurdity of her story struck me so forcibly, I began to laugh, and the more I laughed, the more pained and bewildered was my friend. 'You believed that story?' I asked. 'You *could* believe it?' 'Well,' she replied, 'I was told it, as a fact.'

When I repeated it to Stanley, he smiled and threw out his hand. 'There, you see now why I am silent and reserved. . . . Would you have me reply to such a charge?' And then he told me the story of the little black baby in Central Africa.

As the expedition advanced, we generally found villages abandoned, scouts having warned the natives of our approach. The villagers, of course, were not very far off, and, as soon as the expedition had passed, they stole back to their huts and plantations. On one occasion, so great had been their haste, a black baby of a few months old was left on the ground, forgotten.

They brought the little thing to me; it was just a gobbet of fat, with large, innocent eyes. Holding the baby, I turned to my officers and said in chaff, 'Well, boys, what shall we do with it?' 'Oh! sir,' one wag cried, with a merry twinkle in his eye, 'throw it into the Congo!' Whereupon they all took up the chorus, 'Throw it, throw it, throw it into the Congo!' We were all in high boyish spirits that day!

I should rather have liked to take the baby on with me, and would have done so, had I thought it was abandoned; but I felt sure the mother was not far off, and might, even then, be watching us, with beating heart, from behind a tree. So I ordered a fire to be kindled, as the infant was small and chilly, and I had a sort of cradle-nest scooped out of the earth, beside the fire, so that the little creature could be warm, sheltered, and in no danger of rolling in. I lined the concavity with cotton-cloth, as a gift to the mother; and when we left that encampment, the baby was sleeping as snugly as if with its mother beside it, and I left them a good notion for cradles!

Many children were born during the march of the Emin Relief Expedition; at one time there were over forty babies in camp! The African mothers well knew that their little ones' safety lay with 'Bwana Kuba,' the 'Great Master.'

When the expedition emerged from the Great Forest, a report got about that the expedition was shortly to encounter a tribe of cannibals. That night Stanley retired to rest early, and soon fell asleep, for he was very exhausted. In the middle of the night, he was wakened by a vague plaint, the cry, as he thought, of some wild animal. The wail was taken up by others, and soon the air was filled by cat-like miaouls. Greatly puzzled, Stanley sat up, and then he heard slappings and howlings. Thereupon, he arose and strode out, to find forty or so infants, carefully rolled up, and laid round his tent by the anxious mothers! Bula Matari, they said to themselves, would never allow the dreadful cannibals to eat their little ones, so they agreed together that the night-nursery must be as close as possible to the Great Master's tent! This, however, was forbidden in future, as it made rest impossible.

Now that I am writing of the period of repose and enjoyment which was a kind of Indian summer in Stanley's life, it may be in place to make a comment on his Introduction to the Autobiography. It was the beginning of a work which was broken off and laid aside many years before his death, so that it never received the stamp of his deliberate and final approval before being given to the world.

The crowning thought of the Introduction may be regarded as the key-note of his character: "I was not sent into the world to be happy nor to search for happiness. I was sent for a special work."

But the note of melancholy which runs through the Introduction is to be taken as the expression of a transient mood, and not as a characteristic and habitual trait. Such a passing cloud was not unnatural in a man with great capacity for emotion, and an extraordinary range of experience; and who possessed, as Mr. Sidney Low has reminded us, the Cymric temperament, with its alternations of vivid lights and deep shadows.

I have delayed making any remark on the element of higher and various happiness in his life. I have delayed it until this point in the story, that the reader might view it, not as my own special pleading, but in the light of his self-revelation as scattered through the many pages of this record. They show, with a fulness which needs no recapitulation here, how the cruelties of his youth, as well as the hardships and misconstructions of his later years, had as their counterpoise the noble joys of manly action, in its heroic and victorious phases; the alternations of such rest as only toilers know; the ministrations of natural grandeur and beauty, of literature, of congenial society; the pure delights of friendship and of love.

One passage in the Introduction may sound to the reader, as yet unacquainted with the man, like a cry *de profundis:* "Look...... at any walk of life, and answer the question, as to your own soul, Where shall I find Love?"

Later, he has told us something of where he did find it. He found it in the heart of Africa and of David Livingstone. He found it in his company of Zanzibaris, who, after following him through all the terrors of the Dark Continent, offered to leave their newly-recovered home to escort him in safety to his far-distant home. He found it in such comrades as Mackinnon, Parke, Jephson, and especially Bruce (pages 459-60), of whom he exclaims, "I could have been contented on a desert island with Bruce"; in such men as Sir George Grey, and a few others; and in the sanctuary of his home.

Against the sharp incessant blows which early and long rained on a heart hungry for love, he learned to shield himself by an armour which might easily be mistaken for natural hardness; and that armour was toughened under the discipline of the endless work, and grew yet firmer as he braced himself against the slanders of ignorance and malignity. As his Introduction tells us, he grew fastidious in his affections, and few were those he found worthy of full intimacy.

But, at the touch of a congenial nature, the barriers dissolved. He knew in its fulness the joys of the idealist and the lover. And he knew, too, the homely and tranquil pleasures which serve best for "human nature's daily food." For in his daily life Stanley was really very happy, in a quiet and quite simple way. He was never gloomy or morose, but exceedingly cheerful when he was well. On the approach of illness he was very silent, and then—I knew!

He was extraordinarily modest, and, in a crowd of people enthusiastic about him, felt like running away. He loved quiet hospitality to a few friends, with Denzil and me to back him; then he was a happy boy. To the very end he found real joy in "the doing." He did not look beyond home for happiness; Denzil, Furze Hill, his books, his writing, planning "improvements," filled his cup of happiness—happiness which he had not sought for in life, but accepted simply and thankfully when it came to him.

CHAPTER XXVI

THE CLOSE OF LIFE

THE year 1903 found Stanley very busy making further improvements, building, and planting. The house at Furze Hill, in 1900, had practically been rebuilt by him; every year he added something, and all was done in his own way, perfectly and thoroughly; even the builders learnt from him. After Stanley's death, the builder asked to see me. 'I came that I might tell you how much I owe to Sir Henry; even in my own line he taught me, he made me more thorough, more conscientious. Would you have any objection to my calling my house after his African name?'

In November, 1902, Stanley began drawing plans for enlarging the hall, drawing-room, and other rooms. He made careful measured drawings, to scale. The hall was enlarged for a billiard table and upraised seats. We could neither of us play, but he said, 'I want those who come to stay here, to enjoy themselves.'

The nursery was to have a terraced balcony, built over the hall, and all this was done through the winter months, Stanley constantly there to superintend. When the building was finished, he alone saw to the decorating and furnishing, as it was all to be a surprise for me.

In March, 1903, Stanley first complained of momentary attacks of giddiness; it made me rather uneasy, so I accompanied him everywhere.

Just before Easter, we were walking near the Athenæum Club, when he swayed and caught my arm. My anxiety, though still vague, oppressed me, and I was very unwilling to let him go alone to Furze Hill; but he insisted, as he said there were yet a few 'finishing touches to put,' before we came down for Easter.

Great was my relief when we were summoned to Furze Hill; everything was ready at last!

And there he stood at the entrance to welcome us! He looked so noble and radiant! He took me round, and showed me the new rooms, the fresh decorations and furnishings, all chosen by himself; but — beautiful as everything seemed — it was just Stanley, he who had conceived and carried out all this for my enjoyment, it was Stanley himself I was all the time admiring.

He had thought of everything, even 'fancy trifles,' as he called the delicate vases, and enamelled jars on the mantelpieces and brackets.

There was a new marble mantelpiece in the drawing-room, decorated with sculptured cupids, 'because we both love babies,' he said. Stanley had even replenished the store-room, fitted it up as for an expedition, or to stand a siege. There were great canisters of rice, tapioca, flour enough for a garrison, soap, cheese, groceries of all kinds, everything we could possibly require, and each jar and tin was neatly ticketed in his handwriting, besides careful lists, written in a store-book, so that I might know, at a glance, the goodly contents of the room.

Those fifteen days were wonderfully happy, and the light shining in Stanley's eyes gave me deep inward peace; but it was short-lived, for, on April the 15th, the giddiness returned; and in the night of the 17th, the blow fell, and the joy that had been, could never come again.

Stanley awakened me by a cry, and I found he was without speech, his face drawn, and his body paralysed on the left side.

No sooner had the doctors withdrawn, that first terrible morning, than he made me understand that he wished to be propped up in bed. Now, absolute quiet had been strictly enjoined, as Stanley was only partially conscious, but he always expected to be obeyed, and to have thwarted him at such a time would, I feared, only have agitated him. I therefore raised and supported him, and then he made me understand that he must *shave!* I fetched his razors, brush, soap, and water; I prepared the lather, which he applied himself with trembling hand, the only hand he could use; and then with eyes blood-shot, his noble face drawn, his mind dazed, but his will still indomitable, Stanley commenced shaving. I held his cheek and chin for him; he tried to see himself in the mirror I held, but his eyes could not focus, nevertheless he succeeded in shaving *clean!*

Some days after, when he had recovered complete consciousness and speech, I found he had no recollection of having shaved. I give this account as a typical instance of Stanley's self-control and resolution. He had often told me that, on his various expeditions, he had made it a rule, always to shave carefully. In the Great Forest, in 'Starvation Camp,' on the mornings of battle, he had never neglected this custom, however great the difficulty; he told me he had often shaved with cold water, or with blunt razors: but 'I always presented as decent an appearance as possible, both for self-discipline and for self-respect, and it was also necessary as chief to do so.'

Months passed; spring, summer, autumn, Stanley lay there, steadfast, calm, uncomplaining; never, by word or sigh, did he express grief or regret. He submitted grandly, and never seemed to me greater, or more courageous, than throughout that last year of utter helplessness and deprivation.

Stanley, the very embodiment of proud independence, was as weak and helpless as a little child!

But I had him still. I felt that nothing in the whole world signified since I had him still; and as I looked at his grand head lying on the pillows, I felt I could be happy in a new and more supreme way, if only I need not give him up.

Soon, I learnt to lift him, with someone just to support his feet; but it was I, and I alone, who held him; at times, I had a sort of illusion that I was holding him back from Death! Coleridge wrote to his friend T. Poole, 'I have a sort of sensation, as if, while I was present, none could die whom I intensely loved.'

And so, although the careless confidence of joy was gone, I had the holy, deep exaltation arising from the feeling that he was there, with me.

He got somewhat better as time passed, and spent the greater part of the day on the lawn, in an invalid-chair. His friend, Henry Wellcome, came every week to sit with him, thus breaking the monotony of the unchanging days. By September, Stanley commenced to stand, and to walk a few steps, supported; speech had returned, but close attention quickly wearied him, and fatigue followed any attempt at physical or mental effort.

He would say, that as the stroke had fallen so suddenly, he hoped it might as suddenly be lifted: 'I shall get the message, it may come in the night, in the twinkling of an eye, and then, lo! I shall walk.'

The message came. It came in the final liberation, in the freeing from this mechanism of earth; and Stanley waited, grandly calm, never assuming a cheerfulness he could not feel, his deeply-ingrained truthfulness made that impossible; but he kept a lofty attitude of submission, he was ever a commander, a leader of men, Bula Matari, the Rock-Breaker, who had every courage, even to this last.

In the late autumn of 1903, we returned to London, and there had some months of not unhappy reprieve. I read aloud to him, and we sat together in great peace. We did not talk of the life to come, nor of religion; Stanley had lived his religion, and disliked conjectural talk of the future life; he believed in a life everlasting, but if ever I spoke of it, he dismissed the subject, saying, 'Ah! now you go beyond me.'

At Easter in 1904, Stanley wished to return to Furze Hill, so we went there towards the end of March. The change did him good, he was hopeful, believing himself better; but on the 17th of April, the very anniversary of his first attack, he was smitten again, this time by pleurisy, and suffered very much. He now became most anxious to return to London, and, on the 27th, was taken by ambulance-carriage to town.

As the pleurisy subsided, he revived; and one day he said to me, 'I shall soon walk now, it is all passing from me.' I think he really meant he might recover, I do not think he was speaking of his approaching death; but, after a pause, he said, 'Where will you put me?' Then, seeing that I did not understand, he added, 'When I am—gone?'

I said, 'Stanley, I want to be near you; but they will put your body in Westminster Abbey.'

He smiled lovingly at me, and replied, 'Yes, where we were married; they will put me beside Livingstone'; then, after a pause, he added, 'because it is *right* to do so!'

A few days later, he put out his hand to me and said, 'Good-bye, dear, I am going very soon, I have — done!'

On May the 3rd, Stanley became lethargic; but he roused himself at times. Our little boy came in and gently kissed Stanley's hand; this wakened him, and, as he stroked Denzil's cheek, the child said, 'Father, are you happy?' — 'Always, when I see you, dear,' he replied.

Mr. Wellcome came daily; once Stanley roused himself to talk to him of his dear officer, Mounteney Jephson, who was very ill at the time.

The struggle of life and death commenced on the 5th of May, and lasted long, so great was Stanley's energy and vitality. Day followed night, night followed day, and he lay still, — sometimes quite conscious, but most of the time in a deep dream.

On the last night, the night of Monday, the 9th of May, his mind wandered. He said, 'I have done — all — my work — I have — circumnavigated' — Then, later, with passionate longing, he cried, 'Oh! I want to be free! — I want to go — into the woods — to be free!'

Towards dawn, he turned his noble head to me, and, looking up at me, said, 'I want — I want — to go home.'

At three A. M., he moved his hand on to mine, looking at me quite consciously, and gave me his last message: 'Good-night, dear; go to bed, darling.'

As four o'clock sounded from Big Ben, Stanley opened his eyes and said, 'What is that?' I told him it was four o'clock striking. 'Four o'clock?' he repeated slowly; 'how strange! So that is Time! Strange!' A little later, seeing that he was sinking, I brought stimulant to his lips, but he put up his hand gently, and repelled the cup, saying, 'Enough.'

Then, as six o'clock rang out, Stanley left me, and was admitted into the nearer Presence of God.

On Tuesday, May 17th, Stanley's body was carried to Westminster Abbey. The coffin lay before the altar where we were married, and the Funeral Service was read, after which Henry Morton Stanley, that Man of Men, was buried in the village churchyard of Pirbright, Surrey.

But history will remember that it was the Rev. Joseph Armitage Robinson, Dean of Westminster, who *refused to allow* Stanley to be buried in Westminster Abbey!

Now, however, I am able to quote Sir George Grey's words, and say: —

'I am inclined to think it is best that the matter should stand thus. Yet one thing was wanting to render the great drama complete; would the man who had done all this, and supported such various trials, be subjected to cold neglect for what he had accomplished? And I sit here, not lamenting, but with a feeling that all has taken place for the best, and that this absence of national recognition will only add an interest to Stanley's history in future years.'

'He is gone who seem'd so great.—
Gone; but nothing can bereave him
Of the force he made his own
Being here, and we believe him
Something far advanced in State,
And that he wears a truer crown
Than any wreath that man can weave him.'

I wished to find some great monolith, to mark Stanley's grave; a block of granite, fashioned by the ages, and coloured by time.

Dartmoor was searched for me, by Mr. Edwards of the Art Memorial Company; he visited Moreton, Chagford Gidleigh, Wallabrook, Teigncombe, Castor, Hemstone, Thornworthy, etc., etc.; and, amid thousands of stones, none fulfilled all my requirements. The river stones were too round, those on the moor were too irregular, or too massive.

Owners of moorland farms, and tenants, took the keenest interest in the search; and, at last, a great granite monolith was discovered on Frenchbeer farm; its length was twelve feet, the width four feet.

The owner and tenant gave their consent to its removal, only stipulating that a brass-plate should be fixed to a smaller stone, stating that from that spot was removed the stone which now stands at the head of Stanley's grave. The smaller stones which form the boundary of the enclosure were found quite near.

The following short account of this great headstone to Stanley's grave was printed at the time:—

'These moorland stones are for the great part recumbent. The few which stand to-day were raised as memorials to chieftains; others form circles, huts, and avenues, and remain to us the silent witnesses of a race, of whose history we know so little. Whatever their past history may be, it seems fitting that one should be raised in our time to this great African leader. It has now a definite work to do, and for ages yet to come, will bear the name of that great son to whom the wilds of Dartmoor were as nothing, compared with that vast continent which he opened up, and whose name will live, not

IN THE VILLAGE CHURCHYARD, PIRBRIGHT

by this memorial, but as one of the great Pioneers of Christianity, Civilization, and Hope to that dark land of Africa.'

After much labour, the great stone, weighing six tons, was transported to Pirbright churchyard, where it now stands, imperishable as the name, cut deep into its face.

I desired to record simply his name, 'Henry Morton Stanley,' and beneath it, his great African name, 'Bula Matari,' For epitaph, the single word 'Africa,' and above all, the Emblem and Assurance of Life Everlasting, the Cross of Christ.

CHAPTER XXVII

THOUGHTS FROM NOTE-BOOKS

ON RELIGION

CIVIL law is not sufficient by itself for mankind. It is for the protection of men from abuse, and for the punishment of offenders; but religion teaches just intercourse, unselfishness, self-denial, virtue, just dealing, love of our fellow-creatures, compassion, kindness, forbearance, patience, fortitude, lofty indifference to death by spiritual exaltation. While atheists and heathens would regard only their own self-advantage, opposing craft to an opponent's detriment, a religious man would be persuaded that he could not do so without a sense of wrong-doing, and would strive to act so as to ensure his own good opinion and those of other conscientious, just-minded fellow-men.

Religion is my invisible shield against moral evil, against the corruption of the mind, against the defilement of the soul. As there are specifics for the preserving of cleanliness of the body, so is religion for the preservation of the mind; and it protects the intelligence from becoming encrusted with layer upon layer of sin.

Religion is an invaluable curb on that inner nature of man, which longest remains barbarous and uncivilised.

I am not animated by the hope of a heavenly reward, such as has been promised. It is my reason which tells me that I owe a duty to God as my Maker, and that is, not to offend Him. The Bible tells me, through its writers, of certain instructions and certain Laws that those who desire to please Him should follow and obey. Many of these Laws and instructions appeal to my own sense as being His due; and therefore I shall conform to them as closely as my nature will permit. When I perceive that they are too hard for nature, I will pray for His divine help to withstand the temptations of nature; for more power of restraint; for more docile submission to His will; for more understanding to comprehend what is pleasing to Him, for more gentleness; for moral strength to combat that which my sense assures me is evil, and unworthy of one endowed with such attributes as belong to me, I will keep ever striving to perform acts pleasing to Him, while I have the power, leaving it to Him to judge whether my endeavours to abstain from evil, and perform that which was right, have been according to the intelligence and moral power He entrusted me with. Meantime, I must keep myself open to conviction, so that whenever it shall be my good fortune to light upon that which will clearly inform me as to the exact way to serve and please God, it will be possible for me to conform; and I must by no means offend Him by negligence in doing that which I know ought to be done.

ON THE INFLUENCE OF RELIGION

To relate a little of the instances in my life wherein I have been grateful for the delicate monitions of an inner voice, recalling me, as it were, to 'my true self,' it would be difficult for me to do their importance justice. I, for one, must not, dare not, say that prayers are inefficacious. Where I have been earnest, I have been answered.

What have these earnest prayers consisted of, mainly?

I have repeated the Lord's Prayer a countless number of times; but, I must confess, my thoughts have often wandered from the purport of the words. But when I have prayed for light to guide my followers wisely through perils which beset them, a ray of light has come upon the perplexed mind, and a clear road to deliverance has been pointed out.

In the conduct of the various expeditions into Africa, prayer for patience, which bespoke more than an ordinary desire for patience, has enabled me to view my savage opponents in a humorous light; sometimes, with infinite compassion for their madness; sometimes, with a belief that it would be a pity to punish too severely; and, sometimes, with that contempt which I would bestow upon a pariah dog. Patience has been granted to me, and I have left them storming madly. Without the prayer for it, I doubt that I could have endured the flourish of the spears when they were but half-a-dozen paces off.

When my own people have wilfully misbehaved, after repeated warnings, I have prayed for that patience which would enable me to regard their crimes with mercy, and that my memory of their gross wickedness should be dulled; and, after the prayer, it has appeared to me that their crimes had lost the atrocity that I had previously detected in them. When oft-repeated instances of the efficacy of prayer were remembered, I have marvelled at the mysterious subtleness with which the answer has been delivered.

'Lord God, give me my people, and let me lead them in safety to their homes; then do Thou with me as Thou wilt,' was my prayer the night preceding the day the remnant of the Rear-Column was found. True, they were there, they had not moved since July 17th; but I did not know it.

'Give my people back to me, O Lord. Remember that we are Thy creatures, though our erring nature causes us to forget Thee. Visit not our offences upon our heads, Gracious God!' And thus that night was passed in prayer, until the tired body could pray no more. But the next dawn, a few minutes after the march had begun, my people were restored to me, with food sufficient to save the perishing souls at the camp.

On all my expeditions, prayer made me stronger, morally and mentally, than any of my non-praying companions. It did not blind my eyes, or dull my mind, or close my ears; but, on the contrary, it gave me confidence. It did more: it gave me joy, and pride, in my work, and lifted me hopefully over the one thousand five hundred miles of Forest tracks, eager to face the day's perils and fatigues. You may know when prayer is answered, by that glow of content which fills one who has flung his cause before God, as he rises to his feet. It is the first reward of the righteous act, the act that ought to have been done. When my anticipations were not realised to their fulness, what remained was better than nought; and what is man, that he should quarrel with the Inevitable?

ON PRAYER

I have evidence, satisfactory to myself, that prayers *are* granted. By prayer, the road sought for has become visible, and the danger immediately lessened, not once or twice or thrice, but repeatedly, until the cold, unbelieving heart was impressed.

This much I have derived from many a personal experience.

I have forgotten my prayers; my sensibilities have been so deadened by the sordid scenes around me that my soul was not aroused to feel that there was a refuge for distress. Worldly thoughts absorbed my attention; I became a veritable pagan, ever ready, on occasion, to sneer and express utter disbelief. Finally, I have drawn near a danger, and, in its immediate presence, I have understood its character better; every faculty is then brought to bear upon and around it, and a sense of utter hopelessness takes possession of my mind. There is no cowardice, no thought of retreat; rescue or no rescue, I must face it.

At first, I believe that it will be possible to confront it, go through with it, emerge from it safely. What is wanting, but light? Next, I am reminded that such a scene occurred before, and that prayer relieved me. Ah! but I have so long refrained from prayer, can I believe that, now, prayer would be answered? I have forfeited the right to be heard. Have I not joined the scoffers, and smiled in contempt at such puerile ideas, and said, 'Prayers were well enough when we were children, but not now, when I have lived so long without the sign of a miracle'? And yet—prayer has saved me.

Civilised society rejoices in the protection afforded to it by strong armed law. Those in whom faith in God is strong feel the same sense of security in the deepest wilds. An invisible, Good Influence surrounds them, to Whom they may appeal in distress, an Influence which inspires noble thoughts, comfort in grief, and resolution when weakened by misfortune. I imperfectly understand this myself, but I have faith and believe. I know that, when I have called, I have been answered, strengthened, and assisted. I am prone to forgetfulness, and to much pride; but I cannot forget that, when an accusing thought entered my soul like a sword, I became penitent and responded. Subduing my unbelief, I prayed, and obtained a soothing grace which restored to me a confidence and cheerfulness which was of benefit to myself and others.

ON RELIGIOUS EDUCATION

The white man's child has a more fertile nature than the savage. The two natures differ as much as the fat-soiled garden near the Metropolis differs from the soil of the grassy plains in Africa, the only manure of which has been the ash of scorched grass. The cultivated garden will grow anything almost to perfection; the African prairie will grow but a poor crop of hardy maize or millet. Religion acts as a moral gardener, to weed out, or suppress, evil tendencies, which, like weeds and nettles, would shoot up spontaneously in the wonderful compost of the garden, if unwatched. The surroundings of the child's mind resemble the fertilising constituents of that garden soil.

The demands, by-laws, necessities, of a feverish, yet idle, Society, serve to evolve an abortive man, without truth, honesty, usefulness, or enthusiasm. He has no physical strength, or mental vigour; serious in nothing, not even in the pursuit of variety or frivolity, not a word he utters can be believed, by himself or anybody else; for, simplest words have lost their common meaning, and simplest acts are not to be described by any phrase required by veracity. Religion inspires the moral training requisite to crush these noxious fungi of civilised life. The savage is licensed to kill, to defend his misdeed by simple lying, to steal, in order to supply his daily wants. The white child kills character with his tongue, he robs wholesale where the savage robs by grains.

ON SIR EDWIN ARNOLD'S 'LIGHT OF THE WORLD'

After reading a few hundred lines of Edwin Arnold's new poem,[1] 'The Light of the World,' I perceived that he had not hit the right chord. It is 'The Light of Asia,' in a feeble, vapid style; or, to put it more correctly, it is a Buddhist trying to sing the glories of the Christian's Lord. His soul is not in his song, though there are beautiful passages in it; but it is the tone of an unbeliever. Alas for this! What a poem he could have written, had he but believed in the Saviour of the world!

MIND AND SOUL

My own mind, I know, has been derived from God. Its capacity, in this existence, is measurable. I feel that, up to

[1] Extract from the Journal, dated February 14, 1891.

a certain point, it could expand, but, beyond that, is madness. It can descend to a certain point below normal; below that would be ruin. Being measurable, it is just suited to my limited nature. It is marvellously expansible; it can also descend to that pin-point and faint glimmer of reason at zero which guides the brute. The Intangible, Invisible, yet Almighty Intellect conceived, by knowing, the beginnings of the spacious universe and its countless myriad of things; the brutes cannot comprehend this, but, to me, has been given just enough mind to be impressed by the vast and solemn fact of this immeasurable knowledge. As my mind governs me, and all that belongs to me, in the same manner I conceive that every movement of the universe and its myriad of constituents is subject to some Divine Mind. This Divine Mind is the power of a Personal Spirit which is God, Who has endowed humanity with the necessary, though limited, portion of His own subtle and all-powerful intelligence.

All my instincts warn me that this is so; but that, so long as it is imprisoned by this earthly matter, it cannot give itself that freedom. When freed from it, my spirit will bound to its source.

A contracted, insect-mind, it is often. Fancy it groping with its tentacles, stretched almost to snapping, far into yet further spaces; then, suddenly contracting into apparent mindlessness, at the buzz of a fly, the bite of an insect, the pang of small nerve! With aspirations after a seat in the Heaven of Heavens, yet, more often, content to wallow in the mud — thereby proving its relationship to the noblest and the meanest! Without that portion of Divinity it could not imagine its obligation to the Creator, nor be conscious of its affinity with the brutes.

ON THE FEAR OF DEATH

The weakness of our number against the overpowering force of savages[1] forbade resistance. Against such a multitude, what hope had we? The imminence of death brought with it a strange composure. I did not fear it as I imagined I should; a fortitude to bear anything came to me, and I could actu-

[1] At Bumbireh. See Stanley's *Through the Dark Continent.*

ally smile contemptuously at the former craven fear of its pain and the sudden rupture of life.

ON ILLUSIONS

Though many illusions are of a character we should gladly cherish, yet the sooner we lose some of them, the sooner we gain the power of seeing clearly into things. The one who possesses least has the best chance of becoming wise. The man who travels, and reflects, loses illusions faster than he who stays at home. There are nevertheless some illusions, which, when lost, he bitterly regrets.

To-day, I can feel comfortably at home in almost any country; and can fully appreciate the truth of Shakespeare's words, that 'To a wise man, all places that the eye of Heaven visits are ports and happy havens.' Yet I sympathise still with that belief of my youth, that Wales, being my native-land, possessed for me superior charms to any other.

Had I seen no other wondrous lands, met no other men and women with whom I could sympathise, it is probable that I should have retained the belief that Wales was the finest country in the world, and the Welsh people the best. I used to believe the Bishop was the holiest man living; the Rev. Mr. Smalley, of Cwm, the biggest man; Sam Ellis, of Llanbach, the strongest man; Hicks Owen, the finest preacher; my cousin Moses, the most scholarly; the Vale of Clwyd, the prettiest; Liverpool, the biggest and most populous town; and the Welsh people, the superior of any in the whole world.

Without any effort of mine, or anybody else's, to disabuse me of these illusions, I have seen hundreds just as holy as the Bishop, bigger men than the Cwm rector, stronger men than Sam Ellis, better preachers than Hicks Owen, men more scholarly than Moses Owen, prettier scenery than the Clwyd, richer and more populous towns than Liverpool, and more advanced people than the Welsh!

THE TRAINING OF YOUNG MEN, AND EDUCATION

When I was young, a religious and moral training was considered necessary, as well as an intellectual education, for the improvement of youth; but, since the banishment[1] of the Bible from the schools, it has been deemed wise to pay attention to the training of the intellect alone, while the natural disposition of youth has caused attention to be paid to athletics.

With a few choice natures this might be sufficient, but I observe that the generality of young men have not that respect for moral obligations it would be desirable to foster. The youth whose word is unimpeachable, whose courage is based on a thorough comprehension of his duty, called moral, whose spirit bends before its dictates, yet is capable of being inspired by honour, and swayed by discipline, is far more useful, valuable, and trustworthy than an athlete with all the intellectual attainments of a Senior Wrangler; but an athlete combining such moral and intellectual gifts would inspire love and admiration wherever he went.

When our sons are steady, reliable, and honest, as well as scholars and athletes, this nation will top the list of nations, as there are no excellences superior to these obtainable, and these will lead the world for ages yet. The Presbyterianism of Cromwell did much; but we can beat that, if we aim for the best. The three M's are all that we need — Morals, Mind, and Muscles. These must be cultivated, if we wish to be immortal — we are in danger of paying attention to Mind and Muscle only.

ON EDUCATION

Schools turn out men efficient enough in reading, writing, ciphering, and deportment; they then go forth to face the world, and they find their school education is the smallest part of what they have in future to learn. They are fit for no profession or employment.

The average school-boy and college man cannot understand business, cannot build or make anything, cannot command men; only after long and laborious practice can he be entrusted to do rightly any of these things. Three-fourths of those who came to Africa were qualified only in the accomplishments of the school-boy. They were unpractised in

[1] This is not yet the policy of England. Thus we find Mr. Runciman, President of the Board of Education, saying (February 10, 1909) that he believed that the teachers, as well as the parents, desired that the children should be brought up reverentially and righteously, and there was no better way than basing the teaching upon a Biblical foundation, which had existed from time immemorial, and which it would be foolish and reckless to uproot. — D. S.

authority, untrustworthy as to obedience, ignorant of self-command; they had apparently never sounded their own virtues or capacities; they appeared surprised and incapable when called upon to think for themselves. The public schools and colleges do not teach young men *to think*.

ON LEARNING

Learning, by which is commonly understood the results of assimilation of varied and long years of reading, reflection, and observation, is the capital of intellect, and is an honoured thing. It is composed of literary acquisitions subjected to mental analysis. It certainly contributes to the elevation of man to a lofty sphere; and yet, after all, I am inclined to think that great as a literary man may be from the store of intellectual treasures he may have acquired, he gets an undue proportion of the world's admiration. The master-minds of a nation are many and various. The great statesman, the great administrator, the great inventor, the great man of science, the multitude of nameless, but bold and resolute, pioneers, those, for instance, who made Australasia; our great missionaries, those brave, patient souls who, in distant lands, devote their lives to kindling the fires of Christianity in savage breasts; the missionaries at home, who are unweariedly exhorting and encouraging the poor and despairing, exciting the young and heroic virtue of these, and many more, who go to make the leaders of a civilised nation, — we hear little of these, compared with what we are told of men who write books. But the stones which go to make the palatial edifice have been laid by many hands. Why does most of the honour go to the writer of books?

ON REAL RECREATION

'Joy's Soul lies in the doing,
And the Rapture of pursuing,
Is the prize.'

Even rest is found in occupation, and striving. It is labour which kills discontent, and idle repose which slays content; for it creates a myriad of ills, and a nausea of life, it brings congestion to the organs of the body, and muddles the clear spring of intelligence. The heart is heated by our impatience, while the soul is deflected from its vigorous course by excess of shameful ease. Joy's Soul lies in the doing! The truth which lies in this verse explains that which has caused many a personality to become illustrious. It is an old subject in poetry. Shakespeare, Milton, Wordsworth, Longfellow, and many more have rung the changes, or expressed the idea, in verse.

Milton, though troubled with blindness and domestic misery, was happy in the lofty scenes conjured up by his poetic imagination, and therefore he could have said, 'Joy's Soul lies in the doing, And the Rapture of pursuing is the prize.'

Livingstone was happy in the consciousness that he was engaged in a noble work, and the joy in the grand consequences that would follow. This self-imposed mission banished remembrance of the advance of age, and made him oblivious of the horrors of his position. What supported Gordon during the siege of Khartoum, but this inward joy in his mission which his nature idealised and glorified? Coleridge says: —

> 'Joy, Lady! is the spirit and the power
> Which wedding Nature to us gives in dower.'

ON REVIEWS AND REVIEWERS

The Reviews of my books have sometimes been too one-sided, whether for, or against, me. The Reviewer is either fulsome, or he is a bitter savage, striking stupidly because of blind hate. A Review in the 'New York Tribune,' for instance, or the 'New York Independent,' the American 'Sun,' the 'Times,' 'Morning Post,' or 'Daily Telegraph,' is, however, the disinterested outcome of study, and is really instructive and worth reading.

It was owing to repeated attacks of the Public and Press that I lost the elastic hope of my youth, the hope, and belief, that toil, generosity, devotion to duty, righteous doing, would receive recognition at the hands of my fellow-creatures who had been more happily born, more fortunately endowed, more honoured by circumstances and fate than I. It required much control of natural waywardness to reform the shattered aspirations. For it seemed as though the years of patient watchfulness, the long periods of frugality, the painstaking self-teaching in lessons of manliness, had ended disastrously in failure.

For what was my reward? Resolute devotion to a certain ideal of duty, framed after much self-exhortation to uprightness of conduct, and righteous dealing with my fellow-creatures, had terminated in my being proclaimed to all the world first as a forger, and then as a buccaneer, an adventurer, a fraud, and an impostor! It seemed to reverse all order and sequence, to reverse all I had been taught to expect. Was this what awaited a man who had given up his life for his country and for Africa? He who initiates change must be prepared for opposition; the strong-willed is bound to be hated. But the object need not be sacrificed for this. A man shall not swerve from his path because of the barking of dogs.

Spears in Africa were hurtful things, and so was the calumny of the Press here; but I went on and did my work, the work I was sent into the world to do.

ON READING THE NEWSPAPERS

That which has to be resisted in reading newspapers is the tendency to become too vehement about many things with which really I have no concern. I am excited to scorn and pity, enraged by narratives of petty events of no earthly concern to me, or any friend of mine. I am roused to indignation by ridiculous partisanship, by loose opinions, hastily formed without knowledge of the facts. Columns of the papers are given up to crime, to records of murder, and unctuous leaders on them. Many newspapers are absolutely wanting in patriotism. A week of such reading makes me generally indulgent to moral lapses, inclines me to weak sentimentalism, and causes me to relax in the higher duty I owe to God, my neighbour, and myself; in short, many days must elapse before I can look with my own eyes, weigh with my own mind, and be myself again. In Africa, where I am free of newspapers, the mind has scope in which to revolve, virtuously content. Civilisation never looks more lovely than when surrounded by barbarism; and yet, strange to say, barbarism never looks so inviting to me as when I am surrounded by civilisation.

RETURNING TO ENGLAND

When returning to Britain from the Continent, I am not struck by the great superiority of that land over France, Italy, Belgium, and Germany; in some things it is decidedly inferior, as in the more substantial structure, and more pleasing appearance, of the homes abroad: they are bigger, loftier, cleaner, and handsomer, the public buildings more imposing.

France and Italy shine with whiteness, Britain appears in a half-cleaned-up state, after being drenched with soot; its sky seems more threatening, and though the leafage and grass in the fields are pleasantly green, the stems and twigs are exceedingly black. The white cottages, with red tiles, of France, are more beautiful than the dingy brick and dark slate of England.

The generous union of hearts and hands, loving brotherhood, equality of one sturdy farmer with another, are better exemplified by the open, cultivated fields of Europe, than by the miserable, useless hedges, which, by their crooked lines marking the small properties, tell me which one is poor, which better-off, which rich. Then I hate the waste of good land, and while the island is but small, thousands of square miles are absorbed by the briar and hawthorn-topped dykes, and their muddy ditches, which might be utilised in extending fields to grow corn for man, and grass for cattle.

Then, on reaching London, compare the sad-looking streets, which you look down upon from the lofty railway, with the bright Paris you left in the morning. You may compare the one to a weeping widow, the other to a gay bride; or to a slatternly fishwoman and to a neat grisette. These thoughts tend to make one humble-minded, and admit that, after all you have heard about the superiority of England, Frenchmen, Swiss, Germans, Italians, and Belgians have nothing to deplore at being born in their own lands, whatever some Englishmen may profess to feel for them; but that, rather, we Englishmen ought to grieve that things are so awry with our climate that we have so much to envy our neighbours. However, when we descend from the train, and we mix with our countrymen, and hear their pleasing accents of English, are received with politeness by friends, Custom-house officials, and cabmen, a secret feeling of pleasure takes possession of us, and we rejoice that our native language is English, and that we belong to the big, broad-chested race round about us.

FORTY YEARS AGO

It is the same nation; it is the same Queen; the present Ministers are twin brothers to those who governed then. In the pulpits and the schools the same preachers and teachers preach and teach. One might say that no change has taken place in forty years. It is certainly the same nation, but nevertheless the people of to-day are different from the people of forty years ago.

The captains of ships and officers of the army, the schoolmasters at the schools, and the governors of gaols, have abandoned the birch and the 'cat.' Instead of applying black marks on the bodies of their victims with smiles of content, they put black marks in a book opposite their names — and the curious punishment seems to have good effect, in many cases.

A great change has also been effected in the Provinces. Forty years ago, they were years behind the Metropolis, Liverpool and Manchester were only 'country cousins' to London, and the people of the country were very far behind Liverpool and Manchester; whereas now, a fashion coming out to-day in London will be out, to-morrow, in every village, almost, in Britain.

Of course, the railway, the telegraph, and the Universal Providers are the causes of this universal transmission of metropolitan ideas and tastes. This is desirable in a great measure, because it has a stimulating and quickening tendency on 'provincialism,' and militates against 'stodginess.' If we could only be sure that no matter vitiating the moral fibre of the nation also ran along the arteries of the land from its heart, we should have cause for congratulation; but, if the extremities of the land absorb the impurities of the Metropolis, the strong moral fibre of the nation will soon be destroyed.

There are things characteristic of the masses in towns, and other things which are, or were, characteristic of the country. But now the hot impulse of the city mobs has an appreciable effect on those in the provinces, erstwhile sturdier and more deliberate. If we were always sure that the impulse was good and beneficial, there would be nothing to regret. The frivolities of an aggregate of humanity such as London presents are inseparable from the many millions of people gathered within its walls; but they are out of place under the blue sky, and in the peaceful, green fields of the country. The smoke of the city, and the roar of the traffic, obscure the heavens, and affect the nerves, until we almost forget the God Who rules, and our religious duties.

Outside of London, the smiling fields, and, skywards, the rolling clouds and the shining sun, make us aware that there is a Presence we had almost forgotten.

SOCIALISM

Socialism is a return to primitive conditions. Where it is in force in Africa, on the Congo, especially, we see that their condition is more despicable than in East Africa.

On the Congo, people are afraid to get richer than their neighbours. They would be objects of suspicion; some day the tribe would doom them, and they would be burnt. Property in common has often been tried in America: *e. g.*, the original Virginian settlers, the Pilgrims in Massachusetts, the Shakers, and others; but they have had to abandon the project. Merely by preventing the spoliation of their fellows, and giving each man freedom to develop his powers, we have done a prodigious good in Africa.

Man must be protected from his fellow-man's greed, as well as from his anger. Individuals require to be protected from the rapacity of communities.

LOAFERS

If men who take such pride in cheating their fellows, by doing as little work as possible, were, only for a change, to glory in doing more and better than was expected of them, what a difference, I have often thought, it would make in the feeling between employers and employees!

THE CRY OF 'WALES FOR THE WELSH'

During my residence in Wales every English man or woman I saw has left in my memory an amiable reminder. The Bishop was an Englishman. Captain Thomas, the paternal, fair-minded, hospitable Guardian, was English. Her Majesty's Inspector, learned, polite, benevolent, was English. Brynbella's lessee, generous and kindly, was English. A chance visitor, a lady, who came to sketch in the neighbourhood, sitting on a camp-stool at an easel, was English. I shall never forget her. She painted small water-colours, and gave us all cakes, oranges, and apples, also sixpences to the bigger boys and twopences to the lesser!

The best books, the beautiful stories, the novelettes, our geographies, spelling-books, histories, and school-readers, our Prayer-books and Bibles, were English. Yet the Welsh hated the English, and the reason for it I have never been able to discover, even to this day.

We also detested the Paddys of the Square, because they were ragged, dirty, and quarrelsome, foul of speech, and noisy.

We saw a few French, at least we were told they were French: they were too much despised to be hated. They belonged to that people who were beaten at Crécy, Agincourt, Blenheim, and Waterloo.

I should therefore be false to myself if I stooped to say that the Welsh are the first people under the sun, and that Wales is the most beautiful country in the world.

But, I am quite willing to admit that the Welsh are as good as any, and that they might surpass the majority of people if they tried, and that Wales contains within its limited area as beautiful scenes as any. The result of my observations is that in Nature the large part of humanity is on a pretty even plane, but that some respectable portion of it, thank Goodness! has risen to a higher altitude, owing to the advantages of civilisation. But there is a higher altitude still, which can only be reached by those nations who leave off brooding among traditions, and grasp firmly and gratefully the benefits offered to them by the progress of the age, and follow the precepts of the seers.

'Wales for the Welsh' is as senseless as 'Ireland for the Irish.' A common flag waves over these happy islands, uniting all in a brotherhood sealed by blood. Over what continents has it not streamed aloft? Who can count the victories inscribed on it?

NOTES ON AFRICAN TRAVEL, ETC.

ON STARTING ON AN EXPEDITION

Take an honest, open-eyed view of your surroundings, with as much faith as possible in the God above you, Who knows your heart better than you know it yourself; and consider that you cannot perish unless it is His will. But a man need not let his soul be oppressed by fears, religious, or otherwise, so long as his motives are righteous, his endeavours honest. Let him see also that his actions are just, and his mind free from sordid or selfish passions; and that his whole aim is to be workmanlike and duteous. Thus he is as fit for Heaven as for the world. Then, bidding a glad farewell to the follies and vanities of civilised cities, step out with trustful hearts, souls open as the day, to meet whatever good or evil may be in store for us, perceiving, by many insignificant signs around, that whatever heavenly protection may be vouchsafed to us, it would soon be null and void unless we are watchful, alert, and wise, and unless we learn to do the proper thing at the right moment — for to this end was our intellect and education given us.

Pious missionaries, even while engaged in worship, have been massacred at the altar. The white skin of the baptised European avails nothing against the arrow. Holy amulets and crosses are no protection against the spear. Faith, without awakened faculties and sharp exercise of them, is no shield at all against lawless violence!

WRITTEN IN AFRICA, IN 1876, IN A NOTE-BOOK

One of the first sweet and novel pleasures a man experiences in the wilds of Africa, is the almost perfect independence; the next thing is the indifference to all things earthly outside his camp; and that, let people talk as they may, is one of the most exquisite, soul-lulling pleasures a mortal can enjoy. These two almost balance the pains inflicted by the climate. In Europe, care ages a man soon enough; and it is well known that it was 'care which killed the cat'! In Africa, the harassing, wearisome cares of the European are unknown. It is the fever which ages one. Such care as visits explorers is nothing to the trials of civilisation. In Africa, it is only a healthful exercise of the mind, without some little portion of which, it were really not worth while living.

The other enjoyment is the freedom and independence of mind, which elevates one's thoughts to purer, higher atmospheres. It is not repressed by fear, nor depressed by ridicule and insults. It is not weighed down by sordid thoughts, or petty interests, but now preens itself, and soars free and unrestrained; which liberty, to a vivid mind, imperceptibly changes the whole man after a while.

No luxury in civilisation can be equal to the relief from the tyranny of custom. The wilds of a great city are better than the excruciating tyranny of a small village. The heart of Africa is infinitely preferable to the heart of the world's greatest city. If the way to it was smooth and safe, millions would fly to it. But London is better than Paris, and Paris is better than Berlin, and Berlin is better than St. Petersburg. The West invited thousands from the East of America to be relieved of the grasp of tyrannous custom. The Australians breathe freer after leaving England, and get bigger in body and larger in nature.

I do not remember while here in Africa to have been possessed of many ignoble thoughts; but I do remember, very well, to have had, often and often, very lofty ideas concerning the regeneration, civilisation, and redemption of Africa, and the benefiting of England through her trade and commerce; besides other possible and impossible objects. 'If one had only the means, such and such things would be possible of realisation'! I am continually thinking thus, and I do not doubt they formed principally the dream-life in which Livingstone passed almost all his leisure hours.

Another enduring pleasure is that which is derived from exploration of new, unvisited, and undescribed regions; for, daily, it forms part of my enjoyment, especially while on the march. Each eminence is eagerly climbed in the hope of viewing new prospects, each forest is traversed with a strong idea prevailing that at the other end some grand feature of nature may be revealed; the morrow's journey is longed for, in the hope that something new may be discovered. Then there are the strange and amusing scenes of camp-life in a savage land;

the visits of the natives, whose peculiar customs or dress, and whose remarks on strangers, seldom fail to be entertaining; and, best of all, there is the strong internal satisfaction one feels at the end of each day's labours, and the proud thought that something new has been obtained for general information, and that good will come of it. Lastly, there is the pleasure of hunting the large, noble game of Africa; that truest of sports, *where you hunt for food and of necessity;* to track the elephant, rhinoceros, buffalo, the eland, and other magnificent animals of the antelope species.

It is a keen, delightful feeling which animates the mind of the African hunter, as he leaves his camp full of people, and plunges into the unexplored solitudes, accompanied by only one or two men, in search of game, ignorant of the adventures which lie before him; but with swift pulse, braced nerves, and elated heart, he is ready to try his luck against even the most formidable. The success of the hunt enhances his pleasure, and, on his return to camp, he meets his people, who are all agape with admiration of his prowess, and profuse in thanks for the gift of animal food.

If the traveller's mind is so happily constituted that, in the pursuit of duty, he can also command enjoyment in its pursuit, each day brings its round of single, happy pleasures, often out-balancing the drawbacks of travel in savage Africa.

> 'For such, the rivers dash their foaming tides,
> The mountain swells, the dale subsides;
> E'en thriftless furze detains their wandering sight,
> And the rough, barren rocks grow pregnant with delight.'

If he is a true lover of wild Nature, where can he view her under so many aspects as in the centre of Africa? Where is she so shy, so retired, mysterious, fantastic, and savage as in Africa? Where are her charms so strong, her moods so strange, as in Africa?

One time she appears so stale, flat, and tedious, that the very memory of the scene sickens and disgusts; another time she covers her prospects with such a mysterious veil, that I suffered from protracted fits of melancholy, and depression of spirits, to such a degree I was glad to turn to meditations on the words of the fourteenth chapter of Job. It is when Africa presents vast desolate wastes, without grandeur, beauty, or sublimity, when even animated life appears quite extinct, then it is that the traveller from long contemplating such scenes is liable to become seriously afflicted with sullen, savage humour, as though in accordance with what he beholds.

At another time, Nature in Africa exposes a fair, fresh face to the light of heaven, a very queen in glory, whose grassy dress exhibits its shimmers as it is gently blown by the breeze; soft, swelling hills, and hollows all green with luxuriant leafage; wild flowers and blooming shrubs perfume the air, and beautiful outlines of hills grace the extensive prospect. Oh! at such times I forgot all my toils and privations, I seemed re-created; the mere view around me would send fresh vigour through my nerves.

In her grand and sublime moods, Nature often appears in Africa, her crown, wreathed in verdure, lifted sheer up to the white clouds, the flanks of her hills descending to the verge of her mighty lakes, vast and impenetrable forests spreading for unending miles. These are the traveller's reward; therefore his life in this little-known continent need not be intolerable; it is not merely a life of toil and danger; though constant travel may be fatiguing, thirst oppressive, heat a drawback, and the ever-recurring fever a great evil, he may also find much that is pleasant. If he is fortunate in his travels, he will not regret having undertaken his journey, but will always look back upon it, as I do, as a pleasant period of a useful life; for it will have considerably enlightened and matured him, and renewed his love for his own race, his own land, and the institutions of his country, thus preparing him for the cultivation and enjoyment of more perfect happiness at home.

AFTER ONE OF HIS EXPEDITIONS

Stanley writes: 'When a man returns home and finds for the moment nothing to struggle against, the vast resolve, which has sustained him through a long and difficult enterprise, dies away, burning as it sinks in the heart; and thus the greatest successes are often accompanied by a peculiar melancholy.'

ON THE GOVERNMENT OF THE CONGO

1896. The King of the Belgians has often desired me to go back to the Congo; but to go back, would be to see mistakes consummated, to be tortured daily by seeing the effects of an erring and ignorant policy. I would be tempted to re-constitute a great part of the governmental machine, and this would be to disturb a moral malaria injurious to the re-organiser. We have become used to call vast, deep layers of filth, 'Augean stables': what shall we call years of stupid government, mischievous encroachment on the executive, years of unnecessary, unqualified officers, years of cumbersome administration, years of neglect at every station, years of confusion and waste in every office? These evils have become habitual, and to remove them would entail much worry and dislike, to hear of them would set my nerves on edge, and cause illness.

ON THE VALUE OF THE CONGO AND BRITISH EAST AFRICA

English legislators imagine they exhibit their wisdom by challenging travellers to describe the value of the countries to which they seek to draw attention. Hasty and preliminary exploration of the topographers cannot be expected to discover all the resources of a country. For sixty years the English were in possession of South Africa before either diamonds or gold were found. Nay, England herself was thought by the Romans to produce nothing but sloes! New Zealand was supposed to be destitute of anything but timber. Australia has been frequently contemptuously alluded to.

The Congo possesses splendid inland navigation, abundance of copper, nitre, gold, palm oil, nuts, copal, rubber, ivory, fibre for rope and paper, excellent grasses for matting, nets, and fishing-lines, timber for furniture and ship-building. *All this could have belonged to Great Britain, but was refused. Alas!*

The Duke of Wellington replied to the New Zealand Association, in 1838, that Great Britain had sufficient colonies, even though New Zealand might become a jewel in England's colonial crown!

ON GENERAL GORDON. 1892

I have often wondered at Gordon; in his place I should have acted differently.

It was optional with Gordon to live or die; he preferred to die; I should have lived, if only to get the better of the Mahdi.

With joy of striving, and fierce delight of thwarting, I should have dogged and harassed the Mahdi, like Nemesis, until I had him down.

I maintain that to live is harder and nobler than to die; to bear life's burdens, suffer its sorrows, endure its agonies, is the greater heroism.

The relief of Khartoum, that is to say, removing the garrison and those anxious to leave, was at first, comparatively speaking, an easy task. I should have commenced by rendering my position impregnable, by building triple fortifications *inside* Khartoum, abutting on the Nile, with boats and steamers ever ready. No Mahdist should have got at me or my garrison! I should then have commanded all those civilians desirous of submitting to the Mahdi to leave Khartoum; people do not realise how ready, nay eager, they were to do so. Gordon said to an interviewer, before starting, 'The moment it is known we have given up the game, every man will be only too eager to go over to the Mahdi; all men worship the Rising Sun.'

But I should never have stuck to Khartoum, I would have departed with my garrison to safer lands by the Upper White Nile. It would not have been difficult to get to Berber, if Gordon had started without delay, in fact, as soon as he had fortified himself at Khartoum. My withdrawal would have been to attack the better, 'leaving go of the leg, to fly at the throat'; but if, for some reason, I had decided to stay, my fortified citadel would have held the Mahdists at bay till help came. There would have been no danger of starvation, as I should have turned all undesirables out. Then, as a last resource, there was the Nile.

My one idea would have been to carry out what I had undertaken to do, without any outside help. If I had gone to Khartoum to rescue the garrison, the garrison would have been rescued! When Gordon started, this is what he undertook to do; there was no thought, or question, of sending a rescue expedition. It was failure all round — Gordon failed first, then Gladstone and the Government.

But I have refrained from all public expression of opinion, because it is not permitted in England to criticise Gordon; and, besides, he was a true hero, and he died nobly. That silences one: nevertheless, I hold that Gordon need not have died!

HENRY MORTON STANLEY

LARGE shall his name be writ, with that strong line,
  Of heroes, martyrs, soldiers, saints, who gave
  Their lives to chart the waste, and free the slave,
In the dim Continent where his beacons shine.

Rightly they call him Breaker of the Path,
  Who was no cloistered spirit, remote and sage,
  But a swift swordsman of our wrestling age,
Warm in his love, and sudden in his wrath.

How many a weary league beneath the Sun
  The tireless foot had traced, that lies so still.
  Now sinks the craftsman's hand, the sovereign will;
Now sleeps the unsleeping brain, the day's work done.

Muffle the drums and let the death-notes roll,
  One of the mightier dead is with us here;
  Honour the vanward's Chief, the Pioneer,
Do fitting reverence to a warrior soul.

But far away his monument shall be,
  In the wide lands he opened to the light,
  By the dark Forest of the tropic night,
And his great River winding to the Sea.

SIDNEY LOW.

May 13, 1904.

BIBLIOGRAPHY.

How I Found Livingstone. With maps and illustrations. New York: Charles Scribner's Sons.

My Kalulu: Prince, King, and Slave. Illustrated. New York: Charles Scribner's Sons.

Coomassie and Magdala: the British Campaign in Africa. New York: Harper and Brothers.

Through the Dark Continent. Illustrated. 2 vols. New York: Harper and Brothers.

The Congo and the Founding of its Free State. 2 vols. With maps and Illustrations. New York: Harper and Brothers.

In Darkest Africa: the Quest, Rescue, and Retreat of Emin, Governor of Equatoria. With maps and illustrations. 2 vols. New York: Charles Scribner's Sons.

My Dark Companions and their Strange Stories. Illustrated. New York: Charles Scribner's Sons.

Slavery and the Slave Trade in Africa. Illustrated. New York: Harper and Brothers.

My Early Travels and Adventures in America and Asia. With portraits. 2 vols. New York: Charles Scribner's Sons.

Through South Africa: a Visit to Rhodesia, the Transvaal, Cape Colony, and Natal. With maps and illustrations. New York: Charles Scribner's Sons.

∵ All the above works were published in England by Messrs. Sampson Low, Marston & Co.

Sir H. M. STANLEY'S THREE AFRICAN JOURNEYS

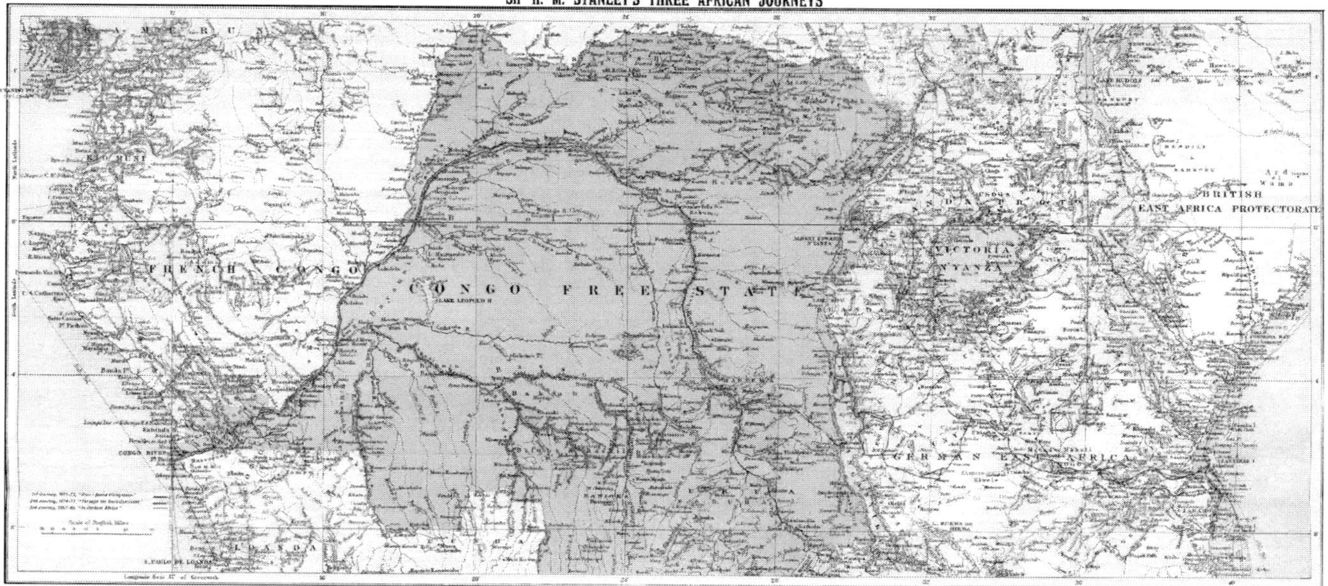

London: Sampson Low, Marston & Company, Ltd.

INDEX

12341216R00335

Printed in Great Britain
by Amazon.co.uk, Ltd.,
Marston Gate.